I0797307

ALSO BY DAN CHIASSON

The Math Campers

Bicentennial

Where's the Moon, There's the Moon

One Kind of Everything: Poem and Person in Contemporary America

Natural History

The Afterlife of Objects

Bernie
for Burlington

Bernie for Burlington

The Rise of the People's Politician and the Transformation of One American Place

DAN CHIASSON

ALFRED A. KNOPF
New York
2026

A BORZOI BOOK
FIRST HARDCOVER EDITION
PUBLISHED BY ALFRED A. KNOPF 2026

Published by Alfred A. Knopf, a division of Penguin Random House LLC, 1745 Broadway, New York, NY 10019.

Knopf, Borzoi Books, and the colophon are registered trademarks of Penguin Random House LLC.

Grateful acknowledgment is made to the following for permission to reprint previously published material:

"Elms" from *The First Four Books of Poems* by Louise Glück. Copyright © 1968, 1971, 1972, 1973, 1974, 1975, 1976, 1977, 1978, 1979, 1980, 1985, 1995 by Louise Glück, used by permission of HarperCollins Publishers and the Wylie Agency LLC.

Library of Congress Cataloging-in-Publication Data
Names: Chiasson, Dan author
Title: Bernie for Burlington : the rise of the people's politician and the transformation of one American place / Dan Chiasson.
Other titles: The rise of the people's politician
Description: First hardcover edition. | New York : Alfred A. Knopf, 2026. | "A Borzoi Book." |
Identifiers: LCCN 2025013635 (print) | LCCN 2025013636 (ebook) | ISBN 9780593317495 hardcover | ISBN 9780593317501 ebook
Subjects: LCSH: Sanders, Bernard http://id.loc.gov/rwo/agents/n79136413 | Sanders, Bernard—Influence | Chiasson, Dan http://id.loc.gov/rwo/agents/n2002029105 | Socialism—Vermont—Burlington—History—20th century | Mayors—Vermont—Burlington—Biography | Burlington (Vt.)—Politics and government—20th century | Burlington (Vt.) —Biography | LCGFT: Biographies http://id.loc.gov/authorities/genreForms/gf2014026049
Classification: LCC F59.B9 C55 2026 (print) | LCC F59.B9 (ebook) | DDC 974.3/17043092 $a B—dc23/eng/20250520
LC record available at https://lccn.loc.gov/2025013635
LC ebook record available at https://lccn.loc.gov/2025013636

penguinrandomhouse.com | aaknopf.com

Printed in the United States of America
1st Printing

The authorized representative in the EU for product safety and compliance is Penguin Random House Ireland, Morrison Chambers, 32 Nassau Street, Dublin D02 YH68, Ireland, https://eu-contact.penguin.ie.

FRONTISPIECE: Mayor Sanders in Managua, Nicaragua, 1985. *Don Melvin*

For my mom, Linda Chiasson,
and for Annie Adams—

this book of people

Twentieth century, go to sleep
You're Pleistocene
That is obscene

—R.E.M., "Electrolite"

O when may it suffice?

—WILLIAM BUTLER YEATS, "Easter, 1916"

Contents

Part I

Natural Histories

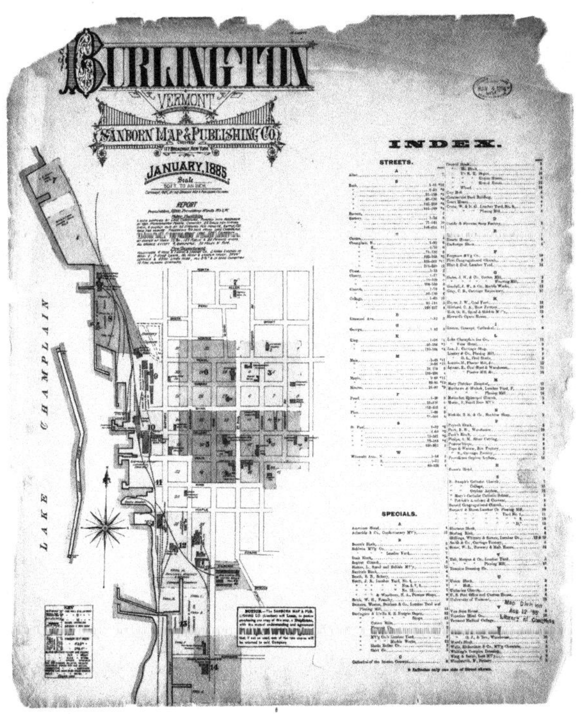

Burlington, Vermont, 1885.
University of Vermont, Special Collections

Prologue: Making a Scene

City Hall vs. Downtown Developers softball game, 1984. *Burlington Free Press*

The Mall Punks

In a video that surfaced during his 2020 presidential campaign, Bernie Sanders, mayor of Burlington, Vermont, stands in a tweed blazer, holding a microphone, near the food court of the Burlington Square Mall. The footage was shot in 1988, as part of a community-access television series that Sanders produced, *Bernie Speaks: The Mayor's Show*. Vermonters in enormous parkas, wool tuques, and moon boots trudge in and out of the frame, gawking at the camera, as Sanders announces the results of twelve ballot items from the recent city election—money for sidewalk repaving, a boost for the library, new equipment for the fire department—then praises the strong showing of Jesse Jackson in the state's recent presidential primary.

Sanders interviews random passersby about their views of government: a soft-spoken visitor from New Hampshire; a shy and thoughtful high school senior concerned about the encroachment of luxury condos; the mall security guard and his friend, a disabled woman named Mary. Then, in the segment that went viral, Sanders stops two teenage punkers with severe piercings, outlandish hairstyles, and heavily zippered black leather jackets. They introduce themselves as "Michele" and "Mike Blair." "Let me start off by saying, it's an interesting hairdo," Sanders teases. "The lipstick is also very interesting." The kids are then asked by their perplexed mayor to decode their looks. "It's just basically saying, 'To heck with society,'" the girl tells Sanders. "Everybody's plastic." Bernie nods and presses gently for some specifics. "Some of the stuff that goes on in this society is basically baloney," Mike Blair interjects. Michele lights up a cigarette, while a third member of their group slouches on the margins, under the sign for Sweet Dreams, the mall candy shop.

I am standing just outside the frame. I can identify almost every person in the video, even the random shoppers streaming by. My friends and I lived at the food court, when not shopping for Japanese throwing stars and nunchucks at the tobacconist upstairs. In a later episode, Sanders interviews my uncle and cousins, out ice-skating one sunny day on Lake Champlain. In an Arbor Day feature, a scout troop plants saplings along a denuded city curb:

The mayor, Mike, and Michele. *CCTV*

there's John, there's Leon, just as I remember them. And Mike Blair, the boy punker? Mike had been among my earliest childhood friends. I published a poem in my first book called "Cicada" about a playdate at Mike's home, a farm outside of Burlington. I was no older than seven or so. My poem is about finding a helpless cicada inside my grown-up New York City apartment, cradling it in my hands, then lifting it out a window to safety. I identified with the cicada: "As a child," I wrote, "I was so scared of my friends' fathers / I would hide when they got home from work."

The footage of the mall punks sat in a dark closet at Channel 15 for decades, before several developments brought it back into the light of day. First, the internet was invented. The very concept was unimaginable for most of us in the 1980s, though the reality was less than a decade away. We had been trained to gaze at the heavens, when lo, the future arrived in our hands. When the technology arrived, though, right away it began to reframe *our past*. The internet served as a powerful memory machine, a time machine. Soon, it began to excavate more and still more of the pre-digital substrate, memorializing even the disposable cultural ephemera of the past. It is uncanny for people about my age—I was born in 1971—to experience the jingles, news sign-offs, local sports broadcasts, all the marginalia of analog life, on small devices we hold in our pockets. For my generation, it is possible even to recover earlier versions of ourselves from the cultural seafloor. My uncle and cousins had never seen their appearance on *The Mayor's Show*: it aired for a week or so in 1987, then vanished. Mike Blair had entirely forgotten about his conversation with Bernie; a friend, he said, had alerted him to its existence on YouTube.

Then, a second development: Bernie Sanders, the socialist mayor of an offbeat city in the second-smallest state in the union, rose to national prominence in a pair of long-shot presidential runs in 2016 and 2020. Sanders is now arguably the most influential leftist politician in the modern history of the nation, and the longest-serving independent in U.S. congressional history. His policy priorities, repeated incessantly for decades, have broken through and redirected mainstream Democratic politics. As of this writing, Sanders, at eighty-three, has begun his fourth term in the United States Senate, where he serves within the Democratic leadership. Whether he will remain in the Democratic Party fold is anybody's guess: at rallies during the spring of 2025, Sanders encouraged audiences in the tens of thousands to look for opportunities outside the corrupt two-party system.

Bernie's impact still cannot be fully measured, since many of those most inspired by him are still quite young. In a 2020 election postmortem issue of *Jacobin*, the democratic socialist monthly, the magazine's young Millennial/Gen Z editors noted that Sanders's support is strongest with "expanding, as opposed to declining, elements of American society"—among others, their own. The principle of generational replacement suggests that Bernie's influence will be long and profound, as his enthusiastic voters age into power and influence; though as people age into power and influence, they sometimes become conservatives.

Nobody anticipated Sanders's rise as a national politician. I have a stack of books about American politics and culture in the 1970s and '80s—David Frum's *How We Got Here: The 70's*, Philip Jenkins's *Decade of Nightmares*, Bruce J. Schulman's *The Seventies*, and several others. Sanders is not mentioned in any of them. Rick Perlstein's magnum opus *Reaganland*, collecting even the tiniest political flotsam, mentions Bernie just once. As teenagers keeping an eye on Mayor Sanders as he bagged garbage outside of city hall, or flew to Nicaragua to meet the Sandinistas, or traveled to Disney World to meet Mickey Mouse, we knew we were witness to something unusual. But the thought that Bernie would eventually break through as a national figure of historic impact would never have occurred to any Burlingtonian of the era—not even to Bernie himself: "People who hold our views," Sanders told his supporters at his mayoral farewell address, "do not hold public office in this country."

MIKE BLAIR AND I drifted apart sometime around second grade; when he next turned up in my life, we were teenagers in Bernie Sanders's Burlington. We had changed, our worlds had changed, but our orbits bisected. His original sweetness remained intact, but now Mike wielded a lethal mohawk and presided over a kind of permanent mosh pit at a boulder across from the entrance to the Burlington Square Mall, which everyone in town called "Punk Rock." Skaters ollied on and off all day long, the clattering of their boards echoing down Church Street. This started a cold war between the merchants and the punks: the preppy clerks from the Benetton store would shoo them away, and the punks, writhing like a nest of eels, would hurl back venomous insults. It was a system in perfect balance.

Around this time, I began to think of myself as a writer. After a beloved English teacher died, I wrote an elegy for him that was printed in the school yearbook; people praised it, so I decided, why not try some more? I made a curriculum for myself and set up shop in the Fletcher Free Library downtown, or in the stacks at the University of Vermont. I was also getting an excellent trickle-down education from my coworkers at a local breakfast place, Sneakers. The waitresses played Bob Dylan, Joni Mitchell, and Joan Armatrading in the front of the house. In the kitchen, I blended the hollandaise and quizzed the cerebral line cooks about literature. Tom, a sinewy marathoner, liked Günter Grass and gave me a copy of *The Tin Drum*. Tom's motto, which I've often repeated to my children, was "Get obsessed and stay obsessed." Kit, whose father was an English professor at Bucknell, stored thick, ruined paperbacks in the cubbies, for reading on his breaks. A little later, one of our regulars was the book critic Dwight Garner, just getting his start in local papers; he met his future wife, the author Cree LeFavour, my favorite person on the wait staff, at Sneakers. Herman Melville said a "whaling ship" was his "Yale College and his Harvard." Mine was Sneakers.

But Burlington itself was an education. One snowy evening in 1986, I went to my first poetry reading, at UVM's Memorial Auditorium: Allen Ginsberg headlined on a weekend bill that also included the then-unknown jam band Phish, billed as a "local percussion ensemble" and backing, beatnik-style, the South African liberationist poet Zenzile. The evening was sponsored by the Mayor's Council on the Arts; before the event, at the Maverick Bookstore in the city's Old North End, Ginsberg, one of the many pilgrims in those days who came to Burlington to experience firsthand an American city run by socialists, presented Bernie with a poem he'd written on the spot, "Burlington Snow," signed and dated 5:30 p.m., February 21, 1986:

Socialist kids sucking socialist lollipops
Socialist poetry in socialist mouths
—aren't the birds frozen socialists?

This is what it felt like to find ourselves, "socialist kids" living in Bernie Sanders's Burlington even in the midst of Ronald Reagan's America. Ginsberg nails the weird wonder of it all. Old Burlington—dowdy, backward, deeply Catholic, ringed by military bases and National Guard barracks—was now a socialist city, an island of reviled and feared ideas. And yet, inheriting a growing local economy that had left Burlington's generational poor behind, by 1986 Sanders had attracted support all up and down the economic ladder, and from voters across the ideological spectrum. "Socialism" had been taught to us, children of the Cold War, as an evil ideology practiced by authoritarians doling out stale bread and block cheese. In many Burlington households—in mine—it meant, simply, Soviet-style communism. Entrusted to our new socialist overlords, however, everything about Burlington was getting obviously, dramatically so much better, crisper, more buoyant, before our eyes—as even the city's businesspeople had to concede.

Though in the video he seems baffled by the mall punks' style, Bernie had a hand in creating it: by 1988, the year the mayor interviewed Mike and Michele, Sanders had transformed our city into a progressive, heterogeneous place that particularly welcomed the young. The punk scene

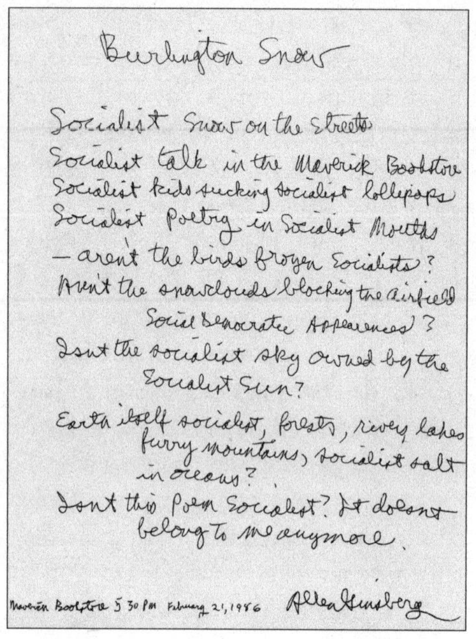

Burlington Snow

Socialist Snow on the Streets
Socialist talk in the Maverick Bookstore
Socialist kids sucking socialist lollipops
Socialist poetry in Socialist Mouths
—aren't the birds frozen Socialists?
Aren't the snowclouds blocking the airfield
Social Democratic Appearances?
Isn't the socialist sky owned by the
Socialist Sun?
Earth itself socialist, forests, rivers lakes
furry mountains, socialist salt
in oceans?
Isn't this Poem Socialist? It doesn't
belong to me anymore.

Maverick Bookstore 5 30 PM February 21, 1986 Allen Ginsberg

"Burlington Snow," by Allen Ginsberg.
Sanders Mayoral Papers, University of Vermont

sprang up in a basement rec space—242 Main—founded by Bernie and Jane Driscoll, who later became Jane O'Meara Sanders. In 2016, *Vice* magazine identified the place as the "oldest all ages music venue" in the country. 242 Main hosted national acts like Fugazi, as well as local thrash, skate, and death metal bands. When its heavy steel door swung open, passersby heard the clamor of bass riffs, bodies colliding, shrieks, roars. This sort of thing did not blossom naturally out of the soil of the Champlain Valley, which nurtured mainly docile folk singers and pale trustafarians playing Bob Marley covers.

242 Main was a place where, as Sanders once put it, the "non-straight-A students" would have a place to hang out. "Everyone yells at teenagers," Bernie wrote in his 1998 book, *Outsider in the White House*. "We offered them a social space, and opportunities for music and dance." I wore blue button-down oxford shirts—then as now—and strove for A's at my Catholic high school. The riotous, frightening "music and dance" at 242 Main was not remotely my scene, but it picked off a few of my best friends. Even to me, it was clear that something important was going down.

I could stay away from 242 Main, but there was no avoiding Bernie. After his mayoral victory by a margin of ten votes on March 3, 1981, we all had a spectacle to behold. To the local press, he was the "ranting and raving" mayor, never far from a bank of microphones, the "avowed socialist," who "crusaded" against the hospital, the governor, the Catholic church, and the business community. Our small-city mayor even boasted that Burlington had "its own foreign policy." He flew to Nicaragua during the heat of the Iran-Contra affair to meet with Daniel Ortega. A few years later, shirtless, he threw back vodka shots in the Soviet Union, bellowing out a Woody Guthrie tune; the footage was beamed back to Burlington to play on Channel 15 and led to one of several mini red scares during Sanders's Burlington years. And yet our sister-cities programs were encouraged by Reagan's State Department as a cunning expression of American soft geopolitical power.

Long before the nuts and bolts of civic transformation fell into place, our mayor had leapfrogged the local press and claimed national attention. It was a novel experience suddenly to have a famous person in our midst. Burlington had produced very few celebrities: Ira Allen, John Dewey. Ted Bundy was born at a home for unwed mothers in town, and was linked, almost proudly, with a brutal unsolved murder in the 1970s. Shirley "Cha Cha" Muldowney, a Burlington native and champion drag racer, sometimes appeared on Johnny Carson's *Tonight Show*. Celebrities would make a stop in Burlington on the road from Boston to Montreal. Somewhere I have the autograph of Brian Setzer of the Stray Cats. My friend got his picture taken with B. B. King. I contend that I saw Dylan checking in at the Radisson Hotel—though my girlfriend said nope, not him. But we all tuned in when Bernie appeared on the *Today* show, in a segment called "Socialism in New England." There was our mayor being interviewed by Phil Donahue, the suave, pewter-maned talk show host. "Are you a capitalist?" Donahue asked Sanders. "No," Bernie replied. "I am not a capitalist." A smile tugged at the edges of his mouth.

Sanders's charisma drove a transformative policy agenda. In this sense,

Some good friends of mine became skaters: Seth, in front, was my best middle school friend; JP, the kid reading the paper, was one of my best elementary school friends. What we see in this photo is "the Bernie effect."
Burlington Free Press

too, he made a scene. The Mayor's Office, newly branded, put its stamp on every initiative and project. These rapid changes in city life, their scope and direction, their implications for our lives and the kind of community we were becoming, drew Burlington into a vital and contentious citywide conversation. The 1970s were a period of demoralizing losses for many communities in our city. A federally funded program of urban renewal had wiped a historic downtown neighborhood off the map, replacing bustling Italian markets and ball fields with brooding parking garages. A string of spectacular arsons had taken some of the city's most magnificent buildings, including, in 1970, its Episcopal cathedral, and, a year later, my family's Catholic church, the Cathedral of the Immaculate Conception. A troubled altar boy whose family was close to mine confessed to the burning of the Catholic cathedral. It was whispered that he had somehow been framed by developers who wanted those vacant lots. When the Diocese of Burlington released its list of priests credibly suspected of abuse in 2019, the conversation about the fires changed yet another time. Those forty familiar names, including a priest who had taken an uncomfortable interest in me but mercifully stopped short of sexual abuse, made many who grew up in the Burlington Catholic community reevaluate the feeling of those times.

Sanders's arrival leveled Burlington's old hierarchies, networks, and institutions. In their place, power was substantially redistributed among ordinary citizens. All of us, Bernie's fans and foes alike, were called on to help imagine and build a new Burlington. In this era of daily cliffhangers, we became aware of ourselves as participants in this wacky, DIY civic experiment. Could Bernie win public access for our waterfront from greedy, mustache-twisting developers? Should Bernie succeed in stripping the kindly doctors at our beloved local hospital of their tax exemption? Should our mayor defy the Reagan administration and fly to Nicaragua to meet with our country's bitter adversaries? Even before I aged into these debates, they trickled down to the playground of Mater Christi School, where we all perfected "Beh-nahhhd Sand-uhhs" impersonations, our nasal, clipped Vermont accents straining toward his broad Brooklynese.

Two Transformations

This book tracks a change within a change: the evolution of Bernie Sanders as a political phenomenon within the shifting political and cultural landscape of his adopted state of Vermont. Sanders, arriving to the state as a part-time resident in 1964 and moving there for good in 1968, simultaneously drove and rode the state's transformation. In a poem or song, the refrain—the unchanging feature of the composition—acts, always, as a measurement of change. Bernie's message has been a refrain, incessant and unchanging, since the early 1970s. His own fixed position within a dynamic system makes him a powerful guage of fluctuations within that system: to see how Vermont changed, simply look at how Bernie's message, reiterated for fifty years, migrated from the fringe to the heart of Vermont's political discourse.

But it is not quite that simple. Bernie did, in important respects, change; and Vermont, in troubling ways, did not. Sanders emerged in the late 1960s as an itinerant carpenter and freelance writer, deeply influenced by the rogue psychoanalyst Wilhelm Reich, who, among other controversial beliefs, connected political liberation with the successful cultivation of cosmos-shattering orgasms. For much of the '70s, Sanders helmed Liberty Union, Vermont's nascent peacenik party. He became the party's superstar, before he bolted in 1977 and ran ever after as an independent. Bernie's status as an independent—and as a withering critic of Democrats—in turn won him strong support within an unlikely constituency: Vermont's rural Republicans. In later days, he has held much of this support even among the MAGA followers of Donald Trump.

And as mayor, the "self-styled socialist" who ran on the slogan "Burlington is not for sale" made controversial alliances with city Republicans and developers. (His primary beef, as we will see, was with Democrats.) He drew the endorsement of the city's patrolmen's union and many in its business community. "Sanders didn't win the Burlington election by saying he would municipalize the phone company," wrote one observer; instead, as Sanders boasted, he "out-Republicaned the Republicans in terms of intelligent, rational responsibility in government."

As a consequence, Sanders attracted vigorous, and often eccentric, opponents to his left, especially among the spurned members of his former party, Liberty Union. Peter Diamondstone, a gadfly who advocated for children's suffrage and the free distribution of narcotics, devoted much of his latter-day political life to torturing his old friend as a "traitor" to leftist ideals. The political scientist Michael Parenti, once a Sanders ally, eventually became a critic of Bernie's accommodation of local capitalists. Murray Bookchin, the anarchist and social theorist, moved to Burlington in the 1970s from New York City to put his theory of "social ecology" into practice; by the mid-'80s, he was Bernie's fiercest local critic. Bea Bookchin, Murray's ex-wife and stalwart political ally, articulated a tough-minded, new-age critique of Sanders that played an important role in halting development of the city's waterfront. Sanders is still resented by members of the Burlington activist community for arresting eighty protesters during a 1983 demonstration at our local GE plant, which manufactured the Gatling-style guns used in

Vietnam and carried by CIA-trained forces in El Salvador. In later years, of course, as a Washington legislator, Bernie caucused with the Democrats, and held positions, especially on gun legislation, to the right of some progressives. The journalist Matthew Zeitlin got it right, I think, in a 2019 piece for *The New Republic*: Sanders sits on "the left wing of the possible in American politics." In many circles in Vermont, that made him a moderate.

On January 31, 1986, a *New York Times* headline announced, "Vermont Shifting to Left in a Flow of Newcomers." The story reported that "until the late 1960's about 90 percent of Vermonters generally voted in Republican primaries." The "flow of newcomers" at one point in the early 1970s numbered as many as one hundred thousand, swelling the state's population by more than 30 percent. Frank Bryan, the foremost analyst of Vermont's rural polity, had predicted the shift more than a decade earlier: "When the only one-party state north of the Mason-Dixon Line and the only one-party *Republican* state anywhere begins to shift gears politically," Bryan wrote, "eyes are turned."

To political scientists like Bryan, Vermont provided "a special opportunity to view close-up the phenomena accompanying political change." But to Yankee Republicans, the shift was an extinction event. Emory Hebard, the state treasurer, a former general store owner and postmaster in the remote Northeast Kingdom town of Charleston, put it bluntly: "The myth of the old-line Vermonter is gone. I think you'd have to say that Vermont has become the most liberal state in the country."

Around 1954, when Bernie, as a teenager, first began to fantasize about the Green Mountains from his family's apartment in Midwood, Brooklyn, Vermont was the most reliably Republican state in the nation. New Hampshire, our neighbor, was a close second. "Anything I can say about New Hampshire / Will serve almost as well about Vermont," Robert Frost wrote in "New Hampshire." Frost kept houses in both states indiscriminately; they amounted to the same place. That was in 1923 or so; by the '70s, after more than one hundred countercultural communes had taken hold in every corner of the state, Vermont had made an abrupt left turn, while New Hampshire, our twin, had become a dense thicket of sprawl, billboards, and fly-by-night development, its tax base decimated by libertarian ideologies. New Hampshire seemed more and more to abide by its bitter, psychotic motto: "Live Free or Die."

The idealistic pilgrims who arrived in Vermont seeking refuge from the "moral and physical blight of urban life" were young and often well educated. Some had money, which helps: living in poverty can be expensive. Many of these shipshape dropouts had arrived from places like New York and Boston, a morning trip away from everything they had renounced, including their parents. They were, therefore, well positioned to assimilate into the small villages whose culture they only sought to preserve. It was what drew them there, not so far from home, in the first place. Looked at in one light, Bernie Sanders is the highest expression of their world and their moment—though in practice, as we will see, Sanders, zigzagging across the state on his endless, low-budget quest to reframe the argument, a fan of basketball and country music, was never a fixture around the fires or in the fields of the hippie scene.

More young people came to Vermont in the 1960s and '70s than to any other rural place—and more of those who came stayed. Soon after their arrival, these neophytes and the primordial Vermonters they met at Sam's Woolen Goods or Woolworth's or the farm supply store often came to like and depend on one another. For decades Vermont had weathered the discouraging loss of many of its most talented young people, who left the state to make their contributions elsewhere. Now hordes of "kids" were coming to make their lives in Vermont. They were unconventional, even radical, but most of them retained manners learned from their parents, along with an instinct toward cooperation. And they needed mentors. In my interviews with these babes in the woods, now in their seventies and eighties, I heard a common note: they were very young, they had bitten off a lot, and, though they distrusted authority, they looked everywhere for parents.

Bernie, too, sought mentorship. Among his first jobs in the state was a stint working for John Rogers, whose construction company still operates in the city of Barre. Sanders learned from Rogers the standard repertoire of hippie carpentry skills, but he also learned, as he said, the "Vermont way of life": Bernie's new mentor knew "every inch of Central Vermont." Rural life depends on an enormous canon of local knowledge, nowhere written down: which dirt roads to avoid in mud season, who to call to fix an alternator, or to plow a long driveway, or to deliver a baby. Bonds of reciprocity bring together people who otherwise might not meet or mix. Rural life is in this sense intensely social: though interactions may be sparse, they are meaningful and crucial.

Many of the new Vermonters had come to make art, in a place where the living was cheap and a community awaited. Old-fashioned Vermont offered these young artists, writers, songwriters, and filmmakers materials and a theme. *Vermont Speaks for Itself*, a traveling show produced in 1973 by a media collective in Monkton, Vermont, celebrated Yankee speech as a kind of found poetry. Bread & Puppet, the anti-capitalist theater troupe, used the existing landscape and natural materials of the Vermont countryside in their Boschian pageants. David Mamet hired Vermont locals as extras in his plays and films. In Bennington, in the 1980s, Jamaica Kincaid recreated the

Antigua of her childhood, both in astonishing, lyrical novels and stories, and in a tropical garden somehow prospering in the temperate microclimate behind her home. Vermont, though, offered inspiration in all seasons: from the winter light in Plainfield, Louise Glück made a poetry of taciturn epiphanies and hoarded silences.

The state also offered these newcomers a political framework to work within. The ethic of rural cooperation is the basis for town meeting, Vermont's strong annual tradition of face-to-face democracy. Most towns in Vermont meet on the first Tuesday in March, right about when the sap begins to run, for open debate of town issues. As the communards became stakeholders in their towns and villages, one path to Vermont's political transformation emerged. Town meeting leads to the school committee and then to the state legislature, and soon higher office comes into view. No other '60s counterculture could aspire to rise through a navigable legislative and judicial infrastructure to sway an entire American state, not merely a city or a region. Vermont was different in this way from the Berkshires or Berkeley. Everything, including the state's representation in Washington, was on the table. Town meeting creates dialogue and consensus across the expected political divisions precisely because its participants are bound by daily cooperation. Bernie did best in his early campaigns in some of the most Republican areas of the state partly because those old-line Vermonters and the radical "kids" who brought them business had met across the fence.

The kids had another advantage: these newcomers were almost all white. By this important measurement of change, the state has remained troublingly static. In 2022, Vermont still ranked as the second-whitest state in America, trailing only West Virginia. Now: Vermont and West Virginia are, in terms of cultural and economic opportunity and political outlook, opposites. How could a wealthy, educated northeastern state full of left-progressives, a few hours' drive for more than 60 million people, remain 96 percent white?

The answer is: only by trying very hard. We will see throughout this book that Vermont's political and cultural transformation, and Bernie's rise within it, transpired in a hothouse world of white progressivism. Vermont's image was intentionally cultivated by its tourism bureau to hearken back to a time before large-scale immigration. Its infrastructure was transformed by wealthy summer homeowners fleeing hot cities where they interacted with Black and brown people. The new Vermonters in Sanders's generation were politically radical but replicated the demographics of that earlier migration almost perfectly: they were white, educated, and from the East Coast, and many of them were rich. When I considered whether Bernie could scale nationally, I figured this, and not socialism, would spell his downfall. Astonishing that he overcame Vermont's elitism and whiteness. Until, that is, he didn't.

Bernie for Burlington

Bernie's political career began in this world of loosely networked rural cooperation, as a new kind of political signal traveled along the state's existing social circuitry, from the general stores, county fairs, and traditional businesses, to town meeting, and eventually to the ballot box.

But anything lacking the bite of confrontation is finally boring to Sanders: to rise, he needed an urban roughhousing politics that was anathema to the mellow farmers' market progressivism reigning elsewhere in the state. When he moved to Burlington in 1971, Bernie encountered a city that was older, poorer, and more culturally backward than the small villages that played host to the countercultural zeitgeist. Many years later, looking back, Sanders recalled a city that was not "very special" in terms of leftist formation, unlike Madison, Wisconsin, or Berkeley, California; its electorate was not yet "politically conscious." Sanders had to cultivate, instead of zealous fellow-travelers, a political base among the poor and working class, the unions, and the elderly, all of whom might be put off by the term *socialism*, if not its underlying values and meanings. His four mayoral victories drew heavily, and in growing numbers, from the city's two poorest wards.

The city did provide convenient political villains: a somnambulant business elite and self-dealing city government, a price-gouging local hospital, a university board and administration run by a monied clique, a powerful Catholic diocese with political sway over its congregants, and deep-pocketed developers eager to privatize the city's most astonishing natural and cultural resource, its waterfront on Lake Champlain. As the '70s unfolded, a small, rowdy leftist intelligentsia at the University of Vermont emerged on the hill, and soon Burlington attracted an emerging activist class, many of whom had come off the farms and out of the woods to found clinics and food

Mayor Sanders, 1985. *Rob Swanson*

co-ops and neighborhood groups. The city's latent political forces—leftists, academics, the elderly, the poor, the unions—were waiting to be drawn into cooperation. None of these groups saw city hall, long the domain of a Democratic machine led by a Falstaffian patronage politician named Gordon Paquette, as a forum for their political work. Bernie rallied them all, but he also rallied Burlington's business and developer class to understand the power of the city's brand—and the central role its cuddly socialism and its telegenic mayor could play in it.

Because I was there, with a front-row seat, I have left my point of view intact throughout this book. I kept finding myself, my family, and my friends inside the story. I was nine when Sanders became mayor in 1981, seventeen when he left city hall in 1989, and nineteen when he was sworn in as Vermont's sole representative to the U.S. Congress, in 1991. These are important years in a person's life, and much about me, including the way I write sentences, was shaped during them. I became aware at some juncture during those years that I was growing up in the middle of a very unusual American experiment. As a low-income Burlingtonian, I was also, in a way, one of its subjects—and one of its beneficiaries.

But the arrival of Bernie Sanders on the scene exposed rifts and tensions in my family. In my earliest memory of Bernie, I am nine years old, growing up in my grandparents' house, my mother's childhood home, where she raised me. I watch from an upstairs window as a wild-looking figure approaches our door, flanked by an aide with a clipboard. The doorbell rings. My grandmother yells across the house, "Milford—It's SANDERS!" My grandfather shouts in reply, "Dorothy—DON'T ANSWER THE DOOR!"

In this vignette I can see the image of an entire place and time. Three generations crowded into our small house. My grandparents had lost their youngest child, Danny, a year before I was born, the third of their children to die before the age of ten. Milford and Dorothy Delorme had hoped to retire to Florida; now they had a new child to help raise, named for a child they mourned. My mom worked long hours to support the two of us. I have an early memory of her operating an old-fashioned switchboard as an ambulance dispatcher. Later, after studying for her associate's degree, she became the business manager of a remote mountain school district, hours away on icy roads. She ended her career as the last superintendent of the drafty Gothic convent where my grandmother, her mother, had been raised as an orphan, a half-dozen elderly nuns still shuffling around inside. My grandparents were middle class, but my mother and I, living under their roof, struggled: I received state and federal support throughout my childhood, including a Pell grant for college. I worked from age twelve on to have money to go to the mall, see a movie, or accept an invitation to visit a friend on Cape Cod.

Mom had been only briefly married to my father, a Canadian citizen who vanished before my first birthday. She had moved back into her childhood bedroom to stay. Cyril Chiasson, my father, was never discussed: in fact, for years I didn't know his name. A scholar of the Jesuit philosopher Pierre Teilhard de Chardin, my father, I learned, had struck out as a professor and made his living as an ESL instructor, moving from Toronto to the Northwest Territories, where he taught the Inuit, and then to Korea and Taiwan. My mother asked me one summer whether I wanted to meet him: he was teaching a summer course at Saint Michael's College, near our home. Her tone indicated that I could certainly refuse, which I did; but I know I saw him that summer, sitting on a bench not far from our front door. I put my head down and bicycled by. The first concrete information I learned about him was that he had died, in the Philippines, in 2009.

Though my tense home quieted me, it made me an observer; Bernie's Burlington gave me something fascinating to observe. I monitored the world through a hairline crack in my extreme shyness, hoping never to anger my grandfather, a heartbroken, brooding man who had helped to develop the state's nuclear readiness plans—bomb shelters, evacuation routes—as its military head of civil defense. Like many in his generation, Milford Delorme had come home from the Second World War to parades and festivities in his honor. Now he felt he was being displaced in the culture, and he blamed the young. My aunts and uncles, his children, whom I adored, followed a range of 1970s paths, often to their parents' dismay. There were perplexing silences, absences, and feuds. My grandmother seemed agonized by all the tensions and prayed throughout the day, even while doing housework. Both of my grandparents saw Bernie Sanders as the final straw in their battle to uphold American values, a literal communist on our streets. Bernie was the candidate of the loathed "students" who lurked behind everything miasmal and seedy in town: Fidel Castro in a household that revered General Patton. Everyone in the home did their best, but it was an uncomfortable place to grow up, and the People's Republic of Burlington was right out my front door. When I passed out of my home and into the wider city, suddenly I was in a place that Sanders had transformed, and, it seemed, just in time for my adolescence.

Looking Forward, Looking Back

The historian of medieval France Jules Michelet wrote that "the nature of things is that they come into being at certain times and in certain ways." For

Michelet, "wherever the same circumstances are present, the same phenomena arise and no others." I have this quotation pinned to my desk. *Bernie for Burlington* is about the alignment of cultural and political circumstances in the twilight of the analog era, and the kinds of political phenomena that were possible only in that now-eclipsed time. The Vermont scene in the 1970s and '80s will never be replicated. Bernie came into being in that lost world of late-twentieth-century opportunities and constraints.

But I wrote this book after Sanders's remarkable national rise in twenty-first-century politics. This consummate analog citizen is among this century's most successful digital politicians: one need only call to mind the parka, the mittens. It was always Bernie's goal to circumvent the corporate media, as we will see. ("The media," like "millionaires and billionaires," is a phrase stitched with Bernie's voice and inflection.) Before Bernie held elected office, he wrote for small papers, founded and edited a newsletter, and built a small, successful media company producing school filmstrips. He produced, directed, and distributed a film about the American socialist Eugene V. Debs. He produced and hosted a show on the local ETV channel about poverty. As mayor, Bernie became a seasoned manipulator of the sometimes-hostile media. He scaled his statewide appeal partly by recording and distributing a gospel album, which received generous, bemused airplay in the late '80s. And on *The Mayor's Show*, Sanders, microphone in hand, gave regular citizens like the mall punks and my cousins a voice. Facebook, Twitter, and other social media platforms as Sanders has used them are continuous with these earlier acts of circumventing the mainstream media to reach people directly. They provide the illusion of intimate presence: Sanders no longer has to hitchhike across the mountains to meet his audience.

This book was, therefore, begun twice: in the 1980s, when I first witnessed Bernie Sanders up close; and in the current era, when he has become a decisive player in American politics, the dean of the American left. It gestated in my adolescence, but it came to life after a dinner party in the spring of 2019. These were the cruel, cold April days after Attorney General William Barr released his tendentious and misleading "summary" of the report of Special Counsel Robert Mueller on Russian interference in the 2016 election. President Donald Trump had been cleared, vindicated—strengthened.

I had carved out a small reputation as a citizen-sleuth, reporting via an email distribution list on sleazy liaisons in the Seychelles, the movement of oligarchs' yachts, backchannels, servers, the pee tape. When word of my research reached Laurence Tribe, the constitutional scholar and Democratic Party operative, Tribe invited me to dinner at his home in Brookline, Massachusetts. He and his wife, the garden historian Elizabeth Westling, warmly welcomed me, and soon we were joined by mutual friends, Jorie

Graham and Peter Sacks, who had been my teachers at Harvard. The final guest, arriving straight from his Kennedy School class, was Ronald Klain, then a close adviser to Joe Biden's presidential campaign and later Biden's chief of staff.

These were the heady days when Pete Buttigieg was quoting Joyce's *Ulysses* and playing white-man collegiate jazz in front of audiences. We were all looking for the solution to Donald Trump. Despite my devotion to Bernie, I was tempted by Buttigieg. Tribe was working in an unofficial capacity for him and invited me to contribute. Klain made what seemed at the time like a lost-cause case for Biden, his longtime mentor and friend. Others argued for Elizabeth Warren or Kamala Harris. But there was one thing on which everyone seemed to agree: Bernie was a threat. At that table he was mocked as an irritant, an interloper—"a *phony*," Tribe interjected. Some at the table wondered if Sanders had even been paid by the Russians to throw the election to Trump. The room full of college professors lamented that Bernie had again captured the imagination of their students: Gen Z was "all in for Bernie," the other grown-ups agreed. The evening ended cheerfully, as Tribe zipped up his tracksuit and headed down to a basement studio for his regular appearance on MSNBC's *The Last Word with Lawrence O'Donnell*. A week after our dinner, Tribe tweeted to his millions of followers, "How can I put it more simply? Based on watching him for decades, I believe @berniesanders is a phony."

Even driving home, I realized that I'd just been in the proverbial smoke-filled room, one of many across the country where powerful Democrats had again mobilized against Sanders. Exactly one year later, with COVID-19 spreading across the land, Ron Klain and others would deliver the nomination to Joe Biden, magically clearing the large field of candidates, including Bernie, in a matter of days. It was 1980s Burlington, all over again: the Democratic machine on one side, working out politics for the rest of the electorate; the naive "students" on the other, demanding their share of power to create a morally intelligible future.

The thing was, I knew what happened next: in Burlington, Bernie, "the avowed socialist," overcame the fears of the establishment with one smart, nonpolitical initiative after another. He brought a professional baseball team to Burlington; he plowed the streets and sidewalks efficiently, prioritizing the poor neighborhoods where people walked to church and school; he got a deal on cable TV for the elderly; he welcomed musicians, poets, and puppeteers to our streets; he built a land trust for affordable homeownership and wealth creation; he and his administration salvaged our city's beautiful waterfront from scrap and toxins. Sanders won over Burlington by making even the businesspeople in our prosperous city feel they had an agile and

Mayor Sanders and his predecessors, 1984. *Rob Swanson*

imaginative government. By the end of his eight years, many of us realized we'd played a role in a one-of-a-kind, historic inquiry into the possibilities for human happiness in an American city.

I am one of the outcomes of that weird, bygone American experiment. But what I feel I mostly did, in those years, was keep quiet, leaning into my shyness, and keep a close eye on things. The Sanders years therefore taught me how to be an observer—that is, a writer. This book is the fruit of that education.

A Note on Methodology

This is a book of stories, and a book about stories. Growing up in Bernie's Burlington, I followed the city's transformation like a thrilling daily serial, narrated by the mayor but interpreted, adapted, and embellished in real time by dozens of reporters, filmmakers, artists, puppeteers, political analysts, demonstrators, dancers, and poets. I've tried to represent the variety and richness of those accounts, their individual distinctness. I've tried as well to convey how it felt to grow up in such a story-rich environment, where we were all, at once, the readers, the protagonists, and in a way the authors of the tale of our cultural and political transformation.

Some of the stories in this book were constructed from my own fallible memories, or from stories told to me during my childhood and upbringing. Others were retrieved from archives—both official collections like the Sanders Mayoral Papers at the University of Vermont and musty hoards preserved in the cellars and attics of the story's important players. I had hundreds of hours of conversations with dozens of individuals, including Bernie's brother, Larry, many of Bernie's oldest and closest friends, most of his living aides and political advisers from his Burlington years, and several of his longtime rivals. A few of these individuals were my friends already, and others became my friends over the course of three or so years of daily work, as I visited contributors in their living rooms or we set out to explore the back roads of Vermont together.

I did not speak with Bernie or Jane Sanders. I made a few polite attempts, but only early on. Those close to Bernie and Jane report that they were aware of my project, intrigued that "a poet was telling the story," and have not sought to interfere with or influence the process in any way. I wondered all throughout the writing of this book what would happen if Bernie suddenly decided to participate: What if one of those emails I receive daily from "Bernie Sanders" had been from Bernie Sanders? But I prefer to think that his refusal to interfere was itself a kind of participation. This skein of historical fact, local lore, best-guesswork, and poetry that I've created and titled *Bernie for Burlington* depended on its subject's remaining silent and on the sidelines. One peep from him, and my whole composition might have unraveled.

1

Welcome to Vermont!

(New York City, 1954)

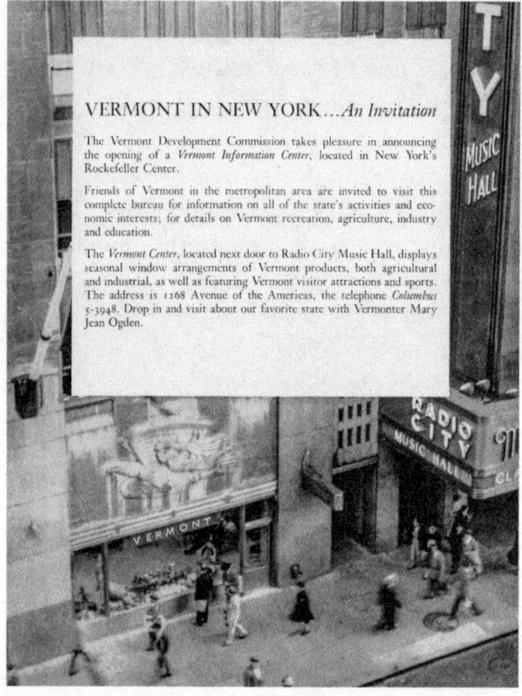

VERMONT IN NEW YORK...*An Invitation*

The Vermont Development Commission takes pleasure in announcing the opening of a *Vermont Information Center*, located in New York's Rockefeller Center.

Friends of Vermont in the metropolitan area are invited to visit this complete bureau for information on all of the state's activities and economic interests; for details on Vermont recreation, agriculture, industry and education.

The *Vermont Center*, located next door to Radio City Music Hall, displays seasonal window arrangements of Vermont products, both agricultural and industrial, as well as featuring Vermont visitor attractions and sports. The address is 1268 Avenue of the Americas, the telephone *Columbus* 5-3948. Drop in and visit about our favorite state with Vermonter Mary Jean Ogden.

Vermont in New York, 1954. *Vermont Life Magazine*

1268 Avenue of the Americas, Manhattan

Once, in Midtown Manhattan, you could visit a shop with a sign that read, simply, VERMONT. Its display windows presented seasonal dioramas. Evenings, the ebullient marquee of Radio City Music Hall shouted out in neon. But Vermont, its cozy neighbor, had gone to bed early. Vermont was dark and silent.

Inside Vermont, the air smelled of woodsmoke, cider, and maple syrup. Vermont boasted that it sold nothing at all, except "the virtues of Vermont."

But Vermont's "virtues" were in fact for sale. In the winter, the shop window was taken over by a large three-dimensional map of the state, with colored bulbs attached where the ski areas were located. It looked like a game show prop. The bulbs shone red, yellow, or green, depending on how much snow had fallen in the real Vermont, far from Midtown. Passing cars slowed as their drivers squinted to make out the map.

Cabbies felt "despair" at driving by, according to *The New York Times*; their fares showed a tendency to cut short their trips, hop out, and study the display. The windows became one of the big city's minor attractions. "There is no official count on the 'window watchers,'" the *Times* reported, "but they are believed to number in the thousands."

Inside Manhattan's Vermont, a staff of Vermonters, mostly young women, greeted visitors, handed out brochures, and answered the phones. Winter was the busiest season. "Between 1000 and 1500 queries a week are received about snow conditions," the *Times* reported. Many young men stopped in just to talk with these delightful, helpful women, who tended their serene island in a sea of noise and traffic.

"Vermont in New York: An Invitation!" read the full-page ad in *Vermont Life* magazine. "Drop in and visit about our favorite State with Vermonter Mary Jean Ogden." "Visit about" was a nice touch: a Yankee speech artifact, suggesting a whole world of front porches and shade trees, and wholesome nontransactional encounters, free of the taint of money.

Outside it was Midtown at mid-century, the world that the poet Frank O'Hara captured on his frantic lunch hour walks: workmen fed "their dirty glistening torsos" between parked cabs, while on "the avenue" women's skirts could be seen "flipping / above heels" and blowing "above grates."

Inside, it was another kind of poem: Robert Frost's "Stopping by Woods on a Snowy Evening," or "An Old Man's Winter Night," with the despair erased, leaving only the ambience: the "snow upon the roof," the "icicles along the wall."

1525 East 26th Street, Brooklyn

In the fall of 1954, nineteen-year-old Larry Sanders took his little brother, Bernard, then thirteen, on the subway from their home in Midwood, Brooklyn, to Midtown Manhattan, a forty-five-minute trip, and visited "Vermont": the Vermont Information Center.

They were not skiers. It might have been an accident: the shop was just to the right of the subway exit. But in 1954, a minor cultural draft blew down from Vermont. Everyone had heard "Moonlight in Vermont," the popular song, beloved of crooners, each verse a woodsy haiku. Hitchcock's *The Trouble with Harry* filmed that fall in the village of Craftsbury, where the foliage stole the spotlight from the cadaver. And Bing Crosby's *White Christmas*, the remake of *Holiday Inn* minus the blackface, now set in a Vermont inn, premiered in November of that year.

Though there were bins of apples and little samplers of maple syrup on offer, the Sanders boys brought a different kind of souvenir back home to Midwood that day. A wire rack presented fliers for "Vermont land," Bernie Sanders recalled in 2015. "We picked up the brochures and we saw farms were for sale."

"It sounds like a made-up story," Larry Sanders told me in the first of our interviews, "but it really happened." On the subway home, Larry and Bernie pored over photos of "farm after farm, pages of farms." The land was beautiful—but more importantly, "it was cheap." "Cheapness," frugality, thrift: these concepts come up over and over as we follow Bernie Sanders's rise. They were yoked early to the idea of the state of Vermont.

There is something funny about two lanky Brooklyn teenagers discussing real estate with the reputable ladies of the Vermont Information Center. But the boys had been primed by attending the Ten Mile River Scout Camp, in Narrowsburg, New York, on the Pennsylvania border: a wild, wooded, "stunning place," according to Larry.

"Bernard loved the countryside," Larry explained. Vermont, he said, was "a fantasy—but an important fantasy."

LARRY SANDERS, whose resemblance to his brother is strong but not uncanny—he is not Larry David—is the keeper of the family's stories. Bernie has made a stand against the politics of folksy charm and personal anecdote, ever since his first races in the early 1970s. In their place he has developed a counter-charisma, an orneriness that in old age makes him seem a flinty, Yankee figure. Bernie's cantankerousness has been very easy to sentimentalize, especially for the young. But it scalded and confused many throughout his political rise.

"The usual path is to begin with biography," Tad Devine, a Bernie aide, told *The New York Observer* in 2015. "I don't see us going there." While Larry very naturally faces backward, Bernie has always barreled ahead. He will not, or perhaps cannot, look back; but he is shaped thoroughly by the braided economic, medical, and emotional traumas of the first little economy he saw up close, that of his childhood home.

The elder Sanders brother has lived mostly in England since 1969, where he is now retired as a Green Party official. Many Americans met him for the first time on the night of July 26, 2016, when, as a delegate for Democrats Abroad, Larry nominated Bernie for president of the United States. The clip can be found easily online: "I want to bring before this convention the names of our parents, Eli Sanders and Dorothy Glassberg Sanders," Larry Sanders begins, his voice breaking and tears welling. "They did not have easy lives, and they died young. They would be immensely proud of their son and his accomplishments. They loved him very much. They loved the New Deal of Franklin Roosevelt, and would be especially proud that Bernard is renewing that vision."

Larry was weeping by then. Bernie had lashed himself to the mast as usual, but soon his own tears began. (I don't believe Bernie had ever cried publicly before that night.) "It was a hectic household," Larry told me. "My mother had a very strong temper." Dorothy Glassberg was born on the Lower East Side in 1912. Home movies from the 1940s show a handsome, stylish woman, at home in a swagger coat and pillbox hat. She waves baby Bernie's hand to the camera, broadly smiling.

But her "hectic household"—three and a half rooms in a tenement—reminded her perhaps too much of her childhood. "She wanted a house," Larry said; she "yearned for status in the synagogue" and in the surrounding community, which came only with having a home where a woman could reciprocate her neighbors' hospitality.

The apartment at 1525 East 26th Street had a bedroom, a bathroom, a kitchen/living room, and a "half room, a widened part of the hall," which, according to Larry, served as a second bedroom. When they were both living at home, Larry and Bernie alternated, the one sleeping in the makeshift bedroom, the other on the living room couch. "They threw a bathroom in as well," Bernie once wrote. "My memory of that one time a fish actually came up through a toilet." The apartment "was incredibly cramped," Larry told me. "Not only didn't we have a room of our own, we didn't have a room together."

In the main room, there was a bookshelf with perhaps twenty books (including a eugenics textbook whose anatomical illustrations were "very popular" with the boys), a radio, and, from 1948 or so on, a TV. The apartment offered "no privacy at all"—no place, Larry added solemnly, that Bernie and Larry "could decorate."

With space indoors scarce, Larry said, "the street was our second home." The rule on the pickup basketball courts was "Make it, take it"—you score a basket, you get the ball back—a brutal capitalistic model for competition, and one that Bernie practiced in his political life, whatever his ideological commitment to the fair distribution of wealth. "We played baseball, softball, punchball, stickball, stoopball, roller hockey, variants of American football, touch football, touch tackle, basketball, marbles," Larry said. "It was a very good way to grow up." Bernie, he added, "might not entirely agree."

IN SOME MARRIAGES, the party that insists on a narrower world automatically wins, though the victory is costly. Dorothy Sanders apparently wanted a broader life.

But three and a half rooms were quite enough for Eli Sanders, who had emigrated to New York from Słopnice, Poland, in 1921, at the age of sixteen. His family in the old country sometimes went without food. "My father's imagination, his life story, was survival," Larry explained. Anything extra was trivial. Larry remembers his father watching a TV show about middle-class "psychological distress" and shaking his head. "But they've got plenty of money," Eli Sanders muttered. "They've got everything they need." Eli had an existential sense of life, drawn in part from his subsistence childhood, and augmented by the news dawning from Europe. Leafing through an old family photograph album, Eli Sanders pointed to one relative after another who'd been killed or lost—"gobbled up," as Larry put it, in the Holocaust.

Eli Sanders was a commissioned paint salesman for the Keystone Paint and Varnish Company. He traveled up and down Long Island for his work and, according to Larry, "probably stopped at every diner along the way." In the home movies I have seen, he is a paunchy man, and ill at ease throwing a ball to his sons. But he had a ready smile and a sweet, gregarious manner. Larry suggests that he spent a lot of his days chatting with his clients, which might have cut into his commissions. In Eli's mind, the family had arrived. In his wife's view, they had stalled out just on the other side of poverty.

In a story both Bernie and Larry tell, their father saw Arthur Miller's *Death of a Salesman* late in its Broadway run and wept for weeks after whenever he thought of Willy Loman, its thwarted protagonist. "He was devastated by it," Larry told me. The play brought home to Eli how close his family had always been to economic collapse. Like many Americans in their precarious position, the Sanders family lived near despair. "The bottom could fall out," as Larry put it. You might be tempted to conclude, as Willy Loman did, that "a man is worth more dead than alive."

So Eli and Dorothy Sanders fought. They fought because they were frightened. The fights were unbearable to the boys, since, as they could plainly see, their parents were closely attached, and loved each other very much.

"My father's thing was, you were spending too much," Larry explained, "and my mother's was, you're not earning enough money." This went round and round and "destroyed what they had." These were "arguments that seared through a little boy's brain, never to be forgotten," Bernie Sanders wrote in *Our Revolution*.

Once, in the 1980s, I saw Bernie shopping at a department store in Burlington, now long gone, called Magrams. He pointed tentatively at the shirt racks, as though trying to make contact with an alien being. A few minutes later, from a second-floor window, I watched him exit the store and storm down Church Street toward city hall, empty-handed. I've always told it as a funny story; but when you hear the brothers discuss the anxiety that money caused them as children, it seems not funny at all.

In *Our Revolution*, Bernie describes an errand he ran for his mother to buy groceries. "I went to the wrong store," he wrote. "I went to the small shop a few blocks away, rather than the Waldbaum's grocery store on Nostrand Avenue. I paid more than I should have. When I returned and my mother realized what I had done, the screaming was horrible."

"The worst of it," Larry told me, still agonizing seventy years later, "wasn't what we didn't have. It was the tensions. The arguments."

I DROVE OUT to Midwood from the Upper West Side one beautiful April afternoon, across Central Park and down FDR Drive, over the Brooklyn Bridge, through a tangle of on- and off-ramps and, at last, out Ocean Avenue. How could it all work so well, said I, a Vermonter, to myself; every bolt

Bernie (left) with mother Dorothy Sanders and Larry. *Sanders Institute*

Bernie (left) and Larry. *Sanders Institute*

and rivet holding as I sped through the balletic chaos of New York's built environment?

The temperature fell several degrees as I neared Sanders's childhood home in a mid-rise tenement on the corner of 26th Street and Kings Highway. Coney Island and Brighton Beach are nearby. You sense the beach in Midwood, in the flat, shadowless glare of the light, and in the gusts of fog that blow across the playgrounds and parks.

The food critic Mimi Sheraton, who grew up in Midwood, described an April day there in 1946. It matched what I saw nearly perfectly: mid-rise brick apartments trellised with black metal fire escapes on the avenues, and "builders' houses, usually duplicated three or four in a row" on the side streets, "brick and stucco affairs." Bright yellow forsythia blazed in many of those small backyards, just as she had described during this same calendar week in 1946.

It was, and is, a middle-class neighborhood with the feeling of an inner suburb. In Bernie's day, it was an enclave of rapidly assimilating Jews within the larger neighborhood of Flatbush. Now the place has been carved out from Flatbush, and attracts a wide array of immigrant families, but especially Orthodox Jews of Russian descent. The day I was there was during Passover; a bunch of guys selling homemade matzoh on the street asked me if I was Jewish.

"Nope, Catholic," I replied, and they waved me off with a chuckle.

1525 East 26th Street, a six-story, yellow-brick tenement, stands apart from the cheerful single-family homes. Many families in the neighborhood began their lives as renters in buildings like this one, aspiring to purchase one of the little houses at its ankles. Bernie's parents dreamed of making that leap, but it never came. In Midwood, in the 1940s and '50s, to own a "private house," as Bernie's parents called them, meant you were seen, your family was acknowledged, you were part of the neighborhood's fabric. Once inside 1525 East 26th Street, though, you vanished.

I walked down 26th Street to James Madison High School. There they remember Bernie Sanders: in the entry hall, just beyond the metal detectors and security guards, is the Madison High School "Wall of Distinction." Bernie Sanders '59 is one in from the lower left corner, next to Beverly Stoll Pepper, the sculptor, who is the mother of the poet and my friend Jorie Graham. They are in distinguished company. Ruth Bader Ginsberg '50 shares the top row with the famed environmentalist Barry Commoner '33, Charles Schumer '67, and Stanley H. Kaplan '35, the founder of the test prep company. Working down the grid, we find Carole Klein King '58, several professional athletes, four Nobel laureates, and Judith Blum Sheindlin '60—"Judge Judy." The roster of graduates is "more distinguished than Eton's," Larry Sanders told me, with a laugh.

What was the secret to the school's success? "It was one of those schools where you felt what the old world was," Jorie Graham told me. "The permission to get an education was an astounding gift because so many had died in Europe."

Bernie entered Madison in the fall of 1954, around the time he and Larry picked up their Vermont brochures. Classmates recall a quiet and serious boy, not terribly political but, as his brother put it, "aware" of politics. "Jewish boys growing up in that time couldn't but be aware just how important politics is," Larry said. "It's a matter of life and death." Sanders eventually ran for student body president, finishing last among three candidates, on a platform to aid orphans of the Korean War.

But sports, and not politics, offered Bernie his first method of channeling his intensity. In a setback, Bernie, always a great pickup player on Brooklyn's "Make it, take it" outdoor courts, was cut from the varsity basketball team. He was a "tremendous player," Larry said. I confirmed that I had seen his game on the pickup courts in Burlington: strong ball handler, solid outside game, and, always, a complete, transforming intensity. Madison "wasn't the skyscraper squad," according to Larry, but they did have one of the "top-ranked teams in the city." If only he'd been "an inch or two taller." (Bernie stands around six feet one.)

Sanders became a standout athlete in track and cross-country, and eventually captained both teams. It baffled me, when Bernie sought to introduce himself to voters in his two presidential runs, that he did not capitalize more

WATCH THAT KICK: Bernie Sanders leads the field in the mile run as Lou Howort trails, a close second.

Sanders finishing strong. *Lou Howart, Madison High School*

on his astonishing high school running career; the ads write themselves. Bernie's best mile was 4:37, which earned him third place in New York City. That's blazing fast, when you consider he ran in it on a cinder track, wearing primitive spikes. Even more impressive, to Larry, was his brother's cross-country prowess. The course, way uptown in Van Cortlandt Park, "was always amazingly muddy," he recalled. The races showed Bernie's "tremendous stamina and dedication."

Practices were just getting underway when I left Madison High that afternoon, April 15, 2022; the courts and fields were filling up with students. Other kids were walking home alone, glued to their phones, or flirting in small, raucous groups. There is really nothing on earth like a high school dismissal, I thought to myself. The teachers and administrators streaming out looked almost as happy as their students, and took me for one of their own.

Theodore Hamm's *Bernie's Brooklyn* describes the strong web of public projects from which the Sanders family benefited as a result of Franklin D. Roosevelt's New Deal, which Larry Sanders also invoked at the 2016 convention: it brought baskets of federal money to New York City, expertly distributed by Roosevelt's local ally, Mayor Fiorello—the name means "little flower"—LaGuardia, who stood only five feet two. Their apartment was rent controlled; Larry guessed the rent was about "fifty bucks a month," perhaps a tenth of his father's pay. Beginning in the 1930s, there were new roads, schools, and swimming pools, and a new campus for Brooklyn College, where Dorothy Sanders eventually organized the Hillel seder every spring.

It was "an environment where New Deal politics were quite normal," Larry said in a 2015 interview with Vermont's *Seven Days*. "It was widely understood that government could do good things."

And yet, anybody who has hefted Robert Caro's *The Power Broker* knows that these anonymized government works had a dark side. Larry Sanders recalls the new public library, which replaced a makeshift space attached to the fire station, a romantic, enchanting hideaway for the neighborhood's kids. The update was a modern, spic-and-span building.

Life in the family apartment seemed alternately clenched and explosive. Outside, though, Brooklyn appeared to be blossoming and changing. Government was indeed doing "good things": Larry points to "a comfortable environment" where the "streets were free and easy and safe." But ordinary families had no say in their neighborhood's transformation. Some were relocated by eminent domain if their buildings blocked construction of an exit ramp. Old homes were now mere feet from the cascading traffic; fragrant blocks were turned into dank, toxic canyons by the new highways.

And none of these grand improvements had eased the worries of Bernie's parents in their small apartment, or altered their wearying daily pattern.

"Nobody would have chosen the new library," Larry Sanders told me. And the concrete of the new city playground was "very destructive to arms and legs." It was mystifying when a new building or playground suddenly materialized where another, beloved structure had been. Who made these decisions? The Midwood families themselves had played no role.

I told Larry that it reminded me of seeing Bernie for the first time on my front porch, when I was nine, as he was priming people for votes. It was a scene that played out over and over in his eight years as mayor. You'd hear about a bond issue coming before the city for some important public works project. Soon, Bernie or one of his disheveled volunteers was out on the street, or in the parks, or at your front door, looking for your support. The skinned knees kids got on those Brooklyn playgrounds stayed with him: a visitor to Burlington, Bernie once boasted, would visit its parks and say, "This is a people's country club. You have tennis, you have swimming, you have softball."

"Inform your parents," Bernie would exclaim, finishing his pitch to a group of disaffected fourteen-year-olds.

Parents

"The train stops somewhere in Brooklyn," Bernie Sanders wrote in 1969, in the *Vermont Freeman*.

> A crowd gets out, someone walks a few blocks into a 3 room apartment, family, dinner, arguments TV and sleep. Eight-thirty the next morning the train is back on 14th street.
>
> The years come and go, suicide, nervous breakdown, cancer, sexual deadness, heart attack, alcoholism, senility at 50. Slow, death, fast death. DEATH.

The piece was published under the headline "The Revolution Is Life Versus Death." It provides a quick montage of Bernie's childhood, inflected by his radical politics in their embryonic, late-1960s form, heavily influenced by his reading of Wilhelm Reich.

While Larry weeps when he shares his childhood stories, Bernie is mostly silent about those years. Larry told me that his brother sometimes accuses him of "minimizing" the degradations of the household. But Bernie's politics clearly began at his parents' breakfast table. Their scorching arguments showed him the emotional and psychological costs of being underpaid. If his hard work didn't pay Eli Sanders enough to support their family's modest needs, who *was* being paid for his father's labor? Where did the money go? Eli and Dorothy Sanders turned those frustrations against each other. "The money question to me has always been very deep and emotional," Bernie wrote in the *Freeman*. As Larry told me, it "ruined" the bond their parents had.

All through their childhoods, the Sanders boys carried the sense that the "bottom could fall out" of their household, as Larry put it. Dorothy and Eli Sanders saw their sons leave home; and then, almost instantly, the bottom did, in fact, fall out. The strain of raising their small family had weakened and sickened them both. Throughout the 1950s, Dorothy Sanders had treated her congenital heart condition with rest and whatever remedies the family could afford, all the while rooting for the rapid advances in open-heart surgery, widely reported in the papers, that would repair her mitral valve and save her life. But this costly, risky surgery would require more than a financial miracle for the hard-pressed Sanders household: Dorothy Sanders had a blood type of AB negative, the rarest variety. A typical open-heart procedure required at least twenty-five pints of fresh blood; banked blood loses oxygen in storage and could not be used.

"19 'Blue-Bloods' Aid Boro Woman Battle for Life," read the punning headline in the March 14, 1960, *Brooklyn Daily*. After her condition dramatically worsened, Dorothy Sanders was rushed to a charity facility, Deborah Hospital in New Jersey, where she awaited a blood donation from the National Rare Blood Club, a Park Avenue philanthropy. The procedure would stand her "in good stead in her efforts to regain her health," according to the paper. But on March 25, Dorothy Sanders succumbed to surgical complications at the age of forty-seven. Bernie, a freshman at Brooklyn College, had coordinated her care and sat by her hospital bed: he was now "destroyed" and "wanted to get away from Brooklyn," his brother said. The experience was Bernie's first with doctors and hospitals, and it left the lasting impression that whether a person lived or died in our medical system was a function, not of the severity of a patient's condition, but of her ability to pay. Of all the stark economic lessons Bernie learned in the family, the last days of his mother's life struck him most powerfully.

Now alone in a silent, darkened apartment, Bernie's father "completely fell apart" after his wife's death, and died just two years later under tragic and strange circumstances, behind the wheel of his car, evidently of a heart attack. From news reports at the time, it can be surmised that he had tried to drive himself from Midwood to the emergency room of New York–Presbyterian Hospital in Manhattan. Eli Sanders, just fifty-eight, was found slumped over his steering wheel, having crashed his car into a bank of construction barriers outside the hospital entrance.

THERE IS A CLIP that can be found online from Bernie's public access show in the 1980s. He's come to Cathedral Square, the mid-rise senior living facility in downtown Burlington where, as it happens, my uncle Esau lived out his final years. Though the apartments are for elderly people on fixed incomes, many have million-dollar views across Lake Champlain. A few times I went along with my mother to bring Uncle Esau a bag of McDonald's for his dinner. I remember baseball on Channel 11 from New York City, on Uncle Esau's dinky TV; and behind it, ravishing purples and oranges of the sunset as it broke apart on the peaks of the Adirondacks.

Bernie is at Cathedral Square to connect with the elderly. He describes a city plan to bring seniors relief from rising taxes, then checks in on whether progress has been made on wiring Cathedral Square for cable TV. The room, I can see, is full of immigrants and children of immigrants, including many likely displaced from Burlington's Little Italy, the thriving neighborhood razed by the city during the 1960s, and located on the very spot where Cathedral Square and the Episcopal Cathedral Church of St. Paul were later built.

The meeting is both funny and poignant. Sanders does not have a special personality reserved for the elderly. Sitting on the edge of a folding table, he spars with the old men and women, pushes back, cross-examines, shows a bit of exasperation and impatience. There is never a note of condescension.

"See, the beauty of the program is, it's called 'bulk billing,'" Sanders explains. Since you likely have heard Bernie's voice, you know how much of Midwood, Brooklyn, enters the room with a word like *beauty*.

A woman interrupts. By her accent I can tell she is from St. Joseph's Parish and grew up in Ward 3, the Old North End. She and Sanders are two working-class people from ostensibly different worlds. But they recognize each other. She begins: "It is my understanding from our meeting that they had to have a good number, not 100 percent, in order to get the low rate, otherwise we would have to pay the $10.50—"

"Nope!" Sanders interjects.

"—let's say like thirty people signed up—"

"Nope! Absolutely not! Is that what they told you?"

Grumbles, nods of assent all around; Bernie, sounding flabbergasted, makes a note, and promises to follow up. The woman seems unconvinced and irritated.

The year is 1987: if they'd lived, Eli Sanders would have been eighty-three, Dorothy Sanders, seventy-five.

2

Welcome to Vermont! (Part 2)

(Hill Towns, Mill Towns, Republicans, Democrats, 1954)

George Aiken at home in Dummerston, 1976.
Michael McDermott

"Farms for Sale"

Those autumn hillsides that enchanted two Brooklyn teenagers in the pages of a glossy tourist brochure were in crisis. "Vermont" bellowed its woodsmoke onto Sixth Avenue in the fall of 1954 to attract tourism and second-homeownership to a place that had made the conscious decision to fight to remain rural. With progress soon barreling toward it on an emerging network of new highways, Vermont wanted to stop time. Embedded in the new federal interstate infrastructure, barely an afternoon's drive from the hectic sidewalks of Manhattan, with a new, modern, international airport serving its very small biggest city, the state chose to pursue a paradox: how to market its isolation; how to make its timeless rural values available to busy twentieth-century Americans.

Vermont Farms and Summer Homes for Sale, the brochure Bernie and Larry took home, was the state's catalog of properties, published "annually on or about April First." The listing for "Old Rixford Orchard" in Franklin, Vermont, on the Quebec border, is typical:

> All equipment necessary to operate. Barn, shop with garage, old style cider mill, packing house, cottage, five rooms, originally log cabin, sheathed and shingled outside, plastered inside, good cellar. No plumbing, but comfortable. Unfailing spring of water on property. Buildings in fairly good repair. There may be 300 to 600 apple trees, 200 planted in 1932 beginning to bear, 265 in 1936 and 80 plum, pears, and cherries—all good varieties and need attention. Old Fameuse (Snow) orchard pretty well run out, trees mostly valuable for firewood . . . There is fairly good hunting all over Franklin County for partridge, woodcock, rabbit, fox and coon, etc. Property would make a pretty good home, furnishing occupation and some income.

The price to become an instant orchardist is $1,500. Interested parties are encouraged to write to the property's owner: Edmund Seymour, 11 Park Place, New York, NY.

By such transactions, Vermont sold off its landscape and history, even as it enforced conservation and preservation of its way of life. The state was in essence recruiting monied stewards for its fields and brooks. It was not merely selling property: it was encouraging city people to dream of a simple life in the country.

Back home, though, these catalogs were part of a fierce political battle over the future of Vermont—and about who could and could not be a Vermonter—that had been waged at least since the 1890s. To keep the state rural required a coordinated strategy involving marketing and publicity, incentives for conservation, and, eventually, legislation to halt development. This process, by which the orchards and cabins and sugarbushes of the state changed hands but did not change character, carried enormous consequences for natives and low-income residents of the V-shaped wedge smack in the middle of the most densely populated corridor in the country.

Nobody who loves the state would entirely begrudge its choice to cultivate itself as a permanently rural place, almost whatever the costs. But in Vermont's efforts to appeal to the fantasies of urban people, many ordinary Vermonters lost out. As its manufacturing base died and tourism replaced it, Vermont marketed the image of a Yankee population unchanged by immigration and the modern economy. The Indigenous Abenaki of the Winooski River Valley were displaced and written out of Vermont's history; Black Vermonters were tokenized and harassed. French-Canadian immigrants were marginalized as rednecks and hillbillies. This last population includes members of my own family—who, as it happens, had settled on poor farms just south of the Quebec border and worked as seasonal pickers in the fields near Franklin, Vermont, perhaps even in the orchards of Mr. Seymour of Park Place.

TO UNDERSTAND WHY the hill farms failed, we must first count sheep. Merino sheep—a variety developed in Spain and Portugal and known for its super-soft wool—were brought to America by a Vermonter named William Jarvis, who happened to be the U.S. consul to Portugal in the early nineteenth century. Napoleon had invaded Spain in 1808; according to the Vermont Historical Society, "Rather than allow Napoleon to squander the Merino flocks, the Spanish lifted the blockade on exporting Merinos." William Jarvis was in the right position to move merino flocks to Vermont.

Vermont's sheep trade boomed. Farms were expanded and improved; the state's big red barns, cathedrals of its built vernacular, sprang up. Then there was a bust: demand changed; tariffs ebbed; industrial manufacturing came into the picture. Sheep farms recovered and expanded during the Civil War, chasing the demand for wool uniforms and field blankets. With the war's end, the barns emptied again. Hill farms, which were ideal for sheep, were bad for just about everything else. The soil was too rocky to cultivate crops, the vegetation often insufficient for grazing cattle: the sheep had munched the land bare. Vermont's hill farms then became sites of poverty, hunger, and disease. Many of the young men who came off the farm to enlist in the First World War were turned down for malnourishment. My great-grandfather, who served in the Great War and was injured in France, once described to me the lines of "ghostly" prospective soldiers—gaunt, baffled, hill farmers—lining up to enlist at Fort Ethan Allen, outside of Burlington.

You can still see abandoned farms from the Vermont interstates. In the late 1990s, I wrote a poem called "Boston" about driving south from Burlington to "the nearest famous city": those beautiful shambles reminded me of "rabbit warren and collapsing domino." By 1900 or so, many farms had been left for dead, mills crumbled into the rivers, fields began to fill in with forest, and stone walls were overtaken by bramble.

The state's scheme to market the old farms to city folk worked. In waves, beginning in the late nineteenth century, Vermont saw its hill villages periodically repopulated by wealthy part-time residents, their taxes filling up the town clerk's coffee cans. A few monied households per village was all it took to bring the desolate parts of the state to life.

Certain changes were immediately made to suit the newcomers. The process of electrification began to light up farmhouse windows in lonely, remote hollows. State highways were rolled out. Secondary town roads were paved, to speed the Friday arrivals and Sunday departures of these new part-time Vermont residents. With the development of the ski industry in the 1930s and '40s, the summer people began to modernize their farms, and Vermont enjoyed a year-round influx of money—and, with it, a new class structure, which reserved a place at the top for the skier from Boston or New York, and a place at the bottom for the Vermonter now plowing the newcomers' driveways or pressing their sheets.

These newly fledged Vermonters, known to all as "flatlanders," were mostly eager to freeze the rural, premodern idyll that drew them to the state. The new orchardists, maple sugarers, llama farmers, and beekeepers began to assert political and economic power to maintain the state as they had fallen for it at first sight. They were often the most zealous traditionalists: their trusts were handled by bankers on State Street or Wall Street, while they trellised the clematis and sugared their trees. In Underhill, Vermont, where my grandmother was raised, there was for generations a family of rich New Yorkers who farmed by horse and plow, even as VWs buzzed by in the summer dusk.

IT IS NO small irony that hill farms marketed to well-heeled city people piqued the interest of a thirteen-year-old Brooklyn Jew and future socialist who would arguably do more to impact Vermont's traditional culture than anyone in the state's history.

The tourist council's fairy-tale Vermont was "timeless": that is, white and Christian. The primeval farmer bent over a milk pail, so familiar from the state's promotional materials, was an Anglo-Saxon icon—"the last of his breed," as *Vermont Life*, the state's quarterly tourist magazine, put it. The landscape he tended hearkened back to an America unaffected by large-scale immigration and industrialization. The messaging was not subtle: into the twentieth century, Vermont inns and resorts stipulated "No Semites" in their advertisements. Black Vermonters were not featured in the pages of *Vermont Life*.

Tourism and summer homeownership became the commercial edge—

the export, if you will—of a state that, despite its apparently wild beauty, had been centrally planned. In 1931, the Vermont Commission on Rural Life published *Rural Vermont: A Program for the Future*, authored by "Two Hundred Vermonters." One of the two hundred was Dorothy Canfield Fisher, the Montessori advocate, novelist, and social reformer, whose book *Vermont Summer Homes*, published in 1937 by the state's tourism council, was part of the same impetus that put farm brochures into Larry and Bernie Sanders's hands.

Rural Vermont was the state's master narrative. It includes sections on Vermont's climate and agriculture, its forests, wildflowers, bugs, and fish, all to be prized and conserved. Among entries on Vermont's cherished flora and fauna, its steeples and stone walls, we meet its summer residents in their habitat:

> Summer homes in Vermont have been established by a very desirable class of summer residents. These people take a real interest in the communities in which they are located. They help the churches, they take an interest in schools and libraries and all community enterprises. Many of these visitors are teachers in schools and colleges, clergymen, lawyers, artists, authors, and other persons who are a distinct asset to any community.

These "Two Hundred Vermonters" had a problem, though: What about the actual, existing Vermonters, currently in the buildings slated for summer guests, the men and women living hand to mouth in those picturesque heaps at the ends of rutted dirt roads?

Vermont had a solution for them, too. *Rural Vermont* is a eugenics study, part of the widespread culture of eugenics in the first decades of the twentieth century. It recommends practical steps to strengthen the state's Anglo-Saxon stock. It speaks of the deterioration of Yankee blood and the problem of towns being overtaken by immigrants who were "failures elsewhere." It recommends that families of "the good old Vermont stock" have more children; it allows for the removal of the indigent and "feeble minded" to asylums.

The shaping force behind *Rural Vermont* was a native Burlingtonian who grew up a block or so from my own childhood home at the rear of the University of Vermont. Henry Perkins went on to be a professor of zoology at UVM, but his passion was eugenics.

In 1925, Perkins instructed one of his field researchers, Harriett Abbott, to "locate, first, the inadequates in the state" and "second, to find out, if possible, why they exist":

> A preliminary classification could well be made on the following basis: Race descent of the four grandparents (or any other good reference that will give racial position); the place or habitat of the individual inadequate; the sort of land he lives on; the sort of communities in which he resides; how he takes part in social community activities; his occupation, his schooling and training, his pedigree or family history. This latter, of course, is very important from the eugenics point of view.

For some of these "inadequates," forced sterilization was recommended. The state of Vermont passed its sterilization law in 1931. It targeted those "outside the accepted moral or social convention of middle-class America," according to Hope Greenberg and Nancy Gallagher. The main groups affected were "the poor, the disabled, French-Canadians, and Native Americans . . . Women were targeted more than men. French-Canadians and Abenakis were seen as a foe and threat to the early colonial settlers of Vermont. These initiatives broke up large French Canadian families, and devastated the Abenaki people."

Growing up in the 1970s on a steep bank that rose from the Winooski River, kids in my neighborhood were warned by the old people about "gypsies" in the wooded ravine behind our houses. Their presence had become, by that point, almost mythic; if they existed at all, I figured they were just hippies, camping on the land.

But in "From Degeneration to Regeneration: The Eugenics Survey of Vermont, 1925–1936," Kevin Dann describes a 1925 address by Professor Perkins. Perkins knew our ravine well, having lived his whole life nearby. His speech, which is satanic, identifies three especially dangerous sorts of Vermont groups: a "pirate" family, whose ranks stole to survive; a "chorea" family, afflicted by a "dreadful form of insanity"; and "the gypsies," who lived around Burlington and counted "seventy-eight paupers" in their ranks.

Who were these "gypsies" slated for sterilization by Perkins? According to the Abenaki scholar Frederick M. Wiseman, they were, in fact, Indigenous people, a community of Abenaki who had lived on the banks of the Winooski River for generations, long before European settlement. My family and I were squatters on their land.

Hills, Mills, Republicans, Democrats

In 1954, the year the Sanders brothers picked up their farm brochures, the old New England saw "You can't get there from here" was in many respects an accurate statement. Well into the 1930s, Vermont counted just twenty or so miles of paved roads. The bedrock was still whole and unblasted where the interstates would eventually run. Retreating glaciers tens of thousands of years before left a crumpled, impassable geography, where towns a few miles apart on a map might be hours apart by car, if they happened to fall on opposite slopes of the same peak. When the interstate highway system came to Vermont in the late 1950s, rural Vermont took even more aggressive steps to protect itself, while Burlington and Chittenden County, the designated urban corridor of the state, absorbed more cars, more development, more federal funds, and faster population growth than it could withstand. Two distinct political cultures emerged: In the hills, you met Republicans. In the valleys, Democrats.

But the state as a whole understood itself in the image of the hill farmer. From the founding of the Republican Party in 1854 until 1958, Vermont elected only Republicans to its state and federal offices. Though "the GOP tent covered almost all shades of the political spectrum," according to the historian Samuel B. Hand, "more Vermonters with progressive leanings found comfort there than with Democrats." The national Republican Party was in turn, in a small way, moderated by the Vermont model of progressivism, thrift, and orneriness. The image of the self-sufficient Yankee Vermonter became part of the iconography of the party in the decades before the rise of Richard Nixon and Ronald Reagan. The Big Business Republicans in Vermont—the quarry owners in Barre and Proctor, the insurance men in Burlington and Rutland—could not sustain such a lasting influence. The "Vermont Republican," distinct even from other moderate New England strains, held a special place in the party and in the nation. Senator George Aiken's tart counsel during the early days of the Vietnam War gives its essential flavor: "Say we won," Aiken advised, "and get out."

Downstream, though, in the valley towns where the woolen mills were built, waves of immigrants came to work for low pay, in brutal circumstances, at ages as young as twelve. They were Irish, Quebecois, Italian, Syrian, and Armenian. The largest mills in the state rose up in Winooski, across the river from Burlington. I owe my existence to those mills. One set of my great-grandparents, Wilfred and Laura Delorme, French Canadians who had grown up on poor farms in the countryside, met there as young teenagers, working at the looms of the Champlain Mill in 1915. In places like the Winooski mills and the Barre granite quarries, a second political culture developed. Vermont's labor history passes from the mill floor to the socialist rec hall to the union, and, eventually, to the Democratic Party, where in turn most of the radical populist energies of its headwaters were siphoned off by corrupt and inefficient political machines. Vermont was Democratic exclusively in its cities, which are scarce and, except for Burlington, small. Only after 1962, two years before Bernie Sanders arrived in the state, did

Democrats begin to make any real headway in Vermont politics, and then only fitfully.

When, in the late 1970s, Howard Dean "moved to Vermont with an idea about having a better life, a more rural life," his natural home, he told me, was the Democratic Party, but in Vermont "the Democratic Party was still probably more conservative, in many respects, than the Republicans." Dean took the slow road, transforming the party from within. But Sanders, by rising on the left outside the Democratic Party, as Dean told me, "created his own path. It would have been, almost anywhere else, a path through Democratic politics." Within the Vermont Democratic Party, the culture clash between people like Howard Dean and old-guard conservative Democrats "took years to resolve," and while it took its time, Bernie built a bridge to progressive Republicans, who, as the national party canted hard right, were soon without a home.

The Rise of George Aiken

If you asked a person now to free-associate on the words *independent* and *Vermont*, they might blurt out the name "Bernie Sanders." But Bernie's "independence" finds a strong antecedent in Vermont's most beloved politician of the twentieth century, a wildflower expert and berry entrepreneur named George Aiken. "Governor" Aiken, as he was called even after more than three decades as a U.S. senator, embodied political independence at home, while in the country at large, Aiken symbolized Vermont's own difference from Washington politics. The support of the hill towns, where the sheep farms had thrived and then died, helped Aiken, the antediluvian Yankee, rise quickly to become Vermont's governor in 1936 and then, beginning in 1941, U.S. senator for thirty-three years, succeeded in 1974 by Patrick Leahy.

Farmers in the Vermont hill towns in the 1930s had plenty of reasons for worry. The eugenics surveyors made fine-grained distinctions between charming country life and immoral squalor. According to Kevin Dann, these polite ladies with clipboards had a "tendency to romanticize rural living" even while rooting out suspected "degeneracy": "Traditional rural occupations such as spruce gum collecting, ferning, berrying, trapping, fishing, and hunting were rendered either romantically or gothically, depending on other aspects of a family's domestic life and 'moral character.'"

The farmer who pickled was singled out for praise; but if he distilled alcohol or hung pelts in the kitchen, the state might sterilize him, or forbid him from marrying, or take away his children. If the young man chopping wood a little slowly was labeled "defective," he might be taken away to

Waterbury, to the state hospital. The category "defective" included "epileptics," people with "harelips," those deemed "queer," "just not right," wild, or "wanderers." In Vermont's Northeast Kingdom, where I spend time in the summer, people still recall families who were broken up by the state, their loved ones taken away "to Waterbury."

If you managed to escape the surveyors, the developers might still find you. Hill farmers in the early 1930s learned from their neighbors of a plan to run a "scenic" automotive skyway for tourists through their land, paying pennies on the dollar. The "Green Mountain Parkway," supported by a confluence of state, federal, and business interests, was to track along the spine of the Green Mountains, riding the ridges and summits like a roller coaster. In 1936, the highway went to a vote on Town Meeting Day and lost in a landslide. Ordinary Vermonters had risen up to keep their mountains pristine.

But the threat of federal control only intensified. In the mid-'30s, land surveyors and inspectors from Washington began to stream into Vermont villages, knocking on the doors of remote farmhouses far from the village greens. These federal agents, working for various departments of FDR's New Deal, had come to condemn entire villages as "submarginal," forcing the hill families to trade their farms for life in a conventional, modern ranch home or efficiency apartment with access to the main roads. According to Sara M. Gregg, in the early '30s more than 35 percent of the state of Vermont was deemed essentially uninhabitable, despite people's having lived for generations in those "submarginal" towns. Under the federal "Farms to Forests" initiative, more than a third of the state would have been sold to the U.S. government. The meadows, slowly filling in with dark, dense forest, would be administered as a national park. These schemes, the brainchild of Washington politicians, hardened Vermont's Republicanism and deepened its distrust of Washington Democrats. In the 1936 presidential election, a referendum on FDR's New Deal, Vermont voted for Alf Landon over Roosevelt in a landslide, joined only by its Yankee cousin, Maine.

The cause of the besieged Yankee hill farmer had always served as proxy for another cause: the unique landscape of rural Vermont, its patchworks of fields and meadows, silos, barns, and white fences. To rally behind the farmer was to save the farms, but often for the delight of tourists. George Aiken reinscribed the right to private property onto this landscape once contemplated for public seizure. "Self-determination"—the right to own your land—became, in many instances, the right to sell it to an out-of-stater. The eighty-five acres that Bernie Sanders purchased in 1964 in Middlesex might not have been for sale were it not for the rise of George Aiken of Dummerston, near Putney, in the southern part of the state. In this mythical Vermont, Norman Rockwell painted his image of a gallant young farmer rising to speak at a town meeting. In the contest between white spires and dark forests, Vermont, and George Aiken, picked a clear favorite.

IN A 1973 INTERVIEW with *Vermont Life*, celebrating his imminent retirement from the Senate, Aiken described growing up on his parents' farm, attending a "little red schoolhouse," traveling four miles each way to school, and tending "the largest tree in Vermont and maybe the largest in New England," a 550-year-old maple that was "seven feet in diameter." The young man interviewing him laps it up—and goads him on.

"How did you get to school?" he asks.

"Walked," Aiken replies.

"Through the snow?"

Through the snow, yes, of course: "Up to your knees."

The interview tells the story of how that barefoot boy became a canny modern entrepreneur. Aiken moved much of his burgeoning berry and perennial business next to the Putney train depot, where he could box and ship his fruit and plants all over New England. Soon he'd developed a catalog mail order business with a slogan known around the Northeast: "It's from Vermont. It's Hardy!" Aiken even went from town to town with a magic lantern, projecting slides of his abundant shrubs. And he shipped his Christmas wreaths, the fullest and most fragrant in the industry, to the street corner markets of New York City and Boston, and along with them the clean smell of pine and juniper from the northern woods.

When he sold his berries and daisies and wreaths, Aiken was selling Vermont itself. "Hardy" in strict botanical terms means a plant can tolerate the winter—much like the state's proud and virtuous rural people. Much like you, the consumer with the good sense to pick a Vermont product. Later Vermont brands, like Ben & Jerry's, have sold an updated, transformed Vermont: tie-dyes, jam bands. Bernie's own political brand, partaking of the entire range of associations with the state, became Vermont's most important export.

In 1938, during his only term as governor, Aiken figured out another Vermont product he could sell: he published a best-selling book, *Speaking from Vermont*, its green covers stamped with the state seal. Aiken's volume, written in shrewd, angular prose, tells the story of how Vermonters beat back the Mephistophelean federal government and took back their state when cranky farmers faced down the "attorneys, theorists, scientists, doctors of all degrees." Aiken extends his rhapsody with a celebration of the Vermont hills and their denizens: the old-timers and, yes, the newcomers, seeking the "acquaintance of a litter of young foxes—all ears and feet" and the "acrid taste of jack-in-the-pulpit bulbs." And he concludes: "There is no place on earth so satisfying, so peaceful, so delightful as the thousands of old farms that the Washington specialists choose to call submarginal." This primordial Yankee was at his heart a canny progressive. "When you can't stop it, you've got to guide it," Aiken told his young interviewer.

THE FREELANCE JOURNALIST sent by *Vermont Life* to interview George Aiken on the eve of his retirement had already made his name as a fringe candidate in two statewide elections. But hippies and peaceniks did not appear in the pages of *Vermont Life*, so its readers were unlikely to have heard of the writer, Bernard Sanders.

The interview is significant—Vermont's version of the famous photo showing a young Bill Clinton shaking President John F. Kennedy's hand. Sanders knew he intended to wage a quixotic campaign for Aiken's open seat in 1974. A young attorney from Chittenden County, Patrick Leahy, won that election. Leahy was the first Democrat Vermont had sent to Washington since 1856. He served until 2022.

I spoke with Stephen Terry, a longtime Vermont journalist and political aide, who joined Aiken's staff straight out of UVM in 1969. By 1972 or so, Terry told me, Aiken and his team had their eye on Bernie: "He was very unusual. He used to hitchhike to debates." Terry coordinated the *Vermont Life* interview in early 1972, and, at Aiken's request, took Sanders to lunch at the "very ornate" Senate dining room. Bernie was "quintessentially Bernie," Terry said. Around the disheveled Sanders, the Senate's lions, among them William Fulbright and Fritz Hollings, feasted on the dining room's famous bean soup.

Aiken was "intrigued," Terry said, to meet "a young radical who was interested in Vermont." And though he saw Bernie's success as "unlikely," according to Terry, by the end of the interview, Aiken seemed almost to be dangling before Sanders the keys to his legacy. Sanders asked the Yankee icon, "What does the philosophy of self-reliance mean to you?" Aiken's answer was remarkable: "Well, I don't think I'm the one to point that out. As I say right now, I'm concerned with the widening spread between the haves and the have nots." He reiterated for effect: "The spread is widening." And to address this crisis, Aiken told his young admirer, "Vermont must change."

3

"Politics Helped"

(Brooklyn College and the University of Chicago, 1959–64)

The mystery man at the CORE sit-in, 1962. *Danny Lyon*

Mistaken Identity

The standing figure at the sit-in for racial justice is dressed in a dark wool boatneck sweater, black dress pants, and round thick-framed glasses. He looks "collegiate," hip, spruce, like he's just back from a Dave Brubeck show. The student activists splayed around his feet are also clean-cut and respectfully dressed. They learned as children how to sit on the floor; some of these kids appear to have brought their homework along.

You can't extrapolate the exact year, but you can get close. The 1960s as we picture them have not yet hatched, but cracks show here and there. These young people, most of them white and prosperous looking, are punctual: they are among the first in line for the revolution. But they've arrived ahead of their style. The corduroy sleeves, the girls' neat buns, the turtlenecks and paperbacks, all suggest a preface. A few years later, young people who look like werewolves and Arthurian damsels will populate these sit-ins, but here, crisscross applesauce is still the rule of the day.

The image was taken in early February of 1962, by Danny Lyon, then a student photographer for the campus paper, *The Chicago Maroon*. The protest against the university's policy of allowing some of its off-campus buildings to segregate by race had ground on for nearly two weeks. Every morning, the university chancellor, a genial Nobel laureate named George Beadle, would tiptoe like a pelican around the protestors, then disappear into his office trailed by scurrying aides.

Lyon's cameras were set up in a corner of the occupied vestibule, but he had set his sights on the horizon. "I remember thinking," he told me, "that this is not the real deal. The real action is in the South." In the summer of 1962, seeking something "dramatic and photographable," Lyon hitchhiked to Cairo, Illinois, 350 miles south of Chicago. Cairo is the town where Huck Finn and Jim were headed to board a steamer to the free state of Ohio, before they hit a fogbank and landed deep in slave territory.

In Cairo, Lyon heard John Lewis speak, then marched alongside Lewis to a segregated swimming pool. The two men became roommates and close friends. Soon after, Lyon took a bus to Atlanta and then to Albany, Georgia, where he was arrested at a sit-in in a pharmacy. Through his cell bars he could see Martin Luther King Jr. in the Black section of the jail, writing his "Albany diary." Lyon went on to capture many of the iconic images of the civil rights movement: King and Ralph Abernathy being released from the Montgomery jail; Bob Dylan and his guitar in a cotton field in Greenwood, Mississippi; the shattered windows of the 16th Street Baptist Church in Birmingham.

I was warned that Danny Lyon was impossible to reach, but he returned my call one morning from a freshwater dock in Maine, where he now spends part of the summer. Swallows twittered in the background as he told me the story of the photo.

Lyon had long since forgotten about the sit-in shoot, which he took to earn a few bucks so he could make his way south to record history. Decades later, history, traveling along another branch, caught up to him. Around 1986, at his home on a farm in the Hudson Valley, Lyon encountered his photo in a newspaper article about a political novelty named Bernie Sanders, the socialist mayor of wacky Burlington, Vermont. "Nancy, I think I took this photo!" Lyon exclaimed to his wife. Lyon remembered Bernie only vaguely, but he liked what he read about his politics, and figured maybe he'd get in touch with him someday. In the meantime, he noted, with irritation, that he had not been credited for the image.

Then another thirty years or so passed, and Danny Lyon again encountered his photo, incorrectly credited ("Grrrr!"), but this time on the internet—and at the center of a controversy. Sanders was running for president, and had begun to outperform expectations in a cycle when Hillary Clinton seemed a lock for the 2016 Democratic nomination. Clinton's campaign felt the winds shift. Her people got down to work.

"This is the below-the-belt stuff," Lyon warned me, with a chuckle. "Did you say you work at Wellesley? Isn't that Hillary's school?"

I confirmed.

"Oh, man. You're going to lose your job!" Lyon laughed so boisterously that I worried he'd fall off his dock.

Danny then told the story of how, in the fall of 2015, an article in *Time* appeared, citing four University of Chicago alumni who claimed that his Bernie photo showed not Sanders but Bruce Rappaport, a fellow activist and student. ("I can tell by the curvature of his spine," one classmate stated.) The University of Chicago's library confirmed that it had changed the caption to correct the perceived error. So Lyon, along with his wife and his dog, scoured his New Mexico darkroom and found negatives and contact sheets that showed several consecutive images of Sanders at the sit-in, seconds apart, many of them full-faced. The standing figure was clearly Bernie.

"This," Lyon told me, "was when I knew I had a hot item."

But the controversy was kept at a low simmer by Clinton's people, until, two days after Sanders won the New Hampshire primary by more than twenty-two percentage points, on February 11, they cranked up the heat. Jonathan Capehart, a *Washington Post* columnist, published an op-ed: "Stop Sending Around This Photo of 'Bernie Sanders,'" its headline demanded. Rappaport's widow was interviewed: she could "tell by his neck," she said, that it was her husband. CNN and MSNBC got hold of the story. John Lewis, Danny Lyon's old friend, announced that he'd "never seen" Sanders during the civil rights struggle.

Danny Lyon then became a somewhat bemused witness to Bernie's civil rights bona fides. Working behind the scenes with the Sanders campaign, he published the evidence on his slumbering blog, which immediately bolted awake with heavy traffic. Arrayed against him was the entire Clinton campaign, including Lewis, and a significant portion of the Clinton-friendly media. Capehart called him at home to cross-examine him; Chris Matthews decried him by name on *Hardball*. Their necessary retractions were eventually made, though late and equivocal. But Danny Lyon had again intervened in the story of the American civil rights era—this time, more than fifty years after the fact.

BEFORE WE HUNG UP, Danny remembered a story. At the start of his 2020 campaign, Bernie asked Lyon to introduce him at a rally in Chicago. Backstage, Sanders teased him: "Can you really make money taking pictures?" ("How Brooklyn was that!" Lyon exclaimed, from his dock in Maine.)

On the way out to the podium, Lyon noted several young people snapping his picture. "The guy from Ben & Jerry's was there, too—what's his name?"

"Ben Cohen," I replied. Cohen and Jerry Greenfield were mixed up in the popular imagination, and my own, with Bernie. All were New York Jews who'd come to Vermont to make their names, while keeping their identities.

"Right! So me, Ben from Ben & Jerry's, and Bernie, all these three Jewish guys, all the same age, all partly bald!"

Lyon told me he turned to Cohen and asked, "Why are they taking pictures of me?"

"It's because they think you're Bernie," Cohen replied.

"Politics Helped"

Once we've determined that the figure in Danny Lyon's 1962 photo was Bernie Sanders, an inevitable question follows: Who was Bernie Sanders?

Jim Rader has known Sanders since Bernie was nineteen and a new transfer student at the University of Chicago. The man that Bernie Sanders calls his "oldest friend" is also his temperamental opposite. Rader was born in 1939 and grew up in a devout Seventh-Day Adventist family, on a farm in the tiny town of Elnora, Indiana. He seems always to have been drawn to high-spirited men. While a student at Wabash College, Rader corresponded with Ezra Pound, who had taught at Wabash for five months in 1907–08, before the young poet was dismissed for cutting chapel and entertaining girls. "Events at Wabash much yes MUCH funnier than any printed version I have seen," Pound wrote, addressing Jim as "RADER." The reclusive poet invited the young man to his castle in Merano, Italy. (Jim declined, but visited Pound's daughter there decades after Pound's death.) An inveterate tinkerer, Rader has invented and patented a three-dimensional word game called Quipto®, and published several volumes of these little verbal thingamajigs. The title of the first book struck me as a motto Rader might have developed while dealing with Bernie all these years: "Never Play Leapfrog With a Unicorn."

Jim moves at a brisk lope and speaks with a Hoosier twang. You could picture him leaning on a shovel. We met the first afternoon for hours on his sunny patio in Burlington, a stone's throw from Lake Champlain. Eventually, Jim and I were joined by his wife, Meg Pond, as well as Meg's daughter and my old friend Emer Pond Feeney, with her husband, Jason, for a memorable dinner of halibut and fresh-picked asparagus. Now in his mid-eighties, Jim has the easygoing vibe of a much younger man. He is one of those types of people George Oppen had in mind when he remarked about growing old, "What a strange thing to happen to a little boy."

There was no flashing sign above Bernie's head indicating that he would someday become a transformative figure. But to Jim Rader, he stood out. Sanders and Rader met on a Friday night in January of 1961, during Bernie's first year at the University of Chicago. Jim and his wife at the time, Diana Maher, were the resident directors of the American Friends Service Committee's Project House in Garfield Park. Their job was to keep the furnace lit and to host weekend workshops for social and racial justice. The couple was just out of college, with a three-month-old baby. Jim and Diana had calibrated their politics to stop short of certain actions like getting arrested, but their living room became an important hub in what Jim calls Chicago's "political ferment."

Rader remembers Bernie stepping away on that January night from the brood of radicals and taking an intensely human interest in Jim and Diana's new baby, Karla, holding her and "interacting with her in a way that was very unusual for a college student." This tender observation is among the very earliest things Jim told me. Sanders had made quite a first impression. Who was this unusual young man?

Sanders had come to Chicago the previous fall as a transfer from Brooklyn College, just a few blocks from his home in Midwood. He "didn't talk much at all about his family," but he did tell his new friends about his political formation. At Brooklyn College, Bernie was surprised to meet "real live socialists, sitting in front of me," members of the Eugene V. Debs Club, manning an orientation table at the freshman activities fair. Socialism was "quite normal" after all, at a college nicknamed "the Little Red Schoolhouse." The text on the student socialists' minds was Albert Einstein's essay "Why Socialism?" first published in 1949. By the early '60s, Einstein's article had lost some of its radical luster and, distributed as a pamphlet, was now a staple of political science classrooms and campus debate nights, where it was often set up as a straw man in defenses of capitalism and the American way.

But the article had nevertheless "deeply impressed" Sanders, as he later told Rader. "Private capital," Einstein wrote, "tends to become concentrated in few hands, partly because of competition among the capitalists, and partly because technological development and the increasing division of labor encourage the formation of larger units of production at the expense of smaller ones":

> The result of these developments is an oligarchy of private capital the enormous power of which cannot be effectively checked even by a democratically organized political society. This is true since the members of legislative bodies are selected by political parties, largely financed or otherwise influenced by private capitalists who, for all practical purposes, separate the electorate from the legislature. The consequence is that the representatives of the people do not in fact sufficiently protect the interests of the underprivileged sections of the population. Moreover, under existing conditions, private capitalists inevitably control, directly or indirectly, the main sources of information (press, radio, education). It is thus extremely difficult, and indeed in most cases quite impossible, for the individual citizen to come to objective conclusions and to make intelligent use of his political rights.

Einstein's case for socialism, grounded in scientific observation and expressed with calm precision, played an important role in mainstreaming, but also defanging, the radical ideas of Karl Marx and the American social scientist Thorstein Veblen. The essay's trenchant critique, propagated by perhaps the most admired man in the world, inspired mainly even-tempered, high-minded discussion.

Sanders "always had a rebellious streak," he said, but he appears to have held it in check; until he arrived at the University of Chicago, it still "hadn't manifested in political activity." On one of his first nights at Chicago, his eyes were opened. As a high school student, Sanders had been deeply inspired by the rise of Fidel Castro in Cuba: it impressed him to witness "poor people very naturally rising up against very ugly rich people." In September of 1960, Sanders and some new friends tuned in from a student lounge to the first-ever televised presidential debate, matching John F. Kennedy against Richard Nixon. The urgent issue was what to do about Soviet incursions into Cuba. Bernie's classmates, mostly fellow Jews from New Deal Democratic households, had lined up behind Kennedy, "the flashy young liberal," who that night played the anti-Fidel hawk, while Nixon, the staid conservative, affected the role of the cautious dove. Bernie "almost got out of the room to go puke" when he realized that both sides "basically agreed" that Castro's revolution should be quickly overturned and a government friendly to U.S. interests efficiently installed. Nixon, as vice president under Dwight Eisenhower, had planned the Bay of Pigs blockade of Castro's Cuba—which Kennedy, his rival, eagerly looked forward to executing once he took power. This sickening dance meant "there was no difference between the two candidates" or between their respective parties. The debate was a coordinated lie.

Friends recall, though, that Sanders targeted his indignation not at Nixon, who seemed distasteful but at least not hypocritical, but instead at Kennedy, whose "liberalism" struck Sanders as a nauseating deception. The color photos that soon made the rounds of Kennedy soaking up the good life in Hyannisport, yachting, cocktailing, carousing—the very images that mythologized the Kennedy family in Americans' eyes—seemed to Sanders a judgment on ordinary people's lives. His thoughts went immediately to the tenement in Brooklyn where his father grieved in darkness for his mother, to the hospital bed where Bernie had spent much of the previous year by her side, and to the humiliations that Dorothy Sanders had suffered as she sought medical care. To Bernie, Nixon and Kennedy were interchangeable, but for one detail: Kennedy claimed to be a man of the people from the deck of a gaff-rigged sloop. "It takes a lot of money to be a liberal," Sanders remarked of a Democratic opponent, thinking back, years later, to the "Camelot" years of the Kennedy White House.

"AS USUAL, TOTALLY BROKE," subsisting on loans and odd jobs, Bernie settled into an apartment far from the University's mazelike limestone campus in Hyde Park, where he roomed with an old elementary school friend from Brooklyn, Ira Churgin. Churgin flipped a coin one night, and Bernie, "always fair," as Churgin told me, accepted the result without protest: he took the smaller of two bedrooms. The messy, long commute to class—"buses and galoshes," according to a friend—demoralized Sanders, who began almost the moment he arrived to consider dropping out.

"We were nobodies," Churgin said, "completely invisible": Sanders had no inherited status, no social or cultural networks, and no safety net. And unlike his classmates at Brooklyn College, Chicago's radicals tended to be "red diaper babies," generational leftists, the children of artists and activists who had a snobbery all their own. Class differences do not disappear in countercultural communities, as Bernie, the perennial outsider, would again learn when he moved to rural Vermont. In a scene often supported by individuals with family wealth and property, Sanders bucked against the unspoken and daunting social codes. Even years after his political rise, Bernie was quick to detect class privilege on the left, and sensitive about being viewed as uncouth.

Sanders was often lonely—and, as he put it, "politics helped." After joining the cross-country team, he sought out all the important campus activist groups: the Young People's Socialist League (YPSL), the Student Peace Union (SPU), and finally the Congress of Racial Equality (CORE), then in the pitch of an important fight. In the fall of 1961, tipped off by campus reporters to the presence of segregation in several university-owned off-campus buildings, CORE had run six test cases. A Black couple would inquire about vacancies and be sent away. A white couple would then approach the same landlord and be shown an open apartment. The findings were leaked to the *Maroon* and presented to President Beadle, who responded by arguing for a policy of "managed integration" in Hyde Park. Beadle asked for patience; CORE mobilized the sit-in; and two weeks later, the university folded, agreeing to bring the community together to discuss "how to end discrimination in university-owned real estate."

The 1962 sit-in was a breakthrough for Sanders; in another of Lyon's photographs, Sanders, victorious, shares the lectern with Beadle. He had quickly risen from the anonymity of his small, off-campus bedroom to become one of the university's leading student activists. Soon he played an instrumental role in uniting the CORE memberships of the college and the city of Chicago at large: in February of 1962, Sanders helped to lead the local protest against Howard Johnson's, which operated segregated restaurants in the South. By May of 1962, recently elected as CORE's chairman, Bernie was negotiating directly with the administration.

The lessons of that negotiation radicalized him. "What I remember most profoundly," Sanders said, was that Beadle, "very distinguished, a Nobel Prize winner," had "lied, cold, right to our face. It was a major, important moment in my life. All these wonderful, important people had lied."

The university never held any community meetings; it had agreed to them cynically to clear the president's foyer of protestors, then gone back to normal business. A skirmish ensued between Sanders and Dean Warner Wick in the pages of the student paper. Wick scolded Sanders for accusing "one of the parties" in the dispute of "dishonesty." Since CORE was opposed in principle to a policy of "managed integration" (that is, continued segregation), there was "no point in further discussion of that question." And then, a sentence that infuriated Sanders: "The University must make its own decisions on specific cases and cannot be accountable to any external body."

From the power structure of a university, Sanders extrapolated the organization of American society at large. Unconscionable decisions are made, in ordinary students' names, by unseen actors behind a secret switchboard. Even to meet with the board of trustees for any activist student, then or now, is all but impossible, and those students with direct access to the trustees are also usually signed into nondisclosure agreements. What a nefarious-seeming body a university is, with its most important decisions made in secret, by individuals whose power is derived from money and influence rather than an intimate concern for or exposure to its community. If you're weaned on this kind of fight, as Bernie was, you're prepared to see vested and veiled power as the source problem in American society, with all the other problems, even intractable ones like racism and sexism, flowing from that spring.

The University of Chicago's reputation is sometimes hard to square: in the American imagination, Chicago is a hotbed of student activism *and* a brutally concentrated corporate power. But in Sanders's evolving worldview, the first nearly always implies, and serves, the second. At the University of Chicago, Bernie noted, people could be as radical as they wanted, unless they expected institutional change. Sanders learned to be suspicious of protest as mere mass catharsis or performance. A deeper analysis of social and political structures was taking shape.

IN THE FIGHT against Beadle and his lieutenants, Sanders also discovered the distinctive pitch of his written voice. "Whose University Is It?" Sanders asked in an editorial on December 4, 1962. The column appears to have been written first as an essay for a class and then printed without adjustment. "The theme of this paper is a simple one," Sanders begins. "It is that the faculty and student body of the University of Chicago are the University of Chicago." A modern university is a bleak model society, in Sanders's account, since the actual students and faculty are given merely the illusion of agency, while shrouded behind the curtain of power and money exists "that august body, the Board of Trustees."

The essay is crude, but it has presence. In fact, a twenty-first-century reader of "Whose University Is It?" might easily guess its author. "What the dean *neglected to mention*," Sanders writes (the emphasis is mine), "is much more interesting and important than what he did say." These kinds of rhetorical flourishes have accompanied Bernie on the presidential debate stage, on the Senate floor, and on the Sunday talk shows.

The comical exasperation in "Whose University Is It?" was, even for so young a man, not merely a rhetorical tool. You sense the coming wear and tear. In his mayoral papers, housed at the University of Vermont, there are pages of drafts of letters to the editor, press releases, op-eds, all on his cherished yellow legal pads. You also find, scrawled in the margins, Bernie's occasional laments about the fruitlessness of it all, all these years: "I have pushed everything, on top of everything, on top of everything," he scribbled in 1985. "Year after year, letter after letter, editorial after editorial." "Whose University Is It?" was the very first, and it already expresses exhaustion.

We detect in the essay some early versions of the all-purpose essentials of Bernie's political strategy. First, find a Goliath: almost any slow-footed institution will do. In 1962, it was the University of Chicago's administration and board of trustees; twenty years later, as Burlington's mayor, Sanders took on the University of Vermont. Next, escalate the conflict from the specific instance to the general principle. If you can manipulate your opponent into making his claim general and categorical, you're in control: by the end of the negotiation with George Beadle's administration, Sanders had forced the university to defend not merely individual instances of segregation but the morality of segregation itself. Negotiation must then unfold in the media, in public view. Bernie understood that if he'd dragged the priggish Dean Wick into the mire of the campus paper, he was by definition winning. "Discussion is no more compatible with deceit than it is with coercion," Wick wrote, in a letter to the editor. And yet there he was, groveling in the pages of the student newspaper, drawn down onto Bernie's turf.

Reading in the Basement

In April of 1963, a year or so after the CORE fracas, the name "Bernard Sanders" appeared for the first time in the national media. Visiting Brooklyn for years afterward, Bernie's old uncle would tease him about the "sex article" that briefly titillated the nation.

"University Slapped Back as Enemy of Free Love," read the syndicated story's headline in the *Dayton Daily News*. Similar headlines ran across the country, in the *Miami Herald*, the *Fort Lauderdale News*, the *Galesburg* (Illinois) *Register-Mail*, and elsewhere. The article pitted "an undergraduate," Sanders, against Dr. Eve Jones, a former faculty member and the author of a syndicated newspaper column on "morality and good parenting." The sexual mores of the rising generation were now under review, and Sanders was portrayed as their decadent spokesman.

Bernie's column was designed to get attention. Sparing no hyperbole, Sanders argued in the pages of *The Chicago Maroon* that the university's parietal rules in dormitories had "the total effect of banning sex at the College":

> In short, if the Administration can not do away with sex as they would like to do, they can take pleasure in adding to the tragic harm which

> comes from the archaic, barbaric, and oppressive "code of morality" of the society at large; that code which shouts out so loudly that there is no such thing as sexual need.

The rules, which set curfews of various kinds in Chicago's dorms, amounted to an "archaic, barbaric, and oppressive" policy of "forced chastity" that threatened students' health: the administration had not consulted university "authorities" who would tell them of the physical ravages of "guilt feelings" over "the beauty and joy" of sex. Sanders concluded with a threat: if the administration wouldn't allow sex in dorms, students would do it "in motels, in cars, on the Midway, or behind the Chancellor's house."

There is, of course, a simple reason a straight male undergraduate would be frustrated over gender parietals. But in spite of the somewhat comical nature of its complaint, the essay conveys a developing, and very serious, worldview. In the basement of the University of Chicago's Harper Library, Bernie was reading "Marx, a lot of Freud," as he told Rick Perlstein. Larry Sanders and Bernie spoke often about Sigmund Freud's ideas; Larry confirmed that Bernie, looking to understand his parents' struggles, was now "very into psychoanalysis" as a method of unspooling the damage wrought by ordinary economic life under capitalism. But Bernie's "sex article" isn't Freudian or Marxist, exactly. It bears the stamp of a controversial thinker excluded from most university curricula, the Austrian psychoanalyst Wilhelm Reich. "The father of free love," as he is sometimes known, was Freud's spurned disciple.

Reich's influence on Bernie's development is something that Larry Sanders told me his brother has since "wanted to downplay." Reich, who trained his disciples to drop their moral "armor" against sexual fulfillment, became a mainstay not at a bastion of the great books like the University of Chicago but on the countercultural fringe. In the radical bookstores and coffee shops near the university, Sanders met fellow Reicheans and discussed the psychoanalyst's theories in late-night conversation groups. The very idea that such a powerful thinker had been kept out of the university classroom was, for Sanders, another indictment of the university. In Reich's ideas, Sanders found a theory of the roots of human misery under capitalism; in the government's persecution of Reich, he learned a lesson about the real danger of holding unorthodox ideas.

Wilhelm Reich moved to the United States in 1939 and became an early guru of the free love movement: he coined the term *sexual revolution*. Reich pioneered a "sex-economic sociology" that attempted to "harmonize Freud's depth psychology with Marx's economic theory." Only this new "sex economy" could break the death spiral of capitalism. When it came to therapeutic praxis, however, Reich struggled to implement his ideas. Reich believed that the traumas of capitalism accumulated in patients' bodies; to undo this damage, Reich broke the psychoanalytic taboo against touching his analysands, and began to employ "body work," complex somatic manipulations of their shoulders, backs, and limbs. For this, he was chased out of Europe and in 1939 turned up in New York City, where he accepted a position at the New School for Social Research.

Sanders discovered in Reich's connection of sexual repression with economic despair "an answer," as he told a friend, to his parents' bleak lives and early deaths. Reich found that his working-class patients, since they were denied the fashionable sexual freedoms and candor enjoyed by the bourgeoisie, suffered from additional physical and psychological ills—and the most important cause of their lethal inhibition was "inadequate housing." In his 1933 essay "The Sexual Misery of the Working Masses and the Difficulties of Sexual Reform," Reich concluded that "civilized living conditions" were essential for "sexual order," and that in Vienna, some 80 to 90 percent of adults "did not have a separate room in which sexual life could take place undisturbed." For Sanders, the University of Chicago's parietals therefore reconstituted the "tragic harm" of his parents' cramped life in a tenement. In their tiny apartment, "there was no privacy, not for us, and really not for our parents," Larry Sanders told me, pausing to suggest the implications. Bernie looked at his parents' bleak lives, their fights over money, their mumbled, impersonal greetings and partings, and their early deaths, and found in Reich a trenchant presentation of the material conditions of their impossible lives.

Out of pure stubbornness at times, Bernie "read Reich deeply, carefully," friends from the era told me. In this he, it must be said, differed from many who professed to be Reicheans. By the late 1960s, Reich, whose books were more carried around than closely examined, had become a pop psych phenomenon, standard fare for many hippie men who wanted to elevate carnal desire by means of a Viennese pedigree—even as the depth and complexity of Reich's theories remained unsounded by these casual acolytes. But the very fact that Reich's ideas lost their distinctive features but lived on, by reputation, in personal testimony tells us that a horizontal information network had come into being. These slow analog networks, almost unimaginable today in our era of instant connectivity, were crucial to Bernie's rise. In the late 1960s, in Vermont, reading and discussing Reich became one of the pathways along which political radicalism traveled.

Sanders also found in Reich's persecution a lifelong political cause. By the 1950s, while his ideas circulated freely, Reich, now prone to delusions, languished in a federal prison. Early in the decade, he had patented his

"Orgone Accumulator," a kind of libidinal phone booth—or "mystical outhouse," as Jack Kerouac put it in *On the Road*. Patients sat inside and collected the energies of the accumulated universe in their bodies. These energies were to be stored up for explosive orgasms and, in aftermath, personal and political liberation. Soon Reich promoted and marketed his new device like a traveling medicine man. Reich combined the Freudian provenance with the entrepreneurial mind-set of a good postwar American: he even persuaded Albert Einstein to take his orgasm cupboard seriously. A distinguished roll call of lusty mid-century men tried out the device, including Saul Bellow, William S. Burroughs, J. D. Salinger, Allen Ginsberg, and Norman Mailer. "Step inside," many women were told, as they stared at a bleak casket. If free love was, as Joni Mitchell once put it, a "ruse for guys," the Orgone Accumulator, premising human survival on vigorous lovemaking, represented the most ludicrous prop in the whole deception.

In 1954, the Food and Drug Administration obtained an injunction against Reich, forbidding him from making medical claims about his device and from shipping Orgone Accumulators across state lines. Reich was jailed for defying the injunction, and died in prison in 1957. The ordeal never left Bernie: when he arrived in Washington in 1991, he told a friend back home that he intended to "immediately look into Reich's imprisonment." Reich was a latter-day incarnation of the American socialist Eugene V. Debs, imprisoned for his political beliefs.

At twenty-two, Bernie Sanders sought a comprehensive theory that could account for all of society's ills and make some sense of the tragedy of his parents' early deaths. Reich's analysis united sexual health with economic fairness and political liberation. What was more primal, more central to political and economic life, than the body and its stigmatized, but perfectly natural, needs? What could be crueler than to deny men and women adequate shelter, including a room apart where intimacy could be explored, then to block their access to restorative medical and psychiatric care? Life had to amount to more than it had for Eli and Dorothy Sanders, whose lives of exhausting work were interrupted only by fights about money. In Reich, Bernie found support for perhaps his most abiding core belief: that ordinary, rational life within American capitalism was an impossibility, and to seek it was a form of insanity.

Reich's ideas also gave Sanders the idea of starting society over from scratch. After many modifications, decades later, Reich's ideas influenced Sanders's bold pitch to an American city: Burlington, Vermont, could become a laboratory, an incubator, for a host of innovative ideas organized under the name "socialism." It helped that in the 1980s, Burlington was home to more Reicheans than perhaps any other place in the country: Reichean mind-body practice became a small, thriving industry in the Queen City. Reich's ideas, in forms modified by his readers, became the basis for policy ideas about reproductive freedom, community health care, affordable day care, family leave, and other priorities that Sanders espoused, even after the Orgone Accumulators were committed to the attic.

"Outsiders"

In the summer of 1963, Chicago's student radicals came out of the foyers and lobbies of their administration buildings to join Black students, parents, and activists in the neighborhoods. Chicago city workers had to be stopped from assembling some two hundred shoddy aluminum trailers in vacant lots along the railroad tracks to accommodate the overflow of students in predominantly Black public schools, just blocks away from new, white schools where empty desks abounded. These "Willis Wagons," named for the superintendent of schools, Benjamin Willis, provoked a growing protest in the weeks leading up to the start of the school year.

On August 12, 1963, Sanders was arrested while blocking a crew of workers putting together the flimsy metal supports of a Willis Wagon, handcuffed, and charged with resisting arrest. One hundred and sixty-nine protestors were taken in; Sanders and three others were charged. The arrests were captured by a student filmmaker named Gordon Quinn, who later directed a masterpiece, *Hoop Dreams* (1994), about a pair of Black high school basketball players caught up in and cast out by the white world of elite sports scouting and recruiting. Stills that circulated from that film, as Danny Lyon told me, are "the best, the most exciting images" from those years.

After attending the March on Washington for Jobs and Freedom in late August—Sanders recalls hearing Martin Luther King's "I Have a Dream" speech firsthand—Bernie returned to Chicago, where he now saw the classroom as a space dissociated from the "reality" pressing in from the streets. Decades later, Sanders explored this notion in, of all places, a classroom, during a University of Vermont class cotaught with his friend Rik Musty. It was an irony that he told the story from behind a lectern, but the primal 1960s scenario—that of the out-of-touch classroom cordoned off from the urgent real world—had evolved, or at least been repressed, by the 1980s. Both Musty and Sanders were '60s activists now ensconced in institutions, imparting the lesson that institutions were essentially illegitimate. Sanders explained to the students diligently taking notes in a classroom that after his experience in "the real world," college courses "were extremely boring." From his seat in the back row of a political science class in the fall of 1963,

Sanders arrested, 1963. *Tom Kinahan, Chicago Tribune*

Sanders noted the split between "what was going on outside my window" and "what was going on inside the classroom." The mismatch between institutional "reality" and the experience of the streets never left him. Outside, where the avenues were erupting in protest, was reality; inside, as Professor Sanders told his UVM class that evening in 1986, "Yadda, yadda, yadda, the professor was going on and on."

Sanders told Russell Banks the story at greater length in a 1985 article commissioned by *The Atlantic* but unpublished until 2015, during Sanders's first presidential run:

> One time there was an incident on the streets that resulted in a picture in *The Chicago Defender*, the black newspaper, of a police officer twisting a young black woman's arm, and we made a poster with it, and I was working near the university pasting up these things to announce a demonstration against police brutality. Unbeknownst to me, a cop car was following along behind me, and as fast as I put the posters up, the cops were pulling them down. Finally, the cop car pulls up to me, and they get out and accost me. Needless to say, I'm terrified. One of the cops puts his finger in my face and says, "It's outside agitators like you who're screwing this city up. The races got along fine before you people came here!" Like this is Alabama or someplace.

"Anyhow," Bernie continued, "I was late for my class, a political science class, and I remember the teacher was talking about local government, and when I walked in and sat down, I saw right then and there the difference between real life and the official version of life."

The unrest outside the window, on that fall day in 1963, was, in fact, history: the Chicago school boycott, when some three hundred thousand protestors filled the streets of Chicago to demand the total desegregation of the city's schools. Sanders, who had played a small but important role in the events that catalyzed the massive protest, was stuck in a classroom. When he graduated from Chicago in the spring of 1964, Bernie, like many in his generation, vowed that he would never be on the wrong side of the glass again.

And yet, a paradox: this restless, talented activist, rising quickly from "nobody" status to become part of a tight network of leftists whose eyes had been opened by racism in Chicago, did not head south to participate in "Freedom Summer," as many of those in Danny Lyon's photo, and as Lyon himself, did. Instead Bernie sought "the real life" on an empty hillside in Vermont, the whitest state in the union, tending a fire over an improvised Sterno rig, with only crickets and katydids for company. Why?

4

The Sugarhouse and the Highway

(Middlesex, Vermont, and Brooklyn, 1964–67)

A Working Honeymoon

In February of 1964, *The Baltimore Sun* announced the engagement of Deborah Shiling, a junior at the University of Chicago and the daughter of a prominent local pulmonologist, to Bernard Sanders. The couple married on September 6, 1964, at the bride's parents' home in Mount Washington, Maryland. Larry Sanders arrived from London with "a very cumbersome wedding gift": Hogarth Press's twenty-four-volume *Complete Psychological Works of Sigmund Freud.* Larry seems somewhat flabbergasted after all these years that the set, which was "a very good buy, but still expensive" from a bookshop near the British Museum, had been "stored somewhere and got badly damaged" and was now he feared, lost. But Bernie did carry the lessons of psychotherapy with him throughout this period, in summer work as a psychological counselor for poor children, and, according to friends, in regular sessions with a Reichean therapist.

The newlyweds decamped for Europe in the fall of 1964 on their honeymoon; though like Bernie's later, working "honeymoon" to the Soviet Union, after his 1988 wedding to Jane Driscoll, this trip followed a curriculum of cultural inquiry and study. The couple met up with Larry in London before visiting A. S. Neill's experimental Summerhill School in Leiston, Suffolk, on England's eastern coast. From there they traveled to Greece, to track down the roots of Western democracy, and finally to Israel, where, for several months, Sanders and Shiling stayed and worked at a socialist kibbutz near Haifa, Sha'ar HaAmakim.

Summerhill was "the priority," Larry told me. Bernie had been reading the 1930s correspondence of Neill and Wilhem Reich, written during the rise of Adolf Hitler. The letters "offered an articulate commentary on the rise of fascism and on the idea of sexual liberation," according to

Christopher Turner in *Adventures in the Orgasmatron*, a study of the weird origins of the sexual revolution. In this searching, rueful correspondence, Neill and Reich connected their own sexual humiliations with the roots of fascism. The damage could only be undone by educating children properly. To Bernie, the Summerhill School was perhaps the only community in existence that had been organized successfully around the ideas of Reich and his circle.

The couple were not alone on the school's verdant campus. By the time Sanders and Shiling visited the school, Summerhill had become a pilgrimage site for readers of Neill's best-selling book, *Summerhill: A Radical Approach to Child Rearing*, who wanted to see firsthand a school founded on the renunciation of "all discipline, all direction, all suggestion, all moral training, all religious instruction." (Summerhill, in fact, had really only one conventional, and very English, rule: tea was served promptly at four.) A brief campaign to found "Summerhill USA" on land in upstate New York might later have caught Bernie's attention. That effort failed, but by the end of the decade, Neill's ideas, spread by pilgrims who'd seen his school in person, had been implemented in countercultural day cares and community schools all across Vermont—as well as in Bernie's own free-range parenting of his son Levi, born in 1969.

After Summerhill and a stop in Greece, where the newlyweds "did the tourist thing and were thrilled by the Parthenon," Sanders and Shiling arrived in Israel. For years it was known only that Bernie had claimed he "worked on a kibbutz"; when the media uncovered the details in 2016, *Haaretz* reported flatly that Sanders had since severed his relationship to "Israel, Zionism, and Judaism." But Sanders visited Sha'ar HaAmakim—meaning "Gate of the Valleys"—in 1964 mainly to witness socialism in daily community practice. "It was the structure of the community that impressed me," Sanders wrote in his 2016 campaign biography, *Our Revolution*:

> People there were living their democratic values. The kibbutz was owned by the people who lived there, the "bosses" were elected by the workers, and overall decisions for the community were made democratically. I recall being impressed by how young-looking and alive the older people there were. Democracy, it seemed, was good for one's health.

The kibbutz, ten miles from Haifa, on the road to Nazareth, was a test case for individual-scale democracy. It had started as a model agricultural community, founded by Romanian and Yugoslavian socialists in 1935: a Vermont-style commune, decades ahead of that cultural vogue. From its beginnings as a farm, the kibbutz had evolved into a small semi-industrial civilization. Sanders and Shiling toured poultry houses, greenhouses where twenty varieties of roses grew, fish farms stocked with trout and salmon, and vast fields planted with cotton, cantaloupes, potatoes, and onions. Energy harvested from solar cells designed on the property was distributed to power mills, factories, and machine shops. The kibbutz made some income from selling its own brand of sunflower seeds, but mainly the people of Ha'ar ShaAmakim lived and thrived by exchanging their work directly for food and shelter. No money changed hands. Weavers laid out their textiles on a wooden table for seamstresses, who sewed dresses and shirts for distribution. Volunteers arose every morning at four and rode out in the back of a pickup truck to shady orchards to pick apples, pears, olives, and grapes until eleven, then ate a communal meal and rested throughout the hot afternoon. At six every night, tea was served; in the evenings, the community enjoyed ping-pong, dancing, storytelling, and poetry recitals.

But Sanders was most curious about the lives of the commune's children. From infancy, the children of Sha'ar HaAmakim lived apart from their parents in dormitories, interacting with their families for a few hours every day. Girls and boys lived together, showering together in communal baths. Sanders had likely read about these "children's houses" of socialist kibbutzim in the work of Bruno Bettelheim, the famed University of Chicago psychologist who had begun an inquiry into a population that he called "the children of the dream." These unique "children's societies" formed entirely outside the patriarchy, apparently free of the economic and sexual traumas that spoil family life under capitalism. Bettelheim concluded that "kibbutz children seem to fare better than do many children raised in underprivileged homes," like Bernie's own in Midwood, and better, even, than some children from middle-class backgrounds.

Sanders returned from Israel eager to purchase land in Vermont, from Vermonters who were eager to sell. The small town of Middlesex, a few miles west of Montpelier, offered several parcels tracking along the new span of I-89, completed in 1960. The highway cut through large farm properties: farmers tended to keep their land only on one side or the other of the road, and cash out the rest. These vast, cheap, and accessible plots, advertised in *Vermont Life* and at the Vermont Information Center in Midtown, beckoned to a new generation of "former scouts and summer campers," as *Vermont Life* put it. Sanders and Shiling had perhaps seen a notice in May of 1964 in *The New York Times* that one such ex-scout, an idealistic professor, Georges de Nagy, and his wife had purchased a four-hundred-acre farm in Middlesex for the founding of a new liberal arts college, which opened in the fall of 1964 and limped along for fifteen years before succumbing to debt and litigation. When a property adjacent to Middlesex College went on the market, the couple made their offer.

Sanders and Shiling paid $2,500 for their eighty-five acres in Middlesex, a farmer's hardwood forest and sugarbush. From Shady Rill Road, you saw only a steeply sloping meadow cresting in dense woods. A timber sugarhouse and a crude A-frame were the only built things on the property. Otherwise, the land seemed mostly untouched by human choices, and by the political priorities that they express. As Sanders told Russell Banks in 1985, "It was just fantastic. I mean, I grew up in a three-and-a-half room apartment, never owned a damn thing, and owning a piece of land I could walk on was just incredible! This brook is my brook! This tree is my tree!"

Pioneers

The young couple was part of a micro-scale generational Vermont migration, somewhat distinct from the hippies who began to arrive only a few summers later. The models available to these new pioneers recommended a kind of monasticism. Helen and Scott Nearing's popular guides to "living the good life," purchased in city bookstores and carried in backpacks to the woods, promised happiness in the cultivation of an ascetic, antisocial existence: the only "fun allowed was picking some onions," according to Peter Schumann, who married Helen and Scott's granddaughter, Elka. The title of the Nearings' 1950 book gives the distinctive flavor of the times: *The Maple Sugar Book: Being a plain practical account of the Art of Sugaring designed to promote an acquaintance with the Ancient as well as the Modern practise, together with remarks on Pioneering as a way of living in the twentieth century.*

But as Sanders soon discovered, Vermont was not any old wilderness: a dense cultural understory, with established political customs and mature social hierarchies, hid in the larkspur. Sanders and his generation of Vermont "pioneers," engaged in their own DIY utopian projects, forging their own new networks, had gone "back to the land," but had nevertheless strayed into the heart of George Aiken's world of Republican politics.

In 1960, Richard Nixon had taken the state of Vermont by seventeen points. In some of the rural counties that would soon overflow with feral hippies and communards, JFK barely cracked 20 percent. In Middlesex, Nixon won 179–138. In Stannard, where Sanders bought a home in 1968, it was Nixon, 26–18. Though Kennedy easily outdrew any previous Democratic presidential candidate in Vermont, still, according to the historian Samuel B. Hand, "a Republican mystique persisted." Though Vermont had essentially only one party, there was great freedom of self-invention within it. The Vermont Republican, absent a predator, had diversified as it evolved, like a Galápagos slug. The national GOP soon became its predator.

In the fall of 1964, soon after Bernie's arrival, Vermont, "the most arch-Republican of all states, from the dawn of political history," as *The Barre-Montpelier Times Argus* put it, voted in a landslide for Lyndon B. Johnson, the first Democrat ever to win the state. It was a form of public grieving, not really an expression of politics. The murder of JFK in November of 1963 had deeply scored Vermont's villages. In the rural post offices, makeshift shrines, palm fronds, and flags were still arranged below Kennedy's portrait, alongside sympathy cards made in bright crayon. Even in conservative Catholic homes like ours, commemorative records of Kennedy's speeches were played for years after while dinner was prepared. And Johnson's opponent, Barry Goldwater, seemed to many an unstable, aggrieved, dangerous man. The American Psychiatric Association's "Goldwater Rule"—which states that psychiatric professionals may not diagnose unless they've conducted an examination—arose after psychiatrists, surveyed as to whether Goldwater was in fact psychotic, said yes; yes he was. (The Goldwater Rule had to be invoked often during the first Trump presidency.)

Johnson's victory could be dismissed as a one-off, but it was not the only proof of life for the Vermont Democratic Party. In 1962, Vermonters had sent a young, Kennedy-like Burlington attorney, Philip Hoff, to the governor's office in Montpelier. Running against an unappealing Republican incumbent and buoyed by JFK's rising star, Hoff—son of Turners Falls, Massachusetts, once a handsome football standout at Williams College, was carried to victory partly by crossover Republicans voting in a third party devised to allow them to vote for Hoff without caucusing with the Democrats. Once Hoff was in, the Independent Party immediately—and, for Phil Hoff, rather ominously—disbanded.

Hoff, playing up the resemblance to JFK, presented his young family as a kind of local Camelot. Hoff's zesty wife, Joan, was touted as "Vermont's Jackie." And it helped in many parts of the state that Hoff was a good Protestant, a Kennedy without the troubling Catholicism. Somehow, supporting the young, affable liberal seemed the nonpolitical choice. But Phil Hoff, despite the benefit of a newly reapportioned legislature concentrating power in Vermont's Democratic-led cities, had merely a probational mandate to transform the state. Republicans still controlled the legislature and retained many de facto life appointments as heads of the state's 126 or so powerful agencies and councils. Hoff soared, but, by 1968, petered out. To be a Democrat in 1968 meant to be allied with draft dodgers, burnouts, and rioters. Vermont's village Republicans returned to the fold, their wild experiment concluded.

But the transformations in the Hoff years were bigger than any one politician. The arrival of the interstate highways began to change the state's physical landscape and its relation to the entire East Coast. Vermont was now part of a central nervous system linking it, by a few hours' drive, to more than 40 million people. When the span between Montpelier and the town of Middlesex opened in 1960, "300 cars lined up to drive the six miles," according to the historian Howard Mansfield. Senator George Aiken blessed the project in the name of traditional Vermont values—even though, as Mansfield points out, a span of the road had "buried the senator's boyhood home."

One domino after another fell. In 1945, Vermont was host to more than twenty-six thousand family farms; twenty years later, the number had plummeted to barely nine thousand. For commuters and vacationers, the interstates meant progress; for Bernie Sanders, they offered easy access to his acres in Middlesex. Yet, for farmers whose ancestral hills and valleys were seized by eminent domain, these same roads meant an abrupt end to an entire civilization and way of life. A roadside marker near Ascutney in southern Vermont commemorates the death of a local dairy farmer, Romaine Tenney, who set fire to his house and barn, then sat down in the burning wreck and put a rifle in his mouth, rather than cede his property. And the roads themselves were still viewed, even in my childhood, as agents of death: even in the '70s, we rarely took I-89 to Smugglers' Notch for fall foliage drives. The "back way," Route 15, was seen as more scenic—and less lethal.

With the world speeding toward it, the state had to consider to what lengths it would go, and what means it would employ, to preserve its traditional and rural character; it also had to decide whether the very *idea* of preservation—by laws, codes, and other sophisticated social and political mechanisms—was itself anathema to its flinty, small-government self-image. During the 1960s, a patchwork of local conservation groups and state agencies succeeded in preserving the corridors tracking directly alongside the new interstates. Anyone who drives Vermont's hundreds of miles of beautifully maintained highway discovers that its exit ramps lead often to a few gas stations, some sheds, perhaps a creemee stand or two. Even a preservationist might see the wisdom in developing the acres surrounding a highway exit—unless, that is, the highway itself was an advertisement for a product called Vermont, its exits deliberately planned to provide access, not to homes and businesses, but to open fields and forests. "All anybody in

Vermont worries about is Vermont," a friend once said to me, after a summer program at Middlebury College. The subtext of that conversation has always been: How much change will be required, and of what kind, for a place to remain the same?

Bernie arrived during this conversation, entirely unaware of it. To Sanders as to so many of the young pilgrims from urban life who followed a few years later, Vermont was woods and fields and flowers: the farthest thing from politics. How could there be politics, when there was almost no population at all in evidence?

Though Sanders didn't yet know the scope of Vermont's political conversation, he soon went on to shape it, and to become one of its most important—and controversial—subjects.

Shady Rill

The early 1960s were a "twilight period between what Vermont had been, and what it would become," according to the Vermont historian Paul M. Searls. It is tempting to mark this crossroads at Bernie's hillside property a few forested miles from the glittering golden dome of the Vermont statehouse in Montpelier.

Jim Rader, Meg Pond, Emer Feeney, and I set out from Burlington to Shady Rill Road on a brilliant August Saturday in 2022, the goldenrod and Joe Pye weed mellowing in tall grasses along the way. We talked about the stretch of I-89 that took us there. My grandfather supervised one of the blasting teams that dynamited a path through the granite ledge and along the Winooski River Valley in the early 1960s. The job put Vermonters in touch with their primordial landscape, even as it represented a new age of progress. In 1960, a mile or so from Bernie's property, crews disturbed a bed of sticky clay at the bottom of an ancient glacial sea, spurring a massive rockslide that slowed the steady assembly, one span clicking into place at a time, of the most dramatic public works project in U.S. history.

The road dug deep trenches into some of the oldest mountains in North America. Actuaries and mystics might agree that human sacrifice would be required in exchange for the permanent alteration of peaks some 150 million years old. In fact, automobile fatalities overall decreased in the state, but the grisly scenes on the new roads became legend. A friend told me about a woman who'd driven all the way from Arizona for a job in Montpelier, only to collide with the newly exposed ledge within a mile or so of her destination. The Vermont papers kept a macabre count of the highways' victims on their front pages: 110, 111, 112.

I-89 is just a hop, skip, and a jump away from Shady Rill, and Montpelier, the state capital with eight thousand or so residents and a thriving professional class, is just over the ridge. But if anything, Shady Rill Road is more forested now than in Bernie's day. There's no driveway anymore; you have to look for a rough opening in the woods. Sanders sold the property to Shiling when they divorced in late 1966. She and her family lived there full-time, entirely off the grid, for more than fifteen years. During the campaigns of 2016 and 2020, reporters showed up and started trespassing on the land; ever since, the family has been wary of people's traipsing on the open hillside that shades into second-growth forest and, eventually, to the clearing where Rader and Bernie used to drink beer, gaze over at Dumpling Hill, and talk about psychoanalysis, politics, and basketball. The property came with a brook for skinny-dipping, a few scrubby outbuildings, and, to Bernie's delight, a specimen of that most storied of all Vermont structures, the old maple sugarhouse built around a central stovepipe where sweet steam boiling up from the sap basin mingled with woodsmoke.

It was never really habitable, but Sanders did seem to enjoy entertaining there, as his mother had dreamed of doing in their small Midwood apartment. Sanders cooked over an open fire or with his improvised Sterno rig, igniting old T-shirts in a coffee can: "Berno," his friends called it. Larry Sanders, who, with his wife, Margaret, spent several months at the sugarhouse one summer, recalls it as "totally idyllic," though "nobody knew what we were going to do for income." The afternoons were spent coaxing Bernie's broken-down van to life, for grocery trips to Montpelier. In the evenings, the Sanders brothers bonded as they hadn't since their parents' deaths. "It was a wonderful summer," Larry told me, wistfully.

But reality awaited back in Brooklyn, where, as Larry told me, Bernie rented "an apartment much like our parents' place," very near their old blocks in Midwood. "I've had some success in my attempts to get into a psychoanalytic institute next year without fulfilling their normal requirement," he wrote to a friend in December of 1965. He dreaded his "exams coming up in miserable school," the New School for Social Research, and said he might take a job at "a private school for bright, but emotionally disturbed kids." A year later, Sanders reported that he had "completed a fairly disastrous term" at the New School, and had taken a leave of absence: "I'll go back next year and finish up for an M.D. which is what I need to fulfill the requirements for the psychoanalytic institute." This flailing between schemes—one year plotting admission to the institute without fulfilling its requirements, the next reporting that he is on his way to a medical degree—suggests that, as of 1966 or so, Sanders had lost his way.

Under the care of his analyst, Sanders interpreted his own behavior with uncharacteristic candor: "I suffer from a peculiar disease which could be called contractitis. Whenever things become difficult for me, instead of attempting to come to terms with them and fight it out, I contract into a ball and go into a deep shell—separating myself from friends, people in general, and the whole world."

Another letter from the period, reporting that "Debby and I will split up," puts Sanders's study of Reich to self-therapeutic use: "I can't talk about it too clearly because my damn body won't allow me to feel it as it should," Bernie wrote, adding that he "doesn't know anything" that his body doesn't tell him: "In other words, my emotions are screwed up and aren't telling me what's happening . . . It isn't something sudden though, we've talked about it for many months."

Sanders lamented that he couldn't "be more human and give more of myself and love more," attributing this paralysis to a kind of sickness that he fears may never be healed, something that is hard to change in oneself, "although this is what Reichean therapy is about." The reckoning with his murky interiority, matched to the necessity of presenting an outward, social persona, troubled Sanders deeply: "One thing I think is certain, though, that most people are very good actors—fooling themselves as well as others. One rarely ever knows what is going on underneath somebody else's outward appearance."

These touching letters, while they confirm how deeply Reich influenced Bernie's worldview, also mark a new development in his politics. By this time, his eighty-five-acre utopia had been "punctured," as Larry said, by the hard reality of rural poverty. While in Middlesex, Bernie "became very close" with a French-Canadian family living at the bottom of his access road, hard on Shady Rill, in a build-as-you-go home with plastic sheeting serving as a crude roof. Bernie told Larry that he "was shocked to see that level of poverty, and the complete inability of the family to access medical care." Larry remembers that his brother struck up a warm friendship with the mother in particular, a quiet woman who cared all day for her young son with an untreated congenital heart condition like the mitral valve defect that killed Dorothy Sanders. This neighbor had confided in Sanders her fear of being unable to have more children. Writing from New York City, though, Bernie broke the good news to his friend:

> Do you recall Debby and I mentioning to you, our Vt neighbor, Shirley, who wanted to have lots of kids but because of a blood type problem with her husband has been able to have only one—along with lots of miscar-

riages. Well, despite her doctor's advice, she became pregnant again and she wrote to us a while ago that she had the baby—a boy. She wanted the baby so much.

This was "the nicest piece of news" Bernie said he'd heard in years. (My quick Google search turned up Shirley's obituary from 2021. Shirley LaPlant of Shady Rill Road, Middlesex, passed away at the age of ninety-five, predeceased by one son—likely the boy with the troubled heart—and leaving five children and "many grandchildren and great-grandchildren.")

Back in Brooklyn, with the goal of a psychoanalytic degree proving elusive, Bernie and a few high school friends started a business called Creative Carpentry—"utility walls, bookcases, toy storage"—out of the classifieds section of *The Village Voice*. The business model was simple: they'd get a call, go look at the job, then scramble out to buy the tools and materials necessary, often teaching themselves the skills on the spot. The idea was to make a little money, but also to make life in Vermont possible on a full-time basis. By 1966, Sanders was counting his property in Middlesex as his rudder in what, year after year, felt more and more like a drifting, wayward life. Bernie "stole away to Middlesex" whenever he could, sometimes "butterflying up the hill through deep snow like an Olympian swimmer," a friend recalled. He'd scavenged boards from a local construction site and was nailing a floor together on top of the frozen dirt. The demands of city life and earning a living wearing away at him, he told friends that he hoped the sugarhouse could become his home base.

In the summer of 1966, newly divorced, Sanders asked Jim Rader to help him remodel the sugarhouse. Jim drew the design for me on a napkin: a modest expansion, but integral to an exciting new plan Bernie devised for his summer getaway. Sanders, Rader, and other guests worked part of the summer framing and roofing the sugarhouse's "new wing."

Bernie appears to have contemplated in passing a kind of progressive school or camp on his hillside, perhaps in coordination with Middlesex College, just over the ridge. He was traveling around to schools founded on the principles of Summerhill, including the Collaberg School in Stony Point, New York, where he and Shiling attended a week of seminars in 1966. In New York, Sanders had taken a job as an Operation Head Start counselor in East Harlem and on the Lower East Side, an eight-week training program designed to help children succeed in the classroom. "Having spent one day" on the job, Sanders wrote to Rader, "I really can't believe it, and I refuse to allow myself to believe it. The children are created by such inhumane contempt." Beginning in the summer of 1966, Sanders began to invite Head Start kids up to the sugarhouse for a few weeks at a time, to experience something like what he'd enjoyed at Boy Scout camp. Rader, then living in nearby Adamant, remembers Sanders's "kids" playing with his own in a scrubby meadow near his small farmhouse. Bernie ran this little exchange program casually, with no thought, apparently, of scaling the experiment. When I suggested to Larry Sanders that Bernie's schemes to host city kids stemmed from a commitment to racial justice, Larry interjected: "No, he was just being a nice guy."

Fair enough. But still, the gesture was not isolated from other such well-intended initiatives, often ending in discouragement or even scandal. In 1965, in Montpelier, a local teacher and civil rights worker, Ted Seaver, had founded "Vermont in Mississippi," an exchange program. Seaver was disciplined by the Montpelier school board for a procedural technicality, was fired from his job, and left the state. Local churches and civic groups all through this period attempted to "integrate" Vermont's villages by essentially importing frightened kids, without much support or guidance once they arrived. After 1968, when Governor Hoff instituted the Vermont–New York Youth Project, a large-scale initiative to bring "inner city" kids for summers in the countryside, this decade-long dream of a new interracial Vermont sputtered out. Facing a racist backlash in the villages, the program folded.

Friends recall, though, one notable long-lasting effect of Bernie's "summer camp": with three or four kids in tow, Sanders for the first time "met Vermont parents, and heard about their struggles" accessing basic care for their families. Bernie and the kids mingled very naturally with poor families at the park and ball field, and gained something of a "non-theoretical, brutally real" sense of children and child care in Vermont. The utopian experiments of Summerhill were not forgotten; the struggle of his neighbors to get their children dental and medical care, though, were the more urgent lesson to heed.

THOUGH HE PRIZED these snack bar, general store, and bowling alley connections to Vermont families, things were different way back on his acres, where the brook ran clear. There, Sanders sought a different kind of of connection entirely.

James Baldwin, in his essay "The New Lost Generation," described a time in the 1960s when "people turned away from the idea of the world being made better through politics to the idea of the world being made better through psychic and sexual health like sinners coming down the aisle at a revival meeting." In Middlesex, discussing spirituality and the more far-out elements of psychoanalysis with Rader, Sanders "recharged" by seeking in the wilderness what Freud called the "oceanic feeling": the sensation of oneness with the world, the ego dissolved into ether. Bernie's goal was what Baldwin described: "psychic and sexual health." On bluebird-blue August afternoons, Bernie described a mystical attachment to the land and sky, and enjoined Rader and his other guests to try to experience the cosmic energy swirling around them.

Occasionally, according to guests who visited the sugarhouse, Bernie would produce "a contraption of some kind." It was not an Orgone Accumulator but "a rectangular kind of device maybe five feet high made of copper wire." One friend described it as "a prayer mat." Its essence was to be inexplicable, indescribable: it struck some as more like "an Indian breastplate." Jim Rader's impression was that Bernie had woven the copper gizmo himself.

"What is that for?" Rader demanded. Sanders, incredulous that his friend needed an explanation, said that he sometimes placed this spiky thing under his back and slept on it, as a way of tapping into or directing orgone energy into the body.

Sanders encouraged Rader to lie back on the hillside and try to "see orgone energy." Jim concentrated on his visual field and stared up into the blue sky. All these years later, Rader swears he saw "something there. I would describe it almost as corpuscles, like paramecia under a microscope."

This was the summer of 1967, the Summer of Love; within a year, these kinds of experiments would become quite common in the fields and forests of the Green Mountain State.

5

“Access to Tools”

(Plainfield and Stannard, Vermont, Late 1960s)

Learning the ropes. *Vermont Historical Society*

Back to the Land

In the summer of 1968, the hippies began to arrive in Vermont “in droves,” as the papers announced. A phrase used often of cattle or salmon, cognate with “drive”: “droves” are compelled, mindless; driven.

The droves drove on Vermont’s new interstates to dells and valleys where the land was cheap and plentiful. “Everyone was fucking done after ’68,” a Burlington activist, Gene Bergman, told me; he meant the 1968 Democratic National Convention in Chicago, when police and National Guard numbering in the tens of thousands were dispatched to batter protestors. The shoulders and exit ramps of Vermont’s highways swelled with hitchhikers and backpackers. Their idea was “to start over, grow everything yourself, barter for your needs, leave no economic trace. Drop out.”

The vision was agrarian, but these new Vermonters knew nothing about the land. They bought up wooded acres for pennies, or pooled their money to rescue the old hill farms collapsing into splinters. They gathered their summer savings, their graduation and bar mitzvah money. The hat was passed in Central Park and Tompkins Square Park in New York City and on the Boston Common.

Hill farmers forced off their land by declining markets for wool or milk now lived on fixed incomes in nursing homes or in efficiency apartments behind the general store. They watched with mixed feelings as the land was taken up again by these strange, rather outlandish-looking, but, as the old-timers had to admit, *industrious* young people.

The "kids," as everyone called them—hippies, puppeteers, foragers, goat farmers, draft dodgers, macrobiotics, potters, glassblowers, poets, underage runaways—arrived in Vermont in astounding numbers: some estimates suggest as many as one hundred thousand young transplants over ten years, from 1965 to 1975. In 1972, a writer for *Playboy* counted precisely "35,800 hippies" in Vermont, or one-third of the state's residents between the ages of eighteen and thirty-four. These new Vermonters fanned out across the state but concentrated in places like the Winooski River Valley around Montpelier; in southern Vermont, near Brattleboro; and in the magnificent, lonely territory of glacial lakes, timber, and tundra just south of the Canadian border, which Senator George Aiken christened "the Northeast Kingdom."

A phenomenon these days understood by a single term—*commune*—was in fact a crazy quilt of notion-based communities. The overall scene was like the deaf-mutes' ball in Thomas Pynchon's *The Crying of Lot 49*: a "mysterious consensus" where "each couple on the floor danced whatever was in the fellow's head: tango, two-step, bossa nova, slop." In *Going Up the Country*, Yvonne Daley estimated that there were seventy-five communes in Vermont around 1970. Joe Sherman, the author of *Fast Lane on a Dirt Road*, put the number at over one hundred.

(But what counted? My aunt and uncle lived communally on a property in Westford, Vermont, without a name or charter. Summer picnics; feral, rather mean children running in packs; volcanic mosquito bites. I heard the property referred to as a "commune" only when we were driving back home and my grandfather wanted to disparage it.)

Some of the dropouts were dialed in. Total Loss Farm in Guilford, just north of the Massachusetts border, sought a media profile almost right away. Its founder Ray Mungo published a best-selling book about the place in 1970, *Total Loss Farm*, which was excerpted in *Harper's*. In the Mad River Valley, near the Sugarbush ski resort, you drove by Prickly Mountain, an architects' commune founded by Yale dropouts. Their homes, which now sell for millions, look like enormous coral accretions or three-dimensional doodles. Farther down Route 100, in Rochester, Irving Fiske, a scholar of the English Renaissance, and Barbara Hall, one of the first female comics illustrators, founded the Quarry Hill community. The Fiskes are the "friends in Vermont" mentioned in Art Spiegelman's *Maus*. When I asked Spiegelman about his time at Quarry Hill, he waved the request away in a friendly manner: "Some things are better forgotten," he wrote.

At the other end of the spectrum, Earth People's Park, the "last left turn" heading north before the Canadian border: a six-hundred-acre preserve of free land marked by hastily drawn and then gradually erased homesites. In 1970, Vermont's conservative governor, Deane C. Davis, responding to complaints about the park, drove up in his Lincoln Continental to interview the young "transients." Davis issued a reassuring press statement about the "hippie invasion." "Like most people," these new Vermonters "go about their business in a self-sufficient, peaceful manner," Davis reported, "although their habits and appearance may not be to our taste."

But trouble at Earth People's Park started almost right away: larcenies, sexual assaults, a dog beaten to death, an arsonist on acid. Communes along the road to the park—Mullein Hill in West Glover and New Hamburger in Plainfield—had to guard against the arrival of pilgrims who'd gotten lost shy of the promised land, and were greedy for housing, food, drugs, or sex.

By the late 1980s, Earth People's Park was known as a place to get magic mushrooms by the wagonload, if you were intrepid enough to find a guy called Nacho who lived in a cabin full of firearms. Drug seizure laws were toughened under Ronald Reagan, and authorities finally confiscated the property, home to fields of untended marijuana long gone to seed, in 1990. It is now one of Vermont's muddiest and loneliest state parks.

AFTER FOUR YEARS dividing his time between Brooklyn and Middlesex, Bernie Sanders moved to Vermont for good in 1968, to join that summer's great migration. Two years after Sanders and Deborah Shiling divorced in 1966, Sanders and Susan Campbell Mott, who had met while working as Head Start counselors, purchased a sagging white farmhouse near what center there is of the remote Northeast Kingdom town of Stannard, population under two hundred. At the nearby Willy's Store in Greensboro, a classic Vermont general store where you can pick up night crawlers, deodorant, and Camembert in a single trip, locals remember Sanders stocking up on necessities and paying the clerks "the way real Vermonters did"—with pockets full of change.

Stannard's population has only declined since 1968. Back on its steep, rutted roads, where there is no cell signal for miles around, life maintains the traditional rhythms and customs that Bernie encountered fifty-five or so years ago as a newcomer. In August of 2023, Jim Rader and I visited Bernie's old eighteenth-century farmhouse, for decades now lovingly tended by the woman who bought it from him in 1978. Asking me not to divulge the address, she told us that Sanders stops by often: "The town has real resonance for him." Across the way, a fading black-and-white picture of Bernie in the town hall shares a wall of fame with legendary plow drivers and pound keepers of old. Of all the Vermont places Sanders lived or stayed in the late '60s—Middlesex, North Montpelier, East Montpelier, Glover, Greensboro Bend, Adamant, Calais, Plainfield—little Stannard, frozen in time, is the town that Sanders acknowledges as his political seedbed.

In July of 2024, I looked on as Bernie, in a wonderfully loose and gregarious mood, picnicked with dozens of his old neighbors at the Stannard town hall, reminiscing very warmly about his years in town. It was in the house up the road from the town hall, he recalled, where he experienced his introduction to fatherhood. Sanders and Mott welcomed their son, Levi Sanders, born in St. Johnsbury on March 21, 1969, just days after buying the deteriorating property with "thousands of beer bottles in the basement." *The Caledonian-Record*, blurring both their unmarried status and Bernie's surname, announced a son born to "Mrs. Susan Saunders." Bernie, whose passionate interest in infants and child development was heretofore merely theoretical, now shared the warmth of the woodstove and the serenity of the late-winter Vermont dawn with a real, crying baby. On that July day in 2024, the fifty-five-year-old Levi Sanders, who often drives his father on these campaign trips around the state, looked on from behind the folding table where his dad held forth about the days of his son's infancy.

Stannard is still reeling from its brief share in the national spotlight. "Bernie Sanders Has a Secret," ran a 2015 headline in *Politico*. The story, by Michael Kruse, was that Sanders had presented Levi to the world as the child of his first marriage. He hadn't, ever, and the scandal, fed by opposition researchers for the Hillary Clinton campaign, flopped. It would be hard to imagine information less scandalous than the fact that unmarried people had a child together in Vermont in the 1960s. Those touched by Kruse's story in 2015 are still scalded by it. Deborah Shiling politely declined to be interviewed for this book, saying she'd had enough.

Piling kindling in the stove, Bernie Sanders was now twenty-seven, with a small family to support and an income derived mainly from carpentry work, newspaper ad sales, and a job registering people for food stamps for the nonprofit Vermont Bread and Law Task Force. The family shivered at home in Stannard, subsisting "on almost nothing," his neighbors say. Tapping away at his IBM Selectric on the kitchen table, Bernie used the time at home with an infant to research and write pieces about the counterculture, with a focus on childbirth and parenting. Sanders held these essays for publication months or years later, in the *Vermont Freeman* and in his own newsletter, *Movement*, but the "man with the yellow legal pads" was well known across Vermont's commune belt. As the network of hippies began to fill in across the state, Sanders understood the revolutionary possibilities of this newly developing civilization, and set himself up to be the scene's Margaret Mead.

He was in fact among the first freelance writers to attempt to make a study of the Vermont communes, but the men and women he chose as his subjects were often wary, perhaps because they could sense his impatience with their scene. Sanders was "unforgettable of course, exactly as he is now," passing through Quarry Hill, or bunking for the night at New Hamburger, according to Kip Parsons, who lived for a time at a commune in Plainfield. But "these places all had their own unique terroir, customs around working, eating, sex, substances, the organization of the day." It was possible to embed with these new civilizations for a spell, but Sanders felt no temptation to go native. He was peripatetic during this period, couch surfing and hitchhiking between stays with Susan and Levi. As a Brooklyn Jew almost ten years older than many of the "kids," a new father, a fan of diner food, basketball, and country music, he was a snag in the countercultural fabric. Many up and down I-89 knew him as a hitchhiker: "My uncle kicked him out of his car," a friend told me. "He was a downer." These kinds of Bernie stories, though impossible to verify, nevertheless have long been part of Vermont's folkways. Hitchhiking had its own code of manners, as well as what we might politely call the expectation of reciprocity. "Gas, Grass, or Ass: Nobody Rides Free" read a once-common bumper sticker. Sanders offered, instead, harangues about Wilhelm Reich or the income tax.

In the summer of 1969, Sanders hitchhiked to a commune in West Glover to report on the phenomenon of home birth, and to test his Reichean theory that the root of politics grew in the composition of the family. "All aspects of life are intimately related," he wrote of his visit to Mullein Hill. "It is only a schizophrenic society such as ours which segregates them and puts them into separate little boxes." In studying the busy, tired, hungry, and cold residents there, Sanders hoped to "get into the areas of feeling and emotion, pain and love—and how people relate to each other, and how people shut off their feelings." Bernie wanted to understand society's drift toward war and violence: "If we want to know, for example, how our nation can napalm children in Vietnam—AND NOT CARE—it is necessary to go well beyond politics." The commune had a strict three-day rule for visitors, according to Kate Daloz, who grew up at Mullein Hill and wrote *We Are As Gods*, a study of the back-to-the-land movement. Exceptions were possible, but none were made for Bernie.

Even as he plumbed the Reichean substrate of political thought, Sanders's own politics during this period became steadily more pragmatic. He had begun to do tax policy research for the state of Vermont, driving the back way to Montpelier on dirt roads through the towns of Woodbury and Calais. The poverty along those rutted roads shook him. Undernourished children stared at passersby from sheds made from corrugated scrap and roofed with garbage bags. Heating and maintaining his home miles from any services, feeding a child on almost no money, Sanders himself lived in poverty, as he would, off and on, for many more years, and contrasted the privilege of the communards with the prowess that generations of Vermont living had bred into his Stannard neighbors. At that Stannard town hall in July of 2024, Sanders provoked a rash of nods when he recalled the punishing winters, "snow so deep it was like driving through a tunnel," and the lessons of the local plow driver, Roscoe Allen, who introduced Sanders and the other hippies in town to the Vermont trick of storing a car battery in a warm oven overnight and reinstalling it every frigid morning. "I was stunned," Bernie told the small audience. "The old-time Vermonters were very welcoming and tolerant of people from all over, people moving in." Without branding itself as a social experiment, the town of Stannard, absorbing the hippies into its weave, was a model for civic cooperation and tolerance.

By contrast, the idea that tens of thousands of talented, privileged, leftist young people were sitting out political life to raise mung beans frustrated him. "He was always Bernie," Lorraine Janowski of Mullein Hill recalled. "He was always organizing." Encountering these mini civilizations run according to wishful thinking and dream logic, Sanders's incredulous response, according to Janowski, was "How come you're not involved with your town government?"

"Jamestown Seventy"

By 1968, then, Sanders was expressing irritation with the low and slow cultural ethos of the counterculture. He was "becoming a political actor in a hurry," making up for the lost years—a "frantic scurrier from one campfire or root cellar to the next," according to an amused friend. He was not yet a candidate for anything, but he could see that political change required these new Vermonters to vote. Sanders knew dozens of hippies in Stannard; but at the polls, the town voted for Richard Nixon in 1968, 13–8. In Glover, near Mullein Hill, Nixon won 160–58. When, in the early 1970s, Sanders eventually became the designated candidate of the counterculture, he never drew more than a few thousand votes in any of his statewide campaigns. Even as Vermont's culture changed, Vermont's electoral politics remained in the hands of the traditional, moderate Republicans, with a culturally conservative Democratic Party still siloed in the state's urban areas. How much conventional political influence did these new Vermonters actually want? Under what conditions could they be coaxed into assuming political power?

On paper it all seemed so straightforward. In a 1972 *Playboy* feature, Richard Pollack fantasized about a Vermont transformed by "a latter-day children's crusade" mobilized to turn what we would now call a red state into blue. Pollack quoted the jurist Oliver Wendell Holmes. "Social experiments that an important part of the community desires," Holmes wrote, might be carried out "in the insulated chambers afforded by the several states."

The potential to transform Vermont politically had begun to attract nationwide attention. Pollack had based his *Playboy* article on a study published in *Law and Social Action*, an upstart journal of the Yale Law School. In "Jamestown Seventy," two law students, James F. Blumstein and James Phelan, called for a reopening of the "American frontier" and the establishment of a "living laboratory for social experiment through Radical Federalism." The alternative, "armed revolution," would be "put down by military might." The article does not single out Vermont, but almost everyone who read it spotted the Eden it envisioned a hundred or so miles up I-91 from New Haven.

The plan was laid out sensibly, including some important caveats. Blumstein and Phelan knew they weren't going to flip a state like Vermont by rounding up frostbitten cavemen and passed-out Pre-Raphaelites. The authors emphasized "ties to society." Previous collectivist experiments were once plentiful in Vermont, but many failed, according to Blumstein and Phelan, because they were too insular, as well as too weird. Communes had to present something to the public to survive. In the nineteenth century, John Humphrey Noyes, the founder of the Oneida Colony, held his own Vermont commune together by inventing "a tantric-like birth-control technique, male continence, which involved the male learning to withhold ejaculation during intercourse." Only when Noyes was chased out of Putney, Vermont, and settled in New York, did his community eventually thrive, by becoming manufacturers of Oneida dishes and flatware, still sold to this day. From withheld ejaculate to flatware was a path few could have mapped out ahead of time. But Vermont's new communards needed to think in terms of similar trajectories.

If this slow-growing "experimental state" envisioned by Blumstein and

Goddard College students in Plainfield, 1971. *Goddard College Archives*

Phelan was seeded in any one Vermont place, it was the fertile Winooski River Valley, in the shadow of the statehouse. There, even before the '60s kids showed up, a DIY ethos inflected the area's arts, goods, and communities. Electoral politics were still downstream, but the current was quickening. At Goddard College, in Plainfield, the new politics came off the commune and expressed itself in unlikely forms: muffins, puppetry, acid-trip architecture, mountain fish farms, and lyric poems.

At Goddard, all the boundaries were porous. "Goddard had a drop-in problem," the actor William H. Macy, a graduate of the school, told me. Macy quoted Timothy Leary: "'Turn on, tune in, drop out.' People were doing the first two, but not the third. Somebody would show up to visit a friend and still be there a year later. The dining hall was feeding four times the student body."

Macy drove up from Maryland in a shiny red VW Karmann Ghia on a sunny spring day, "one of those days when there's still a little snow." He stopped first in Putney, in southern Vermont, "got stoned with those people," and then headed to Goddard, where he saw "beautiful hippie girls and cool dudes with beards." Macy recalled several "standouts," including "a guy who wore a loincloth, summer and winter," and preached a gospel revealed to him through a chasm in the earth. He was regularly admitted for frostbite at the local hospital.

Ginny Callan, a Goddard student from Queens who later owned a legendary vegetarian restaurant, Horn of the Moon Cafe, in Montpelier, remembers a missionary leftist named "Josh" whose arrival was heralded by the appearance of graffiti: "Josh is back." A Weathermen dorm held shooting practices on Saturday mornings, Callan said, "to prepare for the revolution."

"There was another group," Macy told me, "they called themselves 'Man, Woman and Child.'" Callan recalled the same trio, living in a teepee on the outskirts of campus, walking around naked, soliciting "different kinds of relationship possibilities."

Was this what we now would call a throuple?

"Right," Macy said. "They went around together, Man, Woman, and Child. And one time while Man was shaving, Woman got into the shower with me. I remember thinking, 'I really don't have enough life experience to know how to deal with this.'"

It was an incredible place to be high. Once, Macy wandered onto the adjacent property, the Cate Farm, where Bread & Puppet, the experimental theater troupe, was then in residence. Bread & Puppet creates enormous, wildly expressive effigies in papier-mâché: satyrs, monsters, demons, wraiths, U.S. presidents.

"It was one of the most extraordinary things I've ever done in my life," Macy told me. He pried open the barn doors and beheld these gigantic forms, hanging limp and mysterious in the moonlight: it was, he said, "like being in *Where the Wild Things Are*."

THE PEN FOR wild things became a cradle for Bernie Sanders. Bernie had been a fixture on the Goddard campus since the mid-1960s; it was at Goddard that Jim Rader and Sanders again ran into each other, and, five or so years after their last meeting in Chicago, "naturally renewed their friendship." On many mornings, Sanders, though never enrolled at Goddard, made the crawl from Stannard, thirty miles southwest along slow roads, to Plainfield, and set up shop on campus. And it was in Goddard's Haybarn Theatre, as we will see, that Bernie Sanders first raised his hand to run for elected office in 1971.

Sanders needed "to patch together an actual politics out of his scattered beliefs," according to friends from the time. Goddard offered a pathway from the utopianism of the communes to practical political action. The school, founded in 1938, was the pragmatic heart of a grassroots civilization stirring to life in the Winooski River Valley. Its bookstore, stocked with countercultural scriptures like the *Whole Earth Catalog* and *How to Keep Your Volkswagen Alive*, as well as pamphlets on trillium foraging and broadsides on gay liberation, had become the cultural hub of the valley. But the college followed the Yankee principles of its founder, Tim Pitkin, and Pitkin's teacher John Dewey, the American pragmatist philosopher, educational reformer, and ambivalent son of Burlington, Vermont. Goddard's method, which became widely known as "experiential learning," transformed the entire valley into a living laboratory of new, startling ideas and their risky, surprisingly pragmatic applications.

"Access to tools": Goddard's unofficial motto was the slogan of the *Whole Earth Catalog*, a proto-internet where the rudiments of rural life—generators, horseshoes, tool chests, a pig-tooth extractor—shared a platform with guides to vibration cooking and materials for geodesic domes. The Plainfield post office overflowed with packages ordered from the *WEC*, as homesteaders greeted their long-awaited chainsaws and mental travelers pocketed their discreet envelopes stuffed with psilocybin spores. "The era was awash with tinkerers and systems-builders," the historian Erik Davis wrote, "with how-to guides, manuals, teach-ins, cookbooks and catalogs." These highly technical projects led downstream to "understanding and reconfiguring complex interdisciplinary systems, including systems of human togetherness." Stewart Brand, the founder and publisher of the *WEC*, favored a Thoreauvian adage: "We are as gods and might as well get good at it."

Goddard taught the scraggly gods of the Plainfield scene "to get good at" any number of innovative pursuits. The old duffers and tinkerers of the Winooski River Valley inspired them. Among the Yankees working on their John Deere tractors, Macy met a Chicago Jew working on his plays. David Mamet had been at Goddard off and on since graduating from the

Back row: Barbara Greenberg, Robert Hass, Tobias Wolff, Marita Garin, Faye Kicknosway, Ray Carver, Geoffrey Wolff, Donald Hall, Michael Ryan, Stephen Dobyns. Front row: Lisel Mueller, Ann Blackmer, Deborah Tall, Jane Shore, Janet Bloom, Heather McHugh, Gloria Still, Linda Nemec Foster, Louise Glück.
Goddard College Archives

school in 1964. "Everyone wore military clothes," Macy said, "but upon closer inspection, David had had his fatigues laundered and tailored." In a hunting cabin a few towns away, to the accompaniment of owls and hermit thrushes, Mamet, an urban, working-class character, reimagined American banter, cross talk, and repartee, creating his theater of blunt masculinity. By the mid-1980s, Mamet and Macy had founded their innovative troupe, the Atlantic Theater Company. They performed their summer season first in Montpelier and then at Burlington's city hall, in an arrangement brokered by Bernie Sanders. The company was quartered one summer on the campus of Trinity College, a Catholic women's school next to my home, where my grandmother and mother both worked. Mamet and Macy's "go-to for coffees and popsicles," Macy told me, was the convenience store across the way, Kampus Kitchen, where, as I told Macy, in 1980 I first laid eyes on a delicacy known as the bagel, beneath a handmade sign encouraging customers to "Try One!"

Even poetry, among the most recalcitrantly private and solitary of all pursuits, here fortified a community. First in Cabot and then in Plainfield, in a farmhouse set back on a knoll in the center of the village, Louise Glück, who was hired to teach at Goddard when she was twenty-two, expressed the cycles of passion and depletion in lyric poems that bound her own creative process intricately to the rhythms of Vermont days and seasons. Glück's pared-back, elemental lines of this period were akin to seasonal storage, their extreme verbal economy a reflection of how scarce, how difficult to harvest, real insight can be.

I keep near at hand a book given to me by Glück, who died unexpectedly in the fall of 2023 while I was drafting these chapters. Strewn among the backmatter of John Berryman's *Freedom of the Poet*, there are some lines in black ballpoint pen in Louise's hand, crossed out, rewritten, that seem to have begun with the observation of an elm outside her second-floor study window. The metamorphosis of the work is traceable: an image, then a rhythm, then a theme, all emerging on that endpaper. The extraordinary short poem that resulted, one of Glück's finest, is "Elms," and it documents the phases of its own labor:

All day I tried to distinguish
need from desire. Now, in the dark,
I feel only bitter sadness for us,
the builders, the planers of wood,
because I have been looking
steadily at these elms
and seen the process that creates

the writhing, stationary tree
is torment, and have understood
it will make no forms but twisted forms.

The poem is about poetry as a form of work—in fact, it is about the work that went into shaping it, and that the end product does not erase or conceal. "I was probably just fiddling," Louise explained to me, as we drove through the village of Plainfield in the fall of 2022, slowing to look up into the window where she wrote. "I was waiting for the cakes to be finished [Glück supplied a local bakery with desserts during those years] and probably Noah"—Glück's son, then about seven or eight—"was with Jane," his babysitter. A network of single mothers had made child care a community concern. As Glück put it in her biographical remarks after winning the 2020 Nobel Prize in Literature, "in Plainfield, Vermont, in the early 1970s, people were making these choices."

Glück's poems belong to all readers; but to her neighbors and friends in Plainfield, a poem like "Elms" is remarkable for its partial transformation of local materials, like a bench or table made from a single enormous trunk, still bearing its natural grain; as well as for the transubstantiation of ordinary moments within ordinary moments, as when a poem takes shape as a cake takes shape in the oven, or an infant naps. When Glück won the Nobel Prize, Vermonters could boast that they knew where she had found her symbols: the bus stop, the neighbors with their klezmer band, the patch of wild irises that crowd the banks of the Winooski in May, the crocuses

Fourth of July, Plainfield, Vermont. *Goddard College Archives*

breaking frozen ground in March, the deer wandering off bewildered into a thicket of beech.

Bread & Puppet, though, more than any other force in the arts, made the landscape and culture of rural Vermont an expression of their artistic vision of a primal politics based in unconscious drives and appetites. On July 4, 1968, the hoary Yankees of Plainfield, dressed in their World War I and II uniforms and playing their corroded trumpets and tubas, paraded alongside the enormous papier-mâché "wild things" devised by Peter Schumann, a Silesian refugee whose family had fled Allied bombings during World War II, and his wife, Elka, the granddaughter of the back-to-the-land gurus Scott and Helen Nearing. The Schumanns had founded their street theater of Boschian nightmare and confrontation on the Lower East Side of Manhattan in 1962, eventually moving to Goddard in 1966. "The land itself," as Schumann told me, inspired the company to evolve their frightening spectacles for a rural landscape and a pastoral ethos. Like Glück and Mamet, Bread & Puppet understood sparsity and thrift. Their performance gestures and written mottoes—"Courage"; "Revolution"; "Resistance"—were pared back so as to be hyper-legible from a distance, their materials scavenged, foraged, or donated.

In Glück, Mamet, and the Schumanns, all present at Goddard at the same moment, Vermont charted a course toward progressive politics that connected the arts to broader communities and economies. The makers of the Winooski River Valley did not discriminate between high and low forms of craft. Glück's terse poems, Mamet's stark plays, and the Jungian pageants of Bread & Puppet came into being in a loosely confederated network of subcommunities, where bakers, toy makers, doulas, translators, VW mechanics, woodworkers, and gardeners created what can be called the Plainfield scene. Bookstores, cafés, suppliers of paint and lumber, volunteers to drive, midwives, teachers, and others created a network of economic interest. Favors and other forms of barter exchange began to yield to the exchange of U.S. currency; from there, banks, insurance companies, doctors' offices, and schools took over, and electoral politics were the natural next step. The golden dome of Vermont's statehouse, visible from many vantage points in the area, suggested how inevitable it was that some of the wild things would eventually clean up, organize, run a campaign, or run for office.

THE ROUTE FROM domesticity to politics was often blazed by women with young children, who reinvented themselves out of necessity when the men from the hippie scene inevitably "drifted away to other states and other families," according to Yvonne Daley. My own father "drifted away"; my mother, though never a hippie, likewise found herself alone with a child during this period, needing to accommodate her life to the demands of motherhood and economic independence. Hundreds of women's support groups sprang up across the political spectrum in Vermont, from Birthright, an organization of young Catholic mothers looking for alternatives to abortion, to the radical feminist institute known as Sagaris University, cofounded by the poet and activist Grace Paley. Whatever their political alignment, these groups began to channel talented women into policy advocacy and eventually into electoral politics.

This was the path of an important player in our story. Ellen David Friedman, who became the most influential labor organizer in Vermont, and, as the leader of the Vermont Rainbow Coalition, the state chair of the presidential campaigns of Jesse Jackson in 1984 and 1988—as well as the manager of the Bernie Sanders's failed gubernatorial campaign in 1986—started her Vermont journey at Goddard. For people who grew up up in and around New York City, Vermont represented "kind of a frontier," Friedman said, in an interview with the Vermont Historical Society. "I was never that interested in comfort"; instead, Friedman felt "we should be tools, we should be sharp tools." Friedman wanted to live "the idealized socialist life," based partly on her study of the Nearings' homesteader guide, *Living the Good Life*. Life in the cities had become "mostly horrible": "I never really could get," Friedman said, "why people felt the need to divide into smaller and more pure political factions." The Vermont she encountered was by comparison "amazingly commodious and possible."

At eighteen, Friedman "met a group of counterculture architects" who were working at Goddard. The members of the Ant Farm collective—underground architects, thus the name—were "anti-architects," who, visiting Goddard from San Francisco, developed "a technique of inflatables" using industrial-strength rubber and vinyl, hot-welded by Goddard facilities workers after hours. "We were living out in the woods in Plainfield," Friedman explained, "in a giant inflatable octopus," a dome surrounded by tentacle-like sleeping chambers, with "hundreds or thousands of feet" of electrical wires powering the industrial-strength fans that kept these structures inflated.

Friedman's strategic political alliances were not with Ant Farm, but the octopus was not a bad home base. In the summer of 1970, she left her boyfriend and met Stewart and Susan Meacham, "very politically advanced, somewhat older," and a circle of activists surrounding them, known as the Vermont Alliance. Their goal was to draw hippies off the commune to support political change. "Not too many people were interested in electoral politics at that time," Friedman told me in an interview. Vermont Alliance sponsored working groups—on the "deformation" of the Vermont economy by the ski industry, on health care, on women's and reproductive issues. "Eventually we made some money," Friedman reported. "We sold calendars, 'People's History' calendars, at general stores." The money went to hire community organizers; the community organizers, setting up in hard-pressed neighborhoods across Vermont, eventually sought access to political power. Bernie stood out even in the Goddard days, Friedman told me, for the ferocity of his insistence that activists use electoral politics to advance their goals. Like the sap rising through a maple, Friedman's own calling was revealed when the season was due: her involvement in Vermont's Democratic Party, as we will see, shifted it significantly to the left. And many of those community organizers who got their start with Vermont Alliance eventually helped to create the narrow political opportunity that opened for Bernie Sanders in 1981, when he was elected mayor of Burlington by ten votes. You could argue that his victory was nascent in an inflatable octopus, deep in the Plainfield woods.

AROUND 2016, when Donald Trump was first elected president, Vermonters and other deep-blue Americans began to fantasize about seceding from the union, and "Jamestown Seventy"—the Yale Law School paper that plotted a leftist takeover of a rural state like Vermont—again entered political discourse. Sanders, whose rise the 1970 paper uncannily predicted, had come closer to the presidency than anyone could have imagined. Blumstein and Phelan's forty-five-year-old study was circulated in PDF and sparked a renewed discussion of whether individual states like Vermont might operate meaningfully as concentrated sites of resistance to the federal government.

In the fall of 2022, I called Jim Blumstein, the coauthor of "Jamestown Seventy," now a professor of law at Vanderbilt. As a fourth-year student in a multiple-degree program, he and Phelan founded their journal as a leftist alternative to the hoary *Yale Law Journal*. Blumstein told me that the ideas in "Jamestown Seventy" were developed in conversation with another student.

"Hillary Clinton—then Hillary Rodham—was our friend. She helped us a lot. We bounced our ideas off of her."

And so, Bernie's 2016 Democratic primary opponent helped draft the blueprint that anticipated his rise in Vermont politics. Hillary Rodham suggested a new draft of the paper that included a tough, workable praxis. The earlier fantasies of concentrating leftist action in a rural state were merely "mental masturbation," Blumstein told me. "Hillary liked the concept, but her focus was on strategy."

The article was then revised to address Rodham's concerns. Encouraged by her, Blumstein and Phelan began to think in terms of special "methods of communication" that would innovate away from the static opportunities of print and broadcast media. Their "experimental state" would instead be a platform for "symbolic conduct": the authors list flag burning, draft-card burning, and the wearing of armbands in protest as preferable to "eloquent oratory or fancy prose."

And yet, their imagination failed them a little; Blumstein, who grew up in Midwood, Brooklyn, and attended Madison High School several years behind Bernie—I was stunned to learn of this coincidence—told me that he'd left something out of the analysis: the force of pure, animal, incessant tenacity. Cultures didn't mature on their own; like sourdough, they need a starter, a catalyst.

Blumstein used to see Sanders on the courts in Midwood, playing "Make it, take it basketball," Blumstein said, with a laugh. "We all did."

From what Blumstein could tell, Bernie seemed even then to understand innately "the dynamics of having possession."

6

The Vermont Freeman

(The Hanksville Schoolhouse, near Huntington, Vermont)

Networks

In late August of 1968, a transmitter atop Mount Mansfield began to beam the signal of WVNY across the Champlain Valley and into parts of New York, New Hampshire, and southern Quebec. The new network broadcast ABC's national programming—*Peyton Place*, *The Don Rickles Show*, *Bewitched*—along with its own suite of local shows, including "a live bowling alley show" and a variety show for children hosted by Cousin Yancy Stillinger and his Green Mountain Boys and Girls, who treated young Vermonters to a feature about the "history of old Fort Ethan Allen and the cavalry stationed there."

The rabbit ears on the living room TV, if angled properly during favorable weather conditions, could now bring Vermonters the full complement of national offerings: the new ABC affiliate; an NBC network, WPTZ, from Plattsburgh, New York, across Lake Champlain; and Burlington's most influential and distinctive network, and the state's first, the CBS affiliate WCAX. In addition, small transmitters across the state had begun to beam TV-33, Vermont's ETV Network. The networks ran *Gunsmoke*, *Hogan's Heroes*, and Saturday-morning cartoons, in addition to the evening news. ETV offered a documentary on the photographer Dorothea Lange, roundtable discussions on race in Vermont, and a variety of gardening shows.

The skies of Vermont were now loosely thatched by invisible frequencies. Each station required an engineering and technological breakthrough. In 1954, WCAX built a road up Mount Mansfield along a sheer vertical rise of two thousand feet. Crews then hauled the heavy steel for the tower, the fifty-foot-tall steel antenna, and materials to construct Vermont's loneliest residence, a two-bedroom home for the broadcast engineers who lived there in shifts through the winter, when temperatures dipped to near forty below zero.

To plant an enormous steel needle on top of a mountain required messianic leadership and massive investments of time, money, and political capital, as well as military-grade equipment and coordination. The network boards were therefore the redoubts of local business and community leaders: reputable, prudent straight arrows. These decorated war heroes, bank presidents, or insurance men knew how to drive a permit through the local boards and the legislature. When we hear today about "the corporate media"—one of Bernie Sanders's mantras—we needn't imagine distant overlords in gleaming skyscrapers. With the networks' own anodyne offerings setting the pace, it was in the nature of Vermont's fledgling local channels to reflect the most conservative views of the community they served.

What was true on the airwaves was true in the mailboxes. The state's most influential newspaper, the *Burlington Free Press*, functioned as the organ of its owner and publisher, J. Warren McClure, a pro–Vietnam War Nixon Republican. McClure ran a kind of secret intelligence agency out of the downtown offices of the paper. *Free Press* reporters were expected to make regular contributions to the extensive files that McClure kept on everyone in Vermont public life. The files on McClure's perceived enemies on the left were the thickest, and the leftist whom McClure hated the most was the handsome, charming Reverend Roger Albright, the leader of the Vermont Council of Churches.

Albright was the quintessential 1960s Man of God. A peace activist and rugged sex symbol, Albright incessantly criticized McClure's *Free Press* over its support—a steady drumbeat in editorial after editorial—for the Vietnam War. Albright became perhaps the most influential mainstream figure in Vermont to oppose the war. And there were rumors in the state that Albright, a regular presence on the radio call-ins and TV news roundups, had political ambitions of his own. But the *Free Press* was more than equipped to make or break a political career. A decade later, under different ownership, the animosities that the paper trained on Roger Albright were again unleashed on another upstart radical with a dim view of the media, Bernard Sanders.

All throughout the summer of 1968, when the hippies came to establish their lives in an idealized Vermont, tension was building in the real one. On the night of July 20, 1968, the state was forced to abandon its vision of itself as an oasis free of white racism. The notorious "Irasburg affair" led to years of painful introspection. On that moonlit evening, Reverend David Lee Johnson, a Black minister who had moved from California to the remote Northeast Kingdom town of Irasburg, awakened to the sound of gunfire and shattering glass. Johnson rushed downstairs to find his friend and her two daughters crouching on the living room floor, shaken but unharmed. When the minister heard a screeching U-turn, he got his pistol and fired nine shots at the passing marauders as they sped away

A resident of nearby Glover, Larry Conley, an Army veteran who had been arrested two weeks earlier for threatening campers at the local campus of the Vermont–New York Youth Project, was identified as the shooter. But Conley was not immediately apprehended; instead, the state police, with the aid of Warren McClure and his reporters at the *Burlington Free Press*, began to investigate the victim, Reverend Johnson. Two days after Conley was finally charged, the state police made two more arrests: Johnson and his white friend, Barbara Lawrence, were taken at gunpoint and booked on the charge of adultery (Johnson was married). The Irasburg affair has become lore in Vermont: Howard Frank Mosher based his best-selling 2002 novel, *A Stranger in the Kingdom*, on the events of that summer.

When Roger Albright took up Johnson's cause and was photographed on the front porch of his home, McClure weaponized his bursting file on Albright to destroy the young, progressive preacher. "We believe in strict law enforcement," McClure told a dinner crowd at the Vermont Bar Association's annual meeting. "We've got thousands of biography sheets. We've probably got all of you here tonight. Well, maybe not some of you younger members. But—we'll get you." Nervous laughter was heard all around.

McClure then got Albright. After the preacher's extramarital affair came to light, Albright resigned from the Council of Churches, left the ministry, and, as the *Burlington Free Press* described with detectable glee in a news story, traveled to Juarez for a Mexican divorce. "Mrs. Albright retains custody of the couple's five children," the paper reported.

Furious, still brimming with things to say, and now with nothing to lose, Roger Albright resolved that he would, in turn, get McClure. The *Vermont Freeman*, the paper that gave Bernie Sanders his start as a freelance writer, was born out of this complex animus just a few months later.

Freemen and Libertarians

There was a need for a new paper that served all of Vermont, a network to detect the new fragile signals. Information was coming from Goddard College and the Winooski River Valley, from Putney and Brattleboro in the south, from Charlotte in the Champlain Valley. The communes were the heart of something, but no capillaries circulated their values, customs, and goods to the wider scene. "We imagined a collaborative effort, north to south, east to west," Barbara Nolfi, an activist and early leader in Vermont's counterculture, told Yvonne Daley. The communes soon "moved into a loose-knit federation," appointing Robert Houriet as a kind of ambassador from the Vermont commune scene to the world at large. Houriet, smooth and reasonable, even went on the *Today* show and described the scene to a startled, incredulous Hugh Downs. Several communes had begun meeting twice a year, at the solstice. There, according to Houriet, they "sketched a new society" including

> a cooperative system for buying food, primarily grains such as brown rice; a separate children's collective; a medical clinic which would ride circuit between communes to assist at home births and treat all the chronic illnesses and infections; a traveling caravan of people's music and theater; a people's bank, endowed with $5,000 from Red Clover [a collective based in Putney]; a shortwave hookup for communication and defense alert; a car pool of '62 Fords for standardized exchange of parts and mechanics' knowledge.

But no civilization meeting up twice a year according to the position of the celestial bodies would evolve or advance much without a terrestrial matrix of communication: that "shortwave hookup" was good only for faint, blurted syllables. What Erik Davis called "the construction project" of confederating the counterculture was underway. The first real step was Free Vermont, the name of a loose infrastructure connecting communities across the state—by word of mouth, bulletin board, and graffiti. The network began in Putney, on the campus of Windham College, when young people seized several unused acres and established a "Free Farm." The hippie farmers were most concerned about being inadvertently shot: to keep hunters away, John Douglas, a filmmaker and Harvard dropout who was heir to the General Mills fortune, spread word that a nuclear bomber had crashed on the property, and staked homemade "Danger: Radioactivity" signs around its perimeter. Soon Free Vermont founded Common Ground, a vegetarian commissary in Brattleboro, and the Free Garage, for the repair of communally held VWs. The effect of these new networks was to give the communes a public face. They became a social and political interest group as well as an economic force. From the margins, the kids began to drop back in.

ROGER ALBRIGHT ADMIRED the bold social experimentation of the communes and the initiatives that led to Free Vermont, but he believed that the counterculture needed to be connected to the wider community. The key was to present the communes as versions of Vermont's long-standing

Yankee norms and traditions. In formulating this approach, Albright sought an important mentor in the hills of Chittenden County: his neighbor, the scholar of Vermont town meeting and theorist of grassroots democracy, Frank Bryan. Bryan walked with Albright on his back trails and tutored him about the history of town meeting and the dynamics of Yankee ruralism. Bryan encouraged Albright to see the distinctness of Vermont in its total weave of traditional and experimental scenes and institutions. Albright studied the labor struggles of men and women in the quarry belt, near Barre. He met with dairymen struggling to stay on their farms in the Northeast Kingdom. He went to Catholic churches in Newport and Derby Line and heard the congregations praying and keening for the unborn. In Burlington, Albright spent time with poor families on their stoops in the Old North End, with Burlington's Jews, and with African Americans in their small community near the Winooski River. On the hill at UVM, he met the student radicals in Billings Hall, a magnificent H. H. Richardson building constructed from local redstone. Albright also skied at Stowe and Killington, and chatted in the lift line with prosperous second homeowners from Boston, as well as with the hard-pressed natives who cooked their eggs and made their beds. In the north, Albright heard about the asbestos shed by a quarry on Belvedere Mountain. In the south, he learned of a nuclear power plant in the planning stages, destined for a bend in the Connecticut River.

Albright's new venture knit together all of these regions and interests. The *Vermont Freeman*, founded in 1969 with Bernard G. "Bun" O'Shea, a longtime Vermont newspaperman and political figure, was more like a proto internet than a traditional print paper: "an open forum for Vermont," the *Freeman* solicited articles from all Vermonters and promised to print whatever arrived at Albright's doorstep. Editorial offices were set up in a turn-of-the-century schoolhouse in Hanksville, a settlement between the villages of Starksboro and Huntington, in the shadow of Camel's Hump. At first, Albright printed the paper at O'Shea's letterpress in Enosburg Falls, Vermont, near the Canadian border, and distributed it from the back of his VW to town libraries, high schools, bookstores, and general stores. Vermonters all across the state looked forward to the weekly arrival of their own articles, letters to the editor, and classified ads, and those of their neighbors. Vermont saw itself in the *Freeman*.

The early issues of the *Vermont Freeman* established its mix of dogged reporting by Frank Bryan from Montpelier, enticements for new subscribers, lyrical dispatches from sugarers and beekeepers, reports from the communes, roundtables on "issues" like race and poverty. In scanning the *Freeman* you see how the various stances and interests in Vermont might moderate one another. A typical page embodies in its very layout the happy coexistence of contiguous opposites, held in the same loose social net, like farmers and hippies in line at the same pay phone.

The *Vermont Freeman* also introduced Vermont to the voice of Bernard Sanders. Bernie made sporadic freelance contributions to the paper, a dozen or so in all. This small corpus is a hodgepodge. Bernie's prose is strident, didactic, sometimes satirical, and often haranguing. His voice blares beside the mellow dispatches from the beekeepers. Sanders delivered his articles in person to the schoolhouse on yellow lined paper, scrawled in blue ballpoint pen. These pieces are usually rangier, less considered, less composed than the articles set beside them, but, like his early essays in *The Chicago Maroon*, they convey unmistakably his voice. The *Vermont Freeman* allowed him to transmit his presence virtually, with no apparent loss of intensity.

Bernie first broke into print with a letter to the editor in the March 15–17, 1969, issue of the *Freeman*. Writing just weeks before his son Levi was born, Sanders, more than ever dedicated to the theories of Wilhelm Reich, decried America's "destructive schools" where teachers forced their "playful, curious, and loving" five- and six-year-olds to learn "rigid concepts of 'right' and 'wrong' and 'good' and bad.'" Pen and notebook in hand, Sanders had scanned Vermont's commune scene, and felt he could make a prediction: "Many young parents are beginning to feel that, come what may, it is better for their children not to go to school at all."

Sanders's assessment was accurate, but its very appearance in the pages of the *Freeman* suggested that the homeschool movement had, in fact, begun to wane. Kids "from the woods" began to turn up in Burlington schools soon after. I remember the moment in January of second grade, when Sister Theodosia introduced us to a new student and told us with a tense smile how he "had been only with his parents." James Reed was created from scratch, on a small commune in Jericho. The family rejoined civilization together one year when their winter supplies ran short. Soon James's mother became our substitute teacher, a major upgrade from the nuns, and played "Free to Be . . . You and Me" on low while we did our math worksheets. James's father had answered an ad in the *Freeman* and found himself scooping fiddleheads and ramps in the produce section of the Onion River Co-op. The story of the dropouts cannot be told without their necessary and transformative next act, when they all—all at once, it seemed—dropped back in. The *Freeman* itself became a well-trodden path back from the woods and into the public square.

In the pages of the *Vermont Freeman*, many of Sanders's later positions cocooned. In subsequent issues, we find Bernie's consideration of the relationship between cancer and orgasms, citing Reich; the connection is mostly nonsense, but it gave Sanders a starting point for defining the role that social and economic factors play in illness. A defense of Cuba on the anniversary of the revolution hearkens back to Bernie's teenage admiration for Fidel Castro. Sanders has continued to praise aspects of Castro's Cuba throughout his career. Bernie's man-on-the-street interviews with farmers and labor organizers were important early attempts to expand his political constituency to culturally conservative groups. They also foreshadow the roaming-reporter program that he hosted as mayor, *Bernie Speaks: The Mayor's Show*, where Sanders perfected the art of the leading question.

But the *Vermont Freeman* is best known for traveling through time and helping to sink Bernie's 2016 bid for the Democratic nomination for president. The paper was all but forgotten until 2015, when, in the middle of his bruising primary campaign against Hillary Clinton, one of Sanders's *Freeman* pieces was dragged into the light. Like Danny Lyon's photograph of Sanders at the sit-in, the article resurfaced when Sanders's past was harrowed by the opposition. In those days, the Special Collections room at the University of Vermont, where Sanders's papers are held, played host to teams of intense young men working in pairs, there to harvest precious dirt from the old file boxes. When confronted by *Politico* reporters about the nature of their work, these gumshoes became vague, then they scattered.

The offending piece, which appeared under the headline "Man and Woman," opens:

> A man goes home and masturbates his typical fantasy. A woman on her knees, a woman tied up, a woman abused.
>
> A woman enjoys intercourse with her man—as she fantasizes about being raped by 3 men simultaneously.
>
> The man and woman get dressed up on Sunday—and go to church, or maybe to their "revolutionary" political meeting.

What is this, anyway—besides bad, obviously hectoring and didactic satire? Captions for a very nasty cartoon, or stage directions for an ill-conceived black box play, these little bulletins exaggerate for shock value a core belief of Bernie's: that the culture of "revolutionary" politics is as conservative at its heart as a church congregation, preserving, in all but its rhetoric, the deep-seated patriarchal fury and submission that blighted earlier, less "enlightened" institutions.

But "Man and Woman" was portrayed effectively by Clinton's people as the source of a toxin that had spread inside Bernie's presidential campaign. In the spring of 2016, while I was driving in Burlington, a young man pulled up beside me, apparently to ask for directions. He drove a Subaru with an elaborate bike rack and wore the standard Burlington costume of

time to do it again with a co-operative plan to provide this new kind of conservation-oriented park. With the population pressures what they are here in this county, we will be working not only for ourselves, but for the generations to come. This is one we can't afford to lose. ●

Diamonds are forever COMMENT BY BASIL BURSEY

Sean Connery is back on the bandwagon after a five year absence in his sixth appearance as Ian Fleming's super spy. Connery, a little older, heavier and still sporting a hairpiece, is more durable and dashing than ever. He still shows his well-known disdain for the role that made him famous through his liberal use of wry puns, which are honed to a finer edge than in previous Bond films.

With a humorous approach, the plot revolves around the infiltration and destruction of a diamond smuggling ring run by the villain, Ernst Blofeld (Charles Gray), from his Las Vegas headquarters. As usual in a Bond plot, the diamonds figure in a rule-the-world scheme as Blofeld waylays and impersonates a multi-millionaire, recluse tycoon named Willard Whyte (Jimmy Dean) to achieve his dastardly end.

Some of the characters Bond encounters are two comic killer inverts named Wint and Kidd -- Blofeld's hit men. The Bond girls are a little fleshy this time around, but Jill St. John gives a better than usual performance as the treacherous Tiffany Case and Lana Wood (Natalie's sister), as Plenty O'Toole, is given a gratuitous role as a casino gold-digger. The militant Ms will enjoy the two athletic agile female bodyguards, Bambi and Thumper, who kick, throw, and bounce Bond around.

As before in Bond films, the title song was lacking in appropriate quality, with the rest of the score hardly noticeable.

Guy Hamilton directed with action in mind, but with a few visual flaws. Of the action sequences, the chase through the streets of Las Vegas is the most fantastic -- here the flaw being the lines of people on the sidewalks, all intently watching the action being filmed.

But who cares. *Diamonds Are Forever* is one of the best Bond films and offers an evening of action entertainment. ●

"Smile, please!"

H. Kiiy

man-and woman by BERNARD SANDERS

A man goes home and masturbates his typical fantasy. A woman on her knees, a woman tied up, a woman abused.

A woman enjoys intercourse with her man -- as she fantasizes being raped by 3 men simultaneously.

The man and woman get dressed up on Sunday -- and go to Church, or maybe to their "revolutionary" political meeting.

Have you ever looked at the *Stag, Man, Hero, Tough* magazines on the shelf of your local bookstore? Do you know why the newspapers with the articles like "Girl 12 raped by 14 men" sell so well? To what in us are they appealing?

Women, for their own preservation, are trying to pull themselves together. And it's necessary for all of humanity that they do so. Slavishness on one hand breeds pigness on the other hand. Pigness on one hand breeds slavishness on the other. Men and women -- both are losers. Women adapt themselves to fill the needs of men, and men adapt themselves to fill the needs of women. In the beginning there were strong men who killed the animals and brought home the food -- and the dependent women who cooked it. No more! Only the roles remain -- waiting to be shaken off. There are no "human" oppressors. Oppressors have lost their humanity. On one hand "slavishness," on the other hand "pigness." Six of one, half dozen of the other. Who wins?

Many women seem to be walking a tightrope now. Their qualities of love, openness, and gentleness were too deeply enmeshed with qualities of dependency, subservience, and masochism. How do you love -- without being dependent? How do you be gentle -- without being subservient? How do you maintain a relationship without giving up your identity and

In historic Bennington
New Englander MOTOR INN
220 NORTH BENN. ROAD
BENNINGTON, VERMONT 05201
PHONE 802-442-6311
U.S. 7 & 67A

PAGE 20 MID-FEBRUARY, 1972 VERMONT

"Man and Woman." *Vermont Freeman*

a trucker cap, Patagonia fleece, and well-groomed, close-cut beard. He gestured for me to roll down the window, and then, to my eager and smiling face, told me he hoped I would "burn in fucking hell for supporting that fucking bitch."

You know who he meant. By that time in the primary season, with Bernie's defeat all but certain, we'd added a Hillary Clinton sticker to our own Subaru, below the Bernie sticker. Like most normal people, I'd moved on, even as many of Bernie's most ardent supporters were still clinging to a scrap of hope.

The altercation with the Subaru driver was my first experience with the phenomenon known as the "Bernie Bro": progressive in his ostensible politics but authoritarian in temperament, the Bro tapped a deep reservoir of sexism, and, in person and online, sought confrontation with anyone whose reality-based framework, like mine, led him to support the reviled Hillary when the Sanders ship had long ago sunk.

The feral male id unleashed by Bernie's campaigns was then expertly herded by some of his more confrontational advisers, including the combustible David Sirota, who blew up routinely on Twitter at anyone asking that the campaign rein in its Cro-Magnon Bro faction, small but loud. (Sirota, who went on to cowrite the hit film *Don't Look Up*, a flat-footed parable about the climate crisis, blocked me on social media, before a mutual friend intervened.)

Clinton's campaign, seizing on the *Vermont Freeman* "rape fantasy" piece, very effectively reframed Bernie's politics as violently anti-woman. This inflamed young men like my Subaru interlocutor all the more. Many stayed home on Election Day. Some, in those bygone, simpler political days, recognizing in an enemy of their enemy a friend, voted for Donald Trump.

IN THE BROADEST of Bernie's contributions to the *Vermont Freeman*, "Reflections on a Dying Society," in its August 1, 1969, issue, Sanders argues that modern life itself is toxic: "The air is poisonous, the noise deafening, the streets are dangerous to walk." Twenty-three percent of people walking around in Midtown Manhattan are deranged, according to a study that Sanders cites. Our food is cancer on a plate: root beer is carcinogenic, as is most commercially available cheese. It is typical fare—yet one paragraph stands out. "The state is usurping the rights of free choice in many domains of life," Sanders writes, sounding like a fiery Yankee farmer:

> To get an FHA loan one MUST build with specified lumber and materials; to drive an automobile one MUST have insurance and a car which has no rust going through; to run a farm and sell milk one MUST have a bulk tank; to drive a motorcycle one MUST have a helmet—to cite only a few examples.

Sanders, with a rusting car and a series of abandoned construction projects to his name, along with a new baby at home, is clearly drawing his analysis from the issues that irritate him personally. But you see in this branch of his thought the common ground on which Sanders and his Stannard neighbors had met, and which would, in the fullness of time, expand to include the libertarian-leaning rural Vermonters that formed a critical part of Bernie's statewide base.

Frank Bryan noted this left-libertarian strain and began to talk Bernie up in his circles. It was the beginning of a strange but potent alliance between the socialist Sanders and the libertarian Bryan, who had joined the *Vermont Freeman* in 1969 as its Montpelier editor. Sanders, in turn, studied Bryan's pieces to learn about the nuts and bolts of Vermont politics. Bryan's columns offered data-rich analysis of Vermont's political institutions. Some of them went into Bryan's classic book, *Yankee Politics in Rural Vermont*, published in 1974. Bryan did more than any other single Vermonter during this time to connect the hoary institutions and values of Yankee governance to the new ideas of the communes. He viewed these new communities as potential laboratories of democracy, real-time state-of-nature experiments that a political theorist might devise.

Bryan and Sanders were odd allies. But like so many old-line Vermonters—like Senator George Aiken, another conservative Yankee who admired Bernie—Frank Bryan loved Vermont, and he loved people who loved it too. Also like Aiken, he admired, though he did not entirely share, the live-and-let-live political leanings of the communards and hippies, who had come to the Vermont countryside only to reinforce and reanimate its existing rural nature. Though there was plenty in Bernie's thinking to repel Bryan, Sanders's anti-authoritarian streak spoke to him; it had something of the hill farmer in it. During Bernie's later years as mayor, Bryan's soft influence, in the classroom on the hill, on the streets of Burlington, on the radio and TV, and in a funny, cranky best seller coauthored with William Mares, *Real Vermonters Don't Milk Goats*, created the valuable impression that Sanders, an urban Jew, was in a way a Frank Bryan–style, George Aiken–style, rural Yankee. Bernie counted as a "real Vermonter," not an interloper: he almost certainly never milked a goat.

Bryan's blessing was precious. A coiled, compact Golden Glove boxer, Bryan worked out at the Burlington YMCA first thing every morning, then held forth over an enormous breakfast at the Oasis Diner nearby, before his long teaching day got underway. He returned every night to his converted deer camp in the Green Mountains, where he kept livestock and, to the town's dismay, as many as twenty junked Chevy Chevettes, stripped for parts, rusting in an open field. When his neighbors asked him to clean up his junkyard, he immediately agreed. "I am a communitarian," the notorious libertarian told a reporter. For Bryan, one of the great mythographers of rural life, the Chevette dilemma embodied Vermont's founding paradox: Freedom and Unity. To be a libertarian communitarian was to refuse to resolve the paradox.

Bill Mares (foreground) and Frank Bryan, Oasis Diner, Burlington.
Raj Chalwa, Burlington Free Press

Bryan loved paradox, relished it. In fact, Professor Bryan often got closest to what he meant by citing poetry, our most sophisticated verbal system for managing paradox. I used to talk with Bryan at the Oasis about odds and ends, but often about his favorite poet, Robert Frost. It began one summer morning in the early 1990s, when Bryan spotted my Amherst College T-shirt and brought up two poems by Amherst's great sage: "Mending Wall"—the famous poem that includes the misunderstood adage "Good fences make good neighbors," and a lesser-known poem, "A Witness Tree." Both poems are about the importance of boundaries. Both suggest, in complex ways, that the individual functions best in small communities where people are "bound"—perhaps Frost's favorite word, its two senses almost antonyms—to one another, but not to remote, bureaucratic institutions or ideologies. "Good fences make good neighbors," why?

Because, as Bryan explained to me, neighbors make and remake them together, collaborating every spring by filling the breaches in the stone. And the "fences" Frost and his neighbor "made" in Derry, New Hampshire, were barely hip high. A bunny could leap over them. They were therefore primarily symbolic, and what they symbolized was the cooperation that had forged them. And, importantly, they were beautiful, typical, and to some extent tragic, a remnant of an earlier time and ethos.

Bryan is now retired in Starksboro and does not grant interviews, but he has made a permanent mark on Vermont's democracy. For years, Professor Bryan required his students at Saint Michael's College in nearby Colchester, and later at UVM, to attend Vermont's annual town meeting in March. Young people, many of them from out of state, would fan out from Burlington to points all over the region, and listen in drafty church basements as citizens of Pownal or Wolcott worked out their school and road budgets. The students were there as tabulators: Bryan kept strict year-over-year records of citizen participation in the most hallowed of all Vermont traditions, also the most easily sentimentalized, most easily stripped of real and consequential power. Bryan reserved special scorn for "liberals" who treated town meeting as a picturesque civic responsibility. Instead, he wanted the event to be loaded up with nuts-and-bolts issues, so people simply had to attend.

In 1969, sharing the pages of the *Vermont Freeman*, Bryan's "communitarianism" and Bernie's "socialism" looked a lot alike in practice. Both men prized in village governance a high level of citizen participation: in some Vermont villages, attendance at town meeting ran close to 90 percent. Both men feared the encroachment of Montpelier, the capital city, and the influence in the state legislature of businessmen and wealthy transplants to Vermont. Both made a case for direct democracy, unmediated by corporate or bureaucratic interests. Bryan's ideal political scenario was his tiny hometown on the Connecticut River, Newbury, Vermont, where his high school class was composed of seven students. "Keep it small," Bryan told a reporter. "The basketball isn't good, but everyone gets to play." Sanders, blunt and indefatigable, impatient with paradox, and espousing many beliefs simply incompatible with Bryan's Yankee values, was, for Frank Bryan, nevertheless living proof that Vermont democracy worked.

Or perhaps it was simply this: like Frank Bryan, Bernie had been poor. He was at home around low-income people. He simply preferred their company to elites. Sanders and Bryan understood how discouraging poverty was, and also that it was not fated or inevitable. Neither man ever suggested that part of the Yankee code was to force people to fend for themselves. Nor had George Aiken. Vermont, in these men's view, took care of her own.

Finding the Freeman

Most copies of the paper that gave Bernie his start, and then caught up to him, were consigned to the woodbox and long ago met their destiny above a chimney, in the blowing winter clouds. But with the help of the internet, I finally located a pile of them stashed approximately two hundred feet from my childhood bedroom. On an unseasonably warm afternoon in November of 2022, Frank Kochman, the last publisher of the *Vermont Freeman* and Roger Albright's important collaborator, greeted me with an open bottle of Barolo he'd bought at Costco and, tantalizingly, a box full of yellowing newspapers. I then read Bernie's notorious "Man and Woman" on Frank's living room couch, alert to my eerie peripheral view of the house I left when I left Vermont for college in 1989.

A neighborhood is a network. I recognized Kochman, who moved to my street in 1987, from the block: he and his wife, Jennifer, kept a ragged perennial garden in front of their small red ranch house, an homage to their decades living in rural Huntington, one valley over from Hanksville, where Roger Albright published the *Freeman*. Kochman told me how Albright, a stranger acting the part of Good Samaritan, towed Kochman's VW out of a deep snowdrift one frigid night in the winter of 1971, and immediately recruited him to join the paper's staff. Frank and Jennifer Kochman also lived in a converted schoolhouse: in these two schoolhouses, Hanksville and Huntington, the *Vermont Freeman* was relaunched in 1972 after a short hiatus, using a new offset method that lent itself to a more gregarious workspace. The production process itself relied on a network of neighbors and contributors. Bernie, Kochman told me, sometimes came by to assist at crunch time, one of many *Freeman* writers who delivered his copy in person and stayed to paste it up on the printing boards, while mooching off the Kochmans' supply of chips and beer. Others made even more significant contributions: like most burgeoning rural communities in Vermont, at least a few of the local homesteaders had trust funds, and the ethic was to pass such windfalls of capital around.

I was accompanied on the drive from my home in Boston to Frank Kochman's house in Burlington by the voice of Jennifer Kochman, who had died a year before, in 2021. Jennifer was one of many Vermonters recorded in 2017 as part of the Vermont Historical Society's 1970s Counterculture Project. How strange and poignant it was to park my car in front of my childhood home, turn Jennifer Kochman's voice off, and, seconds later, pick up the conversation in Jennifer's home with Frank, who told me that he hadn't heard the recording in a few years. When we parted a few hours later, a little drunk, Frank was about to go listen again to his wife's interview.

Jennifer's voice suggested how in the pages of the *Vermont Freeman* you could find evidence of the very transformation that the paper had helped to catalyze. Frank concurred, and as we looked through the paper, the clue to this *Freeman* feedback loop was in the advertisements. During its first few years, the *Vermont Freeman* sold ads to the establishments that my grandparents frequented. The effect is almost comical: Bernie's screeds on orgasms and political revolution share the page with spots for Jan's Shoes and the Harbor Hide-A-Way, a faux-lighthouse restaurant that served fried scrod under suits of armor and diving bells. Frank told me it was Roger Albright's personal charm that brought such square, old-fashioned businesses to the paper. But then again, there were only square, old-fashioned businesses in Vermont in 1969.

By 1972, the paper's advertising base had changed dramatically, partly because the *Freeman*, which had a subscriber roll of three thousand but an impact on many thousands more, had abetted and accelerated the very civilizational changes that it reported on. Alongside the Sirloin Saloon, with its mile-long salad bar, we now find Origanum Natural Foods in Burlington, advertising "beans," "nuts," "books," "macrobiotic foods," and "much more" (the "much more" would have piqued a young person's curiosity, I think); the hoary old Vermont Bookshop in Middlebury, highlighting its offerings in "The Occult" and "Adult Fantasy"; the Odd Fellows Summer Festival, the Vermont People's Fair, a fiddle maker, and Vermont's foremost local purveyor of tapestries, hanging plants, tribal rugs, and wicker ottomans, "Decorative Things." Most of these businesses were around at least into the 1980s, when I encountered them firsthand. Some still exist today. The counterculture had begun to make strong economic inroads.

The *Vermont Freeman* shut down in late 1974, when Jennifer Kochman found she could no longer tolerate the chaos in her kitchen. The Vietnam War was winding down, and the mainstream networks had begun to acknowledge Vermont's new subcultures. The *Freeman* was a victim of its own success: it had brought the hippies out of the woods, and helped to mature dozens of political alliances, community groups, small businesses, and food and medical co-ops.

But the *Vermont Freeman* did outlast J. Warren McClure's ownership of its rival, the *Burlington Free Press*. McClure kept a stake in the paper but cashed out to the Gannett Corporation. The *Free Press* since has been a kind of customized national paper, rather than a true local paper. An editorial signed by Roger Albright on August 1, 1971, celebrates the exit of Albright's old nemesis: "As a newsman and editorial manipulator of this state's most widely circulated print medium, Mac was too often mistaken in his judgements, sometimes gravely," Albright writes.

He'll be terrific, Albright concludes, in his new role as Gannett's vice president of marketing—far from Vermont, in Columbus, Ohio.

7

We Americans

(Burlington: An Atlas and an Overture)

Queen City Cotton Mill, 1930. *Vermont Historical Society*

The Afterlife of Objects

I began writing poetry in my twenties partly to put my childhood to bed. The method is paradoxical, since first you have to dredge up the material you intend to bury. So I inventoried the household objects from my past that bothered me, summoning them as though before a tribunal. I found them all more or less guilty.

Those poems, published in my first book, *The Afterlife of Objects*, are full of long lists of stuff. Here, a bookshelf in our den:

O mahogany, O birch pipes,
pipe rack, hardcover

books—The Last Convertible, Trinity,
The Royal Wedding,

Biography of Patton.
Railroad spike inscribed

On your thirtieth year
as a soldier, from the 73rd.

Mail-order crest, name etched
in "runic" script.

My grandfather had constructed the bookcase in our garage out of spongy particle board, finished with a splintery maple veneer. In its main bay, three rifles hung above a large aquarium backlit in neon blue. The fish gazed out, through the glass, at my grandfather's medals and trophies: Milford Delorme, known as "Spike" for his marksmanship, was decorated in the Second World War as one of the "skiing soldiers" of the Austrian Alps. But Colonel Delorme brought home battlefield traumas he could not express, along with macabre keepsakes from the liberation. When I was ten, I discovered an SS uniform and steel dagger stored in a steamer trunk in a gambrel-lit attic corner. Also in our attic, I rifled through old clothes and photos, signs of the family losses that were never discussed, though I found signs of them everywhere. Three of my grandparents' children had died before they reached the age of ten, the last, Danny, just a year or so before I was born. I was named Daniel Paul, after their two deceased sons. Among many other emotions, my grandfather perhaps worried that I would die, too. The fear that he would see another child pass away under his roof must have been intolerable. It was no wonder that he sat very silently in front of his aquarium, smoking a pipe. He seemed to prefer silence from others as well, including from me.

The books on those shelves started to offend me, when I was a teenager: I was becoming refined; a scholar, a poet. What the hell was a *Reader's Digest Condensed Book*? How could you "condense" a book? That the emotion survives in the poem, written when I was twenty-seven or so, embarrasses me: it reveals what little distance I had established from this world even years later, when I'd come into a share of cultural power. When I wrote "The Sensible Present Has Duration," I was still mad: not about my grandfather's distance, his silence, or his temper, but about those *Reader's Digest Condensed Books*.

There were a few other books on the shelf that didn't make it into the poem. *Strategy for Survival* was a manual for surviving a nuclear blast: my grandfather worked in civil defense for the Vermont National Guard. We had a cellar fortified for the apocalypse, with metal cabinets full of tinned meats. I inherited the book and keep it close by.

Next to *Strategy for Survival* sat a blue hardbound volume published in 1937, titled *We Americans: A Study of Cleavage in an American City*. It was stamped with the seal of the Burlington Savings Bank, a gift to its new depositors. The title certainly caught my twelve-year-old eye, but the book was a letdown: by "cleavage" the author, Elin L. Anderson, meant only social and class divides.

There was something nevertheless thrilling about it, for the "American City" chosen for study as an illustration of modern social schisms was our very own. I'd never read a book in which Burlington was described for outsiders. I had no idea that outsiders would be in the least interested in Burlington. But here was lavish, rather literary prose, celebrating our city:

> The city rises on a hill that slopes gently upward for a mile from the eastern shore of the Lake. For background it has the sweep of the Green Mountains; for foreground the Lake, and the ever-varied vista of the distant Adirondacks. At the foot of the hill there are the wharves and warehouses, shabby tenement houses, and railroad tracks; halfway up is the business section—one main street running parallel to the Lake and headed by a fine old church; on the upper slope is a residential section of large, comfortable houses and spacious lawns; on the very summit is the University. From the top of the hill one can catch a glimpse of the Lake at its foot, through avenues whose interlocking elms form long aisles of Gothic arches. The unusual beauty of the setting has led many to voice sentiments similar to those expressed by William Dean Howells when, gazing upon the Bay of Naples, he remarked: "The most beautiful view of the world except one—a Lake Champlain sunset as seen from Burlington."

This might as well have been actual cleavage, it was so exciting! That "unusual beauty" of Burlington was part of our consciousness from childhood. Not only was our city beautiful; it was, in a distinction I later learned in English class, sublime: grand, mysterious, almost fearsome. In school we were taught to feel awe at the sight of our surrounding landscape. The mountains rising on both sides of the lake were once the shores of an ancient saltwater sea. The fields outside the city were full of marine fossils, urchins, sponges, whale bones, and other traces of our oceanographic past, like bath toys at the bottom of a drained tub.

Burlington's beauty drew everyone's attention to the horizon, but tended to hide the gnawing social problems right before our eyes. In 1971, when I was born, many of Burlington's neighborhoods had been in long, steady decline. These "shabby," "little known" enclaves were of great sociological interest even to the author of *We Americans*, writing in 1937. Here was my own neighborhood among them:

> All of Burlington, however, is not as lovely as this central area. There is the north end, thickly settled, where there are few elm-arched avenues; where many houses are close together and some are dark, unpainted boxes; where lawns are narrow strips of grass and the children play in the streets for lack of any more suitable playground. This side of the city has its own business section, which is frequented by the "other half" of Burlington only when it seeks a bargain. Then there is the isolated colony around the cotton mill in the south end of town, where uniform company houses shelter a group of workers whose connection with the rest of Burlington is slight. There is also a settlement "under the hill" on the far side of the slope that reaches Winooski, a mill town of 5,000 inhabitants one mile from the center of Burlington. This area, too, especially at its further end, has shabby, narrow houses. These neighborhoods, however, are little known to those who live their lives along the central slope of the hill.

We lived on the downward stretch of the slope that Anderson describes, not quite "under the hill" but heading in that direction. The mills were shuttered in 1954 and later transformed into upscale malls and condos, but in the mid-1970s, kids still scavenged there for rusty metal pipes and glass panes to use in our backyard projects. My neighborhood included a small tent encampment, a cluster of homes inhabited by several interrelated families who were stigmatized as "on welfare," squalid tenements inhabited by wealthy students, the handsome brick mansion of Judge Edward Costello (a wonderful, stately, liberal Republican who stopped to chat with me on his daily walk to work), and the souls residing in Greenmount Cemetery, where a towering obelisk marks the grave of the legendary Ethan Allen. Walking up the "central slope" on my way to school, I approached the magnificent brick and stone edifices of the University of Vermont cresting the hill. Walking home, I returned again to my own "little known" Burlington, invisible to outsiders—yet uncannily mapped in *We Americans*, the book about social class that I found on our very own shelves.

By the 1970s, when I discovered *We Americans*, middle-class Burlingtonians had fled to the suburbs, and city neighborhoods like ours had taken a steep downturn. Even the grand homes slid into disrepair. Slumlords warehoused most of the region's poor and elderly in tinderbox apartments, preying on individuals whose generational poverty was tied to the collapse of local industry and the mills. Students able to tolerate living four or six to a bedroom competed for these houses, and drove up rents all across the city, even as the proud old houses collapsed around them.

After its manufacturing base fell out, the city determined that a certain quotient of squalor and desolation in some of its central neighborhoods was not merely tolerable, but actually desirable: the path forward for the city's revitalization was to lock down federal monies for "urban renewal," the program for slum clearance that demolished many American neighborhoods. The Italian and French-Canadian neighborhood—the area described in *We Americans* as home to "the wharves and warehouses, shabby tenement houses, and railroad tracks"—was, in the early 1960s, encouraged to fail so that it could be condemned. Where parks, schools, and corner stores had been, the city constructed parking garages for suburban commuters and hotels for tourists. The lucky among its displaced found new, inexpensive homes in the city and surrounding towns. But many families dispersed into dangerous, crowded apartments in the Old North End, which was rapidly becoming a slum—and just as rapidly, a target for the next phase of urban renewal.

The city was trying to ruin itself to accommodate people in cars. As with many such public works bonanzas, graft and corruption became the rule. The Adirondacks to our west and the Green Mountains to our east kept their serene watch over it all, but at the bottom of the drained Champlain Sea, where beluga whales had once darted between marsh grasses, Burlington was slowly, neighborhood by neighborhood, block by block, changing from the relatively harmonious and stable city depicted in *We Americans*, to a place permanently scarred by mismanagement.

Sanders became a fixture in Burlington throughout 1970 and moved for good around May of 1971. I was born a few blocks away from his apartment that month. That made us both newcomers to Burlington, at the same moment. But the Burlington we encountered had been decades in the making, or unmaking.

Mills, Malls

A visitor to Burlington today finds sprawling, low-rise development radiating from its city limits: strip malls, gas stations, car dealers, Pizza Huts. You could be anywhere. The mountains are the only clue that you're not, say, in Hagerstown, Maryland. But this was all farmland not long ago: where

Burlington ended, rural Vermont abruptly began, just a short walk from city hall.

One of the nearby farms belonged to my great-grandfather Wilfred Delorme. He would come over on Sunday afternoons for early supper, driving from his small asparagus patch a mile or so away on Dorset Street in South Burlington. Great-Grandpa, a decorated veteran of World War I, was a cheerful tadpole-like man who called me "Danny" in the French-tinged North Country accent once common in our community. My mother speaks with much the same inflection. I like to code-shift, and put that accent on whenever I return home to Burlington.

Great-Grandpa had gone to work as a young teenager in the Winooski mills, sometime around 1915. He met my great-grandmother Laura Lucier on the looms. After the mills closed in 1954, Wilfred Delorme found a job with the state of Vermont and continued to farm his acres in South Burlington, where a Healthy Living supermarket—gorp, kelp, kombucha—now stands. He died in 1982 in an efficiency apartment nearby, surrounded by a few photos and keepsakes, bought off of his farm for pennies by a developer.

He fared okay, all in all. But the closing of the mills had a ghastly impact on many families in Burlington and Winooski, consigning them to generations of poverty relieved only by public assistance. The town of Winooski, the seat of French-Canadian culture in Vermont, was especially hard hit, along with the neighborhood just down the Winooski River, Burlington's Old North End.

The mills closed, the city neighborhoods slumped, the nearby farms were paved, and up sprang a civilization on Burlington's periphery. There, you could go to the buffet at Howard Johnson's, then buy an enormous suit at Gaynes department store to accommodate your new gut. You could live in a new home, modern, comfortable, and rectangular like a Monopoly piece, and drive to your job at the IBM plant in Essex, which in 1999 employed more than seven thousand people. There, transfers from Rochester and Schenectady, New York, joined the old Vermonters who commuted through the mountains every day to assemble superconductors. Mid-century America had bypassed Burlington and settled on its perimeter.

The proud old city was now studied as an urban planner's conundrum: how to move cars in, out, and through Burlington, when Burlington itself was in the way. The solution was to eliminate one of the city's oldest neighborhoods down to its "brick colonials with fan windows, carved windows, and strait-laced New England lines," which, according to the *Burlington Free Press*, "could have been—but never were—restored to dignity." The neighborhood, situated between Church Street, the city's main shopping district, and Lake Champlain, was often known as Little Italy, though it was home to a mix of Italian and French-Canadian families, with small communities of Syrian, Irish, and Armenian immigrants mixed in.

"Urban renewal" was already the subject of national debate when it arrived in Burlington in the 1950s, promising federal monies to combat poverty and decay. City planners in cities like New York and Boston, and in small New England cities like Waterbury, Connecticut, and Pittsfield, Massachusetts, regarded existing communities as unimportant nuisances, holding the threat of eminent domain in their back pocket as they negotiated to purchase families' homes for demolition. A backlash was spurred by Jane Jacobs's *The Death and Life of Great American Cities*, one of the greatest works of American nonfiction. By the mid-'60s, once the concrete set on the lifeless plazas and parking garages that replaced living environments, Jacobs's defense of the "intimate and casual life of cities" had rallied citizens to save what they still could of their historic, human-scaled neighborhoods. For Burlington's downtown, though, the damage was done. We were not a "great American city": while Boston and New York, cities with exponentially more citizens and neighborhoods, might absorb the tragedy of a Government Center or a Lincoln Center, Burlington was and is a city drawn to personal scale, known intimately down to the individual building, its communities numbering hundreds of individuals rather than countless thousands.

"It was cruel," my mother used to say to me when we walked the new blocks where the old shops had been. "They wiped it off the map." I was brought up to admire relatives who had fought the developers to a dramatic stand-off, only to succumb when the threatened summons finally arrived at their front doors. The very last house left standing belonged to Victoria Dutra, my great-uncle Esau's sister, and her family of thirteen. Vicky Dutra was thereafter remembered as the defiant guardian of her own "Ponderosa," a modest wooden frame house surrounded on all sides by construction rubble. In a photo from the time, she sits in her cement driveway in a plastic beach chair, her arms full of children, a crew-cutted husband smoking beside her. A twenty-foot-high pile of debris looms behind them. The wrecking crews had been "swell," Dutra told the *Free Press*: "The dust you can't help. I've prayed for rain." One of her boys had made eight dollars selling old bricks.

The *Burlington Free Press* was hardly neutral in its reporting on the process by which Burlington, over the course of ten agonizing years, from 1958 to 1968, tore out its urban heart. "Urban Renewal: Your Questions Answered" was the headline of its cheerful color feature in February of 1963, a few days ahead of an important vote on the plan. The 27-acre plot, home to "157 families, 67 single persons, and 41 businesses," was blighted,

Enjoying wide open space in Champlain Street Urban Renewal area, Clifford Dutra and grandson, Bobby Dragon, 4, and Mrs. Dutra with granddaughter, Paula Dragon, 13 months, and daughter, Marie, 9.

The Dutras at their "Ponderosa," 1950s.
Burlington Free Press

a "slum" in need of demolition. In its place, the *Free Press* dangled the prospect of a "motor hotel," an "elevator office building," and, most tantalizing of all, "1500 parking spaces." The affected families and businesses would be offered market rates—depressed, of course, by the looming prospect of demolition—to surrender their properties to the steam shovels. There was some urgency, the *Free Press* reported: in 1967, the Montreal World's Fair would attract "some 100 million persons" to the Canadian city to our north, and Burlington was expected to be "ready for business."

Viewfinder

It can be hard for a twenty-first-century American to imagine why cities ever let their waterfronts decline, now that condos with a view sell for millions of dollars. But the neighborhood that Burlington expunged, with its prospect over Lake Champlain, began as cheap housing for workers on Burlington's docks and on its barges. It then became a military encampment for more than four thousand soldiers during the War of 1812, when Burlington saw heavy bombardment. As the city's prosperity grew, the lake was for a century or more regarded as a congested highway for commerce. Burlington was at one time the fifth-busiest lumber port in North America. It was also the hub of a rail system that tracked along Lake Champlain before it deposited its loads of hardwood, slate, slab marble, granite blocks, milk, or hay at points south.

"Nobody ever went west of Church Street," my friend Vince Feeney told me. "There were fires and flaming piles of ash." Vince, the author of the best history of Burlington, described to me how the trains threw sparks and burned long fires all along the track bed. In my childhood in the 1970s and early '80s, Burlington's harbor was still a noisy, dirty, dangerous place. The city, poised over a sheer bluff, is positioned in such a way that you can stand in Battery Park and literally overlook this effluvial zone, while focusing on the scarlet and ochre sunsets on the horizon.

The hub of the city is Battery Park, perched high above a cliff where British cannonballs once rained down from wooden warships in the harbor. I have been every age there: I remember standing eye-to-eye and looking down the chamber of the black iron War of 1812 cannon, three feet or so off the ground; then, forty or so years later, helping my sons to climb its smooth cold flank and ride it like a pony.

Battery Park is hard to know how to see, unless you have layers of memories attached to it. Its nine acres of grass are badly kept, strewn with cigarette butts and the paraphernalia of whatever drug is currently ascendent in the surrounding neighborhoods. A 1970s band shell big enough to accommodate a small orchestra sits cavernously empty almost all the time, ruining many views. A playground, gouged out of the dry dirt, is often littered with broken glass. The expensive hotels a block or two away warn their guests from setting foot in the park at night.

A mounted viewfinder facing the lake, five cents for five minutes, became a childhood attraction. We mainly used it to try to spot the Lake Champlain monster, a Yankee cousin of the Loch Ness monster. "Champ" was rumored to dwell in the murky depths among the celebrated ruins of horse ferries and steamers that make Lake Champlain one of the premier diving spots in the country. A credible photo of the monster emerged in the early 1980s. The creature looked like a whale with the dainty neck of a swan, rising from the blue water. Was it possible that some refugee species had outlived the great Champlain Sea, and hid in a grotto at the lake's bottom, where time cannot be measured? Eminent zoologists from around the world convened nearby, at Shelburne Farms, to study the matter. Nobody ruled anything out. Area schoolchildren were riveted.

We'd often turn the viewfinder around, though, and peer into people's apartments and hotel rooms. Panning across the city, you saw the devastation. To the right, down Battery Street, the new office buildings and hotels where Merola's market had been. Concrete plazas where the old families gathered dandelions for salad. Parking garages, their empty upper floors perfect for high school parties, but also for drug deals and shootings.

Straight ahead is Pearl Street, the old Colchester Turnpike, which divides the city into its North and South Ends, its relatively poor and prosperous zones, with UVM students always straddling both sides of, and blurring, the divide. I lived about a mile up that road, on the north side of the street.

Pan left, and you can see into the homes on Park Street, the hem of the Old North End, where poverty and crime were on the rise. The Old North End thrived while the mills were still operating. Markets and pharmacies lined the streets, serving the needs of small, overlapping communities of African Americans, Chinese and German immigrants, and Jews who'd come to Burlington by way of Montreal. In Moccasin Village, a community of Abenaki lived in tenements on their old ancestral lands. You could find traces of all of these groups into the 1980s. The Old North End, certainly one of the most distinct urban environments in America, has always been a first stop for new immigrants: today the neighborhood has been revitalized by significant communities of Nepalese, Somali, Hmong, Afghans, and Ukrainians.

There was always reason for optimism to be found in the Old North End, but the 1970s were its historic low point. Pockets of the neighborhood looked abandoned. Children were sometimes not formally educated, and their parents often succumbed early in their lives to addiction and illness. The very poor in the Old North End were, by that point, bound by shames, now generations in the making, that kept them from seeking public assistance. To this day when I picture poverty, I picture the worst blocks of Burlington's Old North End, scraped and heaped like a giant salvage yard. Since we were proud of being somewhat better off, I was taught to avoid the neighborhood.

The two areas—the urban renewal zone, to the right, and the Old North End, to the left—were connected by destiny: many of those displaced when the old downtown neighborhood was razed settled in the Old North End, which then quickly deteriorated as its older residents, and the businesses that served them, fled to the city's outskirts. In ripping out one neighborhood, the city had in essence ruined two. As the 1970s wore on, Burlington deliberately concentrated more and more of its poor in an area already blighted by neglect and almost entirely devoid of services. The Old North End had no banks, few remaining markets, crowded and ailing schools, a few dangerous playgrounds, and a rate of poverty that approached, by some measures, 40 percent.

Battery Park itself straddled these worlds. Like the Boston Common, only on a tiny scale, Battery Park was never one place; it was portioned into separate zones just a few feet apart, where hippies got high, elderly people played checkers, parents idled beside their toddlers, teenagers drank and flirted. Everyone convened at the fringe to order fries from a converted school bus, Beansie's, then returned to their squares on the chessboard. The park hosted, in shifts, riots, curfews, demonstrations, band concerts, and fireworks.

Turning our viewfinder around again to face the lake and mountains, we find the dilemma that bedeviled Burlington throughout Bernie's rise, and that continues in later forms to this day. I once wrote a poem in the voice of "Vermont": I cast the state as an aging showgirl, perhaps a little drunk, ruined by her beauty. That's how I think about this view across Lake Champlain. The challenge has been to keep this magnificent attraction free and open to all. People in Burlington quickly pay their restaurant tabs on summer nights, and sprint down College Street to take in the sunset, where a crowd is already gathered. In April of 2024, tens of thousands of sky-watchers converged on Battery Park and the surrounding area to experience "totality," the total eclipse of the sun.

Sanders's first Burlington apartment on Front Street was adjacent to Battery Park, on the fringe of the Old North End. Few physical settings in the United States present such a contrast between agonizing urban problems and almost unreal natural vistas. Bernie's small, rented worker's cottage, his first home in the city, sat on the seam between those two Burlingtons. His challenge was to make the city take its eyes off the sunsets and face itself.

The Cathedral Fires

On January 17, 1970, the *Burlington Free Press* reported on a meeting arranged by the city's mayor, Francis J. Cain, between representatives of the Forbes & Wallace department store chain and the Burlington Downtown Merchants Association. The men from Forbes & Wallace were tempted by downtown Burlington, but wanted certain changes made to the city's development plan. The lot that interested the department store executives sat between Burlington's two magnificent Gothic cathedrals, the Episcopal Cathedral Church of St. Paul and the Catholic Cathedral of the Immaculate Conception, where, in May 1971, I was baptized.

When a group of urban renewal developers boarded a private jet to return to Atlanta and then vanished over Lake Champlain—the small jet fell off the radar, and was found fifty-three years later near Juniper Island—some in Burlington decided that development was cursed. Our beautiful churches would be spared from the steam shovels! Rising up as symbols of resistance, the churches tolled their bells every morning to call straggling parishioners to Mass. Their twin spires a block apart seemed to consecrate the surrounding construction sites for a purpose higher than commerce.

Then, tragically and troublingly, both cathedrals burned to the ground, roughly a year apart. The first fire, at St. Paul's, on February 15, 1971, was investigated only superficially, and attributed to an electrical surge. A year or so later, on March 13, 1972, a former altar boy, Timmy Austin, a friend of our family who had once asked my mother to the prom, was charged with arson for setting the second fire, at the Cathedral of the Immaculate Conception. Austin's mugshot ran on the front page of the *Free Press*: the awkward young man was broadly smiling.

Everyone in Burlington I knew, growing up, simply assumed that the cathedral fires were arranged by developers. This dark insinuation was not dispelled when the Episcopal Diocese of Burlington decided to swap its land with the city for a parcel with less commercial appeal a few blocks away. On the site of the old Cathedral Church of St. Paul, construction eventually began on the Burlington Square Mall—the spot where Bernie, wielding his man-on-the-street microphone, interviewed the mall punks for *The Mayor's Show* in 1988. St. Paul's moved onto a block once dense with colorful homes and businesses, and built a high-rise old folks' home, Cathedral Square, where many of the residents displaced by urban renewal eventually moved.

The suspicion that attended the cathedral fires was not created by them; it had been in the air for at least a decade, as, site by site, the bulldozers made their way across Burlington's downtown. The assumption in the immigrant communities was that city hall and developers were working closely and ruthlessly together. It was a sign—one among many—of how disenfranchised Burlington's voters had become. The spectacle of a city transformed and its population dispersed had done the necessary work of cowing the people of Burlington into submission. Of course the developers would use any means to secure those valuable empty lots in the new, gleaming city.

In a way, though, for the Catholics who had been displaced by urban renewal, this story was preferable to another, much more troubling story, one that was for years impossible to tell. Bernie Sanders would not have risen in Burlington a generation earlier for many reasons. But one main reason was that Bernie Sanders was not a Catholic, and Burlington politics was for decades controlled by men from my world of Catholic parishes and church schools. When our cathedral burned, the end of that particular civilization was nigh at hand, though nobody could predict how swiftly and completely the power of the Catholic Church in Burlington would be undone. By the end of Bernie's terms as mayor, the grip of the Church was broken, and, as priests and bishops retired or died, Burlington's Catholics had begun to express warily, and in code, the secret, tragic fact they'd been hiding even from themselves.

In 2019, the Catholic Diocese of Burlington finally issued its list of priests who had been credibly accused of rape and sexual assault of minors. Ten had served in some capacity at the cathedral, including Father Edward C. Foster, an assistant priest during the time when Timmy Austin was under his supervision as an altar boy. I had come into contact with approximately half of the priests on the list, and knew several personally, and knew very well one in particular: the first name on the list, Father Robert J. Baffa.

I was not abused by Baffa. He had presided at my parents' wedding in 1970; after their divorce, in 1972, the gregarious priest was made available to me as a father figure at times. I strongly disliked his company, for reasons I found hard to explain. "Father Tom" in a poem I published in *The Afterlife of Objects* in 2002 is based on Father Baffa. The scene is my birthday party:

The Lord so loved the world
he sent
a steaming pile of

lasagna for
my ninth birthday.
A plate. Another. One

cascading square
waits on
a spatula; our priest

arrives. My mother greets him.
His peck
on my forehead

is full, unwelcome.
He squires me
from relative

to relative
collecting gifts:
sweater, eight track, monster mask.

Father Tom in ordinary
clothes! I am
a special child.

Later, drunk, cursing
in Latin,
everyone in stitches,

he'll ash
his cigarette
on my bare arm.

The details in this poem have for the most part replaced my firsthand memory of that day, in curious ways. What I still remember firsthand, though, is that I felt, not physical pain, but visceral shame and fear when the hot ash hit my arm: How could I presume to embarrass Father Baffa with my discomfort? What would my punishment be?

There were other incidents with men on the list, as well as incidents with men not on the list, though mercifully in my case none ever went so far as sexual abuse. The churches were full, in those days, of young priests, a little shaggy, with something of the folk singer about them. That was not Father Baffa: he was a bon vivant, a riot, a wit. But the strategy, whatever the predator's chosen style, was to give children a privileged glimpse of the real person underneath the frock. Many priests smoked cigarettes with altar boys, or took them to Montreal and ordered them beers. The feeling you were supposed to have was: "I am / a special child."

When the new church was opened in 1977, there was a feeling among its parishioners of deep confusion and embarrassment. The old cathedral had been underinsured, and of necessity a leaner, cheaper aesthetic was chosen. The new building, designed by Edward Larrabee Barnes, was ambitious and modern, an ersatz-barn-meets-Japanese-temple—and, as everyone admitted, even the priests, it was hideously, shockingly ugly. Light streamed down from its gaudy skylights on a diminished and aged congregation. In its garish architectural nave, the old French-Canadian ladies knelt in the pews, prying their rosaries between thumb and forefinger.

Soon enough, the priest-abuse scandal came to light, and the diocese began to sell off its assets to pay settlements to its victims. The new cathedral, though barely twenty years old, was slated to go. When the end finally came, in 2017, the congregation had dwindled to a double handful of bowed, shuffling old people, solemn with grief. The property, with its beautiful grove of symmetrically placed, still-immature walnut trees, was abandoned, and awaits demolition behind barbed wire. A brief campaign to preserve the Cathedral of the Immaculate Conception for its architectural significance was fought off by victims of the "Cathedral Ten," the ten or so priests who abused children in the parish. "Burn it," one victim wrote in a terse comment on a local paper's website. A curse now hangs low over the building. When I walk by it, I realize that in my lifetime I saw a civilization collapse.

Part II

Bicentennial

Vermont Historical Society

8

The Children's Crusade

(Liberty Union, 1970–71)

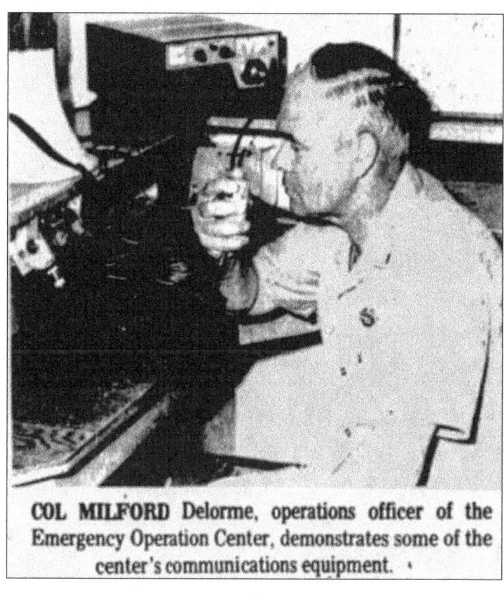
COL MILFORD Delorme, operations officer of the Emergency Operation Center, demonstrates some of the center's communications equipment.

Colonel Milford "Spike" Delorme, 1970.
Burlington Free Press

Kill Your Parents

The article in the *Burlington Free Press* on July 10, 1970, posed a riddle: "What do record snowstorms, student demonstrations and nuclear attacks have in common?"

Give up?

All three would "activate the Vermont National Guard's Emergency Operation Center," located in an underground bunker and linked to a web of tunnels under Camp Johnson, near Burlington. The facility, swaddled in concrete and protected by a thick steel door, was built during the postwar vogue for bomb shelters and blast-proof vaults.

The photo accompanying the article shows a trim, handsome man behind the controls, posing with a Telex handset. According to Colonel Milford Delorme, the operations officer at the bunker, the last time the EOC had been activated was "during involvement-week demonstrations at the University of Vermont." Though the protests had been "low-key," the Vermont National Guard was ready, Delorme advised, to "handle any possible outbreak."

Colonel Delorme's son Philip, my uncle, was at the time a sophomore at the University of Vermont and a student demonstrator. Philip's brother, my uncle Mark, was headed to UVM that fall, to star on the football team. Danny had succumbed to leukemia in April of that year. The man in charge of sending in the troops is furious at one son, proud of another, and grieving for a third.

Was my grandfather's word *handle* a threat, or a message of reassurance? The *Free Press*, our conservative paper, played it as the former. But I think he meant it the other way around: Vermont wouldn't blow up the way Kent State University in Ohio had just two months earlier, when the Ohio National Guard fired sixty-seven rounds into a distant, dispersing crowd of unarmed students on campus, killing four and wounding nine. Vermont, as usual, exempted itself from the national traumas. The University of Vermont was an ag school, full of country valedictorians and village Latin Bee champions, plus a few rich scions who had ski-bummed their way to the bottom of their classes at the New England prep schools. It seemed immune to unrest.

By the summer of 1970, a generational chasm was widening. Action centers were set up at UVM, at Middlebury College, and at Windham College in Putney. Student strikes were called across the state, and sit-ins along the major secondary roads disrupted the passing hay trucks and Karmann Ghias. There were radical actions even at Dartmouth College in New Hampshire, the world of letter sweaters and ice sculptures just across the Connecticut River. Students had become aware of themselves as an organized resistance. At Goddard, firearms training was held on Saturday mornings amid the splendor of the late daffodils.

In early April of that year, Jerry Rubin told the crowd of students at Kent State to kill their parents, "quite literally." A few weeks later, President Richard Nixon, adrenalized by repeated viewings of the film *Patton* starring George C. Scott, announced that to defend the American values under siege at our "great universities," the U.S. would invade Cambodia. As Rick Perlstein put it, "The campuses, Cambodia: it was all the same fight."

But on May 4, at Kent State, it was the kids who were killed, and by the parents' proxies, many of whom, sharpshooters trained in Vietnam, also happened to be kids. Protests flared on campuses across the country that spring. At the University of Illinois at Urbana-Champaign, a cocky political scientist named Michael Parenti found himself one afternoon at the bottom of a scrum of policemen. When his fist located an officer's jaw, Parenti, who had signed a contract to teach at UVM for the coming fall, was arrested, and, while awaiting his hearing, moved to Burlington, where he was greeted by students and faculty as a countercultural hero—and by the UVM trustees as a dangerous agitator. After Parenti led a march of hundreds of students down Main Street waving a Vietcong flag, the Vermont legislature threatened to cut funding to UVM by $2 million, and the trustees, now working with Governor Deane Davis, conspired to find a way to dispose of Michael Parenti.

The "Michael Parenti affair" made national news in the early 1970s. Parenti appeared to relish the attention. First, he began the practice of reading a newspaper with his feet up during his classes, ignoring his students "as a political statement," according to Garrison Nelson. Soon he picked a fight with a nineteen-year-old ROTC cadet bussing his tray in the cafeteria, calling the young man a "fascist" and a "Nazi." The two nearly came to blows. The story was amplified by conservative papers, the matter was debated on the statehouse floor in Montpelier, and the university, under heavy pressure statewide, declined to reappoint Parenti. The "political purge at UVM" then became a cause célèbre: a legal defense fund of $17,000 was raised in his name. The ACLU took up Parenti's cause as a winnable academic freedom case and began the process of moving his name through the courts. Parenti, bored of it all, soon took a settlement from the university and hit the speaking circuit. A political career had been launched.

But Parenti had summoned Burlington's leftists out of obscurity. Sanders soon met this cell of professors and students awakened by the Parenti fracas to the city's political possibilities: Nelson, the political scientist who later became an important behind-the-scenes political player; Huck Gutman, a professor of American poetry who became one of Bernie's closest advisers and friends; John Franco, a brilliant undergraduate gadfly who went on to become Bernie's powerful deputy city attorney; Martha Abbott, a longtime Sanders ally and activist, who worked on his winning 1990 congressional campaign; and, perhaps most important of all, Richard Sugarman, the six-foot-four Orthodox Jew and former football player who was then UVM's "philosopher in residence," but became Bernie's chief strategist during his winning 1981 mayoral campaign. Parenti's legal defense fund was converted into a budget to bring political radicals and intellectuals to lecture at UVM, a current that swelled when the city elected a socialist mayor. And thousands of students now claimed to have been among the hundreds at Parenti's pro-Vietcong march. Sleepy, conservative Burlington detected at its margins an active, restless counterculture.

Liberty Union

In the summer of 1970, after Kent State, Vermont was preparing for midterm elections, and the radical "kids" had no candidate: a population in the tens of thousands with no political home. The leading Democrat to face Senator Winston L. Prouty, a Republican, was Vermont's liberal lion, Philip Hoff. As governor from 1962 to 1968, Hoff had been early in his opposition to Vietnam, a bold and politically risky break from President Lyndon Johnson. He was also deeply troubled by Vermont's whiteness and isolation. But Hoff had overreached: his Vermont–New York Youth Project, which brought hundreds of teenagers to all-white Vermont villages to experience all that a Vermont summer had to offer, including racism, had been an embarrassing failure: the governor had dreamed it up, as the *Vermont Freeman* put it, "full blown before he had talked with any black people."

Hoff, the spruce JFK-era talent, was wrong for the moment, though his political career spanned another two decades. His three terms as governor had weakened Vermont's Democratic Party, which endorsed a Republican, George Aiken, for U.S. Senate in 1968. The prospect of sending a Democrat to the Senate was always a mixed one for Vermont liberals anyway, since, as it was put in the *Freeman*, it would serve only to "strengthen the grip of the conservative Southern democrats on all the key committee chairmanships." In 1970, the Democrats were still, in the South, the party of Dixiecrat segregationists.

By the summer of 1970, Hoff had aged, while Vermont had gotten drastically younger. Hoff drew two challengers in the primary. One was the flamboyant pro-war restaurateur Fiore "Babe" Bove, who called all the ladies "doll" and, well into the 1980s, from behind the fantastic Tiki-style bar of his family's Italian restaurant on Burlington's Pearl Street, doled out little toothpick umbrellas and crazy straws to beguiled children—indeed, to this beguiled child. But the candidate of the counterculture, only then becoming aware of itself as a bloc, was neither Hoff nor Bove, two Burlingtonians, but William H. Meyer, a forester from tiny West Rupert in the far southwest corner of the state, just over the border from New York.

Meyer was known in the state as the political miracle that fizzled fast. In 1958, he made national news when, in what appeared at the time to be a fluke, he was elected to Congress as the first Democrat Vermont had sent to Washington since 1850. A Pennsylvania Quaker who'd been a middleweight boxer, Meyer arrived in Vermont in 1940 to work in FDR's Soil Conservation Service. He was known to everyone in West Rupert for his personal loathing of Richard Nixon, which he carried almost to the point of eccentricity. Soon Meyer had had enough of crabbing about politics at the general store, and, on a shoestring and against an unpopular Republican opponent, ran for Congress. On November 4, 1958, Meyer lost little West Rupert by a wide, friendly margin, but he carried the state of Vermont by a comfortable four thousand votes. *The New Yorker* published Christmas verses to celebrate: "let there be magnificats / And other paeans by the choir" to celebrate "Vermont's landslide—William Meyer!"

Mr. Meyer then went to Washington, spoke his mind, and crashed to earth. Because he advocated complete nuclear disarmament and normalization of relations with red China, Meyer was widely, wrongly assumed to be a communist, as was Bernie a generation later. Embarrassed Democrats primaried Meyer in 1960, and soon Meyer returned to his radish patch and his Nixon fixation in West Rupert, where he pondered his next move.

By 1970, the times, but not the Democratic Party, had caught up to William Meyer. When the *Freeman* called for him to found a third party, a summons was put out in the paper for a summer barbecue at Meyer's home in West Rupert, inviting any like-minded Vermonter to attend. Martha Abbott, then twenty years old, arrived from Burlington to a casual gathering, where a distinctly intergenerational crew of "young men and women with tousled hair, antiwar activists," along with "old radicals, many of them urban dropouts," milled about in the living room of the old farmhouse or on the buggy grounds. All sought a political alternative to the Democratic Party. "Everybody was of one mind," Abbott said. "Let's do this, what will it take to do it."

Bernie Sanders was not a founder of Liberty Union ("deliberately and significantly," according to the *Freeman*, it was "not called a political party"), as many have assumed. In fact, if he'd been at the summer gathering, he would have had to introduce himself to a group whose members were already well acquainted. Many of Liberty Union's founders were rollovers from the New Party, a vestige of Eugene McCarthy's 1968 presidential run. It was a seasoned group. Meyer had a secret weapon in his wife, Bertha, a scholar of Jean-Paul Sartre and a prize gardener who credited her political baptism to a childhood call paid to her parents by the American populist William Jennings Bryan. The Meyers were joined by Dennis Morrisseau, an ambitious Burlington boy of erratic politics, who drew national attention when he protested at the White House in his Army uniform; Abbott, on hiatus from her undergraduate studies in English and theater at UVM; the artist Richard A. Clark and his wife, Betty, of Chittenden; and an obstreperous, outrageous young lawyer and legal aid worker, Peter Diamondstone, of Brattleboro. Diamondstone was a square-jawed raconteur in red suspenders usually accompanied by Saint Bernards. Doris Lake, his beautiful, shy, intellectual wife, who was reluctant to take up politics at all, became one of the party's earliest stars.

The village of West Rupert has a provenance: it played host to the mint for the Vermont Republic, an independent nation from 1776 to 1791. Indeed, Liberty Union suggested a symbolic return to Vermont sovereignty even as its candidates focused the little rural principality on the big national traumas it could no longer afford to ignore. The party's name echoed Vermont's state motto, "Freedom and Unity." The terms of the party's name could be understood as opposites: isn't the test of "liberty" the individual's feeling of autonomy? But nobody snowed into their driveway is "free" until the plow arrives, and the realities of daily life in Vermont meant that a weave of social consideration was necessary for survival. Vermont defines itself as the resolution of this apparent paradox; across the Connecticut River, in New Hampshire, where "Live Free or Die" is the state motto, the crowning value is not paradox, but lethal certainty.

Liberty Union was the first party founded in Vermont for Vermont, but it networked with small leftist parties across the nation, joining an improvised, loose congress of grassroots activists. Vermont had always stood "snugly cocooned from the fractious rhythms of the Republic," according to Jeffrey St. Clair. The state's villages were cells in a hive, and Vermonters tended to burrow in. Local select boards addressed village matters; but what was counted as a village matter, when the hockey stars and Eagle Scouts of Chelsea and Craftsbury were being sent to die in Vietnam? And, if those young Vermonters returned home alive from the war, they encountered an economy tilted to benefit business and development interests. The jobs that awaited, in the granite quarries and asbestos mines, on road crews or seasonal construction crews, were grueling, and fledgling unions tended to be crushed by management. In 1970, eighty-five thousand Vermonters, roughly one in six, lived below the poverty line. Tax breaks for business increased from 1965 to 1970 from $12 million to $81 million, while the tax burden on average Vermonters increased. In Vermont, "the poor subsidize the rich," according to an article by Michael Parenti—who returned to Vermont in the mid-1970s to run for Congress as a Liberty Union candidate.

Though it had support across the state, the heart of Liberty Union was probably Brattleboro, where the Diamondstone family still resides, and near where a finicky, frequently malfunctioning nuclear power plant soon opened. Though Vermont had begun to express itself as the nation's environmental conscience, the state permitted construction of the Vermont Yankee Nuclear Power Station on a crook in the Connecticut River outside of tiny Vernon, on the Massachusetts border. The freezing waters flowed south through its reactor core and emerged fifteen degrees warmer. Fish spawned in the temperate pools, then froze to death. Southern Vermonters tending their early gardens suddenly had to worry whether they fell inside the ten-mile "plume exposure pathway zone," where breathing would be lethal, or the fifty-mile "ingestion pathway zone," where, if the air didn't kill you, the asparagus would.

Vermonters needed to hear what Liberty Union had to say—but how would it get its message out, when the local papers printed mainly stories about high school basketball and bowhunting season? The TV networks beamed canning shows and *Hogan's Heroes* from their antennae high atop Mount Mansfield. On the radio, faint, faraway voices, French voices, drifted by on gusts of static. And the prevailing Yankee style was to say the same kind of thing over and over to your neighbor, every day, so as to express very little at all. Liberty Union had a corps of young, flamboyant, attention-grabbing, and indefatigable talkers: insisters; persuaders. Voices crying in the wilderness.

9

A Special Election

(Sanders for U.S. Senate, January 1972)

Bernie and Levi Sanders, 1971.
Vermont Freeman

A Special Election

In November of 1970, Winston Prouty prevailed in his race for U.S. Congress by a wide margin over Phil Hoff and Hoff's former opponent in the Democratic primary, William Meyer, now running for Liberty Union. Prouty was heir to a lumber fortune from Derby, far to the north on the Canadian border, and had lost part of his hand in a sawmill accident as a child. His tenure in Washington was overshadowed by that of his illustrious senior colleague, George Aiken. Sturdy, reliable, unremarkable, Prouty, widely rumored to be very ill, was nevertheless returned to Washington, and soon after died of complications from gastric cancer, in September of 1971. Governor Deane Davis called a special election for January of 1972. Vermont would now have an immediate second look at its newly fledged nonparty, Liberty Union.

In the meantime, Liberty Union got what appeared to be a big break. During the summer of 1971, the Twenty-sixth Amendment to the U.S. Constitution was ratified in record time, lowering the voting age to eighteen across the land. The Ohio legislature toppled the thirty-eighth and decisive domino. On July 6, Richard Nixon formally witnessed passage of the amendment in a "youth oriented" event at the White House, backed by a stiff, uncomfortable ensemble of eighteen-year-old singers from every state. Back in Vermont, the spray of young people diffusing across the landscape now looked to some like a political juggernaut. Wouldn't Vermont's kids vote to keep themselves out of Vietnam?

But Peter Diamondstone, among others in the party, had his doubts. Liberty Union had deliberately "done no organizing on college campuses and made no attempts to register young people involved in the communes," he boasted to a reporter from Boston's alternative paper, *The Boston Phoenix*. For Diamondstone, it was a waste of time "talking to people already on our side." The goal was to bring culturally conservative working-class Vermonters into a party founded by educated out-of-staters. From the moment he joined Liberty Union in 1971, Sanders "realized that the party itself might be an impediment to realizing such a dream," as one early party member told me. And for Sanders, and the man who later organized college students as part of his winning mayoral coalition, to write off young people was "a travesty."

The Bookchins Take Burlington

By the summer of 1971, Bernie Sanders had moved for good to Burlington. His son Levi, living mainly with his mother in Stannard, often visited his father as part of a casual custody arrangement, but Sanders was solo when he crashed with Jim Rader for a few weeks while getting on his feet. To prepare, Rader tapped the skills he'd used to enlarge Sanders's sugarhouse several years before, and constructed bunk double beds in time to accommodate the new lodger. There was no accommodating Bernie's cooking: to Rader's distaste, Bernie liked to fry thick steaks from Colodney's, the local market, until they were gray and leathery: "a Jewish tradition," as Bernie's friend Richard Sugarman told me. Soon Sanders found a few rooms in the back of an old glass factory worker's cottage a block from Battery Park, on Front Street.

Sanders encountered in Burlington an old-fashioned, stagnating city of lunch counters and blue-plate specials. At Woolworth's on Church Street, the tin ashtrays overflowed, and the old ladies ate toast with marmalade over paper placemats advertising Jan's Shoes, Bailey's Music Rooms, and the Sirloin Saloon. Great War veterans nursed cold coffee from soggy cups in the back of the McDonald's on Bank Street. The '60s had come and gone, and had left the city's barbershop quartets, ladies' auxiliaries, and garden clubs intact. Hippies came to town from the countryside to shoplift at the A&P before fleeing back to the action in the woods, where the zeitgeist awaited its purloined aspirin, tampons, and soap.

It was the sort of town that could be changed permanently by the arrival of a vegetarian restaurant. Burlington's new business, the Fresh Ground Coffee House, had been dreamed up far away, on the Lower East Side of Manhattan. There, in January of 1971, word reached the young members of a collective called the Anarchos Group that "radical ecological consciousness" had taken root in the state of Vermont. Yet when Sandy Brownstein, a member of the group founded by the social theorist Murray Bookchin, scouted Burlington, she encountered very little ecological consciousness in a city full of "bacon-and-egg diners, hardware stores, and gun shops." Brownstein saw her opportunity and returned to New York, where she persuaded Bookchin and his followers to head north to start a new anarchist collective in the dour old northern city. The bacon-and-egg diners were fine, but what Burlington needed, Brownstein told Bookchin's followers, was carrot soup, whole-bean coffee, and a place to gather and organize.

That summer, Bookchin, accompanied by Bea Bookchin—Murray's ex-wife, confidante, and political ally—and their two children, Debbie and Joe, arrived with an entourage in the sleepy Queen City. The Bookchins' friends Michael and Sandy Bass found "an espresso machine in someone's barn," Debbie told me, and opened the Fresh Ground in time for soup weather. Michael and Sandy managed the crowd, a mix of leftist gadflies like Michael Parenti and Bernie Sanders, "obscure people, eccentrics, people writing in notebooks all day or mumbling to themselves," according to Rick Warner, as well as "regular people, even cops." Draft evaders on their way to Canada stopped over at the Fresh Ground, collecting word-of-mouth advice about backroads, border crossings, and safe houses. Once a group of Berkeley poets, including George-Thérèse Dickenson and Anna Blackmer, dropped into town and picked up shifts at the restaurant, taking Debbie Bookchin, then fifteen, under their wing. Warner, who worked on and off at the Fresh

Ground for ten years beginning in 1972, recalled that he twice served Art Garfunkel onion soup. Pete Seeger raved to friends about the coffee, "fifteen and a penny tax, sixteen cents altogether," with refills for "one thin dime." Whether that was Jackson Browne at the table by the stairs, absentmindedly picking at the ratatouille, Bernie Sanders could not have said: he was in the middle of one of his "regular stemwinders" in the raucous smoking section upstairs.

But the star of the show was Murray Bookchin, a dervish in suspenders, obstreperous and iron willed, and at fifty a legend on the anarchist-environmentalist left. Bookchin's political formation, like Bernie's and Diamondstone's, began in New York's outer boroughs. After a hardscrabble childhood in the Bronx, in the 1930s Bookchin organized his coworkers at a New Jersey foundry, where he worked long hours guiding streams of molten metal into the awaiting molds. Bookchin's thinking at the time metamorphosed through the common stages and phases of pre-war leftist formation—he was at times a Stalinist, a Trotskyite, and a member of the Socialist Workers Party; but by 1971, Bookchin was known as the father of "social ecology," a theory of radical localism and environmental care inspired in part by the small-town governance customs of Vermont. In Burlington, Bookchin became a Thomas Paine figure, retailing his revolutionary ideas from park benches, lunch counters, and street corners to young acolytes by day, and to the adult students who enrolled in his seminars in the evenings at the Fresh Ground.

Bookchin's theory of "social ecology" evolved from his early and trailblazing environmental writing. Under a pseudonym, he had published a study of ecological catastrophe, *Our Synthetic Environment*, in 1962, two years before Rachel Carson's *Silent Spring*. A pamphlet, "Ecology and Revolutionary Thought," circulated widely in the communes. Bookchin discovered in Vermont's existing microscale face-to-face political structures, the model for a radically horizontal democracy. He had begun an inquiry into the anthropological and psychic roots of *hierarchy itself*, the trellis upon which power and subjugation was pinned. If he could understand the origins of hierarchy, Bookchin told his students, then he might be able to establish a truly egalitarian society, built across the horizontal axis of human cooperation rather than the vertical slope of subjugation. The existing grid of cooperation in Vermont—gun shops and diners included—was, in Bookchin's view, marvelously visible and intelligible, and sturdy enough to support a new kind of environmentally sensitive, nonhierarchical social habitat.

The Fresh Ground first ran as a collective, as an extension of the Bookchins' communal living pod—"no doors, was the rule"—in a warren of upstairs rooms next to the city's art deco masterpiece, the Flynn Theater, but the news of Bookchin's arrival in Burlington soon hit the Winooski River Valley. Faculty and students at Goddard College heard that Burlington was "potentially happening," Kip Parsons said, and began to gather at the Fresh Ground. Soon, a Goddard anthropologist, Dan Chodorkoff, sought out Bookchin in his smoke-filled study next to the Flynn's marquee, to pitch an idea: a lecture series, followed by the establishment of an Institute for Social Ecology, where experimental biodiversity could be studied in part as a basis for new, human-scale urban habitats. "Complexity, variety, diversity," Bookchin wrote, blurring the lines between animal and human environments, "are a function of stability." Sanders and Bookchin were, from the start, temperamental opposites—Sanders "could never abide the utopian rhetoric," a friend said, "but he agreed with Murray that it would be a good thing for people not to want to dominate each other."

In Plainfield, Bookchin met innovative social theorists like Milton Kotler, the decentralist urban theorist and community organizer, and radical tinkerers like the oceanographer John Todd, whose closed-loop bio shelters collected the sun's rays in massive water tanks filled with tilapia; at night, the water tanks released the concentrated solar energy to nurture vegetables, then were drained to feed the crops with water enriched by the tilapia feces. Soon Bookchin had transformed the Cate Farm—where a stoned William H. Macy beheld Bread & Puppet's "wild things" hung in stalls—into a laboratory for experimental technology. Among the grazing sheep, students encountered a Dr. Seuss world of bio shelters, solar-powered windmills, botanical follies, and geodesic domes. Bookchin presided cheerfully over this remote facility like a countercultural Oppenheimer in Los Alamos—or "like Willy Wonka," as an observer put it.

Between the fish farms in the mountains and the cauldrons of soup at the Fresh Ground Coffee House, a relay ran. Goddard and the Fresh Ground, sixty miles apart, were the transmitting stations for radical ideas about power and subjugation. Sanders, no fan of fish farms or of gourmet coffee, and "ruthlessly sarcastic" about Bookchin's wild-eyed pronouncements, nevertheless participated in the busy traffic moving between the two points, one artery in the larger organism then evolving into a new Vermont.

The left in Burlington now had the beginnings of an infrastructure: in the *Vermont Freeman*, it had a newspaper; in the Fresh Ground, an organizing space and political salon; in the persecution of Michael Parenti, a local cause to rally behind, and a band of leftists stirred to the cause; and in Liberty Union, an upstart political party. VISTA workers and community organizers, fresh from the elite colleges, began to arrive in Burlington's neighborhoods. Because of Parenti, the city also had some unwanted notoriety: the FBI had placed agents on the ground, where they mixed with student demonstrators at UVM and conducted at least one physical search of the Fresh Ground Coffee House. The Fresh Ground was "a known meeting spot for extremists," according to the Bureau.

BERNIE SANDERS HAD become aware of Liberty Union back in September of 1970, when he and Jim Rader attended a two-day conference, "Democratic Change—1970," held at Middlebury College. The event was promoted as an alternative to the revolutionary agendas of the era: its keynote speaker was Phil Hoff, and its sponsor was the Youth Project for Democratic Change, an organization that promised "to assist students and young people who, rejecting both the complacency of the conservatives and the self-defeating and often undemocratic tactics of the extreme left, are working for social change through democratic methods." Off to the side, chain-smoking among the apple-cheeked college Democrats, Peter Diamondstone sat before a pile of leaflets, holding out for the revolution.

Mutual friends saw Sanders and Diamondstone, who met each other for the first time at the fair, as peas in a pod: Diamondstone was an outer-borough Jew who'd attended law school at the University of Chicago, during the time that Sanders was there as an undergraduate. Diamondstone entered Bernie's consciousness when the press reported that this "Brattleboro lawyer" had refused to close his legal aid office on the day of the moon landing and was fired from the organization; Sanders was known to Diamondstone from his *Vermont Freeman* pieces. But what struck the two of them, from the moment they met, were certain intensifying differences. Diamondstone, a merry prankster who spoke in a florid, metaphorical argot and tended a field of junked Volkswagens at his home, was a dentist's son from a middle-class family. It seemed to Sanders an element of his friend's relative privilege that Diamondstone was determined never to win an election. His role inside the electoral system was essentially that of saboteur.

From the Fresh Ground, it was only a stone's throw to an old gas station on Saint Paul Street where, a few years later, Ben Cohen and Jerry Greenfield founded Ben & Jerry's Ice Cream and Soups. There Dennis Morrisseau, the young Liberty Union star, had established a war room, and, meeting Sanders at the Fresh Ground, offered Bernie a desk to write press releases for the party. Sanders produced pages of copy, which Morrisseau, perhaps sensing the threat that his young volunteer presented to his own candidacy, rejected as "too radical." Sanders took it as a dare, and decided "on the spot," friends say, that Liberty Union offered a wide-open lane to Morrisseau's left.

Peter Diamondstone, 1980s. *Brattleboro Reformer*

Liberty Union held its nominating convention at Goddard College on October 23, 1971. Rader volunteered to drive his new compact cherry-red Toyota from Burlington through the mountains, with Bernie and Levi up front and Bernie's girlfriend and her two little girls in the back. When they arrived, according to the *Vermont Freeman*, "about 35 adults and children" had gathered. Levi, then three, squirmed in Bernie's lap and bolted whenever his father stood up to speak. A photo in the *Freeman* shows Sanders struggling to contain the little boy. In another shot, party leaders are pictured "with various children": four exasperated adults, four impatient kids looking ready to cash in on whatever treat they were promised on the ride home. Behind his gesticulating father stands a weirded-out ten-year-old Aaron Diamondstone, who has just turned down the party's prank nomination for the U.S. House. You can see, in Sanders's devolving attempts to control Levi, and in Diamondstone's impulse to run his own son as a practical joke, the coming stylistic fault line in the party. Sanders is headed somewhere in a hurry. Diamondstone has found his paradise.

"Why did I go?" Bernie later wondered. "I really don't know." But he did know; he had practiced his remarks, a version of the stump speech he still delivers, and sussed out his rivals in Diamondstone and Morrisseau. When a candidate for U.S. Senate was sought, Sanders rose, Levi at his hip; winning by unanimous vote in a drafty, vaulted barn-turned-auditorium, Bernie's political career was launched.

The arrival of Sanders to the party immediately fractured its leadership.

Morrisseau abruptly quit Liberty Union to run as a Democrat. Bernie, who would now run as the Liberty Union candidate for Senate, rushed to the media to proclaim Morrisseau's defection "a good thing" and to suggest that he was interested in political "expediencies." This too became the spark of a decades-long animus. In the 1980s, Morrisseau was reincarnated as the tweedy proprietor of an upscale French bistro, Leunig's, just a block or so from Burlington's city hall. There, he set up a kind of shadow administration, delivering, from a corner stool, daily commentary on the Sanders regime to Canadian tourists munching beignets.

For now, in Morrisseau's place, the party recruited Doris Lake to fill in as its candidate for Congress. The "shy, sensitive, and soft-spoken" Lake, who attracted sexist coverage nearly everywhere she went, revealed her fearless streak in a feature article in *The Boston Phoenix*. The article is itself a sign of the immediate success Lake and Sanders had in attracting regional media attention. Zigzagging across the state in an AMC Gremlin, with Diamondstone, who served as her campaign manager, riding shotgun, and anywhere between one and four children in the back seat, Lake, the first woman to run in Vermont for statewide office, sought out unsympathetic audiences and picked issues most likely to draw fire.

One January morning in Newport, a heavily Catholic city on the Canadian border, Lake appeared on a call-in radio show and took calls about abortion. Most candidates found ways to avoid the subject, but Lake, the only woman running for public office during the 1972 special election cycle, sought it out. A farm wife was on the line. "Do you know," she said, sounding shaken, "what it is like to see a three-month-old child with perfectly formed hands and perfect little feet lying on the operating table covered in blood?"

Lake, listening patiently, responded in the firm but calm manner that she'd perfected in many such exchanges across the state: "Ma'am, a pregnancy is part of a woman's body."

The calls had all the hallmarks of having been coordinated by Vermont's "Birthright" movement, which had taken hold in Catholic parishes and made activists of conservative young mothers.

"You could have made your point just as well . . . by leaving word that you couldn't make the show because you had to go down to New York to have an abortion," Diamondstone, the stunt politician, told Lake. But the idea was "to hit all the small towns" where Richard Nixon's "little people"—the white working class—could be engaged, even if in bitter disagreement. "Everywhere she went," according to the *Phoenix*, "Lake set off political timebombs."

Soon Lake and Sanders, the party's candidate for Senate, began to travel around Vermont together. The spectacle of two frazzled parents barnstorming the state could not be ignored. As Lake told me, she and Bernie usually had their children in tow, and would foist them off on one another during joint events. Sanders and Lake were an entirely new political phenomenon: a pair of photogenic young candidates, their unruly children at their ankles and trailing blankets and toys behind them. Many Vermonters had the impression, even long afterward, that Lake and Sanders were a married couple.

They kept up a frantic pace. On one typical campaign day, Sanders and Lake stopped at Mount St. Joseph High School in Rutland, where Bernie found a large crowd of students forced by their teachers to attend, then visited a nearby General Electric plant before finishing the morning at a third stop, Castleton State College. The high school students yawned and fidgeted through a classic Sanders harangue. Think of yourselves as "human beings," Bernie cajoled, "not docile idiots." Only when Sanders suggested that all drugs should be legal did the teenage human beings rouse to loudly cheer.

At the GE plant, Lake and Sanders struggled to keep their children out of the maw of the noisy machinery on the factory floor, and spoke with a few polite but nonplussed workers. Finally, at Castleton State, the pair met with a single student, a reporter. Bernie passionately delivered his stump speech to her alone, and then Sanders and Lake went in search of a few students lounging in the student center who "expressed surprise" when they introduced themselves as political candidates. Animal crackers and campaign literature in hand, their children playing hide-and-seek behind the big couches, Sanders and Lake confronted their potential constituents about the apathy of the young, then pressed their grim leaflets, illustrated with an image of Uncle Sam being lynched with a dollar bill, into the students' hands. "We support action which will do away with all laws relating to the prohibition of abortions, birth control measures, homosexual relationships, and the use of drugs."

"Far out," replied a student.

SANDERS FOR SENATE was a no-frills campaign. Burlington's WJOY AM radio station interviewed Bernie at length one morning in December. Jim Rader, eating lunch in his car next to Henry's Diner in downtown Burlington, heard the segment live. "There was a terrible thumping, all throughout," he told me. Sanders, tucking his lanky frame into a metal chair, was knocking the underside of the flimsy table with his knees. At a debate in Lyndon, Vermont, a "sparse crowd" of twelve or so people heard Sanders answer perhaps his first-ever question about campaign donors and big money. "I have only one donor, and he drove me here," Sanders boasted, pointing at his friend in the back row.

In the special election on Friday, January 7, 1972, Robert Stafford, the Republican, won by a large margin, beating the Democrat, Randy Major, a hale showboat who had cross-country skied the entire length of the state. Sanders for years decried Major's "walkathon" as a bitter example of gimmick politics. He saw his loss to Stafford as fair and square. But after Major's goofy odyssey, Vermont Democrats had begun to get under Sanders's skin in a serious way.

In third place, collecting 2.2 percent of the vote, was the man that the *Burlington Free Press* identified as "Bernard Saunders." Though Bernie's total of 1,571 votes statewide was a disappointment, his opponent was a beloved moderate Yankee Republican in the popular mold of George Aiken. If there were Sanders voters in Stafford's coalition, nobody knew it yet. But within a decade, the Republican Party in Vermont, just years after reaching its apparent apex, had essentially vanished. Only after its collapse, a collapse sped by the cultural transformations that Sanders embodied, did Bernie find a way of pitching his political independence as a Yankee virtue. The Sanders Republican gestated inside Stafford's totals.

A close observer might note one interesting anomaly in the disappointing results. Sanders's support ran about ten times stronger in Burlington than statewide. He found votes in the city's poorer wards and in neighboring, working-class Winooski. A light pencil sketch of his eventual winning coalition could be drawn, though perhaps only in retrospect. Four hundred or so of Bernie's neighbors had voted for him, and they came disproportionately from the working poor in the Old North End. The ward maps did not appear to support the theory, espoused then and throughout Bernie's rise, that he appealed mainly to student radicals and barbarian "out-of-staters" clustered around the University of Vermont.

This was good news, in a way: the brash, disheveled radical had made inroads with Burlington's mainly Catholic, culturally conservative working poor. But it also suggested how hard it would continue to be to lure the young into the political process. Across Vermont, in fact, voters newly enfranchised by the Twenty-sixth Amendment exercised their all-American right to stay home on Election Day. "We did not see young people registering in large numbers," Bernie told an interviewer on WJOY. "I am dismayed by that fact, but obviously we have work to do."

"The Gas Station Method"

Murray Ngoima delivered a suitcase full of old Liberty Union documents and materials to my office at Wellesley College, on a seventy-degree afternoon in February of 2023. Most of the party's records were lost in 2012, when the Diamondstones' old house in Brattleboro burned to the ground. This small archive and a few boxes full of newspaper clippings in Special Collections at the University of Vermont are all that remains.

As we looked through her materials, Ngoima described how Diamondstone "mentored Bernie" on their long drives across the state collecting signatures. But those who knew Bernie at the time say that he already wanted electoral tactics; Diamondstone, in his view, offered mostly irritating, counterproductive antics. As the split between the two men widened, across it many insults were volleyed. By the end of Diamondstone's life, during Sanders's first presidential run in 2016, his old friend had become something like his personal heckler. For years, whenever Sanders found himself at the same events as Diamondstone, he "looked for the exits," according to Ngoima.

Now seventy, Ngoima was one of the earliest members of Liberty Union and remains one of its last perennial candidates. Talking to Ngoima about her upbringing brought into focus the importance of generational leftists in Vermont. Her parents' home in Woodstock was an important base of radical operations, in the years before Laurance Rockefeller, the town's most famous resident, began to curate the village as a kind of quaintness preserve on the Norman Rockwell model. (Rockefeller eventually paid to bury the town's power lines and, with them, any trace of modernity.) Ngoima's father, Byron Thomas, was an artist and an illustrator for *Life* magazine. The butterflies in a 1958 *Life* article about Vladimir Nabokov, the noted author and lepidopterist, were painted by Thomas. Murray's mother, Virginia Beacon Thomas, was educated at the New School in New York, and brought socialite-socialist politics to her ladies' groups and reading circles in well-heeled Woodstock.

Left-wing politics were normal fare at Ngoima's family's elegant columned home near the town green: she first learned about Vietnam around 1964, from an antiwar flier on her parents' kitchen table. Like many a child of well-to-do Bohemians, Murray was sent to the Putney School in southern Vermont, where the faculty included several European Jews who came as refugees. Putney was devoted to cultivated pursuits like poetry, classical music, dance, and ceramics; but when the 1960s happened, Putney students, like students everywhere, wanted to break things, not coax them into shape from clay or molten glass.

Liberty Union did "slow politics" from the beginning. The results of the 1970 and 1972 elections were not disappointing to Ngoima; the party was founded not to "run" candidates in a militaristic race, but to speak the truth. It was assumed that the truth would get drowned out. To lose was a way of winning; this is the circular logic that drove Sanders from the party in 1977.

But Sanders did learn from his allies in Liberty Union where to find "real"—taciturn, conservative, Yankee—Vermonters, and how, as a political radical, to win their trust. In the early 1970s, Sanders sometimes accompanied Diamondstone, his children, and his Saint Bernards all across the state in Diamondstone's VW, looking for voters. Their method was to stop at rural gas stations and talk to the men they'd noticed invariably tended to congregate out front, tinkering under a tractor hood, smoking, and engaging in rural Vermont's laconic equivalent of conversation: one man would make an observation about the coming storm; some time would pass; and then the others would indicate a response by nod or grunt.

"The gas station method" was not efficient. Bernie and Diamondstone sometimes talked for hours before asking these men for their signatures. But by the end of the conversations, they felt they'd established common ground, especially on "conservative" and libertarian issues like taxation and civil liberties. Everyone they met railed against "Montpelier" and the perceived overreach of Vermont's growing state government. "Montpelier's got its hands in our pockets," was the refrain.

I grew up in Vermont being told that Liberty Union was the party of the communes, the draft dodgers, and the strung-out runaways. But when I asked Murray Ngoima where they'd had better luck—at the gas stations or in the communes—she jumped in to correct me.

"We had no luck at the communes," she said. "Those people mostly packed up and went home in the winters. And," Ngoima added, her tone growing sharper, "they had no relationship at all to the poor."

10

Movement

(Sanders for Governor '72)

Marble Bridge, Proctor. *Vermont Historical Society*

Anarchists and Barons

The most beautiful bridge in Vermont can be found in tiny Proctor, just north of Rutland. It was constructed from pure white local marble quarried from the face of a mountain. When the famous quarries of Carrara, Italy, in the Apuan Alps, slowed down in the late nineteenth century, Proctor inherited a significant share of the world's marble business, and welcomed waves of Carrara's quarry workers and stone carvers to the Green Mountains. The earth here yields more marble than can be commercially consumed. Carved stone is used for very ordinary things: benches at bus stops, drinking fountains. Even the sidewalks are done in marble. There are several modest houses in town made of marble, each no bigger than a double-wide trailer. In a shed on the outskirts of the quarry district, carvers here once fashioned the Tomb of the Unknown Soldier for delivery to Washington. The cemeteries elsewhere in Vermont abound with spartan, cold slabs, chiseled with austere names and dates; but in these marble towns, you might see, against the bleak snowy backdrop, a stone corgi so lifelike you want to take him home, or a glorious angel in sumptuous carved robes worthy of Michelangelo.

Because these marble quarries created astonishing wealth for their owners, this part of Vermont was also home to some of the state's stubbornest Republicans. These were not George Aiken Republicans—folksy, front-porch politicians—but Big Business conservatives, union busters, bottom-line men who returned every night to their roaring hearths and their Dickensian ledger books. The marble barons in the Proctor family christened and nurtured the town as "a family fiefdom," according to Samuel B. Hand, and held, during their glory years in the early twentieth century, more political power in the state of Vermont than perhaps any family has, before or since.

In the winter of 1972, decades after the town's period of prosperity, the shaggy-haired high school students of Proctor, Vermont, met Bernard Sanders on one of his campaign swings, and liked what the guy had to say. Young people needed to "take control of their lives," Sanders told a small group near the center of town, as elderly onlookers gawked from passing station wagons. On the radio call-in shows, Bernie had been telling his astonished hosts that he "truly believed" the legal voting age should be fourteen, so "high school students could protect their rights." A decade later, in Burlington, Sanders was still telling groups of teenagers—my friends and me—that we should organize to demand the right to vote. As mayor, Bernie couldn't lower the voting age himself, but he did foster and empower institutions in the city that provided our permanently disenfranchised demographic with, as he put it, "alternative ways to grow up."

The grown-ups in Proctor, though, feared that Sanders had come to town to organize the local workers. Scars of a general quarry strike decades before were not healed. Those gloriously talented stone carvers had brought with them from the Alps a fearsome anarchist politics, plus organizing prowess, and a deep hatred of concentrated wealth and the vanities of the management class. By 1933, conditions in the quarries were abominable. A softball-sized piece of dislodged stone could crush a person's skull. There was no provision for families when a worker was injured or killed. Silicosis, a disease of the lungs caused by aspirating the tiny daggers in stone dust, had ripped up the lungs of the old men. In a 1934 strike, workers blew up the power and railway lines leading into the quarries. The strike was put down at rifle point, the industry collapsed, and many of Vermont's marble workers moved on to places like Mechanicsburg, Pennsylvania, and Paterson, New Jersey. Those left behind were divided permanently into scabs and strikers. The kids in the scrum around Bernie were just two generations downstream from the strike, and they sometimes had to answer for their grandfathers' actions.

All across Vermont's quarry belt, in towns and cities that relied on the punishing work of extracting marble, slate, granite, or asbestos from the earth, Vermont evolved its own regionally distinct socialism, centered at the Socialist Labor Party Hall in Barre, the heart of stone country. That handsome building, built in 1900 and adorned with granite medallions, once housed a busy cooperative market, a raucous dance hall, and rooms where workers could take temporary shelter. It became a regional hub of socialist thought and politics. On July 25, 1912, Barre declared a "Socialist Day" and welcomed the presidential candidate—Sanders's great hero—Eugene V. Debs.

And so, when the senior class of Proctor High School invited Bernie to be its graduation speaker in the spring of 1972, it drew him into a local struggle that went back a hundred years. The Proctor school board met in May of 1972 and revoked the invitation. With the school budget under heavy scrutiny, it was not the time "to have such a controversial man as a speaker."

Sanders, who had been unknown and adrift the previous May, was excited to find that he was newly mildly notorious. The story of the Proctor scandal ran regionally, and was almost certainly placed by Sanders himself: it respectfully summarized his main positions on labor, the utility companies, and the war in Vietnam, and it crescendoed with a zinger from Bernie that felt like it had seen a few drafts: "One of the things that I would have spoken about at the graduation," he remarked, "is the lack of control that young people, especially young people, have over their own lives. And nothing I could have said makes the point more clearly than the cowardly act of the school board."

In early June, the ACLU considered an action against the Proctor school board—until the anonymous plaintiff it had recruited, a Proctor high school senior, backed out of the case, choosing the glories of a Vermont summer over litigation. But Sanders, the pick of 2 percent of Vermonters that previous January, had kept his name in the papers in the fallow period between one election cycle and the next. That's a miracle for a fringe political candidate in Vermont. You could argue that it was Bernie's first political victory.

Movement

Liberty Union tended to scatter after every Election Day. In Brattleboro, Doris Lake took a job in a lens factory, working the 11 p.m. to 7 a.m. shift. "I never dreamed the world needed so many glasses," Lake reported, but at least "one may go to the bathroom at any time." Though part of her was "dead or at least dying fast," the family had debts from their recent campaigns, the house needed painting, and the four Diamondstone children and their two very large dogs needed to eat.

Back home in Burlington, Bernie Sanders struck out on his own. His columns for the *Vermont Freeman* had begun to peter out. Frank Kochman, the publisher, had become wise to Bernie's attempts to make the paper a house organ for Liberty Union. It was the policy of the paper to run virtually any piece of writing delivered to it at the Hanksville Schoolhouse, whether by post or VW Beetle. But even with Bernie dropping by the schoolhouse to help with production—and to raid the refrigerator—the paper clung to its distinct and independent editorial voice, partly by escalating its criticism of the antics of Liberty Union, and especially of its chief jester—by then the author of many angry letters to the editor of the *Freeman*—Peter Diamondstone.

So Sanders founded his own paper. *Movement*, a "newsletter-style periodical" almost identical in layout and design to Ralph Nader and Andrew Kropkind's *Hard Times*, began as a biweekly publication. Sanders converted his rooms near Lake Champlain into a makeshift printing studio. He typed up the articles on his IBM Selectric and hand-designed the graphics. Using a simple waxing device, a sheaf of exacto knives, and a metal brayer, Sanders and Jim Rader laid out the pages and delivered the mock-ups to a local printer. Sanders then distributed *Movement*, a single large sheet of heavy stock folded in half and then in half again, to local libraries and bookstores. Sanders kept a supply in his backpack as he roamed Burlington. Burlingtonians picked up the first issue at the Vermont People's Fair in Burlington's City Hall Park in May of 1972, where Sanders was seated at a card table. Single issues were twenty-five cents. Gradually a few subscription cards floated back home, but the paper could not keep to its goal of biweekly publication, and, in the final issue, published in May of 1973, those who had paid the five-dollar subscription fee for a year's supply were promised "25 issues, however long that may take." Sanders added that *Movement* was the only publication that would show up in your mailbox "when you least expect it." Some are still expecting it.

Though *Movement* announced on its masthead that it was "Published by the Liberty Union," Sanders had editorial control of its contents, which were mostly written by him. An introductory note in the first issue promises a focus beyond politics on "many aspects of our culture and general way of life": "We shall be discussing, for example, hospitals and doctors—and why Western Medicine's response to disease is often similar to the American government's response to the Vietnamese revolution." Childbirth remained one of Bernie's primary themes; he typed up and printed the long interview he'd done with Lorraine Jankowski while staying at Mullein Hill in West Glover in 1969, a two-part feature in the *Movement* issues of early August 1972 and February 1973. Those issues of the "biweekly" paper were consecutive: "One of the more embarrassing aspects of the six-month delay is that we left our readers right in the middle of a natural childbirth."

According to Kate Daloz, Bernie sought out Jankowski because she'd had two children under "vastly different circumstances." It was not unusual in these years to meet women who'd had their first children on one side of the cultural divide, and later children in a new cultural phase, during the fashion for communal birth. Lorraine told Bernie she'd had child number one at the Proctor Hospital, a small facility north of Rutland. "The nurse came in and shoved her hand up my ass," Lorraine said, and then "started punching my stomach." Lorraine was left alone in an antiseptic room "with the big white lights and the white walls." The doctor seemed "a little drunk." Bernie, incredulous, asked, "You mean, they really didn't care how you felt?" Lorraine responded that there was little regard for the "spiritual" elements of giving birth.

By the time she was ready to deliver her second child, Lorraine and her first husband, a folk singer named Peter, had "parted ways," and Lorraine, now living at Mullein Hill, was ready to experience childbirth without the trauma of modern medical care. The process involved the entire community. There were three men who might have been the father, Lorraine reckoned. Two of them stayed with her during the pregnancy. Throughout the long and difficult winter, she did yoga and pilfered dried fruit from the common store. In the spring, she learned the Lamaze method; in early July, when she started having contractions, "some people went running out to get Jack." Sanders inquires, "Who was Jack?" Lorraine replies that Jack, "the guy who lived across the lake," had "delivered one other baby."

Bernie's interjections ("Did you tear?") are rather lacking in bedside manner. He is not the saintly neighbor "Crow," who, Lorraine reported, pressed into her palm a smooth birthing stone to hold during contractions, or her doula, Jack, who had crammed the Lamaze method in his hut across the lake. Sanders was politely shown out after a three-day stay.

But as a record of childbirth before and after the cultural tremors of the late '60s, the interview is fascinating. Who would choose the drunk doctor

Sanders campaigns at South Burlington High School, 1972. *Jym Wilson*

and the roughhousing nurses, when offered raspberry tea and meditation? The article captures what even Lorraine had apparently forgotten. Kate Daloz told me that Lorraine could not recall what was done with the placenta after the birth of her daughter Rahoula. The answer was to be found in Bernie's piece, once she was able to track it down: it turns out, she ate it, as was common in those years.

ON JUNE 17, 1972, Liberty Union held its nominating convention in Rutland. Bernie was chosen as the candidate for governor, with Peter Diamondstone standing for attorney general. A committee of fifteen, including Jim Rader, was picked to recruit candidates for the remaining offices. Liberty Union announced that it would formally endorse the People's Party ticket of Dr. Benjamin Spock, the patrician baby doctor and antiwar activist, for president, and Julius Hobson, the civil rights activist, for vice president. The coming election was, according to Rick Perlstein, "a referendum on the meaning of the 1960s and its toll on institutions."

The '60s changed Spock and his meanings. By 1972, the doctor had reinvented himself as an unlikely shaman in a Brooks Brothers suit. When Spock and four others were convicted in 1968 on federal charges of "conspiracy to counsel, aid and abet resistance to the draft," the spectacular trial in Boston gave Spock his second life in politics. Now, Spock was calling for nothing less than the spiritual and behavioral rewiring of American life. To Dr. Spock, as to Bernie, the typical American childhood was an incubator for sadism. The war in Vietnam was the result of a society that could not show its children love. Liberty Union sensed an opportunity to expand its appeal. "Everyone loves Dr. Spock," Bernie assured people. The party had sponsored Spock's speaking tour across Vermont earlier that spring, in April of 1972. At the first stop, the staunch abortion-rights advocate lectured at Trinity College, the Catholic school next to our home, where my mother and grandmother both worked. There was polite opposition and protest from several activist organizations, including my mother's group, Birthright; though my mother was busy that night with me, an eleven-month-old baby.

The lost kids of Liberty Union thought they had found their father. A strapping WASP from New Haven, Connecticut, and a six-foot-four crew standout at Andover and Yale, Dr. Spock seemed almost predestined for power. But after winning a gold medal at the Paris Olympics, Spock set out to undo the damage done to him by a commanding New England mother, who had required him to live at home during his freshman year at Yale after young Benny confessed to having a crush on a girl. The fruit of this regressive upbringing was Spock's seminal work, *The Common Sense Book of Baby and Child Care*, published in 1946, and for years promoted as "the second best-selling book in America, next to the Bible." Parents learned from it the radical idea that they were not harming their babies by treating them with evident affection. By 1972, the generation brought up on Spock's book had rebelled against some of the assumptions that formed them, especially Spock's vision of women as an omnipresent source of their children's on-demand contentment. But to many on the right, Spock's manual was "the taproot of the new generation's insolence," according to Rick Perlstein. *Newsweek* ran a cover banner asking, "Is Dr. Spock to Blame?" beside a literal flower child: a toddler holding a daisy and wearing a button that read, "Don't Trust Anyone Over 7."

In September of 1972, Sanders and Martha Abbott met Dr. Spock and his wife at Burlington International Airport and took them for steaks at the Holiday Inn nearby, where my great-uncle Esau Olio was tending bar. Esau's bar was the premier watering hole for visiting dignitaries like Louis Armstrong and Perry Como. "The Master of the Mix," whose shifts were advertised in the *Burlington Free Press*, loathed hippies, of course, like everyone in my family of his generation; but he did boast, late in life, of having served drinks to the courtly Spock that night, along with his entourage of "bums." The bums were Sanders, Diamondstone, and Abbott. "I had 1.50 in my pocket," Sanders wrote, as though to confirm Uncle Esau's impression, "and Martha didn't have much more."

Spock and his wife traveled with their own entourage: a Secret Service detail numbering some twenty young men, looking, as Sanders noted, "nothing like" easygoing Burlington people. Spock had requested the maximum protection available to a candidate: threats against his life had dogged him since his conspiracy trial. The twitchy, uneasy group of armed agents sat at the surrounding tables, trying to blend in with the crowd listening to the legendary Goody Goodrow perform numbers by Neil Sedaka and Connie Francis on his organ.

"The whole phenomenon of the Secret Service and their 'professionalism' and discipline, and the guns, and the idea of guarding someone's life 24 hours a day is itself an extraordinary psychological occurrence," Bernie wrote in "Fragments of a Campaign Diary." To Sanders, it was "absurd" and required a "sense of humor." But Peter Diamondstone was "clearly agitated" to be in the midst of those "government guns—neatly strapped across the chest." According to Bernie, Diamondstone's "organism didn't adjust well" to the spectacle.

It was "a fiasco," according to witnesses along the trail. The peacenik party of Vermont rolled through the Green Mountains on that September campaign accompanied by a convoy of black limousines filled with armed men. Liberty Union's great hope, Benjamin Spock, surrounded by this praetorian guard of Secret Service agents, came across as aloof, a bit daffy, and, despite his leftist rebirth, every bit the patrician. When Sanders overheard a factory worker in Brattleboro making fun of Spock, he was astonished: Didn't everyone love Dr. Spock? Everyone, it turned out, did not love Dr. Spock, and the visit augured badly for Bernie and Liberty Union. On Election Day, November 7, 1972, Spock received about 1,000 votes. George McGovern, the Democrat, netted 68,000. Even at the height

Sanders at South Burlington High School, 1972. *Jym Wilson*

of its countercultural ferment, Richard Nixon won Vermont in a landslide, with more than 117,000 votes. Bernie and the other down-ticket candidates fared very poorly. Sanders, with 2,175 votes, badly underperformed even his own low expectations. With the Vietnam War winding down, and with the tolerance for the counterculture's eccentric politics in abeyance, Liberty Union was at a crossroads.

But Sanders found some encouragement in its ranks. At an election forum that fall, Elly Harter, Liberty Union's candidate for lieutenant governor, did not play the hits. Harter didn't argue that young teenagers should vote, or that the highways be widened to accommodate hitchhikers, or that all drugs be immediately legalized and provided safely to addicts free of charge. She did not tie her presentation to Dr. Spock or argue for a radical rewiring of the family unit; she sensed, apparently, the stubborn reality that poor Vermonters often supported the Vietnam War. Instead, she stood up and called for guaranteed free medical and dental care for children. Diamondstone applauded from the gallery, but so did the Republican candidate for attorney general, Kimberly Cheney. There was widespread support for free dental care in Vermont, but only Liberty Union had thought to include it in its platform. Cheney agreed that low-income Vermont children had "deplorable" teeth. (My own teeth were deplorable as a child, and my many fillings would be paid for by the state of Vermont.) Here, then, was another sign that Vermont Republicans and the leftist lunatics of Liberty Union had common ground to explore.

Sanders, who wanted to grow the party's appeal to working people, heard a keynote in Elly Harter's sympathetic approach. Bernie's *Movement* articulated his priorities. The important thing to Bernie was to shed the party's "brown bread and rice image," as Sanders put it. Bernie's own taste for burned steaks made him a natural adversary for the seitan and tempeh crowd, but he was nevertheless frustrated by the problem of drawing together cosmopolitan, educated leftists and the rural working class whose cause they ostensibly championed. Spock hadn't done the trick. In any case, as Bernie told a friend, many of the Vermonters they met along the trail "were expecting the guy on *Star Trek*."

In Saint Albans, one of the state's most conservative and culturally French-Canadian areas, and one where many of my relatives have settled over the years, Sanders conducted a remarkable set of interviews with citizens on the street, discovering among them something dismaying: near-universal sympathy for the former governor of Alabama, George Wallace. Wallace was as close to the face of southern racism as one could conjure, but his bid to redefine himself (he would eventually seek and be granted the forgiveness of many in the Black community, including Jesse Jackson) got a boost when he was gunned down in an assassination attempt in May of 1972. To the white railroad employees, bus drivers, and service station operators Bernie interviewed, Wallace was not the racist governor who stood in the schoolhouse door at the University of Alabama and proclaimed, "Segregation now, segregation tomorrow, segregation forever," but a martyr, a misunderstood culture warrior, a victim of dishonest elites and the media. "By their bumper stickers, you could know them," Rick Perlstein wrote of Wallace's voters: "I FIGHT POVERTY. I WORK; GOD BLESS AMERICA; POW'S NEVER HAVE A NICE DAY; REGISTER COMMUNISTS, NOT FIREARMS."

"He tells the truth and he ain't no yes-man to the big men who own the corporations and ain't paying no income tax," one man told Sanders. This economic populism was something Sanders could work with, but mainly what Bernie encountered, in its larval form, was the grievance politics of the Donald Trump voter, *avant la lettre*: a white working-class man or woman fed up with the "governing elites," as one man told Sanders, and eager to embrace a candidate who stood up for "the little guy."

The conclusions Sanders drew from his field trip to Saint Albans strike us now as prescient. "Democracy in America," Bernie wrote, "just might not make it." Sanders theorized that "a strong man" would rise up to "bring order out of the chaos" and vanquish all of the perceived enemies of his Saint Albans men and women on the street: "blacks; long-hairs," "welfare chiselers," and "political dissidents" could become the new scapegoats, the "Jews and communists of the Nazi experience." Sanders's mind "flashed to scenes of Germany in the late 1920's," and the extermination of his father's relatives in Poland. He had no crystal ball, but the analysis also flashes forward to scenes of America in 2016 and beyond.

The challenge, then as now, was to redirect these grievances away from the desire for a strongman and toward the prospect of a more agile and representative democracy. "These people are disgusted with the double-talk and deceit of the politicians," Sanders wrote. "They admire Wallace's courage and straightforwardness." In a column signed by the "Liberty Union Executive Committee" but written by Bernie, the Vermont legislature is exposed as as "grossly sexist," counting only 22 women among its 180 total members in both chambers. It is also "veritably an old folks' home," including, in the House, 41 out of 150 members who are "retired"—or, as Sanders puts it, "too old to seek gainful employment." Of its six "farmers," Bernie finds that two are bank directors; one is an investment counselor; one, Derick Webb, is a Vanderbilt; and one has a law degree. "It appears that these are not your average Vermont farmers," Sanders, the New York City transplant, comments.

The publication of *Movement* gave Sanders, now officially Liberty Union's chair, de facto control of the party. In the stack of *Movement* issues that Jim Rader loaned to me, a green deposit slip from the Merchants National Bank fell out: it was Bernie Sanders's receipt for a deposit he made to open an account for *Movement* and Liberty Union in his name. In its modest way, the green card signed in ballpoint pen and dated 5/15/72 is a founding document in American politics. It gives the first sign that Sanders will eventually emerge as an independent, freeing himself of the party and its many chaotic, quarreling personalities. Sanders will tolerate Liberty Union for five more years, then leave behind a jilted and diminished party more and more reflecting the whims of Peter Diamondstone.

Liberty Union's radical arguments for hitchhiking, homeschooling, free love, and children's rights notwithstanding, *Movement* showed Sanders carefully addressing issues that might appeal to people like his Saint Albans interview subjects or John Rogers, the construction contractor who drove Bernie around in his pickup in the mid-1960s. Universal dental care was one topic, along with tax relief, legislative reform, and citizen oversight of utilities. Teeth, taxes, and telephones: these were the issues that interested the men and women whose nexus was neither the commune nor the town hall, but the gas station and the general store. And the party could frame all of these issues in terms of individual liberty. Vermont's leftist implants and its native libertarians began, during this period, warily to converge, and Liberty Union was the ground on which they met. Bernie Sanders was the individual candidate who could speak about the overlapping interests of those who favored an activist state government and those who claimed to prefer no government at all. Only in theory, and in the rhetoric of elected politicians, did the two frames of mind conflict.

Pay Phone Socialism

In the lull between campaign seasons, Sanders took stock of Vermont as a whole, which he'd now seen from the roads: the enormous vistas of the surrounding mountains; the huge, dramatic cloudscapes and sunsets; the passing cars taking men and women to early-morning shifts; the wealthy couples coming north from New York or Boston; the busloads of children traveling on icy roads to compete in hockey or basketball; the hitchhikers at the exits with their hopeful thumbs extended.

Though he wrote to Rader that fall that he was "sitting home—doing some reading and writing—and feeling sorry for myself," and feared these restless intervals when "every neurotic aspect of my soul begins to pop up," nevertheless Sanders looked back on the 1972 campaign as "one of the most exciting, interesting, and informative experiences of my life," when he learned "the difference between being a radical and a liberal." He wrote in his "campaign diary":

> Of all the groups that a candidate talks before, I prefer most to talk to low income people. They "know" a lot more than most people because their lives are constantly on the line and they can't escape behind 10,000 a year incomes—as can the good liberals.

Sanders found that he enjoyed traveling with his fellow candidates, whatever their political beliefs; he noted his "very good feeling about Vermont, and even about Vermont politicians." The state was "one of the few places left in America where people with very strong political differences can still talk to each other like human beings."

But the most important lesson was learned between campaign stops. A person driving Vermont's roads, Sanders noted, developed the important knack for finding a pay phone. Most rural gas stations and general stores in Vermont had a pay phone out front, attended by a long line made up of local motley: farmers, runaways, students, traveling salesmen. Telephone service across the state was spotty and subject to being knocked out by storms. Vermonters waiting patiently for service to extend up their steep hillsides had become accustomed to using the pay phone at the bottom of their roads, and still depended entirely on it to stay in regular contact with the outside world.

In the lines for pay phones, Sanders detected an impressive social experiment: communal ties and courtesies were extended even across social groups—even to the dreaded out-of-staters. The line behind a caller meant that he kept his communications short and to the point, by a standard nowhere written down. If you wanted to call your boyfriend just to coo or babytalk into the phone, you found a pay phone in a more discreet place, and probably looked for one of the rare glass booths, like the ones they had in cities: these could be found in the basement of the library or the lobby of an ice rink. Gas stations and general stores had open-air phones for crucial communications. Privacy was granted to you by your neighbors, not taken from them. It was understood not as a right to be hoarded, but as a social good to be distributed to those who were worthy of it.

The phones themselves became a common cause and an important breakthrough item as Liberty Union planned its 1974 campaigns. By late in 1972, Bernie and the other Liberty Union personalities began to push hard against rate increases granted by the Vermont Public Service Board to the New England Telephone and Telegraph Company. The price of toll calls—those made to numbers outside one's calling district—increased by about 20 percent. Pay phones, serving some of the poorest people in the state, in circumstances often urgent, were specially targeted for increases: it cost $1.15 for Bernie Sanders, in Burlington, to call Peter Diamondstone, in Brattleboro, for three minutes. Today, that's an $8 call. Diamondstone took to the press to stand up for "people who use coin phones exclusively," adding that several of Liberty Union's candidates did not have telephones in their homes.

Village pay phones might have united the counterculture and the working class, but the idea of "people's utilities" had to be managed carefully lest it bring up what Sanders called "that horrible word, *socialism*." Though utility companies were a new Goliath for Sanders, his rhetoric and strategy were battle-ready. Readers of *Movement* "might like to know," Bernie wrote, "that despite the fact that this increase . . . affects tens of thousands of Vermonters, there were no consumers at the hearing which granted the increase." The lines of Vermonters waiting to place their calls at the local pay phone could be organized, if only for that moment and that cause, against "the large corporate out of state interests whose main connection with the state is to take Vermonters' money back to New York or Boston to further their own private gain." As long as corporations could be personified as the redoubts of very wealthy out-of-staters, people would hate them even more than they hated government bureaucrats.

In Rutland, in April of 1973, Sanders and Liberty Union, holding more than six thousand signatures from a petition circulated across the state, formed the Vermont Telephone Boycott Committee and began their campaign to support Vermonters who refused the new surcharge. New England Telephone was at a key disadvantage in the dispute: its leverage was located, very inconveniently, on its customers' breakfast counters. In those days, one leased a phone from AT&T, at an eventual cost that far exceeded its value. Would AT&T executives traverse Vermonters' front yards and confiscate the leased phones of the state's proud and ornery citizenry, for principled acts of nonpayment? The specter of phone seizures may have fed blossoming anger at New England Telephone. Sanders and Liberty Union had a winning issue on their hands, and an effective way to keep the party's profile vivid even in the dark corridors between elections.

To everyone's surprise, the threat of boycott worked. The Vermont Public Service Board halted the rate increase; New England Telephone then appealed to the Vermont Supreme Court, which found for the Public Service Board, and required the company to return with data justifying their rate hikes. When on a second attempt the company again fell short, its executives in Boston had a tantrum and churlishly decided to slash the budget in Vermont, laying off dozens of employees and halting future projects that would have employed many more.

Liberty Union had its first significant political victory—and also, with New England Telephone's immediate layoffs and cuts to service, its first experience with unintended political fallout.

AN ARTICLE IN the *Burlington Free Press* expressed Liberty Union's wishful thinking as the party steered into the 1974 election. Sanders had a backchannel to several reporters at the conservative paper, and the article, by Candace Page, repeats the predictions he had been espousing between bites of bread at the Fresh Ground Coffee House. "Liberty Union Party Seeks Coalition of Workers, 'Concerned' Middle Class" read the headline. The focus was now on Burlington, where several Liberty Union candidates had run for seats in the Vermont legislature.

But those 1972 Burlington campaigns delivered a baleful lesson about working people and the limits of Liberty Union's appeal. One candidate was Huck Gutman, the colorful UVM professor of English, a raconteur whose nickname referred to his tendency to walk barefoot like Huck Finn, while chanting lines from Whitman and Yeats. The other was James Girouard, "an unemployed laborer who thinks state ownership of utilities would be 'social communism.'" Gutman, who went on to be Bernie's closest confidant and his Senate chief of staff, ran in Burlington's Hill Section, the seat of the city's small Republican patrician class; Girouard, in the Old North End, stronghold of working-class voters and the center of the city's Democratic machine. Gutman, the eccentric scholar, was greeted with "friendly curiosity, if not admiration," he told me, as he canvased the mansions of Summit Street overlooking Lake Champlain. Yet in the Old North End, Girouard, a native Burlingtonian, met a more hostile response: Liberty Union, he was told, was the party of "socialistic" demonstrators and traitors. If Sanders were ever going to make inroads in Burlington, he would need to appeal to Girouard's neighbors. The prospect looked bleak.

"That's [Dennis] Morrisseau's party," one woman whose brother had died in Vietnam remarked. "I wouldn't vote for any of them since they wouldn't fight for their country."

11

At the Fair

(Sanders for U.S. Senate '74)

Mr. and Mrs. Derick Webb at the fair, 1974. *Shelburne Farms*

The Champlain Valley Fair, in Essex Junction, Vermont, convenes every year for a week before Labor Day, a pent-up spasm of late summer. The air reeks of maple syrup, diesel, and manure. The fair's enormous Ferris wheel, during its mayfly-brief tenure the tallest structure in Vermont, rolls and rolls in place, going nowhere in flamboyant neon. From the top, you have a majestic, ancient view of the Green Mountains and the Adirondacks, before the wheel returns you to the aromas and tantrums of the midway crowds lining up at its base.

When I was growing up, everything led to those fair days. I saved my First Communion money to spend there. I kept my birthday money every year for those few days four months away. When I was six, I remember riding an enormous, saddled pumpkin like a steer. At twelve, my friend Seth and I confronted two carnies who had cheated us out of a plush anaconda we legitimately won at the shooting gallery. One guy lunged at us with his jackknife, and we ran. A few years passed, and the visiting carnies were now welcomed as a dangerous but reliable source of recreational drugs. After a quick transaction behind Mr. Sausage, the cattle in the farm tent seemed to grow in stature and meaning, staring through me with the eyes of Olympian gods. At night, there were concerts in the arena. I caught Bob Dylan on the "Infidels" tour, during his Zionist phase. I applauded as Dee Snider of Twisted Sister took to the stage and snarled, "Helloooo Vermont!"

Everyone went to the fair. In 1974, 116,000 people streamed through its turnstiles. Derick Webb was there, as always, with his prize herd of Brown Swiss cattle. In a typical year, Webb collected every blue ribbon in his division, one year vanquishing a teenage 4-H member with one scrawny heifer.

Webb's animals grazed on the ruins of an old golf course at the estate ten miles south of Burlington well known to the upper classes in Newport and on Park Avenue as Shelburne Farms, but known locally as "The Webbs'." This magnificent but deteriorating property, designed on some four thousand acres by Frederick Law Olmsted for Webb's grandparents, Lila Vanderbilt Webb and Dr. Seward Webb, was home to a 110-room mansion that was later unsuccessfully bid out for demolition, its iron furnaces given away as scrap. Derick Webb, his wife, and their six children lived ascetically in Orchard House, an old colonial on the grounds, while the Brown Swiss herd dozed under the vaulted ceilings of some of the most magnificent barns ever built on American soil. By the early 1970s, those structures were collapsing into the landscape.

Derick Vanderbilt Webb, the first member of his illustrious family truly to farm the land at Shelburne Farms, became a popular legislator and chair of the Vermont Republican Party in the 1960s, during the years when Phil Hoff, the liberal lion, was governor. A decorated World War II veteran and the president of the Vermont Dairy Council, Webb was a kindly, foursquare kind of person, though his tall, rugged frame and his own pedigree implied a fate beyond husbandry. Webb was known in Montpelier for his Cary Grant looks, and often wore a bright lapis tailored suit on the statehouse floor. But the scion of industrialists mainly socialized with a vanishing caste of small-town farmer-lawmakers, and to the detriment of his legislative effectiveness. Webb seemed happier with his cows, anyway. He hosted impromptu tours of his innovative milking parlors and harvesting technology for anybody who turned up on the vast acres of Shelburne Farms.

But Webb was most at home in his private plane, coasting over the foothills near his property. That Cessna, which took off from a gravel airstrip near Orchard House, was often "used for political purposes," Steve Terry told me with an arched eyebrow. It was the only one of its kind in Vermont, and a unique factor in the state's politics. A ride in Webb's plane meant a role in his low-key but effective operation. A friend and protégé, the high-strung local businessman and state Representative Richard Snelling, used to fly with Webb and, according to Terry, would grow alarmed by Webb's nonchalant way of piloting the plane without any thought to planning for an emergency landing.

Webb never crashed: that was "aristocracy in a nutshell," Terry told me. But it was not the amiable and abstract Derick Webb, who seemed born to rule, who would go on to become the governor of Vermont; that role awaited his young friend in the passenger seat, the fiercely competitive Snelling, who later became a rival of Bernie Sanders politically, even as the two men, sharing a cat-and-mouse instinct with the Vermont media as well as unruly heads of curly hair, came to like and admire each other.

Webb's chairmanship was by many measures a success: his Republican Party appeared to be in stronger shape than ever, despite the tremors of the 1960s and the changing face of Vermont. The 1970 census showed that for the first time in one hundred years, more people had moved to Vermont than left the state. The new Vermonters were overwhelmingly young and, one presumed, liberal, but somehow the wave of hippies hadn't made a dent in the state's electoral politics. Liberty Union bled the left flank of the Democratic Party, already weakened by Phil Hoff's sputtering final term as governor. Richard Nixon won Vermont in 1968 and 1972 by wide margins. Webb could return to Shelburne Farms secure in his party's predominance for the future.

But something was different about the fair in 1974, as even Derick Webb could see. In the arts-and-crafts tent, merchants sold hand-blown glass pipes, amulets, and beads. Bread & Puppet performed their anti-capitalist skits along the midway, led by a gaunt, frightening, twenty-foot-tall Uncle Sam. Young Catholic nuns handed out flyers next to a representative of the religion called Eckankar, "The Path of Total Awareness."

Things were different at home, too: Webb's six children, heirs to the farm and the dwindling Vanderbilt fortune, now sported long hair, beards, headbands, bell bottoms. In their own ways, the Webb children had joined their generation and become back-to-the-landers. Alec Webb abruptly dropped out of Groton, the exclusive Episcopal boarding school in Massachusetts, just before graduating. He refused his spot at Yale and began dreaming up environmentally sound uses for his family's estate. Soon, Alec's brother Marshall dropped out of Wesleyan and returned home to stack wood in the fields and forests of the family property. A small corps of friends and friendly interlopers came to stay and work the land. When Alec convened an impromptu summer camp on the estate for kids he'd recruited off the street, word traveled to Newport and the Upper East Side. What had gotten into the Webbs?

George Aiken's Heirs

In election years, the Champlain Valley Fair was the place for candidates to shake hands, pat the heads of babies and calves, and pick apart sticky masses of cotton candy while handing out buttons and literature to nonplussed passersby. Outside the 4-H barn, while Derick Webb kept his head under a cow's belly, the candidates for George Aiken's U.S. Senate seat made their rounds.

Aiken was retiring after thirty-four years as the most popular and effective senator in Vermont's history. His successor had been arranged: U.S. House Representative Richard Mallary, a granite-ribbed Dartmouth man and dairy farmer from little Fairlee on the Connecticut River. In a photo taken at the fair, Mallary hoists an enormous sausage, ready to take a bite. The caption is "Dick Mallary eats it up." Mallary had every reason to believe that Vermont would eat him up, too. And to win Aiken's seat would establish the young, widely admired Mallary in Washington potentially for decades as the heir to Vermont's proud tradition of moderate, maverick Republicans who happened to know the underside of a cow.

The Democrat in the race had made an impression, but nobody in Vermont gave Patrick Leahy much of a chance. The young man, whose family printing business sat across from the statehouse in Montpelier, was appointed state's attorney for Chittenden County in 1966, at the age of twenty-six. In 1971, he led the investigation into the murder of a friend of my mother's, Rita Curran, a quiet young nursing student who, one evening, returned to her apartment in our neighborhood from her barbershop quartet's rehearsal and was tied up, raped, and beaten to death. The killer then smoked a pack of cigarettes over her body.

Growing up, we assumed that the killer had been the serial murderer Ted Bundy, who was born in Burlington and was rumored to have returned. But the murder, unsolved until 2022, was eventually charged to Curran's upstairs neighbor. Leahy used the Curran case and a spate of other violent crimes to establish his bona fides as a very public prosecutor, while consistently taking left-of-center positions on civil rights, abortion, and Vietnam. Though he stood nearly six feet four and was ferocious at trial, it was

Leahy's gentleness, his quickness to laugh and empathize, that seemed the core of the man.

But this was Vermont, and George Aiken, who had not been opposed in an election since 1962, kept up a keen interest in this one. Aiken did not like Patrick Leahy, nor did Leahy particularly like Aiken. According to Leahy's biographer, Philip Baruth, Aiken had once turned a teenage Leahy down for a Senate internship on the grounds that the young man came from a family of Democrats. Leahy's own Senate office ran its internship program, as Leahy has said, "entirely on merit." After Leahy prevailed on Election Day, his team immediately pressured the retiring Aiken to leave early and convey his seniority to the new senator. Aiken very publicly refused: a contract, he said, was a contract. Pat Leahy began his career, therefore, ninety-ninth in seniority out of one hundred lawmakers. He ended it in 2022 as Senate president pro tempore, and the third-longest-serving senator in history.

By late summer, Leahy was gaining ground. The dignified local prosecutor with a Vermont accent thicker than deer hide drove "a battered but technologically enhanced Batmobile," according to Baruth. Leahy's devotion to the caped crusader was already legendary, and as senator, Leahy would go on to several cameo appearances in Batman films, including an important turn as a banker tormented by Heath Ledger's lipstick-smeared and terrifying Joker in Christopher Nolan's *The Dark Knight*. Leahy outfitted his sedan with two Dictaphones (one for the campaign, one for official business), a police radio with a telephone handset, and a siren that Leahy sometimes set off "for the sheer sweet forbidden pleasure of it."

Leahy's most important asset might have been his wife, Marcelle Pomerleau Leahy, a native French speaker who hailed from the railroad town of Newport, just south of the Quebec border. Newport was a boomtown in the nineteenth century, and remained a regional hub for the surrounding communities, some of the poorest and worst-served towns in all the state. In fact many of the towns that Marcelle Leahy visited during the fall of 1974 had only fairly recently been connected to the state's electricity grid. The town of Victory, where Marcelle and her father campaigned in October of 1974, counted seventy residents in the most recent census, all living along three dirt roads. When you pass through Victory, every head turns.

Much of the Northeast Kingdom is like this. The populations of these tiny villages tend to be insular, wherever they fall on the class spectrum. In the nineteenth century, deans from Princeton and Yale set up a summer community around Lake Caspian, in Greensboro, and have kept its glacial waters for the loons and the lucky few with a share in their modest shingled camps. Greta Garbo stayed there one summer in a home behind a screen of aspens. Chief Justice William Rehnquist lived in seclusion in Greensboro, and retirees from the foreign service and the CIA have always loved the anonymity of the place. In nearby Peacham, a row of impressive Greek Revival houses, built during the merino wool boom in the 1840s and '50s and set against the hillside, was reclaimed in the twentieth century by professors from Amherst and Harvard exploring the rural byways off Interstate 91. When the communes arrived, they mimicked the insularity of the existing communities but added their utopian optimism. Bread & Puppet settled in the Northeast Kingdom for good, in Glover, in 1975. It keeps its doors, but never its customs, open to the public.

But the main barrier to outsiders in much of the Northeast Kingdom, as of 1974, was language, and here Marcelle Leahy was the decisive factor. The three northern counties—Orleans, Essex, and Caledonia—are heavily Quebecois, so much so that the region feels not meaningfully a part of the United States. The northern border here is merely notional; at some point, my ancestors unwittingly stepped across it and therefore became American. The signs are bilingual, if not exclusively in French. Marcelle, who spoke French fluently, visited the slaughterhouse workers of Albany, the asbestos miners of Lowell, and the nude sunbathers on the south beach of Lake Willoughby, and conversed with them in the distinct Vermont Franglish of the place. She would then humbly press a glossy campaign brochure into their hands or leave behind a stack at the general store. Marcelle's natural rapport with French Canadians extended to other communities in the state, like Barre and Winooski, which were already heavily Democratic. But in the deeply Republican Northeast Kingdom, her husband's big-city liberal politics never came up. "She's a beautiful woman, that Marcelle Leahy," said a man standing outside the tool-and-die plant in Derby Line. This seemed to be the consensus. Whether inroads were made, inroads were reported; the Vermont press loved the story.

Bernie v. Rocky

George Aiken was no fan of Patrick Leahy, but he liked Sanders. Ever since Bernie had shown up to his office in Washington to conduct his *Vermont Life* interview looking like he'd hitchhiked there, the owlish Aiken had decided he would take the young man seriously. Steve Terry, Aiken's aide, pointed Aiken to Bernie's libertarian streak. Aiken read the anti-authoritarian notes Bernie sounded in his *Vermont Freeman* pieces. Sanders, for his part, had praised Aiken's work for America's farmers: Aiken's rural water bill had brought millions in federal funds to towns in Addison County that had been plagued by drought for many summers in a row. An extensive network of trenches and pumps now brought fresh lake water to the area's parched fields. On a campaign swing, Sanders admired the Tri-Town Water District headquarters in Addison, and told a crowd that Aiken was his kind of man. When word reached Aiken in Washington that Sanders had had kind things to say, the stony Yankee cracked a smile.

The word *Watergate* was on everyone's lips that season, and 1974 was a wave election for Democrats across the country. This was bad news for many of the fledgling third parties that had spawned during the Vietnam era. Sanders and his allies in Liberty Union had made the case for years that the two major parties were indistinguishable—"Democans and Republicrats"—but the electorate was in no mood for such talk. The political moment pitted virtue against corruption; there was no third role. Liberty Union entered the 1974 campaign season hefting a spiral notebook filled with six thousand signatures and some legible phone numbers and home addresses, but no party infrastructure to concentrate its potential new support. And how robust was that support likely to be? Six thousand people had decided that they did not want to pay more for phone service. Some percentage of those people now blamed the party for the telephone company layoffs, and some simply had no interest in politics unless their wallets were involved.

Liberty Union met in a church basement in Burlington in June 1974. The deck chairs were duly shuffled: Sanders would run this time for Senate, Martha Abbott for governor, Nancy Kaufman for attorney general. The caucus did produce a few dramatic surprises. Arthur Deloy, a labor leader who, in 1972, led hundreds of striking hard-hatted construction workers down U.S. 15 to the new IBM plant in Essex Junction, stood for attorney general. Deloy rose to prominence in a strike against Burlington's powerful construction company, Pizzagalli. His was the strongest link to labor groups the Liberty Union had yet forged. And for U.S. House, Peter Diamondstone—"often in disarray," according to Lynn Daley—was defeated by a resurgent Michael Parenti. The controversial professor dismissed by UVM in 1971 was now back on the scene and living in Putney.

In Parenti and Sanders, Liberty Union had its most effective duo since Lake and Sanders dragged their children across the state in 1971. The two men were almost comically intense. Parenti, an off-brand, half-pint Bernie with "a black book of willing dates in every corner of Vermont," had a pugilistic delivery that reminded people he had once punched a guy out, and might again. The candidates were joined along the trail by a brilliant young UVM graduate, John Franco, who'd come into the public eye when he published an investigative report in the university's excellent newspaper, *The*

Vermont Cynic. The story, picked up by the statewide press, exposed the ties of the UVM Board of Trustees to major corporate interests. Franco, foul mouthed, uncouth, and tireless, was running as a Liberty Union candidate for state senate. By day, back in his home city of Barre, Franco sold paint on commission, just like Bernie's dad.

"It was all a little sophomoric in retrospect," Franco told me of his *Cynic* exposé, when we met in his office in downtown Burlington. The 1973–74 OPEC oil embargo had led UVM to the energy-saving measure of running classes on a three-day-a-week schedule, so Franco's two passions that winter dovetailed: he used his spare time to ski at Stowe and do his research. Soon, "we'd gotten our hands on a government report about the disclosure of corporate ownership," Franco said, and "just called all these press conferences. I'd drive up from the paint store in Barre, and we'd meet outside of Bernie's hovel on Maple Street and just hammer the boards of all the Vermont utilities. That was Bernie's answer to everything: a press conference." The press was hooked.

Sanders and Parenti, shadowing Deloy on jobsites and in American Legion halls, wanted to "solve the age-old problem that has dogged the American left," Franco said: they wanted to show "they could talk to average people." Never mind that Parenti was a Yale-trained academic; in Barre, the Italian American quarry workers saw him as one of their own. At a farm in Waterbury, Parenti won over a crowd of farmers by telling them that what they paid for their tractors would once have bought them an entire farm. "These guys were nodding their fucking heads off," Franco said. The rich were doing fine, while average Vermonters "had to tighten their belts." It was "galling," the hypocrisy. In Vermont, weekend visitors "filled up their Saabs next to farmers buying their gas a few gallons at a time, with dimes." Class issues in Vermont are glaring, once you see them. Sanders and Parenti knew just how to shine a spotlight.

To Franco, 1974 was "the first inkling of a breakthrough" for Bernie. But for some, Sanders blew an opportunity. Shaken by the OPEC embargo, Vermonters told Bernie that their minds that summer were on the approaching winter cold. Sanders called before them the specter of Nelson Rockefeller, the patrician governor of New York and a stakeholder in his brother's oil company, Exxon. "I can talk about the Rockefellers until people think I'm out of my mind," Sanders told a reporter, "but if I can convince 1 percent of the people, then I've accomplished something."

One percent is not a winning percentage. But to Bernie, the specter of the coming deep freeze provided the perfect opportunity to attack Governor Rockefeller. And Sanders soon saw reason to go ballistic. When Richard

Nixon resigned the presidency in August of 1974, Gerald Ford took office and chose Rockefeller as his vice president. The appointment required Senate confirmation hearings throughout the fall, to coincide with campaign season. Sanders turned his 1974 campaign into a frantic referendum on the moderate, popular, and charismatic governor of New York, a man widely viewed as decent and statesmanlike. "Rockefeller Republicans," that lamented, now-extinct class, were, like Aiken Republicans, defiant of party power and orthodoxy. But Sanders saw in Nelson Rockefeller something like the end of American democracy.

It was a hard case to make back then, and 1974 could have spelled the end of Bernie Sanders's political career. The first problem was that he seemed at times manic or possessed. Friends from the era report that his obsession with the Rockefeller family's web of connections seemed to consume him. Sanders's darkest suspicions about the cabalistic nature of power and wealth had been proved with Nelson Rockefeller's appointment: the plain and appalling fact was that an oligarch had been set up in the very seat of democracy. (Although this take seemed alarmist at the time, the years, alas, have vindicated Bernie.)

"He didn't so much talk *to* me, but talk *at* me," Garrison Nelson, the UVM political scientist, told me. Nelson dodged Sanders on the university campus—"Everyone did," he told me—but Bernie cornered him in the stacks of the Bailey-Howe Library and "went on and on about the Rockefellers." Nelson had endured the conspiratorial rants of his own father, the handsome, quixotic actor-turned-radical and best-selling novelist Truman Nelson, all throughout his childhood, and connected leftist tirades with the alcohol on his father's breath. He was inured to the kind of dot connecting that Bernie had performed in the pages of the *Vermont Freeman*, where he proposed that Vermonters were suffering because of the greed of one family: "Rockefeller's oil company, Exxon, reported an 80 percent increase in profits for the third quarter of this year," Sanders wrote. "While Vermonters are paying outrageous prices for gas and heating oil, the oil billionaires are getting richer."

Nelson Rockefeller faced televised confirmation hearings on Capitol Hill that fall and performed with unflappable distinction. Sanders tried in vain to tie his Senate opponents, Patrick Leahy and Richard Mallary, to the hearings in Washington. "They are both bought," Bernie told the audience at a debate hosted by WEZF-TV. "They are both clearly within the establishment." Leahy said he opposed Rockefeller; Mallary promised to wait and see. But the telegenic, square-jawed Rockefeller was to many a welcome addition in the White House. The New York governor was confirmed by the Senate in a 90–7 vote that scrambled political divisions: some of his most ardent champions were Democrats.

Liberty Union "was adrift, without the provocation of Vietnam," an observer noted. At forum after forum, Bernie, the third-party candidate, was noted only for his "rapier jabs" against the Rockefeller dynasty, describing in ever greater and more impassioned detail the interlocking directorates of the big oil companies and the six largest banks in the country, all of them in the hands of the Rockefeller family. With Michael Parenti by his side, he was poised to make effective inroads with the construction unions, with dairy farmers, with educated liberals. But he had conditioned support for his candidacy on voters' adherence to a far-fetched creed: the fuel bill, the phone bill, the food bill, all were higher because an insidious cabal had sought to maximize profits. To Garrison Nelson, it was just "downright weird." An image of Sanders as somewhat cracked had by now begun to solidify, with a predictable battery of phrases accompanying press reports about him: the "disheveled," "bombastic," "radical," "perennial candidate" "railed against"—and here Bernie's own predictable and familiar phrases take over—"oligarchs," "bankers," "oil executives," and "billionaires." Stories about Bernie from his previous campaigns reflect the great promise of his outsider status, the intensity and effectiveness of his opposition to the draft, his surprising outreach to rural voters, his "independent streak," his effectiveness with labor groups, his hard-to-place Yankee suspicion of big government and frivolous regulation. Stories from 1974, though, portray him as a bantamweight, red-in-the-face crusader against "Rocky" Rockefeller. He'd gotten himself locked into novelty status.

But Sanders's new hyper-visibility also showed a more promising path forward. Already during this early phase, the fascination with Sanders's appearance and affect began to take hold. With his bracing message boiled down to a few key points, his unforgettable Brooklyn baritone, his mop of black hair and tattered wardrobe, Sanders was from the beginning an analog version of what we would call a meme: a "sameness machine," according to Nico Baumbach, deriving from the French word *même*. Bernie's later success on the internet evolved from the kind of low-fi IRL virality that he perfected in Vermont in the 1970s. Then as now, Sanders symbolized in every aspect of his appearance and self-presentation his core beliefs, which he expressed in a few bare mottoes. Though Sanders still usually went by "Bernard," the "Bernie" phenomenon was born in that 1974 race.

Rocky might have beaten Bernie in this round, but he'd handed him one of the most important effects in his political repertoire: the concept of the "billionaires," individuals whose wealth was itself immoral and incompatible with democracy. Here was a class of people who simply shouldn't exist in this country, Bernie believed. He and the billionaires had, of course, a long, shared road before them.

ON ELECTION NIGHT, Derick Webb and Richard Snelling listened from the kitchen radio in Shelburne as Vermont sent its first Democrat to the Senate since the founding of the Republican Party in 1854. The margin was around four thousand votes. George Aiken had counted on Bernie's being a spoiler for Leahy, but Sanders's roughly six thousand votes drew from several Republican strongholds in the state, where young farmers and culturally conservative blue-collar workers had brightened to his message. Sanders was in fact Mallary's spoiler. It was not the first time, and surely not the last, that Bernie's strength among Republicans surprised the experts. Leahy and Sanders, who went on to serve alongside each other in the Senate, formed a permanent bond during the campaign, when they sometimes split a babysitter for their young children during debates. As Vermont's most powerful senator since Aiken, Leahy directed earmarks to Bernie's Burlington throughout the '80s, and cleared the field of Democrats for Sanders's 1990 winning campaign for Congress.

The news in the House race was surprising as well: Michael Parenti had run well against the victor, James Jeffords, a liberal Republican in the Aiken mold. But Parenti's strong showing triggered an unintended consequence. Parenti finished with about 7 percent of the vote, clearing the threshold of 5 percent that automatically conferred on Liberty Union—which had been founded as a nonparty, an anti-party—the status of a major party in Vermont. Downstream for the chaotic little network of fast-talking dreamers and radicals would be election laws, primaries, and scrutiny of the party's fund-raising.

Reality, not entirely welcome, had now broken on Liberty Union. As a party it now had to function. If it failed to function, it became a drag on its candidates. Parenti's success had crashed Liberty Union down to earth. As Bernie's thoughts turned to the 1976 cycle, he wondered aloud whether Liberty Union had become a liability. In fact, he wondered whether *any* political party would eventually become one.

12

Vermont Vermont

(Act 250)

Shelburne Farms, early 1900s. *Shelburne Farms*

The Fight to Stay Rural, Continued

In 1777, by turning back usurping New Yorkers, Vermont established America's first West Coast, with Burlington, perched on a dramatic rise above Lake Champlain, eventually suggesting a toy San Francisco. Looking across to the Adirondacks, I used to marvel, as I still do when I behold those mountains from Battery Park in Burlington: "That's New York."

Alec Webb's ancestors came from New York City to these shores in the 1880s and eventually bought up thirty adjacent farms. The Webbs were wealthy industrialists but nevertheless part of a generation in search of the pastoral ideal. As Blake Harrison argues in *The View from Vermont: Tourism and the Making of an American Rural Landscape*, middle-class Americans were at the time discovering Vermont farmscapes on "working" vacations. New Hampshire, with its higher, stonier peaks, was sold as a version of the European sublime, and soon, majestic Alpine resorts sprang up in the White Mountains. Vermont captured a more nostalgic yearning for the bygone agrarian past, and offered the traveler, instead of grand vistas, mellow fields and pastures in the company of the thrifty Anglo-Saxons who worked the land. Dr. William Seward Webb and his bride, Lila Vanderbilt Webb, wanted those effects on a grand Victorian scale to suit their Gilded Age ambitions and fortune. Soon after they arrived, the boulder walls running between the old farms were pulled up like stitches yanked out of a garment. The only trace of those old settlements is a beautiful roadside cemetery whose newest occupant arrived in 1866.

By 1976, with the family's resources drawn down, Shelburne Farms was in financial trouble, and Alec Webb and his siblings had a potential devil's bargain in the offing. On a spring walk at the farms, Alec told me that he and his siblings had been shown a map of their estate drawn up by local developers, portioning the land into small lots and promising to return to his family vast wealth on a scale no Webb had enjoyed in three generations. Having made their fortune once from the railroads, these latest Vanderbilts stood to regain it from the automobile, which had brought their verdant pastures within a ten-minute drive of I-89.

Alec and his daughter Heidi, a development officer at the farms, showed me the view across the bay toward Giant Mountain in the Adirondack range. We stood very near the freshly turned earth where Marshall Webb, Shelburne Farms's cofounder, who died suddenly in August of 2022, had recently been buried. A stand of scrub was only partly cleared nearby, where Marshall's work was interrupted.

Alec is a slight, athletic man now in his mid-seventies, endearingly shy. A smile comes to him at the thought of his next remark, a beat before he utters it. He looks like his ancestors in oil portraits I've seen, once adjustments are made for the loss of high collars and muttonchops. I asked him, what would compel six siblings raised in aristocratic austerity to agree to divest themselves of many millions of dollars in awaiting wealth? Alec responded by gesturing toward the bay and toward the meadows all around us that had begun to fill in with purple vetch and fragrant bedstraw. Alec and Marshall's mission was to convert the property from the values of what he called the "showy wealth" embodied by their ancestors to the communal values of their own countercultural generation. He wanted to learn from "what the land had to teach," and he wanted others to come learn as well, especially children.

This was not some utopian plan, but an ingenious adaptation. The costs of owning the property had outstripped the resources of even an aristocratic farmer like Derick Webb; around Shelburne Farms, on every side, a prosperous suburb was growing, with schools and civic amenities that required robust taxation. In 1970, the Webbs decided that they would save their farm. This private refuge of industrialists became a nonprofit, as much of the land passed quickly into the hands of a conservation trust. Shelburne Farms, a property larger than downtown Burlington and double the size of New York's Central Park, shrouded in mystery for decades, now opened its gates.

In an inheritance scene worthy of a Victorian novel, Derick Webb collapsed and died on a Florida golf course in 1984, leaving a surprise in his will: the balance of the acres, along with all the barns and the deteriorating main house, were deeded to his children's nonprofit. This dramatic bequest was the last property melodrama to befall the Webbs, who could have been dealt a lifetime of them. Inside of one hundred years, the most exclusive parcel of land in Vermont, the very signature of hoarded wealth, had been turned over to the people. The property's vast network of trails and country roads have been open to the public for decades, free of charge. Though Shelburne Farms was Alec Webb's inheritance, he is now, as its president, one of many employees who turn up in the office wing of the Farm Barn every morning. During the COVID-19 pandemic, the farms hosted as many as three thousand people per day, including my mom and her walking group, moving in time with the lowing Brown Swiss herds inside the cedar fence.

WHAT THE WEBBS saw hurtling toward their threshold in the early 1970s was evident throughout the state of Vermont. In May of 1969, Governor Deane Davis, a Republican, visited the southern part of the state, where developers were gobbling up farmland to create flimsy town-home ghettos for skiers from New York and Massachusetts. The development scene was "wide open," according to Joe Sherman in *Fast Lane on a Dirt Road*. One project proposed to mine the Mad River near Sugarbush to extract five hundred thousand feet of gravel. Another sought to cut a road up a pristine mountain slope and pack forty-six homes together at its peak. During the boom years, in the greasy dives that surround the ski areas, developers would turn up bearing a suitcase full of standard contracts, then find a barstool and introduce themselves to the local farmers and large landowners who drifted in and were game to accept a round of shots. By this Wild West method and others equally unscrupulous, Vermont was now losing farmland and open space at a greater rate than at any time in its history.

In Davis, Vermont's farms, open hillsides, and riverbeds found a champion. The development rush was occurring "on the most improper basis," without regard to environmental considerations that today seem routine. Builders were breaking ground in fragile soil, along dirt roads deeply rutted during mud season. Davis reported "one development where sewage was running right onto the highway." The governor and his allies were conservationists, but they were also savvy businessmen: Vermont's appeal had by this time become intricately bound to its appeal as a timeless, unspoiled, rural place. For native Vermonters, the bargain was sometimes hard to swallow. Many a struggling Vermonter looking to subdivide his acres has cursed Deane Davis over the years, when told that the distant ridgeline views of second homeowners mattered more than their busted furnaces.

Once the raw sewage washed up on the highway, Vermont's conservation actions were swift and bold. In the late 1960s, the state passed Act 333, banning billboards, a change that first-time visitors notice immediately when they cross into the state. With the so-called Billboard Law, the foreground had been protected, but the background vista of unspoiled ridges required legislative action. Lawmakers in Montpelier were all ears. The "avuncular" Davis, according to Sherman, "disarmed them with his simple language, country wit, and charm." Soon Vermont passed Act 250, which remains the most extensive, and at times the most controversial, land use law in the country. If you want to know why Vermont and New Hampshire look so different, despite landscape and demographic similarities, one reason is Act 250.

The act established nine regional boards to review ten criteria for any development in the state greater than ten acres in size, with tighter rules governing towns without superceding restrictions. The surprising thing is that many of these criteria are not, strictly speaking, "environmental." In addition to soil erosion and wastewater, Act 250 contemplates something it calls "aesthetics" and "scenic beauty." These clauses, flashpoints since 1970, are the main reasons that Act 250 has been perceived, by its critics, as the "postcard law" that doomed Vermont to looking permanently like the cover of *Vermont Life* magazine. Whenever Vermont slumps, Act 250 gets a share of the blame; but ask many Vermonters if they want it abolished, and the answer is more muted.

The values implicit in working a dairy farm are not necessarily those implicit in preserving it as part of a landscape by a web of subsidies, federal support, land use laws, preservation codes, and restrictions on the kinds of things a person can do on property he owns. To freeze Vermont the way Act 250 did was a magic trick of sophisticated progressivism; but many working Vermonters began to wonder whose interests the law had enshrined, if not their own.

Sprawl

As the population in Chittenden County swelled, the pristine acres not an hour's walk from downtown Burlington began to attract the attention of visiting developers on family ski vacations. Act 250, enforcing rurality in Vermont at large, had driven development to the county, the state's only enterprise zone. When, in the fall of 1975, a Boston developer came to call at my great-grandfather's small farm—two acres of asparagus, lettuce, radishes, and potatoes on Dorset Street in South Burlington—Wilfred Delorme shook the man's hand, sat down on the small front porch shaded by October maples, and listened to his story.

The developer described the "inevitable spread" of retail development across my great-grandfather's field and told him that "the sooner he got out, the more his investment would be worth." Already, from one corner of Wilfred's acres, you could make out the sign of a Zayre department store a few thousand feet away. My cousins lived all up and down Dorset Street, in adjacent tidy ranch homes finished with aluminum siding, fronting acres of flat farmland. One by one, they sold. An off-ramp for I-89 was at one end of Dorset Street; at the other end, the University Mall offered thousands of parking spaces for hundreds of stores. And so it was that in the fall of 1975, if the photo albums can be trusted, we drove over to my great-grandpa's farm, rode around on his tractor, collected crabapples for jam, and said goodbye to the modest property that happened to be in the crosshairs of the Rand Development Corporation of Framingham, Massachusetts. Wilfred Delorme took his small payout, moved some framed pictures and his upholstered recliner to an efficiency apartment nearby, and watched as the excavators and steam shovels lumbered past on their way to his home and fields.

"Sprawl" had come to Chittenden County, and the city center took notice: soon Burlington mounted an extensive lobbying campaign to fight development on its fringe, and to spruce itself up to compete for suburban business. The damage seemed contained, as Dorset Street absorbed strip malls, movie theaters, and supermarkets, while downtown Burlington maintained its appeal. Then a field just steps away from the Burlington International Airport caught the eye of executives from the Pyramid Corporation of New York, and the farmer who owned it cashed out gleefully and headed to Florida's Gulf Coast to live out his years in tropical leisure. The proposed Pyramid Mall became the most bitterly contested development plan in Vermont, a metonym for the larger fights that divided the state. Burlington felt it had an ace in the hole: such a large development would trigger Act 250, whose strict conservation criteria had, ironically, driven developers to

Williston in the first place. Now Act 250, "the giant killer," faced its own defining test.

"WHAT MAKES VERMONT SO—VERMONT?" was the question posed by *Brave Little State*, a popular Vermont podcast, in 2024. One answer is that the question itself has been asked continuously for at least one hundred years. Few American places have minded their reputations so zealously. When the sociologists Jason Kaufman and Matthew E. Kaliner published their important study *The Re-Accomplishment of Place in Twentieth Century Vermont and New Hampshire*, comparing Vermont to its estranged sibling across the Connecticut River, they found plenty of comparative data—Birkenstock dealers and food co-ops on one shore; Harley dealerships on the other; gun shops, and guns, on both sides—but their insight about the root cause of the differences strikes a non-sociologist as both very true and very circular: Vermont attracts people who want to live in Vermont.

This self-reinforcing loop is what drew people like Howard Dean to the Green Mountain State. "If you want to see the way Vermont changed, look at Maine and New Hampshire," Dean told me. Dean, Vermont's governor for twelve years and a serious contender for the 2004 Democratic presidential nomination, benefited from those changes, even as he ranks among their catalysts. "New Hampshire was settled by people fleeing taxes," Dean said. But "a political culture" as distinct from an economic culture was spawned when Vermont, unlike its neighbors, made its conditional invitation to the wider world: "Come live here, but leave it exactly as you found it." I used to joke with my fellow Vermonter, the writer Jamaica Kincaid, about a favorite bumper sticker: "Welcome to Vermont: Now Go Home." Kincaid, who moved with her young family to Vermont in 1985, put the paradox this way to me:

> I instinctively knew that Vermont lacked the harsh historical rhetoric of New Hampshire (which is New England's Mississippi or Alabama or someplace nearby) and even Maine. I didn't at the time know how important it was in the Underground Railroad, but I must have just sensed it, so to speak. Later I discovered it was the first republic in the Western world to make owning a person illegal. Then the beauty of it of course: it has no billboards polluting the scenery of the beautiful landscape. And perhaps even more important was the fact that I grew up in a place in which I saw bodies of water, sea and ocean, every day and must have instinctively known the ephemeralness of water, its appearance from a distance of solidness, yet up close was not that at all; the green mountains

> of a place like Vermont [are] part of the ancient geographical makeup of this continent we live on.

The Vermont "difference" has always been as much aspirational as real: Jamaica and her children have faced racism regularly in Vermont since their move to Bennington. But the aspirations *are* real, and they create the impetus for communities to work collaboratively on living up to its ideals.

The answer that *Brave Little State* gave to their question of what makes "Vermont Vermont" was more concrete: it is the effect of Act 250, not merely on the land but also on civic life. "The law encourages participatory democracy in a number of ways," Margaret DeWeese-Boyd wrote in a 2006 article in the *Community Development Journal*, partly by granting statutory party status unusually generously. Few who participate in Act 250 hearings are mere bystanders: instead, a very broad definition of "impacted party" is used to determine who gets a seat at the table. It has meant that neighbors tend to meet one another when confronted with an Act 250 project, and many a Vermont political career has been launched in hearings to defeat some behemoth condo or mall project in a former cornfield. Foes of the law, though, have made the case for years that the statutory standing of virtually anyone who shows up to an Act 250 hearing has empowered random individuals, and some bad actors, to halt housing developments that might benefit communities in need.

The Pyramid Mall rallied Burlington during the mid-1970s, when the city joined the struggle against the project as a statutory party to oppose the giant mall. But the threat of the inevitable—if not this mall, others—also created, in downtown Burlington, a frenzy of new planning and construction. Our own version, the Burlington Square Mall, opened during this hysteria, in 1976; and soon, planning began to turn Church Street, Burlington's main shopping district, into an open-air pedestrian mall. The mayor overseeing it all, Gordon Paquette, wanted to out-develop the suburban developers, but the same adjectives used to tarnish the Pyramid executives of New York were used against Paquette: slimy, greedy, crooked.

Burlington had entered a development spiral. When Act 250 defeated the Pyramid Mall in 1978, the law to protect Vermont's countryside emerged stronger than ever. But it had almost no jurisdiction within the densely zoned city of Burlington. By 1980, Burlington residents looked around and wondered if the pitched battle to save seventy acres four miles away in Williston should have been fought a little closer to home, to save Burlington's neighborhoods; and the fighter they eventually backed was Bernie Sanders.

13

Bicentennial

(Sanders for Governor '76)

Bread & Puppet, bicentennial celebration, summer 1976. *Ron Simon*

Earliest Memory

Two hundred years before the bicentennial summer of 1976, Vermont was still an unincorporated patchwork of grants made by the governor of New Hampshire, Benning Wentworth, to favorites in his circle. Those gifts were made despite contesting contracts on the land held by upper-class New Yorkers, who routinely showed up in Vermont to settle these overlapping claims. Ethan Allen made his name by repelling New York surveyors from the New Hampshire grants, forming, for defense, a loose militia called the Green Mountain Boys, who soon agreed to contribute as freelancers to the Revolutionary War to repel the British at Fort Ticonderoga. The Republic of Vermont was founded in 1777 by the holders of the New Hampshire grants, with the backing of Allen's militia, as an illegal scheme to cheat the New Yorkers—though as *Vermont Life* put it, "some New Yorkers may still persist" in seeing the Green Mountain State as its "most attractive suburb."

And so, in the summer of '76, Vermont gamely celebrated the nation's independence, though reserving some pomp for its own personal bicentennial the following year, as well as for the bicentennial of its statehood in 1991. The 1976 Vermont Bicentennial Commission oversaw distributing some $350,000 in federal monies to Vermont cities and villages. Little Granby got $58 toward historic plaques. The Discovery Museum in Essex, where I used to go to handle geckos and stand within the enormous chamber of a soap bubble, received $8,000. Hippies in Calais got a grant to revive forgotten country dances. Sawmills everywhere were restored; covered bridges were spruced up; in Burlington, a stoner drum corps, the Burlington Beaters, assembled a patriotic program for the holiday. An old steam train running along the old railroad lines was buffed and painted for tourist travel through the mountains. Equipped with federal money, Vermont set out to reconstruct its earliest memories of itself.

The city of Burlington, where I was a five-year-old that summer, spent much of its bicentennial windfall on a July 4 parade, which, to keep holy the sabbath, was held on Saturday, July 3. My own earliest narrative memory (a filmstrip, not a snapshot) is from that day. The parade, led by the actor and Burlington native Orson Bean, went up Church Street, past city hall. Bean, the first cousin of Vermont's famously taciturn president, Calvin Coolidge, was a regular guest on Johnny Carson's show and on Gene Rayburn's *Match Game*, but few Burlingtonians recognized their parade marshal, and when his car passed, a woman accosted him. "Who are you?" she asked. "I know you're important, but for what?" Bean, smiling broadly, responded, "If you find out, will you let me know?"

According to the *Burlington Free Press*, "differing philosophies" were on display at the parade: a "group of feminists may have attracted the most attention." The "well dressed woman on Park Street" who was reported as remarking loudly, "Aren't they a crumbly-looking group of individuals?" was almost certainly my aunt Arlene, who said such things. We watched the parade from Aunt Arlene and Uncle Esau's porch on Park Street, the adults scoffing at the riffraff in the mix alongside Shriners in miniature cars and World War I veterans in dress uniforms.

But my most vivid memory from that day is of the huge party in Battery Park at the end of the parade. I recovered this memory all at once, one afternoon in 2011, while standing at a counter in an apartment I'd rented in Paris for the month. A friend and I had just seen Robert Altman's astonishing bicentennial film, *Nashville*, at a crowded theater in the 6th arrondissement. At the time I had a Ritalin prescription and found that if I took a double dose I could sometimes write very freely. So: down the hatch! What then bubbled to mind was my entire long poem "Bicentennial," written in one fell swoop as the Parisian dusk passed by unnoticed.

The poem jumps around in place and time, but comes to rest in Battery Park, Burlington, July 3, 1976. "I am having / My childhood now," I wrote, the "now" suggesting how abruptly remembered things are experienced, as they were for me that afternoon, as though they were brand new. "That's me; I am at a party // By the lake:

> *. . . the boats jostle for space*
> *Inside the breakwater, a neighbor lifts me*
> *Up to see the band concert, the French horns*
> *Blare, the men wear their war uniforms,*
> *The hippies are riding history, the ferries*
> *Are playing blues for the private parties,*
> *The mountains across the water, that's New York.*

Turning to my right, that afternoon in 1976—it's not in the poem—I saw the nightmare figures of Bread & Puppet's bicentennial entourage: pitiful Founding Fathers looking as though they'd been impaled on stakes; a large, leering, Nosferatu-like Uncle Sam; and a dragon whose abdomen opened and spawned smaller dragons, with the heads of devils.

NINETEEN SEVENTY-SIX WAS a summer for origin stories, and Vermont, its rural landscapes now defended by cutting-edge conservation law, beckoned the entire country to come experience the world as it was before Watergate, OPEC, fuel shortages, and stagflation. Rolled up in the mail cubbies up and down Central Park West, a commemorative summer issue of *Vermont Life*, brought news of the bicentennial festivities up north. One article profiled the Vermont Mozart Festival, a summer company that had begun to perform symphonic works in Derick Webb's enormous, drafty coach barn at Shelburne Farms. Or a visitor could take in the Burlington International Games, which pitted the teenage athletes of Burlington, Vermont, against our peers in the town of Burlington, Ontario. (In the 1980s, I played basketball in the B.I.G. for a badly outmatched team in awe of the agile Canadians who'd come from away to humiliate us in front of our girlfriends. One kid who vaulted effortlessly over our diminutive squad was rumored to be a "recruit," the wisps of a mustache a sign that the guy was easily twenty-one.)

But the centerpiece of the bicentennial issue of *Vermont Life* was an old-timey Vermont broadsheet, printed on yellow-tinted stock with line illustrations of country life. "Vermont Vignettes" was styled to mimic the *Vermont Quarterly Gazetteer*, a legendary work of five volumes and some 4 million words, compiled in the 1870s by "a determined woman," Abby Maria Hemenway. *Hemenway's*, as it was usually called, was a compendium of local lore from every cranny of Vermont: bears in kitchens, barn fires, war stories from Revolutionary War veterans in their dotage. This astounding work, "embracing a history of each town, civil, ecclesiastical, biographical, and military," remains a prized possession of many rural libraries. The bicentennial reboot doesn't merely pick up where *Hemenway's* left off, however. Its author has an argument to make.

At first "Vermont Vignettes" appears to skim the highlights of the state's history and lore; but in addition to the legendary catamount and the noble Morgan horse, the feature explores some lesser-known stories. Its author celebrates the anti-Masonic movement of the nineteenth century for fighting an "undemocratic, elitist institution." Vermont "took the lead in the fight against slavery," and pioneered wind power at Grandpa's Knob, a small mountain outside of Rutland. In the summer of 1883, the copper mine workers of Vershire staged an insurrection against their bosses, who had withheld some $25,000 in back wages. The workers confiscated explosives and threatened to blow up Vershire and neighboring Fairlee before their leaders were arrested and jailed.

These episodes were not depicted on my first-grade classroom's "Bicentennial Wall." Nor did we learn of the visit of Eugene V. Debs to Barre in 1910:

> During the early 1900's, the industrial centers of Vermont, especially Barre and Rutland were part of the national movement for industrial unionization and were the state's centers for radical labor politics. By 1900, Barre was a strong union town, with 95 per cent of its wage earners members of union shops. Eugene Debs' Socialist Party gained strength in Barre's Italian and Scottish communities, becoming a major party in the city and erecting a three-story meeting hall and cooperative which still stands today.

Another entry in "Vermont Vignettes" celebrates the Barre granite strikers, whose uprising was put down by the Vermont National Guard in 1933.

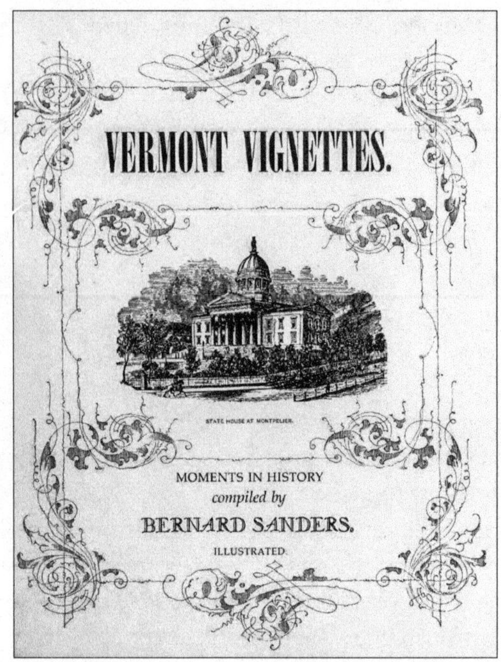

"Vermont Vignettes," 1976. *Vermont Life*

"Vermont Vignettes" adds up to a people's history of the state, smuggled in patriotic garb, and interspersed with obligatory tales of military valor and Yankee ingenuity.

The gazetteer behind "Vermont Vignettes" is, of course, Bernie Sanders, who had begun, in the true spirit of the summer of '76, to frame his politics in terms of Vermont's effaced progressive history. Sanders celebrates the "Bicentennial spirit sweeping the country," and tells Vermont's early stories his way, to reflect his own politics of labor struggle and economic fairness and to frame his 1976 campaign for governor on the Liberty Union ticket. With his contribution to *Vermont Life* in hand, Sanders found support from the Vermont Bicentennial Commission to record radio and TV spots to air across the state. Bernie performed all the parts in his Brooklyn accent: Bernie as Ethan Allen, Bernie as Debs, Bernie as the undersung American Revolution hero Ann Story of little Salisbury, Vermont. "Give me a place among you," Sanders pleaded in the person of this brave young woman, "and see if I am the first to desert my post." This was an earnest attempt to shim a little history between the layers of junk he heard on the broadcast radio and TV networks: "Two hundred years after the American Revolution," Sanders told a reporter, "we should be doing better than having people watching 50 hours a week of hysterical murder shows."

Sanders barnstormed from town to town, using his newfound notoriety to articulate a contrary but sincere "patriotism," as the nation bathed itself in red, white, and blue: "What patriotism means," Sanders told the *Rutland Herald*, "is that you have a respect for humanity and the potential of what people can become. A true patriot has got to say that there is something very wrong in our nation when the entire nation seems to be lacking a sense of purpose." Then it was on to some familiar refrains: "through massive propaganda . . . people identify their needs with Rockefeller's needs." The media was to blame: "We should not have a culture where the three major networks are controlled by the Chase Manhattan Bank."

WITH HISTORY ON HIS MIND, Sanders deputized young John Franco to research Vermont's labor past, for tidbits that Bernie could use on the stump. Franco had left his job selling wallpaper and paint to enroll at Vermont Law School in South Royalton, but he had cut his teeth by exposing the UVM Board of Trustees, and now was diving into his home city of Barre's colorful socialist past. The Debs visit fascinated Bernie, since for years he had admired the Indiana socialist who won almost a million votes for president in 1920, running from prison. And Barre seemed one of America's unacknowledged radical seedbeds. In addition to Debs, the city hosted Emma Goldman, the great anarchist reformer, and "Big Bill" Haywood, the powerful boss of the International Workers of the World. Barre's Socialist Labor Party Hall, constructed in 1900, sheltered dozens of children from Lawrence, Massachusetts, during the 1912 mill strikes in that city. The red socialist flag and the black anarchist flag once flew above its entryway. Barre's socialist publications were produced there, for distribution worldwide.

Bernie had a special interest in Barre's two socialist mayors: Robert Gordon, elected in 1916; and Fred Suitor, elected in 1929. These "municipal socialists"—sometimes called "sewer socialists"—who, according to Robert E. Weir, embodied "socialism as praxis," and were concerned instead with "prosaic tasks" like getting locomotive companies to maintain their crossings on city streets—were part of the blueprint for Sanders's years as mayor. But leading into the campaign season, "the plan was to keep our names in the news," Franco told me. That meant "more frenzied press conferences" in the gravel driveway "in front of Bernie's hovel on Maple Street." The two men hammered away at town clerks across Vermont to bring Liberty Union's tax reform proposal to the people. When Franco presented the requisite signatures before selectmen in Barre, the measure, which called for the elimination of "splinter taxes" that gouge the poor—

cigarette taxes, for example—and the doubling of the corporate rate was rejected by the town selectmen as too "partisan." Franco rejoiced at the opportunity just handed to him, and ran the issue through the courts, with the Vermont press reporting on every twist and turn along the way.

Sanders for Governor. *Vermont Historical Society*

Sanders and Franco ran as a ticket in 1976: Sanders was chosen as Liberty Union's candidate for governor, Franco for lieutenant governor. It was a shoestring operation: in a financial disclosure made that year, Sanders lists his net worth as $1,100, including his car and his savings account, and claims no other possessions. The focus that summer was on labor politics, with Franco working the Italian communities clustered around the Barre quarries and Bernie spending more time than ever in the French-Canadian working-class wards of Burlington and Winooski. The cause of the old Italian men in Barre, their lungs torn apart by gravel dust, "was Vermont's cause," Franco said. In Burlington's Old North End, relentless poverty had taken hold in the neighborhoods where millworkers once brought home a living wage. Some of the old union reps from the shuttered mills were now working to organize the blighted neighborhoods, even as professional organizers, paid by Ellen David Friedman's Vermont Alliance and other activist groups, streamed into Winooski and Burlington. Just five years later, Bernie would unite these community forces as a candidate for mayor.

Franco and Sanders had an inspiring story to tell Barre's disenfranchised union workers. In remote Lowell, Vermont, a group of employees of an asbestos mine had successfully taken ownership away from the GAF Corporation, which planned to close the mine rather than conform to new EPA guidelines in processing asbestos, whose health risks were then coming into focus. But there was a dark irony unexplored in their pitch. In Barre, Franco and Sanders were telling quarry workers whose lungs were ravaged by silicosis a stirring tale about the workers gouging friable asbestos out of the side of Belvedere Mountain. By 1993, asbestos was outlawed, the mine had closed, and the town fell into despair. The defaced mountain continues to shed asbestos and heavy metals into the neighboring streams. Here was an early instance of Sanders's elevation of workers' rights over contesting environmental priorities. Sanders "always detected elitism in environmental causes," his friend Richard Sugarman told me: the conservationists were often hale Ivy League graduates in pressed flannel shirts, their trekking sticks carved with the names of the Rockies they'd scaled.

Bernie campaigned wherever he was invited. In late June he traveled to Norwich University in Northfield, Vermont, the country's oldest private military college, a few miles outside of Montpelier. The teen audience for his speech made up the bicentennial delegation to Green Mountain Boys State, sponsored by the American Legion. Ten years later to the very week, as a rising high school sophomore, I attended Boys State. Those four days were the first occasion I can remember sleeping outside my home. The accommodations were spartan; the rules draconian; the spirit, patriotic verging on militaristic. Bernie, again running for governor after five years as Burlington's mayor, was there shaking our hands and quizzing us about civics with a sarcastic attitude, and I was proud to tell my roommates that I'd often mixed it up with him, even in a small way knew him. My roommates, a farmer's son from Hartland and the son of a gun shop owner from Derby Line, were disgusted by that fact, and asked me if I knew Bernie was a communist. Both aspired to attend Norwich. The old military college sits among green hills in a paradise. I could almost imagine it.

"Is that them? Why are they marching?" Bernie exclaimed, as he approached the campus on the morning of June 26. The *Burlington Free Press* reported that Sanders struck the steering wheel of his "battered '67 Comet" and called out incredulously, "They have them marching already?" In a packed cafeteria, "back in his niche," Sanders told the three hundred young men, among Vermont's most obedient by any measure, "to stand up for your rights" as teenagers, under the thumb of opressive adults. "What people want you to be is good little boys," Bernie told the kids, to growing, if nervous, applause. "It's time you stop being good little boys!"

No rebellion took shape in the crowd, however, even when Sanders began to attack his five rivals in the race, seated on folding chairs behind him. "I'd like to introduce you to Stella Hackel," Sanders said, pointing the boys' attention to his Democratic opponent. Hackel, a lobbyist for the utility companies and a fiscal conservative who had angered many when she compared mothers on welfare to "heiresses," had, according to Bernie, "once tried to raise your parents' phone bills." Hackel and the other candidates, including the Republican Richard Snelling, Derick Webb's protégé and the eventual winner that fall, "exchanged puzzled glances, like people at a party where a drunken guest, for no reason, has just insulted the host."

But Sanders, "surrounded by Boys Staters" after the forum, was pleased: "I'm glad some of them argued with me. Now at least they've had a look at the other side of things."

Train in Vain

By July 4, the bicentennial itself had become a campaign issue. That summer, *The New Yorker* caught up with one E. M. Frimbo—in fact the alter ego of the longtime staff editor Rogers E. M. "Popsie" Whitaker—tucking into a Senegalese soup and broiled scrod at the Lexicographers Club in Manhattan. Frimbo, the world's foremost aficionado of old-fashioned locomotives, reported his excitement about an upcoming trip to Vermont to ride the Bicentennial Steam Train, perhaps the signature attraction of Vermont's Bicentennial Committee—"geared to carry visitors on a 262-mile run through the heart of the State," according to *Vermont Life*, with its "authentic atmosphere complemented by modern amenities which include a comfortable lounge, live entertainment, hosts and hostesses and some of the most beautiful scenery through which a railroad has ever passed."

The steam train of E. M. Frimbo's dreams put Sanders in a bad mood. By midsummer, this train, appealing to a passionate niche of antique locomotive aficionados but few other people, had amassed over $800,000 in losses. Tickets on the one-way train to nowhere were expensive, and a storm washed out the tracks through much of Addison County. Sanders railed against the "waste and stupidity" of the train, sensing a cause that thrifty, commonsensical Vermonters would embrace. Sanders implied that much of the blame fell on Representative Snelling, who, as an influential member of the state's joint fiscal committee, had authorized the program. Contractors along the tracks were now scrambling for payment from the state. "Make Snelling pay them," Sanders blurted out at Boys State.

Even before the bicentennial party was over, then, Vermont had a hangover. All the candidates were pointing fingers, but only Sanders used the debacle to indict "the devastating impact tourism is having on the state's economy." The steam train, Sanders said, was "a perfect example of what happens when the state of Vermont tries to act like a catering service for tourists." Vermont's working people had gone from jobs as "machinists and farmers to being chambermaids and burger flippers." These low-paying, seasonal jobs accounted for 60 percent of new employment in the state, while better-paying and more stable work had stagnated. Driving through Stowe, the candidates saw "cars you never see in Burlington": a Porsche 911, a BMW Bavaria, a rouge Mercedes convertible. Meanwhile workers in the resorts lived in tents in the woods, or commuted hours for minimum-wage jobs cleaning up after arrogant college students.

Before 1976, Vermont's mix of tourists and blue-collar workers was relatively harmonious. But as tourists laid claim to more and more of the state's resources, the balance became tippy, and Bernie Sanders, of Brooklyn, managed to somehow attract to his side of the argument the Vermont natives who, all summer, shouted, "Flatlander, go home" during bicentennial events across the state. Cars bearing the license plates of Massachusetts and New York were regularly vandalized. I can attest to the evolving intensity of these sentiments, since, around 1994, I regularly drove through Vermont with Massachusetts plates, and once attracted an angry horde outside the Rusty Nail on the Mountain Road in Stowe. A truly bizarre scene then unfolded, as four lift operators, their breath reeking of Jägermeister, cross-examined my claim to being a Vermonter. They warmed to me only when I proved my credentials by naming the best local fishing spot—under the train trestle on the Winooski River in Richmond. Then one of the men turned out to be a cousin by marriage, and we returned inside together as a happy band, to order shots of Jäger and tell stories about flatlanders we had met in our lives. A waitress drove me home.

Bread & Puppet's Bicentennial Slaughterhouse

Vermonters had an alternative to the Bicentennial Steam Train. The jesting, leering effigies that frightened me that afternoon in Burlington made their way across Vermont that summer, a traveling satyr play that portrayed America's birthday as a grotesque and absurd sham. "We don't engage in patriotism," Peter Schumann scoffed. "We operate much deeper in the psyche, and farther back inside primal conflicts, night and day, the earth and the sky."

"We were everywhere that summer," Schumann told me on a sunny afternoon outside his studio on a steep rise above the Dopp Farm. He had just celebrated his eighty-eighth birthday. Peter was emerging from a long winter's "half-life" during which he grieved ritually for Elka, who had died the previous August. When my wife, Annie, and I pulled up in our Jeep, Schumann was alone in his studio, a small hut stapled together from scavenged boards, stabbing a housepainter's brush at a bedsheet suspended on the wall by clothespins. The image coming into view was a demented-looking Hamlet for a production of Bread & Puppet's *Ophelia*, a retelling of Shakespeare's tragedy with its suicidal heroine at the center. Schumann, covered in wet paint, embraced us both, and in a Silesian accent not diminished by his many decades in Vermont, invited us to join him for what is known on the farm as "beer o'clock."

From our vantage point, you could see the farmhouse and farmyard below, where Schumann's company of dozens of young performers and countless impromptu volunteers and visitors mingled for a family-style supper. Inside the crumbling red sheep barn, Bread & Puppet keeps its museum, where old papier-mâché puppets are displayed in poignant tableaux, enacting their essences even as they surrender their material bodies to the years and the elements. The surrounding woods and fields, where performances have been held since 1975, are dotted with tents, yurts, old vehicles, and other improvised dwellings. There, young people from all around the world rest after their long workdays spent constructing sets, or learning to walk on stilts or play an array of strange instruments used in the company's performances.

I asked Schumann, the Geppetto of this enormous workshop, what it felt like to have founded, in essence, a small civilization. He paused and considered.

"Do you know Mahler's 'Das Lied von der Erde,' 'The Song of the Earth'?"

I did, a little—from Louise Glück, who wrote her great volume *Averno* while playing this solemn work on a loop, then donated her CD of the recording to the Nobel Prize Museum.

"Mahler used this ancient poetry, ancient Chinese poetry. Drunken poetry. And that's what I hear coming up from the farm, the young people laughing and playing, plus the sounds of crows and jays."

Schumann was now lighting a cigar. "And the second movement, 'Der Einsame im Herbst,' the lonely man, the lonely old man in autumn. Mahler knew." Schumann began to speak whole phrases in German that I did not understand, but, pulling deeply on his cigar, he broke back into an English translation of Mahler's lyrics: "The earth will stay alive, but a man cannot live even one hundred years."

I asked Schumann about the summer of 1976. "The summer we scared you, poor little boy!" he said, with a gravelly chuckle. "Yes, we were doing a pageant, and we did every little town parade, fair, festival. They had us march behind the garbage trucks. Sometimes our part of the parade was twice as long as the entire rest of the parade. So I created a whole race of garbagemen, puppets who could clean up whatever people threw at us. Tomatoes sometimes, only if it was a good season for tomatoes."

Schumann remembered the bicentennial circus held on the farm on the weekend of July 31 and August 1. "We had a boxing match"—research confirms it—"between world leaders, and then shot a crybaby astronaut out of a cannon, weeping, and he is saying, 'Oh, I miss my mother.'" For the finale, Schumann, on stilts and dressed as Uncle Sam, summoned a forty-foot-long papier-mâché dragon representing World War III, tapping out the rhythm of "When the Saints Come Marching In" with his stilts.

I asked Schumann about Bernie. In the 1980s, when Bernie was mayor, he established Bread & Puppet as a regular guest in Burlington. In 1985, the company marched down Church Street bearing the enormous effigy of the martyred Salvadoran Archbishop Óscar Romero, their most distinctive puppet. Sanders stood nearby in the crowd, deeply moved by the sight.

"We launched Bernie out of a cannon, once," Schumann told me, laughing maniacally. He got up, cigar in one hand and beer in the other, and made his eighty-eight-year-old body mimic a tremendous explosion: "Boom!"

He meant a papier-mâché effigy, but didn't say so.

Settling down on his metal chair again, Schumann continued, "He wanted to do a campaign stop here—but we don't engage in politics!"

I responded, surprised, "You mean electoral politics, mainstream politics?"

"No, no. Politics!" Schumann exclaimed, poking the air with his cigar and sounding now quite irritated with me. It was time we let him get back to painting his sheets.

Before we parted, Schumann, strong as an ox, embraced the two of us again, and left me with something I'll never forget.

"The puppets become nothing, they deteriorate. Nothing! Like old men! 'Das Lied von der Erde.' What matters at all is the words! Words!!" Schumann bellowed.

And then, laughing and gesturing to Annie to take our picture, he barked: "Two word-obsessed guys! Two lunatics!"

I would like it to be so.

Part III

Bernie for Burlington

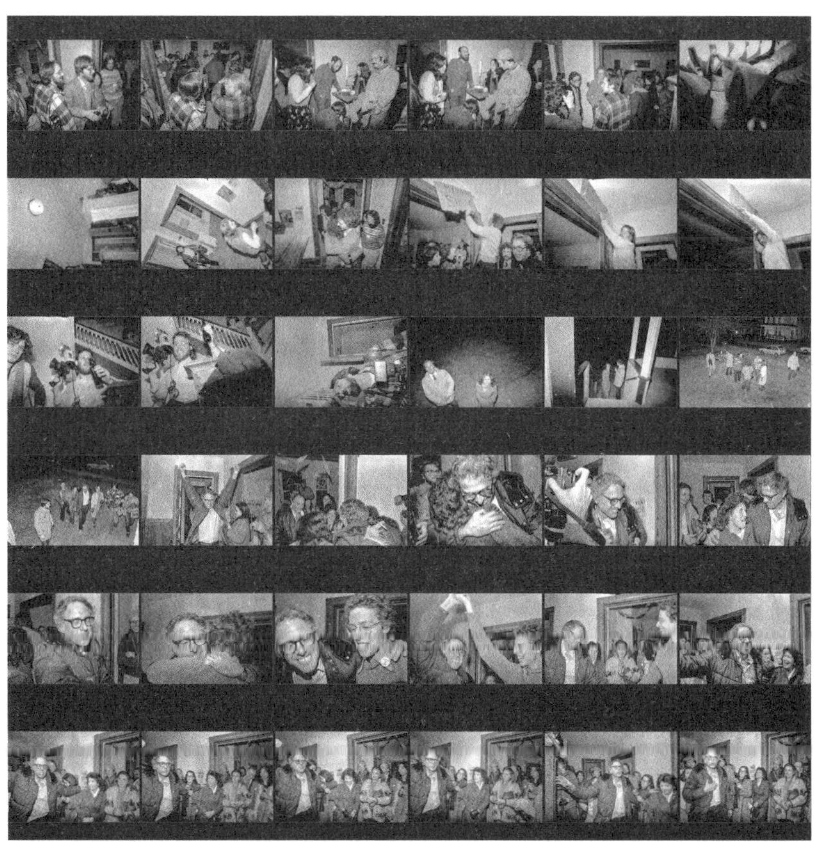

Contact sheet of the roll of film that Jym Wilson used on March 3, 1981

14

Goodbye to Politics

(Burlington, 1976–77)

Sanders and Richard Sugarman, 1980s. *Burlington Free Press*

Perennial Candidate

When you're given an epithet, you know you've become a legend. The epithet clinging to Bernie during his Liberty Union years was "perennial candidate," which, unlike the Homeric epithets for Hektor, "breaker of horses," or Athena, "owl eyed," didn't glorify its bearer. Bernie's epithet had become an albatross.

The *perennial candidate* lost again on Election Night, 1976, to a savvy, indefatigable, and wealthy rival, Dick Snelling, whose frenetic, go-for-broke style Sanders had come to admire. It may have provoked a chuckle among the teenagers at Boys State when Sanders called out the Democrat, Stella Hackel, for her ties to the utility companies. But that criticism stuck, and Snelling never forgot the favor. Hackel lost by eleven points to Snelling.

Sanders, who continued to pull unexpectedly well in traditional Republican towns, finished with his best performance ever, at 6.1 percent of the vote. From that point forward, the socialist got on great with the millionaire capitalist who had made his fortune manufacturing ski racks: these two pugnacious, highly intelligent men were seen regularly laughing, commiserating, gossiping. Those who knew them in the 1980s identify a further strong bond: their mutual fascination with Ronald Reagan and with the political possibilities in opposing him, Sanders as a socialist, Snelling as an independent Vermont Republican.

"I KNOW YOU," Richard Sugarman, a philosopher, said to the stranger seated across from him on the train from New York City to Burlington in October of 1976. "You run for everything. I've voted for you. You're the perennial candidate."

Bernie Sanders winced. He was returning from a family reunion, and "looking very down," Sugarman said. "Nobody in his family seemed to get him. He told me, 'I don't think I was very popular this weekend.'"

Sanders seemed "sad, dejected. We talked about Judaism. I had the impression this guy didn't open up much, with many people, about anything, especially about his Jewish background."

The two men hit it off so well and so instantly that Bernie suggested that his new friend detrain with him at Brattleboro, three hours south of Burlington, where Bernie had parked his car. Sugarman agreed, and together they proceeded to search "for what seemed like a very long time" in the dark for Bernie's battered Comet. The thought was entertained that perhaps it hadn't been Brattleboro at all—but perhaps some other southern Vermont town starting with a *B*? "That's when I knew we weren't so different," Sugarman told me with a chuckle.

"Richard used to get lost in the supermarket," a former student told me. But this time, Professor Sugarman's compass was true. As the two men made the dark drive north in Bernie's car—"a piece of art in itself, with one windshield wiper, which he kept in the glove box"—Sanders told Sugarman about his father's emigration from Poland at the age of seventeen, his own childhood in Midwood, his parents' economic and personal struggles, their early deaths.

When we were talking, Sugarman suddenly remembered the first time he'd ever heard Bernie's name. Sometime in the early 1970s, an old friend and roommate of Richard's from Yale had taken a vacation at the Basin Harbor Club in Vergennes, Vermont, on Lake Champlain. "He called me up," Sugarman said, "and told me he'd heard this guy on the radio in Vermont, this *perennial candidate*, on a call-in show. Sanders was his name. He had just lost some election, but my friend said the guy was the best, the most effective speaker he'd ever heard. He just kept rattling on! The host couldn't shut him off. His prediction was, he told me, this guy was going places."

The Yale roommate so impressed by young Sanders was Joseph Lieberman, who went on to a distinguished career in the Senate from Connecticut and ran for vice president in 2000. So far as is known, Richard Sugarman is the only person in American history to have roomed with two future U.S. senators in the obscurity of their youth.

LONG BEFORE I KNEW who Richard Sugarman was, I noticed him on the streets of Burlington. Like many, I assumed he was a rabbi. When we spoke for this book, I asked him if in the 1970s and '80s he wore a long black cape and walked up and down Church Street with his hands clasped behind his back, deep in thought, or perhaps in prayer.

"That's just what Bernard asked me when we met on the train: 'Aren't you the guy I see walking sometimes, wearing a yarmulke and a long black cape?'"

Sugarman was born in 1944 in Buffalo, New York. One out of every four residents in his childhood neighborhood, he estimates, had survived the Nazi camps. Sugarman became a standout athlete: a football player and a boxer. His intellect, though, took him to Yale, where in the late 1960s a quota still capped the number of Jews in the student body at 12.5 percent. Sugarman then worked his way through college and graduate school, driving a Cambridge taxi during his time as a grad student at Boston University. In between shifts, he read the great postwar Jewish philosopher Emmanual Levinas.

"Richard *is* Emmanual Levinas," his friend Huck Gutman told me. "Sartre said hell is other people. Levinas says, no, we meet one another face-to-face. Other people aren't hell, they are a call to understanding. Richard believes in meeting people, in the deep sense. He became the greatest teacher at UVM because he took every student one at a time, on their terms."

Sugarman was hired by UVM in 1970 in a part-time role in the new Experimental College. "I was asked to be the philosopher in residence," Sugarman told me. "I thought that was better than being a cabbie in residence." There was some teaching, but the main idea seemed to be, like Socrates in the Athenian agora, to nudge people into thought. Soon, though, "I became a bouncer in residence," he told me, when a "psycho from Rice High School"—my high school, twenty years before I graduated, but I think I know who he meant—"an ex-Marine, and a raving anti-Semite, who had been beating up nuns, began to assault women at UVM." Sugarman the philosopher found himself in a "life-and-death" melee with the undergraduate, whom he managed to subdue by bending him backward over a banister, with dozens of students looking on.

By 1976, when he met Bernie on the train, Sugarman had made his peace with Burlington's "really primitive anti-Semitism, redneck stuff, not at all sophisticated like at Yale," found some majesty in the prospect of the Green Mountains, and was living at an illegal apartment on Cherry Street in downtown Burlington, where he kept strictly kosher, smoked abundant marijuana, grappled with the great thinkers, and roamed Burlington's own Athenian agora, Church Street.

One thing that kept Sugarman in the city was an astonishing Gothic jewel box of a synagogue in the Old North End, Ohavi Zedek, built in 1885 for a community of Jews who had come mainly from Lithuania to replicate shtetl life on North Street in Burlington. It is among the oldest synagogue buildings in the United States. In the mid-1970s, its congregation, like the few old ladies who made it up, had drastically shrunk. Richard Sugarman, the young football-playing philosopher, took to this synagogue full of tiny old people with great enthusiasm and charisma, and became its president.

"It meant I knew the Old North End very well," Sugarman told me. He knew its old people especially well, even beyond the intersection of North Street and Archibald Street where the remnants of "Little Jerusalem" could still be detected. "The old Jewish ladies all mixed with the French Canadians at that point," he said. Sugarman, who viewed Burlington from his UVM eyrie on the hill and his garret on Cherry Street, bridging those two distinct scenes, also had perfect access to a third: these elderly folks of the Old North End. His method in getting to know them was simply to "walk extremely slowly" and "offer to go to the pharmacy."

The city of Burlington had let the streets around Ohavi Zedek deteriorate into squalor. The Jewish and French-Canadian old ladies were the last generation to remember working the looms at the Winooski mills. Their small laborers' cottages had been scooped up and subdivided by landlords eager to capitalize on federal housing subsidies. The city ignored the neighborhood except to provide "a few goodies around Election Day, to get out the vote," according to Sugarman. In those days of enormous storms producing many feet of snow, the poorer you were, "the longer you had to wait for the snowplows to come," Sugarman told me. "The plows started at the top of the hill, worked through all the doctors' neighborhoods, and eventually got to North Street. People were trapped inside their homes."

Sugarman told Sanders all of this on their three-hour journey from Brattleboro to Burlington. When I asked Sugarman whether he'd been a kind of mentor to Sanders, I had things like moral philosophy and ethics in mind. I hoped Sugarman would support a theory I had that Levinas's idea of the *rapport en face*—the face-to-face encounter—was, maybe through his mentorship, an important part of Bernie's socialism.

Sugarman laughed. "Did I discuss Levinas with Bernard? Never once. But I did say to him, walk around in this city you live in. I think he only knew where his girlfriend lived and maybe, maybe, where the pickup basketball courts were."

One time, when I was saying goodbye to Richard after a long call, he asked me where in the city I'd grown up. I described the small white colonial hard by the road, across from a convenience store and deli, Kampus Kitchen. He proceeded to recite the names of several of my neighbors and perform an intricate analysis of class and politics in my quite mixed ward, right down to the household. One essence of Sugarman's tutelage, I realized, was his mentorship in Burlington's block-by-block political microcultures.

Another was his observation that 1960s performative politics hadn't worked. Sugarman warned Bernie away from what he calls "symbolic politics" wherever it turned up, and in Burlington in the 1970s, it turned up a lot. Richard cited a demonstration at UVM to protest the 1972 mining of Haiphong Harbor in North Vietnam. Hundreds of students were arrested while occupying the ROTC building and a downtown federal building. One professor of political science, a "Manichean leftist" and a "radical on the academic calendar" was encouraging the students to march to the Chittenden County Jail, then across from the library in downtown Burlington. The idea was to free the prisoners.

This struck Richard as suicidal, and a friend, a disabled political scientist named William Roth, insisted that they stay and persuade the students to stand down. Years later, as mayor of the city, Bernie told Sugarman that he'd looked into it and that the Burlington police, jittery from days of unrest, had placed a mole among the students and planned a swift and severe response. Patrick Leahy was at that point the Chittenden County prosecutor, hoping to raise his political profile, and was out for blood.

"That was when the political scientist and a bunch of other professors of his ilk, you know, 'I hate everything' people, snuck away. You saw them quietly back out of the crowd. Miller said to me, 'I'm up for tenure'—can you believe that?"

I said yes. Yes I could.

"That was symbolic politics. And it was easy, and everywhere in Burlington, and people saw through it. I told Bernard this as my major lesson in his political education," Sugarman said. He and Roth talked the protestors out of marching to the correctional facility and getting themselves arrested or worse. "What the hell was the point supposed to be? *Avoid symbolic politics*, I always said to Bernard. Stay away from symbolic politics."

FROM THE START, the candidates of Liberty Union were too various to coalesce into one symbol. They were different from each other temperamentally, and together they covered the entire state, north to south. Sanders, Diamondstone, Doris Lake, Nancy Kaufman, Martha Abbott, John Franco, and Arthur Deloy had made political gains outside what we might call the lifestyle left. There were quixotic arguments along the way: to allow children to vote, to widen the highway on-ramps to accommodate queuing hitchhikers. Some of these exotic agenda items later became reality: most people in the 1970s would have said the legalization of pot was, well, a pipe dream. But the party knew from the beginning the risk of appealing only to the initiated, and made connecting with working people its priority. For a time, working people in Vermont listened, and some of them showed up to vote.

Then the tide quickly turned. John Franco's 1976 campaign for lieutenant governor had denied the top vote getter, the Democrat John Alden, of a majority. By statute, the election was then decided by the state's general assembly, which sided with the Republican, T. Garry Buckley. Liberty Union had made its first concrete electoral impact in the Green Mountain State: it helped elect a conservative Republican.

By 1977, the left had lost its edge. The hippies were now in their thirties, with families to raise and mortgages to pay. Vermonters with a few acres grew chamomile, borage, or calendula for tea. Demonstrations became regularly scheduled social events—Fridays for peace, Sundays for the planet. Liberty Union, with Peter Diamondstone's influence gaining, had gone from fearless to quirky. The culture of Vermont's lifestyle leftists was diverging swiftly from that of its working people. The gulf that bedevils leftists everywhere, dividing them from economically disadvantaged but culturally conservative voters, had dramatically widened.

The hippies had not made much of a dent electorally, but some of their favorite treats had become mainstream, and in turn the entire scene was named after its most characteristic indulgence, granola. The Grand Union on South Winooski Avenue in Burlington now had bins full of bulk oats, nuts, and carob chips. Protest music by Buffalo Springfield and Canned Heat, arranged for strings, played on WEZF in my grandparents' kitchen. By the mid-1980s, "granolas" had become one of several high school factions, living amicably alongside jocks, nerds, punkers, goths, and all the rest.

"Crunchy" was the affectionate adjective clinging to the granolas, as nostalgia for the '60s spread like a haze all over Vermont.

Soon, crunchiness in all its forms became one of Vermont's most profitable exports and biggest tourist draws, with Ben & Jerry's and, later, the Burlington jam band Phish suggesting a place on the American map where the hippie dream lived on. But Sanders, who liked fried eggs and toast at Henry's Diner, was never part of the cultural left. Richard Sugarman told me that he and Bernie used to laugh at the credentials their radical friends would present at social events. "Who ever thought of going to Woodstock," Sugarman remarked. "Hundreds of thousands of people and four bathrooms? No thank you." After driving Liberty Union toward George Wallace voters, quarry workers, men and women laid off from the mills, and other culturally conservative, economically disadvantaged Vermonters, suddenly Sanders, Liberty Union's standard-bearer, found himself standing atop a mountain of brown rice.

Swan Song

Sanders called a press conference in October of 1977 and announced that he was leaving Liberty Union. The party, he said, "has not remained active on a year-round basis in the struggles of the working people against the banks and corporations which own and control the state and the nation." Liberty Union had failed to hold caucuses and abide by other requirements of its becoming a major party in the state. Sanders had been livid about it for months. Nancy Kaufman resigned from the party the same day, attacking Liberty Union's stance against the Vermont Yankee Nuclear Power Plant, which she contended, in a strong break with most Vermont leftists, was vital for Vermont's energy infrastructure.

Both comments were directed against the southern Vermont wing of Liberty Union, and against Peter Diamondstone in particular. Diamondstone, who had intensified his erratic practical joke politics steadily throughout the decade, made news in the spring of 1977 when he crashed a gathering of "the Decentralist League of Vermont." The group had assembled in Montpelier to discuss the idea of radically local and small-scale government, on the model of the Athenian democratic assembly and its latter-day equivalent, the New England town meeting. There were influential thinkers in the mix: Frank Bryan attended, as did Greg Guma, the activist, journalist, and cultural provocateur from Burlington who would later become a thorn in Bernie's side. Murray Bookchin contributed to the group's charter. Though derided by some as *philosophes*, the decentralists had a serious basis in thought, and a plan to revitalize Vermont's urban neighborhoods.

But Diamondstone, "the Zeno of Brattleboro," as one wag christened him, insisted that the group stop and consider the "paradox of its existence," and "strive for inefficiency," since "efficiency was inhuman." The meeting fell apart after hours of this scholastic debate, when the decentralists could not come to agreement about whether true decentralists could have a central post office box, and where, if anywhere, it should be located. Diamondstone, who had driven the meeting off the rails, beamed. Sanders, reading the news in Burlington, told a friend that imagining Diamondstone among the decentralists made him "want to kill himself." As Liberty Union had atomized into many personalities and individual zones of influence, the party had "reaped little change," Sanders told reporters.

Bernie's announcement that he was leaving Liberty Union implied a second announcement for those listening carefully: he was not defecting to the Democratic Party. As Liberty Union pushed the Vermont Democratic Party farther to the left, many of his old Liberty Union colleagues had become Democrats, and some had maintained footing in the mainstream party all along. But Sanders vowed from this moment forward to be independent. He never joined another political party—even, that is, when the Progressive Coalition formed in Burlington to consolidate his legacy and influence.

Sanders was asked by a reporter what it meant to him, personally, to leave the party that gave him his political start. His answer was uncharacteristically searching. "These things are so deep for me," Bernie said. "It's very hard, and I can't talk about it today."

IN THE FALL OF 1977, Sanders moved into a small apartment in a tumbledown brick carriage house at 295½ Maple Street, on an elegant block in Burlington's Hill Section. What was "hard" and "deep" about this time seems clear enough. Sanders no longer had a political home. He'd grown estranged from his closest political allies. With bushels of new out-of-state money pouring in, and with developers eyeing the empty lots along Lake Champlain, Burlington was more economically stratified than ever. Cultural change had eddied around Sanders and passed downstream. He was discouraged, almost completely broke, and starting over at the age of thirty-seven essentially from scratch.

Bernie's retirement seemed, to those who'd followed his noble, quixotic campaigns around Vermont, to be "the end of an era," as Jim Rader wrote in his journal. Rader watched his friend's "swan song" on the evening news:

> When I called Bernie last night, he said it was a lot like dealing with the end of a failing marriage, with all the ambivalence about whether you

> could have put more effort into [it] or whether you should give it just one more try. Tonite, when I called him, right after watching the news item, I was momentarily surprised that he hadn't even watched it. (So unlike the old days when we rushed into his house & immediately clicked on the TV to see what the newscasters would say!) I sense in Bernie a great sadness; relief, but mainly sadness.

The thought that Bernie Sanders, the indefatigable warrior of the far left, might be done with politics suggested the ephemerality of "institutions (campaigns, political parties, etc.)":

> how easy they are to bring into existence (Bernie's lesson) & how insubstantial & fragile they turn out to be at the other end of the process (the other side of the same coin).

Bernie's "lesson," Jim told me, "was learned from Reich. Bernie believed that by envisioning something to be the case, he could make it so. Not figuratively, but by a process of mental realization."

Sanders also rigidly "connected health with political consciousness" in this period, and "got more than ever into Reich," friends confirmed. Rader, who had taken up running, logged his daily mileage in his journal, but noted that "in spite of his positive verbalizations about my growing 'healthiness,' Bernie feels somewhat judgmental about the direction he feels I am taking—that I am becoming more 'middle-class,' less 'radical,' etc." Rader had fulfilled only one part of the Reichean program, and his old friend expressed his disapproval.

At the bottom of the diary page, Rader composed the epitaph to Bernie's once-promising political career, as well as to Rader's own idealistic hopes for a new political movement in the Green Mountain State:

> Whatever else he does, tonight marks the end of an era for Bernie. And in many ways for me too. (Fitting that that brand-new & luxurious-seeming Toyota Corona we drove over there in that long-ago night is now a heap of junk, mainly a nuisance to be unloaded for a hundred bucks to get it out of the driveway.)

15

The American People's Historical Society

(Sanders as a Small Businessman, Burlington, 1977)

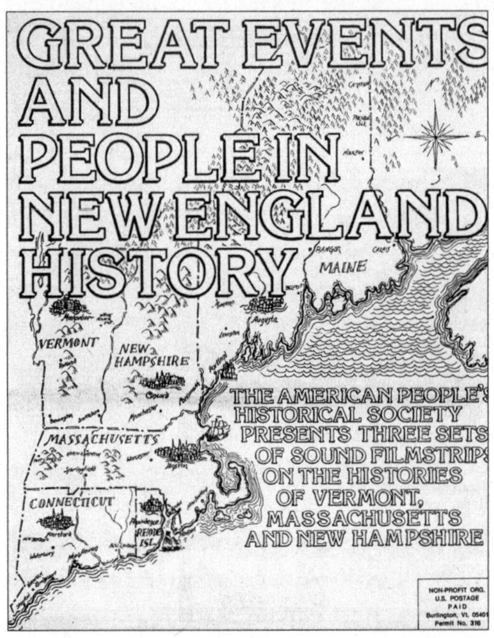

Catalog, "The American People's Historical Society." *Jim Rader*

"He was not a weirdo to me," Nancy Barnett told me. "He was Jewish, and so Brooklyn. The enormous mop of black hair, the dirty T-shirt, the pants hanging a little low, the work boots: these were my people." Barnett, a trompe l'oeil artist who now lives outside of Asheville, North Carolina, moved in with her girlfriend next to Bernie's Maple Street apartment in 1977: "My cousin Linda Niedweske was at UVM," Barnett told me, "and we knew there was a counterculture thing happening." Barnett and Bernie became close friends; he was not guarded around her. When Barnett's parents, Brooklyn folks, visited her from New Jersey, "there they were, on Bernie's front stoop in Burlington, reminiscing about Flatbush," Barnett said. "We could have switched families." Barnett would look through Bernie's family albums with him: "They were iconic, like a dream about old Brooklyn. His mother had the same gap in her grin as my nanna."

From his perch on Maple Street, Sanders saw Burlington's class disparities intensify before his eyes: wealthy doctors from the UVM Medical Center lived up the hill, in elegant, renovated Victorians with cupolas looking across Lake Champlain; a few blocks in the other direction, the King Street neighborhood on the edge of downtown was among the city's poorest and most dangerous. In the narrow alleys between its eighteenth-century saltboxes, just up from Perkins Pier, most of the city's drug deals went down. Pleasure boats from Canada would unload Igloo coolers full of cocaine to the local distribution hub, the Chickenbone Cafe on King Street, where suburban partiers fidgeted and paced while awaiting delivery. Kids in the neighborhood set fires in a nearby freight yard, or shoplifted from businesses on Church Street, divvying up their spoils on the hot sidewalks. An encampment of homeless people lived near the Pine Street Barge Canal, where the mud was contaminated by toxic coal deposits that the neighborhood had lobbied city hall for a decade to clean up.

It gnawed at Bernie to live along this ragged seam between classes. And his own economic position was, if anything, more precarious than ever. Sanders appears to have had little source of income for much of the 1970s. The "freelance writing" cited in his biographies at the time amounted to a few pieces for the *Vermont Freeman* and *Vermont Life*. A few thousand dollars came his way when the farmhouse in Stannard sold in 1978. But what he had, mainly, instead of income, was extraordinary, almost disfiguring thrift. At times he was certainly on public assistance, but the core of the situation is that Sanders appears to have lived on almost nothing for years. He mostly hitchhiked or scavenged another expiring "piece of art" car for hundreds of dollars; he almost never ate out, even at Henry's Diner or the Fresh Ground; his apartment on Maple Street was almost entirely unfurnished, and Sanders siphoned electricity from his neighbor using a Rapunzel system of connected extension cords. "It was an environment I was very accustomed to," Richard Sugarman told me: about all Sanders had in abundance was "books and papers, and yellow legal pads."

Barnett confirmed: "And pens. Pens and legal pads. The place was—it was a pigsty." On those legal pads, Sanders brainstormed his next project, inspired in part by the time he spent with his son, now living in Burlington.

Levi had moved with his mother from Stannard and was enrolled in the Burlington schools. Sanders coached his Little League team, an economically mixed group of children that spanned the households from upper Maple, where the doctors lived, to lower, where evictions were common. "A lot of people met Bernie in the context of Levi, a single father, a coach. Not exactly a radical," said Sugarman. The patriotic radio spots Bernie had created for the bicentennial only tended to reinforce his emerging mainstream image. And Levi "loved it when his father's voice came on the radio," Sugarman said. If Bernie hadn't become a politician, Larry Sanders told me, "he most certainly would have been a teacher."

But Sanders's educational philosophies rendered him almost certainly unemployable in anything like a conventional school. In a 1970 essay in the *Vermont Freeman*, Sanders praised "the radical educator" who "allows children to act naturally and without restraint." In 1972, Jim Rader had recommended Sanders for a job at a day-care center; Sanders was passed over for the work, likely because his antipathy to traditional schooling was a matter of public record. At a commencement ceremony in Wilmington, Vermont, in 1978, Sanders told the graduates that society "wants you to be good girls and boys, docile to your employers." None of them could pursue a life of "meaningful work, like farming or writing." Capitalism hooked kids on television, alcohol, and drugs, he told his audience, so they would be satisfied in an endless depletion loop where they were hired to "make the products, but also to consume them." In fact, as Sanders told the high school graduates, they *were* the products of modern capitalism.

Sanders saw his historical lessons on the radio and TV as cultural deprogramming, a bold counter to the jingoistic curriculum taught in public schools. His new venture would build on their message and their success. In late 1977, Bernie reintroduced himself to Vermont as the president and founder of the American People's Historical Society, "a media company that produced, distributed and sold educational filmstrips to schools and libraries across New England." Some of these strips recycled scripts from Sanders's radio spots. Others were composed by Nancy Barnett, who had obtained a government grant to work as Bernie's research assistant. "Nobody knows what I'm talking about when I say filmstrips now," Barnett told me, laughing, but by the late 1970s, the now-forgotten technology was an established feature of the school day. Soon filmstrips would be eclipsed by VCRs, but in the late '70s it was still a great boredom-alleviating thrill when the teacher rolled out of the AV cabinet a waist-high metal table and assigned a favorite student to run the projector, a magic lantern like the one described in Proust, now beaming summer safety tips and images of Washington crossing the Delaware. While girls enjoyed strips like "The Story of Menstruation," boys, for some reason, were shown "Blood on the Highway," about the dangers of reckless driving. Students then completed the accompanying worksheets in small groups or jammed them into their backpacks to be rushed through later at the dining room table. Helping Levi with these school worksheets, Bernie noted the absence of any lessons in Vermont and New England history, and sensed an opportunity.

Operating under the name Northern Lights Media, Sanders, Barnett, and Ron MacNeil, a photographer friend of John Franco's, created their strips between pickup basketball games on Maple Street. The workday began, according to MacNeil, when the breakfast plates were cleared away from Bernie's one table. Sanders, Barnett, and MacNeil drafted the scripts, then photographed the images with equipment available to the public at the UVM library. Back on Maple Street, Barnett performed the women's speaking parts; Bernie played all the men: "Ethan Allen with a Brooklyn accent!" Barnett exclaimed. Rader, Sugarman, and Gutman were asked to sit on the board of Sanders's new company, though none of them recall ever attending a meeting, or even knowing much about Bernie's plans for the endeavor.

Bernie's filmstrips presented an integrative curriculum for "fourth graders through high school" that blended "people's history" and patriotic standards, "from Ethan Allen and his Green Mountain Boys, to John Stark of New Hampshire, to the saga of Massachusetts and the sea," and on to "the role of the abolitionist movement" and the plight of nineteenth-century women. Each pack contained a set of discussion points, key words, and questions. The strips were offered on a free ten-day trial period, with various incentives to purchase the entire series—a fairly complicated business to run out of a tiny apartment and the media room at a college library, with a permanent staff of two.

"Bernie the small businessman is not an image that comes easily to mind," as Fintan O'Toole wrote, but Sanders, "a frugal manager by nature," according to Jeff Weaver, his longtime aide, ran the American People's Historical Society to make money. "He took to it, very professionally," Barnett told me. At a filmstrip convention in New York, Sanders sought out the Indigenous Canadian actor Jay Silverheels, who was famous for playing Tonto on the TV series *The Lone Ranger*. Silverheels got the attention of Vermonters in a 1972 radio spot he'd recorded for Okemo Ski Resort, which was then promoting an "Indian" aesthetic. "Okemo Sabe" was the slogan devised to echo Tonto's nickname for *The Lone Ranger*, "Kemo Sabe," meaning "loyal scout." Sanders "couldn't get enough of the commercial—he loved it," and he approached Silverheels about narrating his filmstrips. "Silverheels had a great voice," MacNeil told me, "and his involvement really moved strips with some of the school librarians. Once they heard Tonto was in, they bit."

There was one element left to design. "Everyone at the convention told Bernie, 'What you need is a great beep,'" MacNeil reported. The "beep" signaled to the teacher or prize student to advance the strip to the next frame, to sync the images with the narrator's voice-over playing on cassette. When Bernie returned the following year with his finished filmstrips in tow, the conventioneers marveled at his amazing beep and begged to know its secret. "People said I had the best beep, by far!" he exclaimed to MacNeil. Sanders, Barnett, and MacNeil had tested several sound effects: walkie-talkies, a bell, a fork against the rim of a wineglass. The winner was Levi's battery-powered *Star Trek* gun, which Bernie had borrowed after an epiphany one afternoon, hearing Levi scamper around the apartment shooting at things.

Through the spring and summer of 1978, Sanders and his partners drove the filmstrips all around New England. Like his father before him, Sanders was now a kind of traveling salesman. "We did all of Vermont. I mean, every town, every school and library," Barnett said. Nancy drove Bernie's "new" beat-up Volvo while Sanders jotted down ideas on yellow legal pads. They talked "about life, childhood, anxieties, the usual," but also about Emma Goldman, the legendary anarchist, and Eugene V. Debs, Bernie's hero and Barnett's distant cousin.

The filmstrips were a hit: in fact, "we kept running out," Barnett told me. Sanders had trouble keeping up with demand. "He made money at it," Huck Gutman reported. How much? "More than he'd made from anything else he had tried. He made a living." The state of New Hampshire wanted to hire Sanders to produce offerings for its public schools, but as a Vermonter, he recoiled. "Bernie didn't want to make propaganda for New Hampshire," MacNeil said. Only in Boston, where graft was the rule, was Bernie turned away: he'd failed to grease the palm of the superintendent's purchasing representative. "Boston," MacNeil shook his head. "We should have known."

"We Want Debs!"

For the first time in nearly a decade, though, Bernie Sanders looked in vain for his name in the newspapers, and was already growing restless with his premature "retirement" from politics. His next project would be two-phased: first he would make a documentary film, *Eugene V. Debs: Trade Unionist, Socialist, Revolutionary, 1855–1926*; and then Sanders would crusade to get "my Debs movie," as he called it, shown and distributed on public television. If the gambit worked, by the fall of 1978 the name Bernie Sanders would be everywhere back in the news.

That September, Bernie and Jim Rader, Debs's fellow Hoosier, drove west to Chicago, discussing Debs as they went. After Chicago, Bernie continued to the Eugene V. Debs Museum in Terre Haute, Indiana, where he captured photographs of campaign buttons and posters and pennants to use in his film. Back home, Sanders and Barnett readied the script, gathered their materials, and signed out a trunk load of video equipment from the UVM library's AV room.

In October, the small cast of *Eugene V. Debs* assembled in Bernie's Maple Street apartment. Rader, who delivers a single line—"We want Debs!"—was "the only authentic Hoosier voice in the film," as he told me proudly. *Eugene V. Debs* is not a true moving picture, but rather a chain of still images, a kind of moving filmstrip, backed by voice-over narration. The film—recorded on video—begins in a tone, but not a voice, that many Americans would now recognize instantaneously:

> It is very probable, especially if you are a young person, that you have never heard of Eugene Victor Debs. If you are the average American who watches TV forty hours a week, you have probably heard of such important people as Kojak and Wonder Woman, have heard about dozens of different kinds of underarm spray deodorants, every hack politician in your state, and the latest game between the Boston Red Sox and the New York Yankees . . .

The script is unmistakably the work of Bernie Sanders: the ubiquitous intensifier "very," the fixation on the stupidity of TV programming and advertising, and the gratuitous swipe at "hack" politicians. "Strangely enough, however," the narrator continues, "nobody has told you about Gene Debs, one of the most important Americans of the twentieth century. Why? Why haven't they told you about Debs?"

In this topsy-turvy production, Bernie's narration is assigned to a suave Burlington studio actor whose voice was familiar from local Goss Dodge commercials. Bernie, who sounds nothing like a Hoosier, instead reserved for himself the role of Debs, enunciating the great 1918 Canton address of the Indiana socialist in his distinctive Brooklyn accent, hitting pockets of emphasis and inflection completely unknown to any midwesterner.

The ventriloquism somehow works. The words of the Canton address are so strange and thrilling that by the speech's second sentence or so we find ourselves carried away by Bernie's passionate embodiment of his hero. The Canton address—Debs was arrested for giving it, and imprisoned for sedition—crests with an ecstatic vision of "fresh-born manhood" and "glorious vistas" that echoes Walt Whitman's great poem "Song of Myself":

> Socialism has enabled me to hold high communion with you, and made it possible for me to take my place side by side with you in the great struggle for the better day; to multiply myself over and over again, to thrill with a fresh-born manhood; to feel life truly worthwhile; to open new avenues of vision; to spread out glorious vistas; to know that I am kin to all that throbs; to be class-conscious, and to realize that, regardless of nationality, race, creed, color or sex, every man, every woman who toils, who renders useful service, every member of the working class without an exception, is my comrade, my brother and sister—and that to serve them and their cause is the highest duty of my life.

Sanders now had a completed film, but how would he distribute it? In October of 1978, Bernie called up his old rival and friend Peter Diamondstone, and struck up a mutually advantageous deal. Diamondstone was in the midst of his latest quixotic candidacy, this time for U.S. Congress, and agreed to lease the film to use at his own events, if Sanders would edit in a plug for Diamondstone's campaign. Diamondstone and Sanders then bought a thirty-minute block on WCAX-TV to air the film, "Paid for by the Diamondstone for Congress Campaign." On Monday, October 30, Channel 3 presented *Eugene V. Debs* at 9:30 p.m., competing with *Monday Night Football* and *One Day at a Time*. *TV Guide* described the feature inaccurately as "a film essay on the labor and Socialist Party leader who ran for the Vice Presidency."

In November, after Diamondstone's loss, the Debs film reverted to Bernie to use as he pleased—and he used it to test his remaining political reach after two restless years out of politics. WCAX, a commercial network, had charged Sanders and Diamondstone their regular ad rate to air the film. But Sanders next focused on forcing Vermont's fledgling ETV station, Channel 33, to show his documentary for free. He was a Vermonter and a taxpayer, and he demanded it be given airtime. When the station refused, a very public conflict unfolded. In fact, the story of how *Eugene V. Debs* made it to public television during the spring and summer of 1979 is more compelling than the film itself.

Vermont ETV came on the air in 1967, after its four antennae were constructed on mountain summits up and down the state. Its main studio was at Fort Ethan Allen, an old cavalry and artillery training post in Colchester, Vermont, outside of Burlington. Its license was held by the University of Vermont Board of Trustees. The station was in essence a public utility, paid for by taxpayers but held and controlled by the notoriously business-friendly board of a state university that at the time was the most "private"—the most dependent on tuition and gifts, the least supported by the state legislature—of any in the country. Public TV was in essence run as a private corporation.

Here then was another Vermont network held by corporate interests; and this one was founded by and for the people. But by the late 1970s, Channel 33 had become known mainly for its daytime appeal to young children and their caretakers, who tuned in for popular programming like *The Electric Company* and *Sesame Street*, and to an easily mocked class of subdued bookish retirees and intellectuals who tuned in during the daytime and evenings and were known locally as "ETV people." An ETV person cooked soufflés with Julia Child, or stir-fry with Stephen Yan of *Wok with Yan*. In the evenings, classical concerts were beamed from Boston or Philadelphia. ETV's staple was *Masterpiece Theater*, which ran the spicy Edwardian soap opera *Upstairs, Downstairs* for lovers of petticoats, and the Roman-era epic *I, Claudius* for viewers keen on tunics.

ETV turned down *Eugene V. Debs*, on scattershot and contradictory grounds. The film did not "meet the program standards of objectivity and integrity." That meant in part simply that it was bad. But the program director, Gary Simpson, went further: he condemned the film for "emotional editorializing." And because *Debs* was made in coordination with, and broadcast by, Peter Diamondstone's campaign, it was treated as a political ad. Sanders seemed "determined to administer Debs to the viewer as if it were an unpleasant, but necessary, medicine," one viewer of the WCAX broadcast said.

Bernie had drawn another sluggish institution into an embarrassing fight. But unlike the University of Chicago or New England Telephone, ETV was chartered as a public entity, and its highbrow content did not reflect Vermont's realities. There were very few spots in the broadcast day reserved for programming about Vermont, and no preference for Vermont directors. If Bernie prevailed, he would have a significant impact on broadcast media in the state. Sanders and Diamondstone issued a press statement calling for the program director's removal and the immediate reorganization of the station. Sanders threatened "legal action or a sit-in protest at the Colchester studio." In discussions with his inner circle—Gutman, Franco, Sugarman, and others—Bernie worked out a strategy to break up the corporate board, reshuffle the channel's programming, and advance his own work as a writer and filmmaker.

In November of 1978, Sanders brought together a group of Vermont filmmakers at Jim Taylor's Blue J studios on Church Street to form "Concerned Citizens on ETV" and assemble a list of demands. "Something of a mini revolution," according to the *Rutland Herald*, then unfolded: the paper, implying that citizen control of the airwaves gave off the faint aroma of communism, called for a "bloodless, constructive" revolt. Bernie's group countered by citing the 1978 Public Telecommunications Act, which required all PBS stations to set up community advisory boards. Sanders had made *Eugene V. Debs* a very public test case for a new era of "public access to the airwaves." Vermont ETV backed down immediately. Bernie's Debs film was put on the schedule for the spring; ironically, the night it was due to air, Sanders pulled it in solidarity with the employees of Channel 33 who were threatening to strike. *Eugene V. Debs* aired only after the strike was averted.

Sanders and his citizen coalition had also demanded that the station conduct an on-air forum on the future of public access to ETV. At a driveway press conference in January of 1979, his first in two years, Sanders announced "far-reaching changes in the future of television in Vermont" and "significant concessions" on the part of the UVM Board of Trustees. Under pressure from Sanders, ETV broadcast a two-and-a-half-hour feature, *The Public Speaks: Town Meeting*, with Bernie playing a significant role onscreen. Sanders, moderating the program, argued that ETV catered to the wealthy. Faire Edwards, an advocate for the elderly, spoke up for ETV's existing programming: "I like the music," Edwards said, very sweetly. "It's marvelous to have concerts, dance, and symphonies come into your home." Edwards acknowledged that ETV was "a little eggheady" but preferred to accompany her evening bowl of ice cream with egghead content, rather than what Sanders and his allies were demanding: gritty documentaries "by and for working Vermonters," grappling with "real, social issues, poverty, Vermont's inequalities, the money coming in from out of state."

16

Eviction in a Renter's City

(Tenants and Landlords, 1978)

In the fall of 1978, Bernie returned from peddling his filmstrips to find an eviction notice tacked on his apartment door. The rent on his badly maintained apartment had "doubled, or even tripled," according to friends, and Sanders was holding several months back rent in protest. But the landlord appeared to be forcing everybody out to prepare the property for a quick, profitable sale. An elderly neighbor whom Sanders sometimes helped with groceries and errands put him in touch with Gene Bergman, a tenants' rights activist in Burlington. Sanders "went to his playbook," Sugarman said, and began to organize "mass actions" through Bergman's advocacy group, People Acting for Change Together.

He was in those years a "true red," Bergman told me outside Barrio, a bakery and coffee shop in Burlington's Old North End. A trim man and a marathoner, Bergman's excitement is infectious. A little daub of chocolate croissant clung to his tidy gray beard as he gestured animatedly to passing neighbors. Bergman, who now serves on the city council, is something like the mayor of these few blocks, where he has mainly lived and worked for most of fifty years. He was once a very young man here. He became radicalized as a UVM undergrad: in 1972, the student government's initiative to send relief to the Bach Mai Hospital in Vietnam, where an American bombing raid had killed hundreds of children and nurses, was voted down by the student body. Bergman then resolved to join the Venceremos Brigade, a group of Americans, organized by the Students for a Democratic Society, who traveled to Fidel Castro's Cuba to harvest sugarcane. But when "someone handed me Saul Alinsky"—the community organizer and author of *Rules for Radicals*—Bergman decided that his "work was here." He pointed to the sidewalk under us.

"So I paid four hundred dollars to an employment agency, and borrowed a friend's car," Bergman said, to work a night job at a small press in Milton, Vermont, north of Burlington. Bergman was a press operator for two weekly newspapers that were consumed in my household: one was the *Buyer's Digest*, with local coupons, deals, and shopping hints. The other was *The Vermont Catholic Tribune*, where, in 1978, I made my media debut: I was interviewed along with three other children about the meaning and importance of our First Communions. It amused me to think of the young radical feeding rolls of paper into the press as my eight-year-old face was inked, spat out in multiples, and tied in bundles for delivery to the Diocese of Burlington.

Working twelve-hour shifts as a tender at the Milton press, and later at the *Burlington Free Press*, Bergman, who lived in an illegal encampment in the old parking lot of Mazel's department store on North Street, began "very naturally" to organize his neighbors and coworkers as they told their own stories about housing distress in the city. Many worried that they were in a spiral headed toward one inevitable outcome. Bergman's organization, PACT, helped Sanders organize against his landlords, but Sanders "feared homelessness and talked constantly about his fears," according to a friend. He couldn't couch-surf now, with Levi often in tow, as he had around Plainfield and Calais in the '60s. Sanders was a hippie-adjacent socialist moving in a scene where eking out seemed almost chic. But not every Volvo with a duct-taped muffler implies a trust fund, and Bernie, who was plainly unemployable in many types of jobs, was not trying to be chic. "He lacked clothes," Sugarman told me. "I fed him."

Sugarman invited Bernie to stay at his own barely affordable, illegal apartment on Cherry Street. Sugarman had one rule: only kosher food was permitted inside the apartment. Huck Gutman once exclaimed to Bernie, "How the fuck can you live that way?" But Sanders had little choice, and he and Sugarman were almost too busy strategizing to eat anyway. "Tell me we're not crazy," Sanders would say, appearing in the kitchen for his morning coffee. "Do we say good morning at all, Bernard?" was Sugarman's reply.

Levi stayed over for days at a time. Bernie's parenting was free-range and improvised; Sugarman found it "interesting indeed" that the little boy called his father "Bernard or Bernie," at Bernie's own insistence. Though his parenting beliefs were unorthodox, "there was one very conventional and maternal person Bernie listened to about family life," Sugarman told me, "an obscure woman from Philadelphia named Roz. Her son was friends with Levi. Bernie would go by to bring the boys to South Park. 'Why are you late, Bernard?' Roz would say, and Bernie, who usually fought every little comment, Bernie would apologize and shuffle his feet, look down, swear it wouldn't ever happen again. He lived in fear of Roz," Richard told me, with a laugh. Then there was a beat. "I think she reminded him of his own mother."

The phone rang more with Bernie in the apartment: "a lot more, constantly," Sugarman said. Bernie's celebrity on the leftist fringe of American politics was only growing now that he'd "retired from politics." Settling into a new home on Caroline Street, Sugarman had to fend off "at least four people Bernie knew who happened to be running for president of the United States." One was "a Trotskyite, another from the Peace and Freedom Party in California, one other was I think a Marijuana Party candidate."

Sugarman, a very funny guy, slipped naturally into a joke structure to tell the story.

"The first guy comes and stays with us for a week or something. That was fine. I figured Bernie probably only knew one presidential candidate who needed to sleep on our couch.

"Then a few weeks later, another guy, another candidate for U.S. president. Soon there's a third guy, a new candidate sleeping on our couch.

"Finally I got a call from a fourth guy in a phone booth somewhere, 'Is Bernie Sanders there?' I said no, he's out right now. I asked the guy, 'Say, you don't happen to be running for president, do you?'

"'How did you know,' he says to me."

When Bernie arrived home that afternoon, Sugarman told him about the fourth suitor. Sanders drew a line at candidate four. "What the—I hate that guy! If you let him stay over, I'm moving out!" Sugarman assured Bernie that no invitation had been made. And Sanders, given his odds of finding a new place in Burlington, was definitely not moving out.

BURLINGTON WAS A TENANTS' CITY: two-thirds of Burlingtonians rented their homes. Some 40 percent of renters in the city spent more than 30 percent of their income on their often badly maintained properties. They could be moved for the slightest infraction, or none at all, whenever the outermost ripple of gentrification or redevelopment reached their front door. A tenant's call to the city housing inspector usually backfired. Instead of enforcing the housing codes, the inspector often abetted the eviction process; he "sided with landlords," Edward Papin told the *Burlington Free Press*, describing, in lurid detail, the tenant-caused squalor he claimed he encountered. But the reality for low-income working people was that rents were out of reach, and landlords were unscrupulous, if not exploitative. The only squalor most Burlingtonians saw was outside the apartments of rich students, who deposited months of trash on their front lawns as they blew home every May 31 to the suburbs of Boston.

Many of the biggest landlords were from families we knew who had grown up in our school and church circles. After urban renewal displaced households from downtown into the city's adjacent neighborhoods, this tight group of old Burlington Catholic families—their friends and relatives well positioned in the local banks, the fire and police departments, and city hall—found it very easy to purchase up whole blocks of Burlington, push through the necessary permits, subdivide the remaining old houses, and wait for monied UVM students from Massachusetts and Connecticut to sign leases every spring. Areas like King Street and the Old North End, in turn, were set aside for tenants on Section 8, which was implemented in 1974, and other housing subsidies. Both the students and the subsidies were steady profit streams for landlords, who had no incentive to fix up their properties. Their tenants were either too advantaged to care or too disadvantaged to complain. The era of the Burlington slumlord, which continues to this very day, had arrived.

It was a discouraging environment for any tenant seeking safe, clean, and affordable housing; for a divorced woman in her mid-twenties with a young child, the challenge was especially daunting. During these years, my mother would occasionally tell me excitedly that we were finally moving out of her parents' home and "into our own place." Walking around Burlington, I still pause when I pass houses we aspired to live in. They tended to conform to a child's idea of romance and adventure. One house on Pearl Street had a turret, like a castle. Another was no larger than a shed, a kind of doll's house, next to Big Ben's, our neighborhood pizza place. Mom and I often walked by it hand in hand before returning to my grandparents' house, where reality awaited us. At the time, my mother was making minimum wage. She had little savings, and what savings she had was applied to the modest tuition she paid at my Catholic school. We were comfortably housed, living under my grandparents' roof. But with an independent economic life in the city of Burlington well beyond our reach,

Dan Chiasson and Linda Chiasson, 1978.
Dorothy Delorme

the emotional costs, not only of economic precarity but of our dependence on the expiring tolerance of my grandfather for the young family living in his home—a temporary measure that became permanent—became our daily reality.

In the classifieds of the *Burlington Free Press*, the listings for September 1980 usually specify "no children, no pets," and many require either "a working gentleman" or "a married couple." A single woman with a child was almost by definition the poorest prospective tenant, and the presence of a child triggered health and safety codes no landlord wanted to uphold. In the jobs my mother held during those early years, she never made enough to afford an efficiency apartment. Nor did she yet have a driver's license. Our apartment search, if it had ever happened, would have been limited to places within walking distance of her work and my school. The most affordable of these neighborhoods were also, of course, the most dangerous, and the landlords themselves were in some cases the party most to be feared, for landlords did not make exceptions for young mothers without the expectation of quid pro quo. In fact, the threat of a "tenants' blacklist" was often used by landlords to extract sex. That the blacklist existed was reluctantly acknowledged by the head of the landlords' association, Clark Hinsdale, and by Leo Gagner, a Burlington slumlord, who confirmed in a *Burlington Free Press* investigation that "sexual extortion" was sometimes practiced. Gagner added, "We don't know for sure if the landlords are fair in the way they use the list."

My mother knew that they were not "fair," since "sexual extortion" had apparently been demanded by an ex-landlord of the single mother who lived across the chain-link fence from our backyard, whom I will call Sandy. Sandy had been evicted by her boyfriend, people said, which, looking back, made all too clear what had really happened. The mother of two destructive, intimidating children, whom I'll call Jimmy and Robby, Sandy was abused by the men in her life for years. We got used to the cycles: Sandy would dress up and stand at the end of the driveway, waiting for her date to pick her up; later, Sandy would be dropped off, often in tears, or in a state of rage that she expressed by hitting her two young sons. The world next door became an omen for what our life might look like if we left the protective bubble of my grandparents' home. I wonder, too, if the example across the fence kept my mother from dating; surely, I would have been at some risk if she'd become involved with men. Whenever Sandy had a steady boyfriend, he ended up moving in and abusing both Sandy and the two boys. Eventually, when Sandy was arrested for marijuana possession, her boys went into state care. This world played out not ten feet from my bedroom, for we were all of us, my mother and I, my grandparents, Sandy and her kids, living in uncomfortable proximity on a property that was divided only by that rusting fence.

Mom and I were not poor, because of her jobs and the generosity of my grandparents. But Sandy, living on federal and state aid, was poor, and her life was terrifying to behold. In a poem from my first book, "Blueprint"—I quoted it earlier, in relation to Father Baffa—I recall the day that Jimmy and Robby's father turned up. They'd been bragging about him for years, tall tales of a rakish, glamorous motocross racer; Jimmy, the older boy whom everyone described as "slow"—there were many undiagnosed developmental disabilities among the poor in Burlington—would then taunt me: "Who's YOUR fucking father, fucker?" But when the boys' father came, the only time we ever saw him, the man was rowdy, drunk and high, and, confronting something about Jimmy and Robby that set him off, immediately beat the living shit out of them, before pulling out of the driveway, laying on his horn, and threatening to kill our astonished, terrified family, standing on the other side of the fence.

My life then got better. Jimmy and Robby had been brought to heel; from that moment forward, their spirit seemed too low down in their bodies to rise to cruelty. "They were quieter, and I became sole ruler of the neighborhood," is how I put it in my poem.

In young adult life, both brothers were in and out of the "Day in Court" column, a daily feature in the *Free Press*: battery, possession, voyeurism. I felt deep sorrow, then, for both brothers, and began to think back on the ways *I* had taunted *them*. The last notice I saw of Jimmy was a photo of him picking up groceries at the Burlington Emergency Food Shelf. I am told that Robby died in 2007.

"Poverty in Vermont"

Sanders's victory over ETV won him back the notoriety he'd lost in his two-year "retirement"—and some old antagonists were standing by. For a spell in 1979, some Vermonters believed that socialists had somehow gained control of Channel 33. Richard Fletcher, a Burlington resident, expressed the perspective of many in a letter to the *Burlington Free Press*: Vermont ETV had become "a propaganda unit for socialist trivia." There were even some mild, fruitless calls to boycott *The Electric Company*. But it was unforgettable how the UVM board rolled over instantly when attacked by the "shrill" and "overbearing" Sanders. As a rehearsal for battles that Bernie would soon wage as mayor of Burlington against the university and its interests, the skirmish indicated that Sanders would enter with real advantages.

In February, Sanders published an op-ed, "Social Control and the Tube," in *The Vermont Vanguard Press*: "The potential for television, democratically owned and controlled by the people, is literally beyond comprehension," Bernie wrote. By the following month, his "Concerned Citizens on ETV" had gotten everything they'd demanded and then some. The station scheduled five additional forums on issues "of particular interest to the community" produced by local filmmakers. The first such contribution was Bernie's own low-budget interview feature, *Poverty in Vermont*, which Sanders made hastily and with borrowed equipment. The one-hour documentary was first broadcast on March 12, 1979.

It is, in its no-frills way, a powerful work. Wearing a yellow button-down oxford, light blue work pants, and shitkickers, Bernie interviews poor Vermonters at home, or welcomes guests to a studio designed to look like a middle-class living room, his feet up, his right wrist propped on his knee. Throughout, Sanders reminds his viewers not only that poverty exists in Vermont but also that broadcast television could be a powerful mirror of things as they really are. Ordinary people can make contributions. The cheapness of the production is the point.

In the short clips stitched together to create *Poverty in Vermont*, Sanders, though he had not yet considered running for mayor of Burlington, discovers important elements of his eventual winning mayoral coalition. He interviews Ruth Billings, a woman who works at the Old North End Food Co-Op, about federal cuts to food stamps. Two members of the Abenaki tribal council, Richard Phillips and Abner Jerry, discuss poverty in their community. Gene Bergman of PACT argues for rent control; Bernie's longtime allies John Franco and Sandy Baird add their perspectives. A folk singer performs the labor ballad "Joe Hill," named for the great Wobbly activist and songwriter. A poet reads an elegy for a friend who died poor and alone in a trailer in Middlesex, Bernie's first Vermont community. Two UVM professors discuss poverty in terms of social and economic theory. After the closing credits run, a single word in bold flashes on the screen. It is Joe Hill's famous imperative, in the moments before he was martyred: "Organize."

The heart of the film is Bernie's interview with three men from Franklin Square, a housing project in Burlington's New North End. John Bartlett Jr., Carl Billado, and Richard Sartelle describe conditions at the development, where the city built sixty flimsy units in 1971 to accommodate some of the poorest families displaced by urban renewal. The exhaustion in their eyes is generational, a legacy of Burlington's neglect.

By 1979, Franklin Square had become the most notorious address in Burlington. A playground was promised but never funded; on the dismal, muddy quad, where grass was planned but never planted, piles of garbage fed seagulls and rats. Kids played in the graveyard north of the site, while, behind the development, drug addicts and the mentally ill camped in an old buggy swamp.

The sixty units at Franklin Square housed some 250 children. If you had a Franklin Square kid in your homeroom or on your basketball team, everyone, even the teacher or coach, simply referred to the child as "from Franklin Square." On the middle-class streets adjacent to the property, places with names like Sky Drive and Venus Avenue, where many of my friends lived, parents put up high fences, and if a Franklin Square kid showed up at the neighborhood ice cream truck or foursquare court, there were always strict orders to avoid him. I had two good friends from Franklin Square; we would drop them off at the gate, near the main road. We never drove in. I never saw the inside of John's or Steven's homes—and they never saw the inside of mine.

In response to this stigma, children at Franklin Square tended to move as a pack, as they stole bikes, smashed car windows, and went looking for fights. Certain kids had a kind of outlaw reputation in town. At North Beach, on hot August days when the water in Lake Champlain was contaminated with very high levels of fecal coliform bacteria—this was common, in the 1970s—Franklin Square kids with pails and shovels would swim and cavort in the poisoned water, splashing the old people in their lawn chairs. It was a form of empowerment, one of very few available to these kids. Franklin Square was the lowest rung on Burlington's housing ladder; the next stop was homelessness, and many of the project's families, unable to afford the rent increases that inevitably came, ended up in the squalid mosquito-infested encampment behind the low-slung apartments.

"It's a very depressing place," Dick Sartelle, a baby-faced man of fifty explains, in the interview with Sanders. "There's not much encouragement there." Twenty-year-old Carl Billado, who arrived at the interview from a parole meeting, described the cycle of police harassment in Franklin Square: "When they drive in there, they're looking for someone to bust." Consequently, most teenagers in Franklin Square had a juvenile record. "They're looked down on by the community," Billado explains. In fact, by some estimates 90 percent of the children in Franklin Square dropped out of school, and, as Bernie points out in the interview, "not a single child at Franklin Square has gone to college, except for one young guy who went for three weeks."

Franklin Square was constructed during Mayor Gordon Paquette's first term. During his second, according to Billado, surveyors visited Franklin Square and blueprints were ceremoniously unfurled: "They were going to build a park in the backwoods. They had us out there one day, we had a big picnic, helped them cut down trees. Next thing you know, the money comes up. Where is it? Nobody knows." The park was never constructed. During Paquette's third term, when a rash of vandalism in the city was traced back to Franklin Square, Paquette, in an angry mood, called a meeting at city hall with Dick Sartelle and several others. Paquette threatened to close the facility and evict its tenants, and seemed sympathetic to a splinter group of residents who objected to the "youth recreational activities" that Sartelle had valiantly organized.

As a guest on Bernie's ETV program, Sartelle discovered that he and his tenants' group had the attention of Sanders, who struck them as a passionate, articulate young man; and Sanders discovered in Sartelle's group a powerful potential base of support. Sanders's efforts with his Debs film had acted as a culvert, allowing other roads to cross it. The main road running into the March 1981 mayoral election wasn't the impassioned socialist rhetoric of Eugene V. Debs, but the realities of everyday life in the city of Burlington for low-income men and women like Richard Sartelle of Franklin Square.

FRIENDS IN THIS PERIOD describe Bernie's continued "troubled state of mind," "agitation," and "distraction," despite the adventure of his Debs film: a low point that rivals Sanders's wayward period in the mid-1960s, after he and Deborah Shiling divorced. Though his New Year's resolution for 1978 was, as he told a reporter, "to play some role in making working people aware" that their "present-day reality" was "simply a pathetic presentation brought to us by a handful of power-hungry individuals who own and control our economy," Sanders still didn't know what to do, without a home or a job, and politics sometimes seemed beside the point. Rader recorded "a good talk Wednesday afternoon with Bernie":

> He has been reading about hypnotism & getting back in touch with his interest in orgone energy theory & the like. His one real love, he says, is to pursue this area of interest.
>
> As Bernie said, Western science & Western medicine seem to be able to ignore a lot (acupuncture, for example, & hypnotism) until they can't any longer.
>
> To look into [for me]: Mesmer's theory of animal magnetism & the connection between hypnotism & the early work of Freud, et al.

During Bernie's time crashing with Richard Sugarman, Wilhelm Reich was "always on his mind," as was typical of his low periods. To give his friend some perspective, Sugarman took Bernie on long walks, sometimes accompanied by Levi, down Cherry to Battery Street to Perkins Pier and the ferry docks. Sometimes they rode across Lake Champlain and back together on the *M/V Valcour* to take in the sunsets. Sugarman noted that Sanders would pause on these trips and note "the position of his body, the way he held his neck and back." Bernie was taking "a keen interest in his posture and musculature. He'd stop and assess what his body was telling him about his mind." Sugarman, who had read very little of Reich, was nevertheless a curious and open-minded pupil. "It was in line with what I'd studied and believed about the mind-body problem," Sugarman told me. "The French phenomenologists called it *le corps veçu*—the lived body."

Bernie hadn't moved many possessions into Sugarman's apartment. A duffel bag of clothes, "three at most" pairs of shoes, and—hold on, what was this treasure?—a complete Hogarth Press edition of the works of Sigmund Freud in twenty-three volumes. Sugarman brightened when he saw Sanders unbox the handsome editions. "I was delighted to have Bernie's Freud to rifle through" whenever the two men returned to the apartment. Sugarman made the careful study of Freud he'd meant to undertake "for decades." The twenty-three volumes were "better than collecting rent." I perked up when Richard told me this. Was this the edition that Larry Sanders had given Bernie as a wedding present in 1964?

"That was it!" Sugarman interjected. The edition, despite Larry's long-held worries, was safe as of 1978, even through Bernie's nomadic period. Sugarman wanted to email and tell Larry Sanders the good news himself. "He's a lovely man," Sugarman said of the elder Sanders. "In fact I call Bernie *BER*-nard, emphasis on the first syllable, in emulation of his big brother."

17

Longtime Caller

(Sadie's Ladies, Spring 1980)

Sanders with Zoe Breiner, left, and Sadie White, June 7, 1982. *Jym Wilson*

Interlude: Cyndi Lauper and Angela Lansbury

"It looked like a nature show, or *Walt Disney Presents*," is how Cyndi Lauper, the pop star, described seeing Vermont for the first time. Lauper, then eighteen, traveled from New York City to Burlington with a boyfriend in the summer of 1971. Soon she dropped the boyfriend, moved into a hostel downtown, and went on welfare. People who met her around town in those days never forgot her. In Vermont, people called her simply "New York." "'Here comes New York,' they would say," according to Lauper. "They didn't like my accent." There was a rush of wonder back in Burlington when Lauper turned up a decade or so later, spinning, lifting her skirt, and belting out those amazing songs as part of a brand-new phenomenon known as MTV, and looking as though she was designed for the future.

But the winter of 1971 was cold, and Lauper, who spent the days in her room above Church Street painting little landscapes and cityscapes, was lonely: "I remember when it was Christmastime. I kept hearing that Joni Mitchell song 'River' bleed out of the bars on Church Street. You know the one, 'It's coming on Christmas, they're cutting down trees.' It was so sad."

Lauper might have studied her reflection in the big windows of Abernathy's department store at the head of Church Street, but a young woman on welfare would never have dared enter the staid establishment housed in the Richardson Building, a turreted fortress done in the Scottish Baronial Revival style. When, a decade later, the actor Lee Remick peered in its decorated windows, she beheld a beautiful Christmas scene of a snowy Vermont village with tiny toy children and a miniature sleigh. Inside the grand doors, movers were packing up her family's department store. It was the end of an era! At home on Burlington's South Union Street, in the grand Victorian house where my friend Sam lived, Lee Remick's mother, Angela Lansbury, was dying.

This little holiday bauble was *The Gift of Love: A Christmas Story*, a made-for-TV movie filmed in Bernie's Burlington, in 1982. The producers chose Burlington because Abernathy's, the store that anchored business for decades on Church Street, had finally closed. Its shelves and racks and cash registers were still onsite, waiting to be transformed into Angela Lansbury's family's department store as it was put to bed after decades in business. But when Lee Remick peers at the toy Vermont village in its windows, you can see in the reflection the reason why the actual business, Abernathy's, had passed on. The street we can make out behind her is eerily devoid of cars. A pink brick roadway runs underfoot. On the screen and off, it was indeed the end of an era. "We're wasting our time here. Let's try out the new shopping mall," a dejected Salvation Army bell ringer says to his partner, as Remick drops a quarter into his empty cup.

I remember parking on Church Street with my grandmother when I was about seven. It was Good Friday, after Mass. The stores all closed at three p.m. to mark the hour of Christ's crucifixion. At five, they reopened with great fanfare. We were picking up a honey-of-a-ham for Easter supper. A few years later, where our car had been parked, an enormous decorative boulder was set into the brick pavement. Where the ham had been, a gift shop sold wind chimes and Vermont key chains. One by one, the businesses that old Burlingtonians knew were closing. In the Abernathy's building, there was soon a Banana Republic, which did not close on Good Friday at three. Church Street had become an outdoor pedestrian mall intended to counteract retail development in the suburbs. It was now known as the Marketplace.

The metamorphosis of Burlington's old-fashioned shopping street gestated in one man's mind for ten years. The Burlington architect Bill Truex and his wife had visited Copenhagen's Strøget, the city's bustling pedestrian mall, in the early 1960s. A decade later, Truex was the chair of Burlington's planning commission, the agency in charge of urban renewal. Pat Robins, a Burlington boy whose family business, McAuliffe Office Supplies, sat prominently on Church Street, was the chair of the Downtown Merchants Association. Paul Bruhn, who ran Patrick Leahy's 1974 campaign for Senate, was now Leahy's chief of staff. The three men became close friends during the planning phase of the Church Street development: Truex drew up the designs, Robins built support with the merchants, and Bruhn coordinated federal money though Leahy's office. In a masterstroke, they convinced city hall to close off Church Street on a trial basis. Fifty thousand people showed up during one week in August. From there, the transformation of Church Street became a question not of whether, but of when, and of how much. "There was almost no structure in the city of Burlington," Robins said in an interview. "We had a city planner, with very little staff. It was a time when guys like Robins and Truex and Bruhn could just do stuff."

Truex, Robins, and Bruhn returned to Burlington to propose not merely the conversion of Church Street but also the creation of a new, powerful, private agency, the Marketplace Commission, to handle every aspect of the new project. City hall itself would sit on the Marketplace, cheek by jowl with bookstores, sports bars, and arcades. The Church Street merchants, though skeptical at first, understood that they held a strong position. The shopkeepers of Church Street and the politicians in city hall have maintained this tense partnership, co-governing the city's commercial heart, ever since.

That three individuals acting alone could entirely transform our city tells you quite a bit about Burlington politics in the 1970s—and about the circumstances of Bernie Sanders's election on the near horizon. "We had a mayor who was a great guy, Gordy Paquette. We asked him time and time again to do crazy stuff," Pat Robins said. Paquette, a Democrat who served from 1971 until his startling 1981 loss to Sanders, was often in the pew behind my family at church: a jolly Chamber of Commerce type who addressed himself to God as only a dedicated sinner can do. Joe Sherman memorably captured Paquette in his natural habitat, Nectar's restaurant on Main Street:

> A large, flaccid man, Mayor Paquette sat with several city aldermen and a few of their cronies around a table and in a couple of booths along the wall. They talked and joked behind a veil of smoke. A couple of them ogled the occasional coed who walked by. Music drifted in from the barroom, where college students and older hipsters drank and danced. Paquette, oozing overconfidence, suggested a Vermont rendition of Chicago's Mayor Daley, complete with the retinue.

Paquette "oozed overconfidence" by controlling the Burlington Board of Aldermen and the city commissions, which he sometimes staffed with his family and neighbors. Only a man who came up in the stable system of Burlington's Catholic neighborhoods, schools, and parishes could have secured the loyalty of so many in the city. Though he operated behind "a veil of smoke," Paquette was gregarious, approachable, and, like many a man cosseted by long-held power, rather helpless and childlike. On one visit to Washington, D.C., to raise money for the Church Street Marketplace, Paquette and a friend stayed up in their budget hotel room and set up a racetrack for the cockroaches that skittered around their ankles.

Even in Joe Sherman's memorable description of Paquette, the mayor is more a poignant figure than a crook or a bully. The city that he had fed from the back of his family's bread truck during the Depression had changed, and the changes accelerated on his watch. The mayor's old childhood blocks were now among the city's most neglected. As city deficits grew, cuts to services were made, and poverty spiraled. The specter of suburban commercial development had led Paquette to try to turn Burlington into a destination

Mayor Paquette, 1981. *Jym Wilson*

for regional shoppers. Burlington's theory was that it had better become a mall, and fast.

My sense of the mayor echoes still from my childhood living room, where my grandparents kept a running, grumbling commentary over the morning paper. In every household, up and down Burlington's streets, a generational drama was playing out, as the men who'd been welcomed home as heroes in World War II saw their prestige wane and their authority even over their own children crumble. "Paquette," as he was always called in our home, had known my grandfather for years and was owed a grudging respect. Politics had become, for men like Milford Delorme and Gordon Paquette, about defending themselves from young people and their beliefs. The city of Burlington was now said to be "overrun with kids," its downtown, for the first time, viewed as a site not of candy counters and pharmacies but of unruly youth, drugs, unrest, and mayhem.

A sanitized vision of the city, with its city center serving as the jewel in a band of new access highways, began to preoccupy Mayor Paquette, and he took to the airwaves to make his case. *The Jack Barry Show* aired every weekday morning at 9:06 a.m. on Burlington's WJOY AM. Everyone in the city listened to Jack Barry, and many called in regularly to engage his guests, a mix of celebrities passing through town and local politicians. When you skinned your elbow on the playground, the school nurse played *The Jack Barry Show* as she unwrapped the roll of gauze. The line cooks at the Oasis Diner heard Jack Barry over the sizzling in their cast-iron pans. This was before Don Imus or Rush Limbaugh. The intrigue and the outrage were local. My grandmother, doing her housework, carried a small plastic radio from room to room. I could tell she was headed to my bedroom because Jack Barry's voice got louder as she got closer, climbing the stairs.

In the spring of 1980, after years of chaperoning retirees on sightseeing trips to Ireland, Jack Barry had picked up the faintest brogue. And he looked like his voice: cordovan loafers, creased high-waisted trousers, spread collar, an elegant quartz timepiece, fashion eyewear. We'd see him at church. After Mass, in the vestibule, Jack Barry stood opposite the priest and greeted people as they streamed out:

How's the clarinet, young lady?

Is Margaret at Birchwood?

Give Eddie Thibault my best.

Barry's receiving line was longer than the priest's. The priest stood primly by as Barry hugged and backslapped the congregation. Priests came and went, but Jack Barry, beloved of everyone in Burlington, had been at his post for decades.

Richard Sugarman and Bernie Sanders tuned in to *The Jack Barry Show* most mornings, but "turned the radio up" for *The Mayor Speaks*, Barry's Sunday feature with Gordon Paquette. The mayor called it his "Sunday crucifixion": Paquette's catarrhal baritone cracked like an altar boy's when confronted by his angry constituents. But he dragged himself to the studio every Sunday to retail his increasingly desperate vision for new "twenty-first-century Burlington." Paquette "was camped out in Washington" for much of the 1970s, his opponents claimed, "sucking up" to federal officials to bring home huge infrastructure grants. His voters' complaints—crumbling curbs, shuttered pharmacies, broken traffic signals—might have seemed small ball. But to further its redevelopment plans, the city had allowed the neighborhoods along the path of planned highways and off-ramps to deteriorate. Blighted homes and buildings were much cheaper for the city to acquire and raze.

The footprint of Paquette's phantom road tracked along Lake Champlain, and callers on its path now lit up the phone lines at WJOY. Caller number one, a doctor from the South Cove neighborhood in Ward 5, warned of the road's environmental costs. A schoolteacher called in from Lakeside to report that a developer had tried to "low-ball and intimidate" her to sell her family home. A single mother called from King Street, a mile or so up the shore from Lakeside, to say that her landlord had evicted her with three days' notice. Paquette had created an unlikely coalition: none of these callers, all from different socioeconomic bands, likely knew one another. Yet they all lived in fear of redevelopment, and worried for their generational homes, schools, markets, and parks.

Every week, "like clockwork," Sugarman told me, the mayor's archnemesis called in: Sadie White, a seventy-eight-year-old Democratic state representative from Ward 3. Sadie White liked to harass the mayor about the upkeep of Lakeview Cemetery, where, as she reminded Paquette, she "paid a visit to Mr. White" every morning. Mayor Paquette was used to getting an earful about cigarette butts and beer cans, but White's enmity went deeper: she had battled the city for decades as a powerful community activist, liaison to the elderly, and Montpelier legislator. Now that the final piece of the Marketplace puzzle had fallen into place—a $1.5 million bond, passed in 1979—and ground was broken on Church Street, White summoned elderly friends in the Old North End and resolved to make life very difficult for Gordon Paquette.

Sadie White had the regionally distinct sarcastic streak, a coping mechanism for the disempowered, that I noted in my grandmother, who hailed from the exact same neck of the woods. Sanders and Sugarman, listening in, chuckled as White compared the Marketplace to another recent folly, the "Winooski Dome." In 1979, Burlington's neighboring city applied for

Lieutenant Governor Madeleine Kunin, Mayor Gordon Paquette, and Senator Patrick Leahy break ground at the Church Street Marketplace, 1979. *Burlington Free Press*

federal funds to study the feasibility of building an inflatable dome over its central district. Area schoolchildren had followed the news with great ardor. I was assigned to sketch "the dome" in my homeroom: somewhere, in some box, the crayon sketch survives. Soon R. Buckminster Fuller, the noted futurist, visited the city to give the scheme his blessing. The money for the Winooski Dome was allocated by Jimmy Carter but then abruptly canceled when his rival in the 1980 presidential election, Ronald Reagan, began to mock Carter's judgment by citing such expensive, fruitless projects.

Jack Barry, who considered Sadie White as a kind of cohost, readied a stock intro for when she phoned: "Sadie White's on the line, here to talk some sense. Sadie, what's on your mind?" White's "sense" was last deployed against a consultant who proposed to build a scaffolded glass promenade twenty-five feet above the street designed to create entrances to the nineteenth-century buildings on their upper floors: White dubbed him "Judy Jetson," the fashionable, futuristic cartoon wife. Young architects, hearing of the opportunity in Burlington, now arrived to prospect in Burlington from all over, unrolling their blueprints on Tuesday nights before the Burlington planning commission. But even the drastically scaled-back, winning design that Burlington voters agreed to fund—and that my grandparents and their friends derided as "boulders and bricks"—would still "cost my neighbors," as White told Paquette, in the poor neighborhood

Opening ceremonies, Church Street Marketplace, 1980. *Vanguard Press*

most reliant on Church Street pharmacies and cleaners and markets, the Old North End.

Part of White's strategy was to invoke her elderly neighbors by name and address on Barry's show: "Mrs. Limoge on Archibald Street doesn't want a brick mall downtown, and neither does Mrs. Niquette on Blodgett Street." The litany went on. Sugarman and Sanders, listening to White's tirades, were "spellbound." White knew hundreds of old ladies personally and intimately. She had delivered them Meals on Wheels. She provided rides to church, or to the doctor. She brought crullers from Koffee Kup Bakery to people on their birthdays.

Most importantly, though: White boasted that she controlled the "sick ballots" in Ward 3. A justice of the peace under White's control distributed these special ballots to constituents in the hospital or in nursing homes. White coordinated delivery, then nagged the old ladies to fill them out. Accompanied by the justice of the peace, White herself then collected the hundreds of ballots to deliver to city hall. When the mayor heard White read the roll call of her neighbors, he rightly sensed a political challenge on the horizon: Sadie White had told the *Burlington Free Press* that she was considering running against Paquette in the March 1981 mayoral election.

As the roster of "Sadie's Ladies" continued, Sugarman heard a name he recognized from his congregation at Ohavi Zedek: "Molly Wakowski at Fern Hill!" he exclaimed to Sanders: a "not particularly observant" woman, as Sugarman quickly added when he told me, after all these decades. Sugarman realized that White's "gallery of old cronies" included, not just her fellow French Canadians, but also Jewish ladies whom Sugarman knew well, many of them now living side by side in new HUD-subsidized apartments built next to the synagogue. Improbably, Richard Sugarman and Sadie White shared a world. An alliance between the Sanders campaign and Sadie's Ladies might be cemented; and if Sadie's Ladies could be mobilized to oppose the Marketplace, what else might they be called on to do?

"I am frightened by the influence one woman seems to have on Burlington's voters," a *Burlington Free Press* reader complained. White was the most powerful woman in Burlington politics, and by 1980, after she had served in Montpelier for fourteen years, Mayor Paquette's city Democratic machine had had quite enough of her. White was beaten in a 1980 primary by opponents backed by city hall. She then reinvented herself overnight as a candidate for Ward 3 alderman, turning her considerable energies away from Montpelier and toward city electoral politics.

Bernie Sanders and Sadie White appeared to be at similar crossroads as oddball politicians without a party affiliation. At seventy-nine years old, with the birthday of every elderly neighbor noted in her day planner, White was ready for her next act. With Molly Wakowski on his mind, Sugarman gave his friend some advice. "Go direct traffic at a funeral," he told Sanders. "Just show up and volunteer. Sadie White goes to every funeral in the Old North End."

And so, in May of 1980, Bernie Sanders put on the most respectful clothes he owned, and went, as the Good Samaritan, to Ward 3, to help put one of Sadie's Ladies to rest.

AS MUCH AS ANY Burlingtonian in our story, Sadie White played the decisive role in Bernie's rise; and to this day, according to Huck Gutman, Bernie "probably thinks more about Sadie than anyone else from that era." Her life nests snugly inside the twentieth century. She was born Sadie Lucy Tatro, in a town no longer on most maps, Stevensville, Vermont, between Bolton and Underhill. This was 1901, during the William McKinley administration. White died in Burlington in 1999, a year after Bill Clinton's impeachment. At about the halfway point in her life, in 1954, the Champlain Mill, where Sadie White had worked since the age of fourteen, went dark. Her four-decade political career was then all in front of her at the age of fifty-three.

In 1980, the building where teenagers like Sadie White and my great-grandparents had tended the loom, and where Sadie and her husband, William White, organized the workers in the 1940s, became an upscale shopping mall, beautifully renovated to reveal the massive oak posts and beams behind the old walls. Out the enormous leaded windows you saw the rushing Winooski River falls. My friend Vince Feeney opened a store there, Feeney & Daughters (one of the "daughters," Emer Feeney, ended up as Jim Rader's stepdaughter; that connection is one of the origins of this book). Vince sold imported Irish knits and sumptuous tweeds. From age twelve on, I worked across the street, washing dishes, bussing tables, and eventually making omelets at Sneakers, one of the businesses that sprang up in the mill's penumbra. This kind of yuppie progress infuriated White. I remember seeing her at Waterworks, the upscale restaurant in the mill, when she stopped to speak with my grandmother. "Sadie doesn't like this place," my grandmother reported back to us, with that Underhill sarcasm in her voice. "She thinks the food is for *out-of-staters.*"

Vermonters might enjoy an occasional cocoa-crusted loin of pork or a blackened-chicken Caesar, sure; but Sadie White was altogether correct. When its manufacturing base fell out, the new economy ran, in essence, on food for out-of-staters. A decades-long career in the Champlain Mill was no longer available. Instead, intermittent retail and restaurant jobs were about as much as a young person might aspire to find. And the old people whose careers in the mills were cut short were now languishing on fixed incomes.

The path from the farm to the mills to local politics was an arc many Vermont Democrats had followed. Vermont's Democrats were heavily concentrated in mill and quarry towns, where labor organizing metamorphosed naturally into electoral politics. But no woman in Vermont could travel a direct path to public life. Sadie White's improvised route took her from the mill floor to voter registration drives and Election Day volunteer work, to the local VFW, where she became the president of the Ladies Auxiliary, waving to the parade-goers from the hull of a tank.

Her breakthrough came when the Vermont legislature was reappropriated by court order in 1965, and Burlington, under the new scheme to represent the state's population proportionally, gained twelve and a half new seats in Montpelier. White coordinated a modern and streamlined voter registration drive, campaigned on every doorstep, and was elected to the statehouse to represent the Old North End. Proportional representation in Montpelier meant that Vermont's population centers, and with them its Democrats, began to assert new power. Nearly two hundred years of Yankee politics were on the wane.

White had the binocular view of a Montpelier legislator who returned home every afternoon to her hard-pressed neighborhood. In the mid-1960s, as her first significant legislative victory, White led opposition to the construction of the northern spur of the city's new expressway system slated to run straight through her living room. A stripped-down version of "the Beltline," much despised to this day, was eventually built, but White, by amending a transportation and highway bill to force a ballot item before the voters in Burlington, succeeded in delaying the project and rerouting its path to save her neighborhood, making her a legend in Burlington.

But it also made her an outcast in her own political party. City hall Democrats were furious at White's opposition to the northern branch of the highway, on which they'd staked their own reputations. White had somehow risen as a Burlington Democrat outside the Burlington Democratic machine. Since she held no appointment in city hall, White and the city's mayors—Francis Cain in the 1960s, Gordon Paquette in the '70s—kept a suspicious eye on one another.

Sadie White, as a freelance political gadfly, was in a way a test run for Bernie Sanders. The Burlington Democratic machine moved along channels formed exclusively by men in the Catholic parishes and its ancillary institutions: the parochial schools, the Knights of Columbus, the Chamber of Commerce, and a men's-only social club, the Ethan Allen Club. As a working-class woman, White stood outside those networks. She stress-tested them, and they buckled. The networks themselves had been deteriorating, as the Catholic Church's rot began to show. The churches were now full of elderly women and the very poor. Sadie White literally stood out: at the Cathedral of the Immaculate Conception downtown, when I was dragged there for Mass, she was a tall, dignified woman, towering over all the other old French-Canadian ladies kneeling in the pews. When the abuse scandals finally broke in the early 2000s, it was remarked of White, as it was of my own grandparents, how it was a blessing she had passed before the Church's secrets were told.

IN MAY OF 1980, while Bernie Sanders played traffic cop outside St. Joseph's Church, the city's main French-Canadian parish, Richard Sugarman paid a visit to city hall. He was there to test a hypothesis. Soon after the two men met on the train in the fall of 1976, Bernie finished third in the race for governor, with roughly 6 percent of the vote. But the *Burlington Free Press* reported that Sanders significantly outperformed his statewide numbers in Burlington, at 12 percent. The difference was credited to leftists and activists who had streamed into the city in the late 1970s after the rural communes broke apart. Communal life was replicated, now with mortgages and medical bills and child care expenses, in apartments and small homes all through Burlington's neighborhoods.

Burlington's city hall is a compact, classical edifice designed in the late 1920s by McKim, Mead & White, the premier architectural firm of the day. In the city clerk's office on the first floor, Sugarman saw something highly unusual in enormous ledger books of election records. Sanders had indeed done well in Wards 2 and 3, where some of the city's students and activists were concentrated. But there was a secret that nested inside those totals. The difference in these wards was the huge number of absentee and sick ballots that Sadie White, the keen legislator, had personally whipped. "Word had it that she actually stood over her constituents as they filled the ballots out," another skilled legislator, Howard Dean, told me. The source of Bernie's support wasn't only the food co-ops and artists' collaboratives that set up in the old storefronts along North Street, but the dark warrens above them as well, tucked behind fire escapes and sagging balconies, where the poor and elderly lived. And it appeared that these men and women, who would not have voted at all if it weren't for White and her lieutenants, were not Liberty Union voters. They had broken to vote for Bernie but otherwise worked straight down the Democratic column.

Richard Sugarman handed back the ledger book but told the clerk that he would return soon with Sanders. When the two men visited the following week, Sugarman told me, Bernie was encouraged by the evidence but seemed to have "a very negative response to being in the building." By 1980, city hall's marble floors and chandeliers were coated with grime. During the energy crises of the '70s, its drafty, vaulted rooms had been modified with drop ceilings. A corps of city employees had aged and deteriorated along with the building, which smelled of cigarette smoke and, horribly, of cinnamon, from the fragrant sanitary pucks that rested in the banks of urinals in the basement. Sanders didn't want "to shovel snow and worry about budgets" as the city's mayor, he told Richard. He'd barely shoveled his own snow or kept open a checking account. He was finally, precariously, in an apartment of his own.

On the way out of city hall, Sugarman peered into the beds of tulips and daffodils and beheld what appeared as an omen: a twenty-dollar bill poking out of the mulch. Sanders "had a better angle on it"—because, even at six feet one or so, Sugarman told me, Bernie was shorter. Bernie lunged and pocketed the twenty; Sugarman, complaining about the injustice of it all, pressured Bernie to split it. To break the impasse, Sugarman came up with an idea. "I said, you know, I could use a beer. I'll treat you from my half."

Bernie, behind on rent, counting every nickel, was incredulous. "I'm not sure Bernie had ever been to a bar in the city," Sugarman said. "It was completely foreign to him, the idea that you would just go out for a beer, like friends do. I wasn't suggesting an orgy."

Sugarman and Sanders bickered some more, before finding themselves in front of Hannibul's, a riotous downtown bar favored by UVM hockey players. "It's part of your political education, Bernard," Sugarman said, with a firm hand to the small of Bernie's back. Into the dark doorway of Hannibul's the two men went.

18

The Citizens Party

(The Left Outdoes Itself, Summer and Fall 1980)

In the summer of 1980, Burlington's activists lined up to run under the banner of a new political entity, the environmentalist Barry Commoner's Citizens Party. Because Sanders had said goodbye three years before not only to Liberty Union but to party politics itself, he was now in a difficult position. The Citizens Party had organized rapidly and effectively. It appeared to have widespread appeal. The party would almost certainly run its own candidate for mayor of Burlington in March of 1981, rolling its momentum over from the general election just months before. If Sanders wanted Gordon Paquette's job, he would either have to join, or neutralize, the Citizens Party.

Barry Commoner is on the wall of fame, near Bernie and Judge Judy, at Madison High School in Midwood, Brooklyn. Commoner was a 1933 graduate of the school and grew up just blocks away from the Sanders family's apartment. It is strange to think that these two men, separated by a few rows on the wall and a few decades in time, shaped by the same background, years later affected each other's political destinies. Commoner went on to become a PhD biologist who brought the dangers of radioactive fallout to attention. In 1961, Commoner and others published a study showing that a radioactive isotope, strontium 90, was present at alarming levels in the baby teeth of 320,000 St. Louis children after a decade of atomic testing at Los Alamos and other nearby sites. The horror of imagining nuclear fallout in an infant's smile changed public consciousness.

Commoner convened the first Citizens Party convention in April of 1980. Jim Rader and Martha Abbott convoyed out to Cleveland, with Peter Diamondstone and family leading the way in a rickety house trailer. The Burlington left was energized by this midwestern "family affair," but by midsummer, Commoner's own candidacy for president had fizzled as the threat of a Ronald Reagan victory intensified. The campaign is now remembered mainly for an attention-getting radio ad. As Rick Perlstein describes it in *Reaganland*, Commoner exploited an exception for political speech in the FCC's ban on profanity: "Bullshit!" Commoner declares in the ad. A woman's voice replies, "*WHAT?*" Commoner then inveighs against his rivals: "Carter, Reagan, and Anderson—it's all bullshit!"

The Citizens Party made it onto the ballot in twenty-nine states in 1980, but its greatest success was in the city of Burlington, where a talented pair of activists rose to its bait. Robin Lloyd and Greg Guma, sometime romantic partners, lived in separate apartments in a dignified Victorian on Maple Street across from Bernie's old carriage house, raising their young son, Jesse. Lloyd, heir to a cattle fortune, turned up at her parents' farm in Rochester, Vermont, in the early 1970s, where she and Doreen Kraft, who later became the transformative director of the Mayor's Arts Council in Burlington, made "Jungian art films," as she puts it. (When Lloyd's great-great-great-grandfather Sam Maverick refused to brand his cows, he became notorious, and the word *maverick* entered our language.) In emulation of the great experimental filmmaker Maya Deren, Lloyd then went to Haiti, "in search of voodoo," but found, instead, grinding poverty and injustice. Radicalized, and now living in Burlington, Lloyd, in possession of a significant inheritance and boundless commitment, became the city's most important peace activist. If there were times growing up in Burlington when I was more aware of Central American politics than issues closer to home, Lloyd and her allies—including several radical Sisters of Mercy whom I knew from my elementary school—were the reason.

THE SCENE THAT gathered at 300 Maple Street "was an amazing little circle," according to Nancy Barnett, who lived across the way. You tended to meet people who were "awaiting trial," and often very notorious people awaiting very public trials, like Kristina Berster, the West German Baader-Meinhof leftist and alleged terrorist who was detained crossing into Vermont with a forged Iranian passport; or Berster's counsel, the flamboyant activist attorney William Kunstler, whom Barnett once encountered "with his pants down, bathroom door open," mulling over his defense strategy while urinating. The apartment at 300 Maple was part revolutionary cell, part bourgeois salon—and in both of its modes, anathema to Bernie Sanders. "There were endless supplies of drugs," Barnett said, and sometimes a private chef to fuel the boundless energy for what Sanders derided as "middle class" demonstrations. A 1980 photo published in the *Burlington Free Press* shows Lloyd at a die-in on Church Street. She is splayed in the rubble of the ongoing Marketplace renovation, wearing a sign that reads,

"We Are All Hibakusha (Hiroshima Bomb Survivors)." Her son, Jesse, then about three, stands over her, looking solemn in a bowl cut and overalls, and holding an enormous Pepsi.

In November of 1980, Robin Lloyd ran as a Citizens Party candidate against Vermont's popular Republican congressman, James Jeffords, a guy even leftists admired. Lloyd's campaign was in reality waged not against the decent liberal Republican but against his party's frightening standard-bearer, Ronald Reagan. Lloyd carried 12 percent of the vote statewide, but more than 25 percent in Burlington. She and Jeffords danced and laughed at his victory party afterward. There was reason for both to celebrate: Lloyd's showing was proof that the migration of activists from the forests and fields and into the city's neighborhoods had transformed Burlington. The awkward question was whether her 25 percent was a floor or a ceiling. Sanders concluded that the Citizens Party, and its chair, Greg Guma, widely rumored to be considering a run for mayor, needed to be outmaneuvered.

The early advantages were all on the side of Guma and his party. Sanders, at thirty-nine, had a philosopher best friend, an elderly conservative admirer in Sadie White, a disorganized organizer in Richard Sartelle, a reputation as a political loser, a small filmstrip business, and a fraying purchase on precarious financial independence.

GREG GUMA HAD tangled with Bernie for years. In December of 1971, Guma was twenty-four and a newspaper reporter in Bennington in southern Vermont: a "forgotten corner of the state," Guma told me. Bennington College, wide open as to acreage, was very cloistered as to culture; its most famous faculty member was Shirley Jackson, the author of "The Lottery," a dark dream of a short story about a mass stoning in a village square. The town of Bennington peered enviously into the arcadia in its midst, but seemed "lost in time" to Guma and the other radicals and activists just beginning to trickle in.

Guma first met Sanders during Bernie's first campaign swing through in 1971. The encounter did not go well. Sanders, dressed in corduroys and a work shirt, had hitchhiked to a plain ranch home on a rural byway outside the city of Bennington. He stood impatiently in the doorway as he was introduced to the curious crowd of "teachers, craftspeople, and assorted Vermont locals," according to Guma. It was two months to the day since Bernie had raised his hand and agreed to be "a warm body" on the Liberty Union ticket in the special election for U.S. Senate approaching in January of 1971, and, far from acting merely as a warm body, he found he loved campaigning. Over Triscuits and apple juice, Sanders went hammer and tongs against the draft, monopoly capitalism, the rigged banks, the uselessness of the public schools, the rights of children and teenagers. Some Vermonters in the crowd had trouble understanding him, since Sanders "spoke incredibly fast," as one attendee put it. But the centenarian in the room, a schoolteacher from nearby Shaftsbury, nodded vigorously to show she caught the gist.

Guma was intrigued by Sanders, but he had questions. "I wanted to really understand Vermont," Guma told me; Bernie's analysis of class and injustice was stirring, but he seemed "lost in the abstraction" of his argument, and did not know what made Vermont different from other rural places. Guma wanted to learn about Bernie's background, the formative experiences of his life, and what had brought him to Vermont. These were not prying or difficult questions, and they were on the minds of everyone who met Sanders.

"Obviously, you haven't been listening to me," Bernie snapped. "Do you know what the movement is? Have you read the books? Are you against the war in Vietnam?"

"Yes," Guma answered. "But you're a person, not a movement." And Vermont was a place, not a platform.

"You don't understand. It's the movement that's important. Are you for it? If you're not, I don't want your vote."

Guma politely reframed his questions and offered to help. Sanders then retorted, "I don't need your help. We don't have to prove anything to you."

"You have to prove you're a basically good person if you want my vote," Guma replied.

Sanders countered, "I don't want your vote."

The relationship never evolved past that one encounter; instead, it took the form of a series of perfect reiterations, like a stuck needle. Now living a few blocks from Guma, though, Bernie seemed to have lost some of that original edge. By 1980, Guma sympathized with his old antagonist. He thought of Sanders, harried and aimless, barely clinging to life as a single father behind on the rent, as "a lost soul in time." In the clutch of young activists surrounding the Citizens Party, who gathered at Guma and Lloyd's home, Bernie was an outcast. Impatient with even the most abbreviated social banter, Sanders "didn't fit in exactly." At an organizing event for the Citizens Party held at 300 Maple, Bernie stood in the doorway, looking distracted; at some point, nobody knew exactly when, Sanders left.

Access to Records

Like Robin Lloyd, Greg Guma had come to Vermont with the thought of making films, but he ended up with a desk in city hall in the mid-1970s as the administrator of a federal grant working with the city's youth office. After hours, Guma, a dogged gumshoe, made his way to the unlocked file cabinets. "Access to records," Guma wrote, "netted useful information about several city projects."

Guma discovered in his snooping the "true scope of urban redevelopment" in Burlington. Mayor Gordon Paquette had bet all his chips on a scheme intentionally presented piecemeal to Burlington's voters. Few in Burlington understood the plan in its entirety, which would connect Interstate 89 to the heart of downtown Burlington along the city's magnificent waterfront. Sadie White's crusade against the north branch of the road had been but a minor nuisance; city hall held all the cards. The highway would rest on the sedimentary muck running along Lake Champlain, cutting the city off forever from the lake. A Montreal contractor had been retained to design condominiums and shopping on the lake side of the new road. The plan required far more property seizures than officially announced, more neighborhoods destroyed, and more families displaced from their homes. This, in a city already decimated by the previous round of redevelopment.

Guma sounded the alarm about the Southern Connector. By night, Guma, who like Sanders had written for the *Vermont Freeman*, published his own offprint broadside, *Public Occurrence*. Thousands were distributed throughout the city, including a stack in the entry lobby of city hall. Mayor Paquette confronted Guma in an empty city hall one evening about an ad Guma had printed and signed on the back of his paper: "Stop the Southern Connector," it read.

"What is this shit?" Paquette demanded. He "couldn't believe it. Someone working in city hall had attacked the biggest project in city history."

BY THE SUMMER OF 1980, Guma and Lloyd had a political operation that had drawn some of the most talented and energetic young people on Burlington's left, and they had a plan to take city hall. In March, Guma issued a position paper to Citizens Party members. It laid out in detail the conditions that a mayoral candidate on the left could exploit in Burlington. "The current mayor has been in office for nine years, and will either retire or run for reelection next year," Guma wrote. The mayor's pledge to "keep the taxes down and strengthen the tax base through commercial development" has now been "broken" with his call for a citywide tax increase. The "fiscal policies of the city administration have frequently caused confrontation with city workers—municipal, fire, police—and departments—libraries, parks." Guma detailed "escalating financial and curricular woes in the schools," "rioting in the local park," and "widespread resentment among tenants—who are becoming a larger portion of the total population." Mayor Paquette's focus had been exclusively on "redevelopment" while the city's existing institutions imploded.

The strategy presented was essentially the one Bernie eventually followed. Guma suspects that his position paper circulated among Sanders's friends and allies: "Offer a slate of candidates, both for city-wide and ward offices"; "begin to campaign publicly" for the March 1981 town meeting elections "immediately after the November election"; try to register "3 to 5 thousand additional voters"; develop "a precinct system" to drive coordination among wards; and look for ballot items—an unpopular tax increase, or a popular appropriation for parks or beaches—that would swell voter turnout.

Crisis? What Crisis?

If Greg Guma had the name, the organization, the money, and the road map, why didn't he run for mayor? There was one intractable problem, and it involved the British chart-topping pop group Supertramp.

In 1978, Guma had been hired to edit a new alternative paper based in Burlington with a robust investigative unit. *The Vermont Vanguard Press* took over after the demise of a short-lived Burlington publication, *The Eclipse*, founded by UVM grads who had worked on the university's excellent paper, *The Vermont Cynic*. The *Vanguard* corralled some of the longtime freelancers who'd contributed to the *Vermont Freeman*. But the model, and the source of much of the paper's talent, was *The Boston Phoenix*, which reached one hundred thousand readers each week. The *Vanguard* was supported by two talented publishers investing their family's private fortunes. Steve Brown, a ball of big-city energy who had trained as an ad man for the *Phoenix*, seeded the paper with $15,000 from his father's oil shares. Nat Winthrop, the cerebral, ponytailed doppelgänger of his ancestor Governor John Winthrop of the Massachusetts Bay Colony, contributed a large share of his portion of the family's spoils from the China trade. At its height in the mid-1980s, the *Vanguard* counted as many as fifty thousand weekly readers, who plucked the paper from snowbound blue news racks all across Vermont.

Under Guma's editorial direction, the *Vanguard* made an art of harassing Guma's old boss, Mayor Paquette. The mayor and his shadow cabinet combed the paper every Tuesday morning at Nectar's over sour-orange juice and Pall Malls. They had heard that Guma was pursuing a scoop: federal dollars for the Southern Connector, Guma had discovered, had been obtained on a false certification that local matching funds were in place. The mayor was already on edge when, on February 6, 1979, an aide read aloud to him an account by the journalist Frank Kaufman, edited by Guma, of a controversial Supertramp concert two years before that had led to the all-out ban on rock music on city property, a decree enforced by a panel of Paquette-appointed eggheads.

Supertramp was a falsetto-and-synth London hitmaker supporting their record *Crisis? What Crisis?* and poised, with *Breakfast in America* (1979), to become an arena band. Supertramp fans were nine-to-fivers, car salesmen, high school track coaches. A joint in the kitchen drawer, reserved for the weekend; a six-pack of Labatt's: Supertramp fans were weekend warriors, far from unsavory. On the night of the concert, a small group of teenagers sat on the steps outside, smoking and drinking beer; inside, some aisles were blocked, a window was broken, a kid lit off a firecracker in the balcony. Supertramp played on, soaking up the adoration under diffusing bands of orange and white light.

The rowdier event that night might have been at the Elks Club across town, where Mayor Paquette and the city treasurer, Lee Austin, were carousing at the annual retirement party for city employees. Alerted to "a riot" at Memorial Auditorium, Paquette and Austin rushed over to find, instead, a rock concert underway. "I doubt the mayor had ever been to a *controlled* rock concert," a fan said, when it was announced that the show was over, shut down for being "out of control."

The next morning, Susan Green, the *Burlington Free Press* arts reporter, encountered Supertramp's lead singer, Roger Hodgson, and bass player, Dougie Thomson, "squeezing organic grapefruits" at the local health food

Supertramp, Memorial Auditorium. *Jym Wilson*

store, the Onion River Co-op; the reporter and two bandmates adjourned for red clover tea and a cheerful postmortem. The band, "spiritual seekers" who, far from inciting a riot, "hoped to hypnotize" their fans with their futuristic light show, had enjoyed the concert, they said; they hoped to return to the lovely city of Burlington, which reminded them of Bath. Then they were off in their RV to Montreal. The reporter was smitten; the mayor and treasurer convened a meeting and, that afternoon, announced that rock music was banned in Burlington.

In the *Vanguard*, Kaufman reported what was widely rumored around town: Paquette and Austin turned up that night "highly intoxicated" as well as "offensive, absurd, out of control." Paquette, reading this "slander," stewed for a month, then realized he'd been handed a political opportunity. In May of 1979, the mayor filed a libel suit against Kaufman, the publisher Steve Brown, and, amazingly, Greg Guma himself. When asked what damages he had suffered, Paquette gestured vaguely to a federal sinecure he had hoped to win as a reward for his years of loyal work for the Democratic Party. A politically connected judge allowed the suit to stand. *The Vermont Vanguard Press* recognized the suit as an attempt to gag its criticism of city hall. But the paper was itself playing a strong hand: the *Vanguard*'s defense was, simply, that what Kauffman wrote was the truth.

ON A TRIP TO Montpelier in September of 2023, I found what remains of *The Vermont Vanguard Press* in the tidy basement of Nat Winthrop's Victorian house on College Hill. Two months after the floods that devastated the capital city, Montpelier was still struggling. Bear Pond Books had reopened with a small inventory of volumes salvaged from the waters. The Bohemian Bakery, next door, where the cheddar-and-thyme croissants bring a tear to one's eye, was still drying out. The Savoy Theater was closed. There, I saw *Stop Making Sense* for the first time, impressed by the sight of David Byrne's frame in an enormous white suit, like a stick figure inside a marshmallow. The Thai place looked like it would never reopen; the gemstone and bong emporium was wrapped in plastic sheeting. The marquee at the grand old art deco Capitol Theater read, "We Will Be Back After A Brief Intermission."

Nat's basement was dry, thank God. After a contribution to the paper over twelve years that totaled, by his estimate, more than a million dollars, Winthrop has two large plastic bins to show for it, as a souvenir: a mostly complete run of the first few years of a paper that changed Vermont, housed by bins of the kind that we use to keep our kids' first-grade schoolwork.

I was looking for the Kaufman article; Nat pried it out and we read it together in a bright corner, near the stored Halloween decorations. Mayor Paquette's suit was dropped in 1983, but not before the *Vanguard* spent a small fortune defending itself. There were other forms of intimidation: *Vanguard* reporters got threatening notes at home, calls at strange hours. A small fire, attributed to arson, broke out overnight at the paper's headquarters on College Street. But the main casualty of Paquette's libel suit might have been the political career of Greg Guma.

THE NEXT DAY I visited Guma and Robin Lloyd at 300 Maple Street. The old-fashioned house is covered in flowers. An autumn clematis trailed down from the cornice, spilling outrageous perfume into the cool September air. I stood in the doorway for a long time, while Guma, who lives on the second floor, made his way down to me. Through the screen I saw a lifetime of mementos of every emergent cause and struggle to find its way over the years to Burlington, Vermont: the nuclear freeze; boycotts of the local GE weapons plant; a flag of the Nicaraguan Sandinistas. There was also evidence of new fights on display: the F-35, the nuclear bomber stationed at the Vermont Air National Guard that shakes Burlington several times a day on training runs. A Bread & Puppet calendar hung on the wall. Guma's upstairs apartment is like the workroom of Mr. Casaubon in George Eliot's *Middlemarch*—you see the obsessions, the rabbit holes, the commitments of fifty-plus years, in a collection of broadsides, books, videotapes, DVDs, memorabilia, all arranged tidily around a big library table with thick haunches for legs. Guma's dozens of published volumes have pride of place on his writing desk. His first book, distilling and expanding his journalism from the *Vanguard* years, was *The People's Republic*, an early study of Bernie's rise.

An alternative history of Burlington is preserved in this space, a field office for some revolution-in-waiting waiting a long time, with Guma playing the role of its deposed, aging prince. Guma still wonders what if.

"I was vulnerable," Guma told me, "because I'd been promoting the Citizens Party as an editor, while organizing it as a citizen." The appearance of a conflict of interest was enough to make him lose his stomach for a political battle; Gordon Paquette's libel suit would require a discovery phase, and Guma, who had done nothing strictly wrong, would have faced questions about his editorial priorities. Or, he would have had to leave his job, just as the *Vanguard* had begun to attract talented reporters and lucrative ad contracts.

Guma used to hang out with John Franco, Steve Goodkind, and several others in Sanders's circle who would marvel perpetually about Bernie's quixotic political instincts. To Guma, any credible left-wing candidate could have beaten the exhausted and humiliated Paquette. Bernie, Guma felt, just happened to have maneuvered his way into the opportunity.

Guma does not seem bitter; he is kind, funny, rueful, also full of new insights, and promoting two new books that are part of a grassroots history of Vermont. When we finished talking, he took me to the carriage house out back where Robin Lloyd, a beautiful woman in a pinstriped linen shirt, now in her eighties, was sitting at a sunny table, planning a march on Bernie's Burlington Senate office for October 4.

"Tell him about the handshake, Robin," Guma prompted her. Robin had fought Sanders from the left for four decades; Bernie once had both Guma and Lloyd arrested.

I surveyed the room, a bright, bamboo-floored refuge appointed with tapestries and ferns, as Lloyd, a patrician still, despite the class struggles she had fomented, told me the story: When last she saw Bernie, she extended her hand; Sanders, her old adversary, held it a moment, "a little tight for comfort," then released it, as though ridding himself one final time of the woman who never bought what he was selling.

"What manners!" I commented.

Lloyd seemed to relish that comment. "I *concur*," she said, with a smile.

19

Black Faces, White Faces

(Burlington Imagines New York City, Summer 1980)

Eleven Alive

In the summer of 1980, the wider world came to our den in two manifestations: cable television, and a police scanner. The cable box delivered a few blah networks like WMTW from Portland, Maine, an ABC affiliate. But the main windfall was the arrival of an independent network, Channel 11 WPIX out of New York City. "Eleven Alive" was a revelation. *Chiller Theatre* showed B-movies about severed hands that had minds of their own. Burlington boys were always Yankees fans, but now we could recite the ads for Lawn Doctor and the Money Store. We did schoolyard impressions of Crazy Eddie ("His prices are IN-SANE") and the phlegmy spokesman for Carvel ice cream, who described tantalizing ice cream cakes sold nowhere near Vermont: Fudgie the Whale, Cookie Puss.

I began to live that summer in a WPIX of the mind, and though I didn't visit New York City until I was twenty, I came to possess a canon of details that meant nothing whatsoever to me. Yet somehow it was empowering to command them: Mayor Ed Koch was condemning striking transit workers and garbagemen. A cop was shot in Ronkonkoma. There was a fire in Far Rockaway. A brash young playboy "with a smile like Robert Redford's"—we won't utter the syllables of his name—was buying up skyscrapers with the city's assistance and his father's millions. The thoroughbreds were back at the Meadowlands, "and they were racing with the moon."

A decade later, in college, I checked these memories against those of friends who'd grown up in New York. Jeff and I first bonded when we realized we both had aspired (I from 258 Colchester Avenue, Burlington; he from Riverside Drive, New York City) to compete on "PIXX," a primitive call-in video game where one lucky kid selected "from thousands of postcards received every day," and vying for a birthday party at Roller World, released a digital blip, like a stone from a slingshot, by enunciating the command "PIXX!" into the telephone receiver.

Hazy though it was, much of it came back vividly and to stay many decades later on YouTube. Here's Phil Rizzuto for the Money Store. Next up, Croatian separatists claim responsibility for a Midtown bombing. Jimmy Carter and Senator William Proxmire face off over Carter's "timid" budget proposal, against a backdrop of 18 percent inflation. Cookie Puss, Fudgie the Whale, Crazy Eddie: "It avails not, neither time or place—distance avails not," as another New Yorker put it. Like Walt Whitman, Jerry Girard at the sports desk and the meteorologist Roberto Tirado could accurately boast, "I project myself—also I return—I am with you, and know how it is."

But the New York City I'd constructed in my head was an incessant stream of frightening images from the South Bronx, of gangs, fires, collapsed highways, and crowds of Black and Latino kids wandering about the rubble. Teens flipped a broken-down car off the BQE. Girders, tires, rapes, graffiti. This misery was a form of regular entertainment for WPIX's majority-white viewership. Burlington was in this one way a perfect market for WPIX: we were country cousins in whiteness.

It would have shocked most Burlingtonians to be told that their city was racist. Theoretically, diversity was celebrated in Burlington. But Wanda Hines, a local activist and politician, remembers only three other Black families in the city during her own 1970s and '80s childhood. During the '80s there were still private, hush-hush, versions of "Kake Walk," a minstrel show put on before a crowd of thousands for decades as part of UVM's Winter Carnival, before it was shut down in the '60s. These modified events, where frat boys wore green-and-gold face—the school colors—were advertised by word of mouth and performed in the gummy cellars of Delta Psi and Lambda Iota.

To the right of the sofa in my grandparents' home, on a small side table, was the police scanner. It played on low all day long. It sounded sharply scratchy, like someone slowly plying back Velcro, with occasional blurted codes and passwords. It had a sticker on the front with a key to the police argot: 143, hit and run; 148, domestic disturbance. You half-listened for an address you recognized, and hoped to hear one of the more lurid codes: 134, kidnapping; 136, hostages taken. My attention was unevenly distributed between WPIX and the scanner, but I noted every variance in pitch in the dispatcher's voice.

A police scanner is an information network. So are pickup basketball courts. I was playing a lot of ball that summer, perfecting my game on a backboard we'd installed at home. My babysitter took me by bike to shoot HORSE. I used to see Levi Sanders—two years older, tall and gangly, a monster in the key—down at the South Park courts, near Christ the King School. Levi, who was becoming an elite player in town, went on to play at Burlington High School.

I don't know if Levi was there the day my babysitter told a group of us that a friend of his had been beaten down by the barge canal, a godforsaken toxic site that nevertheless offered teenagers a completely private place to get high and fool around. But he described a man emerging from under the canal—"a Black guy," he added—and forcing Alex facedown to the ground with a knee to his back, then attacking him with a tree branch. We shuddered, then resumed our game.

That was May of 1980. By July, summer had taken over, and, though I still sat all day inside in front of the TV, there were popsicles and raspberries. The incident with Alex was a distant memory. But now it was July 17, 1980, around noon. I'd eaten the red tip of the Rocket Pop and was working through the lemon fuselage down to the blue raspberry base. Suddenly the police dispatcher was shouting codes for assault, take cover, reinforcements needed.

As a nine-year-old child, I had no way of understanding why a young man, Louis Hines Jr., who had grown up in a large, close-knit Black family in Burlington, would make a beeline across Pearl Street at lunch hour and bring a lead pipe down repeatedly onto the skull and chest of a young stranger. When Hines approached, Bernadette Lesage was unwrapping her lunch on the lawn of the Unitarian church at the head of Church Street.

Louis Hines on the front page of the *Free Press*, July 17, 1980. *Jym Wilson*

Lesage, twenty-one, my aunt's high school classmate and friend, died from her injuries the next day.

"I am an old hunter," Bernadette's father, Ernest Lesage, told the newspapers, reporting that his daughter had "the glazed eyes" of a dying deer when the family visited the girl's bedside. Ernest Lesage then said that he prayed for the Hines family and bore no anger toward them: the two families "had both lost children" on that horrible afternoon. In fact, "it's kind of odd to say this," Mr. Lesage remarked, "but I'm just sorry this had to happen to a Black man."

I discovered Mr. Lesage's devastating comment while doing research for this book. It has to be one of the bravest things ever said by a grieving father: what had "happened" to his daughter, he suggested, was related to what "happened" to Black men in America. And it was now going to play out in an ugly way in our city. What I remember firsthand from the time confirms Mr. Lesage's implications. On the ball courts and playgrounds, kids were now emboldened to say the *N* word, no doubt having heard it at home. My grandparents never uttered the word, but when my great-uncle freely used it at supper, the conversation continued entirely in that key, with milder terms substituted. The main euphemism used in our home and in much of Burlington was "New York." This city is becoming like New York, my grandfather would say, with WPIX shouting about the South Bronx in the background.

The *Burlington Free Press* stoked the flames with a lurid story about Louis Hines Jr.'s mental condition. "Voice of Dead Father Rules His Actions," the headline read. The family was well known and widely admired in town. The Hineses had relocated to Burlington from Mississippi in the early 1960s, when Louis Hines Sr. accepted a position as an ROTC instructor and bandleader at UVM. In July of 1966, the *Burlington Free Press* reported that Hines Sr. had deployed to Vietnam; just two months later, during his earliest engagement, the young soldier was killed in a firefight at An Khê. Louis Hines Sr. is the first Burlingtonian known to have died in Vietnam.

Now two generations of Black men were held responsible for the murder of a white woman. The paper, deploying a racist trope, added that the young Hines had a "strong taste for marijuana." After a book about astrology was found at Hines's camp by the barge canal, a psychiatrist determined that Hines was "into the occult." As these kinds of stories metastasized, some Burlingtonians blamed the Hines family. Mildred Hines, Louis Jr.'s mother, afterward drove an airport taxi and came to expect a certain diffidence in many of her fares. Wanda Hines, Louis's sister, a community organizer in Burlington, sought a career in city politics, but fell short. Helen

Hines, an unrelated white woman in town, said her family routinely got "really obscene calls, racial names and all that stuff" and feared for her family's business. And the nickname "Leadpipe Louis" has been so persistent in Burlington that when my wife and I named our first son "Louis" in 2004, some of my relatives expressed mild shock.

Wanda Hines politely declined to be interviewed for this book. Louis Hines was released from custody in 2012 and now lives peacefully in central Vermont. His real story has little to do with the voice of his father, the influence of the occult, or reefer madness. In 1977, Hines suffered a nervous collapse and was remanded for treatment at the UVM Medical Center. Upon his release, Judge Edward Costello, who had presided at Hines's hearing—the same judge who used to stop and check on me, another fatherless stray, on his neighborhood walks—took a personal interest in him.

But despite Costello's intervention, Hines next broke into a common room at Trinity, the college next door to our house, just a few doors down from the judge's stately brick home. It seemed like a call for help. He waited quietly for the police to arrive, and, after being found unfit for police custody, was shipped off to the state hospital in Waterbury. There, he was injected regularly with a powerful antipsychotic that caused agonizing and painful side effects. Soon Hines, age twenty, was "introduced to a counselor who taught him about homosexuality," he said. The sessions "invariably consisted of episodes of sex," according to *The Barre-Montpelier Times Argus*. Hines was subjected to these rapes "almost every day," he noted, and, by 1979, back in Burlington, found that he had a consuming hatred of "homosexuals and women."

Black Faces, White Faces

The face of Louis Hines Jr. on the cover of the *Burlington Free Press*—the first Black Burlingtonian I had ever seen—abruptly became the very image of urban violence and danger. As though consigned by our city to one of only two alternatives, Hines had been, before he was mortally feared, totally invisible. His camp near the toxic ooze of the Burlington barge canal, where he had attacked my babysitter's friend back in May, was part of a circuit of woods and watershed mostly known to the city's growing homeless population. Our house backed up to part of this forbidden Burlington: a steep ravine, its banks cut by the roaring Winooski River before it began to recede tens of thousands of years before. When Hines left his contaminated camp site and headed to Church Street wielding a lead pipe, he was passing from Burlington's murky geographic id into its gleaming superego, and just as the

Ben and Jerry, 1980. *Vanguard Press*

city broke ground to transform Church Street into a tourist-facing vision of bubbly capital.

And so the face of Louis Hines, since it could not be integrated into Burlington's representation of itself, was soon repressed. Hines was sent away "for good this time," as it was said, to live in the maximum-security facility at the state hospital in Waterbury. His name was uttered only when he attended regular hearings where a judge considered releasing him, after years of spotless conduct. Then the outraged letters to the paper, the angry radio callers, the gossip on the street, all revved up for another round. Forgotten, along with the real story of Louis Hines, was any opportunity for the city of Burlington to grapple with the racism his crime had surfaced, and his sexual abuse at the hands of the state. Ernest Lesage's compassionate comment—regretting that this had "happened to a Black man"—could have been the spur to a searching, necessary citywide reckoning, but alas, it too was put away, forgotten.

AROUND THIS SAME TIME, a pair of white faces took over Burlingtonians' consciousness. "Pat and I got to know these two guys, one guy Ben, and another guy, his friend, Jerry. Two Jewish guys from Long Island," Nancy Barnett said. She found them, as she found Bernie, adorably familiar: "This is easy," Barnett said to herself. Neither guy cared yet about ice cream: "One did ceramics or something, the other worked in a group home. They were always together, like a package deal: before they had anything to sell, everybody knew them as a pair, Ben and Jerry." Barnett remembers "driving around in Ben and Jerry's van, smoking pot," and later that day cutting Ben's hair on her front porch. As she snipped, Jerry emerged "from out of nowhere" with a spoonful of what looked like ice cream "and was like, hey guys, try this."

Soon everyone in Burlington had. When the conservative writer David Brooks visited Burlington in the 1980s, he noted that the benevolent image of Ben and Jerry, the local "ice cream mavens," was "everywhere," their appealing faces beamed from a billboard inside the Burlington International Airport, from the sides of city buses, from taxis. Though the Carvel man tantalized us on Channel 11 with his unattainable ice cream cakes, Burlington kids were now the envy of America's ice cream lovers. In the converted gas station across from City Hall Park, where Bernie Sanders had once written copy for Liberty Union, Ben Cohen and Jerry Greenfield raced to keep up with demand. Signs greeted you at the front door: "15 Mins to Tennessee Mash," "Chocolate Orange Fudge En Route." My aunt Janet operated one of the shop's first franchises: a cart one block away on Church Street. She wheeled the frosty tubs of ice cream in a cheerful rickshaw across rutted, brick pavement to an awaiting mob.

The arrival of Ben and Jerry's confirmed Burlington's transformation, even as it sped it into a new, more vertiginous phase. Ben and Jerry were childhood friends in Merrick, New York, on Long Island, who had spent the 1970s spottily employed and looking for a way to make their mark. Their first idea was to open a bagel shop in Saratoga Springs, New York, a resort and college town not unlike a sanitized Burlington. After completing a correspondence course in ice cream making, the two men moved to Burlington and opened Ben & Jerry's Ice Cream and Soups—the soups because they feared that Vermont winters would leave them without a cold-weather profit stream.

This was 1978; by 1980, Ben & Jerry's, perched diagonally across from city hall, had set itself up as a kind of independent jurisdiction, keeping its own community calendar of arts programming. The mangy entrepreneurs soon managed to annoy Gordon Paquette and the city board of aldermen, when a "Fall Down" festival featuring jugglers, unicyclists, a frog-jumping competition, and Ben Cohen dressed as an Indian mystic spilled over into St. Paul Street. The following spring, when they wanted to show free outdoor movies projected onto the painted brick wall behind the shop, aldermen fought the idea. The shop wanted to kill the streetlights while the movies showed; the city said crime would run rampant in the shadows. There would "be free movies in Burlington over my dead body," one, very weirdly, proclaimed. Ben and Jerry collected signatures from the surrounding merchants, and the board relented. After a year on the scene, Ben and Jerry held arguably more cultural power on their corner of City Hall Park than the mayor could claim for himself, seated kitty-corner across the way.

Swirled irresistibly into it all was a distinct leftist politics made palatable to all by its pairing with delicious ice cream. The bulletin board at Ben & Jerry's was a cornucopia of goods and services of interest to young leftists: Murray Bookchin's ecology seminar; a die-in for Hiroshima; Reichean bodywork; Transcendental Meditation. The shop became a hub of information, including information about city politics. Ben and Jerry's cozy revolutionary politics all at once erased the view of many that leftists were scolds, or worse, vegans.

Yet, on the eve of Bernie's campaign to be mayor, people in Burlington began to whisper certain coded questions about Ben and Jerry. Weren't they "from New York"? Why was the ice cream so pricey? When Ben & Jerry's started selling pints over their counter, I remember smuggling Chunky Monkey into our freezer, where it sat, immorally small and expensive, next to the Sealtest Neapolitan. It was not hard to decipher any of this: Catholic kids on the playground, repeating the slurs they heard at home, referred to the brand by a range of anti-Semitic nicknames, including "Ben & Jewy's."

We Americans, Redux

What did the term *New York* mean when, in the summer of 1980, it pertained both to a troubled Black Burlingtonian who murdered a local white girl and to two friendly, mischievous white purveyors of ice cream? And what did it mean when it was again wielded against another New Yorker who rose up to become Burlington's mayor, only months later?

In his important study "Vermont and the Imaginative Geographies of American Whiteness," Robert M. Vanderbeck argues that the 2004 presidential candidacy of Howard Dean, the former governor of Vermont and scion of Park Avenue society, drew on "a particular whiteness discursively linked to notions of political liberality/progressiveness." In Burlington, Dean, who drove a battered Toyota truck and jogged in the early mornings along the train tracks on Lake Champlain, was accepted in ways that Ben and Jerry and Bernie Sanders, to say nothing of the Hines family, might never be. To Vermonters, Dean was the right kind of transplant: a WASP doctor, handsome and jovial, who had the compact athletic build of a serious mogul skier. Dean did not arrive in the state to join a commune. He had come to practice medicine. Dean's rise, as we will soon see, transpired alongside, and crossed, Bernie's.

But progressivism was becoming not merely an ideology; it was also a commodity, like whiteness itself. As Vanderbeck argues, "Vermont's whiteness was a marketing tool" in the state's promotional materials for a century or more, and progressive politics rose up naturally within whiteness, especially as it incorporated rural Yankee values and iconography. Meanwhile, for Blacks and other people of color, there seemed to be no role permitted in Vermont except to feature in news stories: the summer campers in Governor Phil Hoff's Vermont–New York Youth Project, harassed by local shop owners; the Reverend David Lee Johnson of Irasburg, fired on in the summer of 1968 by rednecks; Louis Hines Jr., in handcuffs, led away by two white cops.

The study of Burlington I pored over as a kid, Elin Anderson's *We Americans*, which was handed out to new depositors by a local bank in the '40s, was a study of whiteness—but also an artifact of whiteness. Vanderbeck points out the book's origins in Perkins's eugenics survey. Its author recognizes the "patience and faith" of Perkins in her acknowledgments, where she proudly cites its beginnings as a "brief annual report of the Survey." Blacks are mentioned once in the book, as a group Burlingtonians rejected as a type, in lieu of individual instances. When asked, "Whom do you prefer as a neighbor," the persons "questioned in detailed interviews" ranked their own ethnic groups first, then, of the other groups, first Yankees, then the Irish, French Canadians, Jews, and Syrians, with "the Negroes and the Chinese" last.

Ben and Jerry's white faces and sumptuous cones smoothed over, for many but not all, the threat of their difference as Jews and leftists. And as Ben & Jerry's grew, Vermonters began to see this latest export as quintessential, like George Aiken's wreaths and berries, and later, Bernie Sanders's politics. Those two products converged in 2016 and 2020, when Ben & Jerry's issued limited-edition flavors to commemorate Sanders's presidential campaigns.

Though Sanders traveled a path scouted for him by the ice cream impresarios, he was, in fact, never much of a Ben & Jerry's guy. Bernie likes the soft-serve delicacy Vermonters have eaten from time immemorial: the roadside creemee, coaxed upward into a collapsing peak.

20

The Downy-Filled Room

(Halloween Night, 1980)

Franklin Square, 1970s. *Burlington Free Press*

Back to the Future

When clips from the old public access cable program *Bernie Speaks: The Mayor's Show* went viral early in Bernie's second run for president in 2020, I started to see the faces of people I'd grown up with again, for the first time in decades, frozen as they were in the 1980s. Because the clips were so moving to me, I found the discourse surrounding them to be very annoying. Millennials and Gen Z Bernie supporters had constructed the historical Sanders as an adorably cantankerous young fogey, already the ranting uncle at the seder or birthday party. "That's him in the middle?" Mero, of the late-night talk show *Desus & Mero*, asks his cohost. "Damn, he was one hundred then?" Sanders was an athletic-looking forty-five, and sitting, elbows resting on knees, on top of a picnic table surrounded by summer campers.

In the viral clip, Sanders asks the kids, who range from five to fourteen or so, about life back home at Franklin Square. "What about drugs, is that a problem?" Bernie asks. This was 1987, during Ronald and Nancy Reagan's "War on Drugs." Ostensibly to discourage us from a life of addiction, classrooms were plastered with images of fresh, delicious-looking scrambled eggs in a cast-iron skillet, below the slogan "This is your brain on drugs."

One wiseacre sitting at Bernie's ankles pipes up, "I LIKE COKE!" to a chorus of groans and guffaws from the other campers. This was a stock joke in classrooms and playgrounds in the 1980s, meant to trigger in adults Bernie's stock response: "Who said that?"

The scoundrel—I think it's my friend John Abair's little brother Scott—then deals his final card, the standard coup de grâce: "What? I like Coca-Cola!"

"This is Bernie Sanders, the city's socialist mayor," Holly Otterbein wrote in *Politico*. And in the "at times startling" videos, "for some reason, he wants to talk about drugs."

I can supply a few reasons. The kids are at day camp at the Ethan Allen Homestead, a few miles from their troubled home of Franklin Square, because Sanders and his administration scavenged the money to run the camp while heavy machinery built and installed the long-promised playground back home. That playground was the fruit of a yearslong battle that Bernie joined in part as a shrewd political gambit, in part because the development brought to mind the opportunities that such public works provided to his family in 1950s Brooklyn.

If you watch the whole clip, you see Sanders acting as an educator. His method is the opposite of Nancy Reagan's see-ya-wouldn't-wanna-be-ya Just Say No campaign. Some kids lean on him. He tousles one boy's hair. He joshes with them and, when they become a little bananas, he sharpens his tone.

Sanders hands them tools for thought: "Are there any problems at Franklin Square?"

The kids, in unison: "NO."

"Does everybody have enough money?"

More quietly, the children reply, "No."

"And is that a problem?"

"Yes."

There are then lessons in Vermont history, some light class analysis, and a pep talk about the importance of reading.

"Be sympathetic to your counselors," Sanders tells the squirming kids. "I was a counselor once." It is easy to believe.

Then one kid exclaims, "You look like that guy in *Back to the Future*! Not

Michael J. Fox, the other one!": Christopher Lloyd, in the role of "Doc" Brown, the wild-eyed scientist who retrofits a DeLorean to travel back to the year 1955.

The "Bernie video" that delighted his fans in 2020 is also a time machine. For it was at Franklin Square, on Halloween night in 1980, that Sanders's political life started over.

RICHARD SARTELLE GREW UP near the granite quarries in Barre, enlisted at seventeen in the National Guard, and served in Korea, before moving with his young family to Franklin Square in 1971. Sartelle was only six years older than Bernie, but generationally and culturally, Sartelle belonged to the world of Eli and Dorothy Sanders. "Sartelle reminded Bernie of his father," Richard Sugarman told me. The cherubic face, the paunch, the cramped apartment, the antsy kids, the struggle for wages: Bernie saw Eli Sanders in his new friend, and deferred to him at times as would a son.

Sartelle loved a fight, the smaller the better. Sanders had followed some of his crusades: in 1971, Sartelle, who drove long-haul tractor trailers before taking disability, fought to keep the first local Dunkin' Donuts, on Shelburne Road, open all night, calling it a "lighthouse in the dark." He tied his cause to the rights of the truck driver and the night worker. In a small way, the city's enforcement of an old code forbidding twenty-four-hour businesses was a strike at the heart of the workingman. The city relented. Sartelle could celebrate his first political victory with a coffee and a glazed donut at four in the morning.

When Sartelle turned his attention to his own backyard, he made an alliance with Sanders that might have cinched Bernie's startling mayoral victory. Sanders drove out North Avenue to meet Sartelle through streets of tiny, inexpensive, and cheerful postwar ranches. These "Hauke houses" were developed by my friend Martha's grandfather, William Hauke Sr., a beloved and idealistic George Bailey figure. The New North End, where Sanders would eventually settle with Jane Sanders and their children, is the city's most conservative and suburban-seeming area by far. But Franklin Square, a snag in the Kodachrome optimism of the surrounding streets, seemed to Sanders, on first seeing it, more like a kennel than a housing development. Its residents reported to the *Rutland Herald* that they felt "caged" inside the tall chain-link fence surrounding their homes. Bernie reported to Sugarman that he'd seen "Third World poverty" at Franklin Square. The administration of Gordon Paquette had been given enough chances to make it right with Franklin Square. Sanders would get a playground done "if he had to build it himself."

Sugarman, the sworn foe of symbolic politics, was elated to hear Bernie's playground plan: here finally was a "practical, tangible, and winnable battle," he told his friend. Sanders thought back to the endless playgrounds and parks and courts in Brooklyn, a refuge from his dreary, tiny apartment. Bernie began to "talk all the time now about Brooklyn, the ingenuity of how it was put together," Sugarman told me. "The ball courts!" he kept repeating. Franklin Square's one basketball hoop was bent down nearly flush against the backboard. The sight of it inspired Bernie's simplest campaign promise, and the one that shaped my childhood most directly: if he became mayor, Bernie wanted "to give Burlington kids something to do."

Reagan's Inspiration

In the days leading up to the November 1980 general election, Burlington watched the news from Iran, where the release of the fifty-two American hostages held since November of 1979 seemed imminent. Ronald Reagan's campaign operatives, fighting back, spread the word that this release scheme was orchestrated by President Jimmy Carter as a cynical Election Eve ploy. Now the very mention of Iran and Carter in the same breath brought to mind, for many, the fiasco in the deserts of eastern Iran of the previous April, when eight American servicemen had died in a fiery crash during an aborted secret rescue mission. Reagan's people argued that Carter was bound to repeat that tragic failure with a political stunt. And so the "imminent" release of the American hostages was delayed until January 21, 1981, the instant Reagan took office: a backchannel from Reagan's team had intervened to delay for seventy-seven additional days, until the political advantage could accrue to their man.

Yellow ribbons, inspired by the Tony Orlando & Dawn song "Tie a Yellow Ribbon"—recorded years before about a man returning home from prison—were duly tied to every tree and utility pole in downtown Burlington. Since I was told by adults that "Carter was responsible" for the hostage crisis, I remember thinking that the yellow ribbons were expressions of support for Reagan. I had placed Carter somewhere in an intuited countercultural composition that included the Allman Brothers and Bob Dylan, names I had seen in my aunts' stacks of records. The youth culture in our home passed along underground channels, like magma or prairie dogs. When Reagan was shot in March of 1981, I returned home from fourth grade to a celebration in our den. It seemed odd to me, but my aunts were rooting for Reagan to perish from his injuries, so I joined in. We all munched chips together and cheered as the story unfolded. When my grandfather came in from the garage, drying his hands on a dish towel, we instantly became solemn and appropriate.

"Reagan had a lot to do" with Sanders's startling 1981 mayoral victory, according to Sugarman. It was true in several senses. The three-way 1980 presidential race among Carter, Reagan, and a popular independent, John Anderson, resulted in a landslide for Reagan statewide; in Burlington, though, it was a landslide for Carter. Statewide politics still tempted Bernie, but the city of Burlington was now the focus, and Reagan's performance in town provided Sanders with an up-to-date electoral map of the city. It took him inside the voting blocs in the wards in a detailed way. Because Burlington votes for mayor on Town Meeting Day in March, the general election results could be used as a navigation chart. Sanders and his advisers had four months to interpret those numbers. In that time, too, the revulsion over Reagan's election would only intensify Burlington's hard left turn. In one of the first elections held anywhere since Reagan's November victory, Burlington voters, proxies for anti-Reagan voters everywhere, would likely be turning out.

But so would the conservative Democrats who were attracted to Reagan's tax-cutting crusades. These "Reagan Democrats," a nationwide phenomenon, associated the Jimmy Carter's party with bureaucracy, inflation, and taxes. Sanders had his eye on Reagan's showing in the heavily Democratic Ward 2, where Gordon Paquette had once lived and served as city alderman, and Ward 3, where Sadie White was facing a tough primary election to keep her job as state representative. These neighborhoods were once the base of Paquette's working-class support. But the city was running deficits, and Paquette was widely expected to propose a steep property tax hike. If the specter of forfeiting their income to the federal government was enough to sway many lifelong city Democrats to vote for Reagan in November, those voters, faced with a city tax increase for declining services, might be in play for Bernie come March.

In short, although Sanders loathed his politics, Reagan "suddenly expanded the boundaries of what was politically possible," Sugarman told me. It dawned on Sanders and Sugarman during the late summer and early fall of 1980, when they often stayed up late listening to *The Larry King Show*, an all-night call-in show and the precursor to King's CNN program. King would answer the phone himself, greeting callers from Mobile, Dallas, Seattle, or Albany: "Hello, you're on the line." Studs Terkel thought King's show was "a composite of America"; King thought of his lonely callers in the small hours as a version of Walt Whitman's beautiful lists of American types: trappers, joiners, and clamdiggers; cabbies, truckers, stars.

Anyone might call in at any time. One night Milton Berle, the radio comedian, was on the line. Berle told King a story about seeing Reagan backstage at the Friars Club in the 1960s. "You know, Ronnie, you look like a president," Berle said to Reagan. "You should run!"

"This was a guy who could not keep his job as a spokesman for GE, and went on to sell Borax soap!" Sugarman told Bernie. Sanders shook his head.

"I don't know anything about politics. What am I supposed to do? How do I know what to do?" Reagan told Berle.

Berle shot back: "They have people who can take care of that."

A week or so later, Sanders called Sugarman in his UVM office and asked him to come over immediately. Bernie had put on the Peter Sellers film *Being There*, where Sellers plays a simple-minded estate gardener named Chance, who has only experienced the world by seeing it on TV; he rises by a series of picaresque turns and manipulations, until he ends up as president.

Bernie was pointing at the screen "the whole time" in silent amazement. "It's—fucking—Reagan!" Sanders enunciated.

Sanders, Sugarman said, "turned to me then and very abruptly asked me, 'What the fuck do I know about being the mayor of a city?'" Bernie "was worried he was Reagan, or the gardener, Chance."

Sugarman reminded him that to be Reagan was apparently not a political disadvantage. As for governing: "You'll do what everyone does, Bernard," Sugarman replied. "You'll improvise."

On October 23, the *Burlington Free Press* reported that the "historian and film maker" Bernard Sanders was "testing whether he can build a coalition of poor people, blue collar workers and university students for the March 1981 election."

Five men gathered a little more than a week later, on October 31, in the laundry room at Franklin Square: if not a smoke-filled room, "a Downy-filled room," as John Franco put it. Dick Sartelle arranged the venue, two miles and a world away from downtown Burlington. Outside, teenagers aimed Roman candles at each other. Inside, their parents fed quarters into the clothes dryers. A dog barked incessantly at the commotion. "Welcome to the poor part of town," Sartelle told the denizens of a different Burlington entirely.

Jim Rader had lost track of his old friend when Bernie called and invited him to the meeting. Rader was training in Montreal as a counselor for Vietnam veterans. This was the era of *The Deer Hunter*, of hard and lonely homecomings for men who, refusing to be forgotten, thereafter wore only their fatigues. "He's a Vietnam vet," my mom said of a friend's father when he put his fist through the windshield while we rode in his back seat. It meant, *Give him a chance, he's a work in progress*. Rader was moved to be there for these men. He had just helped to open Vermont's first VA-funded Vietnam veterans' rehabilitation center near Burlington. He regarded Bernie "at a distance, with some skepticism" that night.

Rader, Sugarman, Sartelle, and Bernie were joined by John Franco, Bernie's old Liberty Union sidekick, now rising as a hotshot public defender in

Burlington. Franco's name was all over the news the prior spring: he had taken on the high-profile case of one of five members of a motorcycle gang accused of raping two young women in a remote cabin in the woods near Williston. When his client was found guilty, Franco took to the bank of microphones, TV lawyer–style, and promised "to send an appeal to the Supreme Court that will curl its hair." If Franco was initially reluctant to help Bernie out, it might have been because he had his own political rise to consider.

There was still some mystery as to why the conclave had been summoned when Sugarman spoke up. He and Bernie had visited the city clerk's office and looked inside the results of Bernie's 1976 run for governor. The support was there, Sugarman said, especially in the poorer wards. Sugarman, laughing, said he "could personally confirm that Molly Wakowski of Ohavi Zedek, in Ward 2, was a lifelong Democrat, had voted for Bernie Sanders in '76, and was ready to do so again." Sanders had moved to Ward 2, to an apartment on North Union Street, especially to meet the neighbors there. Bernie spoke up about Sadie White, whose defeat in the Ward 3 primary turned her forever after against the Burlington Democratic machine. Sartelle gestured to the surroundings and promised "a bushel of votes" there at Franklin Square, in Ward 4. Franco, the UVM grad, told stories about working the dorms, one pungent doorway at a time, to register students in 1974 and 1976. Now a recent 1979 U.S. Supreme Court decision, *Symm v. United States*, affirmed the right of resident students to vote wherever they attended college. In Sugarman, Huck Gutman, and Mark Stoler, a political science professor, Bernie had a cadre of influential faculty on his side at a time when politics definitely turned up in the classroom. In the old folks' homes in Wards 2 and 3, the housing developments in Ward 4, and the dorms in Ward 1, Bernie's potential voters lived cheek by jowl. Registering them was as easy as going trick-or-treating.

That left Wards 5 and 6, the city's most prosperous neighborhoods. Ward 6, Burlington's Hill Section, bled into UVM; there were students renting in basements and carriage houses all throughout the district. Liberal professors bought fixer-uppers on the side streets. Some of the larger mansions on the hill hosted communes relocated from the forests. In one elegant home, Frank Kochman, publisher of the *Vermont Freeman*, had once lived with a large Philadelphia jazz ensemble, the house band at a summer-only lakeside joint on Malletts Bay, who took regular delivery of heroin from the back of a visiting VW campervan. Ward 6 presented a weird coalition, but it had promise.

Ward 5, the city's South End, was a heavily Irish, middle-class neighborhood, organized in part around Christ the King, a parish school and its grounds. Sugarman still lived in the ward, in the house on Caroline Street that he and Bernie had briefly shared. The neighborhood had always been a lock for Paquette. But Ward 5 was also home to Lakeside, where the mayor's most vocal opponents had organized against the Southern Connector. "Paquette has cousins in Lakeside," Sugarman told the group. "Even they hate him now." Sugarman suggested that Bernie "open a phone book, then get down to Lakeside, and by the way—maybe learn a little French."

When the men and women of Franklin Square roused for their daybreak shifts—coffee, exhaust, scanning headlights, cigarette smoke—the laundry room conspirators packed up and left. Bernie stopped the men, Columbo-style, as they wandered out: "One last thing," he said. "What the fuck happens if I win?"

Sanders invited Guma, now alienated by Bernie's rumored mayoral ambitions, to meet on November 7 at Fresh Ground Coffee House, where Guma and his friends were regulars. These days, Sanders rarely even blew through the store for a plain roll, but he wanted "to slay Guma in his lair," an observer remarked, and in full view of the restaurant's clientele: Burlington's small but growing organized left, a tightly constellated group of pacifists, nuclear freeze proponents, foes of foreign policy in Central America, along with a very small *New York Review of Books* professoriat working at UVM and Middlebury College. The Fresh Ground left was a formidable group, big enough to deny Bernie his opportunity if they so wished; but not big enough, not nearly, to go it alone in the election, since it had no organizing power among the poor. In Sanders's view, the Citizens Party had a low ceiling of support. It was Liberty Union all over again, but without the Vietnam draft to command people's attention.

There was limited small talk that afternoon. Bernie was "an immovable object," Guma told me. Guma's leftists would have to fall in line if they wanted to survive in Bernie's Burlington. Sanders had little regard for "the trust fund babies on the environmental left," and told his friends that Robin Lloyd's inheritance tarnished the whole movement. When Guma pointed out Bernie's lack of an organization or a donor base, Sanders brought up Dick Sartelle and Sadie White, two "real Vermonters with real problems."

"Honestly, he was such an asshole about it," Guma told me, after a pause.

Soon it became clear that Sanders had not come to negotiate. "All he said was, 'I think I'd make a good candidate,'" Guma told me. Then like a gambler anteing up, Sanders pushed his untouched mug of coffee toward the center of the table. It appeared it was time to go.

November: "the Norway of the year," Emily Dickinson wrote. Sanders and Guma exited the Fresh Ground together and went their separate ways, Bernie's hands jammed into his pockets, walking on the balls of his feet into the northern five p.m. dark.

21

"Burlington Is Not for Sale"

(Sanders for Mayor, November 1980–January 1981)

Bernie campaigns on Church Street. *Rob Swanson*

Campaign Manager

"I was totally done with Bernie in 1980," Nancy Barnett told me. "Too much. Always the same. Too much rah-rah. Too much Bernie!"

The conflicts in their working relationship—Barnett had continued to do "whatever research, weird rabbit holes" for Sanders—finally drove her to "overturn a picnic table on Bernie" at a Dairy Queen in the Old North End, to the horror of families standing by. "I was licking my wounds for years after," Barnett said. "There was no working with Bernie. He didn't—he didn't have a good set of emotional tools."

So when Sanders approached Barnett on Church Street and announced, "I'm running for mayor," Barnett knew just what he was proposing. "I said, stop right there. I'm not interested. I'll introduce you to Linda Niedweske, my cousin," adding, "she's tough." What Nancy meant was, "Linda could control Bernie."

Niedweske had arrived at the University of Vermont in 1973 from Westfield, New Jersey, and found a mentor in none other than Richard Sugarman. Though she was "into yoga, meditation, mind/body stuff," Sugarman encouraged her to make a study of her own Jewish faith. Niedweske, an animal sciences and religion major, befriended a Hasidic rabbi, but soon her own spiritual path took her into holistic health. On the side, she did some part-time administrative work for Sugarman and the religion department. "I could type," she told me.

By the late 1970s, the ideas and practices loosely organized under the term *new age*, including holistic healing, had evolved naturally out of recovery groups, which evolved naturally out of addiction—which Vermont, its hippie pilgrims now drying out in their mid-thirties, discovered in spades. What Erik Davis called "consciousness culture" began to exert real power and influence in Burlington in the 1980s. There was always an entrepreneurial dimension. On Church Street, the storefront that had once housed Jan's Shoes, where my grandfather worked before the war, now sold selenite monoliths and agate geodes for many hundreds of dollars. The city drew communities of unlikely small businesspeople: rebirthers, rolfers, channelers, crystal workers, and, mainly from a program at Goddard, Reichean mind-body practitioners. My aunt introduced herself under a new name; we all went with it, even, it appeared, my grandmother. I shared the impulse: there was trauma in the family, and my name carried it.

Niedweske had begun to make a little money giving holistic health classes and seminars around the state. In 1979, this entrepreneurial work took her to the rapidly changing Shelburne Farms, where she presented a talk on alternative diets as part of a program that included presentations in the formal tea room on auras, midnight meditation over candles in the Marble Room, and herbs for health in Lila Vanderbilt Webb's library, beneath the gilt-embossed volumes of Sir Walter Scott. Hundreds of enterprising seekers attended; dozens of microbusinesses were spawned.

Politics travels strange byways in the Queen City, and the Sanders campaign developed from a series of coincidences. Niedweske had found in her academic mentor perhaps the only Jewish mystic in American life who was also a trenchant hobby-strategist for a long-shot political talent. Richard Sugarman had discovered, in his student, the rare young person of spiritual range and openness with the shrewd this-worldly intellect, and the executive functioning of a future attorney. Niedweske is "the reason Bernie won," Sugarman said; Huck Gutman and Jim Rader told me very similar things.

(Niedweske, though, credits Sugarman.) Neither Sugarman nor Niedweske were pledged to any one political program. Niedweske had strong feelings "only about nutrition," she said, with a laugh. Sugarman's fascination with electoral minutiae was, he told me, mostly "a strange pastime." The genuine camaraderie among Sanders, Sugarman, and Niedweske is important to acknowledge as a factor in their successful campaign.

Sugarman called Niedweske a few days after the election in November of 1980, and asked her to meet him and an associate at the greasiest of spoons, Wesson's Diner on Shelburne Road, where "there was nothing I was tempted to eat." Bernie, who struck Niedweske as "serious, but not terribly intense," spoke little, as Sugarman laid out the situation. Burlington's overwhelming rejection of Vermont's presidential winner-by-a-landslide, Ronald Reagan, made it certain that the Citizens Party would seize the moment and draft its own candidates for the city election in March. Democrats would not caucus until the new year; if Sanders declared now, he would beat the Citizens Party to the punch and have a two months' head start on Mayor Paquette. Sadie White's powerful Ward 3 organization was already in touch with Sanders. Dick Sartelle was building a coalition of low-income voters in Ward 4. Gene Bergman was organizing the tenants' groups. A community organizer with outreach across the city, Phil Fiermonte, had phoned Sugarman. Niedweske accepted the men's pitch: "I was looking for a job," she told me. Sanders dropped two quarters on the Formica countertop, and left Wesson's accompanied by his chief aide and campaign manager. Now all he needed was a campaign.

On November 8, Sanders, alerting no one in his tight circle, called a press conference in the foyer of city hall and announced his candidacy for mayor. "If ordinary people are to survive in the coming years," he said, reading from a prepared statement, "it is absolutely imperative that we band together in an organized effort to take control of the institutions which influence how we live." The "we" was notable: Sanders presented himself as a regular working person, not a professional leftist. In hardly his first successful manipulation of the media, Sanders worked his *Free Press* backchannel to place his announcement as front-page news, and, the following day, to help with a report that Greg Guma, his potential rival on the left, would be sitting out the election, since he "did not wish to be in the position of dividing progressives." Guma announced that he wouldn't campaign for Sanders: he planned to take a winter vacation. "I don't think he represents what the majority of people want," Guma told the *Burlington Free Press*. Holding back his support was Guma's only remaining play.

Without a leftist challenger, the number Sugarman had in mind for a win was just 4,040 votes. "It seems doable," Bernie told Sugarman. "He's going to have to knock on every door in Burlington," Niedweske told Sugarman, when she heard that tantalizingly realizable sum.

The magic number was never imagined to be a majority. From the beginning, John Franco told me, the Sanders campaign was picturing a three-way race with Sanders eking out a bare plurality. Gordon Paquette would likely draw a challenger in the January 1981 Democratic caucus; with Sanders already in the race, the second-place Democrat might also hope for a plurality and decide to stay in. Were there opportunities here for political mischief in recruiting and supporting a city Democrat to challenge Paquette? "No," Sugarman told me, after what felt like a lengthy pause.

To win 4,040 votes, Sanders first needed to create in Burlington residents, many of them transient, interest *ex nihilo* in their city government. Turnout in Burlington's mayoral elections was traditionally scant, and Paquette had won all four of his terms by large margins as the consensus candidate of both Democrats and Republicans. Renters rarely voted; students did not vote. Many Burlington leftists—Guma and Lloyd were exceptions—thought in terms of national and global politics; the city of Burlington was a backdrop, a home base. The left-activist networks connected up elsewhere: New York, Havana, Quito. With Sartelle working independently in Franklin Square, and Sadie White nursing her grievance against the mayor in Ward 3, Niedweske got to work in the campaign's unofficial headquarters, her two-room apartment on Loomis Street in Ward 1. Bernie was hungry to organize, but four months out, he figured nobody in Burlington would agree to a meeting. Sugarman suggested to Sanders, "Why not begin with the true believers?" Sanders, bitter and skeptical, responded that if he wanted to lose, he might as well just rejoin Liberty Union.

When Sanders met with a dozen or so longtime supporters in the living room of Mark Stoler, the UVM historian, and his then wife, Jennie, an economist at Saint Michael's College, his fears were realized: there was unanimous, automatic support in the room. "Bernie could have announced he was training for the heavyweight boxing title," Sugarman told me. "It didn't matter. In that crowd, supporting Bernie in whatever he dreamed up was just what was done."

"Every one of us voted for you in every one of your Liberty Union runs," a member of the group told Bernie, expecting a show of gratitude.

Bernie winced, waving his hands frenetically: "This is not Liberty Union! You have to understand me. This is very different. We have a chance to win this."

NO ACTIVIST IN BURLINGTON, Vermont, in 1980 needed to read *Rules for Radicals* to know what it said. Saul Alinsky's treatise on organizing entered the bloodstream of the activist left soon after its publication in 1971. By the mid-1980s, Bygone Books on College Street overflowed with well-worn copies of these slim paperbacks. One tenet of Alinsky's book applied particularly to Burlington, and especially to the Sanders campaign: it was "rare" to find campus activists who "could organize a substantial number of students," and they were "utter failures when it came to trying to communicate with and organize lower-middle-class workers."

Bernie left the meeting with his UVM loyalists worried that in the zero-sum world of local politics, to attract one group was to repel another. Unanimous support in a professor's living room was in fact a baleful omen. UVM was regarded by much of Burlington as a foreign country, if not a hostile power. This was not merely a broad cultural or generational schism. The university's refusal to build housing adequate for its student population blighted much of downtown Burlington, as negligent landlords delivered leases to entitled teenage tenants. Around 1982, the home next to ours passed out of the hands of a big French-Canadian family and into a landlord's possession. Soon there were kegs on the porch, tapestries in the windows, and a junk pickup with Connecticut plates in the drive. I certainly didn't mind, and one high school summer I enjoyed a very intriguing, age-inappropriate flirtation with a UVM girl next door. Though my grandparents blamed Bernie Sanders for these trends, Sanders, the university's chief antagonist from the beginning, in fact took concrete steps to halt them.

The challenge, then, was to oppose the influence of the university while recruiting to his cause its politically energized faculty and student body—whom many working-class Burlingtonians perceived as an occupying force. The lessons of the University of Chicago in the 1960s, and of Bernie's fight against Vermont ETV in the late 1970s, came to hand: Sanders could oppose the corporate entity called the University of Vermont and its conservative board, while working with cells across its communities. But the problem remained that academics and students would not win the trust of Sadie's Ladies, or Dick Sartelle's neighbors, or the isolated poor in Lakeside, or the single mothers of Levi Sanders's friends in apartments on King Street.

Neither would a socialist. To the Paquette voters Bernie had to sway, socialism was synonymous with communism; and Ronald Reagan had revived the fear of communism in the waning days of the Cold War to rally patriotic voters to his side. It was crucial to Bernie's strategy that he sink socialism as an abstract idea or affiliation, while surfacing its powerful class critique. It is a sign of how little his rival engaged with him that Paquette didn't red-bait until late in the race, too late for the message to get through to voters. It wasn't until the days after March 3 that many Burlingtonians realized they had elected a socialist to be their mayor.

A Visit to Mrs. White

Outside the few blocks where he'd lived and the campus of UVM, Bernie Sanders knew well only the bowling lanes and pickup courts of Burlington. Possessing a nature not naturally gregarious, he counted only a few connections to the neighborhoods where he needed to make his name. So Sanders went to see Sadie White at her home in Ward 3. A Christmas tree sagged under the weight of sympathy cards from White's constituents. Mrs. White had been defeated in the Democratic primary to keep her legislative seat after fifteen years of service. Her supporters were dumbfounded. White filed a formal complaint against one of her opponents, Alfred Couture, for an offense that White had been accused of regularly over the years: rigging the absentee vote. Mayor Paquette and his allies in city hall worked against White and cheered the outcome. She was now contemplating her next move, and had told her friends that it would not be retirement.

At seventy-nine, White was almost exactly twice Bernie's age, but Sanders was "unusually natural around her, teased her," his friends say. Though Midwood, Brooklyn, and the Old North End were worlds apart, Sanders and White shared a survivalist ethos and a directness learned the hard way. White, who was childless, would ask Sanders, whose parents had died so many years before, to complete little tasks she'd saved up for him to do—a leaky faucet, a torn window screen—while they talked about the state of his potential support in the ward. Bernie puttered around the small kitchen as White conveyed what was on her neighbors' minds. A looming property tax increase might drive more elderly people out of their homes: Mrs. Limoge had already packed up her house; Arlene Bilodeau collected her photos and keepsakes long before she had imagined selling. These spurned old people were lifelong Democrats. Most knew Mayor Paquette personally, but these days, they considered him to be a stranger.

White told Bernie that she had several friends who'd left the neighborhood and taken apartments in a new subsidized high-rise building in Burlington's urban renewal zone, Cathedral Square. Sanders had wondered about this stark white slab, the second-tallest building in Vermont. The property was built as part of a grand deal with the Episcopal Diocese of Burlington, when the church swapped parcels with the city after its historic Cathedral of St. Paul burned in 1970. Sanders, still learning the basic history of his city he was nevertheless campaigning to lead, asked White to organize a meeting and escort him to Cathedral Square.

White and Sanders met the small group of Sadie White's old constituents in the building's sky-view cinder-block community room, "Top of the Square." Out the big plate glass windows, you could see the band shell in Battery Park and the little row of workers' cottages on Front Street, where Bernie had lived in the early 1970s. The new glass-and-steel Radisson Hotel next door reflected an expanse of parking garages and construction lots where these old men and women in the room had grown up. As kids, some had picked dandelions in those fields for five cents a bag, to deliver to the kitchen door of Bove's restaurant for the old Italian ladies' traditional salads.

Out the window, Lake Champlain and the broad, purple vista of the Adirondack Mountains established the unexpected agenda for the meeting. The spartan ninth-floor community room offered the most dramatic up-close view in Burlington of the city's derelict waterfront. Here was an entirely new prospect on Lake Champlain. The view, followed from north to south along the shore, told the story of generations of successive industrial collapse. The city's steep banks were gouged in the nineteenth century for landfill to create broad railbeds along the marshy shore of Burlington harbor, for the storage of lumber and stone. The railways emerging from the scrub forest, then declined in the first half of the twentieth century, yielding their loads to container ships riding Lake Champlain's broad waterways toward canals at its southern end. The railways then leased their dormant railyards to petroleum companies, whose hulking barges delivered their cargo to newly constructed massive petroleum storage tanks for winter keeping. These tanks, some eighty-three in all, were drained and abandoned once highways were built in the 1950s; oil now sloshed across the Northeast in the backs of tractor trailers. The forsaken tanks leaked their contaminants; the mud beneath them, saturated with fuel, sometimes ignited spontaneously. The largest structure visible on the waterfront, the Moran Municipal Generating Station, had coughed coal smoke into the surrounding neighborhoods for decades: nobody downwind of the plant wanted to hang their laundry out. A huge, dark, terraced structure, the Moran plant resembled a Mesopotamian ziggurat or a giant step stool to nowhere.

Moving southward, a small public boat works shared a cove with the city's antiquated sewage facility, which shed untreated waste into Lake Champlain; nearby, the Pine Street Barge Canal and its drawbridge, where Louis Hines had lived in an area soon to be condemned as a federal Superfund site. Then the eye, readjusting to magnificence, found the pines of Juniper Island and the pristine shores of Shelburne Bay.

IN THE REAGAN ERA, it was widely assumed that the poor vicariously enjoyed extravagant displays of wealth. Burlington's plan was to build three hundred luxury condominiums, tens of thousands of square feet of high-end retail, and a health club on the Burlington waterfront, to give the poor in the adjacent neighborhoods and the elderly in Cathedral Square a front-row seat. Wealthy tourists who had once zipped through the city on their way to the traditional *Vermont Life* villages at its fringe now flocked to downtown Burlington from Montreal, Boston, and New York. The idea was to get them to Burlington on new highways, then persuade them to stay for gleaming lakefront lofts at a fraction of the cost of condos back home, elegant cafés offering city fare, and shelter for their BMWs in a warren of private parking garages. The plan welcomed members of the public to a puny one-acre park, about the size of a typical city dog park, if they could find it in the hedge maze of private amenities.

A powerful local businessman, Antonio Pomerleau, stood patiently by as the Triad Group, a pair of Montreal preppies who kept sailboats on the lake, saw their deal to develop the property snag in a thicket of arcane permitting and regulatory details. These details only he, Antonio Pomerleau, a veteran of Burlington politics and business, could untangle. When the Canadian sailors finally gave up, Pomerleau bought out their contract and negotiated a hold on the purchase of a prime parcel from the Central Vermont Railway. Control of the Burlington waterfront now rested in the hands of the city's most powerful citizen, backed by old friends in the local banks and by Mayor Gordon Paquette. A network of trusted contractors looked forward to breaking ground. Burlington's twentieth-century boom, anticipated since the 1950s, was finally here. The business and development communities contemplated a city on another scale entirely for New England's West Coast.

But the city's poor and elderly residents were, as usual, in the city's way, and now they were angry. Sanders got an earful from the men and women of Cathedral Square who lived on fixed incomes, and who already had to pick their path across the construction rubble on Church Street to find a pharmacy still in business; they would now have to contend with a high-rise condominium building emerging before their eyes, assembled block by block to obstruct their sunsets.

Sanders left the meeting shocked by the cruelty of the waterfront plan, which at that point seemed imminent, inevitable. But Bernie also recognized the opportunity before him. Here was an issue that all of Burlington had started to rally behind. He called Richard Sugarman to brainstorm a new campaign slogan.

A vision of Burlington as seen from that sky-high community room began to guide Sanders's strategy. The planned expressways had spawned dozens of community groups along their proposed track. The waterfront and Church Street Marketplace developments had turned the city's elderly against Mayor Paquette. The flashpoint was a property tax increase widely viewed as a subsidy for developers. "I won't take credit for it," Sugarman told me, taking credit for it. "But I said to Bernard, let's use 'Burlington Is Not for Sale.'"

IN THE FALL OF 1980, Mayor Paquette finally visited Lakeside. He wasn't exactly campaigning; he had not declared an intention to run for a fifth term, and still nurtured dreams of securing a federal position like postmaster to crown his political career, before retiring to play golf among the pelicans in Florida. The biannual March election had become merely a chore, like renewing a driver's license; Paquette had won more than 70 percent of the vote in the 1979 race. Lakeside was once a strong core of his support.

Lakeside was a company neighborhood, its small homes and tenements constructed by the Queen City Cotton Company to house French-Canadian workers. Old photos depict baseball games and First Communions. They do not show accidents at the loom, a woman's hair and scalp pulled off in its heavy machinery, or the waves of work stoppages and layoffs. To be furloughed without pay by your landlord, who nevertheless expects to collect his rent, is a recipe for unrest. In 1937, after decades of turmoil, the Queen City Cotton Company closed, citing the promise of "a cheaper, unorganized workforce in the Southern states." Some Lakeside tenants purchased their homes from the mill, but without steady employment, foreclosures became the rule.

By 1980, General Electric was manufacturing sophisticated weapons systems on U.S. Department of Defense contracts in the old cotton mill building. GE employed few Lakeside people. The old neighborhood, bounded by enormous Mobil Oil tanks to its south and by a Superfund site to its north, was connected to the city by a single, narrow road, prone to flooding. The residents of Lakeside had become enraged.

Paquette met Lakeside's residents at the neighborhood watering hole, the Saint John's Club, a squat barracks on a reef above the lake. Inside, cigarette smoke, Labatt's in bottles, and pine paneling; outside, lawn chairs, dragonflies, sunsets. The club rented out its facilities for banquets and weddings, but to visit you had to breach that dark, pungent sanctum on the way to the back lawn, where the bright balloons and cake were stationed. Paquette was prepared for questions about the Lakeside access road, a steep U dipping under the railroad tracks that became the neighborhood swimming pool after every heavy rainfall. Kids loved the flooded road, where they played Marco Polo in the shoulder-deep water; but their grandparents heading to Mass, or their parents setting out for the morning shift, were cut off from Burlington for days at a time. After dickering for years, Paquette was finally ready to bring before the voters a bond to repair Lakeside Avenue. The mayor had come to the Saint John's Club with good news.

The little access road was a sop. Repair it now, Paquette and his advisers agreed, and Lakeside would forget that Burlington was planning to run a major highway through their backyards. But the residents of Lakeside had not forgotten. Paquette was completely blindsided by the anger he encountered that day at the Saint John's Club, which had been harnessed by his chief antagonist, Joan Beauchemin; she had organized all of Lakeside against the plan, and she'd been given Bernie Sanders's number. "It's putting us in a corner and we'll never get out of here," Rachel Jodoin, a third-generation Lakeside resident, told the mayor. Residents worried about neighborhood children crossing the busy highway at grade. They pushed Paquette to guarantee that overpasses would be part of the design. "Will there have to be a death before something is done?" Jean St. Peter asked the mayor.

There already had been one, and it was on everyone's minds. Near where the Southern Connector was planned, at the corner of Home Avenue and Shelburne Road, a cheerful boy one grade ahead of me was struck by a passing motorist and killed just months before the meeting at the club. The *Burlington Free Press* ran a front-page photo of his small, untied white sneaker left behind on the blacktop. On our playground, it was said that Brett was trying to reach home after "getting an ice cream." The boy's sister Beth, a year below me in school, was the first person I ever saw grieve: I remember how we all solemnly lined up, like Little Leaguers after a game, and touched her shoulder, or lightly hugged her, or shook her hand. We were instructed by the nuns to say something about God's grace. I recall that she seemed very lonely on the playgrounds in the months that followed.

A Neighborhood Movement

By the fall of 1980, Bernie's little campaign seemed ready to rise on a powerful tide of more than a dozen independent neighborhood groups that had formed in response to the city's broken promises. When word of this uprising spread nationally, talented young people working for a federal program,

Volunteers in Service to America (VISTA), began to stream into the poorest areas of the city, organizing for tangible, small improvements: a Stop sign, a spring green-up, tulips, a new basketball hoop. Some of these activists linked up with advocacy groups. The Bread and Law Task Force, Bernie's old employer, had fought successfully for school lunch in Burlington schools. Now Gene Bergman's PACT was working to place a rent control measure on the March ballot, and several of the tenants' groups, organized by Phil Fiermonte, planned to confront the mayor to demand that their representative be appointed to the city's public housing authority.

The mayor got "more than his usual coffee and muffins" at Nectar's that morning, as the *Free Press* put it. Dick Sartelle handed Paquette the group's demands on a picket sign. The mayor, stubbing his cigarette out on a saucer, blurted out his defense, while Nector Rorris, the proprietor, who looked like Mario from the popular arcade game *Donkey Kong*, ushered the unruly tenants out of his establishment, then refilled the mayor's trembling mug. Sanders saw the news of "the Burlington Tea Party" that evening and called a meeting with Bergman and Fiermonte. The meeting apparently went well: Fiermonte stayed with Bernie until 2017, retiring as his longest-serving aide. Bernie's campaign message, "Burlington Is Not for Sale," was easily customized to the individual interest groups. The energy for a small decentralist revolution, deeply resistant to the concentrated power of city hall, was brewing in Burlington.

Now Murray Bookchin was advertising his cautious support for his old sparring partner. "I am seeking direct democracy," Bookchin told Jack Barry one morning on the air, explaining his support for Sanders. "I think we have an opportunity here in Burlington."

Barry seemed convinced. "Murray Bookchin, Burlington's own Thomas Paine, wants to return the power to the people!"

But Bookchin was also putting Bernie on alert. If Sanders took city hall with the neighborhood movement's support, the neighborhoods would be watching as Sanders assembled a government. Bookchin had studied the left, and worried that Bernie was "more committed to accumulating power in the Mayor's Office than in giving it to the people." Bookchin praised the "pepper mix of old Vermonters and new professionals" in the Queen City, and called to mind its "lingering, Libertarian Yankee tradition" against a growing "corrosive, authoritarian corporate reality." "Burlington Is Not for Sale" meant, to Bookchin, "that the city, though not on the auction block, has a genuinely high price tag."

So Bookchin, a natural guru playing the role of disciple, sought out an ally in the great theorist of the New England town meeting, Frank Bryan, at his office in UVM's Old Mill. Bryan "heard this clumping from the two

Murray Bookchin, 1980s. *Courtesy Debbie Bookchin*

stairs, clomp clomp, and in walks this guy. He had on a black leather jacket." The two men, an anarchist from the Bronx and a libertarian from Newbury, Vermont, hit it off, and began a careful study of Burlington's neighborhoods with the goal of draining power away from city hall and back into the six wards. Bookchin wanted to undermine the centralized power of the mayoral machine. That made him Sanders's wary ally during the 1981 campaign. It made him Bernie's bitter nemesis thereafter.

These were the waning years of the Fresh Ground Coffee House, the collective that Bookchin and his friends had founded in 1971. Over soup, Bookchin was telling friends that Bernie reminded him of the guys he knew back at the foundry in the Bronx, where to be a leftist was seen as "macho." His politics, to Bookchin, amounted to mere "bread and butter socialism." Bookchin seemed to sharpen his own Marxist-anarchist-utopian position as Sanders rose: soon, the fiery Bookchin would tell his followers that Sanders's politics had done little more than "rationalize the marketplace." Stirring his own networks to support Bernie, he nevertheless sounded a warning note. Bernie's "well known paranoia and suspicious reclusiveness," Bookchin would soon write, "beclouds the more important fact that he is a centralist."

Sanders and Sugarman ran into Bookchin one freezing night in the winter of 1980 coming out of Bove's restaurant. Sugarman, the philosopher, always checked to see if Bookchin had his talismanic copy of Hegel's *Phenomenology of Spirit* in a leather pouch dangling from his belt. Bookchin flashed the cover and laughed. Bernie was in a great hurry, since as usual he lacked a proper winter coat. "The anarchists are behind you, comrade!"

Bookchin told the shivering "bread and butter socialist" as Sanders bolted away, hands jammed into his corduroys. The expression of support masked a threat: Bookchin and his followers were indeed "behind" Sanders, keeping a watchful eye on his political evolution.

The important detail in this scene, though, is the restaurant itself. As customers streamed out into the frigid night, a political opportunity was taking shape inside. Bove's was as close to a people's commissary as any restaurant Burlington has ever had, then or since: in one booth, you might find Murray Bookchin; in another, a group of nuns in habit; along the back wall, the Burlington High School girls' basketball team. Old, reliable Bove's, the comfort of the workingman, had quietly collected political power for decades, and was about to spend it in Burlington's dawning progressive era.

22

At Bove's

(Burlington, December 1980–February 1981)

Dickie Bove during the dinner rush, 1980s. *Jym Wilson*

Lasagna Night

The gooey square of lasagna dissolving on a spatula in my poem "Blueprint" was not created by the Lord for my ninth birthday, however divine it tasted; it was takeout created by the Bove brothers of Pearl Street, whose classic Italian American restaurant fed Burlington for decades. The restaurant's unofficial charter keyed the price of a plate of basic spaghetti to half the hourly wage of its lowest-paid employee: the overflowing portions could feed two, at half the price of their competitors. Bove's pink and green neon sign lit up the snowy Burlington nights all through the campaign winter of 1980–81. Sanders and his advisers often lined up on Wednesdays for lasagna night, plotting their moves in a booth under the room-length mural of Venice's Grand Canal.

Richard J. "Dickie" Bove, his brother Fiore "Babe" Bove, and eleven siblings grew up in the restaurant, a four-burner operation downstairs from their crowded family apartment in an old-fashioned Burlington house. The restaurant was inextricable from the city's history. Everyone could tell you that it opened the day Pearl Harbor was attacked, and, three years later, fed the returning GIs and their families at homecoming celebrations all across the city. In the late 1940s, Babe Bove installed the city's first TV set behind the bar and wired it to a one-hundred-foot-high antenna, to gather Yankees games from a faint signal diffusing out of Schenectady. Burlingtonians crowded around the bar to watch the dim ghost of Joe DiMaggio cleave the static as he rounded the bases on that Bove's TV.

Urban renewal scattered the restaurant's clientele and left it standing on the lip of a crater. This too was seen as a sign of Bove's almost supernatural hold on the city. The bulldozers approached the shiny front door, saw their reflection, and turned around; everything on the south side of Pearl Street, across the street from Bove's, was demolished; on the north side, staring into the abyss of rubble, Bove's and everything on its side of the line was spared. What dark bargain had the Boves struck with city hall to halt those bulldozers? The Bove brothers fed Burlington's politicians plates of mostaccioli, five-cent glasses of beer, and, after hours, whiskey, cigars, and city gossip. Bove's was simply too valuable to lose.

But Bove's did not remain a politically neutral watering hole. The brothers needed a stake in city politics; their restaurant sat next to a parking lot owned by the city of Burlington at the northern terminus of Pine Street, the major roadway running north through Burlington from I-89. You could draw a straight line from the exit ramp of I-89 along Pine Street and through the Bove's parking lot, to connect up again with the northern spur of the highway. The city dreamed every night about that parking lot.

So, the political banter at Bove's gradually became a little edgier, more partisan. Babe Bove was the state legislator who nearly beat Phil Hoff for the Democratic nomination in 1971, during Bernie's first Liberty Union campaign. Babe's little brother Dickie was a city alderman for several terms during the 1960s. The Boves remained arbiters of city politics, but Mayor Gordon Paquette, once a regular, hadn't been by to tithe in years. He didn't dare: when Pine Street, which delivered customers by the carload to Bove's from points south, was blocked off in the 1970s for the Burlington Square Mall, it was seen as a strike against the family. Bove's watched its business dip; and Dickie, a short, round man cinched in the middle by his apron string, began to denounce the mayor regularly and loudly, for everyone to hear, from behind his steaming cauldrons of sauce. Before I knew who "Paquette" was, I heard my grandparents as they unwrapped the takeout spaghetti, sharing the mayor's latest outrage they'd heard in line at Bove's.

By 1980, then, the Boves had a modest, fragrant resistance operation stationed at Burlington's cultural crossroads, serving a steady flow of patrons that included cops, high school students, UVM professors, hippies, city workers, and the elderly people from Cathedral Square across the way, including many of Sadie White's old neighbors. I ate at Bove's once with four nuns in habits, and next to us was the outlandish local rhinestone cowboy Rick Norcross and his band, the Nashville Ramblers, all in ten-gallon hats. Bernie Sanders came for the lasagna—but he stayed for the cultural amalgam.

IN THE SUMMER OF 1980, Dickie Bove became an unlikely national political celebrity. As an elected delegate for President Jimmy Carter, Bove kept an eye on the economy from his station behind the stove. Out his window, he saw lines forming, not for his food, but for unemployment benefits at the government building across the street. His doubts about Carter's presidency were no longer possible to suppress, and Bove announced that he would attend the 1980 Democratic National Convention in New York City as an unaffiliated delegate: the "pudgy" restaurateur had "developed a hearty appetite" for attention, read a typical news story. In New York, with national media following him, Bove shook Teddy Kennedy's hand in a pew at St. Patrick's Cathedral, then took a call from "someone named Lyndon Larouche." Bove was now angling for a Ted Kennedy/Jesse Jackson ticket. A media tour ensued; all of Burlington watched with amazement as Dickie Bove, one of the best-liked people in town, was interviewed on NBC News.

Brought to heel by the Vermont Democratic Party, Dickie Bove finally fell in line and cast his vote for Jimmy Carter. But life back in the kitchen now seemed a bit boring, and, beginning in the fall of 1980, not long after Sanders announced his candidacy, Bove began to discuss the idea of running against Mayor Paquette in the city's Democratic caucus in January. Sanders egged Dickie on. John Franco had said from the beginning that Bernie could only win in a three-way race. There was no chance that Bove could beat Paquette in the caucus with the city Democratic machine entirely committed to the mayor. But with Republicans refusing to draft their own candidate, what were the odds that Dickie might enter the race as an independent?

"My father liked Bernie a lot," Mark Bove emphasized to me. But he disliked Paquette more.

THE CLICHÉ "to build a coalition" is a mixed metaphor. "Coalition" is related to the word *coalesce*; a coalition is the result of an organic process where elements "grow up" or "grow tall," not as stand-alone entities, but "together." There is no builder in the equation, no architect, no mastermind; the reactions that cause coalitions to form derive from shifting bonds among people and groups. Politicians can catalyze these reactions, but not control them. A coalition might not even be aware of itself as a formal body; coalitions are not built, they are revealed.

In December of 1980, Bernie sent a five-page press release to the local papers and broadcast networks. "The Independent Coalition's primary aim is to make Burlington city government responsive to, and run by, the average citizen, rather than the real estate developers, and their allies, who presently control it." The "coalition" at this point had grown to include a group of UVM allies, including Richard Sugarman, a philosopher, and Joyce Livak, a nutritionist; Richard Sartelle, the erratic hothead who had announced as a candidate for Ward 4 alderman; Sadie White, running for alderman in Ward 3 as a Reagan-style tax slasher; a group of ideologically aligned individuals whose feelings Bernie had hurt, including Greg Guma and Robin Lloyd; Jim Rader, busy counseling vets, when not devising word games and researching the life of Ezra Pound; John Franco, obstreperous, loose-lipped, and likely to offend; and neighborhood rights groups and their organizers, like Phil Fiermonte and Gene Bergman, who operated scrupulously outside the campaign for fear of dividing the working-class Burlingtonians they sought to assist. But the coalition was slowly, imperceptibly expanding: Bergman, then working as a press tender at the *Burlington Free Press*, noted that "the security guards there were all Bernie people from early on."

Sanders's press release promised to "target issues including the $77 million Medical Center redevelopment plan, a city tax reappraisal, Lake Champlain waterfront development and city worker pay." The statement highlighted two men by name: Gordon Paquette and the wealthy developer Pomerleau, whose plan for luxury condominiums on the waterfront had Paquette's support. Sanders challenged Paquette to debate him, and promised "to knock on hundreds and hundreds of doors" before the March 3 election, less than three months away. Bernie's announcement again reiterated that "this was different" from Liberty Union; not a high-minded "educational campaign" or a leftist prank on the electorate. The papers printed quotations from Sanders's announcement at length. An influential anchorman, WCAX's Richard Gallagher, a gravel-voiced local Walter Cronkite, took notice, and invited Sanders on. Jack Barry decided it was time to have

Bernie on his call-in program. Jim Rader ran into Bernie and Linda Niedweske at the Burlington Bagel Bakery, next to the Greyhound bus terminal, and Sanders was "beaming." "I feel like we have a chance to win this," he told his old friends, a month or so out from Election Day.

The campaign, now in its active phase, was entirely coordinated out of Niedweske's two-rooms. "We did everything out of my apartment," she told me, "soliciting, phone calls, small group meetings. If you needed fliers, you rang my doorbell, and I handed you fliers, brochures. Clipboards—I had so many clipboards."

Niedweske also handled donations. "There wasn't much at first," but then donations began to trickle in, a ten-dollar check, or cash jammed in an envelope with a little note. There were five-dollar bills in Christmas cards with March of Dimes return address labels. A fifth-grade class sent tidings, but no money. Some donors itemized their complaints: loud bars, potholes, road salt, delinquents in the alleyways. Sanders took note of how much frustration he stood to inherit from Burlington's voters. Beginning in January of 1981, "we knocked on practically every door in Burlington," Niedweske said, "over and over, until we had a response." Alan D. Abbey, a *Burlington Free Press* reporter who often accompanied Sanders as he slogged his way across the frozen city, recalled the experience years later:

> Time after time, I saw the same result, especially in the city's working-class Old North End. The home's resident, standing in the small vestibule known in Vermont as a mud room, eyed the visitor warily. Bernie's otherness was obvious. The stentorian tone of his Brooklyn accent was decidedly unlike the soft, French-inflected Vermont twang of native Burlingtonians. His rumpled clothes, mop of unruly hair, and tilted eyeglasses gave him the appearance of an absent-minded professor. With only a gruff introduction and hunched into his cloth coat against the biting cold, Bernie would launch into a short speech: Burlington's corrupt politicians helped only their friends. They were in the pockets of local millionaires.

Sanders found "unlikely allies" behind almost every door he approached, according to Abbey. Of course that is an exaggeration; nearly five thousand people eventually voted for his rivals. But "Burlington Is Not For Sale" appeared to have immediate emotional resonance among Burlingtonians of all stripes, who, as Abbey wrote, "felt powerless to stop" Pomerleau's waterfront plan. One elderly woman broke down in tears as she told Sanders she had worked on the paddle-wheel steamer *Ticonderoga* in the 1940s, dealing blackjack on sunset casino cruises. She wanted the lake to remain just as she remembered it. Another man had just returned from his shanty inside the breakwater, ice fishing for northern pike. The thought of luxury housing offended him: "The lake is for the people," he told Sanders, in a French accent.

258 Colchester Avenue

Not every household harbored an ally-in-waiting, or even a willing listener. But in David Clavelle, whose family and mine had been intertwined in Burlington schools and parishes for generations, Bernie found a Burlingtonian who could see the old neighborhoods in generational detail and help him micro-target his approach. Clavelle, an aide to Senator Patrick Leahy, was "the best retail politician I've ever met," Richard Sugarman told me. "David made all the tactical decisions late in the campaign," Linda Niedweske said. Clavelle was "a mastermind," "a savant," and, owing to his work in Washington, "a true political operative, Bernie's first." Clavelle knew the city; but perhaps more importantly, the city knew him and his family.

Clavelle now lives on a mesa outside of Denver, but when we spoke, we connected the Burlington dots. There were at least six Clavelles—David had lost count of the cousins—at Rice Memorial High School in the 1960s, along with six Delormes—my mother and her five surviving siblings. The two families go back at least to the Winooski mills, where our ancestors worked side by side in the 1910s. Clavelle's family rose in the dense urban blocks of Winooski, a mile from our home across the river in Burlington. Working as a staffer in Leahy's Senate office in Washington, Clavelle "got wind of Bernie's transformational campaign" back home. He took a leave from Leahy and returned to Burlington. I wanted to know, from David, how he helped Bernie reach working-class, culturally conservative families like his and mine. "I just said to knock until they answered, and listen to their concerns," Clavelle, who tends to understate his impact, replied.

I am aware of at least one household in Burlington that did not answer the door when Sanders and Niedweske knocked on a bright afternoon in January of 1981. The aluminum-sided white colonial at 258 Colchester Avenue was better kept than its neighbors, with a pair of young crab apple trees flanking its front door. Two figures with clipboards approached the home up a short walkway, then disappeared under its porch. Then, the tense exchange that launched my curiosity about Bernie in the first place, and out of which this book flows: from the kitchen, my grandmother's calling out to my grandfather, "There's someone at the door"; the creak of his recliner swiveling, and his booming voice: "Don't open the door—*it's Sanders*!"

The doorbell rang a second time; there was a loud rapping; then Sanders, the voice unforgettable, called out, "Hello? Hello?" before dropping his literature in the mailbox and retreating. I followed from my second-floor bedroom windows as Sanders and his aide made their way next door, where the neighbor answered the door and stood politely by as Bernie made his pitch. When we spoke forty-two years later, I confirmed with Linda Niedweske that she'd been the sidekick who stood at my front door that day. She covered much of Ward 1, her home turf, with Bernie.

Bernie and Linda had their work cut out for them making contact here. It was a rare occurrence, and to be feared, to hear our doorbell ring. Our front door was rarely breached, except by my grandparents' dwindling set of bridge friends: Dr. and Mrs. Cacavo; Henry and Mrs. Granger; Elizabeth Tilley, a widow; the O'Connors. On Sundays, Uncle Esau and Aunt Arlene. Uncle Philip and Aunt Marge and my cousins, their sons Ian and Luke, still sometimes came by for rushed summer barbecues. After a few swings of the Wiffle bat and a paper plate of jello salad, it was always "back to the woods" for them in their orange VW Thing, and the crickets reclaimed their time.

Our frozen household had inspired a migration to Florida, where my uncle Mark, a charismatic, handsome football standout at UVM, had somehow come into ownership of a society watering hole known as 264. This happy development was nevertheless almost surreal, and I'm not sure anyone asked the details. But soon "the restaurant" became a draw for my three aunts Susan, Paula, and Janet, who, one by one, traveled south from Burlington to work as waitresses and managers at 264, calling home with stories of their illustrious clientele: Richard Gere, Jacqueline Bisset. The restaurant kept secrets; Ted Kennedy partied there. This being the 1980s, the food at 264 faced stiff competition for space on the mirrored tabletops.

With everyone scattered, 258 Colchester Avenue had begun to shadow over with a dark, prayerful Catholicism that made conversation scarce. On one side of our property, Sandy was thrashing her boys; on the other, a family like ours, French-Canadian Catholics with many kids, offered me some refuge. I became close friends with a teenager I'll call Darren. I was not allowed to have Darren, or any friend, inside the house, so Darren and I, seventeen and nine, mostly wandered in the woods. It was a strange relationship, and not one I entirely understand to this day. I was expected to be completely loyal to Darren, to obey his every command. His high school friends were not under any circumstances to see us together. These mysterious rules were enforced by strange punishments. Once, when I interrupted Darren and some older boys smoking pot, Darren made me construct for penance a small diorama of heaven out of a shoebox and cotton balls.

One curious story stands out. Because I lacked a father or siblings, I suppose, Darren asked me one afternoon if I knew how babies were made. We were in the woodshed behind my home, throwing steak knives against the woodpile. I'm not sure how I responded, but Darren then retrieved from his bedroom a stack of magazines. I still do not have conceptual categories for what I was shown, but I am fairly certain that these were not run-of-the-mill porn glossies, *Playboy* or even *Penthouse*—though how would I have known? The women in the photos seemed to be in pain, as I remember; there was some kind of rope around one girl's back, and in another image, a woman's legs seemed to be bent behind her neck. The images were terrifying; the scenario there in the woodshed was truly weird. I began to cry, and Darren, more angry than sympathetic, ordered me, under strict vows, never ever to tell a soul, and especially not his high school friends.

These were the kinds of circumstances that Sanders and Niedweske met, or didn't meet, behind the locked door of 258 Colchester Avenue. But as a result of seeing these interlopers turned away, I remember becoming interested in Sanders just at the moment the 1981 campaign caught a tailwind. I was ten; but I was minimally sapient, and I'd been primed to be curious about what was forbidden from me.

SANDERS LIKED TO TALK about the poor, the working class, and the elderly as though those groups were monolithic blocs. But each category was split along ethnic lines, which over time became political lines. The Irish, rising steadily in Burlington, were Democrats. The French, who had struggled as a community, were not as loyally affiliated, and might be persuadable. David Clavelle knew that in many Burlington neighborhoods, it made sense to campaign with a few French phrases up your sleeve.

Clavelle had studied his boss Patrick Leahy's winning 1974 Senate campaign, when Marcelle Leahy spoke Franglish while visiting the remote villages of the state's Northeast Kingdom. Burlington counted several pockets of French speakers, but the most important was Lakeside, the front lines of the battle over the Southern Connector. Sanders had a presence in the neighborhood already; since the mid-1970s, he and Huck Gutman had been turning up Wednesday nights to play in a pickup league that met in the dark gym behind St. Anthony's Church, under the gaudy crucifixes, where Lakeside went to Mass. Sanders and Gutman arrived at the freezing court, threw some elbows for a few hours, bantered with the other guys, then left; it was not a deep cultural connection. But when Sanders and his aides first visited Lakeside, it "gave him an opening," a friend recalled.

St. Anthony's still held masses in French into the twenty-first century; there were many Gra-meres and Gra-peres in those households, whose English was scant. The politics of the neighborhood were promising: the men and women of Lakeside remembered the malign bosses of the mill, the corporate greed that led to cuts in pay, the layoffs and evictions. Now city hall, with its empty promises to drain a flooded road and its cynical shell game over the Southern Connector, had siphoned all that generational anger back to the surface.

With David Clavelle advising, Bernie's door-to-door work "became more intelligent," volunteers from the time told me. It was the dead of winter, a foot or so of old, dirty, ice-encrusted snow on the ground. Sanders learned from Clavelle that not every working-class household was persuadable. It was not productive to get into a lengthy, heated discussion in every foyer about patriotism; but a working-class Reagan voter—Sanders met many in Lakeside—meant the conversation could be turned to taxes, budgeting, government efficiency. "There were no cultural issues in city politics, as there are now," Clavelle recalled. Occasionally, Bernie's leftist past would come back to haunt him in the form of invective shouted from a rear bedroom or kitchen. When he heard the word *communist*, though, he politely and calmly explained that he was not a communist, but a democratic socialist.

With the days ticking by, it was tempting to steer away from neighborhoods known for their loyalty to the mayor, or for their enthusiastic embrace of Reagan in the recent presidential election; but in one of those neighborhoods, Sanders made perhaps his most important breakthrough. In the New North End, where Mayor Paquette made his home, you found small ranches with single-bay garages used for boats on trailers, jet skis, Ski-Doos—and the family car relegated to the driveway. You learn a lot about people by seeing what they drive. Sanders had the instinct to skip houses with big American sedans, looking for homes with friendlier-looking vehicles out front: Toyota hatchbacks, Subarus, Volvos. Outside a lime-green ranch home, Sanders saw a wood-sided AMC Eagle with a Reagan/Bush sticker on the rear bumper. Though it was mid-January, the waist-high Three Wise Men and their plastic donkeys still stared at the football-sized Baby Jesus in his plastic manger on the front lawn. A gruff man answered the door and introduced himself as Sergeant Moran; from the dark, back hall, beeping loudly, Sanders heard the sound of kids playing Atari. The sergeant welcomed Bernie in and told him that he liked how "he'd been giving Pomerleau hell."

Bernie had been giving Antonio Pomerleau hell exclusively over his waterfront development plan; but Burlington's most decorated citizen was also the longtime appointed chairman of its police commission, acting as the primary liaison between the cops and city hall. Tensions between the police and the mayor ran hot, and had for years. Salaries for all city employees had been frozen. The police would go to a convention in Albany, New York, or Springfield, Massachusetts, and see the new radios and cruisers and holsters and other accessories that small-city policemen elsewhere enjoyed, but where was their new equipment? The force was twenty officers below full strength, with several resignations in the past few months. Cops were ticketing "more dogs than people," Moran said; the city's leash law was easier to enforce than its laws against car theft and break-ins. One officer had lost a carjacker in the woods when reinforcements couldn't be contacted. At a raucous meeting the previous October, Officer Wayne Hunt of the Burlington Patrolmen's Association had pressed Mayor Paquette about his own recent $3,000 pay raise, with Pomerleau sitting in pained silence. Whatever was left of the cops' faith in Pomerleau had eroded as the developer took over the waterfront project; now he and Paquette were practically business partners, and the Burlington Police Department began to watch Mr. Pomerleau very carefully.

Wayne Hunt and his men were not leftists. Bernie Sanders, who as a Liberty Union candidate had spoken colorfully about bad apples in law enforcement—"There is no doubt that there are many Nazis on the force" was the reported quote—was no natural ally of the police, and he risked alienating some in his coalition by courting their support. But to the sound of the bleeping Atari, Sanders and the Burlington cop parted warmly and shook hands, promising to stay in touch.

JANUARY WAS CAUCUS SEASON in Burlington. The Citizens Party met in the wards to choose candidates for alderman. Gary De Carolis, a smart young Citizens Party member moved to run for office by the killing of John Lennon, was picked to battle Sadie White, whose pact of mutual support with Sanders was still a secret, in Ward 3. Among the red onion skins and sawdust at the Onion River Co-Op, Terry Bouricius, a produce worker at the store, got the nomination in Ward 2. Bouricius, a wiry twenty-six-year-old in a wool sweater, was a bit of a mini Bernie, but it was premature to call them political allies. Like everyone in the Citizens Party, Bouricius was stung by Sanders's refusal to seek the party's endorsement for mayor. When the citywide Citizens Party gathered to endorse Sanders nonetheless, Bouricius and Greg Guma, the nominee for alderman in Ward 6, held their noses. Sanders, for his part, barely acknowledged the potentially damaging endorsement. It was a savvy political calculation—not the last Sanders would make in handling gadflies on his left.

The Republicans gathered in an auditorium in city hall on January 19 to nominate, as usual, nobody. "We like the mayor," a party member told the *Burlington Free Press*. "He's pretty conservative." A more eventful meeting transpired upstairs, where Dickie Bove fled the dinner rush at Bove's to join the Democratic caucus and make his stand. The mayor's property tax increase was a dose of poison, he argued; the city wouldn't survive, the people didn't want it, and the expenditures that made it a sudden necessity needed to be reexamined. Paquette, slouching and dragging on a Pall Mall, listened, annoyed at the new effrontery of "the little pizza man," as he called Bove, though Bove's served no pizza. The ballots were cast, and Paquette accepted his party's nomination after a 131–19 vote. Dickie Bove then rushed back to Bove's to pluck his apron from its peg, but told a reporter on the way out to get in touch. "I'm staying in," Bove declared, loudly enough for Paquette to hear.

The race attracted a final candidate: Gordon Paquette's cousin, Joseph McGrath, "a very nice man," Linda Niedweske told me, "but way over his head. Bernie helped him quite a bit." McGrath, whose police scanner was his primary interface with the world, was a one-issue candidate: he wanted the officers in the Burlington Police Department to have snazzier radios. McGrath did supply the press with a steady stream of quips. On the waterfront development proposal: "People shouldn't have to pay to jump in the water." On the Southern Connector: "Take the slow way, is what I say"; on Paquette's sixty-five-cent property tax increase: "Cut it in half, then in half again."

Why was he running? "I thought I'd take my chance, like anyone else," McGrath told reporters: if a spaghetti cook and a socialist could put together campaigns, why not him?

IN MID-FEBRUARY, just weeks away from Election Day, Gordon Paquette "finally acknowledged" his competition in the race for mayor: "Paquette has ceased calling his opponent 'Saunders,'" the *Burlington Free Press* reported, "a sign of his increased respect." The mayor was cornered into participating in three "candidate forums," refusing head-on debates. There were no buttons, no stickers, no fliers for Gordon Paquette's campaign; he wasn't running a campaign, exactly. He was running out his opponents' campaigns.

Paquette's only public statements were long-winded "explanations" of his proposal to raise property taxes by 65 cents for every $100 of a home's assessed value. Adjusting for inflation, the increase would have been over $2,000 in 2023. Paquette took to the airwaves, recording radio spots with his friend Antonio Pomerleau, whose private development of the waterfront stood to enrich him further. "It's a transfer," Sanders told a Burlington audience. "A transfer of wealth from the average homeowner to the bank account of Antonio Pomerleau." It seemed to defy even basic political logic to go on the radio with the wealthiest man in Burlington and tell people they would soon owe hundreds of dollars more to the city, which by the way was passing some of that money along, in the form of tax breaks and city improvements, to that very rich guy.

Paquette had handed Sanders yet another gift with those radio spots. Bernie now called publicly for Pomerleau's removal as police commissioner. He could thus rally opposition to the waterfront and support for the police in one gesture. Sanders was in regular contact with Hunt and Joe Crepeau, the Patrolmen's Association boss. As it happened, he was undergoing a very timely tutelage in police culture: Bernie and Richard Sugarman were devoted viewers of a hit show that debuted in January of 1981, *Hill Street Blues*, a gritty, humanizing look at precinct cops in an unnamed American city. "The police all loved *Hill Street Blues*," according to Sugarman. Burlington officers gathered around and watched the show at the station. In fact, Burlington's police station was grittier than the one on *Hill Street Blues*: Sanders told the press that he was "appalled that police headquarters had no working showers" like the one on TV. Sanders "took a lot of hints from *Hill Street Blues*," Sugarman told me, "right at the moment he needed to understand how to talk to cops." Thereafter he thought of the Burlington police the way they thought of themselves: Officer Friendlies, bighearted working stiffs. Sanders called the city police headquarters "Hill Street," and the Burlington Blues loved it.

LATE FEBRUARY: On the eve of the first of three candidate forums, Bernie was campaigning in the Old North End with the *Burlington Free Press* reporter Alan D. Abbey by his side. Sanders had a new secret weapon: large, sturdy, paper shopping bags emblazoned blue on white, front and back, with campaign slogans: on one side, "FOR THE PEOPLE"; on the other, "SANDERS FOR MAYOR." The idea to print and distribute these bags to the elderly came to Linda Niedweske's father. "I said, 'Dad, it's not really what we're doing, I don't think so,'" Linda told me. But soon a surprise shipment of the bags arrived from the Niedweske household in New Jersey. Sanders loved them. So did the elderly of the Old North End, who had to walk farther to buy necessities after the collapse of their neighborhood and the conversion of Church Street to tourist businesses. The big, strong bags with sturdy rope handles were durable and practical, but they were also a powerful symbol of what Burlington had done to its residents, forcing them to walk miles to obtain basic provisions. The image of old ladies carrying "Bernie Bags" spread on the local news. The bags became a coveted item for years after. I guard mine, a gift from Jim Rader, with my life. When people talk about what made the difference for Bernie in '81, the Bernie Bags often come up.

Sanders and Abbey were approaching Blodgett Street, where Sadie White lived, when a police cruiser slowed beside him. According to Abbey, the officer hailed Bernie and asked him "to phone the police union chief" before he made his remarks at the candidates' forum. Sanders said he already had, "which impressed the officer." Abbey printed the story, and the feedback loop running between Sanders and the police now passed through the pages of the *Burlington Free Press*. In the final week of February of 1981, with the election just days away, the candidates finally met in front of the public. Paquette was "morose," according to Garrison Nelson, who moderated the second of the three forums, held at UVM's Waterman Hall. The mayor had publicly conceded that his tax hike would lose at the polls; his mood was punitive toward the voters, who, he said, "would probably get what they deserved."

At the first forum, held near Lakeside and filled with the activists who had confronted the mayor just months before, Paquette called Sanders "some kind of Robin Hood." Sanders "wants to take from the rich and give to the poor. Well, it didn't work out so well for Robin Hood," the mayor inveighed, creating confusion about what on earth he meant. Pointing at Bove, the mayor cracked that his opponent was "too busy making spaghetti" to succeed in city politics. The crowd applauded as Bove, mimicking the bliss of a satisfied Bove's customer, rubbed his large belly slowly.

At the second forum, a new idea came to Paquette. The mayor and his wife had just seen and enjoyed the Paul Newman film *Fort Apache, The Bronx*, about a burned-out police detective fighting Black and Latino criminals in the South Bronx. The film attracted controversy even before its release for the broad racism of its premise and the grotesque stereotypes among its cast of villains. Citing the bleak dystopia he'd seen in the comfort of Merrill's Theaters 1-2-3 on North Avenue, Paquette told friends that he was going to pin down Sanders "on crime." The mayor blustered his way through an incomprehensible screed against Bernie, muttering a few words about Paul Newman; incredulous, Sanders—who was from Brooklyn, not the Bronx—calmly took the floor to discuss the mayor's tax hike, the Southern Connector, and the crime that had prospered on Paquette's watch while he underfunded the city's police.

Word got around that these solemn-sounding candidates' forums had been in fact quite wild and entertaining. The final event was held at the Unitarian church at the head of Church Street, and broadcast by WDOT Radio. Burlington tuned in to hear Paquette, who had straightened out his

New York City geography, accuse Bernie of wanting to make Burlington "more like Brooklyn." The crowd booed loudly. What did the mayor mean? More diverse? More Jewish? Soon Paquette turned on his hosts, a consortium of neighborhood groups, "some of them I'm just hearing about today." Gene Bergman jeered from the crowd. The Lakeside group booed and shouted obscenities. The mayor thought he'd been "thrown to the lions" and railed against his aides. It was the Supertramp concert all over again: the Sanders "kids" were loud and rude, barbarians at the gates. Sanders, irritated by the entire display, countered by recommending that the Burlington Police Department start an athletic league for children. On his way out of the forum, he told a *Burlington Free Press* reporter, "The thrust of who I am as a human being is totally different from Mayor Gordon Paquette."

The candidates' forum played that night from a transistor in the musty conference room at police headquarters. The Burlington Patrolmen's Association knew it was holding a valuable card. Especially valuable now, since Paquette's only remaining move was to play up Bernie as a "communist." The mayor and his Pall Mall cabinet had discussed the ins and outs of red-baiting Sanders; a cadre of loyal deputies in the wards soon put the word out that Bernie was a Fidel-style revolutionary whose campaign had been funded by violent outsiders. The word certainly reached 258 Colchester Avenue, where Sanders's presence on the evening news elicited howls of anger from my grandfather.

The Patrolmen's Association invited Paquette, Sanders, and Bove to address twenty or so officers and reporters at the station, two days after the candidates' forum, on February 26. Paquette got an earful, but looked bored. Sanders spoke calmly, thanking the officers for volunteering their time with the city's youth. "He was the only candidate in a long time to take an interest in the police," Joe Crepeau said. The door closed on the smoky conference room; Bove, Paquette, and Sanders stood awkwardly outside it, as the vote was taken.

Crepeau and Wayne Hunt emerged and announced that the union had voted unanimously to endorse Bernard Sanders for mayor of Burlington.

"It is a brave act," Sanders said, emotion gathering in his voice. "I am very moved."

23

Apple's House

(Election Day, March 3, 1981)

Victory, March 3, 1981. *Jym Wilson*

Appleton King Jr. was a twenty-four-year-old UVM dropout, living with seven roommates in a grand Victorian on North Prospect Street just off the university green, when he joined Sanders's mayoral campaign. Everyone called Appleton King "Apple," which made him sound less like a Salem witch judge or a long-dead president of Yale, and more like a cool guy you'd meet in a bar in Burlington, Vermont. Apple was a very cool guy, hollow cheeked and handsome, smart and spiritually alert, also a talented raconteur and committed leftist. A lot of people in Burlington had met Apple in bars;

but Sanders, who did not go to bars, first met Apple through John Franco, who did go to bars.

Appleton King—whose sister is Lily King, the novelist—grew up inside a John Updike novel on the North Shore of Boston, in Manchester-by-the Sea, the heart of New England's Gold Coast. His father taught and coached tennis at a local private day school; his mother, a sophisticated woman of evolving political convictions, might have met Updike himself at beach bonfires and Labor Day tennis parties, for many of the pretty young wives of the North Shore eventually met John Updike. Over the years, Gwendolyn King divorced Apple's dad, discovered left-wing politics, and created a big impression on Appleton King Jr. when she became a socialist. Apple's mother was therefore thrilled when her son phoned her in February of 1981 to say that Bernie Sanders had asked Apple to join his mayoral campaign.

As a student reporter, King had covered Bernie's 1976 race for *The Vermont Cynic*. King had loved "Bernie's penchant for broken-record oratory" and "sheer maniac work ethic" in battling the Republican, Dick Snelling, and his opponent, the Democrat Stella Hackel. Apple had a trenchant prose style, but his most impressive talent was for ending up in the right place at the right time. When Franco heard that Apple was back in Burlington in the winter of 1980, holding court nightly at the Millard Fillmore, the hippie-biker-hash bar on North Winooski Avenue, he called his old friend and invited him to meet Sanders in person. "I didn't tend to turn hospitality down," Apple confessed to me from his cabin in Michigan's Upper Peninsula, where he now lives for much of the year, not off the grid, but very near its edge. While we spoke, Apple was holding and comforting his ten-week-old German Shepherd puppy.

Franco, Sanders, and King had breakfast at the Oasis on Bank Street, a classic rail-car diner where Governor Phil Hoff took his morning coffee all through the 1960s. Stratty Lines, the Greek immigrant who had opened the Oasis in 1954, slung corned beef hash and political scuttlebutt from behind the counter in his crisp white uniform. The diner became known as a Democratic redoubt, but, like Bove's, it maintained a strategic independence from city hall; its ties were to Montpelier and even to Washington, through regulars like Senator Patrick Leahy. The Oasis was for generations the obligatory stop for visiting dignitaries. In 1995, Sanders, Leahy, and Bill Clinton lunched there before making their way down Church Street, where my friend Chad and I were waiting to shake their hands.

"I was not ever a big-league player in the campaign," Apple told me; but one night in a friend's coldwater flat, "Bernie showed up and handed me twenty bucks, and told me to put the word out." Sanders would sometimes

Stratty Lines and Friends at the Oasis, 1990s. *Adam Riesner, Burlington Free Press*

breach the banks of smoke to call on Apple in his attic bedroom on North Prospect Street. Sanders talked sports with the roommates, waved away joints and drinks that were offered to him, and got down to the point. He saw Apple as his liaison to Burlington's bar scene. He certainly wasn't going to campaign there himself.

Of course "we went into the bars," Linda Niedweske told me: on any given weekend night in Burlington, thousands of people descended on Burlington's dozens of bars: Finbar's for ferns and third dates; Hannibul's for hockey players; B.T. McGuire's for gaslight-era nostalgia; the Last Chance, where ladies drank for free; What Ales You, the Office, the Rathskeller. None of these spots promised acoustics conducive to in-depth campaigning, but at the denlike, pine-paneled Millard Fillmore, where you could hear yourself think, Apple made Sanders's case, mainly to pretty girls, while Jim Croce covers played from the small stage.

King's wayward role evolved, and by early March, with Election Day looming, Sanders appointed him captain of Ward 1. Apple "got a phone book, and called every number in the Ward 1 directory," including, I am sure, mine; and when Election Day rolled around, Apple turned up at the Ward 1 polling station, Mater Christi School, to observe the action on one side of a collapsible cafeteria wall, where the nuns had set up the long metal voting tables and heavy machines the afternoon before; on my side of the wall, I and my fifth-grade classmates ate Sloppy Joes and drank chocolate milk.

Like my school cafeteria, Apple's attention was divided on Election Day. He had a party to throw that evening. There was still a ping-pong table to be folded up where a dance floor would go. A week or so before, Sanders had found King in his attic room and charged him with an important responsibility: the big house on North Prospect, with its tall ceilings and generous parlors, was perfect for an Election Night celebration. Apple reluctantly agreed, but wondered aloud if the party might be a bit of a downer.

"No way, Apple," Sanders replied. "Plan a victory party."

IN EARLY MARCH OF 1981, as the poor and elderly of old Burlington prepared to vote for their unlikely tribune, the "new Burlington" that had displaced them also got behind Bernie Sanders. More than one thousand new Burlingtonians registered in the months leading up to the election. Once a city of large families, Burlington now had very few children, relative to its size; most of the kids at my Catholic school lived in the suburbs: South Burlington, Essex, Shelburne, Jericho. Their parents' childhood bedrooms in the big houses downtown were rented to grad students, med students, and young professionals. Apple's house at 37 North Prospect Street, then home to a juggler, a guy with a mobile hot tub he rented out for parties, a carpenter, and three former UVM hockey players, was built for a doctor and his large family. Mrs. Florence Perkins of Green Street (Perkins Pier, on the waterfront, was named for her husband, Dr. Charles Perkins) ran an apartment house for young women out of the giant old home, where "lots of Bernie's friends lived," as Julia Alvarez, the writer, told me; Alvarez, who had taken a teaching job at UVM, moved into Mrs. Perkins's house and became one of "Mrs. Perkins's girls" in June of 1981, in what she called "the Bernie aftermath." "These were all Bernie people, right up and down the street," Alvarez said. "Every one of them had campaigned for him."

And so Sanders, who had won the support of the old, alienated Burlington—from Sadie's Ladies to the poor in Franklin Square, from the underpaid cops to the leftists in Greg Guma's circle—also attracted a surprise constituency in these educated transplants in their twenties and thirties, culturally Democrats, who filled the bars and restaurants on Church Street on weekend nights. Some were "professional people who grew up in New York or Boston," according to Garrison Nelson. They didn't see Mayor Gordon Paquette's "economic development as synonymous with progress—that's why they came to Burlington in the first place." Some, like Apple King and his housemates, were college students who stayed, rather than drifting back to the metropolises where they had been raised. This new wave of Vermont transplants was culturally and politically left, but probably to the right of Bernie. Their music was Madonna, Patti Smith, and Talking Heads, along with local equivalents like the Decentz and Pinhead;

they showed up in the bars, among the snowsuits and moon boots, in glossy lipstick, miniskirts, and lollipop earrings from Nuevo Wavo, a downtown purveyor of fishnets and spiked collars. The 1980s had arrived in Burlington. When these young people got to town, part of the Burlington experience was voting for Sanders.

ELECTION DAY WAS raw and cold, in the twenties, with a steady wind blowing off the lake. As the afternoon passed, curious things began to happen at the polls. Mayor Paquette was "camped out" in the lunchroom of the Thayer School in Ward 4; Dick Sartelle, the mayor's old antagonist who was running for alderman as part of Bernie's coalition, then also camped out. The two men were both, as candidates, discouraged from lingering at the polls, and were eventually persuaded to leave the building; Paquette returned late in the afternoon, and joined a corps of poll workers on their break, smoking cigarettes in the school playground. In Ward 3, Burlington's police chief, in a bitter dispute with his union and working behind the scenes for Paquette, had "personally requested" that the old people tramping into the Barnes Elementary School "leave their shopping bags"—that is, their "SANDERS FOR MAYOR" bags—by the door. Some refused and were turned away; Sadie White, holding a sign for her own campaign nearby, encountered a neighbor on his way out and "marched him right back up to the door," a friend said. Polling places, coordinated through Paquette's city clerk, staffed with hired workers he and his neighborhood allies had recruited, were "not friendly to Bernie people," according to Richard Sugarman, who, with John Franco, observed the vote in Ward 5. Paquette's voters were often the election workers' friends, cousins, aunts, neighbors; Bernie's voters were professors, strangers, students, the young, the unshaven. Stationed outside of Ward 3, Gary De Carolis observed as voters who'd accepted rides from the Sanders campaign were "dropped off a block or so away," so as not to be spotted by the Democratic machine, whose workers defended the entryway like a hired patrol.

By seven p.m., when the polls closed, Sanders and his circle knew they had reasons to be vigilant. Citizens voted in curtained voting booths purchased by the city in the 1950s and stored between elections in the cellar of the Burlington Memorial Auditorium, where kids climbed on them or jammed their levers with gum. After the totals were collected from each rickety, malfunctioning machine, a poll worker certified the votes with a handheld tabulator. This process could be observed and checked. But as affidavits from all six wards attest, the absentee ballots—where, in Wards 2 and 3 especially, Bernie would find robust support—had been counted in city hall and reported back to the wards, against the normal procedure. In Ward 5, Richard and Linda Sugarman saw a poll worker take down the wrong figure for Sanders's absentee votes, forcing a correction that netted Bernie five additional votes. Greg Guma, watching his own prospects darken, stood by in Ward 6 as his rival, Chip Wadhams, saw Sanders chip away at Paquette. Both noted that the absentee vote totals appeared lopsided for Paquette. Huck Gutman witnessed a similar problem in Ward 1, and alerted the chief election worker, Sister Margaret, my math teacher.

But there was good news across the city. Sartelle watched in Ward 4 as the numbers climbed for Bernie while his own lagged far behind the incumbent Republican alderman, Allen Gear. Terry Bouricius, helped by a huge Ward 2 turnout for Bernie, was on his way to becoming the first Citizens Party candidate to win an election in the United States. In Ward 3, Sadie White was locked in a tight three-way race while Sanders's totals soared. And under the big gold crucifix at Mater Christi School, Dickie Bove, whose home was in Ward 1, pulled Appleton King aside as the two men observed the count: "You guys are going to win this," he told Apple, flashing a big, satisfied smile.

At five p.m., Garrison Nelson showed up at the WJOY studios to join the legendary Jack Barry for a few hours of broadcast anticlimax. "What's going to happen here, Gary?" Barry asked Nelson, the cranky, potbellied oracle of Burlington politics for decades. Nelson, his accent and attitude hardened by an abusive childhood in Lynn, Massachusetts, could supercharge even the most mundane of local elections with his repertoire of insider political lore, but this one, he was afraid to say, was destined to be a big let-down: "Bernie will get 25 percent, and we'll switch to the Bruins game at eight o'clock," Garry told Barry.

The early word did seem bad for Sanders. Jim Rader, crossing the frigid waters of Lake Champlain on a ferry to meet with a veterans' group in Plattsburgh, New York, tuned in at around five thirty: the turnout in Ward 1, where Apple was stationed in my elementary school gym and where many students and professors voted, had been surprisingly light. To the political analyst and Paquette adviser Vincent Naramore, on the air with Nelson and Barry, this augured well for the mayor. A veteran of four previous Sanders losses, Rader knew just where this night was headed. As the ferry slowed, cut its engines, and shimmied into the dock on the New York side, Rader switched off his radio.

The Boston Bruins were headed for defeat that night to the St. Louis Blues, but in the seven o'clock hour, Bernie and Linda Niedweske, tuning in from campaign headquarters in Linda's living room, were seeing gains. Ward 1 went to Sanders by twelve votes. Garrison Nelson told me he'd be

Eight p.m, awaiting results. *Jym Wilson*

surprised if "even one" of Dickie Bove's 112 votes in his home ward had hurt Sanders. The pattern was set for the night: Bove's votes were shaving Paquette's margins, and Bernie was close on Paquette's turf. Sugarman and his wife, Linda, left Ward 5 elated after it was called for Paquette by a tiny margin of thirty or so. Ward 6, where Barbara Bush sometimes visited old friends from her Smith College days and Reagan/Bush '80 signs still dotted the expansive lawns—"Republican Country," as Chip Wadhams put it—went to Paquette by a tiny margin, around seventy votes. That was a warning flare. Nelson and Barry sat up, perked up, and began to call the night like a World Series game. Our radio at 258 Colchester Avenue went on around this time; I overheard the blended voices downstairs of Nelson, Barry, my grandparents, my mother, and, eventually, Bernie.

The mayor was not tuned into WJOY. He was "sequestered on the ground floor of city hall," according to Alan Abbey: all the doors were locked, and the elevator, the only access to his office, was shut down. Operatives disappeared down a dark hallway to bring the latest bulletins to Paquette. It would be hard to imagine a more striking contrast: Sanders and his supporters gathered all across the city, in fern bars and community rooms and efficiency apartments, while the mayor, bracing for humiliation, brooded in his grotto. Soon the news from Paquette's own neighborhood, Ward 4, arrived: the mayor had won the vote of his friends and neighbors by only a slim margin. Hundreds of former supporters who he saw at the supermarket and in the pews at Mass, who had wished him well, shook his hand, patted him on the back, had then gone and voted against him. It was among the most stinging of Gordon Paquette's many disappointments that night, and it almost certainly indicated that he would go down in defeat. Dickie Bove, "the pizza man" the mayor had taunted as a political naïf, again made the difference; Paquette won the ward by only about 300 votes; Bove had picked off 385.

The strongest Sanders wards were still tabulating. Ward 2, the center of the city, heavily a renter's district, went big for Sanders. But the emotional core of Bernie's support was in Ward 3, where at least five senior centers were under Sadie White's sway. The difference would be in the sick ballots that White had personally distributed to her Ladies. Gary De Carolis, running for alderman in the ward against White, observed the count: the paper sick ballots as reported from city hall put Sanders over the top. De Carolis and White, ostensibly rivals in the race for Ward 3 alderman, were among the first to learn that by winning in "the Bloody Third"—Burlington's most distinctive neighborhood and its most neglected, the Old North End—Sanders had unofficially been elected mayor of Burlington.

Around eight p.m., Richard and Linda Sugarman were in the car on the way to Appleton King's house, feeling good, their radio tuned to WJOY, when Garrison Nelson announced that Sanders was the apparent winner by twenty-two votes, and that an incredulous Paquette was drafting a demand for a recount. Richard let out a whoop of joy; Linda, in the passenger seat, had a different response: "If you want your friend to become the mayor," she said, "you'd better get back to city hall this instant. Didn't Mrs. White warn you about those sick ballots?"

"Sadie White knew everything," Sugarman told me. "She was a scien-

Peter Freyne on the steps of city hall. *Jym Wilson*

tist." Gary De Carolis confirmed: "I called her Professor White." Howard Dean agreed: "Sadie White was a destroyer, an absolute battleship." Sugarman phoned Bernie, who picked up the phone and exclaimed, "I'm on television!" pronouncing the word "the way they do in Brooklyn," Sugarman recalled, laughing. Sugarman and Sanders agreed that they both needed to get to city hall immediately: Mrs. White had told them both that elections this tight had been won and lost for years "in the city clerk's office."

A crowd of Burlington cops were milling about on the steps of city hall and outside their cruisers double-parked along Church Street. "Do you gentlemen want a raise or not?" Sugarman teased them, as he bounded up the stairs. "Make your presence known inside!" They laughed, he laughed; but as Sanders and John Franco worked to get the votes impounded and out of city hall for the coming recount, three police cruisers switched their lights on and circled the building slowly at Sugarman's direction, until Burlington's 9,880 votes, including the all-important sick ballots, were handed over to a marshal of the law and carried out to an awaiting vault at the Chittenden County Courthouse.

NEWBORN STARS FORM in nebulae and reach us thousands of years later in the night sky. Politics form in nebulae as well, and Bernie's star, apparently emerging for the first time at eight p.m. on March 3, 1981, was in fact born a decade earlier in the Haybarn Theatre at Goddard College, in Plainfield, Vermont. Like any new star in the firmament, Sanders was also a time traveler, an embodiment of the past, of 1971. His star had journeyed across time and lodged in the clearing skies above the Queen City.

These are the kinds of thoughts a person might have had upstairs at Appleton King's place, as the bong slowly made its way around a circle of roommates awaiting the arrival of Bernie Sanders. Apple was repeatedly "teeing up 'Rosalita,'" the Bruce Springsteen song, as he told me, to blare the moment Sanders walked in the door. The song played over and over from Apple's old turntable and dented speakers. "I ain't here on business, baby, / I'm only here for fun," Springsteen sang to the eight roommates whose fun and the city's business had, that evening, weirdly and historically aligned.

It was "the strangest, most amazing mix of people at a political event ever," Bernie told his old friend Richard Clarke. From the prow of the stairs, Apple saw the mix assemble: first "gumshoe reporters with pencils behind their ears" and photographers slung like mules with heavy bags set up around the grand entryway, under a chandelier. Murray Bookchin, in a leather jacket and beret, arrived with his several male acolytes and sat "cross legged in a circle." Bernie's UVM supporters—Huck Gutman, Mark and Jennie Stoler, and, eventually, Richard Sugarman—arrived. Terry Bouricius, the new alderman for Ward 2 and Bernie's only certain ally on the board, turned up. Crowds of volunteers and hangers-on streamed in; by the time Sanders was on his way with Franco and Niedweske, at around nine thirty, the house was rollicking and, with outside temperatures dipping into the teens triggering the old hissing radiators to overload, both frigid and sweltering. A group of brothers from Lambda Iota, the neighboring *Animal House* frat from whose roof, in those days, sofas were sometimes catapulted, King Kong–style, onto passing cars, came late in the evening to scavenge pretzels and beer in the thinning crowd.

JYM WILSON AND Rob Swanson were in the scrum of photographers arrayed inside the foyer of Apple's house that night. Wilson grew up in South Burlington and first encountered Sanders in 1972, while a student at South Burlington High School. Bernie railed against corporate greed, income inequality, and "the criminal situation with health care in our country," Wilson remembered, and the students ate it up. Now, not quite a decade later, as a staff photographer for the *Burlington Free Press*, Wilson sat at his desk listening as Garrison Nelson called the race for Bernie, exclaiming, "Burlington will never be the same again!"

"Nobody at the *Free Press* expected Bernie to win," Wilson said; it was likely to be a "relatively slow news night." Wilson got his deployment orders and made his way up the hill to Apple's, where he waited for Sanders and his entourage to enter. The mood was "delirious," Apple recalled. Word spread like a ripple that Sanders, Niedweske, and Franco were approaching the front door; Apple dropped the needle again on "Rosalita."

The iconic moment that Wilson caught on film—Swanson caught it too, nanoseconds later—shows Bernie entering Apple's house like a prizefighter, arms extended, straining the cuffs of a secondhand down parka. Sanders looks all of his six feet one, and yet the ceilings soar above him. The scale of the home is striking, given the images that had been running for weeks of Bernie in dark, narrow entryways or on front porches hung with laundry, pleading for votes. To a Burlingtonian, the interior alone would indicate a home in the Hill Section—"Republican Country"—where Sanders had just come surprisingly close to a victory. The young reporters on either side of Sanders look gleeful—"We were all Sanders voters," Wilson told me. An image of Bernie flashes from the campaign poster tacked to the wall at his triumphant self, fulfilling the slogan printed on the poster: "IT'S TIME FOR CHANGE. REAL CHANGE."

Wilson took one or two more pictures, then raced back to College Street to develop the shots and get them to layout by the midnight deadline. "I had no idea if I'd gotten it," he told me: Bernie's arms rose "only for an instant," then fell to his side. ("He was never very celebratory," Wilson noted.) As he watched the image shimmer into view, Jym Wilson knew he'd captured the most exciting moment in Burlington's political history, and at the fleeting instant when Sanders himself seemed to allow himself not only to realize it, but to enjoy it.

A reporter cornered Sanders in the mob and asked him his immediate plans. "It's too early for that," he said. "First we have to sit down with the people who are going to help us form this administration, lots of people with no previous role in government." Pressed for a concrete agenda, Bernie would only repeat his vow to "provide the quality of life that ordinary people are entitled to," and to "address the problems that face the people of Burlington on a day-to-day level." The reporter asked him to describe his politics in one word.

"Radical," Sanders replied.

"What about 'socialist'?" the reporter asked.

"We're not discussing that now," Sanders said, with some mischief in his tone. "That's not relevant."

JIM RADER WAS hurrying back from his veterans' meeting in Plattsburgh to make the last ferry across Lake Champlain, the 10 p.m., when he switched the radio back on: "Bernie Sanders, the apparent winner in Burlington," is the phrase he heard. "I just about ran off the road," Rader wrote in a memo he composed soon after to memorialize the night. Rader and Bernie "had joked in previous elections, where he clearly had no chance of being elected, about what would happen if he had." A few weeks before, Rader, who'd been supporting his old friend from afar, but had no time or stomach for another campaign, had run into Sanders and Niedweske at the Burlington Bagel Bakery next to the Greyhound station: "We're going to win this thing!" Sanders shouted out, across the café. Rader "entered into the spirit of the prediction" but figured: No way.

Now it was nearing eleven in Burlington, and Rader headed to Bernie's North Union Street apartment, unaware of the raucous party a few blocks away, where Sanders was bantering with Murray Bookchin in a quiet spot of the downstairs parlor, and Apple's girlfriend was framing his bobbing head between her two palms and "guiding a steady stream of vomit out the attic window," as Apple told me, reliving the wildness of the moment.

"Typically," the meticulous Rader wrote, surveying Bernie's empty apartment, "the door was unlocked, all the lights were on, the place was messy, and no one was there."

Rader had heard the discussion on WJOY of the narrowness of the victory, the certainty of a recount, Paquette's refusal to concede, the determination of city Democrats, and the "cockiness" of the newly consecrated "Sanderistas."

Rader stood at his friend's kitchen counter and scribbled a note on an envelope. "Congratulations! It's too bad there has to be *any cloud* over your victory," he wrote, and signed it, "Jim."

24

"A Weak Mayor"

(Awkward Transitions, March–June 1981)

Sanders agonistes, 1981. *Rob Swanson*

In March of 1981, Bernie Sanders received perhaps his first Easter card, from Mrs. Marion T. Bushay of Park Street, Burlington, thanking him for his "victory for all of us." On the front, a baby cottontail bunny hefted a bouquet of tulips. Soon, more Hallmark cards arrived, all from old ladies under Sadie White's sway. Inscribed in a border of spring flowers, one read, "On This Happy Occasion, May God Bless You." The sentiment conveyed by the butterflies and umber foliage on one card seemed more autumnal: "The flower looks up high to see only the light, and never looks down to see its shadow. This is a wisdom which man must learn."

It was advice Sanders could use. With a recount looming and the Democratic establishment uniting against him, he savored the letters of congratulations arriving from near and far. From Miami, Roberto Simeon of the Cuban Democratic Socialist party sent his "socialist solidarity" to "Compañero Bernard Sanders." Tidings arrived from the Berkeley People's Party and, from the Lower East Side, the War Resisters League. Dr. Benjamin Spock, Bernie's old campaign trail sidekick from '74, checked in from the Ozarks, where he'd taken a young bride: "I married an Arkansas woman, Mary Morgan, a ball of fire," Spock wrote. "We live in an all-glass solar heated house hanging over a 70-mile-long lake." Closer to home, Terry Lutius of Williston, Vermont, recalled "Day care! Years gone by!" and celebrated "A single parent father in the Mayoralty!" And Angelo Lio, a barber in West Rutland, Vermont, wrote to offer a miracle cure for Bernie's encroaching baldness: "I singe the hair that is thinning, and have had success doing it." Sanders wrote back: "Your treatment for thinning hair sounds interesting," but "I accept my thinning hair as one of the inevitable consequences of the aging process."

Some well-wishers offered to move to Burlington, or recommended friends who were already on the scene. "Marguerite Crawford of North Avenue might be helpful somewhere," Faire Edwards of Waterbury suggested. "I don't know her well, but she was a bookkeeper and could follow financial things and dig up meanings behind figures. Now widowed and retired, she wants to be an advocate."

It wasn't such a far-fetched suggestion: the mayor-elect, denied the opportunity to form an administration by a bitter cadre of entrenched city Democrats, would need all the help he could get.

The Moonies, Redux

A few days after the election, Greg Guma of *The Vermont Vanguard Press* got up early and headed over to Nectar's, looking for a story. Mayor Gordon Paquette's politburo slumped in its banquette. "We're used to knowing our elected officials," William Blanchard, an alderman, told him, "growing up together and raising families." "I don't even know the man. I'm numb, but trusting in God," Joyce Desautels, the president of the board of aldermen, added.

Desautels had last fought off dangerous newcomers to the city when she and Paquette chased the Moonies out of Burlington in 1976. Followers of the Reverend Sun Myung Moon's Unification Church had been hanging around the UVM green that spring, casting for lost souls. They would scan for emptiness in a young person's eyes and foist a leaflet into her hands. Moon planned a mass summer wedding of new followers on Church Street, to coincide with the city's bicentennial celebration. "You people really frighten me," Desautels told two respectfully dressed Moonies who had called a meeting with city hall to introduce themselves. "It's the fear of the unknown." Desautels "prayed the Moonies out of Burlington," she liked to boast. She hoped to do the same with Bernie Sanders.

To Burlington's Democratic machine politicians, Bernie might as well have been a Moonie: he collected strays and indoctrinated them into a dangerous canon of beliefs. To say that Sanders had "a cult" was not meant entirely as a figure of speech: what else would account for the sudden enthusiasm of the staid, reliable electorate of Burlington for a wild-haired, proselytizing Pied Piper from who-knows-where? Sanders brainwashed the students: this was the armchair analysis heard all over Burlington. To the old men at the VFW or the Knights of Columbus, Bernie's "followers"—never, simply, "voters"—were draft dodgers. At the Rotary Club, Bernie's people were "rabble rousers from New York." At the Ethan Allen Club, where the elite of Burlington's business community met over bowling alley ashtrays and Grey Poupon in jars, Sanders and his circle were simply "an element." Now, with Bernie's election, Desautels began to introduce herself as "a patriotic Christian woman." Moonies, Jews: to some in Burlington, it was all the same. "I think everyone's scared right now," a city official told the UPI.

The mayor's table at Nectar's was now without its mayor. Paquette kept office hours in his city hall crypt a block away, looking drained and baffled as he assured Lattie Coor, the square-jawed president of the University of Vermont, and Hilton Wick, the trusted high-WASP president of Chittenden Trust, the city's primary development lender, of his total confidence that the election results would be overturned upon recount. Paquette was so confident, in fact, that he and his wife were packing the coral slacks for their annual trip to West Palm Beach, Florida, as planned; this fact was reported by the press as a sign of his surrender.

Downtown businessmen gathered at Stratty Lines's Oasis Diner to plan their next moves: at Sadie White's insistence, Sanders had campaigned on a promise to make the merchants of Church Street repay the $1.5 million city bond that financed the construction of the new "brick and boulder" Marketplace, then attracting national attention for its imminent opening. "If Sanders succeeds in putting over his tax proposals, they would shut the business community down," one diner warned, stabbing his poached eggs. "If I was planning a major investment in Burlington, I'd be a little cautious right now," another added. Stratty Lines, dividing the piles of corned beef hash with the side of his metal spatula, toasted his customers: "It's all anybody's talking about in here today!"

On the afternoon following Appleton King's party, Sanders had called a press conference at Franklin Square, the public housing complex whose laundry room had incubated his nascent campaign. He spoke beautifully but rattled many in the city. "I want to see a rebirth of the human spirit in the largest city in the most beautiful state," Sanders proclaimed. He was worn out and hoarse; he seemed both defiant and quite vulnerable. With Richard Sartelle gloating behind him, Sanders promised "to open the door to city hall" to tenants of Franklin Square, the elderly, the poor, artists and intellectuals, children and teenagers. It was impossible for one voice "to single-handedly bring about change," he said; if the board of aldermen wanted a fight, "they will not fight Sanders but all of the people." "Every city project will be reevaluated," Sanders vowed. He promised "no immediate cures to the city's financial problems," but announced that in the meantime, a national spotlight was invited to shine on revolutionary Burlington. "Mr. Reagan," as Bernie always called the president, had shifted the country to the right: Burlington would "go in the opposite direction."

In case prayer didn't work, Joyce Desautels and her fellow aldermen developed a range of plans to thwart Sanders. In Paquette's spring break absence, Desautels, as acting mayor, would preside at the recount, where the Democrats thought they had an even chance of overturning the results. Sanders counted one ally out of thirteen on the board, the newly elected Terry Bouricius, who had beaten a Democrat with a de facto lifetime appointment in Ward 2. In Ward 3, there was the potential for one more: Sadie White faced a runoff election with the Democratic machine candidate, Paul Trepanier. Desautels and her Democrats planned to make that election, two weeks away, into a bitter proxy fight over their future in the city. With Paquette's sixty-five-cent property tax increase losing in a landslide, the mayor told reporters angrily that the books were now Bernie's: "It's his budget now," he snarled. The aldermen claimed emergency power to freeze hiring in city government, just as Sanders began to interview for positions in his administration. They also boasted of the power to vote down his appointments. Though she hadn't yet met Sanders, Desautels told the wire services that she and her fellow aldermen might oppose his hires in principle. "We never questioned them before," she admitted, "but if he brings in a bunch of unknowns from Oosh-Koosh, I'll look at him and say, No way."

If Bernie and his unknowns from Oosh-Koosh weren't Moonies, maybe they were commies. Overnight Sanders went from being "the perennial candidate" to "the avowed socialist" in the papers. "Town Elects a Socialist Mayor," was the UPI headline that confronted readers of Wyoming's *Casper Star-Tribune*. "Socialist Mayor Elected," read the headline in Galveston

Island, Florida. In Bowling Green, Ohio, readers learned that the "rumpled, 39-year-old political activist" was a socialist around the same time that some of Bernie's Burlington voters learned that detail: "I voted for Bernie as a protest against the mayor," a local real estate salesman, Ben Bosher, told the reporter.

Burlington blushed a little when its citizens realized that in the world's eyes we'd elected an "avowed socialist." The adjective implied defiance of decency, if not the law; in fact the Socialist Workers Party, for which Bernie had been a presidential elector in 1980, was at that moment the subject of an FBI investigation. Sugarman told me the campaign feared a runoff if no candidate received a plurality, because in a second round against Paquette "the element of surprise would be missing," and a red-baiting strategy could be used. It was remarkable, in retrospect, that socialism had played such a small role in framing the campaign.

Now, though, socialism—"avowed," shameless, out in the open—became the story. In the vacuum created by Bernie's refusal to introduce himself properly, wild legends circulated. Burlington, it was said, was a vast network of safe houses where fugitives from the 1960s hid out and funneled tote bags full of campaign cash to Sanders. Or, Bernie was a foreign agent, meeting at picnic tables in South Park with comrades from the El Salvadoran rebel party.

On March 13, Joyce Desautels hovered over the tense recount at the courthouse. The morning saw Mayor Paquette chipping away at his twenty-two-vote deficit. Someone called WJOY radio, and "Paquette's steady gains" were reported as harbingers of a shocker; but at eleven a.m., Sanders was proclaimed the victor, holding on by just ten votes. Sanders supporters in the jury room and on the courthouse steps went bananas. "The last two weeks have been a living hell," Franco told reporters. "Before today we really couldn't savor it." Steve Goodkind, Bernie's old VW mechanic, who had become a trusted aide, praised the "lean and mean" campaign. Paquette's attorney, flashing annoyance at his client's absenteeism on the day his political fate was adjudicated, said he would talk to the mayor "once he finds out where [the mayor] is."

It was now time to introduce Bernie Sanders to his constituents. In the *Rutland Herald*, Sanders told Debbie Bookchin that he was a "small *s*" socialist but essentially "a small businessman"—orders for his filmstrips still trickled in, even as the technology petered out—who works "very, very hard" to understand the plight of mom-and-pop businesses. Alan Abbey, the *Burlington Free Press* reporter who had shadowed Bernie, published a two-thousand-word feature story in the March 15 "Vermonter," the paper's weekly magazine section. In "Bernard Sanders: Working Class Hero?" the

Greg Guma (standing, left) and others observe the recount. Joyce Desautels and Frank Austin (in bowtie) look concerned. *Jym Wilson*

word *socialist* appears once, to describe Eugene V. Debs; the word *conservative* appears four times, three to describe Bernie. Bernie had told Burlington nothing personal, nothing about his life or background, during the campaign. This, in a city whose previous mayors had worked in our bakeries and delivered our newspapers as children. Now, Burlingtonians learned for the first time that Sanders's father had been a paint salesman in Brooklyn, "solidly working class"; that Sanders played basketball, ran track, and campaigned for student council in high school; applied to Harvard "with good grades" and was rejected; left Brooklyn College after one year and ran aground in his science classes at the University of Chicago, before making his way to Vermont, where he "banged nails for the summer" with John Rogers of Barre. "He is a very pleasant man. Intelligent. He is easy to get along with," Rogers, a certified blue-collar Yankee, told the paper's readers. The two men riding around in Rogers's pickup "didn't talk much about politics," but Sanders had the man's blessing: "I think he's going to make out well as mayor. I'm kind of pleased."

Burlingtonians also meet Sanders as a single father, playing a game of pickup basketball. Bernie passes the ball to Levi, then eleven, for a sweet layup. "Teamwork!" Bernie exclaims. Sanders points out that he has a pickup game once a week at St. Anthony's Church near Lakeside, where reporters had started turning up. (Sanders would more than once take questions courtside, while toweling off.) Sanders confesses that his "main preoccupation growing up was playing ball." Now that politics has replaced it,

Sanders has keenly synchronized his two passions for a constituency worried about his politics, but eager to believe that Bernie will turn out to be a regular guy, one of us.

Yet Bernie's leftist credentials are not entirely scanted. Readers learn briefly about the CORE sit-in and Sanders's confrontation with the university's administrators. He discloses more than ever—before, or since—about his Vietnam-era service, divulging that his application for conscientious objector status on religious grounds was "investigated for years" by the FBI before being declined on his twenty-sixth birthday, when he was then too old for the draft. (Sanders was told of the wild yarns being spun in Burlington barber shops and diners that he was an ex-Weatherman, wanted by the FBI for draft evasion.) Here and there, we get a hint of Bernie's out-of-the-mainstream ideas about health and medicine, still influenced by Wilhelm Reich. Sanders "worked for a state hospital" in California one summer "and has ever since been interested in the societal causes of illness." He "stays away from most medicines" and once "got a D" from his English professor for a "psychoanalytic interpretation of Shakespeare's Hamlet," the specifics of which, as an English professor, I can only begin to imagine.

But the emphasis remains on Sanders's mainstream, Main Street appeal. Sanders coaches a Parks and Rec team; he's a flinty, New England cheapskate; he's not some '60s burnout. "The truth of the matter is, other than my political point of view, I am quite conservative," he says. "I don't drink beyond having a glass of wine, now and again, with dinner. I don't go to bars." His wardrobe, purchased from Woolworth's on Church Street and Kmart, is corduroy pants and "a button down under a chamois shirt," accented by "three pairs of footwear, waterproof construction boots, regular shoes, and sneakers."

Sanders comes off as a working-class guy whose focus will be on economic justice and "the emotional problems caused by a lack of money." This is not a rigorous socialist analysis; it's a defense of making middle-class pleasures available to more people, and of making those pleasures—parks, clean streets, cheap entertainment, the sunsets as viewed from the waterfront—the business of the city to provide. "Unlike many 'liberals' and 'progressives,'" Abbey writes, "Sanders has genuine ties to poor people, public housing tenants and blue-collar workers."

The article is dense with olive branches. Bernie praises the conservative Republican governor, Richard Snelling, in a telegraphed show of admiration for his soon-to-be sparring partner. During the 1976 gubernatorial campaign, Sanders says, Snelling had shown "genuine feeling" rather than "false political good humor" when booed offstage at a speech that year. Sanders liked Snelling, he told friends, partly because the irascible governor made him, Sanders, look snuggly by comparison. And Bernie has "genuine fondness for Sadie White, the feisty former representative from Burlington's Old North End who almost won a seat on the board of aldermen two weeks ago." White's runoff against Paul Trapinier will pit the city Democratic machine against a woman with "conservative economic and political beliefs." Just as the Democrats were casting him as Che Guevara, Bernie was making a persuasive case for himself as a conservative, Vermont-style. If George Aiken was looking in from Dummerston, he might have approved.

WHILE THE NECTAR'S JUNTO schemed to keep rule in Democratic hands, Sanders made the rounds at his new home, city hall. Desautels and her allies had boasted that Burlington's "weak mayor" system would naturally limit Bernie's influence in city politics. The city's charter was surprisingly undemocratic, vesting almost all governing power—zoning, planning, licensing, ordinances, voting, control of the police and fire departments—in commissions appointed by the board of aldermen. The powerful chairs of these commissions never faced a vote, and so were completely shielded from the public's will. Many had been at their posts for decades, carefully coached by the bosses of the city's Democratic machine. The structure of city government itself required this cronyism: for a mayor to get anything done, he had to have the board of aldermen in his pocket, and, down a rung, a loyal corps of their hand-picked city commissioners.

To rise in this system, you first logged several years on a commission while waiting for a seat on the board of aldermen to open up, then met with the mayor, pledging loyalty. After a decade or so, the mayor would announce that he was stepping down, and from the cast of contestants on the board of aldermen, a successor was chosen. The election was an afterthought; the successor usually ran unopposed. For Bernie to have broken into this system was an outrage. To Paquette's supporters at Nectar's, Sanders was at best a tourist in city government, or perhaps an irritating foreign exchange student, and the city would count down the days until this annoying menace was sent back home. If the board could retain a Democratic majority, Sanders would be completely ineffective in his mayfly-short two-year tenure, and voters would turn him out. A young, liberal alderman, Maurice Mahoney, was waiting in the wings to succeed Gordon Paquette after this surreal interregnum passed. Bernie and his followers would then, like the Moonies, pack up their vans and head to the next town.

The total lack of an inside path meant that Sanders, according to Terry Bouricius in an interview, had to create a "shadow government" working outside the official administrative circuitry of city hall. Sanders met with the city treasurer, Frank Austin, and, realizing the severity of his inherited budget crisis, explored ways "the city can expand its offerings" cheaply: in his modest first actions, he called for a volunteer cleanup day and announced a visiting circus for children. A dedicated corps of unpaid supporters would be empowered to make such events possible. Joyce Desautels, sensing that Bernie had options outside city hall, then decided that the shrewd move was to appear cooperative: "We differ in political philosophy," she said, leaving her first meeting with the mayor-elect, "but we share our love for Burlington and the people in it." She predicted that "we'll be able to work together on some issues," since "he didn't have any green antennas coming out of his head." Once politics came up "in depth," she added, differences "will become apparent." Sanders then announced in the *Burlington Free Press*: "I was not elected to be a weak mayor."

Behind the scenes, Sanders and his attorney had begun to study the city's charter to see what powers he had as of right. With the board of aldermen, who held veto power over his paid appointments, on war footing and organized 11–1 against him (the thirteenth seat was up for grabs, pending the runoff in Sadie White's Ward 3), Sanders appeared to control only a handful of positions: he could appoint two grand jurors, whose roles in the modern era had been assumed by the state's attorney; four constables, in essence bounty hunters who made money by collecting delinquent taxes; a harbormaster, whose job was to putter around in a private craft inside the breakwater in case someone capsized; and a pound keeper, minding stray animals. The situation was humiliating. Every other position was filled with Paquette loyalists, and the city charter appeared to grant the aldermen the power to vote to retain them. Sanders was put on alert that any attempt to fill them with his own appointees would be seen as "cronyism" and "an attempt to plant socialism in the heart of city hall."

Bernie now had to bring his case to the people. The March 24 runoff in Ward 3 was meaningless in terms of Sanders's ability to sustain a veto: even with White on the board, he would be outnumbered 11–2. But as a proxy, it was a chance for Burlington to ratify Bernie's victory over Democrats when there was the growing sense that Paquette's allies would do everything in its power to make him a failed, one-term mayor. Sanders campaigned for White, citing "her links to these people"—the poor, the elderly, the disabled—whom she'd "already brought into the process." Showing off their unusual rapport, Bernie joked, "Despite what you might have heard, Sadie and I are not getting married. She is too young and vigorous and I can't keep up with this woman." When White prevailed by a slimmer-than-expected margin of twenty-four votes, she fled the voting place overwhelmed and in tears. Her political life had been miraculously extended at the age of eighty.

Sadie White, who worked as a weaver in her teens before the First World War, organized the woolen mills in the 1940s, and went to Montpelier in the '60s as Burlington's first woman representative, had helped ring in a new era for Burlington.

WITH SIDES DRAWN over his political appointments, Sanders began to look for political wins outside city hall's bureaucracy. In his spelunking at the city clerk's office, Sanders discovered one enticing power that the mayor of Burlington held in his back pocket: in times of civil emergency, he became "commander of the Burlington Police Force." Mayor Paquette had suspended normal order in 1979 to quash a riot in Battery Park. Bernie saw his first big political opportunity in publicly confronting the University of Vermont over its annual student bacchanalia, "Spring Fling," held on the evening of the last day of classes, in early May. Students in the thousands poured down Main Street, breaking bottles, tearing down road signs, pissing on cars, and shouting insults at random pedestrians, before concentrating at the corner of Main and Church Streets outside the southeast corner of city hall, just a hundred feet or so from the mayor's office. Over the years, the numbers had grown; now Spring Fling was an attraction across the Northeast, with carloads of college students arriving from across New York and New England, along with high school students traveling to join the mayhem from every neck of the Vermont woods.

A year before, in May of 1980, three thousand students had partied all night at Spring Fling. In vain, the city had greased all the utility poles with

Spring Fling gets under way, May 8, 1981. *Jym Wilson*

Vaseline to deter students from climbing and subduing them, like farm boys bending lithesome birch trees. There was little bucolic charm in the sight of a drunken frat brother shimmying up a light post and riding it like a steer, while his comrades heaved their bodies against its base to bring the heavy steel structure down into the dense crowd. But that, and much worse, is what happened at Spring Fling. Reports of sexual assaults had risen over the years, with women reporting that they were groped, forcibly kissed, and digitally penetrated in the terrifying melee. A reporter interviewing students at Spring Fling asked one young man "why he had taken the stoplights apart." Too drunk to respond coherently, the man then "grabbed the hair of a young woman walking past him, and said, 'She's pretty, ain't she!'" Police observed quietly as the party roared on into the morning hours: it was "the easiest night of the year," one officer reported, since all the problems in Burlington had gathered in one place and could therefore be ignored. In an office on the third floor of city hall, Antonio Pomerleau, the police commissioner, looked on without apparent dismay.

The upcoming 1981 Spring Fling promised to be bigger, more frightening, and more violent than ever before. Women at UVM were now in a state of panic. In early March, just a few days before Sanders's election, a student had been tied up and gang-raped at a UVM fraternity, Sigma Nu. There were reports of at least two other rapes in fraternities, and women had been told by frat brothers that they would be beaten if they reported their assaults to the university or the Burlington police. Sanders and his advisers, including Jane Driscoll and Linda Niedweske, were disgusted by the stories coming out of UVM; Driscoll immediately convened, in response, a task force on sexual assault. Friends report that Bernie was "literally nauseous" at the thought of the all-night party happening on his watch, outside his office. The effrontery of wealthy college students damaging city property; the sadism or the outright harassment of ordinary Burlingtonians as these preppy monsters made their way to Church Street; but above all, the injustice of subjecting young women to fear of being attacked, while the university announced that in cases like the fraternity rapes and the Spring Fling assaults, it was genuinely "caught between an obligation to protect students and trying to keep a lid on adverse publicity."

Sanders privately marveled that the city had allowed its student population to go berserk every spring, while cracking down on Supertramp fans at Memorial Auditorium and clearing a crowd of hippies in Battery Park with tear gas and riot gear. He made his first public stand against the university since his election. The issue allowed him to flaunt his politically advantageous relationship with the Burlington police, while giving him an advantage over UVM in battles likely to be much more prolonged. "It is clear that the people of this city have got to be respected," Sanders told reporters on March 17, at his first news conference since winning the recount. "We can't tolerate destruction of property." The mayor-elect's "long-term goal," he announced, was "to make the kids at UVM a part of this community."

Bernie learned over his time in Burlington how to leverage UVM's remarkably chaotic effect on the city, with its many disadvantages for working Burlingtonians. Here was an early opportunity. Sanders had joined a group, led by the former Governor Phil Hoff, opposing the expansion of the UVM Medical Center on the grounds that the cost of the $64 million project would be passed on to patients. Faced with intractable budget problems due to his too-successful campaign to oppose Mayor Paquette's tax increases, Sanders had to find pots of money somewhere. Far from funding the university's expansion, he wanted to bill them. If UVM was going to use city services on its campus, and send its students to destroy downtown, Sanders said, speaking at a hearing before 175 citizens, then he would ask for "substantial payments in lieu of taxes" from the tax-exempt behemoth on the hill in return. To boos and loud heckling, Sanders also attacked "the mentality" of the expansion project, and demanded that poor people be put on the hospital's board of trustees. The new tenor for meetings in Burlington had arrived: on one side, eggheads, bean counters, consultants, engineers, all earnestly making their professional cases. On the other side, Sanders sniping and lashing out at the opposition, with the media lapping it up.

MARCH HAD BEEN an eventful month; the board of aldermen, in essence Mayor Paquette's old cabinet, was strengthening its resistance to Sanders and his socialist cabal; now Paquette himself, tanned and rested from his Florida trip, joined his confederates at Nectar's at their usual table, plotting his restoration. "We just need to hang on for two years," Joyce Desautels told him. The Sanders era "would be a blip."

Sanders had been dodging interview requests from national and international media for weeks. "We'll charge $10 a head to see the freak mayor," he joked—correctly suggesting that he would grow Burlington's economy by becoming one of its main tourist attractions. But when NBC called him from Chicago, Sanders took the bait. Phil Donahue, the schoolboyish, gesticular talk show host with a cumulus-cloud-gray pageboy, wanted Sanders as a guest on his hourlong network program. Donahue had interviewed seemingly everyone in his distinguished career—John F. Kennedy, Malcolm X, Ayn Rand; a true-believer liberal who later campaigned in 2000 for Ralph Nader, Donahue believed that he had discovered in Bernie "an enigma in

Sanders and a spellbound Phil Donahue. *Today*

his own times." Sanders at first demurred: he didn't want to be "the overnight spokesman for socialism," he said, adding, "I'm having a hard enough time keeping my coalition together." He was then approached by Wendy Roth, a producer for the *Today* show, where Donahue had a regular guest spot: to Roth, Sanders was "an offbeat individual in an offbeat town, and seemed to go against the trend in the country, Ronald Reagan and all."

As he boarded a plane from Burlington to Chicago on March 25, Bernie quipped that he was "probably the only person in America who had never watched the *Today* show." The next morning, the rumpled socialist, "sporting tousled hair and no tie," was "given celebrity treatment at the network's plush 19th floor office downtown," the *Burlington Free Press* reported, savoring the hypocrisies as usual. "The thought that you're talking to 10 million people all over the country sits on your stomach," Bernie remarked, but he appeared "nonplussed" and spoke "in his customary rapid-fire manner." Donahue loved it. "He's really very, very good," he told a reporter after the taping, warmly and effusively shaking Bernie's hand as they posed for photos.

The segment, titled "Socialism in New England," began with an intro from Jane Pauley and a slide of a brook gently wandering down a rocky slope. "My goodness, how did this happen in good old conservative Vermont?" Donahue asks Sanders. "Well," Bernie answers, "in Vermont, being conservative is different perhaps than being conservative elsewhere in the country." Sanders then made his argument for the unique amalgam of labor and libertarian ideas that he'd been developing since he wrote for the *Ver-*

mont Freeman. "The cops supported you, didn't they?" Donahue asks. "So, you had police officers voting for you who probably voted for Ronald Reagan?" "Our police are trade unionists," Sanders replied, putting the matter to rest.

Sanders spends far more of the seven-minute segment defending his conservative credentials than making a case for socialism. Vermont conservatism "isn't big-money conservatism. It's not right-wingism and warmongerism. Vermont has always had strong feelings about civil liberties. What conservatism means is 'Leave me alone, get the government off my back.' It's a respect for other people's rights: if we disagree, we'll talk it out." As for "socialism," all it meant, to Sanders, was "democratic participation." George Aiken, taking a break from setting up his bean teepees, tuned in from Dummerston.

Finally, Donahue cut to the chase: "Are you—a capitalist?" he demanded.

Sanders, smiling faintly and lowering his tone, replied, "No, I am not a capitalist."

Donahue: "Yeah, but what about if I build a better mousetrap?"

Sanders: "Do I believe the profit motive is fundamental to human nature? The answer is, no. I believe in the spirit of cooperation, that you and I can work together better, rather than trying to destroy one another."

AT MATER CHRISTI SCHOOL, we tuned in from Miss Rusk's homeroom to see our mayor on what we all called "national television"; everyone in Burlington watched the segment, which aired two weeks after it was shot. On the streets of the city described by Phil Donahue as "a lovely, lovely spot in this country," whatever your politics, the consensus was that it was very nice what Phil Donahue had said about us, and that Bernie really should have worn a tie.

Also tuning in: Edward Williams, the assistant U.S. attorney for the Southern District of New York, a Ronald Reagan appointee. Williams picked up the phone and ordered an FBI agent to Vermont—to flash his badge and ask, as they say, *a couple of questions* of Burlington's new socialist mayor, Bernard Sanders.

Part IV

The People's Republic of Burlington

Sanders and City Attorney Joseph McNeil, 1980s.
Jym Wilson

25

B. S. Sanders, Temporary Mayor

(Red Scare in the Queen City, 1981)

Mayor Sanders in city hall. *Fred Bayles*

Inauguration Day

Burlington had never seen anyone like Bernie Sanders. When they made Bernie, people said, they broke the mold. Sanders's totally unchanging and inimitable personal style—the hair, the clothes, the glasses, the voice—paid political dividends all throughout the 1970s, as people widely dispersed in Vermont experienced nevertheless the same unbelievable phenomenon and heard the same incessant message. There could only be one Bernie.

So, on Inauguration Day, April 7, 1981, what a surprise to meet a second, duplicate Bernie Sanders! Larry Sanders arrived from England, same gap-toothed grin, darker but equally unruly mop of hair, similar horn-rimmed glasses. "The only difference," the *Burlington Free Press* reported, "was their accents." Larry's Brooklyn baritone had an English tint; Bernie, the reporter huffed, had not shown the common decency to pick up even a whiff of Vermont intonation.

Larry had kept a cautious eye on Burlington throughout the winter and spring, from his home in Oxford, England. "Bernard called me during the campaign and said, 'I think I'm going to win this one,'" Larry recalled. "I said, yeah, right." Arriving at the Burlington airport, Larry thought back to the first time he visited Burlington from Brooklyn College in the 1950s, for a debate tournament at UVM. A "kindly, laid-back, very Vermont old bellman" greeted him and his friends at the Hotel Vermont, and chatted amiably with the young visitors, before casually launching into an anti-Semitic lament about the presence of "new immigrants" in town. Twenty-five years later, across from the old Hotel Vermont, on his way to city hall, Larry Sanders happily noted the sign for the Burlington Bagel Bakery. It suddenly began to make sense that one of those "new immigrants" was about to take the oath.

As Bernie and Larry Sanders made their way down Church Street toward the ceremony, an old woman approached: "I voted for you," she exclaimed. Bernie then "got up on the hood of a car," Larry told me, and gave an impromptu speech to a small crowd. "He's so funny," the woman said, tugging at Larry's arm, "and so young—and, he's going to be our mayor!"

Now, three Sanders men, Bernie, Larry, and eleven-year-old Levi, sat in the back of Contois Auditorium in city hall, waiting for the proceedings to begin. With twenty or so minutes to go, Bernie was still writing his speech on a yellow legal pad, fending off admirers and well-wishers. Levi told a reporter he longed to be out "playing hoops." When Bernie was asked if he, too, wished he was playing hoops, he looked up from his pad and answered, "No, I made up my mind a long time ago" that city hall was "the place for me." The answer certainly made it sound like he wished he was playing hoops.

In a gray suit he "had owned for about an hour," purchased from Abernathy's at the head of Church Street and pinned with a pink carnation, Sanders delivered his inaugural address to a crowd of 250. Bernie's proclamation that he "did not have any sadistic desire to destroy the business community—or convert Church Street into a cow pasture" was perhaps a little too fanged to comfort the jittery downtown merchants in the room. Sanders repeated his campaign pledges to stop the UVM Medical Center expansion, the Southern Connector, and the waterfront condos, and announced an advisory committee to devise "new forms of progressive taxation." An olive branch aimed at the seditious Democratic aldermen doubled as a slingshot: "While we have our differences," Sanders said, "let's have them out in the open, and both be able to give a little." He derided "cronyism" and called for wide and enthusiastic citizen participation in city government, and predicted that Burlington would show America "a sense of purpose which we seem to be lacking today as a nation."

After the mayor's speech, city hall, for nearly a decade a dour crypt breached mainly by those seeking the public bathrooms in its basement, invited Burlington in for a community party. Children made their names echo off the marble walls and skimmed Oreos and Hawaiian Punch from folding tables. The generational shift in city politics was immediately apparent: Sanders's closest advisers were in their twenties and thirties, many with young families. Their kids began right from the start to lay claim to the old building as a casual place to hang out, after school or on a snowy weekend day. A metal slinky lurched down the grand staircase of Vermont marble. A superball bounced in the formal foyer. Jane Driscoll's kids played Twister and tag downstairs in the auditorium.

After Sanders had gone and only a few stragglers remained, Jim Rader roamed in the hallway outside the mayor's office, soaking it all in. When the phone on Bernie's desk rang, he decided to answer it: "Mayor's office." An irate woman from Ward 2 was on the line, complaining about a deteriorating curb on lower Church Street and seeking immediate action from the mayor.

For better or worse, as Jim told me, "it was our city now."

AT A DEMOCRATIC SOCIALIST gathering in Springfield, Massachusetts, that spring, Terry Bouricius paraphrased Friedrich Engels: "One of the worst things a socialist can do is get elected before it's time for the revolution." He meant that Sanders had ridden a wave. Others smelled blood in the water.

Bernie sought the national spotlight in part to bring his city hall foes out of the shadows. "We are going to speak out on national and international issues," Sanders told Phil Donahue. "We'll have lots of things to say to Mr. Reagan in due course," he told reporters. To many it seemed grandiose: Sanders was elected by people who didn't want their property taxes to go up, and now he spoke of Burlington, population thirty-eight thousand, as having "its own foreign policy." But Richard Sugarman, mock-inaugurated by Sanders as Burlington's "Commissioner of Reality"—a philosopher friend asked him who would be "Commissioner of Appearances"—thrilled Bernie when he pondered aloud whether maybe even "Mr. Reagan was watching" the little revolution on Lake Champlain.

Mr. Reagan, recovering from the March 30 attempt on his life, was probably not aware that Bernie Sanders had been inaugurated in Burlington; but the Reagan Justice Department, newly emboldened to investigate American leftists, most certainly was. In late March, the president pardoned two FBI officials, Mark Felt (who later admitted to being "Deep Throat," the mysterious informant in the Watergate scandal) and Edward S. Miller, who were responsible for several secret "black bag jobs"—break-ins—at the homes of members of the '60s radical group Weather Underground. The pardon praised the men for acting "in the security interests of the country." Incidents of surveillance and harassment of activists by federal agents were legend in Burlington all through the 1970s but had subsided under Jimmy Carter. Now our city was back in the Bureau's sights.

On April 8, 1981, Bernie's first day in office, an FBI agent arrived in Montpelier and made his way up the statehouse steps to call on Vermont's secretary of state, James Douglas. Badge out, Agent Fred List then told his convoluted story: he was investigating a plaintiff in the Socialist Workers Party's $40 million lawsuit against the FBI, at the time playing out in a Manhattan federal court. Andrew Pulley, the civil rights activist and 1980 presidential candidate, testified that "a party member"—Sanders was not officially a member of the party, but had served as its elector in the 1980 presidential campaign—had "been elected mayor in Vermont." List claimed he had come all the way to Vermont to confirm that Sanders was not a registered party member, in the hopes of discrediting Pulley. Ironically, this was one of the kinds of techniques that prompted the original suit, which alleged decades of FBI secret surveillance and badge-flashing intimidation of Socialist Workers Party members.

When List demanded that Douglas, a Republican, turn over any information he had on Mayor Sanders, Douglas sent him packing, then contacted Vermont's U.S. attorney, who in turn alerted Bernie. The mayor issued a bitter statement: "After one day in office," he said, he could confirm that, like mayors in many other cities across the land, he was "not under FBI investigation." The *Burlington Free Press* called the episode "reprehensible." The federal judge presiding in the suit chided the defendants. "If the FBI goes into places, if they go into the secretary of state in Vermont's office and ask about the mayor of Burlington," Judge Thomas Griesa warned, "that is likely to get ballooned up into something a little more than just checking on the credibility of testimony." He recommended that next time, they save on gas money and simply telephone the mayor: 802-865-7272.

A month later, in May of 1981, Sanders invited Andrew Pulley to Burlington, defying a rapidly expanding red scare in the Queen City. To counter the suit, the FBI had widened its investigation of the party's "subversive activities" and now sought a beachhead in the only city in America with a socialist mayor. The U.S. Immigration and Naturalization Service, whose regional headquarters just happened to be in a Burlington federal building near city hall, announced that it was joining the FBI in its actions to blacklist the Socialist Workers Party as a "proscribed group" whose foreign members could be deported. The FBI now had agents permanently stationed up the block from Sanders. In the newly dedicated Gordon Paquette Reading Room of the Fletcher Free Library, Sanders welcomed Pulley, and defended himself:

> I think the point Andrew will probably deal with is also well known. In the '50s, with McCarthyism, they created a system of bugaboos, with the bugaboo of communism. Any person who stood up for working people, or for low-income people, or for peace, was associated with the "communist front." Now the word is "terrorist."
>
> Now anybody who stands up and fights and says things is automatically a terrorist and to be associated with these people who plant bombs in buses, and murder children and innocent people.
>
> I trust that many of you know how the system works. It happened slightly, in my case. Because I was an elector for the Socialist Workers Party, there was a "non-investigation." I was "non-investigated" by the FBI. The theory is that it was an attempt to smear me.

"I think there's a way to deal with that terrible word," Sanders concluded, suggesting that a grinding investigation into his past might soon be underway, "that pornographic word which they hate in this country—called socialism."

WITH THE BURLINGTON BOARD of Aldermen in Democratic hands, Sanders was powerless to appoint an administration and a staff. Aldermen's meetings eventually became known as "Monday Night at the Fights," as Chip Wadhams told me. At the first meeting, Sadie White and Terry Bouricius, Bernie's only allies on the board, sallied in together, arm in arm, as a show of solidarity. Things degenerated immediately. Late that night, the aldermen fired Bernie's main aide, Linda Niedweske, whom he'd hired as his secretary, then agreed to reappoint her at a lower salary. Two other aides, Richard Sartelle, constituent case manager, and Jane Driscoll, youth liaison, had to be compensated out of Bernie's pocket. Insults flew. Sartelle, who had organized Franklin Square effectively, was simply "a loudmouth, a hanger-on"; Driscoll, a gifted caseworker at the King Street Center, was merely "Bernie's girlfriend." In a subsequent meeting, Democrats delayed consideration of a property tax hike of twenty-five cents—"politically plausible," according to Bernie, who, with Jennie Stoler, had made a careful line-by-line study of the city budget—while they debated into the early morning whether, for the purposes of a two-dollar city surcharge, a refrigerator counted as a plumbing fixture. Sanders twisted and grimaced and sighed. The city coffers were now nearly empty, but at one a.m., the board nonchalantly tabled Bernie's proposal. Sanders raged.

With no possibility of forming a government, Sanders rallied the public to his side. Two hundred citizens crammed into Contois Auditorium for the June 1 aldermen's meeting when Bernie's slate of six city appointees would be considered: "D-Day," one alderman called it. WJOY broadcast the meeting live, with whispered commentary; reporters turned up from all three national networks, *The Boston Globe*, and *The New York Times*. Sanders knew he had a captive audience, and, to loud cheers and some scattered boos, delivered a stemwinder. He condemned the "well-orchestrated campaign" led by "multibillion-dollar corporations to tell us that government is bad," and to return decision-making powers to the private sector. If America wanted to "leave Exxon alone to shape the nation's energy policy," then it was not a surprise that Burlington had entrusted "the future of medical care in Chittenden County" to businessmen, and the fate of the Burlington waterfront to "private developers." Bernie, stressing his "strong political disagreements" with President Reagan and Governor Snelling, called for a revival of democracy in Burlington: "More people, not less, must be brought into the decision-making process." His appointees looked on anx-

"The Day After." William Sessions is to Bernie's left. *Jym Wilson*

iously. It was the speech of a man who, knowing the day's battle was lost, had decided to widen the war.

His opponents countered swiftly. Joyce Desautels announced that "as a woman, a Christian, and a Democrat," she stood against "expanding the base of the socialist party in the city of Burlington." Maurice Mahoney decried Bernie's "reign of terror." William Blanchard complained that Bernie's attitude was "agree or be sued." Every one of Bernie's appointments was voted down 11–2: John Franco for city clerk, Jim Rader for assistant city clerk, Jennie Stoler for treasurer, James Dunn for assistant city attorney, David Clavelle for director of civil defense, and Steve Goodkind as director of public health and safety. The grounds cited for refusal were specious, casual, and deliberately insulting: Stoler, with a PhD in economics, couldn't understand city finances; Franco was a showboat; Rader was demonized as "an attorney"—he wasn't one; Dunn and Clavelle, lifelong Democrats, were "socialists"; Goodkind, a trained engineer who had a walrus mustache, a mullet, and a leather jacket, was derided as a redneck "biker." Sanders, announcing that he would sue the board as he'd warned, stormed off with his attorney, promising "the biggest constitutional crisis in the city's history." Allen Gear, a Republican alderman, crowed, "It's time for the mayor to realize where the power lies, and it's with this board."

The Burlington Flea Press

Burlington's first public Xerox machines crouched in the basement of Capitol Stationers on Church Street. Upstairs, schoolchildren roamed the aisles for markers, sparkle, and glue. Downstairs, at the copiers, metalheads ran off posters for their bands and teenagers occasionally xeroxed their bare asses. The upstairs was wholesome and bright, the downstairs, stygian and edgy. In those days there was something faintly illicit about a copy center and the motives of those who frequented such establishments.

Capitol Stationers, a block and a half from city hall, was a perfect place to produce the *Burlington Flea Press*, an anonymous slander sheet aimed at the city's new mayor. In fact Peter Freyne, the city reporter for *The Vermont Vanguard Press*, an intrepid and tireless curator of scuttlebutt, had thought he saw the traces of a Capitol Stationers job in the material presentation of the *Flea Press*, and stopped by the shop. The copy clerks, who loved gossiping with Freyne, told him of a jowly figure in trench coat and tweed cap who had that afternoon hastily collated and stapled fifty copies of a "confidential document," then vanished into the bright midday Church Street crowd, a bundle tucked under his arm. Ah, but this mysterious figure had left an

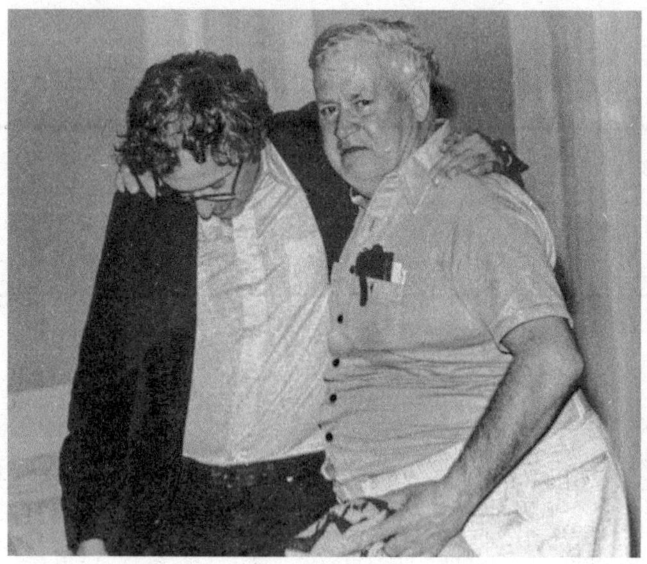

Sanders and Richard Sartelle. *Rob Swanson*

original in the bowels of the big machine! It was a mock-up of page two of the that week's edition of the *Flea Press.*

The public learned of the turmoil convulsing city hall that spring and summer in the pages of the *Burlington Free Press*. But inside city hall, everyone got their news from the *Flea Press*, delivered on Thursdays with a different postmark every week and sealed in a plain manila envelope—"the way porn is delivered," as Greg Guma put it. Sanders received a personal copy, addressed to "B. S. Sanders, Temporary Mayor," or "Burn A. Sunder, Days Numbered." The *Flea Press* went well beyond the bounds of responsible satire, identifying Richard Sartelle as "Pritchard Sauresmail," an "overweight elephant in search of peanuts," and mocking his disability: "We can't imagine that a husky, healthy, ambulatory man could possibly be disabled." A female aide was depicted as "an overweight Venus clad in a flimsy white dress accompanied by six goatish young winos from our Marxist proletariat." Linda Niedweske, called "Glenda Needswitz," was mocked as a spoiled "nutritionist" who couldn't type.

Her portrait was done in verse; whoever was behind the *Flea Press* knew the basics of prosody, and managed to convey his odious ideas in halfway-decent ballad stanzas:

The mayor's typewriter is covered with dust
But sturdy and staunch it stands

Though our middle-class Board thinks typing's a must
It soils nutritional hands.

When a Sanders character appeared in Garry Trudeau's *Doonesbury*, a nationally syndicated strip, the *Flea Press* added its own comic strip, *Goonsbury*, complete with anti-Semitic caricatures of the mayor. Two local attorneys opined that the targets of the *Flea Press* had "grounds for lawsuits against the perpetrator," *The Vermont Vanguard Press* reported.

The author or authors of the *Flea Press* were not just having fun; they intended to destroy Bernie and his allies. I'd heard about the paper for years, but never laid eyes on a copy until Greg Guma—one of its targets, mocked as "Gregg Goona of the Rumpguard Press"—located his stash. It is, in fact, insane. Its author intends to discourage, intimidate, and frighten. As the *Flea Press* became more libelous and seditious, more demented, Bernie's adversaries in city hall began to flaunt their enjoyment of the paper. Allan Gear of Ward 4 distributed it at aldermen's meetings. Its reactionary argot—Bernie's "cadre," his "comrades"—began to seep into mainstream press reports. The paper betrayed "an insider perspective," as Guma put it. "Many people assumed that a city employee was involved."

The shadowy patron who'd left his mock-up behind on the glass was one Vincent Naramore, a math professor at Saint Michael's College, former chair of the Burlington Democratic Party, political commentator and pollster, and one of Gordon Paquette's closest friends. Naramore, in fact, had been on the radio the night of Bernie's victory, spreading disinformation to benefit Paquette about low turnouts in Bernie-friendly wards; it was when he delivered this analysis that Jim Rader, listening on the road to the ferry, wrote the evening off. Naramore had proffered misinformation for years with his patented Vermont Political Poll, which was considered the gold standard until *Free Press* reporters looked at its actual performance and found it to rank near the bottom of all similar polls nationwide.

Naramore therefore had reason to despise the *Free Press* and Sanders both. And though he denied being the *Flea Press*'s author, he had left an additional clue inside its pages. Those demeaning, sexist satirical ballads were clearly the work of an experienced writer of doggerel; it happened that Naramore was an amateur versifier who wrote and published children's songs on the side—including, as Naramore liked to boast, a tune performed on the air by Captain Kangaroo. When confronted by Peter Freyne, Naramore brought up Gordon Paquette's lawsuit against Guma and the *Vanguard*, threatening his own legal action against the paper. Naramore was busted; Freyne's star was on the rise.

DENIED AN ADMINISTRATION, with the FBI on the ground in Burlington and his adversaries threatening him in ways increasingly bizarre and craven, Sanders was ill at ease sitting in his own office. Mayoral power therefore had to be moved outside of city hall. Sanders had a direct feed to the star-struck media, and did much of his governing during that first year in front of a bank of microphones: it seemed almost every night the WCAX news with Richard Gallagher ran clips of Bernie's press conferences, where the sedate announcement of a children's art exhibit at city hall might be followed by a furious condemnation of the CIA. And Bernie "discovered the supply closet," Richard Sugarman said: Bernie had city letterhead, on which he could write appeals to volunteers and philanthropists, as well as outraged screeds to President Reagan, which he sometimes, in turn, announced at his press conferences. The mayor delivered a get-well letter to Pope John Paul II after the attempt on the pope's life, using a go-between, the pope's rumored mistress, who lived in southern Vermont. Sanders then placed the letter in *The Catholic Tribune*. As a strategy to curry support with the city's Catholics, Bernie's letter to the pope made real inroads in parishes like ours, where it was reprinted in the Sunday missal.

But Sanders had, in essence, no government—and no budget. When Bernie visited the statehouse to make a pitch to legislators, a young Republican representative from Burlington, in later years Sanders's opponent in races for governor and U.S. Congress, Peter Smith, presented him with a T-shirt depicting "The People's Republic of Burlington," with fortune-cookie lettering and the city's skyline done in the style of a Chinese take-out container. Sanders loved it; he copied the design and arranged for the shirts to be sold nationally, to benefit his nascent arts council. The gambit raised but a few hundred dollars. Buttons reading "As Goes Burlington, so Goes France," commemorating the elections of Mayor Sanders and French President François Mitterrand, drew the slogan from a line in Trudeau's *Doonesbury* that Bernie inspired. They sold even worse.

Sanders had to siphon authority from the community, bypassing the hostile aldermen and commissioners. He started small, asking bankers like Hilton Wick to support a summer concert series in city hall and uniforms for a new Little League team in the Old North End, where there had never been organized youth baseball. The local burghers generously donated the cash, and Sanders, still the sworn enemy of Burlington's Democrats, began to make inroads with its Republicans, who had been shut out of Gordon Paquette's city hall.

Bernie fielded dozens of letters every week from constituents volunteering to put their talents to work for Burlington and expressing dismay at the aldermen's sedition. Jim Rader, now the city clerk in waiting, coordinated the volunteers using a proto-computational punch card technology. Rader would indicate by punching the hole in a card next to a volunteer's preferred role (parks, budget, elderly outreach, the arts, children's programming); the cards were then stacked, and a long knitting needle inserted through the matched holes would gather them into collated stacks. As Bernie's city clerk, Jim would soon be in charge of elections, where the technology was not much more advanced. But from this primitive beginning sprang a network of task forces and councils that dramatically changed the direction of the new Burlington. The old commissions, still staffed with Paquette's supporters, watched in alarm as Sanders shifted powers away from the smoky redoubts where they'd planned and governed the city for decades.

THE SANDERS ADMINISTRATION in exile met on Sunday evenings at Bernie's apartment on North Union Street, formerly "a FEMA-like disaster site," according to a friend, now hastily spruced up with new rugs, furniture, and houseplants to befit the dignity of the city's chief executive. The tiny space often played host to a crowd of a dozen or so close advisers and representatives of city groups; at one meeting in late August, the minutes show twenty-two people in attendance, including representatives of the police and fire unions, PACT, the King Street Center, and the Church Street Marketplace Commission. The meetings convened at dinnertime, but according to one attendee, "there was not ever any food."

Bernie's staff was therefore a group on the edge, and by the fall it was running short on patience; and Sanders, frustrated by his inability to override the seditious aldermen and seeing his first term slip away, became an impossible boss. A confrontational memo was delivered to Sanders on October 27, 1982, and signed by the core group of Jim Rader, Jim Dunn, Jane Driscoll, Steve Goodkind, Linda Niedweske, Doreen Kraft, Jennie Stoler, and John Franco. While democracy seemed resurgent in Burlington, Bernie's administration complained of being shut out by a crabby despot. "The following comments and suggestions are meant to be constructive statements and not to undermine you as the person or you as the Mayor," the memo read. These suggestions were made by "your greatest and most loyal supporters and advisors":

1. You don't smile at meetings—you look bored and annoyed that you are there—People get the impression that you are doing them a big favor by being there.

2. You are not nice to people—you see people on the street and walk right past them—no hello, handshake, or acknowledgment that they exist—Your bias against young people, women, and wealthy people shows through here—people get really insulted and complain to us.

Item 3 was subdivided into seven points, A–G. Some highlights, though: "you don't read memos," "you don't seem appreciative of the work that is done for you," "you play the martyr that your life is more miserable, hectic, etc. than others," "you lend no support to those around you," and "you have little or no trust that a job will get done quickly and successfully." The back page gave suggestions so basic as to seem appropriate for a middle school kid: plan your days, allocate your time, deal with people and concerns one at a time.

Did the memo have any effect on Bernie's management style? "No," one signer of the letter told me. "It didn't seem to," said another, with a chuckle; but if you knew Bernie well, you weren't at all surprised.

Did anyone resign? Of the seven signatories, three served out Bernie's terms or even beyond, including one, Doreen Kraft, who is still the city's arts coordinator; three more cycled out of the administration but remember the time fondly; and the last, Jane Driscoll, married Bernie.

"It didn't matter," one signatory told me. "When he gave a speech, up there saying all the things we believed, we kind of looked around at each other like: Wow, we are a part of something big."

ON AUGUST 31, Chittenden County Superior Court Judge James B. Morse threw Sanders's lawsuit against the Burlington Board of Aldermen out of court, pronouncing starkly and simply: "This is politics." Sanders vowed to appeal to the Vermont Supreme Court, but the judge's opinion proved all too apt; politics, Queen City–style, continued on apace. Five Democrats on the board, including Joyce Desautels, were up for reelection in March. Less than a year after announcing his campaign for mayor, Sanders needed to run again, and just as hard, on behalf of candidates who would swing the balance of the board in his favor. The incumbents, meanwhile, had a powerful ally embedded in city hall: Frank L. Wagner, Mayor Paquette's city clerk and best friend, and the powerful voter registration board that fell under his influence.

In the early 1980s, the mayor's office and the city clerk's office were next to each other on the second floor of city hall. Sanders had begun to close and lock the door connecting them, sensing that Wagner was eavesdropping on his calls and even entering the office when he stepped out. Wagner was also widely suspected to be the inside source for the *Burlington Flea Press*—Wagner's second assistant clerk was the sister-in-law of its publisher, Vincent Naramore. In July, Wagner intercepted a letter addressed to Sanders critical of Wagner; when Sanders caught him, the city clerk, a bow-tied, apple-cheeked bureaucrat, was put on unpaid leave for three weeks. He returned cheerfully to his bailiwick just five feet from Bernie's desk once his sentence was served, whistling while he worked. Now, emboldened by the failure of Sanders's lawsuit, Wagner sought to interfere in the March city election that would determine the partisan spread of the board of aldermen—and therefore his own future in city hall.

Lacking a party infrastructure, Sanders grudgingly delegated to the Citizens Party—whose endorsement just months before he had downplayed—the job of recruiting a slate of progressive candidates for alderman. Caucuses would soon be held; in the meantime, Seth Lipschutz and others from the party registered some five hundred new voters for the March contest. When Wagner reviewed the list of names, he counted one hundred or so students living in UVM dormitories. Abetted by his cronies on the voter registration board, and assuming that those were one hundred votes for Sanders's allies, the city clerk announced a new policy: students living in dorms would have to come to city hall in person to certify their residency by a six-step process if they wished to vote. A hearing was scheduled for the Monday before Thanksgiving, when many of those students would be home in their childhood bedrooms in Massachusetts and New Jersey, reuniting with the KISS dolls, Shaun Cassidy posters, and stuffed animals of their childhood years.

"The students": old-guard Burlington assumed they'd put Bernie over the top, even though turnout in the student wards was down on Election Day 1981. "Anyone under thirty with a beard," Garrison Nelson said, "was assumed to be a student." The term was a messy shorthand for "leftist," since the actual students at UVM, many of them party animals and frat brothers who spent much of their time skiing at Stowe and Sugarbush, were apolitical. But Wagner and his allies on the board even floated the idea of moving city elections from March to May, when UVM was on summer break. In Ward 1, my ward and the main turf of the university, Joyce Desautels rallied voters like my grandparents to support her on March 5. "We're going to need your support against the students!" she wrote in a Christmas card.

With weeks to go before an all-important election, dozens of registrations in Ward 1 were still held up; but in late February, a U.S. district court judge issued an injunction halting the voter registration board's six-step residency test. It would be hard to imagine that any of these contested votes went to Desautels over Rik Musty, the Citizens Party candidate. Musty was the chair of the UVM psychology department, a wry, lanky Minnesotan with a background in leftist politics, cannabis research, and ice hockey. In corduroy blazers and jeans, Musty seemed the very image of the cool professor. You could see just why a small group of students in Ward 1 fought so hard for the vote; you might even wonder to what extent they had enjoyed their professor's indulgence and guidance.

IN MARCH OF 1982, the beginnings of a new political party began to emerge. The Progressive Coalition was not formed until two years later, with cautious support from Bernie, its figurehead; but its origins are found in the slate of six candidates recruited by Sanders, vetted by him in one-on-one meetings, and presented to the voters as a bloc, under the slogan "Burlington Moving Forward."

Three of Bernie's candidates ousted old-line Burlington Democrats. In Ward 1, Rik Musty turned aside Joyce Desautels by forty-five votes, ending her political career. In Ward 2, Zoe Breiner, "a completely nonpolitical person," as she admitted, running mainly to oppose a wood chip–generating plant planned in her backyard, defeated Russell Niquette, a machine Democrat. In Ward 3, Gary De Carolis defeated Ronald Paquette, the ex-mayor's cousin. With Terry Bouricius and Sadie White, that made five votes on the board for Sanders, enough to sustain his veto but insufficient to generate or advance much legislation of their own. There were no two alike among these five, and they disagreed with one another, and with Sanders, frequently. But there were also odd allegiances: Bouricius, the farthest left and most ideological of the group, was closest personally to White, a conservative democrat. Bouricius, De Carolis, Breiner, and Musty were representatives of the Citizens Party, which was allied closely to the Burlington Peace Coalition, though none of them were active in the antiwar movement. Sanders's initiatives divided the five: Breiner was against Bernie's wood chip plant; Musty was against his attempts to extort revenues from Musty's employer, the University of Vermont, and against rent control; De Carolis opposed Bernie's fiscal austerity measures; White, the former chair of the VFW Ladies Auxiliary, was culturally of another era, and kept her distance from anything approaching radicalism.

This motley group found surprising points of contact with the Republican bloc, newly resurgent and also internally varied. Musty, hailing from a big Republican family outside of Minneapolis, became close friends with Bob Paterson, the Republican alderman known at the Burlington Tennis Club as a gracious doubles partner. "They've kept us out of the conversation for years," Paterson told Musty, who sat beside him at the horseshoe-shaped aldermen's table, whispering jokes and passing jotted notes. Both men considered themselves progressives. And this confluence was not merely terminological: both Bernie's progressives and their Republican counterparts favored an expansion of individual rights, the creation of a rational and modern bureaucracy, policy innovation driven by citizen input, and public-private development partnerships. The devil would be, of course, in the details. But Sanders entered the second year of his term with a tenuous governing coalition made up of people purportedly on opposite sides of the political spectrum who nevertheless seemed to like one another—and to revile, in Burlington's Democrats, the same enemy.

26

The People's Republic of Burlington

(Pilgrims, Artists, and Monsters in the New Burlington)

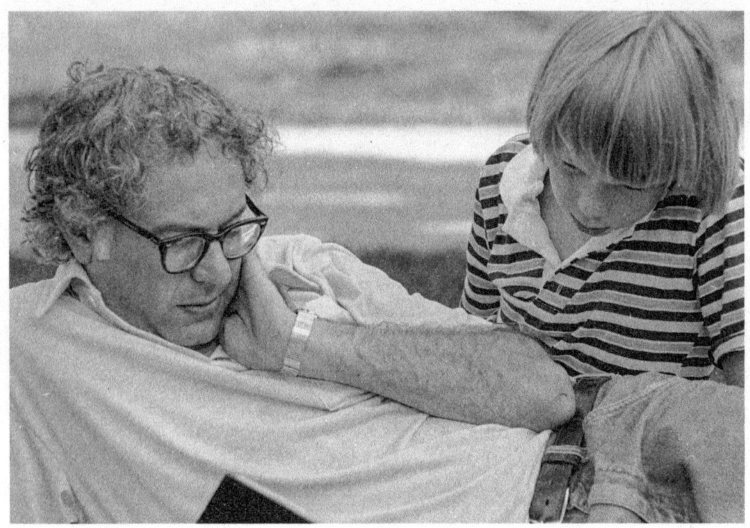

Bernie and Levi Sanders, City Hall Park, 1981. *Jym Wilson*

Though Cyndi Lauper quickly came and went, and Supertramp was banned, a vibrant scene of artists, writers, and performers matured organically in Burlington throughout the seventies, awaiting a champion in city hall. When Bernie emerged, this eager community was there to greet him, and to help him. In mid-March of 1981, Sanders sat down with Doreen Kraft and others to create a task force on the arts, as his first official act as mayor-elect of the city of Burlington. With scarcely a week to plan it, Sanders announced a free festival in the gymnasium of Edmunds Middle School for late March, headlined by old friends from the Winooski River Valley. Donny Osman's "Two Penny Circus," an eight-member troupe of volunteer acrobats and mimes, performed in Vermont schools, jails, and nursing homes, with shows like "Mission: Nutrition." On March 27, 1981, when a spotlit mime fluttered out of a papier-mâché cocoon at half-court, the Sanders era in Burlington was underway.

Now Sanders and Kraft planned a free summer concert series in Battery Park, to complement the Sunday-night Lawrence Welk–style band concerts played before a crowd of dozing old people in lawn chairs. Sanders wanted to "rehabilitate the atmosphere" of the troubled park, which had seen another downturn: pot smoke, petty crime, muscle cars, tank tops. Bernie promised to serve "many different tastes. We'll have classical, folk, country, jazz. Even rock, which I personally have a hard time with." Appealing to local Republican businessmen for sponsorship, Kraft and Sanders soon booked their first act, the Birchwood Bell Ringers from the Birchwood nursing home, where Sadie White had connections.

The next letter went to a Cadillac salesman on Lyman Street in the city's South End, Wilfred Beaudoin. Willie Beaudoin's Jazz Band had for years played supper-hour music at the Burlington Country Club, breaking only for lobster Newburg and a brandy sour. Jazz and Cadillacs, though, were only Willie's ways of paying the bills. Willie and his family, performing as La Famille Beaudoin, were the greatest living performers of traditional French-Canadian mountain music, learned from their parents and grandparents during "kitchen junkets" in their childhood home, nearby in Lakeside. The family had kept a canon of songs and performance styles from vanishing. Their reels, hornpipes, and jigs originated in the wild, steep Laurentian town of Sainte-Émélie-de-l'Énergie, ninety miles north of Montreal. After emigrating to work in the mills of Lowell, Massachusetts, the Beaudoins arrived in Burlington in 1937, to join the large French-speaking community that fought to elect Sanders in 1981.

During the '81 campaign, a Sanders volunteer met Willie Beaudoin in his vestibule, and persuaded him to play a little of "La Bastringue," a traditional tune. The Beaudoins were not an obscure act, except at home: the family had played at one of Jimmy Carter's inaugural balls in 1976, and again that year on the National Mall, for the bicentennial. Bob Hope had them on a TV special. Andy Williams had welcomed them for a Christmas telecast. But the family had never once performed in their home city of Burlington, where French-Canadian culture lingered in pockets like Lakeside but elsewhere dried up, as people like my great-grandparents assimilated. "I've always had a hang-up about that," Willie told a reporter, "a fear that we'd be better accepted away from home. But this time I felt that, if it will help to clean up the park, I want to do my part."

Eight hundred people crowded Battery Park to see La Famille Beaudoin perform in July of 1981, welcomed to their lawn chairs by the newly established Mayor's Council on the Arts, with Doreen Kraft as its indefatigable director. The three living Beaudoin brothers (Louis, the eldest, had just died) and their children and grandchildren performed on fiddle, harp, spoons, and guitar, the time set by traditional step dances for loud wooden clogs. "Just to get out, see Burlington, I guess," Willie Beaudoin told WCAX, when asked his favorite part of the evening. "Just get out and have a look around. Haven't been downtown much in a long time, I suppose." Burlington saw quite a bit of the Beaudoins after that. Mayor Sanders had invited them home.

"I CAN'T BELIEVE they elected you," Henny Youngman exclaimed when he greeted Bernie at the Burlington International Airport. A local rug installer unrolled a three-foot-wide strip of red carpet for Youngman to walk down, then handed the comedian a business card. The seventy-six-year-old Borscht Belt legend greeted dozens of awaiting fans: "I do banquets, sales meetings, outdoor fairs, bar mitzvahs, colleges, conventions, trade shows," he told a reporter, "anywhere they need a guy like me!"

Burlington evidently needed a guy like Henny Youngman. At the Holiday Inn on Williston Road, the marquee spelled out, "Henny Youngman knows that fiddling goes with a paucity of prose." "What the hell does that mean?" Youngman demanded. "I don't know about this town!" At the UVM Medical Center, Youngman was presented with an engraved bedpan noting his "bedpan humor." Arriving at city hall, Youngman approached Linda Niedweske at the receptionist's desk and demanded to see a foot doctor. "What does a guy have to do to get a foot doctor in this city?" Youngman kept saying throughout the afternoon. "I need a chiropodist!"

It became clear that he was not entirely joking, but Sanders, proclaiming "Henny Youngman Day in Burlington," was "guffawing the whole time" and "never had so much fun in his life," according to Richard Sugarman, who accompanied Bernie and Henny on their whirlwind tour, culminating in a reception at the Burlington Bagel Bakery. "Do you guys serve scrambled eggs?" Youngman asked the bagel people, prompting cascades of laughter in the crowd; once again, it was not clear whether he was joking, but Sanders clasped his shoulder and side-hugged him, absolutely shining with admiration for the man.

"EVERYONE WAS CALLING ME: Should I move to Burlington?" Sugarman told me. "Like it was fin de siècle Vienna or Sartre's left bank." Julia Alvarez, the Dominican American poet and novelist, was among the very first artists to take the measure of Bernie's Burlington. Alvarez moved to Burlington in June of 1981, to teach at UVM; by the summer of 1982, she was living in Mrs. Florence Perkins's boardinghouse on Greene Street. Mrs. Perkins was "a Burlington institution. When she died at 109, they had a parade," Alvarez said. "She vetted us. It was girls only. You didn't do anything so crass as slip the rent money under her door," Alvarez reported. "You visited with her, she dressed up as Mrs. Santa Claus on Christmas, she distributed little dish towels as gifts, Irish dish towels with the next year's calendar."

"I became an osmosis hippie in Burlington," Alvarez told me. "All my friends were coming home from hearing Bernie, going to Bernie events, going to city hall to see Bernie in a meeting, or at a press conference." Alvarez's sonnet sequence "33," in her first book, *Homecoming* ("My Burlington book," as she wrote in an inscription to me), was mostly composed in her room on Greene Street. The poems are an exquisite emotional calendar, marking the days as Alvarez, "divorced at twenty-nine," now "thirty- / three without a husband, house, or children" and "ill with acute loneliness," gradually puts a new life together in the city, one fourteen-line block at a time.

Alvarez's romantic improvisations keep malfunctioning: she has a boring date at the Sirloin Saloon, where I had my First Communion reception, and flirts with the UPS guy ("surprised / that he's a decade younger") on her birthday. But the poet's formal improvisations within the patriarchal framework of the sonnet end up fortifying her: "I've tried my moves out here instead, / getting as close as I can in this poem, / and now, closer." In

A page from Julia Alvarez's "Burlington Scrapbook."
Courtesy Julia Alvarez

"Housekeeping Cages," a prose work, Alvarez described her ambition to write "33" in "a woman's voice" like the one she would use, perhaps, sitting in the Greene Street kitchen "with a close friend, talking womanstuff."

Homecoming is perhaps the first, and among the most durable, on-the-ground dispatches from the new Burlington, tracking its revolutionary-seeming opportunities for life and expression. Burlington had become "Bernie's city," as Julia told me. The excitement of generational change and political possibility—the forces that brought young, dynamic women like her to elderly Mrs. Perkins's rooming house—registers throughout the book as the sudden flash of attraction between writer and reader, paired across silence like smitten strangers on the bus or the sidewalk. To me, growing up a few blocks from where the sonnet sequence was written, "33" reads like an homage to Alvarez's adopted city. The poet might have been addressing Burlington itself when she wrote, "There's nothing you can do, / by now, I am already inside you."

WHAT WAS IT like "inside" Burlington? People around the world wanted to know, and they wrote to Bernie to ask. A woman from Belgium inquired about the Fletcher Free Library: "Does it have an extensive cookbook section?" A couple from Baltimore asked about the public kindergartens. A socialist couple from Abilene, Texas, worried about the winters. These letters were a constant during the Sanders years, as were Bernie's prompt and thorough responses on city letterhead.

Some who arrived in Burlington asked to be compelled to stay, so intense was their commitment. "I am writing to you because I want to make my permanent residency in Burlington as official as possible," Betsy Carter of North Carolina explained. "I have enclosed a document (which I created myself) establishing Burlington as my one true home. If you would sign it and return it to me in the enclosed self-addressed stamped envelope before January 1, I would greatly appreciate it." Sanders dutifully signed and returned, and Betsy Carter invited Bernie to a "small, candlelit ceremony (complete with readings from Plato and vows)" to mark her arrival.

Burlington, Vermont, was the place to see socialism in action. The French philosopher Michel Foucault visited UVM for three weeks in November of 1982, traveling from Berkeley to Burlington, lured in part by the desire to behold this unique American experiment firsthand. At Leunig's on College and Church Streets—"a replica of Paris!" he told his hosts, Huck Gutman and Kenneth Rothwell—he could jot down notes in peace all day, entirely unrecognized in the throngs on the Church Street Marketplace.

In UVM's Bailey-Howe Library, where Bernie spent much of the 1970s reading leftist paraphernalia, Foucault "had managed to locate a book unobtainable in all of Paris," as he told a reporter: the *Oneirocritica* of Artemidorus, a second-century Roman guide to dream interpretation and a subject of *The Care of the Self*, the third volume of Foucault's magisterial *History of Sexuality*. Day after day, revisiting this cursed tome, with its detailed dreams of incest, spiders, and horses, Foucault sat at a corner table at Leunig's or on the orange sectionals in the lounge at UVM's Living/Learning Center, where my mother recruited many of my early babysitters. When I read Foucault, I often think of the loud vending machines in Living/Learning, dispensing bottles of Fanta Orange or Grape for a quarter.

Sanders introduced Foucault at a public lecture in early November, reading a speech written by Huck Gutman. He then sat uncomfortably through Foucault's talk, whispering to Sugarman, "Do you think anyone in this audience knows what the fuck he's talking about?"

And yet Foucault's address, titled "Technologies of the Self," seemed chosen to speak directly to Bernie and Burlington. In opposition to the ancient Delphic oracle, which mandated "know thyself," Foucault described a higher, more communitarian ideal: "to be concerned with yourself" or "to take care of yourself" in the interest of social and political organization. Speaking slowly, and pausing to allow his words to settle, Foucault seemed to call on Burlington to revive this forgotten principle: "The precept 'to be concerned with oneself' was, for the Greeks, one of the main principles of cities, one of the main rules for social and personal conduct and for the art of life. For us now this notion is rather obscure and faded."

Despite his impatience throughout Foucault's address, Sanders beamed at a reception afterward, joking with Foucault: "Did Huck write your speech, too?" Foucault seemed "perturbed" by that, according to Gutman. In a seminar for faculty, Sugarman found Foucault "slippery" and impossible to engage: when challenged about his interpretation of a "spurious dialogue of Plato," Foucault barked, "Technicalities!" When asked his opinion of Levinas, Foucault said, "How can one even attempt to describe such a man?" Sugarman responded, "Why not try?" But the great man's visit was in many ways poignant, for reasons only a few in the community knew. The UVM visit was Foucault's last extended public appearance before his death from AIDS in 1984.

BERNIE'S BURLINGTON MOVED to a distinctive, new sound. This sound made a leap from the existing Burlington styles: the "jazzgrass" outfit Pine Island, playing at the Opry on Main, later Hunt's; the nouveau-Celtic band Colcannon at the Millard Fillmore, later the OP; Banjo Dan and the Midnite Plowboys downstairs at Nectar's; the singer-songwriter Jon Gailmor at the Fresh Ground; the high school arena-rock knockoff groups playing Toto and Journey covers at North Beach; or the N-Zones, a rowdy white rhythm-and-blues ensemble, playing the paddle-wheel party boats in the harbor. Clearly something had been laced into the product: the new sound had a jackhammer beat, bright vocals, and curt, coy lyrics. It was sometimes simply called "new wave," but not by those who made the sound or danced to it.

The new sound was boinging, bubbly, frazzled, danceable, and urban by way of Montreal, just eighty-seven miles to our north. But the fashions associated with the "Burlington sound" could be purchased locally: beach ball chokers and arachnoid earrings from kiosks downstairs at the Burlington Square Mall; checkered ties and miniskirts from Nuevo Wavo on Church Street; military surplus gas masks and flak jackets, old watches and brooches, or Little League jerseys to wear with a skirt, from Old Gold on Main Street. The Burlington look was not an up-country cosplay of CBGB on the Bowery or the Rat in Boston: it incorporated New England elements—skiwear, puffy parkas, L.L. Bean sweaters, moon boots. "Miniskirts are MADE for Moon Boots" read a local ad from the era, since inside every Burlington club, the temperature on a below-zero January night was hotter than the equator. The freezing and sweating crowds assembled at the Mill restaurant in Winooski, a dive with a stage; or, nearby, at Sneakers, by day a brunch spot, by night a mirrored neon jamboree that hosted some of the first gay nights in the area; or at the Daily Planet in Burlington, where the Clark Kents and Lois Lanes from *The Vermont Vanguard Press* met in the steampunk solarium designed by Vermont's dean of space-age backwoods architecture, David Sellers of Prickly Mountain.

The Burlington sound played all during Bernie's early mayoral years, and at many of his mayoral events—and its most distinctive talent was Pamela Polston, a grad student at UVM hailing from Omaha and Lincoln, Nebraska. Polston formed the Decentz with veterans of the "bluegrass wimp-rock group Nicky and the Nightboys," including Gordon Stone, who went on to play with Phish. Stone played pedal steel guitar; Jimmy Ryan played banjo. These were not customary instruments in the new wave, and the Decentz were sometimes billed as a "country wave" act. Burlington clubs were still booking "what's left of Little Feat" and "warmed over hippy-dippy" downers, but the Decentz carried new wave, punk, and ska sounds down the hill and into the bars. Polston's group became the city's new-wave welcoming committee for the big touring bands: Talking Heads, the English Beat, the Ramones. Polston once watched Dee Dee Ramone emerge from the locker room at UVM's Patrick Gymnasium "so stoned he was moving in slow motion, or like a wind-up toy": Ramone, attempting to navigate a hallway, bounced into a cinder-block wall, backed up, shook it off, walked into it again, backed up again, and gave it another try, before resigning himself to turning right through the double doors to take the stage.

But the secret ingredient in the Burlington sound had been imported from Jamaica. "We were all listening to *Trenchtown Rock*," Polston said, referring to the long-running Friday-night reggae show on WRUV, hosted by Jay Strausser. The broadcast, among the first reggae shows in the U.S., made Burlington, one of the whitest small cities in America, an unlikely incubator for reggae. In 1978, the Jamaican government sent its "reggae ambassador" to two specially selected American cities: Detroit, "Motown," of course; and—what? why?—Burlington. John Wakeling arrived to promote Reggae Sunsplash, a festival back home, with suitcases full of records and tapes unavailable anywhere in America, including rare demos and interviews with Bob Marley. Wakeling took over Strausser's show for a week, exploring Burlington in his free time. "I have rarely been to a place where I feel so welcome," Wakeling told a reporter. "There must be few places in America where the general attitude is so easy." Arriving from Jamaica, "physically a paradise, to be struck this forcefully by another place is amazing." Wakeling took in some local country and bluegrass downtown, praising the "people's music" and pointing to the similarities between "reggae riffs" and "country pickin'."

Bernie rides Burlington's reggae boom, 1983.
Vanguard Press

In 1981, Strausser opened Pure Pop Records in downtown Burlington, where, selling eight-tracks, then LPs, then cassettes, then CDs, and then LPs again, for decades, the reggae DJ silently sorted and scrutinized his collection behind the counter to the warm beats of Wakeling's rare records. You could hear reggae while walking by the underground shop, even on a cold February day. Pure Pop was my generation's musical education: the line of development from reggae and ska to the Decentz and Pinhead to Black Flag and Minutemen to local thrash bands like Screaming Broccoli could be traced simply by shopping there, where it was always tempting to buy whatever Strausser was playing—unless it was one of a kind, a gift carried directly from Kingstown.

WHEN THE ENCHANTING Nastassja Kinski came to town to shoot a film with Rudolf Nureyev and Harvey Keitel at UVM's Williams Hall, across from my elementary school, Burlingtonians lined up to be extras. Kinski, who was spotted in line at Ben & Jerry's, was a "star like nobody had seen in fifteen years, like Dietrich or Deneuve," according to the *Burlington Free Press*, and Nureyev was the ballet legend who had defected from the Soviet Union in a dramatic scene at the Paris airport. At the new arthouse movie theater downtown, the Nickelodeon, Kinski had beguiled audiences in *Tess* and *Cat People*. The shoot a block away created some wild energy at recess for a week: the crews parked on Mansfield Avenue, across from our flag football game. We saw Kinski smoking outside her trailer from the windows of my sixth-grade classroom.

The film, *Exposed*, directed by James Toback, was an erotic thriller filmed in Burlington, New York, and Paris; Toback, who acted in the film as a sleazy English professor, was later accused of multiple acts of sexual harassment on set, and the movie has been forgotten, even by Burlingtonians. I don't know if my schoolmate Alessandro Nivola got the idea of becoming a movie star from the Hollywood vibe that had overtaken Mater Christi School that winter—or even the following, when Angela Lansbury and Lee Remick turned up in town to shoot their Hallmark Christmas movie, *The Gift of Love*. Both films showed Burlington itself on the screen for the first time in decades, though *Exposed* was supposed to be set in Wisconsin. It didn't matter: the stars were flocking to Burlington! A few years later, Bernie himself acted in a cameo in a Don Johnson film shot in the area, *Sweet Hearts Dance*. That film auditioned high school students as extras: I was rejected, but my friend Seth Feeley got a credited speaking part. Though all of these movies left a lot to be desired, the People's Republic of Burlington was itself becoming a star.

Yet nobody, not Nureyev, not Kinski, not Lansbury, not even Bernie Sanders, could compete with the area's biggest celebrity. In the summer of 1981, two months after Sanders took office, the mayor was upstaged on the national scene by a phenomenon even rarer than an elected socialist. On June 30, *The New York Times* ran the story of a curious photograph taken by a Connecticut woman vacationing on Lake Champlain near Saint Albans, Vermont, thirty miles north of Burlington. The image appeared to show the long neck and broad back of a creature rising from the serene waters of the lake, its head turned in profile, as though acknowledging the paparazzi. The photo, authenticated by experts at the University of Arizona Optical Sciences Center, was greeted as proof that a prehistoric monster lived in the four-hundred-foot-deep waters of Lake Champlain; it is still considered the premier piece of evidence ever collected for the existence of lake monsters. The biologist Roy P. Mackal of the University of Chicago hypothesized that the photo showed "some kind of rare, elusive mammal, probably related to the zeuglodon, which was one episode in the evolution of the whale." After thousands of sightings over hundreds of years, the Lake Champlain Monster, or Champ, as he is called, had now been captured on film.

It is hard to overstate the effect this news had on kids' lives that summer and in the years after. We'd been prepared for it. On regular field trips to UVM's Perkins Museum of Geology, area schoolchildren were shown the skeleton of "the Charlotte whale," a small beluga whale discovered in a field in the nearby town of Charlotte one morning in 1849, by men digging Vermont's first railroad tracks. The fragile skeleton floats in a glass case. Its skull is repaired from the blow struck by the railroad man's shovel upon discovery.

Champ emerges. *Sandra Mansi*

What was a whale doing in a cornfield, hundreds of miles from the nearest ocean? The docent explained to our spellbound second-grade class: Lake Champlain had once been a vast saltwater sea, the surrounding mountains its shore. Our lake was the vestige of this broad, prehistoric ocean; our inland fields, enriched with marine minerals, were once its sunken bed. It was not a leap to imagine that a community of primordial creatures had withstood the sea change at the lake's murky bottom, surfacing every now and then to have a look around. Perhaps Champ was as curious as everyone else about the new political scene in town—or wanted to meet Nastassja Kinski.

In July of 1981, Champ appeared again, this time near Shelburne Farms. Seven witnesses, including Sansea Sparling, the manager of the 108-room Webb family mansion known as Shelburne House, watched for nearly a half hour as a creature "deep and fast and very long" cavorted in the water just off Shelburne Point, before swimming westward toward the Adirondacks. Sparling was clipping herbs on the sloping lawn, she told me, when she heard "screaming, I mean incredible screaming" coming off the curved beach below, as a group of people emerged from the steep bank, pointing at "six humps, with six individual wakes, quite far apart." By the behavior of the wakes, the creature was figured to be over sixty feet long. "This will make my career!" a woman exclaimed, and produced a camera. A blurry image, hard to make out, appeared in the *Burlington Free Press*. But Sparling's incredibly detailed and vivid description of what she witnessed traveled widely by word of mouth.

Notice was put out: Shelburne Farms "is not open to the public for monster sightings." But a month later, 150 people jammed into the property's Coach Barn, where the great carriage horses of the Webbs' guests once chomped salt hay, to hear the testimony of esteemed scientists and eyewitnesses. "Does Champ Exist: A Scientific Seminar" brought together experts like Chicago's Roy Mackal and J. Richard Greenwell of the University of Arizona. Mackal held the room spellbound as he described a shy and intelligent creature, a cousin to the Loch Ness Monster, who communicated in intricate squeaks like a dolphin and, landlocked herself, fed mainly on landlocked salmon. Some in the room wept as what they'd seen with their own eyes was at last confirmed by respected professionals or seconded by credible eyewitnesses. Sandra Mansi, the photographer who'd captured the shot, described a creature "slimy and slow moving" and "quite majestic." At one point she worried that the monster "had legs" and was headed onto shore. Mansi expressed her concern that she'd "opened up Pandora's Box," and pleaded with the group to do something, anything, "to protect this beautiful creature from man."

Vermonters were in awe of Mansi's image of the monster—but also of the rumored conditions of its sale to *The New York Times*. The sum was not disclosed, but Mansi suggested that it had been significant. What if Champ could be caught, somehow? P. T. Barnum had offered $50,000 in 1873 for "the hide of the great Champlain serpent to add to my mammoth World's Fair!" The fantasy was expressed mainly in the form of corny dockside jokes, but the idea spread that a very big prize now awaited wily anglers on Lake Champlain: Champ's image, if not his carcass, was the trophy. Champ fever took over the lake! There were more than thirty recorded sightings of the monster in 1981. Joseph W. Zarzynski, a schoolteacher from Wilton, New York, who had been searching for a decade for the monster at great personal expense, expressed the fear that the proof of Champ's existence would arrive "on a flatbed truck."

In June of 1982, with a bill moving through the Vermont legislature to enroll our ancient plesiosaur on the endangered species list, every fish in the lake had a bounty put on its head. The first annual Lake Champlain International Fishing Derby awarded prizes in seven categories. Three thousand entrants vied for hundreds of thousands of dollars in potential prizes. By arrangement with Lloyd's of London, two fish in particular, a trout and a walleye, were tagged and guaranteed to pay $50,000 each if an angler made the lucky catch. Bernie stood on Perkins Pier and made small talk with the contestants as they loaded in their coolers of Molson and worms. Told about the prize money, Sanders shook his head: the way the city's budgets looked, he said, "I should have chartered a boat." Then Sanders shook the hand of the derby's founder and coordinator, my great-uncle John Delorme, and advised Captain John "to be on the lookout for Champ." Uncle John didn't hear it as a joke: he "knew where to find him," he said, near the schools of landlocked salmon in the shallows by the Champlain Islands. Sanders, chuckling, looked a little concerned.

Bernie had reason for worry. Captain John, newly retired from driving a cab in the mountain town of Duxbury, Vermont, was my grandfather's younger brother, as well as a family hero: John Delorme had been anointed by Clarence "Bish" Bishop, the *Free Press*'s revered outdoors columnist, as "the most knowledgeable fisherman on Lake Champlain." John was a natural, and his big brother Milford, to keep up, outfitted his thirty-foot walkaround with banks of technology—depth finders, fish finders.

In my mind I'd pitted Uncle John against Champ, like Ahab against the white whale. But nobody hauled in Champ that weekend, or the two tagged fish worth $100,000. Vermonters caught the usual bony varieties, walleye, pike, and perch, and then the community's attention turned back from the uncollected spoils at the bottom of the lake to the ongoing shoestring operation two hundred feet above sea level, in Bernie's broke, and broken, city hall.

27

City Hall

(Good Bureaucrats, 1981–83)

The Sanders administration. *Courtesy Jim Rader*

Across the street from city hall, on the corner of Church and Main, Upton's Ice Cream Circus scooped freezer-burned Praline Pecan or Hawaiian Sherbet flecked with candy-colored pineapple bits to a pre–Ben and Jerry's Burlington. Little kids were officially forbidden from going in, because Upton's main profit stream wasn't ice cream but pinball; and pinball machines, in the mid-1970s, had become rather sexual. "We're into fantasy here," Howard Goldberg, Upton's owner, told the *Burlington Free Press*: on "Wizard," a machine based on the film version of the Who's rock opera *Tommy*, a "seductive woman" with "a snake shaped belt-buckle pointing between her legs" sat on the lap of a clearly aroused Elton John. This was fantasy, indeed! According to the *Free Press*, "four of the eleven machines" depicted busty, half-naked girls. If you were the right height—that is, the appropriate age—the machine's playboard met you right at the belt, and you could buck your crotch against the equipment to influence the path the metal ball took between the flashing paddles and bells. But if you were, say, eight, and therefore short, and had snuck in, you had to peer over the machine and across a vast bonging and ringing apparatus at eye level. The game was over before it started.

When Burlington's new city clerk, Jim Rader, showed up for work on a Monday morning in April to his office across from Upton's, his disgraced predecessor had taken most of the details of how to run this most complex and challenging of all municipal departments along with him into retirement. And it was like showing up to run a restaurant for the first time during the dinner service: the city clerk's office was the public-facing division of Burlington's government, keeping regular hours, like a post office, to fulfill requests for vital records. From this cramped warren, a staff of amateurs now coordinated Burlington's democracy. It was up to Rader, a veterans' counselor, and his assistant city clerk, Jeanne Keller, an official with the Vermont Public Interest Research Group (VPIRG), to figure out, without much "element of orientation," as Rader told me, how to fulfill the duties laid out in the city charter: running elections, keeping public records, presiding over board of aldermen proceedings, managing licensing, and disseminating public information. These elements were among the foundation blocks of the community's trust in its government.

Rader was hired, he reckons, to be "a good bureaucrat" in the "highly partisan environment of city hall." He inherited an office of six or so sleepy lifers and, remaining in his post while Keller finished up at VPIRG, the old assistant city clerk, Andrew "Pat" Sullivan. The name rang a bell. Sullivan had been in the news a year before when he and the city constable busted an eleven-year-old who'd snuck into Upton's to play pinball. In the process, the two men discovered perhaps the world's most wholesome illegal pool hall on the second floor: five tables surrounded by middle schoolers, a pile of *Star Wars* backpacks in the corner. The board of aldermen considered pulling Upton's permits, but Upton's had an ace up its sleeve. With the city's action pending, Upton's raced into the future: both the lusty pinball machines and the upstairs pool tables were exchanged for bright, beeping stand-up arcade games: *Asteroid*, *Centipede*, *Space Invaders*, *Pac-Man*. The establishment renamed itself "Upton's Arcade." The city had no rules regarding *Pac-Man*, a phenomenon unimaginable when the narrow pinball ordinance passed in the 1950s; and so, beginning at age twelve or so, my friends and I flocked to Upton's, where we ended up spending the good part of our early adolescence. Pat Sullivan could bust an eleven-year-old, but in terms of running the city clerk's office, Jim told me, "he had little to impart."

The Hoosier tinkerer now faced a daunting problem: how to tune up Burlington's democracy after years of neglect. The November election was the first test. Frank Wagner had never bothered to audit the voter rolls: some thirty-three thousand names swelled the list in a city of approximately thirty-eight thousand. Thousands of dead people and long-fledged students needed to be culled, and thousands of new residents added. Rader announced an ambitious registration drive in the *Free Press*, and a corps of volunteers representing all of the city's political factions added some two thousand new voters in time to create, on Primary Day in early September, "a complete catastrophe," as Jim put it. Many voters gave up before they got their chance to breach, one at a time, the curtain of the old, cantankerous voting machines, with their sticky levers and loose knobs. The new city clerks failed to vote in their first election: dashing out in a short window before the absentee ballots arrived in their office, Rader and Keller met lines around the block and decided, as Rader told me, to "forget it."

The fall elections were trial runs for March 1983, just months away, when Bernie would face a tense and tight reelection, and Rader needed funds to buy new machines. But everyone needed funds: the parks department for new benches and bleachers; the public works department for curbs and sidewalks; the police and fire departments, for officers' salaries; and the schools, for Burlington's first computers. The loose web of volunteer task forces and councils was coming apart as its bright initiatives remained unscheduled and unfunded. Sanders had gone a few too many times to the city's plutocrats to pay the city's banjo pickers, storytellers, and yodelers. The kids of the Old North End had a Little League team, but as one of its first coaches told me, the twelve-year-olds were showing up with jackknives and taking smoke breaks in between innings. The People's Republic was an innovator in the eyes of the world, but some of Burlington's worst problems had not yet been addressed by its famous mayor. In short, socialism was badly in need of capital.

Windfall

In the late 1970s, Jonathan Leopold, a prince of the Vermont Democratic Party, worked as a young bean counter in the Massachusetts statehouse for Governor Michael Dukakis. Leopold's father was Vermont's first commissioner of mental health under Governor Phil Hoff. Dr. Jonathan Leopold led the agency that brought psychiatric services into the dark back bedrooms and attics in the loneliest and most forsaken corners of Vermont, and in so doing overcame some of the most deep-seated fears Vermonters held about the role of the state in their local communities. Governor Hoff was "like a member of the family" and ate supper with the Leopolds "four or five times a month" during Hoff's historic tenure, from 1962 to 1968, as Vermont's first Democratic governor. After rising quickly in Democratic politics under the "squeaky clean" Dukakis, Leopold soon found himself working for "the most spectacularly corrupt politician I've ever witnessed," Dukakis's rival and successor, Governor Ed King. When the extent of King's rot became impossible to ignore, Leopold resigned. Biding his time as a financial analyst in downtown Boston but keeping an eye on the socialist revolution back home, the whiz kid answered Bernie's ad in *The Boston Globe* for a new city treasurer.

Leopold, who seemed to spring from the pages of Lisa Birnbach's *Preppy Handbook*, that season's best seller, wore a billowing red-striped bow tie and button-down oxford from the Harvard Coop when he met Sanders in city hall in June of 1982. The contrast between Leopold's nattiness and Bernie's disarray, noted that day and ever afterward, presented a strategic advantage: for Burlington now had a treasurer whom "the Republicans liked"—partly, Leopold told me, "because I looked like a Republican." In those days Bernie sat with his back to the big window in his corner office looking out at the intersection of Church and Main. A red, white, and blue sign for the deli across the way seemed to capture the ironies of the moment when Sanders, the socialist, offered Leopold, the scion of Vermont Democrats, the job. The sandwich shop banner spelled it out: "The All-American Hero."

Like Rader, Leopold inherited from his predecessor a single primitive computer and bound folios inscribed with the city's handwritten records. The outgoing treasurer, F. Lee Austin—he was the city's rock-n-roll czar, in charge of implementing Gordon Paquette's Supertramp ban—proudly displayed the computer bearing "early spreadsheets of the city's deposits, but little else." Austin was astounded when he prompted Leopold to "guess the five-letter password" and the young man, by some dark gift of prophecy, nailed it on the first try: "MONEY." Finances were otherwise handled in an enormous ledger recording only cash expenditures and returns; no record had been made of the city's complex web of annuities, loans, and investments. "This was general ledger accounting," Leopold said, "like Bob Cratchit in Dickens's *A Christmas Carol.*" For the fiscal year 1981, though, as a nod to modern life, Austin had outsourced the city's annual budget audit to a group of UVM students as part of their class project.

It seemed there might have been good reasons for city hall to have kept such spotty records all those years. Starr Farm, in the city's New North End, was a premier stretch of shore for sunsets and fishing; over the decades, high-ranking city officials had built lake camps (the term, like "cottages" in Maine, is the local name for "summer houses") with no-interest mortgages issued from the city's cemetery endowment. A depositor securing a plot at Lakewood Cemetery might have been surprised to learn that his somber investment had financed a cedar deck just north of his final resting place, upon which Burlington's parks commissioner blared Lionel Richie and mixed up the daiquiris. Worse, the city's pension plan had been engineered to pay out "the correct amount to three individuals out of one hundred and sixty-six pensioners"—those three were Mayor Paquette's closest allies; the other pensioners had been chronically underpaid for years. There appeared to be small loans made out of obscure pockets of money all over Burlington's accounts. The city's insurance policies were written by politically connected local businessmen, some of them, like Antonio Pomerleau, who served as city commissioners: this cartel charged the city $100,000 in 1981 to pay claims of $177,000. "Where I come from, that's a lot of money," Sanders said. Leopold soon realized that by merely scrubbing Burlington's books he might have found a solution to the city's deficits, and just in time for the opening bells of Bernie's 1983 reelection campaign.

In September, a sympathetic reporter at the *Burlington Free Press*, Scott MacKay, ran a feature story about the savings in city hall. Though Sanders "is known for his adherence to socialist causes," MacKay wrote, the mayor was "using free market principles that Adam Smith or any corporate chieftain would applaud." By managing, rather than simply depositing, its funds, and by incorporating competitive bidding across the city's bureaucracy, the administration would save the city between $400,000 and $600,000—in today's dollars, between $2 and $3 million. Sanders "could run his reelection campaign as a fiscal conservative," according to Leopold: an astonishing, in some ways almost embarrassing, turnabout for a politician whose distrust of the free market had spooked Burlington's business class into despair.

But there was more to come. Throughout the fall, with Sanders's Republican opponent already actively campaigning, Democrats and Republicans were in talks to unite behind James Gilson, the mild-mannered proprietor of our neighborhood pizza place, Big Ben's. The *Centipede* machine at Big Ben's was a gathering spot for me and a few buddies: Jean Paul, whose dad had his dental office down the block, and Brian, whose dad taught English in the Old Mill building at UVM. Gilson would sometimes give the three of us quarters, or bring over slices of pizza, as we gazed spellbound at the high scores racked up by high school kids. Now Mr. Gilson, a staunch fiscal conservative from Ohio and chair of the Burlington School Board, was on WCAX and in the *Free Press* crusading against Mayor Sanders. Big Ben's became the headquarters of the Bernie resistance, though in its mixed clientele of teenage arcade rats, nuns from Trinity College across the street, and nurses from the UVM Medical Center, it was not Bove's or the Oasis.

Sanders certainly looked vulnerable in a two-way race. Then in December, a miracle: after a simple audit, Jonathan Leopold and Barr Swennerfelt discovered in the city's books a windfall of approximately $1.9 million, more than $6 million today. Delinquent tax payments in the hundreds of thousands, never assigned to the previous years' annual reports, made up the largest share of the surplus. The irony was delectable: Mayor Paquette in fact hadn't needed to propose the crushing property tax increase that tipped the '81 election to Sanders. Whether he truly did not know, or for some reason would not say, that there was hidden money in the city's coffers, was never investigated. Paquette, on the sidelines, raged against Sanders, and tried to blame a situation decades in the making on his successor. Bernie announced that he was now seriously considering a property tax *decrease* for the coming year. "It's a good Christmas present," the mayor said.

But there were still a few days before Christmas. On December 22, the *Burlington Free Press* announced that Jim Gilson's school board was "using improper accounting practices" and ran a significant deficit. Gilson was outraged at the "political smear" spread by his rival. In fact, Leopold told me, it was Scott MacKay, the *Free Press* reporter, who'd made the discovery: "We taught him a little too well how to decipher the books." Sanders was insistent that MacKay kill the story, fearing the backlash if the mayor appeared to be using his new accountants to take down a political rival. Gilson, the fiscal hawk, looked foolish; Sanders, Leopold, and Barr Wright were praised by Republicans and Democrats alike; and now a poll showed Sanders easily beating all but a single potential challenger: the outgoing lieutenant governor and the fastest rising star in Vermont politics, Madeleine Kunin.

Kunin, her sights set on Montpelier, had "no interest" in becoming Burlington's mayor; after losing to Richard Snelling in 1982, she was regrouping for a successful gubernatorial run in 1984. At the *Centipede* machine one afternoon, Brian, operating the trackball, blurted out, "My mom is going to beat Bernie for mayor." We all spontaneously broke into our Bernie impressions, like a flock of hungry Brooklyn geese. But sure enough, in January, Brian's mom, Judy Stephany, a popular Democratic legislator in Montpelier representing Burlington's New North End, made the surprising announcement that she was stepping down from her elected post to run full-time for mayor of Burlington "at the urging of party officials." Sanders entered the prime stretch of his reelection campaign liking his chances in another three-way race, against two candidates both hoping to force each other out of an eventual runoff.

All that winter, very weirdly, my friends and I lived the ups and downs of the campaign in the rhythm of our days. On our daily walk from Mater Christi School to the *Centipede* machine at Big Ben's, we shuttled between an environment pulling heavily for Stephany, a smart anti-abortion Democrat with huge support among Burlington's Catholics, and the headquarters of Jim Gilson, who had by then grown his political and customer base by extending discounts to members of UVM's fraternities. After alienating the frat kids with one anti-partying measure after another, Sanders now threatened to tax their huge houses as real property. The frat boys swarmed Big Ben's, coupons in hand; and they took over our *Centipede*.

THE LIGHTS IN the city clerk's office went on every morning long before the building opened to the public at eight thirty. Jim Rader inherited from his Indiana farm forebears a taste for working as the sun came up. Rader was at his office "by six thirty" every morning, according to colleagues; when I asked Jim to confirm, he very characteristically demurred. "Early," he answered. "Ask Meg"—Jim's wife—"for the specifics."

Jim's business that winter was brisk. He and his office managed the enormous response to the voter registration drive, while answering a surge of requests for absentee ballots. With city finances flush, Rader oversaw the purchase and delivery of ten new voting machines, to accommodate the new era in Burlington's citizen participation ushered in by the Sanders administration. The new machines were lighter and more compact: one of the old machines "almost killed me," Rader said, when the 850-pound contraption rolled down a ramp and nearly flattened the slight man of five feet seven.

The city clerk's office, handling birth certificates, death certificates, marriage licenses, and the mechanics of voter registration, determined who counted as a Burlingtonian. Rader and his office were in the business of turning persons into citizens, and citizens into voters. It pained Sanders "perhaps more than anything else" in public life, according to Richard Sugarman, that so many citizens did not vote; and so it was in Rader's office more than any other that Bernie felt his success could be measured.

The numbers did not lie. By February of 1983, fifteen hundred Burlingtonians had requested absentee ballots, double the usual number. The voter checklist surged by more than 5 percent that year. From 1982 to 1988, Burlington added about nine thousand new voters to its rolls. Participation was up across all types of elections, including special elections, which became routine as Sanders brought ballot referenda before the public on issues of ongoing city business, as well as matters beyond: the U.S. invasion of Grenada, CIA actions in El Salvador. (Julia Alvarez spoke powerfully at a hearing on U.S. imperialism in Latin America, before the Grenada vote; a photo of her, mic in hand, ran in the *Free Press*.) The electorate in Burlington grew, and grew more engaged and passionate, almost overnight.

While counting these new voters, Sanders was keeping another, more difficult, count. City hall sits at the intersection of Church and Main, between the lowest Marketplace block of Church Street—at the time, usually open to cars—and City Hall Park, an eight-acre, gently sloping rectangle with garden beds and paths converging on a central fountain. Across the park, in those days, was the Vermont Transit bus station, open all night. Burlington's homeless population, growing with every passing season, congregated in this central area very openly. In the dead of winter, Burlington's overnight temperatures sometimes reached thirty below zero. Darting from his parking space to his office in the frozen dawn, Sanders encountered these men and women clustered together in the park under layers of blankets and tarps. It was a miracle every morning that they'd made it through another night in one of the coldest cities in America.

Homelessness in its current form was created by Ronald Reagan, by

Clean-Up Burlington! 1985. *Rob Swanson*

callous negligence if not by design: the homeless were sometimes called "Reagan Refugees." Urban poverty was a political winner for the Republicans, then as now. The president "owed little," according to *Shelterforce*, "to urban voters, big city mayors, black or Hispanic leaders, or labor unions—the major advocates for metropolitan concerns." Reagan cut federal revenue sharing to cities, announcing that "there is no revenue to share," even as his cuts to other federal programs made the burden of care that much more onerous for places like Burlington. Funds for public service careers, job training, food stamps, and public transit were dramatically reduced. In 1980, the federal government picked up 22 percent of urban budgets; by 1988, that figure was 6 percent. According to Sheldon Danziger and Robert Haveman, these cuts particularly devastated the group with "the lowest mean census income—households headed by women with children."

After the murder of Bernadette Lesage in the summer of 1980, Burlington was tense about its population of "street people," a term formerly used to indicate panhandlers, hippies, eccentrics, buskers, and the generally benign. But with Reagan's election that fall, many more seriously mentally ill people were stranded on Burlington's streets. Holding up the specter of the country's sanitariums—rusted iron beds, torn wallpaper—Reagan accelerated the trend toward deinstitutionalizing the mentally ill, and then, as his second act, repealed the law (the Mental Health Systems Act of 1980) that had provided federal support to community shelters and clinics. The message delivered over and over by the White House was that poverty was shameful, grotesque, immoral; particularly urban poverty, and especially urban poverty in northeastern cities like Burlington, where Reagan was beaten by thirty percentage points in 1980.

Burlington suffered under Reagan as all cities suffered; but Burlington is small: people new to town are noticed in any case. And Burlington is the regional capital of a profoundly rural corridor: it is the only city with extensive services north of Albany, assuming a much greater regional importance and presence. And so, it acted for the surrounding oblivion like a small-scale San Francisco, a destination where services were conceivable and the stigma of living out in the open was less severe. In short, there were many good reasons for a homeless person to come to Burlington. But the main reason was simple: now there was a growing community. It was why many individuals who might have felt stranded and alone in Burlington ten years before now began to arrive; but the homeless were the only community forming in Burlington whose lives were in immediate jeopardy.

Word spread across the region's homeless communities that Burlington had beds available. As an extension of his work counseling Vietnam veterans, Jim Rader and others had been involved with a small shelter in the late 1970s. The space offered room for fifteen individuals, "which about met demand," Rader said. Bernie began to hear from community and religious leaders in the fall of 1981 that there was now a need for a permanent emergency shelter accommodating up to one hundred people. As the homeless community grew, though, so did the fear that "a massive effort to provide additional beds will be known as far away as Florida and the West Coast," as Peter Whitaker, the director of the Burlington YMCA, put it, citing "a highly effective network maintained by the nation's street people and drifter population." Soon Church Street merchants expressed their own fears that the broad brick pedestrian mall that had just opened to shoppers was attracting the homeless in large numbers to its covered alleyways and awnings. The parking garages built to accommodate suburban shoppers now hosted several small encampments. Sanders and Rader had on their hands a potentially combustible political issue in one of the first versions of what has become a dismal American theme. No more than one hundred individuals, the vast majority of these souls entirely private and courteous, distressed a city of thirty-eight thousand.

"Bernie Brought in the Bums," read a mailer that arrived at our home in January of 1983. It became a common slogan, as downtown merchants began to refer to homeless men and women as "Bernie Bums." When, on Christmas Eve 1982, the Waystation opened its doors, Sanders was credited, or blamed, depending on one's view, for expanding services to homeless addicts and alcoholics without requiring sobriety, or Jesus. Rader told the *Free Press* the inconvenient truth: that the new shelter would undoubtedly act as a magnet drawing homeless people to Burlington. "Our concern from the beginning is that nobody freeze to death," Jim said.

Sadie White Street

In the fall of 1982, Sadie White decided she'd had enough of the "foolish antics" of the Burlington Board of Aldermen, and, at eighty-one, won back her old seat in the statehouse. For two months in early 1983, then, White served both as alderwoman and state representative for her neighborhood in the Old North End, the first Burlingtonian ever to play such a dual role. Sanders was delighted, and pushed the aldermen to rename a short block of downtown Burlington that ran by White's parish, the Cathedral of the Immaculate Conception, "Sadie White Street." White loved the idea: "I've been around the area for quite some time," she said.

White and Gary De Carolis had initially fought the new emergency shelter in their Ward 3, but were persuaded to drop their opposition. Instead, with Bernie's support, White spent her last months in city hall fighting an

X-rated bookstore planning to open down the block. V-T Books and Movie Arcade had been forced out of its location in nearby Williston, when its landlord learned that it was selling "explicit books and sexual devices" and offering "coin-operated movies." V-T Books sued, and the matter was making its way to the Vermont Supreme Court. As the new location on North Street opened and the case began to attract the attention of civil liberties lawyers and activists, Sadie White told the *Free Press* that the store would remain in her neighborhood "over my dead body." The word among teenagers at Upton's was that V-T would sell porn "to anybody," but a store employee, holding a vibrator that he identified as a "martial arts item," reassured the community: "We don't sell to juveniles, unless they got a fake ID or something." After a neighborhood petition drive collected more than one thousand signatures, Sanders backed White and instructed the city attorneys, Joseph McNeil and John Franco, to seek an injunction to close the shop for zoning violations. In January of 1983, Bernie Sanders and Sadie White, teaming up one last time, banished the peep shows and dildos of V-T Books to an obscure strip mall north of the city, and welcomed the homeless to a clean and warm space on the block.

Meanwhile, the snow was piling up in Sadie White's driveway, and the juveniles outside of Upton's were looking for something to do now that copies of *Bust Out* and *Nylon Naughties* were scarce in Burlington. Richard Sugarman, "being from Buffalo, after all," had apprised Sanders of the "political possibilities of snow, a major civic and municipal issue that made careers," as he told me. Sanders piloted a program the previous winter, "Project Snowshovel"—Jim Rader came up with the name—that matched elderly and disabled people in need of shoveling with teenagers eager, as my friend Emily Lawrence told a reporter, to do something "kind." The program was coordinated by Marcy Ryan, a local advocate for the disabled: Ryan worked a switchboard and "hitched" callers in need with young volunteers. Seniors were "enamored" with the "clean cut young people" who turned up to dig them out. One woman praised four "lovely young men" from Phi Delta Theta who scaled her roof to clear an ice jam, tipped their caps, and went on their way. "They came to the rescue of a little old lady in tears," the woman said. "This is something I've never heard of in Burlington before."

"WARNING: If Sanders is reelected this could happen here," read Jim Gilson's full-page ad in the *Free Press*, describing a nightmare vision of urban despair, not the optimistic, newly prosperous city that he fed every day from his ovens on Colchester Avenue. "Mayor Sanders is an AVOWED

SOCIALIST," the ad warned. "Socialist principles have not worked anywhere in the world . . . they won't in Burlington either!"

In late February of 1983, running not as a brash revolutionary socialist but as a good government fiscal conservative who chased vice, debauchery, and rudeness out of the city of Burlington, made peace with developers, and shoveled every driveway, Sanders faced his frustrated opponents in a debate at the Burlington Rotary Club. The Rotarians were united against him, but the hissing ceased when Sanders boasted that he'd brought 44 percent more commercial development into the city and had proposed "an ongoing venture capital fund" to bring more business into Burlington. President Reagan's approval rating was stalled somewhere near 40 percent, unemployment nationally was around 10 percent, and the economy was just showing the first signs of expanding after the worst economic downturn since the Great Depression; but the People's Republic of Burlington was thriving. An ad taken out by the Burlington Small Business Community showed empty storefronts, but the block depicted was destroyed by fire in 1971 and had been a vacant lot for nearly a decade before Bernie became mayor. "I might have done many terrible things as mayor," Sanders told the Rotarians, "but, really, I did not burn down the Strong Theater."

To Greg Guma and the city's activist class, Sanders's reinvention was troubling. "Bernie Sanders wants to stay in office," Guma said in a radio commentary on WDEV. "He has surrounded himself with professionals and the academic crowd. He talks about efficiency and lower property taxes" but "takes few risks." "There will be no revolution—that simply isn't what is happening in the Queen City," Guma concluded. "The establishment has little to fear."

"He'll get his 40 percent," Garrison Nelson told Jack Barry on the air on Election Night, again underestimating Bernie's support. In Ward 6, "Republican Country" and home to Jim Gilson, Guma spent the day working the polls, an experience the city clerk's office "had streamlined." The ward exceeded its previous record turnout by four p.m. with hours still to go. To Guma, "it was extraordinary, and the pattern was the same all over town." Republicans "were voting for Sanders, then returning to their own straight ticket." The machine totals in Ward 4 were 1,042 votes for Bernie, 621 for Gilson, and 540 for Judy Stephany. Guma and the other workers "were startled."

At the election party at Minerva's Rest, the mood was ecstatic. Pamela Polston looked out from the stage between numbers, surveying the crowd: Sanders arrived, pumping his fists, and the Decentz launched into "Seems So Strange," their bounciest number. Jane Driscoll approached Appleton

King, who'd strayed in with a few friends, and yelled over the music, "You helped do this!" When the eleven o'clock news came on, Guma observed the crowd growing silent. Sanders had won the three-way contest with an astonishing majority of 50.2 percent. Bernie looked "almost humble." Guma, though a skeptic about the drift toward business and fiscal discipline during Sanders's first term, had to admit: "The event felt historic. Burlingtonians had elected a socialist and evidently rejected the two major parties." And yet Guma wondered if Sanders had built much more than "an election machine, able to beat the establishment at its own game."

By powerfully ratifying Sanders's 1981 election that many still characterized as a fluke, Burlington had laid a claim to being America's "most unusual city," as Guma put it. The next day at *The Vermont Vanguard Press*, Guma noted that the paper seemed "unable to join the joy of the progressive opening it had done so much to create." Noting the malaise, Guma circulated a petition to protest the paper's commercial drift, and was fired instantly. The radical years of the paper had come to a close; the *Vanguard*, like many a Burlington institution, had matured, and was now at the mercy of profits. Were Burlington's own radical years also on the wane? Its socialist mayor had run, and won, as an innovative capitalist.

Lawyers, Guns, and Money

(Burlington's Foreign Policy)

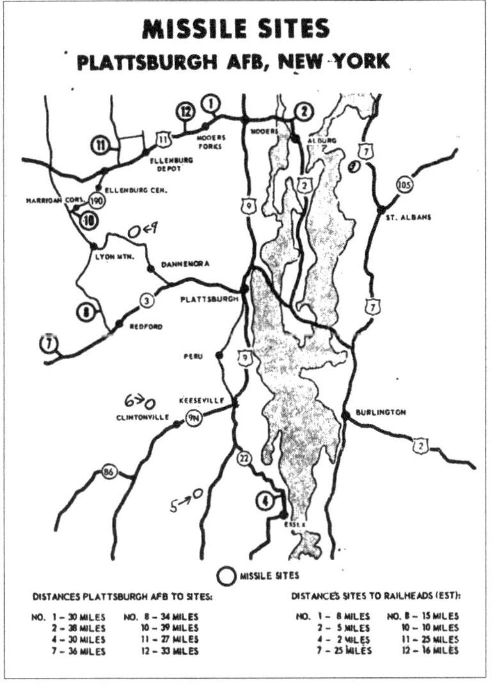

Figure 31, Strategy for Survival. *Courtesy the author*

The Story of a Gun

Mayor Bernie Sanders owed the people of Lakeside, the poor community built by the Queen City Cotton Mill, who had rallied to help elect him in 1981, and felt genuine affection for the vinyl-siding and chain-link neighborhood with the sublime views across Lake Champlain. As its tenements and frame houses came on the market, several of Sanders's aides and allies scooped them up. By 1983, Lakeside was a neighborhood in transition: the old Burlington and the new lived side by side in these dense city blocks. The young progressives blended easily with the French-Canadian families who'd made a home there for generations. Their kids played together on the cheerful central playground and swam at the hidden beach behind the parking lot of the Blodgett oven factory.

But the neighborhood's glowering mill building had become more nightmarish and secretive over the decades, and was now protected by a security barrier designed and managed in cooperation with the U.S. Department of Defense. Some 3,700 employees were buzzed in every day at the plant's height of production in the late 1960s. Many were specialized engineers, scientists, and machinists who had trained to do one thing: to design, manufacture, and test one of the deadliest light weapons in the military's arsenal, GE's Vulcan Minigun, a Gatling-style mounted machine gun. You can picture the gun: A UH-1 "Huey" helicopter door slides open, low above Vietnam; from the air, a door gunner fires six thousand rounds per minute into a fleeing crowd of unarmed villagers. The door slides shut, and the Huey peels away into the clouds. The gun used was the Vulcan Minigun, manufactured in only one facility: General Electric's missile and armament division, on Lakeside Avenue in the People's Republic of Burlington.

The Vulcan systems were pioneered in Burlington in the 1950s, but initial demand for the guns was low, and GE laid off hundreds every year to protect its profits while it awaited the next big government contract: that is, the next war. It would not need to wait long. By 1964, General Electric was producing thousands of its lightweight, lethal Miniguns per year. In a 1969 classified report, the U.S. Army Concept Team described the Vulcan's "cyclic rate of high explosive fire" as "unsurpassed" in a range of Vietnam combat scenarios, including "convoy security," "perimeter defense," "ambush patrols," and "show-of-force runs." The Vulcan was recommended for "inundated rice paddies and gently rolling hills" as well as "heavily jungled areas and open forests."

One would expect that a gun optimized for rice paddies and jungles would fall out of production after the Vietnam War ended in 1975, and Burlington's GE would slump. In fact, by 1978, GE boasted of its state-of-the-art production facility in Burlington, including "machine shops, an engineering development lab with Adage computer display, R&D prototype manufacturing, heat treating, welding, deburring, a 'dome trainer,' a plating room, and paint booths, all of which were utilized in the manufacture of the land based Vulcan Air Defense system, the EX-83 for the Navy, and the GAU-8/A Avenger, mounted on A-10 aircraft." All through the 1970s and early '80s, Burlingtonians wondered at the market for these "Vietnam guns," as we called them. As a result, we had a sneak preview of the nation's foreign policy in the Reagan years, when there were new jungles, and new wars, awaiting discovery.

THESE GUNS WERE everywhere when I was growing up. At the Champlain Valley Fair, Vulcan systems were displayed with red ribbons tied around their barrels. Twenty miles outside of Burlington, at my family's plot in St. Thomas Cemetery in the town of Underhill, the sound of Vulcans sometimes punctuated the rural silence. In the 1970s, we made trips up to the cemetery as a family to lay flowers on the graves of my uncles Danny and Paul and my aunt Joanne. Through the dense woods you could hear artillery fire echoing from the Vermont National Guard's Ethan Allen Firing Range, where General Electric leased several hundred acres to test the guns. The low chattering of the Vulcans answered the hollow boom of mortar explosions and the *snap-snap-snap* of M-16s in a grim symphony. When the performance subsided, the metallic tang of gunpowder in the air, the chickadees took over.

In 1980, Burlington began to grapple with the fact that its biggest private employer and largest corporate taxpayer produced a weapon designed for indiscriminate mass killing of the poor. Ronald Reagan's increases in defense spending had the local GE plant "bouncing off the ceiling," according to David Goodman, a defense analyst: "There's so much business they can't keep up with it all." By the time of Bernie Sanders's election in 1981 as Burlington's mayor, part of GE's "business" was supplying arms to government death squads in El Salvador.

Two atrocities far from Burlington quickly changed the politics around the GE plant and its Vulcan systems. On March 24, 1980, in San Salvador, a government assassin stepped into a small hospital chapel and fired a bullet into the heart of Archbishop Óscar Romero, murdering him while he was saying Mass. Romero was targeted because he had begun reading the names of his dead and disappeared countrymen on his weekly radio broadcasts. The archbishop's funeral in San Salvador, attended by 250,000 mourners, was called the largest demonstration in Latin American history. Later that year, on December 2, three American nuns and a Catholic lay worker, all with ties to the local Catholic community in Burlington, were beaten, raped, and murdered by El Salvadoran soldiers, their bodies buried in a shallow mass grave near the San Salvador airport. The Reagan administration's response to these murders was to increase military aid to the murderers. GE's local payroll swelled to some $50 million, and the economy of Mayor Sanders's Burlington boomed as a result.

Sanders and the weapons manufacturer were on a collision course. GE's heavy machinery, valued in the hundreds of millions of dollars, was taxed by Burlington as business inventory. Its employees spent their ample paychecks in Burlington's shops and restaurants. The weapons engineers at GE coached soccer teams, and their kids won science fairs. GE was, in short, a model community-within-a-community and a valued employer, the second largest in the state of Vermont. GE was also home to Burlington's biggest and most robust union, the International Union of Electrical Workers Local 248, with more than one thousand members. And yet: to put guns made in Burlington into the hands of soldiers who raped and murdered nuns seemed grotesque to regular Burlingtonians, even those outside the normal activist circles. At Mater Christi School, the Sisters of Mercy prayed every morning for the souls of the slain sisters. Sanders had a very narrow strait to navigate in this conflict, with peace activists on one side, a union on the other: allies, and danger, on both shores.

"A Foreign Policy"

"How many cities of 40,000 have a foreign policy?" Bernie Sanders wrote in *Outsider in the House*. "I saw no magic in separating local, state, national and international issues." Yet Sanders's "foreign policy" risked ruining the delicate coalition, broad but shallow, that brought the mayor to power. When the interior minister of Augusto Pinochet's repressive regime in Chile visited nearby Charlotte to "study American democracy," at the invitation of the State Department, Sanders lashed out at Juan Garcia: "The irony is, they should be giving PhD courses in how to destroy democracy." Sanders made the statement in defiance of his own aides, who had informed him "that it was a bad idea that I hold a press conference on Chile." Bernie responded in a blistering memo: "I do not intend to be told by this group what I may, or may not, do as Mayor."

But Burlingtonians who were not actively grateful for Sanders's regular diatribes mostly just ignored them. Bernie's "foreign policy" was seen as "just part of the package," according to Walter Shapiro: "The aw-that's-just-Bernie syndrome helps explain the schizophrenia" among Sanders's more culturally conservative supporters. In my experience, many of those old Burlingtonians in fact welcomed Bernie's flamboyant opposition to Reagan's reckless military buildup. Global politics was local for us. Burlington was a primary target in thermonuclear war, and the knowledge that we might any day be instantly obliterated was intrinsic to Burlingtonians' lives. It had weighed on the city for decades. Long before it was known for ice cream, sunsets, and socialism, Burlington had been a strategic military outpost. In the twentieth century, the region became a showcase for Cold War weapons and civil defense technology. When ABC broadcast *The Day After* in the fall of 1983, the film depicting in lurid detail the aftermath of a nuclear holocaust shook Burlington in a very personal way. Our city would be "one of the first to go," my grandfather told me, the day after *The Day After*. He sounded agonized, mournful.

Colonel Delorme's blueprint for nuclear emergency was contained in a yellow-jacket-striped hardback book, kept out for casual perusal in our home. *Strategy for Survival*, by Thomas L. Martin and Donald C. Latham, listed our city among the 303 American communities most likely to be attacked by Soviet ICBMs. A ring of twelve Atlas F missile launch sites, ten in New York, two in Vermont, had been constructed in the 1960s. These eighty-one-foot, four-megaton missiles, buried deep in the earth, carried a range of six thousand miles. They were the only ICBMs ever constructed east of the Mississippi, and, though decommissioned a few years after they were built, they still weighed heavily on the mind, since the strategic reasons they were constructed in the first place had not changed: the Air Force base located in Plattsburgh, New York, our dour, old-fashioned twin across Lake Champlain, ranked among the first targets in Moscow's sights.

"Civil defense" was the Cold War project to make nuclear war imaginable and ultimately winnable, and Burlington became one of its exhibition grounds. Many families had a root cellar or basement like mine, outfitted with a heavy door and, inside, a "mother's pantry," as they were known: a cabinet full of corroding tins of tuna, boxes of biscuits, Tang, iodine, vitamins, and a bible.

Figure 31 in *Strategy for Survival*, a map of the Champlain Valley, depicts Burlington at the bull's-eye of concentric blast circles. I studied the page with a mixture of horror and titillation: it was nice to feel important. But it was also nice, at the age of thirteen, to find a "starter" political issue that a young teenager could understand: in the 2020s, climate politics plays this role for many middle schoolers. In 1982, the nuclear freeze movement was at its height, and children were invited to play an important role in anti-nuke actions in Vermont: after all, we were the living demonstration of life's promise and fragility. When Bernie talked about taxing the hospital or developing the waterfront, these issues passed seventh graders by; but when he scolded "Mr. Reagan" about the folly of American policy on the global stage, in an important way he was speaking directly to Burlington's children. My first political possession was a "No Nukes" button, worn on my backpack strap. Bernie's foreign policy, broad and bold, spoke our language; it even seemed conducted on our behalf.

In March of 1982, President Reagan approved the $4.2 billion Crisis

Relocation Program, coordinated by FEMA, to evacuate certain cities and metropolitan areas in the event of a nuclear war. A network of blast shelters and evacuation pipelines would be built, a new civil defense infrastructure that would allow Americans to flee the incoming ICBMs in middle-class comfort. Sanders was enraged when he was informed that our city would be on the list. The plan, a FEMA official told him, was to move ninety thousand people in Chittenden County thirty miles north to Saint Albans. There, Mayor Floyd E. Handy, signaling that he would roll out the red carpet for these nuclear refugees, began to leverage the absurd scheme to attract publicity for his struggling city. Seventy-five communities in Vermont were informed that they would host hundreds of thousands of Connecticut residents, some of whom began, in the summer and fall of 1982, to explore the rural hillsides where eventually perhaps they would contend for acorns in hungry packs. Judy O'Leary of Trumbull, Connecticut, heading up to her assigned community of Randolph, Vermont, called the plan "incredible." In Randolph, the local coordinator for crisis relocation planned a "pre-war pot-luck brunch" for the pilgrims. "Evacuation tourism" was rural Vermont's latest outreach to wealthy daytrippers, a macabre twist on the annual rite of "leaf peeping" that brought our lowland neighbors north.

"Utterly and completely absurd," Terry Bouricius told the board of aldermen, calling for a city resolution opposing Reagan's relocation scheme. Bouricius had standing in this fight: he'd grown up outside of Los Alamos, New Mexico, where his father, a brilliant scientist, worked on the Manhattan Project. The entire plan was "irresponsible idiocy": Bouricius, Zoe Breiner, and Gary De Carolis led the opposition on the board, but even the Republicans opposed the ghoulish plan to commit "national suicide." The resolution passed unanimously, and Sanders drafted one of his "Dear Mr. Reagan" letters: "It seems to me that the major point our city is making," Sanders patiently explained to the president, "is that we believe it to be totally irresponsible to allow people the false hope that they could survive a nuclear war."

IT WAS EASY to imagine the Cold War as a Manichean wrestling match between superpowers, as in the MTV video for Frankie Goes to Hollywood's "Two Tribes": a WWE-style rumble between a Ronald Reagan lookalike and a stand-in for the Soviet premier, Konstantin Chernenko. But Burlington, a city where F-15s on daily training drills shook our homes, was an important tributary that fed into the larger horror. All throughout 1982, as Salvadoran soldiers trained at Fort Benning, Georgia, and American civilian "advisers" in El Salvador began to receive bonuses set aside for combat fighters, GE loaded its weapons onto camouflaged convoys: the frightening cortege moved through Burlington toward the firing range in Underhill for target practice. Vietnam II seemed to be underway. "We are headed, I am concerned, into another Vietnam," Sanders said, at a press conference. "The horror must end. Burlington will not stand by and watch as our country drags us into another tragic adventure."

The murder of the churchwomen in El Salvador had changed the equation in our community. A socially conscious group of Catholics, led by a radical nun, Sister Miriam Ward, and her friend Marmete Hayes, broadened the issue beyond the usual ambit of Burlington leftists and activists. Hayes founded a local chapter of Pax Christi, the Catholic peace group, and worked in conjunction with the social justice committee of the Sisters of Mercy, my elementary school teachers, to frame the issue in clear moral terms. These women made a strong, tempting case for a leftist Jesus, the most compelling argument for worshiping Christ I'd heard after years of mumbled prayers and priestly folderol. Sister Miriam, my grandmother's oldest friend from convent school, would drop by our house, "back from the Holy Land!" as it was always said. Suppressing her radical revolutionary ties, her uncompromising pro-Palestinian allegiances, Sister Miriam, a compact, no-nonsense lady with a boy's regular haircut, sat quietly with my grandmother over Sanka, reminiscing about the dark barracks and watery gruel of the convent where these two women had been received, sixty years before, as frightened orphans. Sister Miriam sometimes brought little mementos of "the Holy Land" for me, including a small straw donkey with a blue design on its bright red caparison: Arabic script, I later realized. Sister Miriam would then say her goodbyes, disappear from our back porch, and, lo, reappear in the pages of the *Free Press* or on the TV news, testifying righteously to U.S.-sponsored violence she'd seen firsthand in Gaza and the West Bank, or in El Salvador, Nicaragua, and Honduras. "Sister Miriam is back in the Holy Land!" my grandmother would proclaim cheerfully, seeing her old friend's byline on the editorial pages.

It was strange to follow the bloodshed in El Salvador within the context of Burlington Catholicism, where a gulf was opening between the culture of the young priests, egotistical, coddled, and, as we already knew, predatory; and that of the nuns, politically aware, leftist, and often happily and discreetly paired, shopping for pies at the farmers' market. Our French and Latin teachers were now on the evening news, praying the rosary among the anti-nuke activists in Montpelier and in City Hall Park, cheering as Sanders and others decried U.S. intervention in the region, and circulating their petitions in the swelling crowds. On Election Day in November, voters in Burlington and Saint Albans, the cities bound by Reagan's risible evacuation scheme, overwhelmingly passed resolutions condemning U.S. policy in El Salvador. All eyes were now on the GE plant.

In the Ward 1 polling place, our school cafeteria, the nuns then folded up the voting tables and rolled the voting machines onto the flatbeds for return to Memorial Auditorium, readying the lunchroom for their next big event: the annual holiday fund-raising bazaar, where fudge and maple candy replaced radical politics as the order of the day.

Bernie fired off another "Dear Mr. Reagan" missive, but now the fight had come to him.

Civil Disobedience

David Dellinger, the Chicago Seven defendant and legendary peace activist, was also a New England mage, the Massachusetts scion of an old-line Republican family with ties to the founding of the nation. Dellinger had the "hard working, modestly gregarious, and absolutely devoted sense of how mission and detail interlock," as Norman Mailer wrote in *Armies of the Night*, his account of the March on Washington. "He could easily have been taken for Class Agent of his fellow graduates at Yale." In 1981, Dellinger, "fed up with working in radical enclaves," as he said, moved with his wife to Peacham, a white-spired *Vermont Life* village in the Northeast Kingdom, population 530, to "make connections." Strange impulse, to move to the middle of nowhere in order to connect, but a version of this paradox had driven an entire generation to this region a decade before, and the old networks offered an opportunity to return to first principles. Dellinger told friends that he had another reason for moving to Vermont: he wanted to meet and work beside Bernie Sanders.

By 1983, Dellinger, then sixty-seven, was a legend on the American left, a Thoreauvian courage teacher with desirable non-Thoreauvian traits like a rowdy sense of humor and a penchant for Beefeater martinis. Dellinger moved to Peacham just as the nuclear freeze movement swept Vermont on Town Meeting Day in March of 1982. Of Vermont's 252 towns, 155 approved of the resolution demanding an immediate halt to the nuclear arms race. The leftist networks, maturing over a decade, a few committed individuals per shire, now linked towns from Peacham to Putney, north to south. Dellinger recognized that Vermont had become the premier organizing framework for left-wing political action perhaps anywhere in the country.

Dellinger met Greg Guma, Robin Lloyd, Sister Miriam, and others in Burlington in early 1983 to plan the "biggest act of civil disobedience" in the city's history. From the beginning the organizers knew that their plans would put Sanders in a bind. Phase one would be a rally, a march through town, and a final jamboree with bands and speeches calling for "a nuclear freeze, opposition to Euromissiles, nonintervention in Central America, and jobs with peace," according to Guma. In phase two, two days later, a human chain would blockade General Electric's loading gates, to draw arrests. The latter action would pit Bernie's supporters in the peace community against his allies in the GE workers' union. Few who knew Bernie well doubted that he would stand with the workers, and a pantomimed negotiation ensued, with Sanders seeming to relish the public role into which he'd been cast.

On June 8, Guma, Lloyd, and Dellinger met Bernie in city hall. The focus was the guns, not the workers, the activists promised. Guma and Lloyd described their meetings with GE management to discuss conversion of the plant to peacetime uses. "What are they going to do, make toasters?" Sanders snapped. Guma explained that such a large employer, so critical to the economy of the region, shouldn't depend on fickle defense contracts tied to illegal covert wars. Sanders was silent. Dellinger had come, as Guma told me, "to inform Sanders what we were planning. Not," he stressed, "to ask permission." Somewhat chastened by the presence of the leftist demiurge, Bernie suggested that the group gather instead at a federal building or at the office of Vermont's Republican U.S. senator, Robert Stafford. "Those people make the laws," Bernie said. "I'm not going to blame the workers." Sanders "would have no choice but to arrest" the protestors, a group likely to include members of his own administration.

The stand-off could not have been more effectively staged had Sanders orchestrated it himself. Bernie had been looking for opportunities to demonstrate his loyalty to organized workers in a city where labor unions were somewhat scarce. The 1981 endorsement by the Burlington Patrolmen's Association had been "a highlight of his political career," Richard Sugarman said, and Sanders sought another opportunity to distinguish his politics from the bourgeois orthodoxies of the activist left. "It wasn't even a calculation for him," the labor activist Ellen David Friedman told me. "He knew precisely where he needed to come down."

On June 9, Sanders stood beside the union chief at a press conference. "The result of what they are doing is to point the finger of guilt at working people," Sanders said. "Not everybody has the luxury of choosing where they are going to work, or the money not to work." It was a low blow, aimed especially at Robin Lloyd, the heiress whose inheritance had by now been widely distributed among peace and social justice causes. Lloyd struck back: "I feel he has polarized a situation between two of his major allies, working people and the peace movement." Murray Bookchin agreed: Sanders was "acting as a publicity man for GE, not the socialist mayor of Burlington."

The crowds of teenagers and children tie-dyeing T-shirts in City Hall Park were excited about the protest. Sanders was alone in drawing such a dramatic line and insisting on a binary choice.

On June 18, Bernie joined hundreds of demonstrators as they marched through Burlington to South Park. The mayor was "sullen and distracted," according to Greg Guma. Public opinion had turned against him: the line he wished to draw between pampered demonstrators and oppressed factory workers had not held. Some of the GE workers supported the protests, and the police were now speaking directly to the union, cutting the mayor out of the talks. Several members of his administration now planned to join the GE sit-in. It appeared that Burlington wasn't the kind of community where a cultural schism like "activist" versus "worker" could easily be created and exploited. When Bernie spotted a policeman filming the march, he lashed out at the officer and, attempting to regain the trust of the peace community and draw the public back to his side, ordered the police to desist from South Park and promised an investigation.

Then Sanders bolted from the park, the strains of "We Shall Overcome" fading as he drove down Pine Street to join the crowds at Perkins Pier, where he found a scene to lift his mood: thousands of anglers weighing their catches at the second annual Lake Champlain Fishing Derby. The proud fishermen displaying prize walleyes, pikes, and bass welcomed the mayor, a mile and a world away from the tense politics of the day.

On June 20, 1983, the morning of the sit-in, protestors, union workers,

Rice High School counterprotestors, left; Lucy Gluck, a protestor, right.
Jym Wilson

and police all very comfortably took on their assigned roles, while Sanders, arms crossed, stewed behind the police line, perhaps regretting the role he'd created for himself. Four dozen Burlington police officers met 150 demonstrators, issuing 114 citations and arresting 88. Several protestors returned after being booked and released in order to be arrested a second and even a third time. It became "a pavement picnic," according to Guma, who was among those arrested. As on a movie set, where a vampire might chat between takes with his buxom victim, or a lion share a cigarette with a Roman while awaiting their scene, cops and peace activists mingled cheerfully between orchestrated periods of antagonism. Police Chief Richard Beaulieu invited the protestors to join the police in a makeshift canteen, where our tax dollars had provided a modest spread of cold cuts, coffee, and doughnuts: "a little happy hour," the chief said. A group billed as "counter-protestors" were in fact conservative jocks from my high school, who admitted to the *Rutland Herald* that they'd mainly counterprotested "at a party the night before." These guys used the occasion of the protest to exchange views respectfully with the peace activists: "They made some really good points," a hockey player conceded.

Only one figure stood apart, outside the little human ecosystem that had sprung to life on Pine Street: Mayor Sanders, leaning silently against a guardrail. Sanders was "pleased with the actions of police and protestors," he said, as the union workers—the faction whose "right to earn a living" was so loudly defended by the mayor—greeted neighbors and cousins among the protestors, and both groups recognized familiar faces among the police. "We had protests in the '60s, but nothing like this," Chief Beaulieu beamed, complimenting the activists. Burlington, it turned out, just wasn't a place where people liked to stay in character.

The assistant city treasurer was working overtime in her silent city hall office when the clamorous June 18 march passed below her window. Barr Swennerfelt was no longer happy to be considered "the Jane Fonda of Coopers & Lybrand," she told me: her emerging radical politics seemed incompatible with her reputation as "the most brilliant accountant of her generation," as her boss, Jonathan Leopold, described her. "I'd like to be considered a brilliant peace activist," Swennerfelt said, with a laugh. Her first step was to ditch the partner track in Boston and take a job with the only socialist mayor in America. Other, more dramatic steps, would soon follow. "Why am I here, and not with them?" Swennerfelt thought as she pored over the city's books, while the protestors marched by. "It was a little twinkling."

Swennerfelt, a single mother of three young children, soon became a leader in Burlington's peace community. A Quaker, she stressed to me the

"A pavement picnic."
Jym Wilson

"necessity and art of friendship" as it was gradually revealed during the course of a ten-year-long vigil that she and others held, every Friday morning, outside the GE gates. The protestors and workers got to know one another well during this period. They had kids in the same classes and on the same sports teams. Birthdays were acknowledged through the chain-link fence. Swennerfelt, who taught basic accounting in the evenings at the Community College of Vermont, recognized some of her pupils among the GE workers. When she was arrested by the new chief of police, Kevin

Scully, he greeted her warmly: "a wonderful man," she told me, "we used to sit down together and work on the police budgets together." Swennerfelt was arrested several times in the 1980s for trespassing at GE. During a sentence of eight days, she shared a cell with a developmentally disabled woman being held for allegedly murdering her boyfriend. If you knew Vermont in those years, you knew there was a lot more to the story. "I testified at the woman's trial, on her behalf. The judge told me that he was glad something good had come out of my imprisonment."

AFTER GE, Burlington's peace community became a kind of rapid-response cell, as Ronald Reagan widened our country's butchery in Central America. In March of 1984, I joined a group of students and teachers in a crowd of 150 outside of the Champlain Mill in Winooski. The nuns led the group in prayer for the people of El Salvador and Nicaragua, then we shouted the slogans of the day toward the upstairs offices of Robert Stafford, Vermont's senior U.S. senator. Stafford, a moderate Republican, was a favorite in our home: my grandfather had known him since World War II, and often accompanied the senator as a military escort on excursions to view blizzard or hurricane damage. Sanders spoke, followed by David Dellinger and others. When the protest trailed off, sixty or so protestors, including Dellinger and, from the Sanders administration, Swennerfelt, Jeanne Keller, and Phil Fiermonte, entered the building and occupied the senator's suite of offices for three days. The occupation led to the case of the "Winooski 44," when

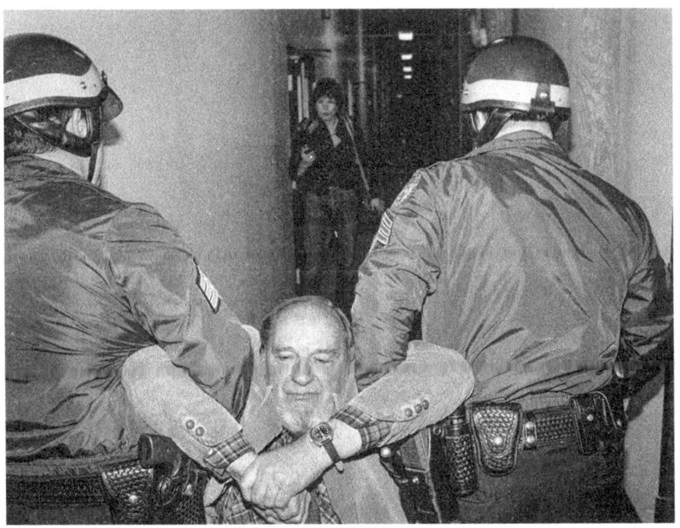

David Dellinger arrested in Winooski. *Jym Wilson*

26 defendants—"44" had caught on as a nice round number—were tried for unlawful trespass and defended by attorneys using a novel interpretation of the "necessity defense."

"It was as necessary for us to 'trespass' in Senator Stafford's office," Dellinger wrote, "as it would be to 'trespass' in a burning building to save its sleeping occupants." Swennerfelt, who was not a defendant in the trial, looked around in the gallery and saw "Howard Zinn on one side of me, Ramsey Clark, a former attorney general under Lyndon Johnson, on the other, and realized, wow, this might be historic." Zinn, the author of *A People's History of the United States*, testified to the role that "social movements all throughout American history" play to ratify the promise of the Declaration of Independence: "They start small," he told the jury, when "the legal channels do not seem to permit the voice of the public to be heard very well."

On November 18, a jury of twelve Vermonters, none of whom appeared to David Dellinger to betray the "taint" of leftist political beliefs, returned twenty-six not-guilty verdicts. To Ramsey Clark, the jurors looked "like Reagan voters." "We got international law into Vermont District Court," Jeanne Keller proclaimed, triumphantly. The *Burlington Free Press* reported on "shock waves from coast to coast." The average Burlingtonian believed that American conduct in Central America was sufficient "emergency" to justify taking over the office of a United States senator.

The senator himself appeared to agree. In 1985, Robert Stafford, who told activists that "Central America hadn't been an area of focus," and that he "only knew what he read in the papers," withdrew his support for Ronald Reagan's aid package to the Nicaraguan Contras.

29

Neither Out Far nor In Deep

(Burlington Imagines Its Horizons, 1983–84)

Burlington waterfront, 1970s. Mobil Oil tanks in foreground; Moran Generating Plant in background. *Art Huse*

The Ghost of Timothy Follett

The grandest building in Burlington crowns a steep rise at the base of College Street overlooking Lake Champlain. Follett House is a Doric temple to the god of commerce, its six white granite columns suggesting the toothy grin of a man counting his fortune. When Timothy Follett, a local judge, built the home in 1843, he had reason to smile: Follet's rough-hewn stone warehouse a block away on Battery Street now stored cargo for hundreds of barges passing Burlington harbor daily as they made their way to the new Champlain Canal at the lake's southern point; from there, Vermont lumber and stone traveled down the Hudson River to New York City and the wider world. Follett established the Merchants National Bank of Burlington to capitalize his busy pass-through, then dreamed up an east–west line linking Lake Champlain to the Connecticut River and ultimately to Boston. But the Burlington–Rutland line proved to be too late and too slow, its route threading a dangerous path between mountains. When it failed in 1853, Judge Follett lost his fortune and sold Follett House to a bitter rival. Four years later, a probate notice appeared in the *Burlington Free Press* on behalf of a ward seeking license to liquidate "the whole of the real estate" remaining under the name of "Timothy Follett, insane person" in order "to pay said ward." Follett died a lonely, impoverished man in a sanitarium; but it is still a Burlington tradition to watch for his ghost pacing behind the curtains of his magnificent home, as though the poor man were still agonized by his downfall.

In the late 1960s, the sagging Follett House seemed fated for demolition as a part of the city's program of urban renewal; but the owner of the historic wreck, a hidebound local chapter of the VFW, where both my grandfather and great-grandfather were members, refused to sell to the city; and therefore the spread of progress was halted before Follett House and the historic buildings along Battery Street to its south could be destroyed. The members of the VFW smoked and played bingo while the city, licking its wounds, went back to the drawing board.

When Antonio Pomerleau, Burlington's wealthiest citizen and largest single taxpayer, approached the VFW to purchase Follett House in 1977, his intention was nothing short of restoring the ruin to its original 1843 grandeur. When the VFW was persuaded to move their bingo game to a new clubhouse subsidized by the family, Tony Pomerleau, along with his son Ernest, began to "catalog and study every single piece" of the building, according to Pomerleau: boards, nails, carpets, shingles, tiles. When the building nearly burned down in 1979, Pomerleau said it felt like losing a child. But the restoration continued, and in 1980 the public was invited to a gala day of events at the new Follett House. "My family and I treasure our life here in Burlington," the invitation read. Tony Pomerleau wept as the doors were thrown open to families and neighbors on a hot August afternoon. From his new office behind pillars, Pomerleau planned the future of the Burlington waterfront, which now spread out before him like an architect's diorama. It was not in his plans, however, for Bernie Sanders to be elected mayor.

Tony Pomerleau is already a character in our story: the shrewd waterfront developer in cahoots with Mayor Gordon Paquette; the police commissioner presiding over an underpaid, angry rank and file. This was the narrative that Sanders and his allies promoted all through the bitter campaign winter of 1980–81. With Pomerleau as the public face of both police frustration and greedy development—two of Bernie's most effective issues—it was the story necessary for Sanders to tell, and it worked.

Privately, though, even during the heat of the campaign, Tony always had a warm word for Bernie when they passed each other on Church Street or at Bove's. "Dad and Bernie got along famously," Ernie Pomerleau said. "They always did." It wasn't only that Pomerleau was a pragmatist, and that Bernie might become the mayor; there were deeper affinities. Both men could see that the other had been poor. Born in Quebec, Pomerleau was raised on a hard-pressed dairy farm in Newport, Vermont, on the Canadian border. At two, he fell into a cellar hole and nearly died from injuries to his back. At twelve, after casting aside the metal corset he'd been told he would wear his entire life, this destitute farm boy, speaking only French, was hired by the local five-and-dime to stage holiday window displays. The community loved little Tony's windows, his toy sleighs parting the banks of cotton snow under a tinfoil moon. Ten years later, as a new employee of Endicott Johnson, the shoe company, Pomerleau was again put in charge of windows, and this time "revolutionized" the retail display of shoes by composing little humorous, festive, and patriotic narrative scenarios. Pomerleau then built his empire of strip malls and grocery stores on Burlington's periphery, while focusing his political and philanthropic efforts on the center of the city. Sanders praised Pomerleau as "a self-made capitalist, not a corporate capitalist." As Steven Soifer put it in his early study of the Sanders administration, *The Socialist Mayor*, "This is not the sort of distinction one expects a socialist to make."

Tony Pomerleau, claiming more power than any mayor and operating from a grand pillared mansion that many newcomers to Burlington assumed was city hall, watched as his network of bankers and contractors and city commissioners froze up in the weeks after Bernie's startling 1981 election victory; but while the aldermen plotted and the banks fretted, Pomerleau paid Bernie a visit in city hall, and both men approached the *Burlington Free Press* after a two-hour meeting to report on "a surprisingly pleasant conversation." Sanders and Pomerleau, acting in his role as police commissioner, coordinated a series of actions together: they gave each other credit for "the quietest Spring Fling" in years; they pantomimed a dispute over police salaries that allowed Pomerleau to claim he'd gone to the mat for his officers; they agreed to divert money from parking meters directly into the police department's coffers, over the public objection of former mayor Paquette, who was now attending budget committee meetings to brood and scowl at Bernie. These victories assigned to Pomerleau as commissioner set up an astounding concession made by Pomerleau the developer. After Pomerleau indicated that he was willing to withdraw his plans for two eighteen-story towers, he and Sanders began very publicly, and weirdly amicably, discussing the fate of the waterfront. Pomerleau told friends that his new perch on Lake Champlain had made him suddenly "contemplative" about his prior plans "to build high." He held the option on his prime parcel for one more year, after which he would need to pay $100,000 to renew it. So Tony Pomerleau began to bargain against himself, to save his sunset views.

Pomerleau's friendship was the best gift the mayor had yet received. Pomerleau "always dressed down" for his regular meetings with Bernie to indicate the new spirit of cooperation, according to friends. "I get along better with him," Pomerleau told a reporter, "than I ever did with Paquette." The Burlington press loved "the odd couple," and Sanders's aides were in on the joke: Linda Niedweske noted that Pomerleau, waiting humbly in the reception area for his meeting with the mayor, was "a very calm, gracious" presence, "very in control. I never saw him angry." The implication was that Pomerleau's negotiating partner had no such equanimity.

The two men were both "streetwise loners," Pomerleau said. Their bond seemed sealed by fate—or what passes for it in a small city like Burlington, coincidence. An apartment at 143 North Union Street had been Tony Pomerleau's first family home in the city, its two small rooms filling up with the first several of Pomerleau's ten children. This tiny apartment brimming with babies was an integral part of Pomerleau's rags-to-riches story; he would return sometimes, introducing himself to the current tenants and wishing them well.

Now, sitting in his office in Follett House and watching the sun disappear behind the Adirondacks, he drew a reporter close and asked, "Guess who lives there now? The mayor!"

The Paths of Dean and Sharp

In these years a paralysis in Burlington lifted, as citizens found they no longer needed to accept the vast anonymous life-altering public works projects that had fed their city's coffers, and scrambled their city's neighborhoods, for decades. In the South End, the beleaguered residents of Lakeside got an unexpected break: when ground was broken for the highway that was to pass through their tranquil corridor, pockets of benzene, a deadly carcinogen, wafted across Blodgett Beach from the Pine Street Barge Canal. The Southern Connector was, for the near future, dead. What years of citizen protest couldn't achieve, these deep contaminated tar pits, the remnants of a nineteenth-century gasworks that threatened the entire lake's ecology if disturbed, finally accomplished.

With construction of the Southern Connector tied up in a lengthy Superfund cleanup, Burlington now turned its attention to its downtown wasteland by the water. Tony Pomerleau was still holding his option, apparently to give Sanders a chance to assemble his own counterproposal. The coordination between the two seemed to include a choreography of bitter public spats followed by warm reconciliations. "I can't stay mad at this guy!" Sanders told reporters, clasping a beaming Pomerleau by the shoulders. In November of 1982, Pomerleau dissolved his option on the twelve acres of prime waterfront, citing the city's "changed political climate." The land reverted back to the railroads, which immediately shopped for a new buyer. Sanders floated the idea that the city should buy it outright; Pomerleau supported him.

Burlington, having been bailed out of debt by a miracle windfall, felt it had been given a tabula rasa. The city began to imagine its shore collectively, and in doing so it created, in the years between 1982 and 1985, a vital community brainstorm where even children played a role. Tables were laid out in City Hall Park with markers and paper. Kids submitted their visions: a Ferris wheel, a roller coaster, a zoo; a boardwalk with cotton candy, bumper cars, and Soak-the-Bloke; an aquarium "for Champ," the fabled lake monster. Sanders set the tone when, in the summer of 1983, he retained as his architect the irrepressible David Sellers of Prickly Mountain in Warren, a red-haired child of a man who had created in clapboard and shingle and glass some of the strangest improvisations in the history of American architecture on his steep hillside in the Mad River Valley. Sellers proclaimed the Burlington waterfront to be "the best site in North America." Holding forth at the Daily Planet, inside the strange urban terrarium that he had designed for the restaurant, Sellers invited input from all. He was the coordinator, the impresario, the host of Burlington's dreams.

The truth was that Burlingtonians knew very little about their waterfront. Sanders didn't walk the Burlington shore very much; nobody did. Larry Sanders remembered visiting his brother in the 1970s. "It was actually almost crazy," Larry said. "Bernard kept trying to show me the lake, but it couldn't really be visited. We kept hitting obstacles." Staring down at the shorefront rubble from Battery Park, Bernie exclaimed, "Jesus, what the hell kind of city is this?" So when asked whether they wanted to pay a little more in property taxes to own this godforsaken mess, many Burlingtonians stopped Sanders on Church Street to tell him a firm no. A public purchase of the land was off the table, and David Sellers returned to Warren to play in the woods.

Of course, nobody consulted the people who'd made their home on the waterfront for generations. From the broad lake, out fishing with my grandfather, I remember seeing semipermanent settlements all up and down the Burlington shore, oriented away from downtown and toward the shallows. At the base of College Street near the Naval Reserve Station, a family of

Robar Family Houseboats, 1950s. *Vermont Historical Society*

Indigenous St. Regis Mohawk, hailing from Whitehall, New York, at the southern tip of Lake Champlain, had shared a network of houseboats for decades. In the old days, the Robar family had run lines and dinghies for its grand neighbor, the Lake Champlain Yacht Club, now long ago abandoned and razed. By 1981, ice fishermen and wanderers knew them best. The Robars sold minnows, nightcrawlers, worms, and perch for bait, and rented rowboats for a nickel "sunup to sundown," as Rita Robar said, as well as a spare bedroom to souls down on their luck. The Robars' houseboat village was a liminal world all to itself, neither shore nor lake. In a CCTV interview, Rita Robar recalled seeing the grand steamboat *Ticonderoga*—these days, dry-docked as the main attraction at the Shelburne Museum, ten miles south of town—pass by twice a day.

How did it feel to see the big paddleboat glide by, its decks crowded with partiers? "Often as a child, I'd get upset," Robar lamented. "I used to watch a little mother sunfish who made her nest under our gangplank." When the tourist boat passed, "that would cause like a tide, and all the mud would go over her little nest."

RICK SHARP HAD VISITED Burlington as a kid from his dreary hometown of Bellows Falls, Vermont, and recalled a city "something like Oz." Home was not easy for Sharp: his mother had died when he was an infant; when Rick was fourteen, his father, a screen printer, killed himself using his son's rifle. Burlington was "where I wanted to spend the rest of my life."

One warm, glorious May afternoon in 1978, the young attorney thought he would take a dip in Lake Champlain. At the base of every steeply sloping street, Sharp found the elements of "an industrial wasteland," including a "tank farm containing large stainless-steel structures surrounded by chain link fences topped with barbed wire stretched to the horizon." Sharp "couldn't even get to the water, much less swim in it."

As he describes it in *The Burlington Bike Path and Waterfront Park*, Sharp spent the summer of 1978 delivering pizzas and studying for the bar exam, while clerking for the Vermont Department of Environmental Conservation. At a Democratic picnic in the Old North End, Sharp met a young doctor just finishing his residency at UVM. Howard Brush Dean III stood out from the crowd: the son of a wealthy stockbroker and an art appraiser, Dean had been brought up in splendor on the Upper East Side of Manhattan, with summers in East Hampton and schooling at St. George's and Yale. Dean's lockjaw betrayed his privilege, but the formative event of the young doctor's life was a tragedy: while backpacking in Southeast Asia in 1974, Dean's younger brother Charlie was kidnapped and executed by Laotian guerillas. Howard wore Charlie's leather belt everywhere in his brother's honor. The doctor seemed consecrated for politics by personal loss.

Dean and Sharp began regularly walking the Burlington shore along the old Rutland Railroad tracks, badly overgrown with bramble. "You took your life in your hands," Dean told me: the roaring up ahead in the trees, growing louder and angrier as it approached, was a neon green ATV speeding through the thick brush, or a swarm of whizzing motocross racers. Over the years, though, the ATVs and dirt bikes and snowmobiles had exposed the old railbed, and now walkers along the trail became more common. The process of clearing and reclaiming two miles of magnificent shoreline had begun, one step at a time. "We took a look at it," Dean said to me, "and decided right then we wanted a bike path."

A BIKE PATH TRAVELS three overlapping routes on its way to fruition: one is topographical; the second is political; and the third is legal. The Burlington Bike Path in its proposed form connected Leddy Beach to Oakledge Beach, along two miles of the disused railbed of the Rutland Railroad purchased in 1964 by the state of Vermont. Dean and Sharp hosted "several tie removal parties during the summers of 1981 and 1982," as Sharp wrote. A Boy Scout troop turned up with crowbars. A UVM frat hazed its pledges by forcing them to pull up ties. Soon the path was even and clear.

Now, though, a thorny political path came into view. "Rick was very aggressive," Dean told me. "Very, very aggressive." In 1980, Dean and Sharp left a meeting with Mayor Paquette "scratching our heads": the mayor offered no support, and seemed to expect loyalty, nonetheless. Volunteers then collected thousands of signatures to bring support for a bike path to the voters of Burlington in the fateful city elections of March 1981, on the same ballot with Sanders and Paquette. Rick Sharp believes that his energized recruits, heading to the polls en masse to defy Paquette's city hall, were the decisive factor in Bernie's narrow victory. Sanders, who had campaigned on a promise of open and free access to the lake, seemed a born champion for the narrow ribbon of public land that Burlington's citizens had demanded.

Just as the political route seemed clear, though, the bike path became entangled in bitter litigation that "changed the equation," according to Dean. The old tracks crossed private parcels belonging to Little Eagle Bay, a luxury condominium development, and its neighbors, the Burlington Elks Club and the Episcopal Diocese of Burlington. At Little Eagle Bay, a lawyer named Clarke Gravel, representing the developer, Paul Preseault, stood sentry on his balcony, noting an eerie quiet since the walkers had replaced the motocross bikes. A public grab of this valuable land was already underway. The abutters at Little Eagle Bay organized to fight the public's assertion of a right by presumptive easement on the abandoned land.

In the summer of 1981, after the success of Dean and Sharp's ballot question, Preseault and Gravel filed a lawsuit against the city, drawing the Elks Club and the Episcopal Church into the complaint. "I left the Episcopal Church over it," Howard Dean told me. "I became a Congregationalist, which is more New England anyway." All the plaintiffs imagined glorious private benefit accruing from the disused railbed, which Gravel, citing English Common Law, argued should revert to abutters, and not the general public. If Preseault and Gravel had their way, the astonishing network of 270,000 rail lines crisscrossing the United States would be swiftly and permanently dissolved by private landowners. The U.S. Congress, responding to the dispute in Burlington, acted quickly to establish the 1983 Railbanking Act. Preseault then sued in federal court to overturn the law, arguing that the Interstate Commerce Commission's confiscation of the abandoned tracks amounted to an illegal seizure of property. In 1990, the U.S. Supreme Court found for the government in the case of *Preseault v. Interstate Commerce Commission*. Howard Dean celebrated that day from his office at the statehouse in Montpelier; rising steadily in state politics after his debut as the "bike path guy," Dean was elected lieutenant governor in 1987.

In working out the relations among land, law, and politics, Burlington also worked out its future. Dean, the cheerful, hale crusader, became first a foe, and then a cautious Montpelier ally, of Bernie's city hall. Sanders, bending the legal delays to his advantage, co-opted the bike path as a card in larger negotiations with potential waterfront developers. In the process, Howard Dean and Bernie Sanders, Vermont's most important twenty-first-century politicians on the national stage, met as rivals, and used the bike path as a proxy for much larger questions about the drift of statewide politics.

HOWARD DEAN AND Rick Sharp were die-hard Democrats, out of step on a new day in Burlington. "I figured maybe Bernie was going to win when my wife told me she was voting for him," Dean told me, "but then when my mailman Tony said he was voting for Sanders, I knew it." The candidate that appealed to a Princeton-educated young doctor, Judith Steinberg, and a French-Canadian mailman, nevertheless did not sway Howard Dean: "Of course not," he told me. "I was a Democrat."

Sanders, at that point in his first term busy fighting the Nectar's junto and the *Burlington Flea Press*, had little time for two preppies and their lark. Dean and Sharp found "an unresponsive" Bernie, "a closed door" where they had expected a warm welcome. It did not help their case that Sharp and Dean, as Bernie knew, were rising in Democratic politics outside the viper's nest of city government. Dean worked for Jimmy Carter's campaign in 1980, unofficially headquartered at his neighbor Esther Sorrell's house in the Old North End. Over cookies and gossip, Sorrell, who was known as the "mother of the Democratic Party in Vermont," gave the young man "a crash course" in the state's politics: the same lessons she'd given to two other future Vermont governors, Phil Hoff in the 1960s and Madeleine Kunin in the '80s. Sorrell, the party kingmaker, spotted Dean even before he'd imagined a political career.

So had Sanders. "You're a liar. You've been lying!" Bernie shouted at Dean, by then the chair of the Chittenden County Democratic Party, when the two future presidential hopefuls met for the first time in city hall.

With Dean contributing op-eds regularly to the *Burlington Free Press* and planning his run for state legislature, Sanders decided that the bike path issue had been "politicized" by Dean and Sharp—and began to slow-walk any related business that crossed his desk. Bernie saw the path as a back-channel for Democrats to defy him once again: "This group is being used as a partisan arm of the Democratic Party," Sanders charged. Whether or not Sanders was correct, the bike path was now entangled with the larger politics of waterfront development. The titans, Sanders and Tony Pomerleau, nominally at odds but actually cooperating, worked together against Dean and Sharp's ragged citizen's group.

So Dean and Sharp escalated. The two men went back to work on the waterfront, using elbow grease to transform another small area, a "spit of crap, rocks, and junk," as Dean put it, at the base of College Street where the Burlington Community Boathouse now sits. "Rick had some construction equipment," Dean said, chuckling, and knew "where to find stockpiles of old fill and bricks" left over from the construction of the Church Street Marketplace. The friends laid a brick path, planted a few trees, and made a point of hanging out there. "I'm sure it was illegal," Dean said, "maybe even in violation of several federal statutes." Soon "over 200 loads of urban excavation" had been brought in, and the Army Corps of Engineers showed up "in a friendly mood" to halt the project, but not to order it dismantled. At a party for the finished park, now planted with lilacs and tulips, and fortified against beavers, Mrs. Dorothy Hunt brought lemonade, cookies, and a sapling locust from her yard.

Dean told me that planning and installing the little peninsula park helped him to determine "the facts on the ground" in city politics as they became increasingly wrapped up with waterfront development. It was clear that Bernie intended to "use the bike path as a political football," Dean said, and that the credit for any form of public access to the waterfront would accrue to him and his administration. "I'm disturbed that the mayor has an attitude that nobody but Bernie Sanders has a good idea about what should be done on the waterfront," Dean said. Co-opting the bike path was entirely a "political maneuver," Dean told me, sounding, despite himself, a little impressed.

THE FIGHT NOW broadened from the ribbon of old railroad tracks to the surrounding acres, a level barrens where the railways had built their freight yards. In August of 1983, Mayor Sanders announced that he and John Franco had been "quietly grappling" with "a little-known law that requires public use of the prime lakefront property," according to an article by Debbie Bookchin in the *Rutland Herald*. "Research suggests," Franco said, "that the state is not competent to convey outright interest in the lake bottom." According to the public trust doctrine, the filled land on which the railroads built their business before abandoning it to the elements was legally no different from the lake bed. "It's just not something that can be sold," Franco said. Sanders and Franco began to make plans to seize the land from the railroads. Rick Sharp rejoiced: now the entire waterfront, and not just the narrow strip where the tracks ran, would revert to the people of Vermont. The lakefront belonged "to all Vermonters," he liked to say.

And yet, that summer, several discreet purchases were made along the Burlington harbor by a mysterious group of investors. The Alden Waterfront Group, represented by John Osgood of Warren, Vermont, would not disclose its partners, but their pockets were apparently deep. By September, Alden had negotiated options to buy five waterfront acres, and had designs on twenty-six more. Before anyone knew much about the dark money behind these arrangements, Alden had hired the country's foremost architect of reclaimed urban spaces, Ben Thompson of Cambridge, Massachusetts. Thompson's renowned firm had transformed Boston's Faneuil Hall and Quincy Market, South Street Seaport in New York, and Baltimore's Inner Harbor. On "secret missions to Burlington," he said, he'd fallen in love with the city. Handsome, gregarious, and patrician, admired for his periwinkle seersucker jackets and trousers in lilac or bubblegum, Ben Thompson sometimes did business from his wood-burning Baltic sauna on the harbor of Barnstable, Massachusetts. Thompson was the latest settler to arrive in Burlington and decide that he had discovered paradise.

In the fall of 1983, the city of Burlington entered an unorthodox development partnership with the mysterious Alden group. Sanders and Peter Clavelle met with Thompson in his offices off Brattle Street in Cambridge, Massachusetts, impressed by the bright, festive world that the brilliant man had created in his working environment. Nearby was the showroom of Design Research, the retail store Thompson founded, and the finest American source for modern design. Toys by Charles and Ray Eames—elephants, spinning tops, a house of cards—sat atop the buttery Alvar Aalto tables. A Marimekko throw, pink daisies on an aubergine field, draped over a Bertoia wire lounge chair. It was all very Cambridge, distinctly Brattle Street, in its vision of domestic life as composed of conversation, cocktails, jazz, a few perfect artifacts, some perfect children, and the possibility of tacit sexual adventure. The life of a Harvard professor, perhaps; but available to anyone with a little income and an apartment to fill.

The meeting was "thrilling," according to Clavelle. Thompson presented a little model Burlington, its shoreline development expanding into the lake along a newly constructed breakwater: "a floating park," as he called it. The old Burlington breakwater, an underwater New England stone wall that rises six feet above the lake's surface, was built in the nineteenth century, over decades, by dropping rubble and boulders into sunken wooden cribs, a feat almost ancient Egyptian in scale. This new breakwater would come together—presto!—in a matter of months. The wizardly Thompson seemed to operate in the zone of magic or dream. Sanders and Clavelle left the meeting in no mood to be disenchanted.

MY FRIENDS MELINDA and Rick Moulton hand-built their stone-and-timber house in the mountains as part of the hippie wave of the early 1970s, felling trees and sledding boulders down from the hillside. Inside their home, a massive oak trunk, still rooted in the soil, polished smooth and hung with family photos, acts as a central column. When, one morning in 1984, Eli Moulton, my high school buddy and teammate on the Rice Memorial High School tennis team, saw an Alden helicopter descend into his parents' meadow against the foothills of Camel's Hump, open its bay doors, and carry his mother away, it was clear that a new era had dawned in Burlington.

Melinda Moulton was hired in 1983 as operations director for Alden. Its main investor was her friend Lisa Steele, a quiet local entrepreneur whose family owned Dow Jones and Company and controlled *The Wall Street Journal* until its sale to Rupert Murdoch in 2007. "We were going to bring Burlington into the twenty-first century," Melinda told me, over tuna sandwiches. "This was major-league stuff. I secured financing from seventeen banks, the project was $100 million, there was going to be a marina, a children's museum, and a new breakwater constructed as a public park." I expressed surprise that Bernie Sanders, who ran on the slogan "No enclaves for the rich," was behind such a dreamworld transformation of the gritty shoreline. "Bernie understood economics," she said, and "he understood that public access was better negotiated with developers who had truly deep pockets." In addition, she added, Ben Thompson "was an amazing guy," a visionary who had revitalized the windswept wastelands of three major American cities.

In the winter of 1983–84, Burlington was at a crossroads. New England, lopsided toward the Atlantic, lacked a metropolis on its west coast. With new infrastructure waiting to be exploited, a reputation for easygoing, outdoor-centered living, and modern amenities to spare—the best hospital outside of Boston, the best public university in New England, jobs metastasizing faster than workers—Burlington looked like it might become the last great small American city of the twentieth century.

But as the details of the so-called Alden Plan leaked, two things became clear: the essence of the new Burlington was public conversation; and the essence of the new Burlington's public conversation was whether the city really wanted to become a different sort of place entirely, a JV San Francisco.

THE NEW YEAR'S EVE lights and banners still hung in city hall when Burlington met the Alden architect Ben Thompson in late January of 1984. Thompson had spent the day on Church Street, drinking Lillet Blanc and Aquavit at Leunig's and regaling curious passers-by with an exclusive sneak peek at the details of the evening's presentation. By the time the meeting rolled around, Thompson was in high spirits. Burlingtonians entered the Contois Auditorium, the old battle-ax where city aldermen met on Mondays to plead and cajole, to discover a mellow moodscape with dimmed lighting and smooth jazz piped in over the loudspeakers. Thompson told the *Burlington Free Press* that he played music at these community meetings to keep people from caucusing against his plans before he could present them. Thompson was a shy man, a little rambling in public, even before the Aquavit. Unless you sedated the crowd with a little Chet Baker, "everybody jumps on your head," Thompson told the reporter.

Bernie had been dreaming big ever since he had parted ways amicably with David Sellers the previous year. But the talk in frozen Burlington that winter was Disney's new EPCOT center, where Vermonters, on their annual Florida trips, had experienced a simulated India, Holland, and China, before returning home to road salt and heating bills. What Thompson showed Burlington that evening "looked like EPCOT," one woman pointed out, not sounding pleased. She meant phony, uncanny, not-of-this-place. The marinas, the two-hundred-bed hotel, the little villages for artists, the "Heritage Center" and condominiums for the wealthy: the project that Thompson gleefully presented "was something out of fantasyland," Wanda Loney told a reporter. It's "more like EPCOT," the man beside her added, to vigorous nods of agreement. Jada Wood, a student at Champlain College, attended the meeting "with one concern": sitting in her wheelchair in the Contois balcony, Wood "wanted to make sure that anyone with a mobility problem would have access."

The meeting was indeed spirited; and the bike path activists, seeing their dream of public access to the shore's edge jeopardized, jumped on Ben Thompson's head. Bea Bookchin stood up to decry the lack of a proper setback. Rick Sharp, seated next to Howard Dean, threatened a lawsuit if the buildings were not moved off the hem of the shore. Dean intended to be "neutral," he told me: the project was "promising," but the buildings loomed over the water. And the entire scheme appeared to hinge on whether Burlington could secure a federal grant in the neighborhood of $23 million, a long shot when the entire state of Vermont had netted less than $10 million in such grants in the previous five years. "It's very, very big," Dean told a reporter, attempting to stake out a position on the fence. Sanders, leaving city hall, sounded cautious: "It was an impressive evening. Now we take it on the road, take it to the people."

30

Coming Out

(Prosperity and the Progressive Coalition, 1984)

First Night

Burlington's New Year's Eve, 1983, began at six a.m. in a snow-locked barn in Glover, Vermont, two icy hours away from the Queen City, where Peter Schumann selected papier-mâché hands and heads and masks for our city's Grand Processional: a ritual pageant banishing the old year and welcoming the new. For this joyous night, Schumann chose only the jolliest and friendliest of his creations. For himself, Peter picked an enormous white Sunbird; for the other performers, Schumann packed dozens of costumes—zebras and reindeer and owls and angels—and loaded into the flower-power school bus all the brass instruments for the marching band. Last, he packed his stilts.

Bread & Puppet's Grand Processional was the main event at Burlington's inaugural First Night celebration, when eight thousand people traversed the snowdrifts downtown to experience Vermont acts like the St. Andrew's Highland Dancers, the Ketch Modern Dance Company, "Jugglers from Mars," and the Unknown Blues Band. Burlington's restaurants piled their boards with delicacies unheard of on ordinary nights. The Ice House offered chateaubriand for two, rack of venison, and a caviar fountain. Pearls featured "hot and sour consommé made with duck, gravlax with Italian mustard fruit, and cranberry sorbet between courses." At midnight, the temperature dipping below twenty degrees, a shower of fireworks would rain down over frozen Lake Champlain. Then it would be 1984, Orwell's year.

Schumann's school bus pulled into the Edmunds Middle School parking lot around three p.m., where Bread & Puppet met a crowd of volunteers, mostly children. The masks and banners and wands were passed out, the kids given basic lessons in marching and twirling, and, at five p.m., the parade began, hundreds of people beheld by thousands along the route. My friends and I came prepared to join the "kazoo chorus" at the rear, as the parade passed. The buzzing intensified as more children joined from the banks of the road. In Battery Park, at the parade's end, Schumann and company performed heathen rites to ritually turn the hours, and the year 1983 was burned in effigy in a bonfire.

The parade route took Bread & Puppet on a tour of Burlington's transformation. When Schumann had last performed on Church Street, in the bicentennial year of 1976, all the old family businesses—Jan's Shoes, Bailey's Music Rooms, Kelley Pharmacy, Abernathy's—still clung to life. Now, Schumann's papier-mâché angels and zebras encountered modern corporate capitalism in a faux hometown guise: on the new brick blocks of the Church Street Marketplace, the androgenes on the Benetton poster silently disdained the passing kazoos, the maidens at Laura Ashley found no prince among the puppeteers, and a pith-helmeted mannequin in the new Banana Republic store—in the early 1980s, the chain was still a purveyor of safari fashions—looked eager to net one of Bread & Puppet's papier-mâché tigers.

These were the kinds of changes that modern prosperity brings to a place. But where were the changes that socialism promised to bring—that Bernie had promised to bring? To Murray Bookchin and others on the left, Sanders and his administration favored "a sharp 'business' orientation to Burlington as a well-managed corporate enterprise." After nearly three years in office, Sanders brooded on a set of paradoxes. Since 52 percent of the real property in his city was tax exempt, Burlington's tax base needed to grow by attracting businesses of all types. The city hosted sprawling nonprofit institutions like UVM, which brought Michel Foucault to town but paid no taxes, and profitable employers like GE, which fortified the tax base but manufactured mass-murdering machine guns. The mayor seemed, at times, guided by one principle to the exclusion of others: he would not raise property taxes on Sadie White and her neighbors.

Already there was an enormous burden on poor and elderly Burlington homeowners, who'd stood by helplessly as Burlington metamorphosed; and now, with Vermont requiring the booming Queen City to reappraise its property or lose its share of the state's aid to education, eight loathed appraisers roamed the neighborhoods, knocking on doors. My grandparents pulled the curtains; some people hid in their garages. Everyone tried to make their properties look as weatherbeaten as possible. Our neighbors hauled a moldy fishing boat out of their barn and into their driveway. It was all fruitless. White called Bernie to complain that her tiny home had increased "overnight" from a valuation of $8,900 to nearly $50,000. Sanders repeated in nearly every press conference on the issue of gentrification that "in America, a working person should be able to own a house, and a retired person should be able to keep their home."

So, the answer was more business and more tourism, which could only mean, eventually, still higher appraisals. The shops of the Church Street Marketplace sold the kinds of things that drove Sanders crazy, and the desire to purchase them, and to consign oneself to a life of debt to do so, seemed to him a human sickness. But tourists loved the Marketplace, and these merchants selling products that few Burlington families could afford had nevertheless chipped in to create First Night out of their growing profits. The cycle left many behind. Richard Sartelle, home in Franklin Square and on the outs with his old ally—Sanders now "wouldn't take my calls," he told the *Burlington Free Press*—stayed in that New Year's Eve, smoking one Lucky Strike after another, and wondering where the promise of Franklin Square's playground had gone.

INSIDE MEMORIAL AUDITORIUM, Bernie Sanders and Jane Driscoll danced to the brass and banjo jazz of Bob Connors' New Yankee Rhythm Kings. Sanders was "bobbing and twisting," according to the *Rutland Herald*: the image brings to mind bait on a hook. Bernie's shitkickers, jeans, and special-occasion moth-eaten gray crewneck indicated less than total commitment to the festivities. By ten o'clock, as usual, the mayor was checking his watch. Soon, having conditioned his friends to abrupt goodbyes, Bernie scrammed. But the band played on as Gary De Carolis chatted with Zoe Breiner and Rik Musty and their spouses and families. Peter Lackowski, an activist and schoolteacher, joined their small circle. Terry Bouricius, according to the *Herald*, "jitterbugged the night away in a tux with tails and white gloves."

The group of five that Bernie left behind—known to friends as "Sanderistas," to foes as the "five blind mice"—had convened the previous October for midnight beers and roast beef sandwiches at B.T. McGuire's, the dusty fern bar on Church Street, across from city hall. David Clavelle explained to them the current political state of play. After five terms, Dick Snelling was burned out in Montpelier, and would likely not seek another term as governor. Snelling "wasted tremendous energy on controversies that stemmed from an attitude of superiority," as Joe Sherman put it: he had not been the same man since the suicide of a state trooper from St. Johnsbury, accused by Snelling of playing a role in a scheme to steal drill bits. Sergeant Howard Gould walked into the dense woods behind the Vermont statehouse one evening and shot himself in the chest, leaving Snelling a note: "I hope you sleep well at night." ("Dick Snelling didn't, ever," Stephen Terry told me.)

Sanders and Snelling admired one another: Bernie had his own tendencies toward squandering his might on petty squabbles. Clavelle had polled Sanders's chances in a statewide race and "was not discouraged." If Bernie ran, it would leave at least a temporary vacuum in city hall while the mayor, who'd ventured out of Burlington only rarely during his time in office, reintroduced himself to the state of Vermont.

The Burlington Progressive Coalition—and with it, the dominant, Bernie Sanders strain of twenty-first-century American progressivism—was born on Halloween night, 1983. "'Progressive' wasn't that often used, in those days," Terry Bouricius told me. "David Clavelle gave us the idea. It was a way of saying 'socialist,' without—in both senses of the phrase—flying a red flag." Clavelle confirmed, but added, "It was also a way of saying, we're making progress." The term called to mind the populist Progressive Party of Wisconsin's Robert La Follette in the 1920s and George Aiken's grassroots Vermont progressivism, as well as Henry Wallace's national Progressive Party in the '50s. But Burlington's new progressives didn't evolve out of those movements, so much as rehab an abandoned term whose vague positive vibes still hung around. The twenty-first-century association of the term *progressive* with Bernie Sanders began, therefore, at this midnight conclave at B.T. McGuire's, with Sanders nowhere in sight. At last call, the five blind mice straggled out of the bar as a new, leaderless political entity, ready for the next phase of the movement.

Small-stakes city politics had "begun to wear on my friend, to be sure," Richard Sugarman told me. Bernie's voice began to sound a little loud and grating in his ears for the "small rooms and tiny crowds" he addressed. The ironies of his role as socialist mayor of a boomtown confronted Bernie when his economy car—the first new car he'd ever owned—was rear-ended by a BMW. Sanders worried that the crash was brought on by his hubris: "I should never have bought it," he exclaimed. Bernie didn't like chateaubriand or caviar, and had begun to identify the problems of Burlington's poor as intractable unless they were addressed at the higher levels of government.

The mayor confided his state of mind to the pages of a yellow legal pad otherwise filled with the season's to-do lists, drafts of press releases, and preliminary agenda:

> I am unable to look in the mirror—and see how I am. How am I? I don't know. I don't know who "I" am.
>
> For years now, I have not lived a normal emotional life. My relationship to J. remains unclear. We pass time together, but the relationship doesn't [grow], mature or deepen.
>
> I have pushed everything, on top of everything, on top of everything.

> My ability to think, to cry, to laugh, to relate to other human beings, is strained. Year after year, editorial after editorial, letter after letter, media bullshit after media bullshit.

The passage trails off, Sanders draws a line across the page, and, like a puppy bringing its leash to her master, city business again presents itself. The window for self-reflection has closed. Bernie writes down some figures next to two phrases: "Vermont Gas Co" and "Water Resources."

Bernie worried that his popularity was in fact a measure of how little he'd done. A poll taken in the fall of 1984 put his approval among Burlingtonians at 67 percent. Some 57 percent of Burlington's scarce Reagan voters, self-identified, approved of Bernie's job performance. His approval among high-income Burlingtonians stood at 65 percent. Two-thirds of Burlingtonians "said the economic climate was improved," since Bernie's 1981 election, according to the *Free Press*. When the journalist Walter Shapiro visited Burlington, he found "a mood of civic satisfaction and mutual accommodation" between Sanders and his old adversaries, evidence that the city had "embraced its radical conqueror, reveled in its newfound civic celebrity, and ended up neither Red nor dead." By 1984, most Burlingtonians could recite while blowing snow Bernie's tirades, and his revolutionary mottoes were by now so familiar that they could have been framed in needlepoint on the walls of the Birchwood nursing home. Bernie's rhetoric, and to some extent even his politics, had lost its tang and became essentially neutral—even in negotiations, where, as a business leader said, "you just took the abuse, waited for it to subside, and then began the conversation. Bernie was ultimately very pleasant."

When Vermont families arrived in Burlington on New Year's Eve—the Bourbeaus from Fairfax, the Angolanos from Swanton, Nate and Marcy Threlwell from Barre—they saw a city at its historic highwater mark, almost flaunting its success. For three bucks, Brad Angolano got a First Night button, got to march with Bread & Puppet, and learned to juggle in a church basement. His parents warmed up with a hot toddy at Leunig's, then saw a fireworks display in the middle of the winter. The downtown hotels were full, the university on the hill had been proclaimed a "public Ivy," the Vermont Youth Orchestra filled the Flynn, the Shakespeare Festival brought tunics and swordplay to the Royall Tyler Theatre. And it all felt like a buoyant, humanistic repudiation of the national meanness and stupidity brought in by President Ronald Reagan, already cruising toward his landslide reelection in the fall.

With Burlington prospering, Sanders posed a question to himself in the yellow legal pad: "Do I have the right not to run for governor?"

The Reds Arrive

In March of 1984, Sanders surprised even many of his aides by announcing that he would not join the "exceptionally weak field of candidates" running for governor of Vermont. From Montpelier, the Senate minority leader, Peter Welch, who now serves in Washington as Vermont's junior senator, sent Bernie a curious note on statehouse letterhead: "While I understand your recent decision," the rising Democratic star wrote to the socialist, Democrat-baiting independent, "many had looked forward to your campaign. Perhaps another day." It marked the beginning of an intricate, tense courtship dance—or was it a dance to the death?—between Sanders and Vermont Democrats. "There is no doubt that a campaign would affect my ability to give 100 percent in Burlington," Sanders told the press, adding, perhaps for Welch's ears, "our time will come." With the Alden Plan requiring intricate daily stewardship, Sanders would be kept busy all summer and fall. But what finally persuaded him to stay home during the summer of 1984, Richard Sugarman guessed, "was probably baseball."

"Longing on a large scale makes history," Don DeLillo wrote in *Underworld*. It is a frightening notion when considered in its entirety, but DeLillo's immediate subject was a baseball game: the deciding contest of the 1951 National League Championships, when Bobby Thomson of the New York Giants blasted a walk-off home run into the Polo Grounds' outfield bleachers: the "shot heard round the world" that cost the children of Brooklyn a pennant. Bernie and Larry Sanders were listening in on their parents' radio. Bernie had just turned ten.

Opening Day, 1984. *Vanguard Press*

In April of 1984, while the Burlington waterfront overflowed on the back burner, Bernie and a group of allies brought a professional baseball team to Burlington. The AA Vermont Reds of the Eastern League took to UVM's Centennial Field, directly across from my home, on April 18, 1984, with Sanders pitching a ceremonial strike to open the game. My bedroom glowed from the new 1,500-watt lights installed by a group of private boosters. After the third inning, the lights shorted out and the crowd sat in total darkness for fifty-four minutes. After the fifth inning, I watched from my front porch as cars all up and down Colchester Avenue were towed from the lawns and curbs where fans had dumped them. The sneers of Billy Idol's "Rebel Yell" between innings drove my grandparents crazy. "Bernie's Reds" were not appreciated in our home.

But having a professional baseball team in the neighborhood became a lesson in microeconomics, as Colchester Avenue turned its pique into profit. All the neighbors got into the parking business. The Bilodeaus on Thibault Parkway rented their attic to several lean and silent players, who shoveled down slices at Big Ben's. In the neighborhood, we knew where the holes in the fence were, so we never paid a dime. Little kids set up folding tables and sold the foul balls that blossomed in their backyards. Even my grandparents saw that in economic terms, the external benefits outweighed the costs. My friends and I were thirteen, too old and jaded to cheer, so we mainly used the games as a place to meet up with groups of girls, stand around by the concessions, and act obnoxiously within earshot of the eager families who had driven from all over Vermont to see their team. Bernie was there many nights, often sitting beside Levi, then about fifteen. He made the rounds and greeted the players. I remember seeing him high-five the ubiquitous Dancing Chicken, the mascot of Mountain Wings N' Things, who got the wave going in the bleachers and leered at the female fans. "I think if you asked Bernie now," Huck Gutman told me, "he would point to those Reds games as among his happiest moments."

Larry and Bernard Sanders, like all Midwood boys, "obsessively followed the Brooklyn Dodgers," Larry said. The team was an education: the Sanders brothers learned math by calculating players' batting averages. They also learned about social justice by cheering for Jackie Robinson, the first Black player in the majors, and Sandy Koufax, the Dodgers' great Jewish left-hander. "Baseball was absolutely essential to Bernard's socialism," Larry told me. "The solidarity we felt, the sense of a community pulling together, even suffering together." When the Dodgers were moved to Los Angeles in 1957, "it was like they would move the Brooklyn Bridge to California," Bernie told *The New York Times*. "How can you move the Brooklyn Bridge to California?" In 1960, Ebbets Field, the Dodgers' beloved ballpark, was demolished with a wrecking ball painted to look like a baseball. The obscenity of it all gave Sanders an early lesson in corporate greed. Gutman and Sugarman, the core of Bernie's "Professional Baseball Committee," created early in his first term, had also grown up as Dodgers fans. Sugarman recalled for me his childhood in Buffalo: "We were a city of underdogs, and strongly identified with the Dodgers." In Brooklyn, Sugarman said, "the three most hated men were Hitler, Stalin, and Walter O'Malley"—the Dodgers owner who took the beloved team away—"though not necessarily in that order." For Bernie, betrayal and renewal were both bound up with baseball.

In a 2020 interview, Bernie Sanders could still recite the Dodgers' entire starting lineup: Gil Hodges, Junior Gilliam, Gene Hermanski, and all the rest. Now Burlington would have an opportunity to cheer for up-and-coming players like Barry Larkin, just months away from stardom with the Cincinnati Reds, and Paul O'Neill, who, like David Mamet and William H. Macy, in town and staying in the dorms next door at Trinity College, enjoyed the subs at Kampus Kitchen, across from our home. The young players were a racially mixed group of men who stuck together in our crushingly white city, greeting admirers politely but shyly in line at Merrill's Showcase or Ben & Jerry's. "It's not a bad thing for kids to have heroes who are baseball players," Bernie said. Seeing a young fan approach Chris Sabo for an autograph, Sanders beamed and admitted that he was in "seventh heaven."

LURING THE REDS to town was a triumph for Sanders, and not only because the team brought home three championships during their four seasons in Burlington. Sanders was a natural for the baseball business, where he came off not as a leftist lunatic but as a city kid still dusty and scrappy from the block. By the summer of 1983, after several false starts, Burlington finally had a team in its sights: the Lynn Pirates of Lynn, Massachusetts, a hardscrabble immigrant community north of Boston, whose owner, Mike Agganis, hailed from a storied Greek family in that town. Harry Agganis, Mike's uncle, was a Lynn sports legend who played several seasons for the Boston Red Sox before succumbing to illness at the age of twenty-six. It was a big deal for an Agganis to own the ball team in Lynn, and a big deal for Mike to agree to move his team to a town he'd never visited. "I did it for you!" he often reminded Bernie in those days. But Agganis was "a car guy," he told me. "Ferraris, Porsches. I drove up through the mountains, on those beautiful roads, going about a hundred miles an hour." Once in Burlington, he said, "I grabbed a coffee and sat on a bench downtown. What a beautiful city, I said to myself, right out loud.

"I'm a ghetto kid," Agganis, who is now retired and lives on a golf course in Delray Beach, Florida, told me. "You don't ever get it out of you. I'm eighty-one. You should see the road rage." But Agganis recognized Bernie as a fellow ghetto kid. Sanders seemed "very passionate, very truthful," to Agganis, whose politics were "night and day" from Bernie's. "We respected each other," Agganis said. He was given the red carpet treatment on a tour of Burlington with Sanders and Tom Racine, a Burlington merchant and the chair of the baseball boosters. "The local Kentucky Fried Chicken guy was a fellow Greek," Agganis said. John Hanzas, my friend Mike's dad, offered Agganis "free fried chicken for all Greeks!" The boosters' effort was run partly out of Racine's intimate apparel store on the Marketplace, Bertha Church. A woman interrupted her purchase of a cream-colored satin teddy to write Racine a check for improvements to Centennial Field. "What people, what an incredible community!" Agganis exclaimed, calling the moment back to mind.

"IT'S A NON-POLITICAL THING," Tom Racine told *The Vermont Vanguard Press*. "I can see some walls coming down between Bernie and business-people because of this." After a failed attempt to model public ownership of the team by selling low-cost shares, Sanders turned to the city's merchants, who raised $30,000 to spruce up Centennial Field: the ballpark, built in 1902, is older than Fenway Park or Wrigley Field. When Roger Angell of *The New Yorker* visited, he captured its essence: "an ancient dark green beauty, the outfield terminating in a grove of handsome old trees." Neighborhood teens found it to be perfect for wiffle ball and hand jobs, but for it to become suitable for professional baseball, Agganis demanded "extensive renovations."

UVM had initially balked at allowing the team to use their rickety field at all. It was Richard Sugarman, working the sidelines at a university reception for Michel Foucault, who persuaded the UVM president, Lattie Coor, to sign the contract in exchange for a few concessions from Sanders. The mayor had been threatening to levy charges against UVM for city services in lieu of taxes: Bernie temporarily dropped the demands and changed his tone, and in the fall of 1983, Sanders, Coor, and Agganis announced that the Lynn Pirates would play their 1984 season in Burlington. Then a last-minute setback: when the *Burlington Free Press* ran an editorial criticizing the contract, the Pirates abruptly pulled out of the deal, and for three weeks in September Burlington had a franchise, but not a team. As though irony wanted a say, the organization that came to the city's rescue was the Cincinnati Reds, whose AA team was the laughingstock of Waterbury, Connecticut. America's socialist mayor brought baseball to the city by wooing its businessmen, while, as Burlington's most famous red, Bernie became something like the team's unofficial mascot. Socialism was apparently ready to play ball.

A BASEBALL SEASON IS a timepiece, consulted by an entire community, measuring the passing of spring into summer into fall, the gradually lengthening, then gradually shortening days, the dance of sunset and moonrise. The Reds games brought crowds—eight hundred, nine hundred, a thousand people, night after night—to the "ancient dark green beauty." On the field, the polite young strangers of the Vermont Reds soared into first place. At the concession stand, you saw kids you hadn't seen since kindergarten and met people's one-hundred-year-old aunts.

Behind the scenes, the two ghetto characters, Agganis and Sanders, scrapped over everything: the lights, the locker rooms, the concessions, the parking, the dust. Agganis's threats to leave the city began almost the moment the lights went on, then immediately went off, at lowly little Centennial Field. Bernie "worked nonstop," Larry Sanders told me. "I visited him in the summer of 1984, and he was on the phone with the Reds' owner morning, noon, and night." But in their correspondence, Sanders mostly defends himself by rope-a-dope, encouraging his business partner to trust the big picture. The strategy didn't work. During the dramatic playoff stretch of fall 1984, the Vermont Reds returned victorious to Burlington to find that their locker room had been reclaimed by the UVM girls' soccer team. In 1987, Sanders wrote to Agganis that he had "heard rumors about baseball leaving Burlington." Agganis appears to have responded only through an assistant. The Reds moved on after 1987. Agganis's franchise stayed one more season, hosting a nomadic Seattle Mariners team, in between parks: we got a look at the amazing Ken Griffey Jr., and then big-league baseball left Burlington.

Was Burlington merely a stopgap for Agganis all along? "Look, I'm a businessman," Mike told me. Like a character from folklore, Bernie had made a wish imprudently, inadvertently summoning corporate capitalism and the ghost of Walter O'Malley along with his baseball dream. Agganis and his franchise, under pressure from the league to maximize their championship appeal, opened the 1989 season in front of five thousand fans in Canton, Ohio, at a new stadium named for the great Yankee catcher Thurman Munson.

The Dancing Chicken's glory days were past; he got a series of depressing gigs at the Midas and AAMCO on Shelburne Road, then hung up his beak for good.

The Progressives Gather at Pearls

From the bleachers of Centennial Field, you could make out the Greenmount Cemetery just behind the outfield fence, where a Carrara marble figure of Ethan Allen floated in the junipers atop a thirty-five-foot Doric column. Sword in his right hand, Ethan Allen raises his left to demand the surrender of the shifting clouds and darting crows, backed by his army of the dead. The commander's left forefinger extends into the sky as though he'd just licked it to test the direction and intensity of the prevailing winds. After four baseball summers, what kind of place was Burlington becoming?

Since Ethan Allen could not be reached, people asked Sanders. A gay psychoanalyst wrote from Columbus Avenue in New York City, hoping to move to Burlington but concerned about the scarcity of both gays and psychoanalysts in town. Linda Niedweske responded on Bernie's behalf:

> Needless to say, Burlington, Vermont (pop. 38,000) could not possibly compare to New York with respect to the range of activities offered and the size of the gay community. The following is the information that was told to me:
>
> 1. It is a good sized community for a small city;
> 2. There are limited activities compared to New York;
> 3. Pearls is the only gay bar/restaurant in the area, but it is very attractive and usually quite crowded;
> 4. There are organized volleyball games;
> 5. There is a gay students' union at the University of Vermont;
> 6. There is a gay Episcopal group called Integrity—coordinated by Bruce Howden;
> 7. A small gay rights political organization exists;
> 8. The Burlington Board of Aldermen recently passed an ordinance prohibiting housing discrimination which included sexual preference;
> 9. There is a Gay and Lesbian rights parade every June.

"The people of Burlington and Vermont are known for their openness and 'live and let live' attitude," Niedweske concluded. "Our mayor," she wrote, as though it was not widely known, "is a socialist."

One source of Linda's prudent advice was her cousin and Bernie's old research assistant, Nancy Barnett, who had mercifully broken free from Sanders's orbit and "cooked up something new"—something, in fact, even more exciting than the Vermont Reds. In June of 1983, Burlington hosted its first Pride parade, drawing 350 participants from small towns across New

England, as well as from Boston, Montreal, and New York. "There was suddenly momentum," Barnett told me, and that October she and three friends—Ed Packen, Barbara Volz, and Jimmy Moyer—opened northern New England's first gay bar. Pearls was indeed "very attractive and usually quite crowded," as busy and friendly as Bove's, its neighbor down the block. There was a family resemblance: Pearls felt like Bove's gay little brother. Both establishments occupied old-fashioned New England houses hard by the road; both served crowd-pleasing food in bustling rooms where, when the door swung open, the mayor might enter. "We did regular spaghetti nights," Barnett said, in homage to their Italian neighbor: "red-checked napkins, candles in empty bottles of chianti." Otherwise, the downstairs restaurant's pale pink tablecloths were set every morning with vases of fresh flowers to welcome the entire Burlington community. "We had the contract to feed juries on recess from the federal courthouse across the street," Barnett recalled, with a laugh. "The gay bar fed the juries." Upstairs, Barnett poured drinks in a wood-paneled saloon, open all day: she called it a "gay *Cheers*," referring to the hit sitcom about a Boston bar "where everybody knows your name."

I could see in our conversation that the famous slogan, once she'd uttered it, gave a moment's pause. Barnett then told me that she did the payroll behind the bar when business was slow. "We had twenty-three employees,"

Opening night at Pearls. L-R: Nancy Barnett, Jimmy Moyer, Chef Connie Jacobs, a waiter, Ed Packen, Barbara Volz. *Courtesy Nancy Barnett*

she said. "I did all the payroll by hand. I could recite those names for you right now." Once AIDS made its sweep through Burlington, Barnett "began recognizing a lot of names in the obituaries. Most of those people are gone."

At night, "the food got pushed aside," Nancy said, and Pearls became a disco. Burlington's gay community had for decades gathered quietly in living rooms, or in failing restaurants eager to attract a clientele and willing to keep secrets: the Hi Hat on Main Street in the 1960s, or the Taj Mahal on College Street, by day an Indian restaurant. "I had no intention of opening a bar," Barnett told me, but Moyer, who'd been working at an expense account brasserie on Madison Avenue, and Packen, part of the Studio 54 diaspora who left New York City after the club was shut down in 1980, persuaded her. The idea was simply "to have fun," Barnett said, waving away my suggestion that what she and her partners did was revolutionary. At a time when gay men feared the inevitable day when they would be told "to go home and get their affairs in order," Barnett said she saw Pearls as a riotous, intersectional "version of the *Star Wars* bar scene": gay men and lesbians, "Montreal boys mixed with hayseeds," Vietnamese people from the resettlement community, Burlington accountants, Franconia bikers, "people's old mothers at Christmas," even a drag version of Burlington's legendary "hot dog lady," Lois Bodoky, who served dripping franks out of her Church Street cauldron in a beehive hairdo and granny glasses. "Ron Connor was his name," Barnett told me, "a beautiful soul. His life was our bar."

Barnett recalls very few incidents of harassment at first: "a redneck driving by and yelling faggot, sure," but the crowds spilling out onto Pearl Street knew "that the Burlington police considered us the best-mannered bar in the city." Over time, however, as Pearls became a destination for New York and Quebec revelers, it also attracted a sickening drive-by gay-bashing scene: liquored-up bumpkins honked and gunned their engines as they passed, or shouted slurs out their windows just for the thrill of it. High school kids did it too, including kids I knew well. The patrons of Pearls, gathered outside in groups to smoke and flirt away from the strobes and bass, mostly gave back as good as they got, shouting, "Fuck you, redneck" or mooning the revving muscle cars. But soon the *Free Press* and the *Vanguard* began to report trouble outside of Pearls, incidents where gay men were chased, or their tires slashed. Then in 1990, a man was beaten in the alleyway next door and left for dead. His skull had partly collapsed. The assailant, a drywall installer from the nearby farm town of Hinesburg, told police that he "went looking for it. I went to Pearls, found a fag, and kicked the shit out of him." Witnesses reported that the assailant was performing oral sex on the victim before the assault. The man's arrest was followed by two attempts by arsonists to burn Pearls down, and increased tire slashing in the nearby parking lot. These incidents made Pearls "a war zone," Nancy Barnett told a reporter, and they helped to frame Vermont's passage of a groundbreaking hate crimes law in 1991. Less than a decade later, on July 1, 2000, Vermont became the first state in the union to legalize civil unions. You could make the claim that it started at Pearls.

But in 1984, working-class Catholics still heard Sunday sermons proclaiming that AIDS was a plague sent from God to wipe away homosexuals: Brother Adrian, my religion teacher, told me so, while tickling my earlobe with his index finger. The *Free Press* happily printed what we would now call hate speech in its letters to the editor. In this climate, "our bar became the progressives' hangout," Nancy Barnett told me. It was at Pearls that the progressives planned their next initiative. In October, an aldermanic committee led by Gary De Carolis and Rik Musty passed Vermont's first ordinance forbidding discrimination against tenants based on a list of what was then called "sexual preference." Sanders, recalling his days leading the CORE sit-in at the University of Chicago, compared the discrimination faced by gays to bias against Blacks and Jews. Had the "gay Cheers" on Pearl Street changed Bernie's Burlington?

"Not intentionally," Barnett said. "But maybe just by existing."

A CROWD OF PROGRESSIVES gathered at Pearls on Election Night, November 6, 1984. This was the Reagan landslide: 49 states, 525 electoral votes. Walter Mondale, the Democrat, a former senator and Jimmy Carter's vice president, won only the District of Columbia and his home state of Minnesota. Mondale's finish in Vermont suggested that Vermont's much-touted "turn to the left" was more like a hesitant lane change on I-89. Reagan beat Mondale by seventeen points in Vermont, winning only Chittenden County. Mondale had "no political operation in Vermont," according to Garrison Nelson. Why would a Democrat try to win in the Green Mountain State? Mondale never visited Vermont: he sent, in his stead, Ed Asner, the comedian.

The mood at Pearls was dejected, and yet the results showed Democrats making "surprising gains," according to the *Burlington Free Press*. Madeleine Kunin won by a tiny margin, becoming the state's first female governor and only the third Democrat elected to the post. Control of the Vermont Senate passed to Democrats, who came within four votes of taking the House. Seventy percent of registered voters in the state turned up to cast a ballot. Sanders had a surprising reaction to Reagan's landslide. There seemed to Bernie "some encouragement," according to an adviser, in the results. He'd begun to see Reagan's popularity and his own as uncannily connected, even down to individual voters. "You have to remember," Peter Clavelle told me, "that Bernie and Reagan coincide almost perfectly. Without Reagan, there is no Bernie." Adding Reagan's victory to the Democrats' down-ticket gains, you could see an emerging dynamic in Vermont: the state had become more Democratic, but almost as a consequence it retained its devotion to politicians who fell outside of, and corrected, that drift. Vermont voters liked to leave the polling place secure in the feeling that they were fundamentally independent. David Clavelle, already planning Bernie's March 1985 reelection campaign, saw in the phenomenon of the Reagan-Sanders voter an opportunity to win the heavily conservative Ward 4. And Burlington would not be deprived of its favorite David and Goliath show: the "Dear Mr. Reagan" letters would continue. It was last call at Pearls, and Bernie Sanders came away from Election Night feeling "pretty good, all in all," about the broadened prospect of his political future.

31

"A Wonder of the World"

(Burlington Comes to Its Senses: 1984–85)

In the 1960s, the trauma of federally subsidized slum clearance created a Burlington folk hero in the person of Vicki Dutra, my great-uncle's sister, who presided over a Victorian coop surrounded by construction debris on South Champlain Street. Dutra's household had a bad reputation: it was described by the *Burlington Free Press* as a crossroads for "thirteen or so family members and others." But the property soon became known throughout Burlington as "Dutra's Ponderosa," the last house standing; and in 1967, Vicki Dutra, in a housedress and rollers, a cigarette bobbing and teetering on her lip as she spoke to a battery of reporters, held her ground against the approaching steam shovels. The Dutras then sold their home to the Burlington Planning Commission under duress; when they surveyed the spreading rubble where Merola's market had been, they bitterly regretted their decision. Their anger was shared by an entire community that felt it had been fooled by "bigwig" developers and politicians. The planning commission came to stand in for everything the city had done to ruin itself.

In 1974, the $53 billion in federal grants that required Burlington and other cities to demolish their historic downtown neighborhoods dried up. According to a study by William J. Collins and Katharine L. Chester, well over three hundred thousand Americans had been forcibly relocated under urban renewal, about half of whom were nonwhite. Now a new set of federal grants became available to cities to undo the agony created by those decades of slum clearance. In 1977, the Department of Housing and Urban Development established a new federal program "for the purpose of revitalizing distressed cities," according to a study by Ingrid W. Reed. Urban Development Action Grants, or UDAGs, funded partnerships with private builders on the basis of a "but for" rationale: the private project wouldn't go forward but for the federal boost. Cities were invited to dream big, and, by

1983, to act fast: these UDAGs were a vestige of the Carter administration, and becoming scarcer with every new Reagan budget. The UDAG program folded in 1986.

A window therefore opened when Sanders took office. The planning commission had largely slept on these UDAG opportunities, while Burlington's haggard neighbor, Winooski, a federal "Model City," became a showcase for new planning and development. "Winooski brought in more federal dollars per capita than any city in the country," according to Peter Clavelle, its energetic town manager in those years. But the "Winooski Dome" scheme, and the municipal hubris it suggested, had ended Winooski's boom years. One little boy interviewed on the nightly news expressed the feelings of most Vermonters, rooting for its demise: "I'd miss feeling the snowflakes." Soon, the dream of a dome was shattered, and the snowflakes drifted to hand.

By 1981, the little hardscrabble city of Winooski had substantially transformed itself, with its new brick sidewalks, riverside lookouts, and renovated factory buildings, now filling up with treadmills and saunas. But behind the scenes, a cabal of old-timers eager to undermine the transformation of their city starved the city budget so that the new Washington-funded wonderland couldn't be properly maintained: snow piled up in the winter as the plows broke down; in the summer, the town pool had to be drained, and playgrounds were closed for overdue repairs. Winooski's schools stood on the brink of discreditation. Clavelle, the twenty-five-year-old town manager who'd helped bring in the Washington money, found himself in the middle of a class war between old and new Winooski.

PETER CLAVELLE WAS not some interloper in town. The son of a Winooski small grocer whose shop functioned after hours as a social club for city Democrats, Clavelle, now in his seventies, retired after seven nonconsecutive terms succeeding Bernie as Burlington's mayor. He described himself to me cheerfully as a "river rat," a slur everyone used to identify Winooski River people.

Sanders met Clavelle, who'd taken a job tending bar at local dive, in the fall of 1982. "I know nothing about city government," Bernie confessed, ordering a Coke, "so I came to see you." Sanders had spent the afternoon strolling through the renovated Champlain Mill, trying to look right at home in its boutiques selling vanilla candles, rosemary sachets, and wind chimes. Bernie marveled that an innovative public-private partnership facilitated by young Peter Clavelle had restored this terrifying wreck, long the very image of manufacturing decline. Now, old men and women who had worked in the mill as teenagers walked its broad planks again for the first time in decades. Some of them even recognized themselves in the large photographs of baby-faced millworkers that lined the brick walls. The Champlain Mill was an urban triumph, and Peter Clavelle had helped to make it happen.

Clavelle wanted "to get back into politics," he told me, but he was not an automatic Bernie enthusiast: like his grandmother, he was a lifetime "Blue Dog Democrat." (That meant "she would vote for a blue dog before she'd vote for a Republican," Clavelle said.) But Clavelle had washed his hands of Winooski's Democratic machine, and he and Sanders agreed on most policy goals. In 1982, he joined his Winooski cousin David, a fellow river rat and Blue Dog Democrat, in Burlington city hall, as a volunteer member of the mayor's cost-cutting committee. In these lean years, Peter and David Clavelle, John Franco, and Barr Swennerfelt worked around Peter's dining room table putting together the city's annual budget.

This volunteer role was Peter's foot in the door. In May of 1983, when a blue-ribbon panel of local businessmen, hand assembled by Sanders, recommended that the city form a nonprofit development company to capture UDAGs, an odd coalition of progressives and Republicans on the board of aldermen approved. Burlington's Community and Economic Development Office, newly established, hired Peter as its first director. CEDO was soon the city's single most powerful municipal entity and arguably the most effective of its kind in the United States, usurping much of the power of the spurned planning commission—whose leader, William Aswad, became Bernie's angriest adversary. Soon CEDO, in control of millions of dollars in grants, ran completely independently of the city's budget, even paying its officials out of federal money. In the race to compete for those funds, Burlington had found a winner in Clavelle. "Peter had the magic touch," Garrison Nelson told me.

Howard Dean and Rick Sharp's bike path was among the first and most popular initiatives that CEDO gobbled up, but soon the new office had dozens of projects under its control: a revolving loan program for small businesses, a land trust to spur city homeownership, and the renovations of some of Burlington's grandest, most badly neglected commercial buildings. These included the Maltex building on Pine Street, where Maypo, the artificially flavored maple cereal, was manufactured, and the Wells-Richardson building, where a wildly popular patent medicine, Paine's Celery Compound, was produced. The companies had gone the way of malt cereal and snake-oil remedies, but the magnificent structures built to house them reopened for business. "If you drive along Pine Street today," Clavelle told me, of the main road passing through the city's South End, "you see what CEDO has accomplished." Businesses like Champlain Chocolates, with $22 million in annual revenue, operate in what was once a lonely barrens where cattails grew through the floors of junked cars.

These projects were all training runs, however, for the most ambitious enterprise in Burlington's history: for CEDO had also been given control of the Alden Plan. Suddenly it was "game on," according to Melinda Moulton. Bernie Sanders had become a classic ribbon-cutting mayor, and the site was one of the most exciting opportunities for urban transformation anywhere. It was curious, though, that nobody in city hall mentioned the possibility that CEDO's signature project might have been literally built on sand. Only Peter Freyne, in *The Vermont Vanguard Press*, drew attention week after week to Alden's failure to obtain a title for the waterfront acres from the railroad. It appeared that a kind of folie à deux took over: Sanders, believing he could use the "public trust doctrine" later in the process to negotiate for more public access in the plan, held it in his back pocket. The lawyers for the Alden group, considering cases in Boston and elsewhere, concluded that their interests were secure. All of Boston's Back Bay, after all, was built on fill; was the state of Massachusetts going to seize the grand townhomes lining Beacon Street and Commonwealth Avenue, and evict the Cabots and Lowells? This hoary law was rarely invoked; and since it benefited both parties to ignore it, Sanders and the Alden partners tried to make the public trust doctrine vanish from discussion.

But discussion in Burlington was not so easily suppressed. Under Sanders, in fact, discussion had become Burlington's favorite pastime; and the "expanded democracy" that Bernie touted as his signature municipal accomplishment would soon be summoned to work against him.

The Neighborhoods Revolt

If Burlington could get a coveted federal UDAG grant, Burlingtonians would be given a freebie of $23 million. Many embraced the project in that spirit. "It isn't going to cost us a dime," my mother said. Disney World was coming to us! But without the UDAG money, Bernie would need to bring the financing before the voters in the form of a proposed bond. The more democratic process was obviously the latter, where the project itself would essentially come up for a vote. But, as one game-show fan told WCAX news: Why not "spin the wheel for" the federal money?

The gamble was a long shot. The $23 million that Burlington planned to request was a little more than 5 percent of the annual budget for the entire UDAG program to aid "distressed" cities. Burlington was booming; the willingness of several private developers to finance renovation of the waterfront was proof alone that Burlington was not the distressed community envisioned in the UDAGs. But CEDO had already far outperformed expectations, Peter Clavelle had excellent contacts in Washington, and Alden had on its staff a local political operator, Paul Bruhn, whose main ties were to Senator Patrick Leahy. Why not spin for it, indeed?

When Burlington filed its scaled-down request of $17.5 million, Peter Clavelle, in line for waffles at the annual city Chew Chew festival, admitted that "Burlington is not that depressed," but hinted at close collaboration with the grant writers in Washington, who were "enthusiastic about the project." The "spin for it" caucus initially drove close to 75 percent approval for the plan in the neighborhood meetings. But behind the scenes, all through 1984, contingency plans were being dreamed up. The Alden Plan was shrinking, even as the city's prospective share of the bill was growing. Bernie found himself arguing ever harder for a program likely far smaller and, for Burlingtonians, probably more expensive.

As our miracle grant stalled in Washington, Burlington grew less and less suitable for it: the U.S. Conference of Mayors proclaimed the city to be among the nation's "most livable" in June of 1984, and touted its soaring economy. On the streets, you could feel the enthusiasm draining out of the Alden Plan. Local architects were angry they hadn't been hired. Local contractors wondered whether they'd be cut out of the work. Burlington was just warming up to the Church Street Marketplace, which sketches of this new project resembled. At Bove's, Babe and Dickie called the Alden Plan "Atlantic City." Stratty Lines at the Oasis told his breakfast crowd to oppose the plan. Peter Freyne, the intrepid *Vanguard Press* reporter, mocked the vanity of Burlington's new self-image: a "baked potato in a fur coat."

THE VISITS FROM SURVEYORS, architects, planners, and developers, the endless sketches and slides, the hairsplitting over acreage and square footage, setbacks and soil tests, the plans for marinas, tennis courts, brasseries, promenades, and condos, had wearied Burlington, and in the legal squabbles over individual puzzle pieces, a game of inches fought by powerful interests on every side, something important had been lost: the overall grandeur and magnificence of our lake and its views, which had lured so many to visit the city, and tempted many who visited to stay.

America's great poet of urban waterfronts, Walt Whitman, discovered the majesty of those vistas on an 1871 visit to his cousin, the landscape painter Charles Louis Heyde. From his home and studio on lower Pearl Street, marked with a sign "C.L. Heyde, Painter of Vermont Scenery," Heyde made a daily study of the lake, in all its seasons and moods, peddling his romantic landscapes to the city's newly prosperous residents for the grand parlors of their Hill Section homes. After passing through "a captivating wild region" on the Central Vermont Railway, Whitman rested a week in Heyde's studio, and painted his own landscape in words:

> & so to Burlington, & about Lake Champlain where I spent a week, filling myself every day, (especially mornings & sunsets) with the grandest ensembles of the Adirondacks always on one side, and the Green Mountains on the other—

Burlington needed to be reminded not only of the beauty of its setting, but of how many people its "grandest ensembles" had "filled" over the years. The story of Whitman's visit to Burlington became a powerful rhetorical tool for those fighting the Alden Plan. I am almost certain that I first encountered the name "Walt Whitman" on a circular or poster invoking the bard's eerie, posthumous disapproval of the Alden waterfront bond. In any case, to oppose the waterfront development took more than legal cunning. It required Whitman's human assessment of all that we stood to lose if something so spiritually "filling" was taken away by the city.

In the fall of 1985, Rick Sharp, along with Bea Bookchin, Sandy Baird, and others, formed Citizens for a Better Waterfront, a group that cut across the city's political factions. Sharp and his crew then treated Burlington to a history lesson. Old city maps, they explained, told the story of how, over many decades between 1810 and 1880, Burlington created an entirely new shoreline. Gradually, as Sharp and his team determined, "60 acres of land in Burlington Harbor was created by filling the lake." That sixty acres included the twelve acres that the city envisioned as its new gateway. The public could sue to stop any development of the waterfront for commercial purposes, the group told Burlington's citizens. The land could not be titled as property: the city had a legal responsibility to protect it for "public use." This meant,

Charles Louis Heyde, *View of Burlington Bay*, 1880s. *Skinner Auctioneers*

simply and shockingly, that since it could never be titled, therefore it could never be sold. In 1874, the Vermont Supreme Court established the public trust doctrine as law. That old law, Sharp wrote, "had never been reversed or challenged."

Sandy Baird was a Green Party activist and lawyer, one of many on the left who felt spurned and abandoned by Mayor Sanders. She and Sharp were formidable, but they thought the way lawyers think. Bea Bookchin, on the other hand, was in a position to argue for Walt Whitman's sense of the lake's grandeur: "Our lake," Bookchin reminded Burlington, "is one of the great wonders of the world." It became hard for me, from that day forward, to see it any other way. Trained in computational linguistics, Bookchin had become "deeply influenced by her study of Wilhelm Reich," her daughter Debbie Bookchin told me; she and her colleagues had found in Burlington "the formation of a subculture of people who shared a deeply held theoretical view: the separation between mind and body—which is another way that capitalism alienates us from ourselves—had to be overcome as part of our politics." She had worked on the backs and bodies of thousands of Burlingtonians in her massage practice above the Fresh Ground Coffee House, creating a well of trust that cut across city factions. Now Bea Bookchin saw the waterfront as a wider battle for "the Body Politic": she set out to "dethrone the ego" at work in destructive capitalism, and "return power to the body, to the imagination, to the moods." Sanders no doubt detected in these terms the influence of Reich, his favorite psychoanalyst, now, ironically, weaponized against his signature project.

Opposition to the Alden Plan soon became a referendum on democracy itself in the city of Burlington. When Peter Clavelle set up his easel in front of the city's six Neighborhood Planning Assemblies, the Citizens for a Better Waterfront widened their fight to oppose not just the underlying plan, but also the misuse of the NPAs as "mere focus groups" for the city's schemes. In 1982, the NPAs had been introduced to great fanfare as a "people's parliament" by Sanders, quickly ratified by the board of aldermen—and, to the horror of Murray Bookchin, immediately turned over to CEDO, a "quasi-private development fund," in his dim view, which starved these little democratic cells by meting out their budgets. Bookchin now reminded the city that these fragile experiments in face-to-face democracy traced their origins not "to Bernie Sanders's brain" but to ancient Athens, and should never have been centralized under mayoral power. Sanders "had not made these up in his head," Bookchin said, but had "drawn on a welter of ideas" bouncing around Burlington in the 1970s. The NPAs indeed had their roots in the Tilapia tanks in the woods of Plainfield, the Decentralist League, the social ecology seminars and debates held in the early days of the Fresh

Ground Coffee House, and the "communitarian" writings and teachings of Professor Frank Bryan of UVM, who'd taught generations of students to revere town meeting. Sanders had "coopted" the NPAs, Bookchin charged, to capture and direct democratic participation in the city's plans. Here it was at last: the leftist power grab that Bookchin and others had feared since March of 1981.

When the disconnect between city hall's waterfront plans and Burlington's waterfront wishes seemed to widen, the Sanders administration found that it had a grassroots uprising on its hands, and the Bookchins had the showdown with Sanders they'd been craving for years. But Sanders struck first: "There are some people of the Green Variety," Bernie told a scrum of reporters, "who are essentially anti-development and come up with a long philosophical position as to why almost any development is bad." Murray and Bea Bookchin and their followers, Bernie implied, were among those with a "back-to-the-woods mentality that life should be simpler." Sanders was clear: "We don't share that view."

"Tell Your Parents"

With a federal UDAG now appearing doomed, Bernie Sanders and Peter Clavelle called a vote for December 10, 1985, on a bond of $6 million to meet the city's share on the much-scaled-back Alden Plan, with most of Ben Thompson's razzle-dazzle pared away. Citizens, armed with fliers prepared by Baird, Bookchin, and Sharp, took to the microphones with their questions about the public trust doctrine, that obscure legal artifact from the time of Robin Hood now impacting our community's future. Sanders and Clavelle headed into the neighborhoods and began to knock on doors. The two-thirds majority required to pass a bond seemed to be slipping away, one front porch at a time.

As Burlington fought its quixotic battle, Howard Dean, in Montpelier, took a more aggressive role in promoting Bernie's vision. "I was politic about Alden," Dean admitted to me. He believed that "it was our best chance. If Alden backed away, the waterfront might never be developed." Sanders and Dean had put their differences aside as Dean worked in Montpelier to the benefit of Burlington's urban goals: Dean now found Bernie "very easy to work with, very straightforward. He didn't lie, which is refreshing in politics."

At inflection points like this, Bernie, who usually weaved and darted around the crowds on Church Street like a point guard evading the defense, became suddenly expansive and accessible. The first time I remember speaking with him, in fact, was in September of 1985, when he approached a group of teenage rugrats on Church Street to ask us to remind our parents about the Alden bond. My friend Scott, a wise guy, told Bernie that the plan needed a skate park. "You like to skate?" Sanders asked us.

It seemed clear that he thought we meant ice skating. In a scene that feels like an outtake from a bad '80s movie, Scott, the Ralph Macchio character in the sequence, then noisily threw down his board and ollied off the steps of city hall. I think it was the first time Sanders had seen a skateboard, because he seemed genuinely curious and surprised. Within a year skaters were bounding off of every curb and platform on the Church Street Marketplace, and merchants led a crackdown.

"Tell your parents to vote," Bernie said, waving off our teenage nonsense.

ON DECEMBER 2, 1985, the Citizens for a Better Waterfront held a dramatic public meeting at Burlington's Fletcher Free Library. Addressing a crowd of two hundred or so, Rick Sharp charged Sanders with a "conspiracy to withhold information" about the public trust doctrine from Burlington's voters. Since Sanders had brought the issue to the public's attention in the first place, his subsequent silence about it hardly seemed like a cover-up, and there was some laughter in the room. While not quite a conspiracy, silence was a political strategy, and, it turned out, a bad one. Clavelle and Sanders's refusal to respond to Sharp's attacks proved to be a fatal error: in the vacuum, Sharp had put the phrase "public trust doctrine" on the lips of every Burlingtonian.

Bea Bookchin then spoke, calling for a "people-oriented waterfront": "I think that plain, ordinary people should have some amount of park space up close to the water, where they can walk or bike or sit or talk." The importance was to give "ordinary people"—the phrase conveyed an entire moral vision of what a city was, and how humans should exist within the city—"access to the shore." It wasn't enough to see the water from twenty or fifty feet back: citizens needed to experience "the edge of the water," surrounded by "five dozen species of trees, a hundred species of birds." Burlingtonians left the meeting with a sense of what it means to open their senses to the shore and its "varied strange sensations": Whitman's "fragrance of salt-marsh and shoremud," "the briny and damp smell of sedgy grass and fields by the shore."

Did Walt Whitman's vision, distilled by Bea Bookchin, bring us back to our senses and rescue Burlington's waterfront from the yuppies? The voters of Burlington went to the polls on December 10 and defeated the Alden bond, and with it the Alden Plan, by a minority: 53.4 percent in favor, 46.6 percent opposed, enough to keep it from the two-thirds required. Rick

Sharp, in victory, seemed a little concerned he'd "become the goat of Burlington" if the waterfront remained undeveloped for very long. Howard Dean walked the shore alone one afternoon, heard the gulls, skipped some stones, and returned home, relieved. Peter Clavelle, when I asked him whether he regretted that the Alden Plan had not passed, said he felt "we'd gotten something better, in the end."

It eventually fell to Clavelle's administration, post Bernie, to create much of what Burlington now enjoys: a large park on the public trust lands, host to hundreds of picnickers on warm spring days. The finish line of the Vermont City Marathon crosses the site where luxury condominiums were once planned. Burlington had beaten back its own grandiose fantasies and temptations. And Bernie, resetting his record for a 1986 run for governor, told Vermont that he had fought to keep that land open "for the use of the entire state." For now, the fur coat had come off the baked potato.

32

I Want My MTV

(Burlington's Pragmatic Socialism, 1985)

In January of 1985, as the waterfront debate reminded Burlingtonians of the allure of long July nights by the lake, the city settled into its main winter activity, which was watching television. Bernie Sanders was also keeping an eye on the screen. Sanders and John Franco had been plotting for two years to accomplish a classic socialist goal, to municipalize a major utility. To the question posed by a visiting group from Finland—"Where can we find socialism in America's socialist city?"—Burlington's fight for cable TV offered one answer.

Fourteen-year-olds followed this story in the news for a reason: we wanted our MTV. In Burlington, music videos still circulated as samizdat on VHS tapes recorded by visiting cousins from Michigan or New Jersey. We'd pop the contraband into Seth's VCR and curse the backwater where destiny had stranded us, away from our generation's defining entertainment: David Lee Roth on all fours, prancing across the video for Van Halen's "Jump" like a mating panther, or ZZ Top rescuing a pallid wallflower from sexual irrelevance by performing a rock-and-roll makeover on the terrified girl, to the strains of their number one hit, "Legs."

While the eighth graders of America gorged on twenty-four-hour videos, Burlington kids flipped among twelve stations: four separate ABC affiliates from other backwaters like Schenectady, New York, and Poland Springs, Maine; two different Montreal CBC channels; two CTV affiliates from Ontario; and, since the cable company, Cox Communications, was from Atlanta, a very lo-fi, larval WTBS. The only bright spot on the dial was Channel 11 out of New York City, for *Chiller Theatre* and Yankees games. Where was *our* MTV?

ZZ Top was caught in the middle of a yearslong negotiation in which Sanders's dreaded "socialism" again functioned as a market tool. Bernie inherited a city whose ninety miles of streets had not been repaved since the 1940s, a $7 million anticipated bill to repair them, and an absentee cable company, granted a monopoly by the state, that charged the highest fees in the nation for some of the worst service. Now Cox Communications, rebranded locally as "Green Mountain Cable," was intending to upgrade its offerings by tearing up one-quarter of the city's already crumbling blocks, and billing the city's taxpayers. "A turkey," John Franco said. "It was obviously not tenable." By late August of 1983, Burlington's coffers had again been drawn down, and the city needed revenue. Kicking a pile of broken asphalt on his way into a budget meeting, Bernie dreamed up a plan to levy an excavation fee against the cable company. A rate of $10.30 per square foot was determined by the city; William Gilbert of Green Mountain Cable opposed the fee as outrageous: "There are works of art that sell for less than ten dollars and thirty cents a square foot."

Eighth graders wanted MTV, Sadie White and her friends wanted reruns of *Gunsmoke* and Lucille Ball, fans of the Red Sox wanted regular broadcasts from Boston to even out the preponderance of Yankees games on the dial. Everyone wanted to pay less. Everyone dreaded the long winter indoors. So, with the cable company taking the city to court over the digging fees, Sanders and Franco decided to go big. Bernie had appointed Huck Gutman in 1983 to chair a committee to study whether it would be feasible to municipalize cable services in Burlington. Now the city commissioned a professional review; the blue-ribbon panel found the answer to be, emphatically, yes; the board of aldermen unanimously agreed; the Vermont Public Service Board appeared to greenlight the plan. Over 50 percent of Burlingtonians were in favor. The electric department, already a municipal agency, seemed eager to administer the new utility. The estimated profits for the city would run into the millions per year. Burlington, the only American city run by socialists, looked to be ready, as the *Burlington Free Press* put it, "to take over the airwaves."

Burlington then predictably went through another red scare, with our MTV hanging in the balance. The *Free Press* ran a scorching editorial, suggesting that Bernie and his fellow socialists wanted "to bring their message to a larger audience about the utopian paradise they had fashioned in Burlington." Sanders's 1979 coup against ETV seemed now a premonition of the authoritarian drive to control not merely the medium but the message. When both the board of aldermen and the Burlington Electric Commission abruptly withdrew their support, the city's scheme to wire its own cable network appeared, for the moment, dead. Never mind that other communities, like Shrewsbury, Massachusetts, near Worcester, had municipalized their own cable services: those places were not in the grips of a socialist overlord.

When the Public Service Board looked likely to approve Green Mountain Cable's plans to dig Burlington up, Sanders then did what he'd done many times before when he found himself in a jam: he put John Franco to work. Franco sequestered himself in the main floor vault where Burlington's city records are housed. There he discovered that the cable company's contract with Burlington had, in fact, lapsed: "According to the city charter," Franco announced, "there is no valid cable franchise." Before Green Mountain Cable could tear up the city's streets for its new lines, an entirely new contract negotiation would need to take place. The cable company still appeared to have the upper hand: Burlington "doesn't want its cable hijacked by socialism," one man said. A mailer appeared at our home: "Cable TV—or Bernie TV?" Burlingtonians had grown tired of the fight. Sanders now had a political problem on his hands.

AS I VEGETATED in front of Canadian Chrysler-Plymouth commercials, the city lured one group of teenagers off the couch. For months, Burlington followed the revitalization of 81 Manhattan Drive, a deteriorating Victorian in a quiet corner of Ward 3. In these teenagers' slow, learn-on-the-job renovation of the home, many strands of our story converge. The house and property on the banks of the Burlington Intervale was purchased by the Burlington Community Land Trust, a program seeded by $200,000 in funds from the Leopold/Swennerfelt windfall of 1982. The kids were hired by the Burlington Youth Employment Program, a new venture administered by the Mayor's Youth Office. The land trust and the Youth Employment Program were both, in turn, run by CEDO. "There was nothing terribly 'socialistic' we could do," Terry Bouricius said. "We weren't going to take over the banks." But by 1985, CEDO was coordinating the area's development lenders and controlling its own multimillion-dollar federal kitty. In essence, Sanders *had* taken over the banks. Next—the airwaves!

The job site on Manhattan Drive expressed two of Bernie Sanders's campaign promises: to control "youth vagrancy," as it was then known; and to halt the sprint toward gentrification now pacing many of Burlington's traditional neighborhoods. Nailing new siding to the studs, Leon, Cindy, and a bunch of other slightly older kids I knew were changing the nature of property in the Queen City. The land trust worked by a simple strategy: the city would locate a distressed building, purchase it, train people who wanted to enter the workforce—including teenagers and women—to fix it up, then sell the home itself to a buyer, while retaining ownership of the land. Since buyers owned only the structures, these properties became available for a fraction of their market value; when a home was resold to the land trust, the owner's profits were capped at 25 percent of the purchase price. Bernie, sounding not at all like a socialist, initially opposed the equity-sharing arrangement: "My issue is that home equity is the path to the American dream," he told Meg Pond, then the land trust's director.

One parcel at a time, though, Burlington bought up nearly a quarter of its residential property, as the hundreds of houses and apartments enrolled in the program created a permanent, low-cost path to ownership and equity for Burlingtonians. Soon area banks and investors began to support the land trust, which had a foreclosure rate of zero, as a no-risk venture. With the city acting essentially as a mortgage cosigner, buyers with the land trust were given the lowest rates and the best terms. The city led regular evening seminars on home buying. Several of my relatives used the program and its spin-off, the Champlain Housing Trust; several others opposed the program as a form of communism.

Becky Premo "got the paperwork in order, signed with the lawyers" and moved into 81 Manhattan Drive with her husband and daughter the minute the teenagers in hard hats packed up their lunch pails. By the time the family furnished their new home, a backlash had taken hold. The Sanders administration had extended its "socialistic land grab" into Ward 4, the city's most conservative neighborhood. Sanders had enticed developers of luxury units there to swap acres of property into the land trust in exchange for shore rights on Lake Champlain; but the lakefront abutters, who might have been among America's first NIMBYs, defending their exclusive enclave by citing the patriotic, all-American, "God given" right to private property. This ideological skirmish caught residents like the Premos in the middle: homebuyers were called freeloaders, charity cases, welfare queens.

The NIMBYs and the foes of city-owned cable TV now joined forces, an angry cell opposing "government control"—Bernie was buying up city blocks, and now he wanted to own the airwaves!—but in fact were frustrated that their dictator had never materialized in the new Burlington. Lacking a Stalin, they would have to contend against Bernie.

SANDERS SURPRISED SOME in December of 1984 when he announced that he would seek a third term as Burlington's mayor, running "for the first time as a true incumbent," and borrowing elements of Ronald Reagan's reelection strategy. Bernie told aides he would remind Burlington, as Reagan had reminded the nation, "of everything we're doing right." The mayor even appeared to praise Reagan at an aldermen's meeting: confessing his "extreme distaste" for the president, Sanders nevertheless pointed to the local economic boom and the 1984 Eastern League champion Vermont Reds as reasons to herald a Reagan-like "Morning in Burlington." Terry

Bouricius was troubled: "I was not particularly impressed" by Bernie's talk about Reagan, Bouricius told the *Burlington Free Press*. It seemed to open up an obvious line of attack for Sanders's foes, who noted a few differences in the two men. "You're talking about apples and oranges in terms of personality," said Caryl Stewart, the chair of the city's Democratic Party. Bemoaning "the mayor's personal style," one Republican called for "a healing process" in the city.

Because polling showed Sanders to be essentially unbeatable, there was no pressure for his foes to consolidate behind a single opponent. Instead, six candidates—all, initially, with rather nice things to say about Bernie—rushed into the race. William Murray, a libertarian, admitted that he'd moved to Burlington partly because he admired Sanders. "When the mayor said we in Burlington should determine our own destiny, I felt like cheering," Murray said. "Hallelujah, let's have a little revolt!" Murray correctly saw "a lot of libertarian" in Sanders, as many others had, going back to Senator George Aiken: "He's on my long-range conversion list," the jovial oil and gas distributor told the papers. John Tatro ran as a one-issue candidate, calling for a cleanup of the city's putrefying landfill: Tatro "would favor using an Australian flower which loves garbage, it survives on impurities." Michael Hackett, running as a "neutralist"—Bernie had co-opted the term *independent*, he complained—was in it because he "needed a job." Diane Gallagher, a well-heeled, Hill Section Republican alderman (she created a small scandal when she refused the term *alderwoman*) who spoke of a warm personal rapport with the mayor, drew Bernie's flirtatious teasing. "Give Diane the job," Sanders told reporters, his arm around his beaming rival. "She deserves it." Brian Burns, the Democrat, had been an effective Montpelier legislator and Jimmy Carter appointee to the Farmers Home Administration. Burns sponsored the bill creating Vermont's "Tooth Fairy Project," which paid for low-income kids like me to get our teeth cleaned. Though he could name few policy differences from Sanders, he did accuse the mayor, perhaps the world's least social politician, of throwing wild parties "at Northgate and Franklin Square," the city's large housing developments.

The remaining candidate happened to be Franklin Square's best-known resident and one of Bernie's most important political allies. Dick Sartelle had hosted Bernie's Halloween laundry room conclave in 1980, and campaigned assiduously for him in '81 and '83. But despite Bernie's "baffling" and "weird" but "total" devotion to Sartelle's advancement, Sartelle had begun to cultivate the press with nasty off-the-record tidbits. Though Bernie paid Sartelle out of his own pocket, Sartelle complained that he was never allowed to join the "Sanders clique," and decried the infestation of "yuppies" in Bernie's Burlington. Privately, Bernie told aides that Sartelle

Skaters and Jane Driscoll, city hall, 1985. *Jym Wilson*

was a *Free Press* source for dirt. A sinecure arranged by Bernie at a local employment agency, designed to get Sartelle out of city hall, soon dried up. Now Sartelle, smoking a Lucky Strike and pacing around the Burlington Boys Club while he watched the press straggle in, hours late, introduced himself as an ordinary workingman who'd been thrown overboard by his glamorous friend. "It hurt Bernie a lot," when Sartelle defected, David Clavelle told me. Diane Gallagher and Brian Burns, Bernie's two plausible contenders, seized Sartelle's rebellion as an opportunity to portray Sanders as a traitor to Burlington's poor. Sartelle, now wearing his Sunday outfit seven days a week—wool slacks, a kelly-green cardigan, and a Tyrolean cap with a bright red feather—stood in the cold outside city hall day after day, distributing his handmade leaflets, as though what he really wanted was for his old friend to invite him back in.

"SANDERS FOR MAYOR" headquarters was above Upton's Arcade, across from city hall, in the brick-and-beam loft that housed the middle school pool parlor raided by Mayor Gordon Paquette. Jane Driscoll, the ambassador to Burlington's teens, put the call out for volunteers among the *Karate Champ* and *Galaga* contenders downstairs, and soon we found ourselves with bags of campaign paraphernalia to distribute in our home wards. I felt distinctly odd, a little disobedient, approaching the front doors of our neighbors, who had known me since I was a baby. I spent my summers swimming at the

Suprenaults' pool; Henry and Bea Granger were my grandparents' bridge rivals; Leona, a solitary woman who lived above the Kampus Kitchen, had been befriended by my mother; Judge Costello was Olympian, above political shenanigans. I doubt there was a single Bernie voter in any of these households. I aborted my leafleting very early in the process and left my stash on a card table in the vestibule of the Fletcher Free Library. I was still too shy for politics.

But for many in the city, to support Bernie's reelection seemed a natural, almost a nonpolitical, thing to do. The "political" energy was on the side of the opposition, who soon became more hell-bent, more ideological, and more unhinged. Brian Burns told WCAX that Sanders and his allies were "interlopers in Burlington." Dick Sartelle hammered Sanders as "no better than Paquette" for poor and working people. Diane Gallagher shocked the city when she told reporters that "she had seen and lived through this kind of mass control" and compared Burlington under Bernie to "Nazi-occupied Poland, where my family helped many people evacuate" and where "people were forced to sit in the mud and excrement" while the Gestapo "painted yellow stars on the wall and doors." An incredulous reporter gave Gallagher, who was normally a levelheaded, dignified person, a chance to refine or retract her statement, and instead she doubled down: "The methods of mass control are not that different."

Sanders, appearing shaken by the remarks, privately worried for Gallagher's sanity. "As someone whose father's family was totally annihilated by the Nazis, I find Mrs. Gallagher's remarks reprehensible, inexcusable, and unbelievable," Bernie responded. Gallagher accused Sanders of portraying her as "this rich bitch, the girl with the pearls, Lady Di, and that image is false." "That image" was in fact the brainchild of the *Vanguard Press*'s Peter Freyne, who'd coined the durable "Lady Di" smear in columns that winter. Freyne was no kinder to Sanders, calling him "Ol' Bernardo" and referring to Jane Driscoll as "Bernadine," among many other insulting nicknames. At a tense candidates' forum the day after Gallagher had made her strange comments, Gallagher accused the *Burlington Free Press* of fabricating her quotes. When the paper stood by its story, Gallagher seemed even more deranged. Sanders, expressing concern for his rival and friend, said he hoped "in calmer times" Diane Gallagher would apologize.

Gallagher's distressing flameout strengthened Bernie's campaign. With just two weeks to go before the election, the adult in the race was now polling twenty-five points ahead of Burns and thirty-five ahead of Gallagher, with Sartelle and the other candidates showing barely a blip. Bernie was therefore in relaxed spirits on the night of February 22, when he joined a fund-raiser, "Poets Reading for Bernie," held at the city's German Club in the Old North End. "We read our poems, and it was nice enough, sort of like a coffeehouse event from the '60s," according to T. Alan Broughton, a Burlington poet and novelist. Soon, "we passed the hat, and then Bernie got up to say a few words, of thanks, we figured. He started talking about how much he liked poetry, how much it had always meant to him, like we all expected him to do, and then, before we knew it, he was reading a couple of his own poems, which weren't really all that great, but they had a passionate Beat Generation kind of intensity to them, about the poor, of course, and the evils of capitalism."

In grainy footage of the event that can be viewed online, Sanders passionately defends the importance of poets and poetry: "In truth I envy the poets," Bernie says. "They have the opportunity to do what many of us in politics cannot do, and that is to be honest." Bernie then revisits Wilhelm Reich:

> It is not inappropriate for political people to talk about love, or hate, or death, or sexuality. This should not just be the province of poets . . . To me what's important, is not just the abolition of poverty and war, so on and so forth, but to try to create a society where people can love fully, where energy can move, where people are not emotionally constipated. If we can create a society where people are feeling reasonably good about life, they will not be quite so desirous of marching off to war.

Sanders ends by reading a poem in tribute to his father, freshly brought to mind, perhaps, by Gallagher's baffling attack: Dylan Thomas's villanelle, "Do Not Go Gently Into That Good Night." His voice breaks a little as he recites its famous conclusion:

> *And you my father, there on the sad height:*
> *Curse, bless, me now with your fierce tears, I pray.*
> *Do not go gentle into that good night.*
> *Rage, rage, against the dying of the light.*

The Kaypro and the Door Hangers

With the election days away, Nat Ayer, a videographer, brought his handheld camcorder to the upstairs headquarters of the Sanders campaign and inadvertently captured the future as it wriggled out of its egg. The date on a wall calendar is March 1, 1985. Reams of paper pile up on the folding tables, as a volunteer collates newsletters and fliers. Couriers and UPS drivers appear with packages; a young campaign worker shows up looking for a check to pay the printer for door hangers. "What I need is sticks!" another worker demands, "forty inch, one by one, that come to a point!" The famous Bernie shopping bags—leftover blue-lettered bags, stored in Bernie's trunk since the '81 campaign, and new, red-lettered bags for '85—hang from pegs on the brick walls. The camera pans slowly across a wall of black-and-white photos, the iconic images, already well known, that document our city's remarkable civic transformation. Bernie, in plaid flannel, hauls a trash bag; Bernie gesticulates at a conference table; Bernie enters Appleton King's house, arms extended in his prizefighter pose. These images, like the paper they're printed on, are envoys from the past. The '85 campaign was retrospective; beyond retrospective, it was nostalgic. The camcorder is the first sign we've breached a new technological age, but the surplus printed matter tells you we haven't made it very far into this brave new world. A sign on the exit door pleads: "PLEASE TAKE POSTERS OR LEAFLETS BEFORE LEAVING."

The campaign is last minute, because Sanders declared late and without much passion. We see the group working on various crunch-time fund-raising schemes. Leather '80s-style skinny ties, the kind worn by Ric Ocasek, signed in silver Sharpie by Bernie; a Bernie "fashion show" concept; Bernie impersonators.

In the corner of the room, a campaign worker pecks away at the first computer in Burlington politics, a Kaypro 10 purchased by David Clavelle, the '85 campaign manager, with his own funds. The Kaypro, an eight-bit portable computer that retailed for around $2,795 in 1985, allowed Clavelle and the campaign to input voter data supplied by Jim Rader in the city clerk's office and store the information on the computer's built-in hard disk drive. Nat Ayer, behind the camera, asks the person doing data entry what he's up to: "It's hard to explain. Trust me," the man says. Ayer takes it as a cue to bug off.

"It was a big step," Clavelle told me. "It allowed us to maximize our time, and our money." Prior to 1985, he said, "we had tremendous amounts of information, on little slips of paper. The work of entering that stuff into the Kaypro was time-consuming," but a stream of volunteers "did the drudgery" in shifts, and soon a database of voting patterns was in place. The Sanders campaign "was the first at our level, the first in the city," to create a digital map of the Burlington electorate. With Bernie cruising to victory, the Kaypro told the campaign where down-ticket progressives needed his help and support.

The Kaypro knew the neighborhoods, but only its programmer, David Clavelle, understood the Kaypro. "Where's David? David, David, David," the guy at the keyboard mutters. Soon Clavelle arrives, in a down jacket and a ponytail, slugging back an Orangina. The new door hangers have not arrived. "It's a slow process," a worker says. "They have to cut that hole." The demand for door hangers is keenest in Ward 3: "We could either not hit all the doors, or be overzealous, and order more." All of these last-minute decisions about paper material—how much of it to order, where to distribute it, given the pressures of scarcity—were driven, as Clavelle told me, by the mysterious computer in the corner, its screen glowing with green text. "Before that we were blind," he said. "We either way over-, or way under-, estimated." Viewing the video, I feel terrible that I had not done my part and dropped those leaflets off with Henry and Bea Granger: "There's a shortage in Ward 1," Clavelle tells a colleague; I could have informed them where to find an additional hundred or so. "I tell you, fifteen thousand doesn't even cover the city anymore," he complains. The other guy shakes his head: "What's happened to this city?"

THE DOTS CONNECT across time: Nat Ayer's footage of the primitive portable Kaypro computer decades later found a permanent home on the internet. I viewed it on my laptop. The technological steps in between Kaypro and Apple were, however, slippery. The footage was first broadcast on Burlington's fledgling public access channel. The fate of little CCTV, like that of MTV, was bound up in the cable battle that was still unfolding as Election Day approached.

A subdued Sanders celebrated his landslide victory at Minerva's Rest on March 5, 1985. His main opponents were sullen. Diane Gallagher refused to come to the phone to comment; Brian Burns told reporters, "I'm a stranger in my own town. I'm outnumbered, because I was born here." The Progressive Coalition had come up one seat short of a majority on the board of aldermen, but four changes to the city's charter promoted by Sanders and the progressives passed, and by huge margins. Together these four initiatives were a significant shot across Montpelier's bow. They represented a challenge to the state of Vermont's authority over cities and towns, and particularly to the power of our popular chief executive, the Democrat Madeleine Kunin. Sanders and Kunin shook hands politely outside Governor Kunin's Ward 5 polling place on Election Day. The image was captured by the *Burlington Free Press*. Everyone could see the subtext. Kunin, who viewed Bernie as a nuisance but not a threat, read those proposed charter changes on her ballot and knew Bernie had his eye on her job.

Days after the election, Burlington's cable fight brought the fate of MTV and CCTV before the Vermont Supreme Court. Burlington's case looked weak; but the cable company, its leverage ruined by a change in

FCC law, its attempts to raise capital from Wall Street thwarted, suddenly announced an agreement to sell its Burlington service to a local company. In Atlanta, Cox Communications had run out of money to litigate its distant Vermont claims. Sanders extorted a payment of $1 million from the new buyer, Mountain Cable of Vermont, in exchange for dropping Burlington's legal challenges. And so, a deal was signed. Sanders, "delighted" to make such a shrewd bargain, announced in late March that the new service would soon be available. A win for socialism? Or for capitalism? What was the lesson here? "A bird in hand," said John Franco.

The city, hard pressed for revenue as always, was now $1 million richer, and some of that new windfall would go straight to the Burlington Community Land Trust. The NIMBYs dropped their public opposition to the land trust and returned to their condos to sulk. Bernie's socialism had again proved to be a force that could rack up wins in the free market. A satisfied Burlington welcomed the steam shovels as they gobbled up our streets; and by May, the month of my fourteenth birthday, I had my MTV.

Associated Press Photo by TOBY TALBOT

Pressing the Flesh

Gov. Madeleine M. Kunin, a Burlington resident, shakes hands with Mayor Bernard Sanders, a candidate for re-election, outside St. Anthony's Parish Hall during city voting Tuesday.

Sanders and Governor Madeleine Kunin, "Pressing the Flesh," 1987. *Toby Talbot, Associated Press via Burlington Free Press*

33

Sandinista!

(Managua, Puerto Cabezas, Burlington, 1985)

Archbishop Oscár Romero in his stall at the Bread and Puppet Museum, Glover VT.
Author photo.

Managua, Open City

In January of 1985, Peter Schumann brought the Bread & Puppet Theater to Nicaragua to perform the troupe's astonishing pageant, *The Nativity, Crucifixion, and Resurrection of Archbishop Oscar Romero of El Salvador*. A pair of filmmakers, René de Carufel and Ron Levine, along with Susan Green, an arts writer for the *Burlington Free Press* and *The Vermont Vanguard Press*, shadowed the company for three weeks. On the ground in Managua, Green and her companions found rooms in "a small *hospidaje* with cockroaches the size of cigars" and met "numerous *internacionales*—Danes, Brits, Germans, whatever" in town for the inauguration of President Daniel Ortega, the young leader of the Sandinista National Liberation Front (FSLN), which had overthrown the American-backed Samoza regime in 1979. In November of 1984, Ortega prevailed in Nicaragua's first-ever free and fair election, with a majority of 67 percent. The international community expressed faith in the election. The Ortega regime had arranged its own birth! Now, hordes of Americans came to Nicaragua to witness the baptism. Back home, the growing Nicaragua solidarity movement counted thousands of young Americans, including many Burlington teenagers, among its ranks.

Schumann and his company arrived in Managua with a payload of heads, hands, wings, and stilts. Romero's face shared a packing crate with a monstrous, carbuncular Uncle Sam, looking like a cannibal out of Goya. When I visited Schumann in the summer of 2022, he showed me how he and his puppeteers created Óscar Romero's face out of clay, baked it in their ovens in Glover, Vermont, and created the prelate's kind visage by wrapping the figure in papier-mâché and Celastic. That original puppet presides at an altar in the hayloft of Bread & Puppet's roadside museum in Glover, located in an old red barn. In the opposite stall, a puppet of Lieutenant William Calley, the American war criminal who burned the Vietnamese village of My Lai, bathes in blood and viscera, the martyr and the murderer staring each other down for four decades now.

To perform in El Salvador, Romero's home country, was "not possible, since we would have been killed," Schumann explained to me, with a rueful chuckle. "And also it made sense, because, you see, Nicaragua was Romero's resurrection." Seventeen members of Bread & Puppet descended on Managua and joined performers from across Central America, including a brass band from El Salvador. The improvised company immediately got down to work. In the film, *Bread and Puppet Theater: A Song for Nicaragua*, which soon screened in Burlington's city hall, Schumann is a latter-day Hamlet instructing the players of his patched-together troupe:

> The idea is that there should be some technique before one starts. But there is no technique. It's not true. There is no technique. There is no technique how to make a poem, there is no technique how to make a piece of music, there is no technique how to make a piece of theater. You have to understand your social situation. Hopefully you have something that you want to say to your neighbors. And then you have to invent the means of how to say it.

"I don't know if you have access to cardboard?" Schumann asks a host. "It's difficult, but you can find it," the man responds. After a week building puppets and sets out of scavenged materials, Schumann and his company, joined by hundreds of Nicaraguan volunteers, "invented the means" to perform *The Nativity, Crucifixion, and Resurrection* in and around the ruins of the city's Gran Hotel, before an audience that included Father Ernesto Cardenal, the Nicaraguan poet and minister of culture, and Abbie Hoffman, the American activist and radical. Fidel Castro did not attend, but Green and her crew ran into him, "charisma oozing from every pore," outside the Palacio Nacional, addressing a small group. Hoffman spoke for all the pilgrims who'd made the dangerous trip to a war-scarred city still struggling to rebuild after a 1972 earthquake: "Managua's the place to be. I think Nicaragua is the most exciting experiment in human living taking place on the planet."

THOUGH MANAGUA WAS "the place to be," Burlington's own intimate ties were to a place 230 miles across the forests from Nicaragua's capital. The city of Puerto Cabezas, population fourteen thousand or so, occupies a bluff overlooking the Atlantic Ocean, surrounded by pine savannas. In 1984, the Sanders administration established Burlington's sister-city relationship with this remote community, even as our GE plant armed the Nicaraguan Contras stationed nearby. The Contras, still loyal to the deposed regime, carried on Somoza's methods of indiscriminate killing, looting, and harassment of local towns. Burlington sent letters and cards to the schoolchildren of Puerto Cabezas, and welcomed the city's poets, artists, and medical personnel to work beside us in Vermont. Meanwhile, friendly Puerto Cabezas was in fact a strategic command post for the Contras, who, according to *The New York Times*, planned to seize the port city as its base of operations on the Atlantic coast.

The city was a good candidate for "seizure" by the Contras, since its population included pockets of strong resistance to the Sandinista government. One clue could be found in the request published in our local papers for books and media in English, "to preserve our culture." Locals returned from Puerto Cabezas surprised to find a mixed population composed of gringos descended from American and British industrialists, Creoles, and Miskito Indians united in their disdain for the "Spaniards" in Managua and, according to the reporter Stephen Kinzer, by their admiration for the United States. When word of the Sanders administration's support for Ortega spread among some Indigenous activists in Puerto Cabezas, Burlington became the site of a testy conversation about just what our sister-city arrangement might accomplish.

The pro-Sandinista left in Burlington had "closed its eyes to atrocity," according to John Mohawk, an Indigenous activist who visited the Queen City in 1984. "The West has no consciousness of the struggle of the tribal people and Central American governments," Mohawk told a somewhat perplexed crowd at a peace rally in Battery Park. The Sandinistas had displaced thousands of Miskito from their timber- and gold-rich tribal lands and relocated them to what Mohawk called "concentration camps," to turn them into productive citizens. Miskito leaders were disappeared, arrested, and killed, and their tribal territory was mined in case of their return. Soon, the Reagan administration realized its opportunity and adopted the Miskito as "freedom fighting" mascots. Ronald Reagan even declared, ludicrously, "I am a Miskito Indian." The CIA "trained and armed groups of Miskito fighters and encouraged them to join the contra war," according to Kinzer, at the time the Central America correspondent for *The Washington Post*. The Sandinistas, in turn, stepped up their indiscriminate attacks against Miskito communities. American intervention had turned "the lush Mosquito Coast into a brutal battleground."

The smiling faces of Puerto Cabezans and Burlingtonians hung side by side in a photographic study that later made the rounds, curated by Dan Higgins, the Winooski photographer and arts impresario whose dedication to the program has kept it going over the years. Here were the Lines broth-

Sister cities, side by side. *Dan Higgins*

ers of the Oasis Diner next to the proprietors of a Puerto Cabezas *cafetería*. Our hot dog lady, Lois Bodoky, hung next to the image of a Puerto Cabezas tamale vendor. We understood the barbarity of our government's war on these good people, but perhaps not the entirety of the complex geopolitical tangle in which they, and we, were now ensnared. When Managua eagerly authorized this sister-city arrangement between a sympathetic American city and a Contra stronghold, was it a soft expansion of Sandinista influence on the Mosquito Coast? When Burlington rallied to the call, printed in a full-page ad in *The Vermont Vanguard Press*, for materials to aid "return to the Miskito homeland"—nails, saws, hinges, hammers, machetes—how many of us knew that it was the Sandinistas who had displaced them to begin with?

ON JUNE 8, a letter arrived in city hall from the Nicaraguan embassy, relaying a cable from "Mr. Carlos Nuñez, Commander of the Revolution." The message thanked Sanders for his "sincere support and friendship" over "the past six years," and invited Bernie to Managua to attend the Sixth Anniversary of the triumph of the Sandinista Popular Revolution:

> It would be a great honor for all Nicaraguans if you could take part in these celebrations, which will once again reaffirm the decision of our people to continue, without vacillations, our struggle in defense of sovereignty and national dignity.

"Sovereignty" meant, simply, freedom from American imperialism, but "the defense of sovereignty" suggested armed struggle. On July 7, as the proxy war between Soviet-supplied Sandinista fighters and CIA-backed Contras boiled over in Puerto Cabezas, Bernie Sanders announced that he would travel alone to Nicaragua as the honored guest of President Ortega and Commander Nuñez, on tracks laid down by Bread & Puppet during their extraordinary visit the previous January. "It is my strong belief that we in the United States must exercise greater care and concern in understanding the problems and needs of other nations," Bernie told Nuñez. "I am delighted by your invitation and welcome the opportunity to be a part of your important and historic celebration." Sanders, the highest-ranking U.S. official to take part in the celebrations, would pay for his own flights, but the Sandinistas covered the rest.

Bernie's announcement divided Burlington, but mainly along lines already long established. Terry Bouricius, who had toured Nicaragua in 1983 as part of a humanitarian group, expressed his strong support: Bernie's visit was "just a decent thing to do." Bouricius described for me crossing paths with Henry Kissinger at the Managua airport, and realizing then the "extent of our covert involvement with the forces trying to overthrow a popular movement." While the progressives' backing was expected, Sanders also drew strong and unexpected support for his mission—both personal encouragement, and tactical aid—from Senator Patrick Leahy, an influential member of the Senate Committee on Foreign Affairs. Peter Freyne told the crowd at the Daily Planet that he swore Bernie was acting as a kind of secret attaché for Senate Democrats.

Some who were opposed to Bernie's trip tried a little light red-baiting; alas, the routine had gotten old at this point. But rising Burlington politicians, eager to test-run the city while Bernie slept under the Nicaraguan stars, found an angle they liked. William Skelton, the Republican president of the board of aldermen, acting as mayor in Bernie's absence, practically dared his rival to run for governor. "It should tell people where his real interests lie," Skelton told a reporter, while shelving fatigues at his downtown business, Skelton's Army Navy. "Burlington is nothing but a steppingstone in his long-range ambitions and plans."

Garrison Nelson, the UVM political analyst, felt the Nicaragua trip "would certainly hurt Bernie, unless it would prove that nothing could ever hurt Bernie." But Burlingtonians, surveyed on a glorious July morning on the Church Street Marketplace, were mostly unfazed. "There's nothing wrong with being friendly," Phil Barry said. "I think it's terrific," Pat Gunelic chimed in. Dana Lubitz, a UVM student, thought it was "a good idea. He's encouraging the idea that sisters may be different, but we understand, we don't all have to operate the same way." On the eve of Sanders's trip, Bernie took in a Vermont Reds game and mingled with fans at the hot dog line. They congratulated him for his victory over the Goliaths at the cable company, and joked about how to spend the crisp $1 million windfall the city had just collected. While aides like David Clavelle agonized about the political fallout, Sanders projected the confident air of a politician on the rise, making all the right moves.

There was a curious news item on the morning wire. As Sanders prepared for the trip, the *Burlington Free Press* announced that a second Vermonter would be joining the anniversary festivities in Managua: Stewart Meacham, the chair of Vermont's Rainbow Coalition, the organization founded to support Jesse Jackson's 1984 Democratic primary campaign. Peter Freyne disparaged this "alliance of ex-hippies, peace activists and progressives who have kissed third-party politics goodbye and joined the Democratic fold," but in fact the Rainbow Coalition had begun to change the Vermont Democratic Party from inside. The group had elected several candidates to the state legislature, and managed to change the rules of Vermont's Democratic primary to advantage Jackson. And Ellen David Friedman—we last saw her in the late 1960s, living in an inflatable octopus on the fringes of Goddard College's campus—was now rising within the Rainbow Coalition and led what many considered to be a hostile takeover of the Vermont Democratic Party, serving as its national committeewoman. As Sanders eyed a run for governor, Meacham and his organization eyed Sanders: here was a politician who might turn the Democratic Party into a powerful labor and progressive force just as the party, under Governor Madeleine Kunin, carved out a position as the sensible, liberal, and fiscally prudent redoubt of prosperous Vermonters. The Rainbow Coalition, with its troubling liminal position both in and out of the Democratic Party, needed Bernie. And Bernie, with no statewide organization and a busy Burlington progressive base fearful of losing its leader, soon concluded that, even if he wasn't ready to "join the Democratic fold," he might soon need the Rainbow Coalition.

The City Hall Beat

As the *Burlington Free Press*'s new city hall reporter, Don Melvin understood that his job was "to cover the mayor. Where he goes, I go." Most days, Melvin went to city hall, lingered in the vestibule under the fluorescent lights and drop ceilings, and bolted to attention whenever Bernie emerged to make a statement. On July 15, though, Melvin's beat took him a little farther afield. Melvin and Sanders flew from Burlington to Miami, where they boarded a puddle skipper that "banked a turn over the Orange Bowl and out over the Bermuda Triangle," before making a beeline "into the unknown": first Belize, then El Salvador, and finally Managua. Sanders and Melvin sat beside a Salvadoran student whose Nicaraguan friends, she said, had warned her of new dangers in that country. "Somoza, the former dictator, was bad," the young woman told them, tracing the outline of a mask: the Sandinistas were "the same" but "with a different face." When Melvin asked, "Is there no middle?" the girl responded, "In the middle is the people."

Sanders and Melvin met Sandinista officials on the tarmac and were shown to a VIP airport lounge (air conditioning, paper napkins, Pepsi) before a car whisked them through the Managua darkness to the Hotel InterContinental. Hours later, Sanders, "stimulated and sleepless," summoned Melvin for an impulsive hike around the city, where they met children playing basketball under a mural depicting the dramatic events of the revolution. "The mayor in him came out" at moments like these, Melvin noticed. Sanders was always happiest and most himself on a pickup basketball court. "They're Americans," he told a group of reporters back home. "They play basketball."

Melvin prolonged the evening at the "run-down, slightly faded" hotel bar, where he found "a scene out of *Casablanca*": rattan chairs, potted palms, an old, drunk British journalist holding up the bar and "bemoaning the fate that brought him to a Central American backwater." Throwing down another double whiskey, the man "could not understand why the United States was frightened by this tiny country," run by "a bunch of incompetents." This boozy wag continued: "The Sandinistas are middle-class kids, children of '68, who fancy themselves Marxist-Leninists."

The next morning, Sanders and Melvin awaited "the permission," as it was everywhere known, to fly over "the steaming lip of the Santiago volcano, over the farmland, across the mountains" and into Puerto Cabezas, landing at the little airport with the very long runway recently optimized for warplanes. The details of this leg of Sanders's visit were not reported in Melvin's regular daily bulletin in the morning *Burlington Free Press*; instead, a vague pre-filed piece bought Melvin time: "Phone service to Puerto Cabezas is believed to have been cut recently," he wrote, so "no report of Sanders's trip to the Caribbean was available late Tuesday." Reporting from Nicaragua was never straightforward. Armed government officials had already harassed Melvin near the hotel: "Pictures can be only taken with permission," the men scolded him, flashing their submachine guns. Hearing nothing from Puerto Cabezas, Bernie's friends at home became worried. A detailed account of Sanders's visit to our sister city appeared only several days later, once Bernie had secured a meeting with Daniel Ortega in a side room of the seized country club where Ortega held court. During the "largely formal," on-the-record part of the meeting, Sanders presented Ortega with a Vermont Reds jersey and asked broad, softball questions about poverty, literacy, and nutrition in the country. Melvin agreed to keep the first half hour off the record, but it is tempting to wonder whether the two men discussed what transpired in that reporting gap, during Bernie's harrowing sixteen-hour trip to Puerto Cabezas.

"WE ENDED UP as roommates that night," Melvin told me. After a day of touring the barrios, "the permission" to return from the Atlantic Coast to Managua as planned was denied, and Sanders and Melvin found themselves sharing a shed on stilts in the heart of Puerto Cabezas, the blue waters of the Atlantic lapping at its ankles. The two men split the light from the one swinging lamp: Melvin jotted down notes for a story; Sanders drafted speeches and statements on a fresh legal pad. At eleven p.m., Sanders heard a group of women outside wailing. Out on the muddy street, he learned that a truck carrying the bodies of six Miskito men would soon arrive in Puerto Cabezas. The men had been killed by a mine while clearing the banks of the Rio Coco—as part of an agreement with the Sandinistas that allowed them to resettle in tribal lands—which had been booby-trapped by both Contra and Sandinista fighters. Their bodies were ferried up the river and laid in a shady grove, while men hiked twenty-five miles through the forest to obtain a truck. The coroner, gesturing to his nose, warned the crowd that the bodies had likely started to decompose. Sanders fastened a bandanna to his face as the truck pulled into Puerto Cabezas, the wailing intensifying as it approached. "I tried to insulate myself from the horror," Melvin wrote, "interviewing the undertaker, watching as the bodies roped to stretchers were unloaded from the truck, snapping pictures that were in the end too gruesome to use." Sanders stood very quietly behind the villagers, slowly shaking his head. When the two men returned to their beach shed, Melvin stayed up to write the very story that I have been quoting, "as the bugs flitted around the lightbulb." He wondered how long he and the mayor would now be stranded in a war zone without telephone service. The trajectory of their trip seemed dangerously in flux, now that the two men had heard "the wailing and the death chants" of the Miskito women and witnessed what Sanders called "a sight almost beyond belief."

SANDERS AND MELVIN FLEW from Puerto Cabezas to Managua on a six-seater Cessna at five the next morning. Sanders, astonished that he could "go anywhere, talk to anyone" in those total-access days of the revolution, now prepared to meet the national heroes he called Nicaragua's own revolutionary "founding fathers." These men had been "among the most jailed, tortured people in the world," Sanders remarked, and under the last and most sinister of all of the Somozas: Anastasio "Tachito" Somoza Debayle. A pudgy, pampered, U.S.-educated dauphin, Tachito was almost literally a vampire: he owned a blood and plasma trafficking business, paying a pittance to harvest vital fluids from the villagers he'd impoverished, and selling his product on an international black market for blood. The rubble on Managua's streets was a sign that Tachito had looted the city's emergency aid after the 1972 earthquake. The only building left standing was the twenty-story headquarters of the Bank of America.

The men disparaged by Ronald Reagan as "looney tunes and squalid criminals" were among the bravest individuals Bernie had ever met. In Managua, Sanders approached the foreign minister, Father Miguel d'Escoto, in a dark bedroom behind a sooty, nondescript church. Father d'Escoto was frail and confused on the tenth day of his monthlong fast to protest American imperialism. A "lover of the good life," according to Stephen Kinzer, Father d'Escoto had once been the target of an alleged CIA plot to kill him with a poisoned bottle of Benedictine. Sanders was deeply moved by the twenty-five-minute meeting for which he "was invited to sit on d'Escoto's bed" as the two men discussed "a fundamental reassessment" of U.S. policy in the region. "If Nicaragua is supposed to be an aggressive and warlike country, they have chosen the wrong man to head the foreign ministry, because he is one of the gentlest men I have ever met," Sanders told reporters.

The next day Father Ernesto Cardenal visited Bernie's Managua hotel room, a classic Bernie disaster area "festooned with papers and documents all over the bed and everywhere else," as Melvin told me. Sanders prepared carefully for the conversation with Cardenal, a legendary poet-priest from a dignified family who had trained with Thomas Merton at the Abbey of Gethsemani. Among the island's windswept pottery studios and weaving rooms, Cardenal "directed long consciousness-raising sessions with altruistic young people," as Kinzer wrote, "to persuade them that the way to live a Christian life at this moment was to become a Sandinista fighter." Burlington's leftist bookshops were well stocked with volumes of Cardenal's poetry. The priest's tranquil mien graced the back covers of these slim volumes jammed with hard-boiled, militant imagery:

Managua the target of machine guns
from the chocolate-cookie palace
and steel helmets patrolling the streets
"Zero Hour"

Cardenal, wearing a white smock and black jeans, his snow-white hair spilling out of a black beret, "kissed, embraced, and patted his way" through the lobby on the way to Bernie's room. There, he told Sanders that a U.S. air invasion from a staging ground in Panama was certain, and promised "too many American deaths" to count. Cardenal handed Sanders a bizarre diplomatic cable sent to the Sandinistas by the Pentagon, establishing as grounds for the coming invasion an intelligence report referring to an imminent "attack against American personnel" in Honduras. After their meeting, Sanders, one of the only elected American officials currently in Central America, ran to a microphone, sounding more than a little troubled beneath his sarcastic veneer: "God forbid that I or one of the American delegates have a heart attack and drop dead. I presume the government of Nicaragua would be held responsible and we'd start World War III."

Sanders, Ortega, and an interpreter. *Don Melvin, Burlington Free Press*

On July 21, a tense Sanders, fearful that his own government had positioned "American personnel" as geopolitical pawns, met Daniel Ortega at the presidential country club. Ortega seemed ill at ease in the meeting, possibly because his own distrust of Americans was at this moment extreme. His wary smile belied a brutal history. After serving as director of the Sandinistas' "urban resistance" in Managua, Ortega was arrested in 1967 on a charge of bank robbery, beaten by his government interrogators, and jailed for seven years. People sitting a few feet from Ortega tended to notice the deep scar from the beatings, near his right eye; but Stephen Kinzer pondered "other, less visible scars" on Ortega's psyche. He spoke quietly to Sanders about the ruinous effects of Reagan's embargo on Nicaraguan goods, and said that "President Reagan, full of the best intentions, has profaned the patriotic image of your founding fathers" by praising the "freedom fighters" of the Contra resistance. Sanders asked whether Ortega thought "invasion of this country is a likelihood." Ortega calmly replied that "an invasion could happen at any time" and that military action would "convert all of Central America to a theater of war. We are certain that it would be worse than Vietnam." A brief Q&A was cut short when Melvin asked Ortega a tough question about the Sandinistas' treatment of Miskito communities. Sanders would soon need to parry such questions on his arrival back home in Burlington.

THE CROWD AWAITING Bernie's return at the Burlington International Airport was a roster of progressives and old friends who had begun, during Bernie's seven-day absence, to take the measure of the city without its usually omnipresent mayor. The commissioner of reality, Richard Sugarman, towered over the group in a black fedora. Jim Rader, ever the navigator, scrutinized maps and itineraries on the edge of the gang. John Franco gossiped with Peter Freyne, tiptoeing outside the range of the live microphones. The network reporters straightened their ties and reapplied their makeup. Lauren-Glenn Davitian, the founder of Burlington's CCTV, was there to capture this slightly tipsy-seeming welcome wagon as it awaited Bernie's eleven-thirty arrival. She holds up for her cameraman a copy of the very first issue of the *Burlington Progressive*, a twelve-page tabloid edited in city hall by Jane Driscoll and staffed by Progressive Coalition volunteers. The symbolism could not be ignored: the paper had been mocked up and distributed in Bernie's absence as proof that the movement was greater than one man.

The mayor seemed eager, for his part, to prove the opposite: he was greater than, or at least independent of, the progressive movement. Bernie arrived after the fourteen-hour flight tanned, his mop of graying hair windswept, his collar flapping. Driscoll met his small plane on the runway and walked Bernie back to the press scrum. Bernie addressed the awaiting microphones with the flair of some swashbuckling aviator who'd traversed the Atlantic. From his nemesis, President Reagan, he'd learned to sprinkle some patriotic sugar on his remarks: "It is totally amazing," Sanders said, "considering the fact that they are now fighting a war supported and financed by the United States government, the lack of anti-Americanism." Sanders was in part deflecting reports he'd read of the celebration in Managua, where chants of "Kill the Americans," and "Death to Yankees" were heard. "In fact," he continued, "They play baseball. They play basketball. They watch the same stupid American television programs that we watch. You feel a real kinship."

On his way out the airport doors, Sanders was stopped by Debbie Bookchin, reporting for the *Rutland Herald*: "Bernie," she began, "Burlington's sister city is inhabited by a population of Miskito Indians." Sanders waved the question away, but Bookchin persevered: "What about the charge that the government has not been responsive to their needs?"

"Fourteen hours, Debbie!" a woman's voice, probably Driscoll's, responded.

Bookchin sharpened her question but was drowned out by an indignant chorus of replies: "Debbie, fourteen!" "Fourteen hours!" "Fourteen, Debbie!"

Bookchin, whom Bernie hired just six years later as his Washington press secretary during his first term in Congress, might have gotten the job that night.

The Sticker Dumpster

Buoyed by our brave mayor, Burlington enjoyed its new regional status as the epicenter of the anti-imperialist, anti-Reagan, left. Next door to my home, the nuns at Trinity College held weekly peace vigils in their little stained-glass chapel, strumming along to a mixture of Catholic folk songs and '60s-era protest music, with Latin American traditional tunes worked into the mix. Down at Pure Pop, Black Flag and Minutemen replaced reggae and Madonna on the speakers. The basement shop filled up with snarling hardcore anti-anthems in defiance of American jingoism. In "The Big Stick," Minutemen raged:

Now over there in Managua Square
There's American-made bombs falling everywhere
Kill women and children and animals too
These bombs are made by people like me and you

"These bombs" were indeed made by people "like me and you" and like my friend's father, a GE products engineer. Mr. Stossel forbade his son from playing this new, angry, thrilling music at home, so Jan, like many area kids whose punk cassettes were banned in their homes, took to the street, where Burlington's nest of fledgling skate-punks, formerly altar boys, oboists, and Little League pitchers, awaited them. The steps and railings of city hall became the center of local skate culture. Dead Kennedys now thundered from a boombox permanently stationed in the beds, among the hollies.

The skateboards themselves supplied a busy new platform for political expression, and stickers emerged as its definitive medium. My friends and I knew where to find them in enormous rolls, for free. Down by the Winooski River, behind the Chase Mill, the unrenovated twin of the Champlain Mill on the opposite shore, a custom sticker business disposed of its factory seconds in a designated dumpster teetering on the Winooski's rocky banks. Sticker printing must require great precision, because the sticker dumpster overflowed weekly with fresh duds. Our main desiderata were the rolls of mildly defective blank stickers. The opportunity afforded by a blank sticker inspired the creation of several Burlington teen bands. With a roll of blank stickers, my friends and I, none of us musicians of any kind, "founded" a "band" called "Parts of a Dog." We wrote some lyrics, but we never performed a note.

Around September or October of 1985, at the very beginning of high school for me, a group of us found a roll of white stickers with red script printed off-kilter, reading, "Sanders for Governor." These were no ordinary duds! We grabbed the roll and plastered the stickers on our binders, notebooks, and skateboards, as well as on telephone poles and curbs all over the city. The mystery of these castoffs didn't confront me until I was researching this book. I think at the time we just assumed, well, Bernie was running for governor, and here were some factory-second stickers for our use and enjoyment. But Bernie wasn't yet running for governor in October of 1985; he announced in May of 1986, after months of handwringing. By plastering the stickers all over the city, it appears that we were acting, perhaps by someone's cunning design, as a kind of advance campaign team. Everyone knew the sticker dumpster kids and city hall were closely connected. Levi Sanders, as well as Jane Driscoll's children, were part of the extended group that loitered on Church Street or ollied off the city hall steps. I know it sounds far-fetched, but Burlington politics, as we know from these pages, did indeed travel along some very strange byways.

34

Welcome to Vermont! (Part 3)

(Sanders for Governor, 1986)

Sanders, Bruce Seifer, and Jim Schumacher, 1986. *Rob Swanson*

The writer Joe Sherman lives in the shadow of Jay Peak, in the cold, northern town of Montgomery, about eight miles south of the Quebec border and sixty miles from Burlington. When I visited Joe in the summer of 2022, delivering a bag of Myer's Bagels, he reminded me of a story in his classic history of late-twentieth-century Vermont, *Fast Lane on a Dirt Road*. Montgomery's postmistress, the story goes, was just back from a day trip to Burlington with her teenage son, Frankie, and a friend. The boys had never been to Burlington: walking around the glittering streets "in kind of a daze," and flashing big smiles, Frankie and his buddy kept "saying to people as they passed, 'We're from Vermont!' "

In the spring of 1986, planning to run for governor over the strong objections of his friends and political allies, Bernard Sanders of Burlington reintroduced himself to Frankie's Vermont. On road trips to places like Montgomery, Sanders got to know the distinct character, and characters, of every village. Montgomery had several: on "an elevated slice of wilderness," the area known as Avery's Gore, Joe Sherman and his wife rented an outbuilding from Chuck Trois, a member of the Soul Survivors, a flash-in-the-pan white R&B group. Trois displayed his eight gold records in a remote castle built from stones burgled from the local farmers' walls. Every town now boasted of something distinctive: an eccentric, a recluse, a poet, a sculptor in stone or metal, a puppeteer or acrobat spun off from Bread & Puppet. Limestone bowls were sanded in New Haven, truffles were dug behind an old orchard in Shoreham, baguettes were baked in a fieldstone oven in Plainfield, built and tended by Jules and Helen Rabin.

There was only one way to see Vermont, and that was very, very slowly. Wending along the old forest roads, a stream playing hide-and-seek in the trees, you drove until you caught the spires of the next village and then the next. To get a sense of the place—swimming holes, apiaries—you pulled into the local general store, and asked around, or read the postings on the bulletin board: healers, lawyers, dowsers, psychics, snowmobile parts. One time at a general store near Cavendish, I spotted that town's attraction, Aleksandr Solzhenitsyn, the dissident Russian writer, buying groceries; it was like running into Tolstoy. The protocol with Solzhenitsyn, everyone knew, was to leave him alone, since he'd moved to Cavendish to hide from the KGB. I thought of trying to speak to him, but didn't want him to think I was a potential assassin.

By the mid-1980s, village life in Vermont tended to spotlight the local cornucopia of eccentrics, and hide the poor. Just over the covered bridges, down the logging roads, Vermont's rural poor remained among the nation's most underserved populations. Vermont was by certain measures the poorest New England state. On drives through Stannard, his old Northeast Kingdom town, Sanders saw families barely clinging to the electric grid, their phones disconnected, their boilers running dry as the oil and propane trucks canceled delivery in the dead of winter. The basics of survival were glaringly simple and few for these Vermont families: food, warmth, power, medical care. Sanders knew that the only way to break through to the rural poor was to do as he'd done in Burlington, speak to people face-to-face, door-to-door: "Do you have enough to live on? Do you see a doctor?" But the doors in a statewide "door-to-door" campaign might be twenty or thirty miles apart. Sanders did now have a working car and, in a young aide, Brian

Pine, a volunteer driver. At times these seemed his only advantages over the Liberty Union campaigns of yore.

A landscape perfect for road trips is terrible for efficient gubernatorial campaigning, and Sanders, approaching the most important political decision of his life, realized, on these long drives, that he had no statewide operation to deliver him from village to far-flung village, regional microculture to microculture. Liberty Union had provided Sanders with a fringe but working network during his last statewide campaign, way back in the bicentennial summer of 1976: a couch, a coffee maker, a shower, a kitchen phone. Those bonds had broken, and none had replaced them. Sanders now could count on few close contacts outside of Burlington.

In Middlesex, Sanders called up a neighbor from his sugarhouse days, Jim Buckley, "an old leftie, and a classic Winooski Valley tinkerer type," according to friends. Buckley, in work shirt and suspenders, appeared as a "Farmer" in Bernie's 1979 ETV special, *Poverty in Vermont*, where he was flanked by Holsteins. Sanders ran into Buckley on the street in Montpelier, where his old friend had started a business, "Auggie's Doggies," a hot dog stand in front of the statehouse that did a brisk trade with scurrying legislators and lobbyists. "Our man in Montpelier!" Sanders exclaimed to Buckley, only half-joking. Sanders planned to check in with Buckley all through the summer and fall. Who knows what the hot dog vendor might hear. "On the street, where I sell my hot dogs, Bernie is the overwhelming favorite!" Buckley reported.

IN BURLINGTON, Bernie couldn't cross Church Street to the Red Onion Deli without being hailed a half-dozen times. A vendor on College Street sold crocheted dolls of Sanders; another sold Sanders caricatures in charcoal. Stickers spanning three campaigns were layered in palimpsest on light poles throughout Burlington. Sanders was nearly this famous outside of Vermont, in places like Berkeley, California; Ann Arbor, Michigan; Amherst, Massachusetts; and the Upper West Side of Manhattan. Bernie had begun to travel to these places, to raise money and give speeches, and there, in the soap bubble of the left, he had good reason to believe he was a star.

In much of Vermont, though, Sanders was a ghost. Blank stares met him at the Willey's Store in Greensboro. There was "not even a nod on the streets of Brattleboro"; quarry workers in Barre barely looked up from their smoke breaks. "This is a fucking disaster," Sanders told Brian Pine at a diner in White River Junction. Pine looked around at old Vermonters munching their breakfasts and Dartmouth students sitting on enormous backpacks and suitcases as they waited for the Vermont Transit buses to pull into the depot next door. A mounted TV showed the ABC affiliate reporting from Manchester, New Hampshire. What, Pine wondered, was the problem?

This was late April; Sanders had told the media to expect an announcement in the second week of May. "It's a fucking disaster. I'm about to announce I'm running for governor, and not a single person in this entire place recognizes me."

Pine, who went on to run Burlington's Community and Economic Development Office, told me he "tried to reassure Bernie. They will know you, I said. They have different TV down here, and different newspapers. They don't know you yet. That's why you do the campaign."

Sanders shook his head, repeating under his breath: "What a fucking disaster."

"EVERYONE THOUGHT it was crazy," Jim Schumacher told me. "Jonathan Leopold, David Clavelle, Jane Driscoll, Bernie's future wife. They all thought it was crazy." Schumacher rose in Burlington politics while working at the Burlington Bagel Bakery, across City Hall Park, where he'd "gotten to know the progressives." One afternoon he ran across David Clavelle. "I'd seen this interview in the *Vanguard Press*," Schumacher said, "where Bernie was asked why he was thinking of running for governor, and he's talking about Nicaragua." Schumacher asked Clavelle, "What is this, what's Bernie doing?"

"This fucking guy!" Clavelle responded, echoing the frustration of most of Bernie's aides. "All he's talking about is Nicaragua, and he wants to be the fucking governor of Vermont."

In April, Jonathan Leopold hosted an "intervention" at his large Victorian home on South Union Street: fifty progressives and administration members gathered to stop Bernie's "kamikaze mission to Montpelier," as Leopold called it. Sanders arrived and made his intentions plain. "Not a single one of us supported. It was 'no,' 'no,' 'no' all around the room, fifty nos." Leopold told him, "We're not finished here. Let's focus on what we're doing here in Burlington." Peter Clavelle told me his perspective, as the administration member perhaps most dependent on relations with Madeleine Kunin and her administration in Montpelier: "What the fuck. We need to work with these people." A poll released in February had shown that Sanders remained popular in the city but would fare poorly in a statewide race. The same poll revealed that "Sanders's strong popularity apparently does not carry over to his Progressive Coalition," as Debbie Bookchin wrote. Just 8.3 percent of Burlingtonians said they would vote for any progressive for mayor other than Bernie. A Sanders run for governor looked like a political extinction event both for Burlington progressives and for the candidate himself. Richard Sugarman, whose political advice had never been discounted, "stared at Sanders the whole time, as though to say, 'What are you doing? What are you doing?'"

What he was doing, in part, was honoring an agreement made over the winter with Ellen David Friedman and the Rainbow Coalition. Friedman had first met Bernie in the 1960s at Goddard, where, as Friedman told me, Sanders "was the only one of us interested in electoral politics"—in fact, he was "only interested in electoral politics." While Friedman, Stewart Meacham, and others grew the Vermont Alliance into a network of activist and community groups, Sanders, impatient as ever with slow-boil organizing, was "not ever a factor." As the village networks strengthened, Sanders was in Burlington, raising Levi, bowling, making filmstrips, and studying hypnosis. "For those Vermont progressives with a commitment to left independent politics," Friedman wrote in 1990, "there is a strong appetite for bottom-up, grassroots democracy. Sanders is widely understood to be—by his own choice and description—outside this trend, leaving him oddly isolated from his best natural base of progressive issue activists."

The Rainbow Coalition now wanted to stage a fight for the future of the Vermont Democratic Party, and they understood their once-in-an-era opportunity to ally with one of the most dynamic, articulate, and effective advocates for progressive and labor values that had emerged in modern politics. Friedman and others were "compelled by Bernie's program, his powerful rhetoric, and his unique ability to reach poor and working-class people with the zeal of a class fighter." Organizing on the left, Friedman had made real inroads with Vermont's organized labor groups, few and scattered though they were. Sanders seemed to be "one of the only elected politicians who could bridge poor people, working people, and the activist left," Friedman told me.

Sanders is a "complicated player in a complicated game," as Friedman put it, and his own calculation was complex. Insiders like Peter Freyne of the *Vanguard Press* had long expected that Bernie would ultimately join, or at least work closely with, the Vermont Democratic Party. Such an ulterior plan to shelter with the enemy would explain a tense appointment that Friedman described for me. She set up the meeting in Bernie's office with Jesse Jackson, the progressive civil rights activist, just as Jackson's 1984 outsider candidacy for the Democratic nomination appeared to be gaining steam. Friedman "had prepared Jackson" for an enthusiastic mayoral reception capped by Bernie's endorsement. Yet Sanders was "distracted and vague" in the meeting, which was cut short when "Bernie kept staring out the window." On the eve of the meeting, Jackson was hit by a damaging scandal: a hot mic caught him referring to New York City as "hymietown." Leaving city hall, Jackson wondered if Sanders, a New York Jew, had taken offense.

It seems unlikely; Sanders considered all such scandals to be equally stupid. The fact was that Bernie had already decided to build a profile in the party by throwing his support behind its moderate front-runner, the former vice president and Minnesota senator, Walter Mondale. Bernie stood out as "about the only elected official in Vermont" to campaign for Mondale, Friedman told me, laughing. When I asked why he did it, she thought for a moment: "He just was being very, very cautious about the party" in that cycle.

In October of 1984, Sanders fired up a large Burlington audience to welcome Mondale's running mate, New York Representative Geraldine Ferraro. The crowd of Democrats at Memorial Auditorium seemed "wild about Bernie." Freyne put it simply: "Bernie has been running all over the state lately, ostensibly on behalf of [Mondale]. What Bernie's actually doing is building a statewide organization that will get him into the Governor's seat in 1986."

There was "only one roadblock in his way—Madeleine Kunin," Freyne cautioned. If Kunin lost a second time—she was beaten in 1982 by Richard Snelling—this time around she would be "political dead meat" and Sanders would enjoy an inside lane to the statehouse in 1986. But when Kunin, a Burlingtonian, eked out a narrow win, it shone a spotlight on her hometown. Trailing her Republican rival, John J. Eastman, by a single vote as the papers went to press, by sunrise Kunin had won by three thousand votes, mostly from late-reporting Burlington wards. This "drove Sanders crazy," an aide said; he "swore up and down" that the support for Kunin was "soft" and then worked steadily to oppose, and annoy, the governor throughout her first term. Bernie had enjoyed an amiable rivalry with Dick Snelling, Kunin's predecessor; with the formal and dignified Kunin, relations were arctic. The governor made it plain that she found Bernie basically intolerable. In her memoir, *Living a Political Life*, Kunin recalled run-ins with Sanders going back to the 1970s. "My rise to power was different than his. So were my issues and style. As a woman, I could never sound and act like Bernie, whose daily diet consisted of vitriol."

And so, when, in early 1985, an opportunity to pick a high-profile fight with the governor presented itself, Bernie grabbed it. The issue was the city's right to raise revenue by any other means than the single method permitted by the Vermont constitution, the property tax. Montpelier had just made that tax much more regressive for Bernie's constituents. The state's mandated property reappraisal was "the absolute worst thing I've had to deal with in five years as mayor," Sanders told Russell Banks. The effect of the reappraisal was to triple or quadruple the valuation of some of the city's oldest homes, and thus the tax burden on many of the poorest homeowners. Bernie had made reducing property taxes a signature issue, and one that cut across politics and class. Now Montpelier had done an end run around these measures. Bernie's answer was to lobby Montpelier to approve changes to the city charter, granting Burlington "home rule" to soften the effects of the reappraisal. If Burlington won, the state lost: Kunin's administration would be embarrassed, Sadie White could stay in her home, and Bernie Sanders could make the case that he was a champion of that most mythologized of all Yankee virtues, local control. It was a fight with statewide resonance, a showdown that Vermonters had long wanted to have. The frustration with Montpelier had been building for decades. Ever since the legislature was reapportioned by court order in 1965, Vermont villages that had lost their representatives felt that their representation itself had been confiscated. For Murray Bookchin and Frank Bryan, the amendment to the Vermont constitution that enshrined reapportionment—only the second time that the revered, two-hundred-year-old document had been amended—was a travesty. Villages yoked to their neighbors in sprawling congressional districts had lost their culture of sovereignty. "Zombie legislators," stripped of their seats, railed against the state on Town Meeting Day. The state had aggrandized its bureaucracy. The hill towns again awaited their champion.

AFTER A SPECTACULAR overreach by the previous governor, trust in Montpelier was, in the villages, now at an all-time low. On June 22, 1984, Dick Snelling had ordered the Vermont State Police to raid the remote village of Island Pond. The bearded, braided members of the Northeast Kingdom Community Church—some called it a commune, others called it a cult—looked like hippies, but, as the state alleged, practiced strict forms of Old Testament discipline that amounted to child abuse. Ninety Vermont state troopers and fifty social workers appeared in Island Pond and removed 112 children from their homes. The kids were bussed to the city of Newport, where they were held in a sweltering gymnasium, as Judge Frank A. Mahady—the judge who presided at the Winooski 44 trial—decided on their fate. Mahady immediately threw the state's cases against the church out of court in a pointed rebuke of the governor. First reapportionment, then Act 250, then the Island Pond raid, and now the state's mandated reappraisal: in "woodchuck Vermont," as Bernie called the rural villages, Sanders saw an opportunity to channel the spirit of George Aiken, the champion of the poor farmer, the citizen legislator, and the rights of towns to take care of their own people. "I find it ironic that I'm arguing the conservative position of 'Get government off our backs,'" Bernie told the *Free Press*. His spats with Montpelier set up a campaign in which he hoped he could claim to be more progressive than his opponents, as the socialist mayor of Burlington, while still being more conservative, as the defender of local control. The strategy began to implode when Burlington's Montpelier delegation, headed by Howard Dean, successfully pushed Burlington's most important charter change through the legislature: the measure, backed by the city's merchants, taxed business and industrial property at 120 percent of fair market value. Sanders had counted on Kunin's churlish veto, but the governor backed the change, cheerfully shedding some of her leverage over cities and towns in the process.

When, as her coup de grâce, Kunin scheduled the bill-signing ceremony at Burlington's city hall, Sanders and his allies boycotted the event just twenty feet from where they sat, calling Kunin's visit a stunt and "cheap politics." The governor, charging that a "childish" Sanders was "pouting" that his political ploy had backfired, now claimed the upper hand; but Sanders saw an opening. The mayor and a young Republican alderman, Fred Bailey, joined by others across the political spectrum, addressed the media, proclaiming "a day for Burlington more than a day for the governor's office."

The socialist had a lot of friends among Republicans, and he began to reach out to them. In May, Sanders met Dick Snelling and an awaiting scrum of reporters for a very public lunch date. Snelling had launched his own campaign for Senate against Patrick Leahy. Snelling and Sanders, conspirators across the political aisle, left the tuna sandwich summit "practically arm in arm," a reporter said. It was great politics. Snelling figured that there was a Snelling-Sanders voter that Bernie's race would lure to the polls. One way to attract these voters was for Sanders to embrace an issue that resonated with "woodchuck Vermont" and young people in the cities alike: opposing Governor Kunin's plan to cleave to federal pressure and raise the state's drinking age to twenty-one, as forty-eight other states had done. This was the era of Mothers Against Drunk Driving, when a totaled pickup truck splattered in fake blood might at any moment materialize on our high school's fifty-yard line, much to our amusement. Sanders very shrewdly framed his opposition in the libertarian terms that came naturally to hand: How dare the federal government "impinge on the rights of states and individuals?" A pro-partying position was a new stance for the old buzzkill, but it was good for at least five hundred votes from UVM alone, where popped collars and the Beemers indicated the new '80s-era yuppie drift of the student body.

On May 9, 1986, Sanders announced his run for governor, already not-so-secretly underway. Despite protesting all spring that he was "still undecided, despite what the media wants to believe," Bernie's campaign office above a pizza place in Montpelier had been staffed and furnished weeks earlier, and his campaign hotline (1-800-BERNIE3) already buzzed through to volunteers. The tables were scattered with brochures for upcoming fairs, parades, farmers' markets, field days, stock car races, town picnics: Bernie's "face-to-face, one voter at a time" onslaught had begun. Deciding to bypass the media in this era before widespread use of email, Sanders announced that forty thousand letters would be mailed directly to Vermont households, explaining his campaign themes: property tax reform; money for elderly services, public schools, and the arts; a promise to lower utility rates and bring the "thieves at the telephone company"—Bernie called it "the most despised entity in Vermont"—to heel; support for family farmers; and local control for cities and towns against the behemoth in Montpelier.

Sanders ran as an independent within the Rainbow Coalition, but the race was initially framed as a decision that Democrats had to make about their future. Governor Kunin was irate that a Democrat was managing Bernie's campaign, and, through surrogates, began to pressure Ellen David Friedman to quit her elected post in the party. When she refused, the Sanders campaign was treated as a dangerous coup. These dynamics presaged Sanders's 2016 and 2020 independent campaigns for the Democratic nomination for president of the United States. The parallel with 2016 is especially strong. Kunin had gone further in Vermont than any woman before her. In fact, until Becca Balint was elected to the U.S. House of Representatives in 2022, Kunin remained the only woman to rise to the top tier of Vermont politics. Her positions were to the right of the Rainbow Coalition, but Kunin, as a Jewish woman, was herself a living embodiment of Jesse Jackson's call, at the 1984 Democratic National Convention, for "a quilt" made of "many patches, many pieces, many colors, many sizes, all woven and held together by a common thread. The white, the Hispanic, the black, the Arab, the Jew, the woman, the native American, the small farmer, the businessperson, the environmentalist, the peace activist, the young, the old, the lesbian, the gay, and the disabled."

Bernie's Republican opponent, Lieutenant Governor Peter Plympton Smith—in Vermont, governors and lieutenant governors are elected separately and often represent rival parties—was the preppiest Burlingtonian alive, the young scion of a local banking family, and a graduate of Andover and Princeton. Smith "was literally the Princeton fucking Tiger"—the university's football mascot—Garrison Nelson told me, "running up and down the sidelines in his orange pajamas." Smith was also a progressive

Republican, one of the last of his breed in a state where he would have been welcomed, just a decade before, as the herald of Vermont's political future. Smith and Kunin clashed often in the statehouse—Kunin, one observer said, treated her lieutenant governor "like a page"—while Smith and Sanders got along like old tennis partners.

After a spasm of national news—a socialist was running for governor in quirky Vermont!—Bernie's campaign "fizzled at the starting line," according to Andy Potter, a longtime Vermont reporter. The factions within the Rainbow Coalition "were set at furious odds with one another when the question of supporting Sanders for Governor came up," Friedman wrote, in a searching postmortem. The activists at the core of his support "just didn't show up," she told me. "He was seen as a one-man show." A Rainbow Coalition member in White River Junction complained to Debbie Bookchin that Sanders was "not accountable to any movement." What Sanders was doing "was substituting himself for a radical movement," Howard Hawkins said. Bernie's politics were "I stand up for the little guy. Give me power instead of the other guy. It's not that different from George Wallace." A state of "frozen ambivalence" took over on the left, Friedman noted. In Burlington, some progressives quietly worked for Governor Kunin behind the scenes.

The long, warm nights of June allowed Sanders to traverse the state, looking for puddles of support in traditional communities like Morrisville, in Lamoille County, where Sanders told the crowd of farmers and laborers that he was "opposed to gun control, period." In Wells River, he played up Burlington's David and Goliath battles against Montpelier. In Swanton, he told the crowd that he opposed Vermont's seat belt law and Governor Kunin's proposal to raise the drinking age. "I don't think government should tell you what to do . . . in the area of individual and civil liberties," Sanders explained, to loud applause. In Saint Albans, in Franklin County, where Sanders had interviewed George Wallace supporters in 1972 for his short-lived periodical *Movement*, Sanders found the same kinds of voters suddenly receptive to his message. "He says 'socialism' and I want to see him deported," a machinist told the *Saint Albans Messenger*, "but if you stick around and listen some more, he starts to make sense." At the Thunder Road Speedbowl, in Barre, Sanders explained the intricacies of his property tax plan over the roar of the stock cars. When he was welcomed between heats, the working-class, conservative crowd loudly cheered. Sanders was thrilled: he'd been booed at the Speedbowl in the past.

As enthusiasm on the left sputtered, Sanders picked up the support of a voting bloc that once belonged to George Aiken: the farmers of the Northeast Kingdom, who loved his "Robin Hood rhetoric of justice for all," as

Peter Freyne put it. The numbers here were tiny: the village of Albany had perhaps three hundred voters; Bernie's old town of Stannard offered no more than sixty; in Westmore on, the northern shore of Lake Willoughby, Bernie contended for his share of one hundred and fifty votes.

But the political importance of this region, the state's poorest and most beautiful, was bound up with symbolism: the besieged dairy farmer was now fighting for the very life of his cows. Meeting at the end of their long, dirt driveways, dairy farmers in towns like West Glover, Craftsbury, Hardwick, and Barton told Sanders about the dark incentives offered by the U.S. Department of Agriculture under its whole-herd buyout program, coordinated with the state of Vermont. Under the program, farmers, facing record low prices for their milk and struggling to survive, were paid to sell their dairy cows for slaughter, as a way of gaming supply and demand. The plan to kill one-tenth of the country's dairy cows accelerated the loss of farming in Vermont. It was savage in its methods: federal agents went from farm to farm, branding the cows' delicate faces with hot irons to mark them for destruction. The Humane Society of the United States sought a temporary injunction, but the relentless branding continued. Farmers didn't blame each other for accepting the satanic terms of this bargain; they blamed the government for putting the incentives in place to begin with. Only Bernie, of the three candidates, understood the anger these farmers directed against the government for the cruelty visited upon their herds. "Don't be surprised to see Ol' Bernardo draw a lot of votes from folks who just want to flip the bird at the status quo in Montpelier," Freyne predicted.

Inside Track

Peter Freyne was a regular at Sneakers, the Winooski restaurant where, in the summer of 1986, I was promoted to bussing tables after three years of "pearl diving," washing dishes. Bussing was better, since it involved less intimate exposure to the messes on customers' plates. As a dishwasher, my job was to collect from the front of the house the galvanized dish tub, then pry apart the piles of glass plates smeared with egg yolk, ketchup, or maple syrup, always with cigarette butts and ashes mixed in. It was better to stack these appalling plates than to separate them, but both tasks gave me a dim view of brunch that I've carried forward into my adult life. The two jobs roughly corresponded to the inner and the outer person. Elbow deep in the frothing dishwater all day, you were radically alone with your thoughts. Out front, clearing tables in the busiest restaurant in town, the job demanded social gifts like quickness and charm, since you had to banter with some of Burlington's finest, and Peter Freyne was the finest of all banterers.

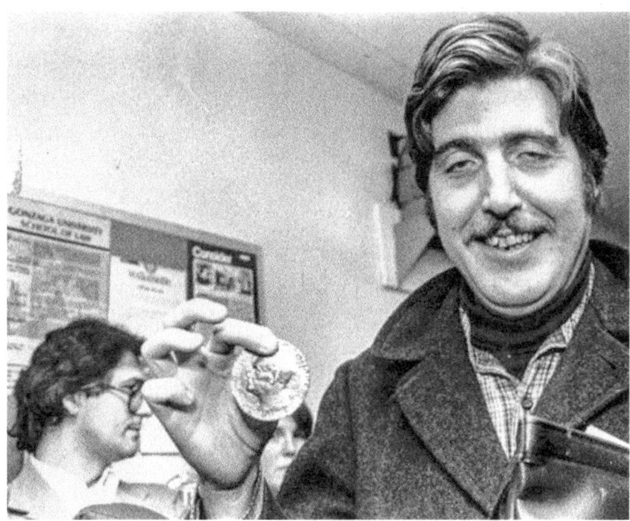

Peter Freyne, 1986. *Rob Swanson*

In the years before the members of Phish started eating at Sneakers, Freyne was probably our most famous regular. A bearlike Chicago native and ex-cabbie, precarious on the spindly ten-speed bicycle he rode from venue to venue, Freyne often claimed a whole booth for himself, and for a time kept his own Big Gulp coffee mug behind our counter—an arrangement he'd worked out with the wait staff, since they'd gotten worn out refilling the svelte porcelain diner mugs we supplied. Freyne was the same way with information, glugging it back, expecting an unbroken stream. His column, "Inside Track," ran weekly in *The Vermont Vanguard Press*, and drew from conversations Freyne had, or overheard, at Sneakers over coffee and, later in the day, over bourbons at the Daily Planet. When the week's crop of bold-faced gossip appeared in his Tuesday column, I wondered how much he'd gleaned from his Sneakers booth. Politicians feared Freyne, irascible, mercurial, ruthless; but he was perfectly kind to a fifteen-year-old in a *London Calling* T-shirt.

"Inside Track" captured the political summer of 1986, perhaps the most thrilling electoral season in Vermont's history. Freyne's nicknames for the major players caught on: Ol' Bernardo, Queen Madeleine, and Preppy Peter, in the governor's race; King Richard (or the "Earl of Shelburne") versus Prince Patrick in the Senate contest. By July, though, some of the fireworks had fizzled. Dick Snelling, the Earl of Shelburne, had let the darkness in his character consume him, and hired the notorious smear shop of Black, Manafort, and Stone—Paul Manafort and Roger Stone, of course, later became notorious collaborators with Donald Trump—to attack his unimpugnable opponent, the Eagle Scout Patrick Leahy. Freyne had the scoop.

Freyne was flying high. When Superman himself, Christopher Reeve, turned up at a rally in City Hall Park to stump for Leahy, praising the senator for his work "on the finance committee," Freyne cornered the man of steel and pointed out that Leahy wasn't on the finance committee. Reeve, "suffering from kryptonite poisoning," according to Freyne, said he'd meant "the arms committee," which, as Freyne pointed out, does not exist. "I mean, the arms control aspect of the debate in the House," Reeve replied, intending to refer to the Senate. "Superman then jumped into his waiting car," Freyne wrote. It didn't matter: by midsummer, Leahy was up ten or more in the polls.

Freyne loved to recite Irish poetry, and his "Inside Track" was the city's oracle. So I took to heart his rather runic statement as I cleared his omelet plate. Freyne rarely said much to me, but that morning he pointed to my "Bernie '86" pin and, lowering his voice, intoned the phrase "darkening skies." I knew I would soon learn what he'd meant by reading his columns. In early July, with the campaign nearly broke, Jim Schumacher and George Thabault, Bernie's assistant and an old beach volleyball teammate, were dispatched by Jane Driscoll to meet in Montpelier with Bernie's campaign staff. Ellen David Friedman welcomed them to the office above the pizza place. The Burlingtonians met a listless, wan "field director" who "didn't look like he'd been out in the sun for a long, long time," Schumacher said. "He didn't look like he'd knocked on a lot of doors." Pointing to an easel pinned with newspaper articles, the field director explained the entirety of the campaign's strategy as it entered the critical stretch: "We're going to go out and visit every trailer park in Vermont," he promised, "and we're going to register ten thousand Vermonters and that would be enough to win the campaign." Schumacher knew from his own failed races for alderman, and from canvassing for Bernie, that "you can register a lot of people to vote," but "what's the turnout machine?"

In mid-July, Peter Freyne reported that Ellen David Friedman had stepped down as Bernie's campaign manager. Soon Sanders's press secretary also quit. All seven of Bernie's paid campaign staff were gone by August, and the Montpelier office was shuttered. The Rainbow Coalition focused on down-ticket races, withdrawing its support for Sanders. Bernie's only liaison in Montpelier was now Jim Buckley at Auggie's Doggies, "the Capital's best franks."

"It was enormously painful," Ellen David Friedman told me. The donors stayed home: Sanders had spent most of the pittance he'd raised by late summer. "Interest flowed into a much cleaner race" between Snelling and Leahy. "Ellen met us for a tearful lunch," Jonathan Leopold said, "announcing that she was turning the campaign over to the progressives." Several people I interviewed told me the story of a Democratic henchman who threatened Friedman with the "loss of her career" unless she pulled the plug on Bernie; none of them wanted this reaper's name, well known still in Vermont politics, to be revealed. But the "main force behind" the campaign to shut Sanders down was no doubt Governor Kunin herself.

"THERE WAS A REALIZATION," Jim Schumacher told me, "especially among Jonathan, Jane, and George and me, that this was probably going to be a disaster, and if Bernie got humiliated it would be a disaster for the Burlington progressives and his ability to stay on as mayor, when he's up for reelection in 1987."

So Leopold and Driscoll asked Schumacher what he thought he could do. "I'll tell you what, I mean I'll, I know there's no money so nobody's going to pay me anything, but here's what I'll do. I will see if I can revive this."

Schumacher adjusted his hours at the Bagel Bakery. The campaign hired a twenty-year-old Boston University student from Swanton, Vermont, Jeff Weaver, to work out of Burlington as its single paid staffer, in a donated office above Nectar's "that smelled like beer." (Weaver rose with Sanders, and eventually managed Bernie's 2016 presidential campaign.) George Thabault designed an eye-catching, interactive quiz for voters, inviting them to tabulate their gains under Bernie's plan to reduce property taxes. One hundred thousand of these ingenious fliers found their way into Vermonters' hands. Schumacher, John Franco, Driscoll, Leopold, and Doreen Kraft called a list of three hundred volunteers collected by the Montpelier staff and then entirely ignored. County fair season approached, with the first cold mornings in late August. At a beer tent in Tunbridge, Sanders and Schumacher met legions of inebriated farmers who clasped Sanders's hands and promised their votes. When the fairs closed, new volunteers fanned out to the regional malls. "At some point during the campaign, a fax machine appeared," Thabault told me. "Bernie was beside himself," and began to draft and fax press releases to every news outlet in the state. The goal was not to win; the goal was to save face.

"I ran into Garrison Nelson," Schumacher told me. "You'll get 10 percent," the UVM prognosticator said, with a laugh. Somebody must have told Peter Freyne the story, because "Inside Track" now reported clearing skies: "Bernie Sanders is picking up the pace," Freyne wrote. "Bettors, who just a couple of weeks ago were predicting he wouldn't get ten percent of the vote, are having second thoughts." Freyne's dark prophecies of August turned, in September, to the story of a corps of scrappy realists building momentum for Bernie's next run.

On Election Night, Madeleine Kunin won easily, though she fell short of a majority, and the election was decided in the legislature. But Sanders, who won only 14.4 percent, saw plenty of encouragement inside the results. "Working people voted for me," Sanders told *The Vermont Vanguard Press*. "Who did not vote for me, was liberals. That makes sense. It takes money to be a liberal."

Sanders, thinking of his warm welcome at the Tunbridge beer tent, told his aides that the campaign confirmed for him the existence in Vermont of a white working-class voter—the George Wallace voter, later the Donald Trump voter—who was "open to socialism." If that view underestimated the power of Bernie's libertarian rhetoric to supersede his socialism, it did appear that Sanders was right when he told an interviewer, "I think we are the only state in the United States where socialism is not automatically thought of as a negative." The heart of that paradox and possibility was in places like Tunbridge and the Northeast Kingdom. The Associated Press's Chris Graff broke down the core of Bernie's support. "It came from the conservative hill towns," Graff wrote, "the Republican strongholds, the farming communities":

> Windham County, Vermont's fastest growing area for progressive candidates, gave Sanders his lowest county total, while his greatest countywide support—19 percent—came in the conservative Northeast Kingdom county of Orleans.

"It is clear that Sanders drew some of his support from progressives," Graff concluded, "but it is equally clear that there is a receptive audience for his call to arms" among traditional rural Republicans.

"Not to be disparaging to any of these people," Jim Schumacher told me of Bernie's campaign office, "but I do feel for those of us who were really doing grassroots, door-to-door electoral politics, it felt like the folks in Montpelier were a bunch of theoretical activists." The fourth-down play run by Burlington progressives, eager to save their own hides, reset the game and "assembled the beginnings of a statewide organization for Bernie."

Peter Freyne celebrated a "revived, refreshed, Bernardo." At a "victory party" for the badly beaten Bernie, the cameras from WCAX captured a new rallying cry in the tight-knit salvage crew: "We got a date in '88!"

35

The Same River, Twice

(Flowing and Colliding in the Queen City, 1987)

Πάντα ῥεῖ

In May of 1987, when I turned sixteen, I converted the labor of many summers and weekends into a twelve-year-old Volvo that I soon discovered had been welded together from two salvaged chassis, its engine parts scavenged from a junkyard. I had studied the classifieds all winter: in the mid-1980s, a lot of great two- or three-owner 1970s cars were put on the market for one last time. I checked out a 1974 BMW 2002 the color of a tennis ball, with 150,000 miles on the odometer; a fern-green Saab 99 with a stuck odometer showing 120,000 miles, "clean and inspected," but with a badly slipping clutch; and a 1975 MGB in a shade of cantaloupe that convulsed in third gear. But my vehicle awaited me at Countryside Motors in Milton, Vermont, a salvage yard in back, a sales lot up front. The proprietor showed me and my mom the newly painted burgundy 1975 Volvo 145 Wagon with purple vinyl seats and a tape deck. We did the paperwork in his trailer office among *Hustlers* and taxidermy. I handed over my entire savings of $2,800, and drove away into the freedom of a Vermont summer.

By August I noticed a slight crack in the paint under the driver's-side door. By September, the entire driver's side sagged, and I began to enter and exit the car gingerly through the passenger side. In October, driving to Ryan's in Charlotte, the undercarriage of the Volvo scraped the pavement the whole way, sending off sparks. A mechanic at the Swedish Pit emerged with the prognosis: "Your car is breaking in half. They made it"—he was wincing in horror now—"out of two different cars. It is not safe. The car is dead." My Volvo was towed away before Christmas. Every Saturday and Sunday at six a.m., I was back at Sneakers, rebuilding my savings from zero.

But that summer had been idyllic. Growing up, I'd been outside of Burlington mainly for basketball tournaments in places like Rutland and St.

Johnsbury. Now my girlfriend and I were bathing in the cold, clear waters of the New Haven River, at the base of the Lincoln Gap, just downstream from a rushing waterfall that emptied into a tranquil blue-green pool. Of all the swimming holes in the Green Mountains, Bartlett Falls was the best, since, though it was very beautiful, it was not very deadly. Huntington Gorge, a few ridges away, was more dramatic, but drunk thrill-seekers diving from the cliffs made it terrifying even to picnic on the forested banks above its narrow, fleet channels. Almost every summer someone drowned there. The saddest roadside marker in all Vermont, erected in 1995, memorializes eighteen young people by first name: Dennis, Scott, Rosemary, Brian, Kevin.

It is a miracle I had a girlfriend, since my favorite cassette to play while driving to Bartlett Falls was a recording of T. S. Eliot's "The Waste Land," performed by Eliot himself, sounding like the world's undertaker. I cranked up the bleakest, the most unspeakably frightening lines: *bats with baby faces in the violet light / Whistled, and beat their wings.* The poem's vision of personal horror accompanied me on those blissful drives down Route 116, and when I arrived in Bristol, I often set up a blanket by the falls to read my paperback *Collected Poems of T. S. Eliot*: underlining, reciting aloud, memorizing. Many decades later, after we had introduced our sons to the falls, I wrote a poem that tries to capture the feeling of returning to Bartlett Falls day after day, for years:

The waterfall runs all day and night,
shedding big self on the rocks below,
refilling with more self, more self, more self,
while bathers visit in small groups, never
the same bathers, always the same river—
my local, inverted, redneck pre-Socratic.
"Falls, Bristol, VT"

It was Heraclitus, the ancient Greek philosopher (a favorite of Eliot's that I discovered in Eliot's great poem "Burnt Norton"), who claimed, "You can never step into the same river twice." In my poem, I view myself as a monotonous, vain version of the river, ponderously wrapped up in my own endless self-definition and refinement: "more self, more self, more self," and yet "always the same." I'm the "redneck pre-Socratic" unable to accept refreshment from the waters upstream. The bathers, or readers, come by to gawk at the spectacle.

———

"ALL THINGS FLOW" (*Πάντα ῥεῖ*) is the other famous Heraclitean maxim. Burlington, alas, could confirm. It was why, in fact, Bartlett Falls was so jammed with swimmers in the summer of '87. By then, most Burlingtonians told stories of encountering untreated human waste while swimming or boating on Lake Champlain. We are talking about actual human turds bobbing along on the surface of the water. I once encountered one while kayaking out to Juniper Island: when my paddle sent a very large turd skipping across the water, I was officially done with Lake Champlain for the summer. Hello, Green Mountains! Hello, Bartlett Falls!

"The Waste Land," indeed: Lake Champlain was used by Burlington as a toilet until 1953, when the city opened its first wastewater treatment plant. The small, nifty facility—we toured it, with our noses plugged, in fourth grade—screened solid waste out, dried it by burning the methane emissions naturally released in the process, chlorinated the wastewater, and sent a stream of chemically purified liquid into the lake. The byproduct—cooked human feces—was used as fill. These advances came with a cost: while it was odorless to dispose of raw waste in the lake, the new handling and treatment process reeked horribly, and its funk rode the prevailing winds when they wafted through downtown. My grandfather, the city's harbormaster during the 1950s, had presided over an uptick in boating and fishing off Burlington's shore, and complained that the airborne stench made hot August days intolerable. By the mid-1980s, despite some upgrades, Burlington still sent 170 million gallons of untreated sewage annually into Lake Champlain, from pipes overwhelmed by summer storms. The beaches, teeming with fecal coliform, closed for some of the most beautiful summer days, and residents who lived near the city's "sewer relief points"—underground overflow tanks distributed throughout the city—would sometimes return home to find their cellars soaking in the backup of human filth.

Sanders inherited this problem, along with an overflowing city landfill that leaked methane gas into the Old North End and leached toxins into the lake. Our dump came out of the shadows when the city built the Burlington Beltline. This new road sliced through the dump's steep banks and revealed a heap of old boats, junked cars, refrigerators, and mattresses nearly outnumbering trees. The site had been used for illegal dumping for decades. In 1984, a bulldozer operator punctured a barrel of ferrous chloride and was hospitalized for exposure to toxic gas. The landfill, on wetlands adjacent to the Burlington Intervale, drained into the Winooski River and then to Lake Champlain, where the toxic goo met and mingled with the human waste.

The outside world had taken notice of our city as a model of progress in the arts, in democratic participation, in services for the poor and elderly, and in the visible elements of infrastructure. But from underground, waste and sludge were rising up to assert their own claims on our little utopia.

The state of Vermont, meanwhile, saw a point of leverage over disobedient Burlington when, in testimony during a lawsuit filed by an abutter to the landfill, the site's manager admitted that "loads were not inspected" and never had been, even in this era when asbestos was being scraped out of every Burlington building and deposited illegally in our dump. The plaintiffs' home was full of methane gas; the couple was afraid to turn on their stove, for fear the entire home would explode in a fireball. Burlington's expiring landfill now became a pawn in the Sanders administration's ongoing battle with Montpelier, just as Burlington sought state funds to modernize its sewage treatment plant. Earth, air, fire, and water, the four elements of the ancient universe, brought Burlington, and Bernie Sanders, back to square one.

IN MARCH OF 1987, Sanders had defeated a kind and honorable local painting contractor from an old Burlington family, Paul Lafayette, in Bernie's fourth and final mayoral campaign. Lafayette, known to everyone as "Paul the Painter," was a character out of a Richard Scarry picture book for children, a friendly bunny of a guy in white pants, a white smock, and a white cap, who drove a white truck emblazoned with his name on the side. The Sanders campaign, managed by Jim Schumacher, was initially concerned about Lafayette, partly because Paul's red-lettered "Lafayette Painting" truck spread his name far and wide, partly because Paul the Painter had been in everyone's homes—he was a classmate of my uncle's, and had painted our back porch, shooting hoops with me after the workday—but mainly because Bernie liked and respected Paul Lafayette, a Sadie White–style working-class French-Canadian Democrat, and a talented politician. It turned out that Lafayette seemed to like Sanders quite a bit too. Both candidates pulled their punches in a "polite snoozefest," as Garrison Nelson described the race. Bernie won this, his first head-to-head mayoral contest, 55 to 45 percent.

After six years of Bernie, the People's Republic of Burlington had matured into a new phase of self-reflection. The institution created to be its mirror was Chittenden County Television (CCTV), founded and directed by Lauren-Glenn Davitian, a trained anthropologist who stayed in Burlington after graduating from UVM in order to "document the community," and Nat Ayer, the scion of an old New England family who'd made his name as a collector and distributor of Bob Dylan bootlegs. Ayer and Davitian recognized the mid-1980s in Vermont as a transformative time and place.

Cable companies were required by law to make resources available to the public under "public service" requirements won by activists at the dawn of the medium. In Vermont, as in few states, a citizen could make herself a legal party in regulatory hearings; Davitian headed to the statehouse, where the future of cable TV in Vermont was being charted. Now that audio and video equipment was light and portable, Davitian, a committed Marxist, was inspired to "try to put the means of production and distribution" in the hands of ordinary people, as she said, and in doing so "to radically change the nature of storytelling." Sanders, who had fought ETV in the 1970s for a version of public access TV, and had dreamed since the '60s of wresting power from the corporate media, implored Burlington "to use the channel, use the technology. We're waiting to see what you make."

I made a big mess. Somewhere in the archives of CCTV, as yet undigitized, there is a recording of Sanders introducing me and my rivals at a "roadkill-eating contest" held in City Hall Park in July of 1987. I won the opportunity by being the eleventh caller to a promotion on Burlington's home for the hits, Q99. Larry, Darryl, and Darryl, the Vermont bumpkins on TV's *Newhart*, served as the judges: the three actors, William Sanderson, John Voldstad, and Tony Papenfuss, surprised me by being completely normal and out of character when we met, snapping into their yokel personae only at the last possible moment. The three were evidently tired of playing dimwitted factotums for a living: Vermont's busy schedule of festivals and fairs kept Larry, Darryl, and Darryl in the state all summer. It was as though they were running for governor. I dove into my "roadkill" (an ice cream cake formed to look like a flattened beaver), came in third, won a Ben & Jerry's gift certificate, and headed back to Sneakers to finish my Saturday shift.

The pie eating, tree planting, and square dancing on CCTV was immediately condemned by Bernie's antagonists as agitprop for the progressives. Sanders, adding fuel to the flames, soon became the network's biggest star. *Bernie Speaks with the Community*—the title shifted several times over the years—debuted in late 1986, and in the summer of 1987, Bernie became ubiquitous on the streets of Burlington, microphone in hand, Nat Ayer stationed with his camera nearby. This canon of footage was digitized as Bernie's star rose, sorted for its most amusing moments and broken into viral clips during Bernie's 2020 presidential campaign, when many Burlingtonians saw it, and themselves, for the first time. My cousins Jenn and Kelly, interviewed by Bernie while strapping on their skates, were six and eight, and barely recall the afternoon Bernie interviewed them with their father, my uncle Steve. The community as a whole recovered its memories when these episodes made their miraculous return. The viral video on which this book began shows my friend Mike Blair, who, when I knew him in second grade, did not yet have a sharp mohawk and multiple facial piercings. *Bernie Speaks* documents Burlington's transformations, which were visible down to individual styles, bodies, sexualities, forms of artistic and social expression on casual display. But what role had Burlington played in Mike's mohawk?

The city's changes and Mike's fed one another in a dark basement room where blood-streaked teenagers collided every Friday. In 242 Main, the city's teen center, the Sanders administration incubated a scene probably unique in the entire country. Burlington teenagers planned, built, and helped to run the center and its programs, and soon, they bled together in the violent mosh pit that took over the space during twice-weekly hardcore shows. As 242 Main became a regional magnet for hardcore and skate punk, city hall did not back away from its promise to provide teenagers with "a place to hang out and listen to their music, loud and miserable as it may be," as Sanders once put it. Those of us who liked other kinds of music mostly stopped going to 242 Main once we'd aged out of after-school air hockey and grilled cheese. Occasionally, though, I would breach the steel door and stand awkwardly on the fringe of the pit. It was like Ned Flanders had turned up at CBGB. Mike Blair stage-dived into the scrum. Brad from CYO basketball was covered in lacerations. I felt like saying, "Hi Mike! Hiya Brad! Give my best to your parents!" But my Burlington generation, the Bernie generation, had been sucked into this angry, ecstatic vortex.

242 Main was managed by the city's beloved arts coordinator, the late

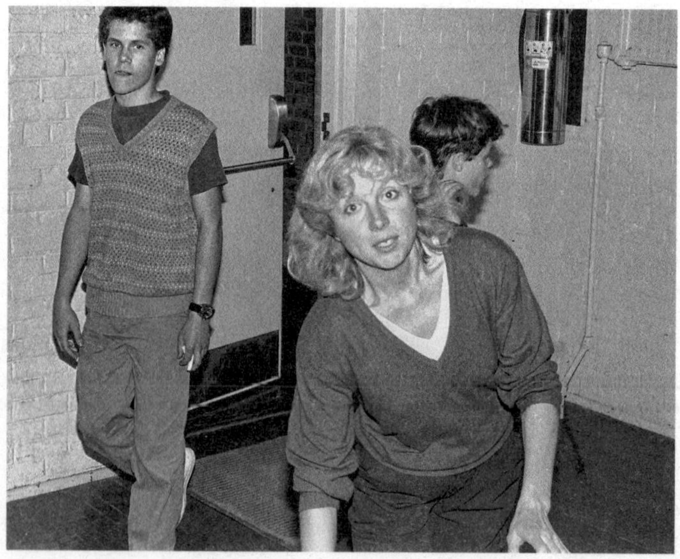

Kathy Lawrence, at 242 Main, 1988. *Burlington Free Press*

Kathy Lawrence, whose daughter Emily was my good friend, and Jane Driscoll, soon to be Jane Sanders, the founder and director of the Mayor's Youth Office. Both women could sometimes locate their own children in the snarling, thrashing energy of the pit. It was integral to the strange mix of wholesomeness and degeneracy that these two young, cool, beautiful moms ran the place, and that by day, 242 Main was transformed back into a *Leave It to Beaver*–type venue for hot dogs and egg creams (Driscoll, nostalgic for her own Brooklyn childhood, introduced the old soda fountain favorite to Burlington kids). Most teenagers want to shuttle dramatically between innocence and risk, childhood and adulthood. 242 Main, spic-and-span by day, dank and dangerous by night, embodied those impulses.

Many of the punkers now ramming their bodies into one another had come of age in children's programs that Driscoll introduced to the city, working for years as a volunteer in city hall in an office so understaffed that kids ran their own programs, by necessity. Dance, poetry, puppetry, ceramics, theater: Driscoll had curated it all, but she credits the kids: "The youth office couldn't have gone anywhere; the teen center couldn't have gone anywhere," she said in an interview, "without their active participation. It wasn't, 'We can do this for you. Come and be part of it.' It was, "What do you want? What do you want?'" So they said, "We want a newspaper."

That short-lived newspaper fed the emergence of 242 Main. *The Queen City Special*, mocked up by high schoolers on a light board in the basement of city hall, was condemned by the *Burlington Free Press* as "a political instrument for Sanders and his allies," in a blistering attack by a syndicated corporate newspaper on a broadsheet written and produced by fourteen-year-olds. But the idea that the kids' paper spread mind-controlling Sanders propaganda gave the cub reporters of *The Queen City Special* some actual clout. Soon its arts team covered Burlington's Battle of the Bands, when teenage Rick Springfields and Pat Methenys performed for a full house in Memorial Auditorium. To host these teen bands, Sanders had to cancel the city's Supertramp-inspired rock embargo: "One of the first things we did," Jane Sanders said, "was to lift the ban on rock music in city hall facilities."

Battle of the Bands showcased a teen music scene initially quite varied: the Boyz, Duran Duran–style heartthrobs, played pin-up pop; Siddhartha performed jazz fusion and ELO-like space jams; Jeff Wick, a teenage Eric Clapton, carved guitar riffs for "the Imaginites." But the future arrived in the form of the 1985 winner of city hall's "Basement Placement" contest, in which eight novice bands competed for one final spot on the bill with more experienced teen ensembles. "Nobody knew who it was until Big Transitions stepped on stage," Jessica Bernstein reported in *The Queen City Special*. After a surf number, for "twenty minutes, Battle of the Bands burned into a hardcore show, complete with slamming, stage dives, and a sticker toss." I was among those in the audience who, as Bernstein noted, "were not so fond of the music, and loudly voiced their disapproval." The jazz cats of Siddhartha won the evening's prize—a session in Todd Lockwood's White Crow studios, and money to distribute their tape—but all anybody could talk about was the strange riot or spasm or dance—so new to many of us that we didn't know the term for it, "mosh pit"—that broke out during Big Transitions' set.

Teen sounds that had evolved freely in the city now had, in hardcore, attracted an apex predator; and most perished. But when the mosh pit moved to 242 Main, lo, a scene was born. That pit, nurtured and overseen by two cool moms—one of whom dated the mayor—offered kids an entirely new path through a Burlington adolescence: not flow, but collision. This had to be one of the most distinctive cultural interventions of the Sanders era, for it could not be ignored that Mike Blair and his friends now roamed Church Street looking, as James Wolcott described the early East Village punkers, like "crashed UFOs, bondage queens, and Iroquois warriors." Some of these kids returned at night to comfortably appointed bedrooms in the Hill Section; I know, because just a year or two earlier, I'd been in their bedrooms playing *Intellivision* and making prank calls to girls. It seemed naive to suggest, as Bernie sometimes did, sounding at least a generation older, that the "music and dancing" at 242 Main saved at-risk kids from a life of vagrancy. Whatever was going on there and in the library parking lot next door, where overspill teenagers skated and smoked, this was not dancing school. I associated the teen center not with kids at risk, but with kids whose parents' dental plans could, if necessary, pay to replace a mouthful of teeth. It was a good thing, I remember thinking, as the crowds spilled out onto Main Street, that so many of the punks' parents worked in city hall.

THE CIVILIZATION EVOLVING in the basement of Memorial Auditorium developed its own customs and codes; these days, in Jim Lockridge, a veteran of 242 Main, the teen center has its own historian and anthropologist. Lockridge shared with me the astounding archive he has compiled for a documentary film in progress, *No Stage Diving: The Story of 242 Main*. In one interview, Bobby Hackney Jr. recalled his first visit to 242: "I was scared," he said. "It was really intimidating to me because it was this dark room—no windows, it was just like a basement. I saw some people that I've just never seen before—people with piercings on their faces, tattoos, different-colored hair." Hackney, a high school junior at the time, had joined the parental "ride train" to Burlington from the country town of Jericho in the foothills of the Green Mountains. But Hackney's fear matured into curiosity: "There was something about the energy in there that was really off-putting to me, but it was really intriguing, and I was really interested."

As "one of the few Black kids in an all-white town in Vermont," Hackney said, "I always feel like an outcast wherever I go." But at 242, "everybody felt like they had issues with society or the outside world and when they were all in that room together, everybody could see each other and we still noticed each other's differences—like you don't have to ignore your differences, but we all felt like we were in it together and we're all kinda the same." When 242 Main briefly attracted a group of white supremacist skinheads, Hackney and others at the center put together a group called Anti-Racist Action. The skinheads "fizzled out, or decided maybe not to be skinheads anymore." Rednecks used to post up across from 242 Main, at a Mobil station, known to everyone, following a grisly double homicide, as the Murder Mart. The rednecks glared at the punkers from across Main Street, leaning on their "Honda Civics, all souped-up with spoilers and rims and the lights on the bottom." I remember strolling through the crossfire of those volleyed taunts and insults, utterly invisible to both gangs.

While 242 Main changed Burlington visibly, some changes took decades to unfold. "When we were kids," Hackney explained, "we just knew our father and uncle as reggae musicians." The Hackney brothers' father and uncles, Bobby Sr., Dannis, and David Hackney, had arrived in Burlington from Detroit in 1977, "to clear their heads for a few weeks." They performed as a gospel act, the 4th Movement, but soon the elder Hackneys met Jay Stauffer at Pure Pop, where Stauffer turned them on to Jamaican music. "We were a bassist and a drummer," Bobby Sr. said. "Reggae was a natural choice." Bobby and Dannis Hackney soon formed Lambsbread, Burlington's biggest and longest-running reggae act. Lambsbread played a particularly spacious and improvisational sort of feel-good reggae, often for white audiences that were very, very stoned. Members of a new Burlington band, Phish, were often in those audiences, learned from the sound, and joined forces with Lambsbread for many of their earliest shows at Burlington frats and bars.

As his father played reggae at Hunt's on Lower Main Street, Bobby Hackney Jr. played punk up the hill at 242 Main. One day Bobby Sr. "was like, yeah, when we were younger, your uncles and I used to play this kind of music," said Bobby Jr. "I was like, nah. Nah, man." Years passed, and Julian Hackney heard a raw, ragged punk song at a party in San Francisco. He recognized his father's voice immediately. Back in Jericho, Bobby Sr. found the masters for a long-forgotten recording by their first band, Death, which by 2009 or so had been rediscovered by Jack White of the White Stripes.

"I couldn't believe what I was hearing," White told *The New York Times*. "When I was told the history of the band and what year they recorded this music, it just didn't make sense. Ahead of punk, and ahead of their time." The history of American punk, one of the whitest of all genres, now needed to be rewritten, with a Black group at the starting line.

In 2009, the younger Hackney brothers formed Rough Francis, a band devoted to playing the recovered punk of Death. Rough Francis became a fixture at 242 Main in its last phase, before it closed for good in 2016. This uncanny collaboration across time, between two generations of three Hackney brothers, could only have formed from the basement punk scene curated by Kathy Lawrence and Jane Sanders. "I've always thought of doing a longitudinal study," Sanders told Jim Lockridge, "to see where all those kids are now, see what became of them." Jane's timeline would need to include a portal back to the year 1976, where, far from Burlington, in a recording booth in the Motor City, the ultimate impact of 242 Main was realized, long before its existence.

Bug Off, Bernie

The homegrown din at 242 Main drew the city's sanction and support. The racket up the hill, from UVM house parties and fraternity parties, triggered a different response from the mayor. To distinguish between the two kinds of noise, and the two drastically different kinds of reactions from Bernie's city hall, is to understand something about Burlington politics as Sanders collided into his final mayoral term on his path to a historic campaign, in 1988, for Vermont's open seat in the U.S. Congress.

The controlled burn at 242 Main was put out every night around midnight, when the punks clattered away on their boards or piled into their parents' minivans. The noise and chaos then moved a few blocks up the hill and settled in the ransacked Victorian mansions of Ward 1, their proud facades hidden under fire escapes. Parties along College Street in Burlington got going around two a.m. when the bars downtown closed, continuing until dawn. Mrs. Elizabeth Tilley, a dignified friend of my grandmother's, had to tolerate the pandemonium outside her College Street apartment until the closing of her days. Some of her neighbors were not willing to be so long-suffering, and the elderly of Wards 1 and 2 began to use their neighborhood association to pressure city hall to shut those parties down. "People become physically ill," one woman told Bernie. "I know a man who was so exasperated by the party taking place next door to him that he had a heart attack and died."

Sanders, who wanted to widen his multifront war against the univer-

THE VERMONT
CYNIC

News
Arts
Student Life
Sports

UNIVERSITY OF VERMONT STUDENT NEWSPAPER

Bernie v. students

The debate over quiet

Conference held in Sanders' office last Friday with UVM and city officials.

Bernie v. students! *Vermont Cynic*

sity, welcomed this new theater of battle. From the mayor's earliest days in office, he'd been furious at UVM, the independent principality on the hill that fell within the city's boundaries but fell entirely outside his mayoral jurisdiction. To Bernie, UVM was an attack on Burlington's sovereignty by the state of Vermont. He "saw it as an occupation," an adviser told me. "It drove him nuts," UVM's own Richard Sugarman said, that Bernie's power ended at UVM's green. To the rest of the state, and to most Burlingtonians, "it seemed more like Burlington was very fortunate to have the university." There was a lot to love about UVM: the dairy bar, the library, the hockey games, the winter carnival. As a child, I stopped after school to visit the mummy and the suits of armor at UVM's Fleming Museum. In eighth grade I saw REM at Patrick Gymnasium. I discovered poetry in the stacks of UVM's library, where, forty years later, I wrote much of this book. And in the summer of 1987, I began to crash college parties with my high school friends. Some details are here redacted. We loved UVM!

To secure access to Centennial Field for the Vermont Reds, Bernie had temporarily backed off his incessant demand that UVM "pay its fair share" for the city services—fire, police, roads, snowplowing, utilities—that it drained. But when the Reds were long gone, and cataracts of waste flowed downhill from UVM into the lake, and discarded couches, aquariums, litter boxes, and other dorm room essentials crowded our dump. When Burlington voters approved, and Montpelier rejected, a charter change to allow city hall to tax UVM, Sanders and John Franco rummaged far and wide for leverage to compel the university to cough up payments in lieu of taxes. UVM came to the table only when Sanders threatened to cut off fire department services to the campus, and the university agreed to pay the city on a "per fire" basis. Sanders and Franco then sought to change the city's zoning ordinances to make development on UVM's campus "conditional on social, economic and environmental impact," and entered as parties into a state of Vermont Act 250 review of the university's proposed expansion. If he couldn't extract taxes from the school, Bernie would instead draw blood.

"For those of you who are students at our local colleges, welcome back," Peter Freyne wrote in September of 1987. "Not a whole lot has happened while you were gone." Freyne recalled "a great summer for swimming . . . if you have a pool. Around these parts there was a problem with too much 'caca' in beautiful Lake Champlain." The students could look forward to beefed-up parking enforcement, aimed by Sanders directly at their vehicles: "Out of state plates won't keep the tow truck from hauling your Saab to the pound," Freyne warned. Other than that, "Bernie Sanders is still the mayor and he's been spending his summer slapping around the Medical Center Hospital of Vermont."

In the summer of 1987, Sanders renewed his old crusade against the university's state-of-the-art hospital, the largest and best in New England outside the medical metropolis of Boston. The battle to tax the UVM Medical Center carried implications affecting the tax status of nonprofit medical care across the country. Burlington was a promising test case, since Burlington doctors flaunted a very visible position at the apex of the city's economic and social classes. The city didn't play host to a broad upper class drawn from a full range of professions; the presence of the enormous, thriving hospital, and the absence of a commensurate financial elite, meant that the wealthiest Burlingtonians were usually doctors. They'd made their money from the hearts, gall bladders, and knees of people they ran into every day, in our small city. As the costs of these procedures climbed, so did the number of Audis in the UVM Medical Center's parking lot. Sanders and Franco pulled data to support their charge that UVM did not satisfy the charitable obligations required by its tax-exempt status. But everyone could see the lifestyle that doctors—almost exclusively doctors—enjoyed in Burlington, even as many of us had bills from the hospital we couldn't pay. The logic that says "tax the hospital" is the same logic that says "socialize medicine." In Burlington, people noted the unfairness of seeing your surgeon drive by in a Mercedes while you paid the interest on a new hip. The memory of these conflicts drove Sanders, decades later, to propose his signature policy priority, Medicare for all.

The battle against the doctors quickly escalated when, in May of 1987, Sanders held a group of nurses hostage. The Visiting Nurse Association of Vermont had long depended on supplemental funding from the city of Burlington; Sanders withheld the money until the UVM Medical Center, whose claim to being a "charity" rested on such gestures of outreach into the community, matched the city's $15,000 share. Burlingtonians were chilled by this tactic: the visiting nurses "came to your home and cooked your elderly father a meal while they cared for your dying mother," Freyne wrote. When the Medical Center laughed him off, Sanders played his next card: he presented the hospital with a tax bill for $2.8 million. The hospital sued, the Chittenden County Superior Court found for the Medical Center, and Sanders, organizing the city's appeal to the Vermont Supreme Court, decided in the meantime to bolster his case against UVM with a little mayoral intimidation.

"Ol' Bernardo had even taken to riding in the front seat of the police car and threatening UVM students with eviction," Peter Freyne reported. "If necessary," the mayor had even "threatened to confiscate stereo equipment." On a Saturday night in September, Sanders stood outside the dilapidated brick mansion at the corner of College and South Willard and "kind of threatened me," said a student tenant, Cindy Rosengard. "He asked me to promise never to have a party like that again."

Sanders and Chief Kevin Scully conducted a sweep of UVM's fraternities, where Bernie had made many enemies after years of harassing the "zoos," "sties," and "animal pens," as he called them, on the hill. By the end of the evening, Bernie had handed out dozens of noise citations carrying fines up to $200 each. The next week he convened a public conference, summoning the young men of Lambda Iota, Kappa Sigma, and several other fraternities to sit across his conference table from the elderly neighbors whose sleep they'd interrupted, before a battery of cameras and reporters. Sanders ripped into the sullen frat brothers, their hair feathered, Aviators dangling from their necks: "People have the right to enjoy a good night's sleep," Sanders scolded them. "Without a good night's sleep, people can get physically ill, or lose the security of their job."

After issuing some 210 citations, Bernie's "anti-noise" campaign moved into the courts. The mayor ordered the three local judges who would preside over the students' hearings to attend a meeting in city hall, where he planned to pressure them to enforce the city's maximum penalty. When the judges balked, Sanders threatened to turn up in the courtroom of Judge Edward Cashman to argue that the city's "credibility" was at stake: "People will say, if you can't enforce a noise ordinance, what can you do?" Cashman retorted. "The last thing I want to do is to create an impression that I'm

Sanders, McGruff the Crime Dog, and Chief Kevin Scully, 1987.
Burlington Free Press

responding to the mayor of Burlington in how I make decisions." When the *Burlington Free Press* published a lead editorial swatting at Burlington's self-appointed sleep czar, the students borrowed its headline. "Bug Off, Bernie" shirts, sold at fraternity parties and in the downtown bars, now enjoyed a brief vogue in the Queen City.

IN SEPTEMBER, the Vermont Supreme Court handed the city of Burlington a bitter defeat, finding that the University of Vermont Medical Center was a legitimate tax-exempt charitable organization. The hospital president, James Taylor, boasted that he'd "earned his salary" of $140,000 just that summer, fighting Bernie's tax bill. "I may even ask for a raise," Taylor joked. Sanders was not amused: "From a commonsense point of view," he said, "I have a very hard time understanding what the word *charitable* means" when applied to an institution "that spends a great deal of time hounding people for payment."

Losing the war, though, Sanders had at least won the battle against pandemonium, for the time being. Noise complaints plummeted as fall turned to winter. "It's not Bernie," a student told the *Cynic*, "it just became too cold. I can't wait to graduate. I'm moving somewhere warm."

TODD LOCKWOOD, a Burlington musician and producer, was drinking coffee at Leunig's that fall when an idea came to him. Lockwood's White Crow Audio had recorded albums by Alice Cooper and Odetta, as well as the first Phish records, in their studios off Pine Street. Lockwood drained his mug and headed to city hall. He approached the mayor with a proposition: Would Burlington's biggest celebrity like to record an album? Sanders was immediately "enthusiastic about the project," the mayor told the *Burlington Free Press*: "Music, especially folk music and gospel music, has always been important to me."

In November, Sanders set up in Studio A2 to sing "We Shall Overcome" and several other inspirational classics, backed by a gospel chorus of twenty Vermont musicians. Wearing a gray hoodie, and holding hands with the local country star Rick Norcross, Sanders sang the choruses. "He's probably a tenor," Douglas Jaffe, the co-producer, said. Bernie spoke the verses, some of them improvised. "It's more like rap," a pianist said, struggling for the words. "It's like early rap," an arranger interjected. The producers self-comforted by boasting of their post-production options: "We could make him sound like a chipmunk or a woman, or we could have him played backwards."

"What I love," Sanders told his fellow musicians, is "when music or poetry comes from people. It doesn't matter if it's good or bad. When kids, for example, express their feelings and their perception of the world, almost by definition, that's good." Sanders predicted that the songs "about peace" might get some airtime, but those "about class struggle" would never be

Sanders performs "We Shall Overcome." *Sanders Institute*

played by "the corporate media." It becomes clear, in this footage broadcast on *Bernie Speaks with the Community*, that Bernie thought of this project as a hack to circumvent the Vermont news media—his latest innovation, however modest, in direct communication with voters.

Bernie's rinky-dink spoken-word project worked. "We Shall Overcome" was an enormous novelty hit in Burlington. "It's this year's pet rock," its faddish gift, Todd Lockwood told *The Vermont Vanguard Press*. Lockwood drove the cassette all around the state. The single became a Vermont radio standard, partly for its absurdity. It was the era of "We Are the World": with its chorus of voices accommodating a poor singer, Bernie's "We Shall Overcome" sounded in a way like an odd outtake from that iconic recording session. Soon the song was ubiquitous, and even Bernie's detractors—musical, political—at this point had to recognize the transformative value of the mayor's sincerity, if not his musical gifts. The conviction in Bernie's voice quieted rooms in far-flung Brattleboro, Springfield, and Newport. People across the state listened, and they spread the word, giving him a taste of the statewide exposure—as a novelty, as a celebrity, as a truth teller—that had eluded him in 1986.

A local DJ, Louis Mano, suggested a follow up: *The Bernie Sanders Christmas Album*. Mano and Jim Condon of Q99 recorded a mock commercial for the record. The track list neatly summarizes the state of Burlington politics, heading into 1988: "Rudolph the Left Wing Reindeer," "Sewage Smells" (to the tune of "Silver Bells") and a song everyone had heard: "It's Beginning to Look a Lot Like Congress."

"Making History in Vermont"

(Sanders for Congress, Winter–Spring 1988)

Sanders on the campaign trail. *Rob Swanson*

Miss Piggy's *Payload*

Burlington's summer of '88 began in November of 1987, near Galveston, Texas, where marine surveyors hired by the Sanders administration inspected a hulking steel oil barge. The gently used specimen was 30 feet by 120 feet, in "new condition," and a bargain at $41,000. Burlington's new barge was towed to West Palm Beach, Florida, where it met the *Miss Piggy*, a push boat owned by Ray Pecor, the Burlington businessman who owned Lake Champlain Ferries. *Miss Piggy* nudged Burlington's barge along the Atlantic coast, into New York Harbor, and up the Hudson River to the Champlain

Canal at Troy, New York. In 1823, this canal opened Burlington up to prosperity: "The connection of Lake Champlain with the Hudson, by means of a canal," speculators determined at the time, "would greatly enhance the value of the northern lands." Iron, salt, gypsum, marble, granite, lumber for masts and clapboards, all the spoils of the Vermont and New York wilderness now trundled south from Burlington Bay to New York City and beyond. The new railroads linked to the canals, and the busy port of Burlington grew in nineteenth-century wealth and influence, before slipping into twentieth-century industrial ruin and abandonment. The Galveston barge docked in Burlington near torn-up railroad ties, rusted wire fences, and collapsing freight cars; but the railroads, still fighting their claim in the courts, were not quite done with Burlington's waterfront.

"We are gathered here today on the shores of Lake Champlain to announce the arrival of the barge for the Community Boathouse," Bernie proclaimed on the first day of December 1987. "Like the notion of Vermonters going south and picking up that inexpensive and rust-free automobile, we've gone south and found ourselves a 'cherry.'" The boathouse, Bernie promised the small crowd, would be constructed in time for July 4, 1988, using a $2.9 million bond approved by Burlington voters. In August, the city would enjoy sailboat rentals; in January, hot cocoa; in every season, sunsets. A reporter shouted from the edge of the scrum: "Bernie, can you discuss why it needs to float?"

The design of a floating boathouse was in fact an ingenious practical and political stroke. With this bobbing secondhand raft, Bernie, John Franco, Peter Clavelle, and Michael Monte, Clavelle's CEDO deputy, laid claim to the shore still owned by the Central Vermont Railway, and just as the company broadcast its intention to ignore a pending suit and market its waterfront acres to a high-rise developer. The Community Boathouse, anchored to the little "spit of land" at the foot of College Street where Howard Dean and Rick Sharp had constructed their peninsula park, was the boldest declaration yet that the waterfront belonged to us, and the Sanders administration would fight for it. Beside the boathouse, the decaying Naval Reserve building, surrounded by a six-foot-high chain-link fence, would be the next domino to fall: Monte announced in January that the city had come to terms with the Navy for a land swap. With these adjacent parcels in place, Burlington readied itself one last time to defend its sunsets.

"Waterfront Truce Disintegrates," *The Vermont Vanguard Press* reported in October. A Chittenden County District Court judge ruled that the thirty-one acres belonged to the railroad but had been "impressed with the public trust doctrine" and could indeed be developed—but "only for public uses." This should have been good news for all parties: the executives at Central

Vermont Railway could now profit from the acres, and, because the court judgment depressed the land's value, the city of Burlington could count on a bargain. But the railroad tycoons spied some wiggle room, and argued that "public use" included hotels and condos, appealing the matter to the Vermont Supreme Court. This situation was rather incredible. After years of public consideration, several judgments, many ballot issues, the work of Howard Dean, Rick Sharp, Murray and Bea Bookchin, Peter Clavelle, and Bernie Sanders, the railroad sought to overrule all of it and build whatever they wished. These petty barons, caricatures from a Monopoly set, plotted to deny a city its public park. Sanders easily united Burlington's disparate political factions and drew support, brokered by Howard Dean, from Montpelier. The city, playing a strong hand, announced its plans for a new three-acre waterfront park, already zoned in by a unanimous vote. Central Vermont Railway decried the zoning as "confiscatory," and threatened a separate legal action. With the matter before the supreme court, the city's public relations battle expanded to include soil scientists, whose petri dishes showed that the petroleum-saturated acres on Burlington's waterfront should never be breached for construction, and an Abenaki elder, who reminded all parties that the land was sacred to the god Odzihozo, who had turned himself into a small island, Rock Dunder, just off Burlington Bay. From that vantage point, Odzihozo kept an eye on Burlington's shenanigans. What a view; what a show.

IN THE WINTER of 1988, Sanders kept his own eye on the airfares from Burlington International Airport to Washington, D.C.'s Dulles Airport. Following the deregulation of the airline industry in 1985, People Express, a low-budget carrier, took Burlington by storm. We were suddenly minutes away from much, much more exciting places! Burlingtonians now flew to New York for Sunday-afternoon Yankees games and back that night, for about forty bucks. After years of suffering for sixteen hours on Vermont Transit buses—gum in the ashtray, smoke in the upholstery—Vermont eighth graders now flew in style to wade through the cherry petals on field trips to the Washington Mall. The mayor deserved some credit for luring People Express to the city, and Bernie Sanders hoped soon to become a regular commuter.

The job in Washington was one of a kind. When Robert Stafford, Vermont's senior senator, announced his retirement, Representative James Jeffords—Peter Freyne dubbed him "Jeezum Jim" for his Vermont twang and aw-shucks, Mayberry persona—presented himself as Stafford's heir. I met Jeffords, whose defection from the Republican Party in 2002 threw control of the Senate to the Democrats, along with Sanders, when the two men visited Green Mountain Boys State in '86 and mingled with the teenage politicos. I got a nice backslap from Bernie but had a long conversation with Jeffords, who invited us all to describe our career dreams. I announced that I wanted to be a poet; Jeffords found it incredible, a riot. The expression on his face was of joy mixed with bewilderment. I think it's one of the reasons I followed through.

By the time Stafford's seat opened, people were practically pining for Jeffords to be our senator. I know few Vermont leftists who would disagree. He was, after all, a dying species, and therefore an automatic object of curiosity and sympathy. There have been Vermont Republicans since, of course, but Jeffords was the last of a certain type: the rural legislator, stepping outside the state only for college, before dashing back to milk cows and pass bills. Jeffords became more liberal with every passing session. It was thrilling to see how far he'd go. Eventually, when he left the Republican Party in 2001 and tipped the Senate to Democrats, Jeffords went so far as to change the balance of American political power.

In 1988, Vermont's sole seat in Congress had been held by Republicans for all but four of the previous 132 years. It was tradition to hand the seat down, like an all-club tennis trophy, to the next Republican in line; and Peter Smith, Bernie's handsome, progressive, patrician rival in the 1986 gubernatorial race, stood ready to collect his prize. As Vermont tilted left, so did its Republicans; Smith, a popular lieutenant governor, was probably the most liberal Republican ever to run for office in Vermont. But Smith was not quite in the Jeffords mold. The son of a prominent Burlington

Peter Plympton Smith and George H. W. Bush, cut from the same cloth.
Jym Wilson

banker, Smith read as "professional" and "urban." He made some of the mistakes blue bloods make. Sanders noted the painful spectacle of Smith's attempts to bond with farmers, quarry workers, and checkout clerks across Vermont. Peter Smith was Vermont's version of George Herbert Walker Bush, his own presidential candidacy then underway: an Ivy League golden boy stumped by the cost of a gallon of milk. Smith and Bush alike suffered from what Peter Freyne called the "noblesse oblige disease." (But it should be noted that Bush won in Vermont in 1988, by a solid margin.)

Sanders now had to consider Vermont Democrats, who were in a "pitiful, pitiful" state in this cycle, as Garrison Nelson told me. There was no path to Congress for a centrist or moderate Democrat against the presumptive Republican, a liberal and likable and smart person, Peter Smith; and yet four candidates lined up. The only open lane was on the left, and it passed directly through Vermont's Rainbow Coalition, which had reconvened and expanded to support the ascendant candidacy of the Reverend Jesse Jackson for the 1988 Democratic nomination. Sanders swore he would never again trust the Rainbow Coalition after their feckless campaign organization crumbled in the home stretch, back in '86. A move toward Jackson and the Rainbow Coalition was by no means without risk.

IN JANUARY, Sanders appeared on a C-SPAN national call-in show and fielded a convenient question about his plans, posed by a caller from South Burlington: "It's no secret in Vermont that I am giving some thought to running for Congress." His decision would depend on whether his campaign "could raise the kinds of money that we'll need," after being "outspent 10–1 last time."

Throughout January and February, Jesse Jackson's campaign, staffed by sixty or so volunteers in Vermont, found in Bernie a charismatic surrogate; and Sanders found in Jackson's organization a trellis to climb toward his long-anticipated announcement in March. Vermont was an important test for Jackson: as though designed by a campaign strategist or science fiction writer, our state provided the candidate a virtually all-white civilization on which to demonstrate his appeal beyond urban Black voters. The candidate's race had drawn commentary across the political spectrum, and racism from the right: Jackson "will not be the Democratic nominee," the conservative William F. Buckley wrote in his syndicated column, "and his *disqualifications go beyond* the coincidental color of his skin." (The emphasis is mine.) Despite the "hegemonic support of black Americans," Buckley continued, "the non-black population is not going to vote for Jesse Jackson." But DeWayne Wickham, a Black syndicated columnist, more or less

Sanders and Jesse Jackson, Burlington, 1988. *Jym Wilson*

concurred: "There simply aren't very many white voters willing to entrust their political fortunes to black office holders." Exit polls in Iowa and New Hampshire showed that "white voters in these states liked the message but rejected the messenger." Why would Vermont be any different?

By 1988, Vermont, though still nearly entirely white, *was* different; it had become different over time and by degree. Jackson's performance in its phased nominating contest was an important test of the state's political transformation, advertised for more than two decades but as yet mostly unrealized. In early February, Sanders welcomed Jackson for a day of events in Burlington. The two men first held a press conference at the city-owned day-care center, surrounded by crying, shouting, sneezing toddlers. Over the din, Jackson refused to say whether Bernie should run for Congress: "a personal decision," Jackson said, appearing to surprise Bernie, who smiled enigmatically at the choice of phrase. Then it was on to UVM's Ira Allen Chapel, where I waited outdoors in the overflow group of hundreds who'd been turned away from the jammed pews. Jackson, in a banker's coat and leather gloves, spoke forcefully to our shivering group, and then joined the raucous crowd inside for a warm-up performance by the San Francisco Mime Troupe ("loud mime, not pantomime"). A white actor playing the colonial governor of a fictional African nation, Mozangola, performed a satirical rap before the mostly white crowd, to the visible discomfort of the Black students and dignitaries seated on the stage behind him. (CCTV captured the afternoon's events; I am describing the recording.)

Sanders, introduced by Ellen David Friedman, then took the rostrum, sounding like a candidate for Congress, or, as Vermont pundits openly wondered, even Jackson's potential running mate. "Fellow Vermonters," he began, "today is a very exciting day for the city of Burlington, and for the state of Vermont." Jackson had "made history" by assembling a coalition of "Black workers and white workers," of "Hispanics and Orientals" (the offensive term provoked eyerolls), of "young people who want the right to get a higher education without having to bankrupt their families," of "elderly people, who want and are entitled to decent Social Security benefits, decent health care benefits," and of "farmers, who all over America today are being thrown off their land." The crowd erupted in applause as Bernie hit a familiar crescendo: "Let's take America back from the millionaires and corporations that dominate it."

Jackson had done his part to make history, by staging the first credible candidacy for president by a Black American. Now it was Vermont's turn. "As some of you may know," Bernie continued, "the state of Vermont happens to be the whitest state in the United States of America. That happens to be a demographic fact." Though "the great political geniuses have decided that our candidate can't become the president of the United States," Vermont would send a message: "If Jesse Jackson can carry Vermont on March 1, the message will go out," Bernie concluded, "that this man is going to be the next president of the United States of America."

Jackson then treated Ira Allen Chapel to a performance of oratory, and political organizing, probably unprecedented in the building's distinguished history. Calling out to the unconverted, Reverend Jackson beckoned even those from "the balcony" who "would register to vote today, to come right on down into the aisles." A crowd of fifty or so young people joined Jackson and, heads bowed, right hands raised, took the Freeman's Oath, administered by a volunteer. "Welcome to America!" Jackson exclaimed. "You do not have to vote for me, but you ought to! Say *I do*!" The scattered, muttered "I do"s suggest a crowd unaccustomed to the Black church, so Jackson's next request might have come as a surprise: "Each of you have envelopes," Reverend Jackson said. "There is ten thousand dollars in this room."

Jackson started at one thousand dollars, inviting donors to "come right on down," and reading the names of the pledges as they appeared at his knees. "Shush now, be orderly," the minister implored his entirely silent and obedient flock, now reading the names of his new converts: "Anne Rothwell, twenty-five dollars!"

IN 1988, Vermont Democrats expressed their presidential preferences in a two-stage process: first, a nonbinding beauty-contest primary on March 1, in which Jackson exceeded expectations but lost decisively to the Democrats' well-financed front-runner, Governor Michael Dukakis of Massachusetts; then, binding caucuses on April 19 to assign delegates. Between the two phases was an opportunity for growth. Jackson's passionate volunteers understood the mechanisms of a caucus—a social process, where high school gyms and library reading rooms transform into a living organism, oozing, growing, shrinking, toward consensus. Caucuses always favor grassroots campaigns. Here was a dramatic opportunity in seven weeks to show that the Rainbow Coalition could tap a "well of populism," as Ellen David Friedman put it, "that is, minimally, neither racist nor reactionary (as some tendencies of American populism have been)." Bernie Sanders, now rising along with Jackson's campaign, staged his announcement between the primary and the caucuses. Jackson's primary tally had established the floor of his support. His gains seven weeks later in the caucuses would measure the difference Sanders had made.

On March 11, Bernie declared his candidacy for the U.S. House of Representatives at a news conference in Montpelier, invoking the owlish Yankee elder whom Sanders, as a freelance reporter wearing a backpack, had interviewed in the Senate building in 1973. "The state of Vermont has a history of sending unconventional representatives, mavericks, to Washington. Over forty years ago, we sent George Aiken there." Sanders joined four Democrats and two Republicans waiting to be winnowed by far-off September primaries, plus a perennial libertarian candidate, James Hedbor. Bernie's presence in the race shifted the parties' political calculus: the Democrats' liberal rising star, Peter Welch, who now serves beside Bernie as Vermont's junior senator, fell, and a "conservative" option, a working-class high school teacher and hockey coach from Barre, Paul Poirier, rose. On the Republican side, Peter Smith now seemed inevitable in his race against a far-right newcomer, James Gates. Running as an independent, Bernie had a head start, but the Rainbow Coalition, still a Democratic entity working within the party infrastructure, could not endorse him until their own convention in July. So Bernie again barged into a campaign without a dedicated staff or corps of volunteers, no money, and no plan to raise money. He did not recruit the Burlington progressives to his campaign. He had not reached out to his 1986 rescue team, whose last-ditch effort had salvaged his dignity. His oldest friends and political advisers were in the dark. Jim Rader, Huck Gutman, and Richard Sugarman saw it on the news, the way the rest of us did.

In April of 1988, Jim Schumacher was chilling out in Arizona, "looking for something different," he told me. "Looking to make some money," Debbie Bookchin added, with a laugh. I sat with Bookchin and Schumacher one Sunday afternoon at their dining room table in Albany, New York, near the campus of SUNY Albany. The couple's binocular perspective on Bernie's 1988 and 1990 races for Congress, which transpired long before they married, came together for the first time over a beautiful lunch of a winter salad and fresh bread, along with a pecorino tartufo I'd brought from Boston. "You have to understand," Schumacher, the insider, said. "There was nothing." Bookchin, the reporter and analyst, interjected: "He was never building an organization." A volunteer strategist like Jim Schumacher would have had "at least some kind of party sinecure waiting for him" after running two campaigns, but with Sanders, there "was no party," and also no memory of gratitude. Schumacher's only real tie back to Burlington was his job at the Burlington Bagel Bakery, where, he said sardonically, "the door was always open." When Schumacher heard Bernie's news, first he called the Bagel Bakery to get back on the schedule, then he called Jonathan Leopold in city hall. "Is this a real campaign or not?" Schumacher demanded. The answer, at that point, was no: no money, no staff, no plan. "You can't run a statewide campaign without money and staff," Schumacher told me. "I think we all sort of said, 'We're not going to do this again for free.'"

With his allies scheming behind the scenes to stage a real statewide campaign, Sanders focused on what he did best: he picked a fight with Democrats. The Burlington Democratic Party Caucus met on the evening of April 19 at Burlington High School, and Sanders, representing the Jackson campaign, planned to crash the party's party. Officials worked behind the scenes for weeks to keep Sanders away; Sanders said he "found it amusing" that the party was still conniving to undermine him, eight years after he'd wrested their power away. Democratic foes lined up in the cinder-block high school lobby: the commissioners who'd clung to the low-hanging fruit of city bureaucracy, who'd hoarded their pensions and patronage networks long after the will of Burlington voters was made clear; the wags behind the *Burlington Flea Press*, who had red-baited and slandered Sanders for sport; the officials who had stolen his mail and towed his car from the mayor's designated spot behind city hall. For decades, the party had enriched its loyalists through development deals, no-interest mortgages, no-bid contracts, and insurance monopolies. This routed machine was now the minority party in a three-party city. The cause of their dramatic collapse sauntered past these embittered Democrats and into the auditorium, surrounded by supporters.

As a klatch of Burlington progressives took their seats, Governor Madeleine Kunin, supporting Michael Dukakis, told Lauren-Glenn Davitian, reporting for CCTV, that she "hoped people were here for the Democratic Party." Democrats expressed "surprise" at the enormous turnout, but dismissed the Jackson supporters as interlopers and "students," that old Burlington term of abuse. From the stage, Kunin and Howard Dean mocked the progressives in the room, before Sanders, wearing a "Bernie '88" pin, rose to speak on behalf of Jackson and "the real people of America," to raucous applause from progressives and boos from many Democrats. Both groups heard Bernie's address correctly, as a "Sanders for Congress" campaign speech.

In the lull after Bernie's stemwinder, a small, old-fashioned man in tweed rose to the podium. Lyman C. Hunt Jr. was known to many Burlingtonians only from the local school named for his father, the city's longtime superintendent. Hunt Jr. had made his own distinguished career in education: a renowned professor at UVM, Hunt reformed elementary education in Vermont by proving that children needed "sustained periods of silent reading in the classroom." His curriculum was adopted by all the area schools, but Hunt was not silent tonight. Nominating Al Gore for president, Hunt insisted that "the issue" was not which candidate won, "but whether the Democratic Party wins." The soft-spoken educator then became impassioned: "I do not wish to see the Democratic Party self-destruct again." Hunt struck the podium: "I resent intruders who would undermine and destroy the Democratic Party." Into the growing chaos, Hunt shouted, "If a vote for Jackson is a vote for Bernie, I will not vote for Jackson!" A Democratic Party official leaped to the stage, as Hunt continued: "Burlington is *my hometown*! I can remember Church Street in the '20s and '30s!" Lyman C. Hunt Jr., the silent reading advocate and friend to Burlington's children, then took his seat. But he had lit a fuse.

It was all too much for Mrs. Helen Malloy of Dorset Street. The elderly woman made her way up the central aisle, called out to Sanders as he returned to his seat after voting, and, planting her feet for maximum impact, slapped the mayor hard across the face. Sanders, appearing shaken, told Mrs. Malloy, "I don't think that was very nice." Reached for comment that night by the *Burlington Free Press*, Mrs. Malloy claimed she'd just "lost her footing," but still seemed unapologetic: "It's impossible to get any kind of unity when you have somebody like Bernie Sanders trying to break up the party by passing himself off as a Democrat." The *Free Press* added its own slap: "Sanders describes himself as a socialist."

It was Jesse Jackson's night in Burlington and all across Vermont: the political outsider, gaining steam across the nation, beat the Democrats' anointed front-runner in a show of grassroots power. The nominating season lurched ahead toward a tense Democratic National Convention in July. As the nights lengthened in Vermont, a campaign summer now beckoned to Sanders from the county fairs and farmers' markets, where Bernie would dust off his square-dancing, udder-pulling, and radish-tasting skills as his biggest political test awaited him.

First, though, a vernal interlude: a proposal, a wedding, and what Sanders called "a very strange honeymoon."

Spring Fling

In early April, Bernie approached Jim Rader in the city clerk's office with a happy request: he wanted his oldest friend to officiate at his wedding. Peter Freyne had the scoop, which Jane Sanders confirmed years later to *People* magazine: after sundaes at the Shelburne Road Friendly's, Sanders proposed in the parking lot—twice, in fact. When Bernie asked, "You wanna get married?" Driscoll thought he was just checking to confirm her position: "You know I do," she responded. Clutching her by the shoulders, Sanders then made himself clear: "Will. You. Marry. Me." The couple took a week's engagement trip in St. Lucia, and returned home to plan the day. The papers made jokes about its being our low-budget version of the Royal Wedding, and asked whether Jane would now have to resign her post in city hall. A Memorial Day weekend wedding was planned on North Beach. The public was cordially invited. I was working that day at Sneakers, but my friend George, who'd been hired as a summer "baby cop" patrolling the beaches (mountain bike, billy club, biceps), said he would pedal by and give Bernie and Jane my blessings.

On May 28, 1988. Bernie and his best man, Levi Sanders, waited in the

Bernie Sanders marries Jane Driscoll, 1988. Jim Rader performing the ceremony.
Burlington Free Press

sunshine as Driscoll's bridesmaids, her two daughters, Heather and Carina, approached; Driscoll followed, escorted down the aisle by her young son, David. The new blended family stood together before hundreds of guests in a scrubby grove among hibachis and picnic tables. Residents of North Beach Campground, where Canadians, hippies, and the homeless set up shop for the summer, filled in the back rows. One man looked on in a wetsuit. Judy Collins's "Since You've Asked" warbled from the upright speakers, accompanied by robins and motorboats. The setting in Burlington's imperfect arcadia was "about as Bernie and Jane as you could get," Rader told me: a public beach and busy park, just steps from the contested acres on Burlington's waterfront and the new, bobbing boathouse down the shore. With our city clerk presiding, and the local networks and reporters on hand, the wedding was a tribute to Bernie and Jane's Burlington.

Rader welcomed the crowd of "friends, family, and coworkers" to "the shore of our beautiful lake" and shared "a few personal comments about Bernie and Jane," beginning with his recollection of first meeting Bernie when he was nineteen, "the age that Levi is now," in Chicago:

> What most impressed me was not your politics, though you were a political activist even then. It was not your tremendous energy, though you've always had that. What impressed me then was your ease with children, and your caring about children.

Rader "was thinking of that first night," he told me, "when Bernie held our daughter," stepping away from the group of young activists in Rader's Chicago living room. He recalled the improvised summer camp Bernie ran for three city kids on the Middlesex property, and of Bernie's "pickup games with Levi" on Burlington's rutted asphalt courts. Jane, who had fostered teenagers in her home, worked with young people at the King Street Center, raised three children of her own, and now ran the city's transformative youth office, had "seen in Bernie," as Bernie had seen in her, work with children as "an area of common interest and concern."

Their relationship began as political kinship, this "Che Guevara type in Yankee Vermont" and his "grassroots Jane Fonda," as Joe Sherman memorably described them. Jane had first heard Bernie's name on the lips of his disgraced predecessor, Mayor Gordon Paquette. She turned up in Paquette's office as an organizer for the King Street Center; the mayor listened impatiently to Jane Driscoll's harangue and then dismissed her rudely: "You sound like Bernie Sanders," he said. "Who's that?" Driscoll wondered.

Soon she knew, and soon after that, they were dating. Their lives had since then played out in full view of the People's Republic of Burlington. Rader hoped that the couple would now enjoy "a home base and a refuge" in family life. Roxanne Leopold then stood up to acknowledge "the private moments" she and Jonathan had shared with Jane and Bernie: "We wish you both a home, not simply a structure of stone and wood," but "a home with books, and music, and poetry, all the things which represent the highest strivings of men and women." After an exchange of rings and a chaste kiss, the newlyweds headed to Jane's minivan for the getaway, past the baby cops, through the campground, and out to North Avenue.

Their "refuge" lasted seventy-two hours. Three days later, accompanied by a delegation of ten Burlingtonians, Ol' Bernardo and Queen Jane popped up in the Soviet Union: their itinerary took them to Leningrad, Moscow, and, finally, a city 272 kilometers northeast of Red Square, the borough of Yaroslavl.

IN MARCH OF 2020, in the last days before COVID-19 shut the world down and the Democratic Party closed ranks around the presidential candidacy of Joe Biden, *The New York Times*'s Moscow bureau chief Anton Troianovski returned from Yaroslavl with a story in his maw: "Previously unseen documents from a Soviet archive show how hard Mr. Sanders worked to find a sister city in Russia when he was mayor in the 1980s. Moscow saw a chance for propaganda."

A supplementary article recounted Troianovski's lionhearted retrieval of these "previously unseen documents," which, it turned out, nobody had ever requested: a "researcher from our bureau" had uncovered "a wealth of documents in Yaroslavl," and implored the reporter to brave the four-hour morning train ride to one of the Soviet Union's most picturesque and historic cities, a trip just as uncertain and perilous as an Amtrak journey from New York to Boston. Come at once, the researcher implored: "While it might take time to get access, I think it is worth it."

The New Yorker's Masha Gessen, who was raised in the Soviet Union, noted a few oddities in the *Times* story:

> The reporter, Anton Troianovski, described the search for the documents, which involved taking a train, visiting the archive, and physically paging through catalogues until he found a reference to the Burlington files. (Alternatively, he could have logged on to the Web site of Yaroslavl's regional archives and tried typing "Берлингтон"—"Burlington"—or "дружественный"—"friendly"—into the search field, and he would

have located the call numbers for the folder containing the documents from 1988.)

Gessen then pointed out that the Russian term for "propaganda" meant "any effort to promote a point of view." And the "point of view" being promoted during the summer of 1988 was, according to the Sovietologist David Brandenberger, "a lot closer to relationship-building and cooperation than some sort of dogmatic messaging." In fact, the kinds of exchanges and sister-city relationships that Bernie and the Burlington delegation forged with Yaroslavl were "an important part of our effort to expand and broaden contacts and communications between the people of the United States and the Soviet Union," according to a 1986 declaration by President Ronald Reagan. "People-to-people programs can help build better understanding and genuine constituencies for peace."

The trip that *The New York Times* red-baited as Bernie rose in the polls was about as radical as a Chamber of Commerce luncheon. It was expedited to overlap with the Moscow summit where President Reagan and Mikhail Gorbachev, the Soviet premier, worked out the terms of a new geopolitical cordiality. The Russian policy of glasnost meant "openness to consultation," but was usually translated as "democratization." It meant that the Cold War had thawed. I remember thinking, well, you have to hand it to Reagan this time. At a table in the Kremlin, the ink dried on a new intermediate-range nuclear weapons treaty that made the world instantly and significantly safer, while in Yaroslavl, a bit of glasnost appears to have gotten into Sanders and his group. Footage from the trip played on WCAX: was that Bernie, shirtless at a long banquet table, doing vodka shots and belting out "This Land Is Your Land"?

I remember Peter Freyne's reaction in his Sneakers booth: "I have never once, in eight years, seen him have such fun in Burlington!" We were all a little jealous that the Soviet Union had brought out this loose, freewheeling Mayor Sanders.

37

"Give 'Em Hell"

(Sanders for Congress, Summer–Fall 1988)

Burlington Community Boathouse, summer 1988. *Vanguard Press*

One July afternoon in 1988, I headed down the steep slope of College Street, crossed Battery Street, and stepped onto the brand-new Burlington Community Boathouse. Burnouts played hacky sack on the lower deck; seagulls contended for a toddler's ice cream cone. Along the long dock-porch, an Adonis from Sailworks rented Sunfish for a few dollars, to anyone, without any kind of lesson, and so the harbor was full of bright capsized vessels and laughing, frustrated sailors. On the opposite end of the porch, the Burlington Dive Center offered scuba and snorkeling gear. I paid five dollars for three hours, snapped on a mask, snorkel, and fins, and set out to explore the habitat of the bony Lake Champlain perch, flashing among old bottles and tires in the breakwater.

When I resurfaced on the dock, dripping and squeaking, the first sight I beheld was Bernie Sanders standing nearby, shaking hands and passing out campaign literature. Toweled off, with my sneakers jammed under my armpit, I approached Bernie and gestured widely to the signs of human life and enjoyment surrounding us, as though to say, "Congratulations. Can you believe this?" He smiled a moment and took it all in. Then I got what most Burlingtonians had come to expect when running into Bernie: a slap on the back, warm but final, as though to say, "Our interaction has concluded." That my T-shirt was still damp from lakewater made the point of contact, and the moment, memorable.

As I could see from the materials that I carried away, Bernie '88 was a different sort of campaign. For one thing, here was an envelope, self-addressed to campaign headquarters at 209 College Street. Within that hectic upstairs room a paid staff processed donations from all around the country. "Money was pouring in," Jim Schumacher told me, "we were astounded. It kept us going. We were like, 'What's going to be in the mail today?'" The campaign manager, Rachel Levin, "hired someone just to open the mail, endorse the checks—big checks, like five hundred dollars, and get them to the bank." The hold on checks was in some cases a week in those days: the campaign was racing to make those funds available, to scale its operations in this, the twilight of analog politics. When a check cleared, the campaign raced to Laser Image, Burlington's first retail graphic design shop, mocked up a campaign flier, printed tens of thousands of copies, and loaded them into the bed of Schumacher's Toyota pickup for distribution across the state.

How many of those donations came from Vermont? Schumacher laughed: "Almost none." The Sanders campaign had found in Doug Boucher, an ecology professor at the University of Montreal, the architect of its direct mailing strategy. Boucher was an unlikely finance director. An adviser to the Nicaraguan Alliance, a Washington, D.C., advocacy group, Boucher likely had met Sanders in the lead-up to Bernie's 1985 visit to Managua. The nuttiest, riskiest stunt of Bernie's political career was now, three years later, paying a concrete dividend in the work of Boucher, who was networked across the nation with leftists who'd sought to join forces with Sanders since the first days after his 1981 victory. The Sanders files at the University of Vermont overflow with letters expressing solidarity from socialist organizers, Green Party officials, citizens' advocates, peace workers, and fellow-travelers from Bernie's Liberty Union years. And as Bernie's profile rose, though, well-positioned and influential figures on the left also monitored his career: people like I. F. Stone, the journalist and gadfly; Alice Walker, the novelist; Ed Asner, the actor; Danny Lyon, the legendary photographer who'd captured Bernie at the sit-in, in 1962; and Bernie's old friend from the campaign trail, the baby doctor Dr. Benjamin Spock.

In 1988, it was still a novelty to open a letter and be personally addressed—"Dear Dan," etc.—by Dr. Spock or Lou Grant from *The Mary Tyler Moore Show*. This magic trick was courtesy of a method called direct mail; its techniques, especially as they have migrated to the new technology of email, no longer cast any kind of spell. Direct mail had come of age in the 1970s as a political tool on the right, but had never been practiced by a Vermont political campaign before 1988. It required two things: an eye-catching name, and a list of the addresses of likely donors. When Bernie's campaign reached the octogenarian Dr. Spock in his Ozarks cabin, Spock cheerfully recalled the halcyon days of 1972, when he and Bernie traversed Vermont together. Spock was in; now the campaign needed addresses. "We bought *The Nation*'s list," Schumacher told me, "and stuffed envelopes, one at a time, in our office on College Street."

By 1988, the '60s diaspora had stranded leftists in professional careers across the country, fondly remembering their hippie days on campuses and in communes in places like Vermont. The irony of Bernie's fund-raising strength during the 1988 campaign is that he tapped into Reagan-era nostalgia for the barnstorming, hitchhiking campaigns, fruitless but noble, of his Liberty Union years—as well as Reagan-era prosperity. Levin, his campaign manager, was the daughter of Liberty Union activists. To reach the farms and state fairs of Vermont, Bernie plugged into this network of nostalgic leftists stationed in places like Omaha, Oakland, Portland, Maine, and Portland, Oregon. These donors were "repeat people": the better Bernie did, the more likely Bernie's supporters on the diasporic left would open their wallets a second or third time: "It kept us going," Schumacher said. "By the fall, we were able to do real advertising."

"SANDERS IN 1988 had a summer and fall most politicians can only dream of," Chris Graff wrote in *Dateline Vermont*. Bernie's fund-raising kept pace with his two main rivals, the Republican Smith and the Democrat, Poirier, a respected legislator and hockey dad from Barre who argued, even as Sanders passed him in the polls, that Bernie was a spoiler. In fact, Poirier was the spoiler, as Sanders kept saying, the near rhyme emphasized for effect. As Jim Schumacher's field operation of hundreds worked the creemee stands and country fairs, Bernie's radio and TV spots, highlighting his Burlington successes, became ubiquitous: "Bernie Sanders, Independent for Congress. For Once, a Voice for Real Change." A local songwriter, Bill Cleary, contributed a jingle so infectious that I can hum it now as I type its refrain: "We Are Sending Bernie Sanders to the Congress!" In several televised debates, Sanders benefited from the Vermont custom of including all candidates on the ballot, no matter how bizarre or obscure. If you worried that Vermont might squander its tiny share of congressional power on a political novelty, it helped that Sanders, looking sound and in command, shared the dais with eccentrics like the country barrister and nature poet Morris Earle of Vermont's "Small Is Beautiful" movement and, down at the end of the long table, Peter Diamondstone, Bernie's old mentor from Liberty Union, still arguing for the party's groovy platform of children's suffrage, the abolition of the military, and the legalization of cocaine. In these forums, Poirier weakly echoed Bernie's own stands; Smith, in trying to differentiate himself, kept inadvertently agreeing with his socialist rival. "Not again," Smith exclaimed, slapping his forehead.

The race attracted national attention. In early October, Harry Reasoner of the CBS program *60 Minutes* arrived in Burlington to profile Vermont's rising socialist phenomenon. Reasoner was known in network news circles for his seasoned reporting as well as his love of martinis. In Burlington for three days, the broadcast veteran found a suitable pour across from city hall, at B. T. McGuire's, where the Progressive Coalition had been born four years earlier over roast beef and beers. "After a hectic interview in Burlington's City Hall," Peter Freyne told readers of "Inside Track," Reasoner "drifted across the street for a little liquid refreshment—parched throat, you know." By midafternoon, Reasoner had attracted a crowd of fans to the bar, signing autographs and ordering rounds for his new Burlington friends. The veteran newsman normally slept off his lunch martinis on a metal cot stored in his network office. Without his cot, Reasoner did not take his customary siesta; and without his siesta, Reasoner was transformed into "one of the most companionable fellows I've ever known," as Morley Safer once said of his longtime colleague. By the time Sanders showed up to collect Reasoner, the bedlam had spilled onto Church Street, where, according to Freyne, "countless passersby stopped to greet the very familiar" Reasoner. The phrase "very familiar" was a considered touch.

Sanders seized the opportunity of the *60 Minutes* visit. As Paul Poirier fell in the polls, the Democrat had made a fatal error: Poirier withdrew his support for federal subsidies for Vermont's beleaguered dairy farmers. It was confounding; even Poirier had a hard time believing he'd said it. It appears that he simply choked. ("There is only one rule in Vermont politics," Richard Sugarman told me: "Praise the farmers.") So Sanders, accompanied by Reasoner and his crew, staged a last-minute press conference in front of a herd of Holsteins in Plainfield, near Goddard, to attack his opponent; then, at Reasoner's suggestion, they headed to Montpelier, where the two men executed a classic *60 Minutes*–style unannounced drop-in at the offices of the Vermont Bureau of the Associated Press.

With *60 Minutes* in tow, "I could expose the AP to the world," Sanders recalled in *Outsider in the House*. "It was delicious." Bernie wanted to know, "How come you never come to my press conferences?" Chris Graff, the AP bureau chief, bolted back from his lunch hour to find Sanders and the *60 Minutes* crew in his office. "It didn't faze me in the least that Bernie marched in that way," Graff told the *Rutland Herald*. "It's just what we expect from Bernie."

60 Minutes never ran the segment, but the showdown made headlines in Vermont, as new polls showed Bernie closing in on Peter Smith. When several prominent Vermont Democrats abandoned Poirier for Sanders, Bernie's Democratic rival scaled back his campaign, and was rumored to be preparing to drop out. The news of Bernie's surge reached the Democratic National Committee: with about four weeks to go, the Dukakis campaign abruptly suspended its voter drive in Vermont because of all the new Sanders voters they were inadvertently registering. Bernie was indignant. "I think it's pathetic," Sanders told a reporter. "I literally cannot understand why a candidate running for president of the United States is more worried about Bernie Sanders than he is about his desire to win."

With Dukakis's candidacy fizzling as he neared the finish line, Sanders now relished the opportunity to wash his hands of both Washington political parties. In September, the "diminutive governor of Massachusetts," as Dukakis was often called, had made perhaps the funniest campaign gaffe in American history, when, looking like a prairie dog popping up from its burrow, the governor, an enormous helmet accentuating his large head, posed in the belly of 68-ton M1A1 battle tank, and immediately fell behind—"tanked" was the low-hanging pun—in the polls. Sanders "was dying of laughter" and "couldn't get enough" of the Dukakis tank debacle. With the feckless Michael Dukakis and the cosseted George H. W. Bush exemplifying their parties' most loathed characteristics, Vermonters saw in Bernie their chance at independence.

Trouble Down South

Vermont's interstates run up the Connecticut River on the eastern border with New Hampshire, and then branch across the Green Mountains like forked lightning or a cursive Y. A four-lane divided highway planned along the state's western flank, connecting to Interstate 89 in Burlington, was never built; in the decade that it took the state to finally appropriate the funds, Vermont had become a leader in conservation, and the window for such projects had closed. When activists sued the highway department in 1972, they found in the local judge a sympathetic rhapsode. "In wildness is the preservation of the world," Judge James J. Oakes intoned, quoting

Thoreau: the "little limestone hill" that conservationists sued to protect was "covered with basil and marjoram and creeping thyme, with columbine and yellow ragwort in dramatic abundance." An ancient byway, Route 7, was thereafter developed piecemeal, and much of it remains a slow, two-lane road wending through farmland and village centers. Southwestern Vermont is closer to the rest of the world, tracking along the New York border, but seems farther from the rest of Vermont. Geologically, this region is New York State: its mountains are part of the Taconic Range, and its wealth lay in the slate beds that straddle both sides of the border. In the fall of 1988, the region seemed especially remote from Burlington, and stubbornly impervious to the charms of the man that the *Rutland Herald* condemned as a "political curiosity" overseeing a "garbage can" of a city.

When internal polling showed Bernie "really struggling in southern Vermont," Jim Schumacher "camped out" in the working-class city of Rutland, but the microculture of the region proved hard to breach, and the campaign office hard to staff. With two weeks to go, Schumacher found himself at a kind of rave in Montreal—a "dance thing, a building-was-shaking kind of thing"—where he met fifteen or so strobe-lit Quebecois leftists willing to come to Rutland and volunteer across southern Vermont. It was unlikely that these Canadian ravers ("prone to lunch breaks") would win over the rural poor or the working people of Rutland, Springfield, and Bennington, but the Sanders campaign needed bodies. When a local physician offered his prop plane to shuttle Sanders between Burlington and Bennington, Bernie hopped on board and "became a fixture in the southern part of the state."

There, an old friend, now a bitter foe, had been expecting him. As the race's one resident of southern Vermont, Peter Diamondstone knew Sanders was struggling in his neck of the woods, and stepped up his attacks on his former comrade. In the years since Diamondstone had traversed the state in a VW Beetle covered in enigmatic slogans, an unruly Saint Bernard riding shotgun, his true-believer persona had changed only fractionally: he now drove a VW Rabbit, and the hand-scrawled graffiti covering his latest jalopy now targeted Sanders. Spray-painted letters spelled out, "Bernie Is a Quisling!" as well as such slogans as "Lettuce Is Murder." Diamondstone's method was to park this attention-grabbing vehicle on Main Streets across southern Vermont, wherever Sanders was due, and stand beside it, cheerfully fielding questions like "What is a quisling?" and "Why is lettuce murder?" from curious passersby. (A quisling is a traitor; commercial lettuce is farmed with pesticides.) When Diamondstone baited Sanders to attend a televised debate, Bernie turned up to find only Diamondstone in the studio, and vanished out the rear door. For years now, Diamondstone had trailed Bernie across the state, heckling and taunting him. Now Diamondstone, praising Peter Smith as the "true radical," even as Smith hosted Gerald Ford for a fund-raiser at the Ramada Inn, was intent on checking Bernie's momentum. At the margins, this relentless performance-art politics might have made a difference: the major southern papers ran stories on Diamondstone's Main Street installations, with photos of the street-corner radical proselytizing beside his derelict Rabbit.

AS ELECTION DAY APPROACHED, a refrain could be heard across Vermont. "I think he'll give 'em hell," a dockworker in Grand Isle said, while knotting a line. "I think Bernie will raise a lot of hell," a Barre quarry worker told the *Rutland Herald*. A second granite worker chimed in: Bernie would "give us a little leverage" in Washington, he said. At Sneakers, as I checked in the cases of eggs one November morning at five thirty, I noted that the egg farmer, Mr. Gadue, wore a "Bernie '88" pin for his morning rounds. "Give 'em hell," the farmer said, in response to my thumbs-up. Peter Smith couldn't find a worksite in the state that was safe to visit with the cameras rolling: in Barre, the sight of Smith, in khakis and a chamois, provoked several workers to pledge their vote for Sanders. Smith's attempts to shame Sanders for raising "out-of-state money"—some 70 percent of Bernie's donations came from his network of diasporic leftists—also failed. "Nothing was working," Garrison Nelson told me. "People just wanted to send Bernie to Washington." Sanders's old adviser David Clavelle put it this way: "People vote their gut. It's ideology, but it's also emotion. It involves trust. It involves charisma. If there's any ideology, it's that 'He's here for me.'"

Little Vermont just "wants to be heard," Peter Freyne wrote. "It seems like Ol' Bernardo is the megaphone of the moment." As Jim Schumacher and his volunteers swarmed every on-ramp and rotary south of Rutland, Bernie spent Election Day mainly in Chittenden County, where 25 percent of the state's voters resided, and where he hoped to gain nearly 50 percent of the vote. A band of working-class towns along the Connecticut River looked to be in play for Bernie, even as Paul Poirier, hoping to sweep his home city of Barre, fought hard to stem Bernie's momentum in a community where socialist dances and raffles and picnics of the 1920s were still fondly remembered among the old quarry workers. The farmers of the Northeast Kingdom had adopted the Brooklyn Jew as one of their own, while Peter Smith, the small-government Republican who had forged his political persona in their image, stumbled. In Franklin County and Grand Isle County, where French was heard in the supermarkets and laundromats, Sanders had the edge. But the signal was jammed south of Rutland, where the Bush signs outnumbered Dukakis placards "probably 2–1." Sanders knew he could count on some Bush voters splitting their votes; but to sway enough of them would take a miracle.

The polls closed at seven p.m., and Bernie's supporters looked around in horror as they streamed into the Election Night party: What had happened to Hunt's? The mellow, scuffed venue, site of Bernie's 1983 victory party and the incubator of Burlington's music scene, home to Pinhead, the Decentz, Lambsbread, and Phish, had been bought by a pair of Rhode Island DJs and converted into a 1950s-themed nightclub, Sha-na-na's. The honeyed wood floors were now tiled in shiny black and white; a '57 Chevy gleamed in one corner, and the buxom waitresses wore their hair like Lucille Ball. The cultural upheavals and revolutionary politics of the '60s, the era whose ideals had birthed Burlington's progressive movement, had been purged entirely from the space. None of it ever happened. As Bernie's supporters hollered and cheered, the stereo played Bill Haley and His Comets. Some of Sha-na-na's usual Tuesday patrons arrived, expecting the weekly hula-hoop contest, while their husbands smoked outside, leaning on their finned Chevys and Fords. Inside this ersatz sock hop, Sanders and his ponytailed, beaded, bearded, braided supporters looked like creatures from some *Star Trek* planet or interlopers from an alternate reality whose timeline had crossed into the cotton candy and motor oil world of Sha-na-na's.

As the first results from Burlington rolled in, the crowd erupted: Sanders was way up in all of the city's Democratic strongholds. WCAX had Bernie ahead by ten points at eight forty-five, but Jim Schumacher was driving some bad news north. Setting out from Bennington and "stopping along the way at every little radio station" to collect the local results, Schumacher knew that Sanders "had gotten his clock cleaned" in southern Vermont. In Bennington, Smith was up by a thousand votes. In Manchester, Smith's totals doubled Bernie's. In Dorset, in Dover, in Pawlet, Smith extended his lead by hundreds and hundreds of votes. Sanders did not take a single town along the Route 7 corridor south of Middlebury. He had lost Bennington County by 30 percent. At ten thirty, Schumacher arrived in Burlington with the bleak totals. At ten forty-five, Sanders took the mic at Sha-na-na's, standing in front of the '57 Chevy, and uttered the words politicians use when they've narrowly lost: "I think we're going to have a long night ahead of us." Looking "exhausted, disappointed, crushed," Bernie offered some perspective: "What we have done is historical. We have raised the issues no one else would raise. We had to put our whole movement together from scratch. It's not easy changing the world."

Sanders canceled his morning flight to LaGuardia and called off a rendezvous with Jane Pauley on the *Today* show. At 1:05 a.m., Bernie conceded.

"I admire you," Peter Smith told him. "You've run a beautiful race." The final tally was Smith, 42 percent, Sanders, 39 percent, Poirier, 16 percent.

BERNIE'S "primary mode is repetition, not variation," Fintan O'Toole wrote in *The New York Review of Books*. But Sanders, "the outstanding entrepreneur of our time," knew that change hides inside repetition. What was historic, if not "historical," about Bernie's narrow, three-point loss to an appealing, progressive, talented Republican in a solidly Republican state? Sanders visited the same town halls and county fairs where he'd campaigned in 1971, 1972, 1974, 1976, and 1986. He said the same kinds of things, in the same pitch, in many of the same clothes, altering his approach only at the extremes. His totals in those elections tell the tale: 1 percent, 2 percent, 4 percent, 6 percent, 15 percent, 39 percent. That trend represents significant variation emerging inside of apparent repetition. Expressed as an SAT problem, the next term in the sequence would certainly be north of 50 percent. Repetition is how we measure change. What changes—in Bernie, in Vermont—did the 1988 near miss reveal?

"Ideology has replaced party," Garrison Nelson argued. "Sanders has demonstrated there is a substantial progressive ideology in Vermont." To Eric Davis, a political scientist at Middlebury College, the hard lessons awaited Vermont Democrats: "The established Democratic structure is so weak that the Rainbow Coalition could move in and take over the Democratic Party." Many Democrats agreed. The Vermont House speaker, Ralph Wright, once a bitter opponent, conceded: "Maybe at some point what the Democrats have got to say is 'All right, Bernie, we've got to stop this. We're going to embrace you and back you, and we want you to run against Peter in two years.'" The *Burlington Free Press* called it "a sad fate for the party of Lyndon Johnson and Franklin Roosevelt."

For their part, Vermont Republicans "despaired in their victory," Garrison Nelson told me. "Peter Smith's days in politics were almost certainly numbered," even as the young congressman-elect packed up and headed to Washington. Vermont's "Republican hegemony," eroding since at least 1974, had now been washed nearly completely away; granite-ribbed hill country Republicans found in supporting the Brooklyn socialist an unlikely expression of their ornery anti-government streak. Farmers in Hardwick, Wolcott, Greensboro, and Woodbury kept their "Bernie '88" signs up through the winter, a spot of bright red visible in the banks of drifting snow.

River Rat

(Mayor Clavelle Takes Over the People's Republic, 1989)

Nov. 24, 1971

Nov. 2, 1976

Dec. 6, 1982

June 8, 1982

Oct. 4, 1988

Through the years

• Sept. 8, 1941: Bernard Sanders is born in Brooklyn, N.Y.

• 1964: Sanders graduates from the University of Chicago with a bachelor's degree in political science.

• Jan. 7, 1972: Sanders is the Liberty Union candidate in a special election for U.S. Senate. "As for my qualifications, I am not a politician," Sanders says. He gets 1,571 votes, or 2 percent.

• Nov. 7, 1972: Sanders is the Liberty Union candidate for governor. He gets 2,175 votes, or 1 percent.

• Nov. 5, 1974: Sanders is the Liberty Union candidate for U.S. Senate. He gets 5,901 votes.

• Nov. 2, 1976: Sanders is the Liberty Union candidate for governor. He receives 11,317 votes.

• March 3, 1981: Sanders beats five-term incumbent Gordon Paquette by 10 votes and becomes mayor of Burlington.

• March 1, 1983: Sanders wins re-election with 52 percent of the vote.

• March 5, 1985: Sanders is re-elected mayor with 55 percent of the vote.

• Nov. 4, 1986: Sanders runs for governor and wins 15 percent of the vote.

• March 3, 1987: Sanders is re-elected mayor with 55 percent of the vote.

• May 28, 1988: Sanders marries Youth Office Director Jane Driscoll in a public ceremony at North Beach.

• Nov. 8, 1988: Sanders is an independent candidate for the U.S. House. He wins 38 percent of the vote, 3 percent less than Republican winner Peter Smith.

Sanders records folk songs in 1987

Sanders celebrates his first victory in 1981

Sanders pitches for a City Hall softball team

The mayor accompanies Burlington children to Disney World in 1988

All photos from Free Press files

The Free Press looks back on the Sanders Years, 1989.

The People's Republic of Winooski

In March of 2024, I met Peter Clavelle, Bernie's successor and the longest-serving mayor in Burlington's history, in the parking lot behind Winooski's city hall, a squat, modern brick building constructed on the site where Clavelle's father and uncle once ran a small market and after-hours political club. Clavelle is a shy man of medium build, known since childhood as "Moonie" for his round face and enormous, accommodating smile. As we drove through his old neighborhood, Clavelle pointed to several small frame houses where he and his family had lived. The nineteenth-century homes here are updated in Easter-egg colors of yellow, white, and baby-blue aluminum siding. Many share their small plots with a metal swing set, a boat, or an aboveground pool. Shade is scarce on these blocks where there is more asphalt than grass, but this is Winooski's middle-class neighborhood, where firemen and shopkeepers once raised enormous families: five children, eight children, "fifteen children, can you believe that?" Clavelle marveled, pointing to a modest colonial.

The residents of "p'tit Canada" now share these streets with refugee families resettled in Winooski since the 1980s. Many of these new Americans, arriving here from Laos, the Congo, Afghanistan, Vietnam, Somalia, Vietnam, and Nepal, followed the path laid out by the Quebecois: by moving here, they have entered the middle class. We passed the elementary school a block or so away, where 46 percent of the students are multilingual. The hallway chatter blends English, Somali, Nepali, Swahili, Rundi, French, and Lingala. The corner stores sell momos, lassi, and fermented cassava. This city of 7,400 is home to nearly 2,000 refugees, who work as dental hygienists, bus drivers, nurses, machinists, entrepreneurs, and teachers. A quiet civic experiment transformed Winooski over thirty years, while, rising on the steep banks across the river, the city of Burlington hogged the limelight.

"We went over there to get school clothes, that's about it," Peter told me. Burlington was a "completely different place" for the "river rats" of Winooski, Vermont's most densely settled square mile. And yet this hardscrabble city, the center of Democratic politics in Vermont, has been exporting talented politicians to Burlington for decades. The childhood home of Francis Cain, Burlington's mayor in the 1960s, faces Clavelle's. Down the street is George Thabault's childhood home. David Clavelle's is nearby. These Winooski Blue Dog Democrats have worked both in and out of the Democratic Party over the years, but they played pivotal roles in Bernie's rise. An arguable point: when the Brooklyn socialist met the Winooski Democrats, Burlington's progressivism was the result.

Peter Clavelle's upbringing resembled in some respects Bernie and Larry Sanders's life in Midwood, Brooklyn: Clavelle's father "worked as many as four jobs" at one time to support the family's modest needs. His parents, like Bernie's, "revered Franklin Roosevelt" and saw an ambitious, activist government as essential to their lives. Like Brooklyn, Winooski lost much of its old housing stock and community infrastructure to federal urban renewal, as its displaced residents looked on in fear and horror. In both of these immigrant communities, the church or synagogue offered a formal script for life's milestones—bar mitzvahs, First Communions—and supplied a web of connections among families bound by faith, and by FDR.

But the differences between the two places are at least as salient, and they explain, in a way, the differences between a rocket like Sanders and a rock like Clavelle. Midwood was a place of great social mobility and optimism: as families rose in economic power, they tended to leave. But when Clavelle was a Winooski kid "collecting frogs, roaming around in the woods," his community's poverty rate hovered around 25 percent. "When the mills closed, it was the beginning of the disintegration of the city of Winooski," Clavelle said. The city settled into a decades-long depression. Bernie Sanders left Brooklyn more or less for good after one year at Brooklyn College. Peter Clavelle, the native who was called back home to become city manager at the age of twenty-five, helped to turn Winooski around.

"Never thought I'd make it over the river," Clavelle told me as we drove across the Winooski Bridge. On either side of us stood the mill buildings where our ancestors had gone to work as young teenagers before the First World War, buildings that, in the 1970s, Clavelle and his colleagues at the Winooski Development Corporation had revitalized. The conversion of the Winooski mills became the blueprint for Burlington's own industrial transformation. As we toured Burlington's streets, passing one converted industrial site after another, Clavelle told me that he knew how to get the federal grants, but he also knew, going back to Little League and high school, the local developers and contractors and small businesspeople who could make those projects a reality. These were not "Bernie people," Clavelle said, but the Community and Economic Development Office had the federal matching monies to bring the city's business class to the table. Once Clavelle had their attention, CEDO would broker innovative trades. If a developer wanted the federal cash, well then, the city wanted a few acres of green space, or a few extra units of affordable housing, in return. The "community" items and the "economic" items in CEDO's portfolio thereby advanced in lockstep together. Little by little, block by block, the river rat transformed the big city across the way.

Lessons that Clavelle had learned in Winooski guided his work in Burlington. As its federal projects advanced, Winooski's mill district became a draw for tourists and young professionals, but the "Winooski Renaissance" left the poor behind. In the 1980s, at Sneakers on Main Street in Winooski, I worked beside a man in his sixties named Kenny, whose home for much of the year was an encampment by the Winooski lower falls. When Kenny was late to work, one of us would scramble down the boulders under the Winooski Bridge and rouse him. I figured a day would come when we would find him dead. Kenny had originally fallen into despair after the mills closed and his tenement was razed. For decades he'd done stints as a dishwasher in the small dives along Main Street, spending his day's wages that night on cigarettes and whiskey. His life had played out entirely in these few Winooski blocks; like many in his generation, he was a part of the story of the city's decline, but not of its revitalization. Sneakers, where our boss John, a brusque, warmhearted Navy veteran, had more or less adopted him, was Kenny's only real share in the Winooski Renaissance. Clavelle had seen people like Kenny jettisoned by progress as "an entire culture vanished, language vanished, traditions collapsed" in his home city. The new Americans on Winooski's streets and playgrounds testified to the community's bright future, but few here remembered its past.

"A city needs a moral vision," Clavelle said. "Sanders was a moral visionary, articulating the goals, the moral goals, of the community," Clavelle said of the man he "doesn't consider a friend, exactly, in the sense of calling each other up, or going out for beers." But a city like Burlington also needs a local face to implement the nuts and bolts of that "moral vision." It would be hard to find someone less radical seeming than "Moonie" Clavelle, who speaks slowly in a Quebecois dialect and accent preserved from the days when his grandparents fed the looms. I slipped into the hometown accent, too, as we got to know each other. As Clavelle and I drove by my childhood home, we compared stories of the Sisters of Mercy we'd both had in school, one generation apart. As mayor, Clavelle would sometimes get letters in city hall from these nuns, cheering him on or scolding him. After a public health event where Clavelle distributed free condoms, the mayor received a polite reprimand on Sisters of Mercy letterhead.

After a tour of the waterfront, Peter Clavelle and I sat down at the Formica horseshoe counter of Handy's Lunch, a Burlington favorite since 1945: pine paneling, a mounted Rossignol ski, scrumptious burgers and chili dogs served in plastic baskets. Earl Handy, the diner's charismatic third-generation proprietor and head cook, greeted Clavelle warmly: "Mr. Mayor! You came out of retirement!" Before long, Handy and Clavelle were discussing the design of a front window deemed out of code by the outgoing mayor, the Democrat Miro Weinberger, and his

"Jake," holding an onion in the Onion City, by Dan Higgins

Dan Higgins and Jake, Winooski. *Dan Higgins*

building inspector. "I showed up one morning and it was shattered," Earl told Peter, "so I went to Lowe's and replaced it. Next thing I know, I get a notice from the city in the mail. They drove by, took a picture, and issued me a citation. We've been operating in this city for eighty years! Come in, sit down, have a patty melt and fries, and discuss it with me." Clavelle shook his head and exhaled a deep sigh. "Wouldn't have happened under this guy," Handy said, his hand on Mayor Clavelle's shoulder.

The Soviets Invade

In October of 1988, with Bernie's congressional campaign racing toward the finish, the apparatchiks of Yaroslavl arrived in Burlington to sign the papers on our sister-city arrangement and to sample the benefits of American free enterprise, Burlington-style. Terry Bouricius, who spoke "passable Russian," seized the opportunity to make "болтовня"—small talk—with the Soviets on their way to Ben & Jerry's. The Soviet delegation toured the UVM Medical Center, the shops of Church Street, the CEDO-funded industrial conversions of Pine Street, the Community Boathouse, and the waterfront. The Soviets loved these photo-ops with ice cream cones, pancakes, and baseball hats, and, through an interpreter, praised Burlington's "variety of goods" and "quality of medical equipment," even as they vigorously defended their own "society, way of life, and culture." At a mini summit in city hall, Sanders was statesmanlike as he passed the Cross pen to Yaroslavl's mayor, Aleksandr Ryabkov, to sign the "treaty" connecting their two communities. Sanders then "read aloud from the golden-sealed document," Debbie Bookchin reported, and presented the Soviet mayor with a best-selling coffee table book, *A Day in the Life of America*. In return, Ryabkov "presented the city with a hand-carved wooden bear" and, leaning in as though to hear the bear's whispered secrets, told Burlington, "He is inviting all the citizens of Burlington, all the citizens of Vermont, to the city of Yaroslavl." The crowd applauded, and then the bear delivered his final insinuation, in a distinctly Cold War accent: "He says, 'We will be very happy to take you in.'"

Why would Burlingtonians want to defect to the Soviet Union? In the fall of 1988, after Bernie rebuffed an effort to draft him for a fifth term, the mayor's potential successors lined up to inherit a thriving, dynamic city, near its historic peak of prosperity and appeal. Burlington boasted among the lowest unemployment rates in the country, and was chosen in several national surveys as America's "Most Livable City." Dizzy Gillespie, strolling down Church Street on his 1988 visit to Burlington, beamed, "This is America?" Did Yaroslavl have the Beansie's Bus or Al's French Frys? In Yaroslavl, was there a local Cajun restaurant like ours, Bourbon Street Grill, that would serve Xingu Brazilian beers to high school juniors, just minutes after the dismissal bell rang? To a country mouse like Joe Sherman, Burlington had become a "dreamy, ethereal" place:

> Maybe it was the altitude, or the sunsets over the Lake, or the High Peaks of the Adirondacks rising to the West. Burlington had the allure, particularly to urban types. City blocks, cafés, and festivals reminded them a little of back home.

My friend George and I, seventeen, drunk, and flirting with the waitress on a September Tuesday, our stomachs full of pitch-black Amazonian beer, were not even considering defecting to the Soviet Union!

The progressives would now learn whether their entire movement was simply the "manifestation of one person's charisma," Garrison Nelson told me. Terry Bouricius positioned himself on the left, and reached out to the activist and peace communities; Jonathan Leopold, who enjoyed the support of the city's business class, offered himself up as the more "conservative" choice still within the Progressive Coalition. Peter Clavelle was the wild card. If "charisma" was required to spruce up progressive politics, Clavelle, whom the *Free Press* described as "sleepy" and "a mumbler," was doomed. As CEDO director, Clavelle's presentations to the city conveyed all the passion of a high school geography class taught by the football coach. In interviews, Clavelle sometimes seemed to drift away, as though back in the Winooski mud looking for tadpoles. It was hard to identify his natural base. Some in the business community saw him as Bernie 2, "but worse," as one banker said: "With Bernie you know where you stand." On the left, the Greens remembered him as the losing-side cheerleader for the Alden waterfront plan. And he was happy in his current job: dozens of new projects at CEDO were shovel ready. Not to mention, as he told CCTV, he "had three kids at home, the oldest being four years old."

But Peter Clavelle's record was hard to dismiss. His "hunters and gatherers" at CEDO had brought home some six thousand new jobs, matching local investors and federal dollars, and created hundreds of units of affordable housing, without raising property taxes. All of Pine Street now smelled pleasantly of cocoa from the new headquarters of Lake Champlain Chocolates, in the renovated Maltex building. The old Vermont Maid Syrup building—Satan invented fake maple syrup here in the 1920s—became a funky vintage store. Jogging on the bike path past the boathouse, you were in a world CEDO had created. Clavelle's reach could be felt even on Johnson Street, where elderly residents for years had locked themselves inside their efficiency units, while the narrow lane hosted late-night open-air dogfights. The dogs yelped and writhed in agony, and their handlers threatened to assault the old ladies if they snitched. By paving the street and planting trees, the city suddenly had a presence on Johnson Street. The Johnson Street Revitalization Project became the model for tiny enclaves facing scary problems throughout Burlington. Clavelle's figures were impressive; but more impressive, the sedate bureaucrat, whom *Newsweek* introduced to the world as "balding, paunchy, and colorless," was a hero on Johnson Street.

IN LATE NOVEMBER, Debbie Bookchin encountered Bernie Sanders in city hall, "in relaxation mode" after a week's Florida vacation. Feet up on the mayor's desk, sporting a yellow oxford shirt, Sanders reflected on a poll showing that 60 percent of Burlingtonians wanted him to run again for reelection. "I'm not running," Sanders told Bookchin. "I've clearly made my mark on the city." Since 1971, Sanders had endured ten elections, including six in the past eight years: "That's a lot of elections. I think it's appropriate to take a break." Sanders had been telling friends he hoped to "teach, write, and study" in his time away from politics.

The mayor continued: "In the politics I believe in, you just don't want one person dominating the political scene." Bernie refused to be "a kingmaker," and pledged to "knock his brains out" supporting the choice of the Progressive Coalition, which would caucus on December 8. Now that Burlington had "seen the difference with what progressive government can do, its responsiveness and its ability to fight for ordinary people," the people of the city did not "want to go back." Bernie echoed the inspiring sentiments he'd expressed at his first inauguration in 1981: his government had led a "rebirth in the human spirit in the largest city in the most beautiful state." Burlington hadn't yet "changed the world," but Sanders promised that his "political revolution" was on the way.

The next day, Peter Clavelle addressed a crowd of 250 jammed into the upper deck of the Community Boathouse, announcing his candidacy for mayor of the city of Burlington. "This election is a referendum on progressive government," Clavelle told his supporters. His script echoed Debbie Bookchin's interview with Sanders, which had appeared in that morning's *Rutland Herald*. But there was an important difference: "If I am nominated," Clavelle told a crowd that included his parents, holding their squirming grandchildren, "the progressives will be in the unique position of fielding the native-son candidate." Clavelle recalled his childhood in a home without hot water, the trials of his grandparents in the Winooski mills, and the efforts of his dad, "Old Moonie here, next to the balloons," to provide for Clavelle and his siblings. "Half of the people in this room are family," Clavelle joked. "Too bad most of them don't vote in Burlington." The situation was indeed "unique," because this "native son" stood to command what many in the old-guard working-class communities still called "Bernie's Army" of occupying leftists. French Canadians like Sadie White and Dick Sartelle had been a part of Bernie's winning coalition. Now the river rat, rising along ancient political paths branching toward the new routes cut by Sanders and his allies, stood atop the Progressive Coalition.

Clavelle ran unopposed at the December 8 caucuses, but Mayor Sanders stole the show. Bernie was now in "city upon a hill" mode, Nelson said, referring to the language that Ronald Reagan had co-opted from the first governor of the Massachusetts Bay Colony, John Winthrop. "We are a symbol of hope," Sanders said, "that ordinary people can come together in a democratic manner, develop an agenda and together can stand up to the big money interests dominating America's politics." The crowd rose to its feet as Bernie concluded: "We believe in the brotherhood and the sisterhood of all people. We believe that men, women, and children can come together in relationships that are not based on greed, exploitation, and domination—but on love, cooperation, and mutual respect." Rising to accept the Progressive Coalition's nomination, a low-key Clavelle addressed the elephant in the room: "You know that I am not Bernie Sanders. I'm Peter Clavelle. I'm different from Bernie in style, temperament, and my roots are different. Our accents are different, our hairlines are a bit different. Bernie has two ties," Clavelle said, pausing for the laughter to subside: "I have three."

The election was "about what Burlington is going to be in the '90s,"

Nelson told the *Free Press*. Clavelle's opponents, the Green Party activist Sandy Baird and the Democrat Nancy Cioffi, who also secured the support of the city's Republicans, enjoyed some advantages right out of the blocks. Baird was a litigator by profession, brilliant, impassioned, and supported by a well-funded activist network. Her radical environmental and human rights agenda might tempt a city ever poised to bank left. Cioffi's advantage was more tangible: she and her husband ran a delightful retail store, Apple Mountain, that drew shoppers to the top block of Church Street with its inventory of Levi's, flannel pajamas, maple candy, Champ T-shirts, and Bernie Sanders souvenirs. Apple Mountain sold Bernie's Burlington to the wider world: if you'd spent the day on the Marketplace and wanted to return home with a memento, your Bernie bobblehead awaited you there. Why did Cioffi, who served also as the Democratic alderwoman from Ward 5, want "fundamental change" in a city that had benefited her store and her family? Cioffi and her husband, Bob, had moved to Burlington during Bernie's second term, after "falling in love with the city," she said. Late in the campaign, Cioffi disclosed that she and her husband had written checks to support Bernie's 1986 gubernatorial race.

Baird and Cioffi were tough candidates, probably more formidable than any Sanders had faced in his own mayoral campaigns. In debates, Cioffi, a Wellesley College graduate and gifted raconteur, tied Clavelle in knots over tiny inconsistencies, as Baird prosecuted her case against the city's human rights and environmental record. Clavelle, a man of many layers, seemed to search deeper than necessary for the simple response, and to get lost on his way back to the surface. But Cioffi, who was just too new in town to know where the trip wires might be, offended one of the city's most powerful Democrats when she criticized his business for its recycling practices. As her attacks on Clavelle became more personal—she seemed to imply that he'd left Winooski under the cloud of scandal, calling him "soft on drugs"—public sentiment began to turn against her. Even though Cioffi sold maple candy and tie-dyed "I Love Vermont" T-shirts, she failed to absorb an important rule of Vermont politics: Do nothing that the opponent can characterize as "negative campaigning." And yet, in January, the race was still a dead heat between Cioffi and Clavelle, "a candidate with a personality and no record and a candidate with a record and no personality," as Garrison Nelson put it.

In late December of 1988, the political winds began to blow toward city hall from the New North End, where some thirteen hundred Burlingtonians lived at Northgate, a subsidized townhome complex abutting the lake shore. At Handy's Lunch, Peter Clavelle told me about the "very, very unique arrangement" that saved those families. Northgate's developers, Fairfield Associates of Connecticut, had financed the complex in the late 1960s with low-interest loans from the federal Department of Housing and Urban Development. The instrument that created Northgate, though, also spelled its demise. Once the twenty-year HUD mortgages were settled, Donald Tarinelli of Fairfield Associates, who had gone on to buy Haystack Mountain Ski Resort and develop the flimsy vacation village at its base, was free to convert his 336 units to condos and sell them on the open market. You could skip a stone in Lake Champlain from the back porch of your Northgate apartment: with Burlington's high-end real estate booming, time was running out for these homes, which contributed one-quarter of all the affordable housing units in the city. Northgate was designed "to fall apart," Clavelle said, once its mortgage expired. But it remained a desirable option, one of the few in the city, for low-income people. "There was no way we were losing those units," Clavelle said, while munching Handy's Wednesday special of grilled chicken and mortadella. "It probably would have cost you the election," I suggested. Clavelle nodded, while continuing to destroy his sandwich. His political future, and the future of the Progressive Coalition, passed straight through the Northgate deal.

In early January of 1989, a flare went up. From slopeside, Don Tarinelli, who had harassed his tenants for years with threats of eviction, announced drastic rent increases at Northgate, intended to empty out most of the units for quick renovation and sale. Sanders, in his last important action as mayor of Burlington, brought a fight years in the making to the absentee slumlord ensconced in his faraway ski chalet. The board of aldermen voted unanimously to use every measure to oppose the rent increase. The city threw its support behind a nonprofit tenants' group attempting to buy Northgate. Sanders roared and raged and condemned the developers, backed by the entire city. Clavelle, along with Brenda Torpy, a Burlington housing administrator who went on to lead the city's land trust, put together the pieces. On March 4, three days before Election Day, the Vermont Housing and Conservation Board pledged $3.1 million to the tenants' group, Northgate Non-Profit, to be augmented with a HUD loan of $2 million and money from several private investors, for a total deal of more than $20 million. Clavelle had coordinated this intricate financing package to preserve the largest affordable housing complex in the state, with Patrick Leahy working in Washington to pry money out of his Republican friend, HUD Secretary Jack Kemp. The sum also paid for improvements to windows, foundations, roofs, and appliances in these units long neglected by design. A playground blossomed when the ground thawed in May. "If you dream it, as they say . . ." Clavelle chuckled, quoting Kevin Costner.

While the Northgate deal came together, Sanders and Clavelle received

Sanders congratulates Peter Clavelle.
Burlington Free Press

another political windfall. In December 1988, executives from the Central Vermont Railway had begun to lobby Burlington aldermen individually with a go-for-broke, last-ditch scheme for their disputed parcel on the waterfront: 2 marinas, a hotel, a 150-seat restaurant, 500 condominiums, 1,700 parking spaces, and 55,000 square feet of office space. Gene Bergman, alderman from Ward 2, met them for lunch. "They stated explicitly that they would rather not deal with the mayor or Peter Clavelle," Bergman said. In the evenings, the railway executives dangled their plans before hand-selected groups of Burlington contractors, merchants, and attorneys, over prime rib and Châteauneuf-du-Pape at the Ice House, while gazing out on Perkins Pier and the Burlington breakwater. Burlington's city attorney, Joseph McNeil, called the plans "a proposed settlement"; but a "settlement" pursued secretly, in violation of the city's code of conduct, seemed to many in city hall to be something more nefarious. "Why don't they just bring a suitcase of hundreds!" Sanders was heard to exclaim.

"Let's have some daylight," Bernie told the aldermen: rather than chase these cartoon barons out of town, the city invited the Central Vermont Railway to come out of the shadows and present their illegal scheme to the board in January. The railway executives rushed right into the trap. On January 18, the *Burlington Free Press* tattled on its own advertiser, which had arrived in town "armed with wall-sized drawings and colorful brochures—inserted in today's editions of The Free Press at a cost of 2,300 dollars." Bergman censured the rail company for "a subversion of democracy." John Franco accused the executives of "trying to create a psychological climate whereby the expectation is the city and state will lose the public trust suit." Sandy Baird called the plans "a moral abomination." Clavelle and Sanders coordinated a cooler response: "The city of Burlington strongly believes that the land belongs to the citizens of Vermont," Bernie said. Clavelle agreed: "Until this very basic ownership question is resolved, it's impossible to seriously entertain this proposal." The judgment of the Vermont

Supreme Court was still months away, but now that the railway executives had telegraphed their intention to defy the will of the people and destroy the most precious parcel of land in the state of Vermont, their odds of a favorable verdict "became next to nil," Clavelle told me.

UNITED AGAINST THE Northgate developers and the waterfront raiders, Burlingtonians went to the polls on March 7, 1989, in below-zero temperatures, to elect Peter Clavelle as their mayor. The margin rivaled that of Bernie's biggest victories, 55 percent for Clavelle, 44 percent for Nancy Cioffi, and just 3.5 percent for the passionate leftist, Sandy Baird. The progressive experiment was now in the hands of Moonie Clavelle, the standout guard for the Rice Memorial High School football team and erstwhile Winooski bartender. "A party guy, always a big party guy," George Thabault told me. He didn't mean political parties, but the talk in Burlington had turned to forming a statewide Progressive Party on the near horizon, in time to support a 1990 rematch between Bernie and Peter Smith for U.S. Congress. "What happened today was not the election of Peter Clavelle as mayor," Clavelle told his supporters, "today was a referendum on progressive government, and we won it!" Bernie then took the stage, agreeing that today's victory was not merely, or not entirely, Clavelle's: "We took on not just the Democratic Party, not just the Republican Party, but both of them combined," Sanders said. It was "a message to the entire United States of America," that Burlington progressivism "is not just a one-man show—it's a movement."

The next morning Peter Clavelle got his usual black coffee across from city hall, at the Red Onion, and greeted well-wishers. "Balding, paunchy, colorless," he laughed, as an old neighbor shook his hand. Strolling up Church Street with an Associated Press reporter, the world's second-most-powerful elected progressive remarked, "I love Vermont. I'll live here all my life. I'm a basic woodchuck." The reporter reminded him that Burlington was Vermont's largest city. "I'm an urban woodchuck," Clavelle replied.

Farewell Address

Toward the end, George Thabault told me, Sanders would say to him, "Pinch me, George. You have to pinch me, George. I can't believe I'm the mayor of this city." Bernie's young assistant loved these retrospective moments when "Sanders let his hair down a little," and talked openly about his life and career. Their colleagues from that time still speak of the "unusually warm and trusting, even easygoing" relationship that Sanders and Thabault shared. Bernie laughed with George about his quixotic battles, and the "ups and downs of his relentless personality" in the "amazing, amazing city" that "welcomed him, tolerated him, took an interest in his ideas, didn't write him off."

I headed to Contois Auditorium on April 3, 1989, to witness the swearing-in of Peter Clavelle and to hear Bernie's farewell tribute to the city. The Bernie Sanders that addressed us that evening was very much in "Pinch me" mode. "This will shock people," Sanders began, "but I'm not sure what I can say." He praised his colleagues on the board of aldermen, the city commissioners, and the members of his administration. But "his highest praise," Debbie Bookchin wrote, "was reserved for the people of Burlington." Sanders thanked us "for allowing me to be your mayor":

> The people of this city have had to deal with unusual concepts like socialism, but they have had the courage to look at the issues, and look at the programs, and look at the ideas, and judge me not on ideology alone or on what the newspapers wrote. They had the courage—and it took a lot of courage—to look at what we were trying to do and to vote their consciences. And that's not easy.
>
> I honestly know how hard it has been for some of those people, waking up and reading the paper and saying, God, what's going to happen next, why our city, there are thousands of cities, what did we do to deserve this?

When the applause and laughter subsided, Sanders again thanked us for "giving me personally the opportunity to do something that I never dreamed in a million years that I would personally have an opportunity to do." He concluded, "Most people who hold our views do not hold public office in this country."

And so, the eight-year-old municipal experiment ended how it began, with a low-budget party: Hawaiian Punch, Oreos, photo ops, streamers, balloons. It was as though the city's dramatic transformation had been staged as a third-grade play, and here was its closing-night celebration.

Why our city? What *did* we do to deserve this?

At the reception following Sanders's remarks, I looked around the room full of Burlington celebrities and wondered how many small cities there had ever been in America where politics had expressed itself so intimately, colorfully, and dramatically. Our mayor was a rising star, but also a local character. Even the side players—the city clerk, the city attorney, the deputy city attorney, the treasurer, the youth office director—were widely recognized by the citizens who paid their salaries. If I'd grown up across the lake, in our tarnished mirror-image city of Plattsburgh, New York, I am sure that as an eighteen-year-old I wouldn't know or care much about property taxes or waterfront zoning.

But Bernie had electrified these micro dramas and educated us all. He'd cast our struggle in the highest moral terms but fought like a dog for every remnant and scrap. He had given the people of the city of Burlington, "waking up and reading the paper," a thrilling narrative to follow from day to day, even through all its wacky side plots and digressions: and since the theme of the story was our city's transformation, eerily and amazingly we could all locate ourselves inside the story, even as we followed the story. *We were* the story. Its protagonist wasn't Sanders, but, as Sanders recognized in his farewell address, the average citizen of Burlington and the city itself: its people, its institutions, its landscape, its very existence in time and place, now suddenly a memory.

Because I knew I'd be leaving Burlington soon to attend college in faraway Massachusetts, I happened to be curating my days for maximum retrospective meaning and poignancy. Anticipated nostalgia was the reason I attended the city hall ceremony in the first place. But I now had to shape an ending. I thought of going over and trying to greet Bernie, but it seemed such an unsatisfying narrative resolution, really no more than a gimmick. Once I'd ruled out that obvious choice, though, I was stumped about how to conclude; for the city of Burlington offered too many potential endings to this story.

A stroll along the transformed waterfront? A trip to Pure Pop, where new CDs by the Pixies, De La Soul, and Beastie Boys were on my shopping list? A burger at Leunig's? A visit to the Peace on Earth Store for some radical bumper stickers? A Xingu at the bar at Bourbon Street? A drive out to Bristol, for a moonlit April dip in the falls?

It all seemed somehow so cheesy. The problem might have been, though, that all the elements of the narrative had been constructed, all along, too consciously *as* narrative. Maybe it was too late, and the ending of such a story, no matter what ending I chose, would have to be cheesy.

But it wasn't the end, not quite yet. The story had one more chapter.

39

One Small City, One Small State

(Rematch, 1990)

Some by Virtue Fall

Republican Representative Peter Plympton Smith arrived in Washington in January of 1989, eager to work across the aisle with like-minded Democrats, but pessimistic about winning favor inside his own caucus. Newt Gingrich, the Georgia conservative, was gobbling up influence along his slither to power, "uniting the caucus," as Gingrich claimed, by bullying its new members behind the scenes. Smith, once a teen standout on the green clay mountain-view courts at the Burlington Tennis Club, modeled his own Washington strategy on the hard-fought but collegial skirmishes of a doubles match. When he "bonded with a Democrat who'd been born on the very same day," Smith and Indiana Representative Glenn Poshard cohosted a breakfast for college-bound teenagers from Anacostia, the poor neighborhood in the shadow of the U.S. Capitol. The kids were asked "what one thing" they felt they needed, back in their neighborhood. "I figured they'd say opportunity, or resources, or some such," Smith told me, "but I'll never forget one kid's answer: 'courage.'" The girl had feared gun violence since she was a child, she told the congressmen, and carried "in her body, in the way she breathed," the certainty that before college ever came around, "she would be killed."

It had been a tense January in America. A week or so before, Smith arrived from Vermont to his Capitol Hill apartment and flipped on CNN. He initially had trouble conceptualizing the horror that confronted him. Stretchers were laid out side by side in a school playground. A paramedic called his dispatcher: "We've got children scattered all around this school." Hysterical teachers told reporters that "it smelled like firecrackers." One woman described a child running out into the hall, unaware of the blood streaming behind him before he collapsed. Police tracked the blood trails into closets and cabinets where children hid. The shooter, Patrick Purdy, a racist drifter with a history of violence, had fired at least 106 rounds from an AK-47-style assault rifle into his old elementary school, targeting "Hindus and boat people." Five children—all of them Cambodian and Vietnamese refugees—were killed, and thirty-two were wounded. We all know what happened next. The unimaginable in America soon became routine. The Stockton, California, schoolyard shooting, the first in a series still ongoing, was the benchmark that later mass school shooters wanted to surpass.

"I was shaving, as I recall it," Smith told me. "I thought, you need to actually like this person because you're going to see him in the mirror the rest of your life." Smith was trained as a middle school social studies teacher before he began his political career. So, when the congressman was approached to cosponsor a bill banning certain kinds of assault weapons, it was "not even a decision," Smith said. "I felt I had no choice." Smith's "staff was very nervous about it," warning him of the political fallout in the Republican Party, where the National Rifle Association had begun to exert its suffocating influence.

On March 4, Smith held a news conference in Montpelier. Lifting up first his father's Winchester 30-30 rifle, typically used for hunting, and then a Chinese-made assault rifle like the one fired in the Stockton shooting, he declared that "assault weapons are not sporting guns or self-defense weapons—they are the weapons of choice in the criminal world." A local NRA official in attendance, Creighton Audette of Springfield, Vermont, approached reporters afterward to announce that Smith was now his group's "primary target." In the summer of 1988, Smith had pledged in writing to oppose all new federal gun legislation, and collected the NRA's endorsement. Vermont gun owners sought vengeance. "He lied to us," Audette said. Smith's courageous cosponsorship of H.R. 1190, the Semiautomatic Assault Weapons Act of 1989, received praise on the editorial pages of many Vermont papers, while letters to the editor expressed a decidedly more mixed reception among his constituents. "To put it mildly, all hell broke loose" back home, Smith told me. In a state where rates of gun ownership exceeded 50 percent, and where gun laws were among the loosest in the nation, Smith was now, three months into his term, "a marked man."

Neighbors

Gordon Paquette had savored his retirement years, shuttling between his condominium in Florida and his longtime Burlington home in a neighborhood built to deliver suburban comforts within city limits. The former mayor and his wife welcomed their grandchildren to a tidy ranch home on

Killarney Drive in the New North End, for pool parties and cookouts. He was still greeted as "Mr. Mayor" at the Ethan Allen Shopping Plaza, just steps from his backyard paradise. The Mayor and Mrs. Paquette, movie buffs, especially enjoyed strolling to Merrill's Ethan Allen Cinemas, Burlington's "cheap seats" theater where second-run films screened for $1.50 a ticket. In February of 1989, the cheap seats showed *The 'Burbs*, a Tom Hanks comedy about a suburban homeowner driven mad by his obsession with the new "neighbors from hell"—who turn out to be a family of ritualistic murderers.

When the mirror-image ranch home next door went on the market, Gordon and Mary Paquette toured the open house, admiring its spacious bedrooms, the large, well-tended pool, and the generous plantings. Real estate agents came and went, but nobody had yet snapped up the home, priced at $175,000. But on this cheerful, middle-class block, where kids played kick the can out in the road, surely it was only a matter of time before Paquettes met a new young family next door, and gained some new playmates for their grandchildren.

In late February, a "Sold" sign went up. "On the housing front this week," Peter Freyne told the readers of "Inside Track," "the natives of Killarney Drive were buzzing over a certain couple about to move to the neighborhood—Mr. and Mrs. Bernie Sanders!" What's more, Bernie and Jane "picked as their dream home" the listing "right next door to the home of the man Ol' Bernardo beat by ten votes back in 1981—Mayor Gordon Paquette!" A beside-himself Peter Freyne raced out North Avenue to pay a visit to Paquette, and to peer across the fence at "the opulent new Sanders residence." Freyne "pointed out that the swimming pool would make a great location for teen center parties this summer," imagining a backyard mosh pit next to the home of the mayor who banned Supertramp. "Thank God we've got that noise ordinance," Paquette replied, with a mischievous grin. Freyne's article implied that Bernie's loyal friend Tony Pomerleau might have helped the couple secure a home where they could spread out a little and "properly entertain." As for the mortgage, "it'll be tough doing without those two city hall paychecks, but somehow we know they'll do just fine." Mayor Paquette seemed uninterested in the irony that he and his radical adversary would now be greeting one another across the hedges. "Anyone can go live anywhere they want to live," Paquette told Freyne, with a shrug.

From the comfort of his new living room, Sanders watched his political fortunes rise as those of his once-and-future rival spectacularly crashed. In the spring of 1989, Smith's "unconscionable betrayal" of gun owners rallied a constellation of local sportsmen's groups, fish and game clubs, and trappers' associations, to gather in piney lodges from Newport in the north to

Pawlet in the south. This "Elmer Fudd Federation," as Peter Freyne called it, organized under the statewide banner of the Sporting Alliance for Vermont's Environment. SAVE's only political action prior to opposing Smith had been its ongoing efforts to defend the local practice of fish shooting, an obscure method, indigenous to the Lake Champlain region: a fisherman fired into the spawning grounds of native pike or walleye, then collected by the dozens the stunned fish that floated belly-up to the surface.

In March, SAVE waded out of the marsh and took aim at Peter Smith. With the support of NRA's national leadership, the Elmer Fudd Federation mounted a relentless, NRA-funded campaign to recall the congressman on the grounds that he had "obtained his office under false pretenses." Smith's Washington aides persuaded him to frame his position as a fight against "drug dealers" and "gang members," but even this race-baiting strategy failed to calm the opposition. SAVE and its confederated groups had thousands of signatures, and soon bumper stickers and lawn signs cropped up all across Vermont: "Dump Smith," "Smith and Wesson? Yes. Peter Smith? No." Smith doubled down on his stance: "There are some issues that define a politician," he told the *Burlington Free Press*. In the eyes of the NRA and its Vermont members, Peter Smith had indeed been defined—and so had Bernie Sanders.

THAT WINTER, Professor Dennis Gilbert had received a letter addressed to "Chairperson, Department of Sociology, Hamilton College, Clinton, NY." The writer identified himself as "the only socialist mayor in America," and, inquiring about employment for the following academic year, concluded, "I think that I could give your students an unusual academic perspective."

Gilbert, a scholar of the American class system and a credentialed man of the left, had read about Bernie Sanders's 1985 mission to Nicaragua and seen his face on the news during family ski trips to Vermont. He interviewed Bernie by telephone and found him "well qualified" to teach two courses in the spring of 1990: "The Problems and Potential of Urban Life" (Sociology 335) and "Democracy and Socialism" (Sociology 235). Sanders could now show proof of employment to a mortgage lender, and look forward to planning a campaign from a perch four and a half hours from the hothouse environment of Burlington politics, though connected to the news back home by telephone, fax, and a new technology: the internet.

Hamilton is an elite liberal arts college, known at the time as a magnet for boarding school jocks with their sights set on Wall Street. In 1981, Lisa Birnbach's *Preppy Handbook* named Hamilton the second-preppiest college in America. Sanders welcomed his appointment at "a lovely school with a tremendous reputation, and really fine students and faculty," still many months away. But the announcement, in May of 1989, immediately scrambled Vermont's political playbook. Frank Bryan told the *Burlington Free Press* that Sanders had nothing to lose: "His kind of organization doesn't need pampering. He doesn't have to build up name recognition." For hopeful Vermont Democrats, Bernie's news implied that he would not enter the 1990 race for governor, since he was sitting out the prime season for in-state fund-raising. Madeleine Kunin's chief of staff seemed to flatter Sanders: "He doesn't play by any of the usual rules." Howard Dean, considering his own run for governor, also nudged Bernie a little: "For other candidates it might hurt not to be in the public eye. But people don't forget someone like Bernie Sanders very easily." The messaging was coming down from on high: "Saint Patrick" Leahy, according to Peter Freyne, had begun making calls to clear rising Democrats out of Bernie's lane, and to keep Bernie out of theirs. In a two-way race against Smith, Senator Leahy saw Bernie as unbeatable.

In the fall of 1989, Sanders was a fellow at Harvard's Institute of Politics, where he led a not-for-credit study group on third parties and hosted a cast of visiting lecturers, including his old Liberty Union ally Michael Parenti. Bulletins from Cambridge began to roll in from Vermonters. "I saw him at Au Bon Pain, wearing his backpack," my friend, a freshman at Harvard, reported, happy to have a fellow Burlingtonian on the scene; Sanders wrote that he'd "become addicted to the cinnamon raisin buns" at the Harvard Square chain restaurant. He recalled his term at Harvard years later, in *Outsider in the House*: "I know that conservatives worry a great deal about Harvard. They see it as a bastion of progressive thought, a brain trust for the revolution. They can stop worrying. Harvard has many wonderful attributes, but the revolution will not begin at Harvard University."

It did, however, in a way, begin at little Hamilton College. In January of 1990, Sanders moved into the parlor floor of a college-owned mansion near campus, and became a fixture in the department mailroom, where he made daily use of the college's franking privileges, and in the faculty dining hall, where Dennis Gilbert sometimes encountered him animatedly "discussing the complexities of human behavior with a colleague in our psychology department, which was a rats-and-stimuli sort of department."

His students recall Sanders as a "fish out of water" at preppy Hamilton, but a committed and innovative teacher, and, zipping along the shaded paths in work boots and corduroys, "something of a campus celebrity." Sanders taught "The Problems and Potential of Urban Life" to a class of forty or so in the college's "Red Pit," a sunken auditorium carpeted in ruby shag. "He was keen to kick us off campus and get us into Utica," Brett Mandel told me. "Hamilton is an ivory tower, so it was refreshing." Mandel, the author of several books about urban policy and Philadelphia history, recalls Sanders often asking his students first to "visualize the problems of the working person," using Wilhelm Reich's method and imparting its mental steps, before they set out into the deteriorating city next door to witness economic despair firsthand. The students met with Utica's city officials and social workers, returning to the Red Pit to "debate with Professor Sanders." Mandel and Sanders once argued after class about a civic center planned in Mandel's neighborhood back in Philly. "He thought it was a terrible idea," Mandel told me. Recalling the human costs of urban renewal in Burlington, Sanders challenged his pupil: "What about the people displaced? What about the neighborhoods displaced?"

In his low-key, tweedy new friend Dennis Gilbert, Sanders found an unlikely bridge back to politics. "It was pretty clear to me right away that he intended to run again," Gilbert said. Over dinners at Friendly's, Sanders told Gilbert about "the burden" of his new home and mortgage, his threadbare, almost nonexistent political organization, and his fear that he'd worn out many of his old city hall allies who "weren't willing to work with him" now that Burlington was theirs to run. Sanders was often "glum" about his political prospects, but "when he was feeling good," he spoke about how much he'd done in Burlington, and how Burlington had been transformed into a laboratory where "things could be tried out," almost like "an alternative state capital." He told Gilbert that he hoped "a congressional office could perform a similar function."

On March 19, back home in Vermont, Sanders announced his campaign for U.S. Congress. Citing statewide polls, Bernie claimed that he would "run strong against Smith in a two-way race." As though to confirm it, Peter Smith welcomed Sanders, "and anyone else who might get in the race down the road." A three-way race was Smith's to lose. Against Sanders alone, as he knew, the freshman congressman faced an uphill climb. One after another potential Democratic opponent then rushed to the media to announce that they were sitting out the race for Congress. In a turn of events unimaginable to those who had followed his rise, Bernie Sanders, the slayer of Vermont Democrats, was the de facto Democrat in the race to become the state's sole U.S. representative.

In a second unforeseeable development, technology now made it possible for Sanders to be in two places at once. "They were sitting there one day, in late March, in the registrar's office," Gilbert told me, "and all of a sudden, the fax machine pipes up. It was the design for our campaign poster." Brett Mandell, Bernie's student, "had an on-campus job working in the college computer lab where I would lend out software discs to students, un-jam dot-matrix printers, and remind users to save their work on backup discs," rituals that today "must seem as ridiculous as churning butter." Mandell had "to jump to attention anytime the giant tractor-feed printer behind me roared to life so I could tear off the printed pages and file them for pick up," he recalled. "It seems that this printer was connected to what we now know as the internet." With his campaign rolling forward in Vermont, Sanders camped out in the computer room. Once, Mandell told me, Bernie "appeared at my window rather excited to get something that had been spat out by my printer. Maybe it was polling or some other data." The printout was so important that Sanders "had to splay the accordion-folded pages on my desk to devour the information." From his campus work study job, Mandell concluded that this "was no quixotic quest. It was a real political campaign focused on data and intent on winning an election."

"LIKE SOME KID who runs away with the circus," Dennis Gilbert arrived in Burlington in late May, to put his stamp on "the strangest election Vermont had ever seen," as Garrison Nelson described it. "Smith was an incumbent with a party, but without a constituency; Bernie had a constituency without a party." Gilbert, offering to work "for not much money," was hired as the campaign's pollster and lead researcher, and assigned to a second-floor nook at 104 Church Street, the old Vermont Reds season ticket office, its front window drawing the smoke of clove cigarettes up from the Marketplace like a fireplace flue. Gilbert learned right away that "the care and maintenance of Bernie was a major preoccupation," of the campaign staff, including Rachel Levin, serving again in the role of campaign manager; Martha Abbott, Bernie's old Liberty Union ticket mate, acting as field director; and a young Middlebury College graduate and investigative reporter, Steven Rosenfeld, who would work on "media and issues" along with Gilbert. Jane Sanders coordinated the staff and ran interference with her husband. "I can't work with everyone," Bernie told Gilbert. "I'm a weird animal," he told Rosenfeld. "I am strange. It's a family of sorts."

As the incumbent, Peter Smith could count on the advantages of his office, the support of the National Republican Campaign Committee, and a network of PACs; Bernie had only what Gilbert described as "a bunch of amateurs," already sparring. "The organization wasn't coming together," Bernie told him, because he'd hired "the wrong people"; Rachel Levin, confiding in Gilbert, seemed to agree, but placed "some of the blame" on Bernie, who "always wanted to run off and give speeches and see people." Sanders soon "began to distrust" Steve Rosenfeld, whose investigative focus seemed to be turning inward toward the campaign itself. By June, Sanders was telling people that Steve "couldn't be fired," since he already knew too much and lived with a reporter at the *Rutland Herald.* Sanders's instincts were sharp: soon after the campaign ended, Rosenfeld published his four-hundred-page tell-all, *Making History in Vermont*, an eyewitness account to minutiae that left out one important detail: the manuscript itself, and the effect Rosenfeld's writing it in real, unfolding campaign time had on day-to-day operations.

But Smith's incumbency was no simple advantage: "It hung on me, everywhere I went," Smith told me. The daily death threats against him had subsided a little, but in Washington, the Capitol Police still "felt they had to put some guys on me," Smith said. "Some nut calling me up and saying 'I'm going to fucking kill you,' that became predictable. What you worried about was the quiet nut in the crowd." At a Memorial Day parade in working-class Vergennes, Smith looked "beleaguered," Rosenfeld wrote. "His stride was lanky and tired." The congressman heard the mutterings in the crowd as he passed: traitor, coward, liar. "All you hunters," one woman said, "he's the one you don't want." A painted bedsheet hung from the branches of an elm tree along the route: it depicted Smith as Pinocchio in a rifle's crosshairs, with the message "Aim to Fire Peter Smith" scrawled beneath.

The first televised debate of the campaign was scheduled for June 15, hosted by the Vermont Federation of Sportsmen's Clubs. Smith sensed a trap. The VFSC was a network of fifty or so clubs across the state: in Manchester, the Rod & Gun Club fished for rainbow trout on the Battenkill River. In Stowe, the Lake Champlain Retriever Club hiked with their dogs on the Long Trail. Bowhunters, trappers, owners of bear hounds and beagles: Vermont's sports clubs were varied, passionate, and organized. All the candidates but Smith had confirmed their participation: Sanders; Tim Philbin, a bespectacled Republican insurance agent and gun rights activist; Dolores Sandoval, a UVM professor and the first Black woman to run for higher office in Vermont, vying as a Democrat without her party's support; and Bernie's old tormentor, Peter Diamondstone. Representative Smith was "elusive" in the lead-up, according to the *Rutland Herald*, and refused to commit until just days before.

"I thought I was handling it," Smith told me, of the threats to his life. "I clearly was not handling it." Sanders seemed to walk a fine line in his own taunts against the congressman. "I hope Peter Smith is not going to run away from debates," Sanders said. "I hope he will defend his record." Privately, Sanders told aides that "the gun support" made him "very, very nervous": his campaign had been assured by an NRA member that the gun rights group "was supporting Tim Philbin in the primary, and Bernie in the general." Imagining the backlash on the left, Sanders told Rosenfeld that it was "not our issue to win, but it was our issue to lose."

SANDERS ARRIVED AT the Colchester studios of Vermont ETV to find the entrance blocked by a sheriff's cruiser flanked by two armed deputies. Smith's reports of death threats back in Washington had triggered the local response. To Bernie's staff, it was transparently a political maneuver: Smith's strategy would be to tie Sanders to the NRA, while seeming to put his own life on the line to oppose weapons of mass murder. The five candidates and the moderator were escorted in and seated at a small table, their elbows nearly touching.

The first question: How would each candidate define a sportsman? Sanders, sitting a foot or so away from the patrician incumbent, found the class angle: "Sportsmen, and sportswomen, enjoy communion with nature. Very often, these are people who do not have the sums of money to go to the yachting clubs, or the country clubs, or to buy big boats, but they enjoy what nature has given us." Philbin dug in on constitutional grounds: Sportsmen were "people like you and I," he asserted, "and their biggest concern is to maintain freedoms that they have fought long and so hard for." Sandoval invoked "sportsmanship" and the virtues of fairness, underscoring her campaign's message that women were "peacemakers." Diamondstone churlishly refused to answer. Smith, hewing to his script, praised hunters and fishermen as "the true conservationists."

When the focus shifted to "the firearms issue," Sanders leaped into the fray:

> I believe in hunting. I will not support any legislation which limits the rights of Vermont's hunters to practice what they have enjoyed for decades. I do have concerns about certain types of assault weapons.
>
> I said this *before* the 1988 election. The Vermont sportspeople, as is their right, made their endorsements. They endorsed Peter Smith, they endorsed Paul Poirier; now, I lost that election by about three and one half percentage points, a very close election. Was my failure to get that endorsement pivotal? It might have been, you never know. Maybe it wasn't. All I can say is I told the sportspeople of Vermont what I believed before the election, and I will say it again.

Bernie's objective was to say as little as possible about guns, and portray Smith as, simply, a "Washington politician": slippery, dishonest, ambitious. Smith, hoping to drive some of Bernie's voters to Sandoval, countered by linking Sanders to the NRA: "What you are saying is absolute political garbage," Smith inveighed, while staring directly into his opponent's eyes. "I am surprised to see you buying the national NRA's strategy. They said the same thing about George Bush and Ronald Reagan and Barry Goldwater when they changed their position on semiautomatic weapons . . . These weapons are in a class by themselves. I am disappointed." Philbin, "doing our work of attacking Smith," as Rosenfeld put it, then got the last word: "You answered the question. You made the promise. You told them. You signed it. And you went back on it." The candidates packed up, but the debate lived on. A VHS recording went out to all of the state's sportsmen's lodges, where, accompanied by the buzzing of mosquitoes and the calls of loons, it played on a loop throughout the summer.

Sanders was now delighted that "he could be completely consistent" on guns, and defended a position he had held since the early 1970s: except in extraordinary cases, gun legislation should be passed only by the states. The federal government should not take guns away from its citizens. This stance put Bernie strongly at odds with 90 percent of his voters, but his consistency and his candor neutralized any real damage on the left. Meanwhile, for men like John Alderman of Bennington, a service station manager and a Republican, the time had come "to see if Bernie at least will stick to his word and fight for the little guy in Washington like he always says he will."

Sanders greeted these newly attentive Vermonters with a stripped-down message: "If you like what's happening in Washington, vote for my opponent. If you don't, give me a chance." By midsummer, "it was almost too easy," Dennis Gilbert told me. The campaign had internal polls showing Sanders up by five, even ten points. Gilbert pointed me to this passage in his campaign diary, describing a dairy fair in Franklin County, near the Canadian border:

> I recall a woman who came out from behind her store counter to give Bernie a hug. She thinks she knows him because she sees him on TV. He conveys something to people that they like. (I've also seen little kids in Burlington jump up and down for joy, screaming "Bernie! Bernie!") An old guy who Bernie identified as the head of the Democratic Party—or former—greeted Bernie warmly. Encouraged us in the race against Smith, mentioning two issues that were for him red hot: "Smith lied to us about gun control," and "the corporations are pushing people around."

A man "pulled 10 dollars out of his pocket for gas—as a campaign contribution." To Gilbert, the fair suggested an "an odd juxtaposition of issues," but the subtext of such afternoons was clear: "Much of the male population of the state is enraged at Smith."

Grant Street

Sanders for Congress '90 was run out of three Burlington locations: Dennis Gilbert's little nook on Church Street; Bernie and Jane's home on Killarney Drive; and the main campaign office in a run-down former florist's shop on the corner of Grant Street and South Winooski Avenue in the Old North End. The Grant Street office accepted drop-in volunteers, and offered the rare Burlington benefit of window-mounted air conditioning. By the front door, a card table awaited anybody who wandered in off the street to receive their orders from Shari, the cheerful office manager. On many summer afternoons, inches from the hot sidewalk, I licked envelopes. Most days I spaced out to REM's *Murmur* on my Discman. There was always a bin of outgoing mail waiting to be carried a few blocks away to the post office on Elmwood Avenue, or a copy job needing to be picked up on Church Street. The campaign was sending out Bernie's 1987 cassette tape of *We Shall Overcome* in exchange for donations of fifty dollars or more: hundreds of shrink-wrapped cassettes were lined up on a rack of DIY pine-and-cinder-block bookcases, next to slender phone books from every town in Vermont. The more seasoned volunteers phone-banked or headed out into the neighborhoods to knock on doors. I recall one near miss with the candidate: a senior volunteer asked the envelope stuffers, "Who has wheels, and could pick Bernie up at Midas Muffler on Shelburne Road?" I kept my head down. The hours passed without much conversation: our mouths were occupied with licking. Intense-looking people would blow in from the sidewalk, traverse the linoleum, and disappear into the campaign's engine room, a basement warren of offices where the senior staff discussed strategy. My mind was mostly on Robert Frost that summer, so I listened from above for the campaign's muffled "sentence sounds"—urgent, animated "tones of meaning," as Frost put it, "but without the words."

ONLY THIRTY-FOUR YEARS LATER, speaking with Dennis Gilbert, did I fill in what could be faintly overheard. The campaign was in chaos. Some of those official-looking people trudging through Grant Street were auditors from the Vermont Department of Education and Training. Sanders '90 had commissioned its own audit to counter charges from Peter Smith that it had hired workers as consultants deliberately to avoid paying payroll taxes. It turned out to be a smear: this was a common campaign practice, used even by Smith. But Sanders, incensed, "reacting, overreacting, to every little provocation," kept the story in the news. By mid-August, the campaign was "terribly disorganized," Gilbert told me, while the candidate was "unfocused, impatient." Larry Sanders, heading back to Oxford after three weeks of campaigning with his little brother, put it this way: "He'll win if he can keep his temper."

The Sanders campaign then got a reset. David Clavelle stormed into Grant Street, his faint smile communicating: *Not again.* The mender, the minder, always summoned late in the game, Clavelle was a liaison to both the thousands of Winooski Democrats who had issues with Bernie's socialism and to Senator Patrick Leahy in Washington. "It's fucking August 15, and we don't have a strategy," Clavelle told the basement conclave. Levin worried she was on the outs: Rosenfeld "was twisting in the wind"; Gilbert, who in his diary expresses confidence in his job security, appears in Rosenfeld's telling to be equally precarious. Meanwhile, Smith's campaign went negative, shaming Sanders for accepting unemployment insurance in the 1970s and implying that he, personally, was under IRS investigation. Bernie dictated to Gilbert an enraged response: "SANDERS RESPONDS TO PERSONAL ATTACK." Smith's charge was "vulgar," "deep in the mud," and "desperate," and he had "received hundreds of thousands of dollars in earned income from stocks, bonds, and other investments," Sanders said. In contrast, Bernie continued,

> I have had to work for a living my entire life, and like many people in this country I have had, on occasion, financial problems. The Smith campaign thinks it's odd that I could run for statewide office in 1974 while being unemployed. I know that this must come as a shock to them, given that the Republican president is a millionaire, the Republican vice president is a millionaire, and my Republican opponent for Congress is a millionaire. The law still permits people to run for office even if they are not millionaires. I know this is hard for our Republican friends to believe, but it is true.

"Bernie was out campaigning, exhausted," Gilbert wrote in his diary; when the staff told him the statement was "angry," "defensive," and "counterproductive," Sanders at first "seemed like he was going to explode." Levin and Gilbert patched Sanders through to "the campaign's crisis hotline," Senator Patrick Leahy's longtime press secretary, Deborah Graham, who was mentoring the campaign from behind the scenes. "He did call Deborah, who got Bernie to put out a short, matter-of-fact statement in Rachel's name." This was "regarded as an enormous victory, even a turning point." Bernie had kept his temper, according to his brother's prescription, and the "bunch of amateurs" kept their jobs.

The Lay of the Last Republican

"I'd touched the third rail of American politics," Peter Smith told me from his home in Santa Fe, New Mexico, where he has retired after a distinguished career in higher education. He was quoting Stephen Terry, the former George Aiken aide and biographer, who has kept vigil over the Vermont Republican Party for three decades.

In August of 1990, Wayne LaPierre of the National Rifle Association instructed its members to vote for Bernie Sanders as "the lesser of two evils," and added, as though he would know how to gauge it, that Sanders exemplified "integrity in politics." Behind the scenes, it troubled Bernie, who "detested the NRA," an aide said; yet the endorsement also buoyed him, since, as his friend Richard Sugarman told me, Sanders "doesn't care about guns, he cares about the elitism of people who think they're above the gun owners." Like the Patrolmen's Association endorsement in his 1981 mayoral race, the NRA's statement inoculated Sanders against the idea that he was a dangerous leftist. And it solidified in Vermonters' minds the qualities of "authenticity, honesty, and consistency" that Dennis Gilbert's polls showed were popular with voters. Contempt for Peter Smith had spiraled away from guns. As a hunter from Saint Albans told Steve Rosenfeld, "Bernie Sanders isn't going to cause the demise of the country. The Republicans and Democrats together are doing a good job of it themselves."

On Labor Day, Smith told me, "I was still ahead. I'd parried the gun issue for fifteen, sixteen months." But something "was different in the air," on the campaign trail, where having an R next to your name was suddenly like the scarlet letter. The fall phase of the 1990 campaign, with the Republican National Committee hedging its support, felt like "swimming against the tide of history," Smith explained. "I could go down to Washington and vote to the left of 50 percent of my party, which I did, and which the Bush White House went out of its way to remind me I did. And that"—Smith hesitated for a moment—"was okay. But it changed quickly thereafter." It changed in two ways: in Washington, it meant Peter Smith was ostracized by Republican leadership; and at home, it meant he was tied to the policies of a party running as fast as it could to the right, and taking President Bush, moderate in instinct but weak of will, along for the ride.

"That sound you could hear was the toilet flushing," Smith said, with a rueful chuckle. "My mother called from Burlington and said, 'Peter, dear, people won't talk to me anymore at the grocery store. I think you're going to lose.'" Smith's internal polls now had him "going from twelve up to seventeen points down." With Sanders calling bingo games and sampling venison pie at the VFW, the "little old ladies and gun nuts were going to win this thing for us," Gilbert wrote. Smith, meanwhile, was stuck in Washington, where he found himself on the losing side of a controversial House vote for Bush's budget—which, among other unpopular initiatives, called for an increase in the gasoline tax of twelve cents per gallon. After hunting season in Vermont, it becomes snowmobile season, and snowmobilers like to complain about one thing more than any other: the price of gas. Smith's vote seemed intended to further inflame a constituency now understood as symbolic of the state's electorate as a whole: the hard-pressed Vermont sportsman, defending his way of life. There was a little of his noble spirit in every Vermonter.

With its candidate stuck in Washington budget talks, Smith's campaign triggered Armageddon mode back in Vermont. Smith was reluctant, but "we had nothing left": the new message was that Sanders was a socialist, opposed to our way of life. In his closing remarks at a debate on October 14, Smith, who could have chosen to tarnish his opponent with Bernie's praise for Cuba, the Soviet Union, or Nicaragua, instead opted for Sweden: "My opponent glorifies in being an outsider," Smith began. Bernie's people beamed: "outsider" was one of their best-polling adjectives. "What he advocates for is Swedish-style socialism," Smith went on. The parking lot was full of Volvos and Saabs. Smith quoted some data about the Swedish economy, including a figure meant to instill terror in Vermonters: "A loaf of bread in Sweden is four dollars." Gilbert "wasted a day on the phone with the Swedish embassy" to rebut the charge, but Vermonters liked Sweden, thought the bread was probably very good there, well worth the cost. In any case, voters seemed mainly to share the sentiments of "a little old lady in Montpelier" who was "more concerned with the price of medical care in the U.S., and trusted Bernie to help her."

On the morning of October 23, Representative Peter Smith flew from Washington to Burlington on Air Force One, alongside his prep school classmate's dad, a man he first met on the campus of Phillips Academy in tenth grade. "We called it shared heritage, without the money on my side," Smith laughed. "I told him on the plane on the way up, I may need to give you a little room." President Bush chuckled: "That's okay, I think I can use it." The exchange spoke to the trouble that both men knew awaited them in the political near future. At the $500-per-plate breakfast, Smith stood up from his apple-stuffed pancakes and shocked the well-heeled crowd of bankers and local politicians: "My specific disagreements with this administration are a matter of record," Smith began, looking back at the president, who loudly munched an apple. Smith then reeled off quite a few "disagreements," on civil rights, on abortion, on the budget, and left some in the crowd wondering when, or if, he would pivot to anything resembling praise. "I said it, I did it," Smith told me. "And then I got the shit kicked out of me."

Bush was gracious, but both men were under considerable political strain at the time, and Smith's remarks seemed to touch a nerve. "Like all Vermonters, he is a man of independent mind," the president began. "I wish he'd stop reminding me that we do have a few differences. There are 435 of these people serving in the U.S. Congress"—Bush hit the phrase "these people" uncomfortably hard before returning to the script. "This one votes his conscience." The press was not as kind as the president: Smith's takedown of the commander in chief seemed staged to some, unhinged to others. But Smith found he couldn't conceal his contempt for the forces acting on Bush and on the party of his father and grandfather: "They'd begun to warp language," he said, "under the mentorship of Gingrich. To use words that I had been raised to believe meant one thing, now they were using to mean the opposite." I asked Smith for some examples. "Oh, compassion. That would be one. That's a big one. Women's health, that was another." Two days earlier, Bush had vetoed the Civil Rights Act of 1990, under pressure from the right. "Racial equality would be another," Smith added, shaking his head in disgust.

Smith campaigned the next day in Rutland. "I was above the fold in all the major papers, the headlines all saying essentially, 'Smith pisses Bush off.' My cousin, working in Hanoi at the time, called and said, 'Peter, what's up? You're on the front of the *International Herald Tribune*.'" With two weeks to go, down by double digits, Smith began a whistle-stop tour of Vermont in a secondhand camper dubbed the "War Wagon" and emblazoned with fine print about the cost of eggs and milk in Sweden. In an attempt to bring the working classes back into the fold, Smith "stressed that beer is more expensive in Swedish bars because of a state tax designed to discourage public drinking," according to the *Burlington Free Press*. Sanders, looking amused but incredulous that his opponent's closing argument was "Don't let Vermont become Sweden," pointed to the absurdity of it all: "If I was running for prime minister of Sweden, it might be relevant." The old woman in Montpelier, shaking her head in confusion, asked, "What does Sweden have to do with anything?"

"Needless to say, at that point, it was over," Smith told me.

NOW A BOYISH MAN in his late seventies, Peter Smith expressed gratitude that he "got to do what I was put on this earth to do," after his loss to Sanders by a margin of seventeen points. The former congressman went on to "expand access to education for thousands of adults," serving as the dean of George Washington University's College of Education and the founding president of California State University, Monterey Bay, before working for UNESCO and writing several books about education reform.

But more importantly, Smith told me, "Bernie Sanders got to do what *he* was put on the earth to do." Describing his old rival as "one of ten, maybe five, most influential American politicians alive," Smith said he had "come around, over the years, to Bernie's understanding of power, his hatred of disenfranchisement." Smith is that rare phenomenon, a person who has grown progressively more liberal as he has aged.

Back in Washington after the 1990 campaign ended, Smith ran into Senator Leahy. "We had to do that to you," Leahy told him, describing the bargain Vermont Democrats had made to keep a viable Democratic candidate out of the race, as long as Bernie worked within the Democratic caucus: "You were the future of the Vermont Republican Party."

Smith now sees it another way. "I was the end of the Vermont Republican Party," he said. To hold high office in Vermont since then, Republicans have worked outside of the ancient, collapsing party structure, and only after years of cultivating "their own unique personal brand and appeal." One hundred and thirty or so years of Republican hegemony in Vermont ended on the night of November 6, 1990.

"I was roadkill," Smith said. "Is it strange to say you're proud to be roadkill?"

Polyphony

Tuesday, November 6, 1990. I have stationed myself in Frost Library at Amherst College, on a high floor where my Walkman picks up the clear signal of WKVT Brattleboro. In 1990, you still can't remain in one place and be everywhere. I am thirty miles south of the Vermont border, but I want to be told a story about Vermont.

The polls close at seven, and then full coverage will begin. Throughout the afternoon, Bernie's final radio spots come across as soft-spoken, confiding, comforting. He'd known economic despair in his life. Living paycheck to paycheck ruined his parents' lives. He's been enormously moved to share the struggles of ordinary Vermonters. He would be grateful to be given an opportunity to fight for us in Washington.

I do my Ancient Greek 111 worksheets as the pale November sun goes down around four thirty. I watch a "far, slow, violet gaze" take over the mountains of the Holyoke Range, Emily Dickinson's very own, beloved "old Mountains":

How the old Mountains drip with Sunset
How the Hemlocks burn—
How the Dun Brake is draped in Cinder
By the Wizard Sun—

Garrison Nelson's voice in my ears prepares me, far from home, for "Burlington's biggest political night since"—Nelson pauses—"since, well, since March of 1981, when our wild ride with Mr. Sanders began." On that night, when I was nine, Nelson's voice had thundered from my grandparents' kitchen radio, while I lay in bed upstairs.

It is possible, right now, to forget where I am in time.

By seven p.m. or so, I have memorized the definitions of several ancient Greek words, ducked out to grab a chicken puck and some tater tots, and returned to set up shop for the evening in my carrel. Now Jack Barry is in the studio to tell his part of the story. Barry has "followed every political potboiler in our little state for forty years," he says, "and followed this particular political yarn, this wild, unlikely caper, the story of Bernard Sanders, who is now poised to become Vermont's sole representative in the United States Congress—since the early '70s." Barry reminds us of those "barnstorming days," when Sanders would hitchhike to debates: "And you know what—he's still the same man, love him or leave him, he's the same guy. The signs suggest that there will soon be a socialist from our state, our state of Vermont, serving in the United States Congress."

The story now becomes *polyphonic*, a useful term from Mikhail Bakhtin that I have just learned in my literary theory class. The story has no single narrator. Joe Sherman turns up in Burlington from Montgomery with his eight-year-old son, Andrew, seeking "a political cheap thrill," dancing and swaying along to the zydeco band. The microphone gets passed around the floor of Memorial Auditorium. I know that building so well that I find I can station each voice precisely in a mental model of the room. The broadcast finds familiar Burlington voices: Richard Sugarman, Sadie White, and then Ben Cohen of Ben & Jerry's, scooping Mint Oreo into Dixie cups. "He's our fighter, we're sending him to Washington!"

The broadcast then breaks off for a word from our sponsors.

> Concern for the self always refers to an active political and erotic state. [The Greek verb] "*epimelesthai*" expresses something much more serious than the simple fact of paying attention. It involves various things: taking pains with one's holdings and one's health. It is always a real activity

and not just an attitude. It is used in reference to the activity of a farmer tending his fields, his cattle, and his house, or to the job of the leader in taking care of his city and citizens, or to the worship of ancestors or gods, or as a medical term to signify the fact of caring.

It is highly significant that the concern for the self is directly related to political ambition at a specific moment of life.

—Michel Foucault, addressing Bernie Sanders and the city of Burlington at UVM's Ira Allen Chapel, October 1982

~*Πόλις* (noun): A city, a citadel, a community of people.

Politics (noun): pertaining to public affairs, concerning the governance of a country or people; from Old French politique, "political" (14c.) and directly from Latin *politicus* "of citizens or the state, civil, civic"; from Greek *politikos*, "of citizens, pertaining to the state and its administration; pertaining to public life," from *polites* "citizen," derived from *polis*, "city."

At around ten o'clock, Bernie's voice takes over: hoarse, exhausted. "The evening is not over yet," he tells the crowd, to loud groans.

"We have won a beautiful victory in our home city," Sanders says.

"Ber-nie, Ber-nie, Ber-nie!" the crowd cheers.

"We have won in Rutland. We have won in Essex Junction."

Roars in my headphones; silence all around me. A few weary stragglers arrive to burn the midnight oil. One, as I can smell, has smuggled in a thermos of soup.

"We have—" Sanders stops himself: "We all went through something two years ago."

At 10:10, Sanders again takes the stage: "As I understand it, Congressman Smith has just conceded. Two years ago, we conceded. And I know the pain that he feels. But now our job is not to look back on the past, but to go forward, and to show the country that the state of Vermont is prepared to lead the nation."

Roars, cheers; Sanders is quiet for what seems like a long time. The audio picks up more from the crowd than from the congressman-elect.

"... the courage ..." "... the two party system ..."

"... the courage ... Congress is out of touch ..."

"We are prepared to lead ..."

"Ber-nie, Ber-nie, Ber-nie!"

"I remember, back in 1981, when we won in Burlington, and I was thinking at that point that the city of Burlington, one small city, could play a role in changing the value system of this country ..."

I lose it when I hear him say, "Burlington."

"One small state, our state, might go down as being the leading state in the fight for a political revolution."

Back in Crossett dorm, I encounter my roommates, Jeff, Rob, and Bodhi, watching local returns. William Weld, the liberal, affable, high-WASP Republican, has beaten the Democrat, the frightening, much-despised despotic president of Boston University, John Silber, and been elected governor of Massachusetts.

Rob, then the president of the College Republicans, now, in 2025, a man without a political party, worked hard on the Weld campaign. I liked Weld; we all did. I congratulate Rob on the victory.

"And your guy, huh? Your guy won!" Rob exclaims.

My guy won.

Epilogue: The Stannard Family Picnic

(Summer, 2024)

Structures of Feeling

None of the people portrayed in this book foresaw the enormous changes to personal and community life that would arrive in the new millennium. "We are really living in a world now that no one in the '80s or '90s could have even imagined," Debbie Bookchin remarked to me. "Everything about it, from the internet to social media and the ubiquity of iPhones, to AI and the speeding up of capitalism itself, has profoundly transformed the way people think and feel." This was an astonishing thing for Debbie to say, since her own distinguished parents had, in their different ways, as we have seen in these pages, devoted much of their lives to thinking about the possible futures that awaited humankind.

I lived my own late-twentieth-century life mostly ignorant of the changes hiding inside the frame. Around 2000, I "went online" mainly in the cheesy internet cafés springing up along Bleecker Street in Manhattan (an hour online and a latte for ten dollars) or at metered terminals in the Hasidim-owned copy centers near my apartment under the Manhattan Bridge in Brooklyn. Surfing Craigslist for sublets, futons, or "missed connections" ("Inbound F Train, York Street. We were so cute and embarrassed! Another try?"), I thought of the internet as a boost to twentieth-century life, which I intended to continue living offscreen.

"Twentieth century, go to sleep," Michael Stipe sang in REM's beautiful, mournful fin-de-siecle lullaby, "Electrolite." But Bernie Sanders did not sleepwalk into the twenty-first century and its new technological opportunities. Instead, by 2020, Sanders had set the pace as the most successful digital campaigner of the social media era. "As much as any political figure," Gilad Edelman wrote in *Wired*, "Sanders showed how politics could work in the age of YouTube, Instagram, and the smartphone." Daniel Kreiss, a political scientist at the University of North Carolina at Chapel Hill, agreed: "In so many ways, Bernie Sanders' run in 2016 and, less so, in 2020, cemented the fact that insurgent candidates running a strong, robust challenge to institutionally validated candidates can use the internet as an extremely powerful tool." In 2015, I attended a parents' workshop at our children's elementary school, where we were warned of the dangers of Snapchat, the social media platform then favored by teens and tweens. Later that week, the Sanders campaign debuted on Snapchat, and quickly drew legions of followers.

Though vivid only in retrospect, forerunners of Sanders's twenty-first-century media breakthrough can be found in these pages. The internet itself enters the story only very late and very marginally, buzzing to life during Bernie's 1990 congressional campaign; yet it is present from at least the early 1960s, not as a technology per se, but as a raw "structure of feeling" in search of its eventual technological embodiment. The phrase was coined by the Marxist critic Raymond Williams to describe the "emergent and pre-emergent" relational and social phenomena in a given era:

> We are talking about characteristic elements of impulse, restraint, and tone; specifically affective elements of consciousness and relationships; not feeling against thought, but thought as felt and feeling as thought; practical consciousness of a present kind, in a living and interrelating continuity.

The elements of a "structure of feeling," must be, according to Williams, hard to identify, hard to get a grasp on: you don't find them in the explicit statements or ideas of an era, but rather its distinctive nuances of "impulse, restraint, and tone." Oxford Reference suggests that "if the term is vague" it is because "it is used to name something that can only be regarded as a trajectory." Poets, not surprisingly, play an outsized role in divining this ghostly trajectory—what John Ashbery, in 1970, called "The New Spirit." "Outside," Ashbery wrote, "can't you hear it, the traffic, the trees, everything getting nearer." But David Byrne of Talking Heads put it best, in "The New Feeling": "It's not yesterday anymore."

The word *happening*, with its etymological connection to luck and chance, was all over the culture in the last decades of the century ("There's something happening here, but you don't know what it is," Bob Dylan taunted his clueless interlocutor: "Do you, Mr. Jones?"). Countless performers from the period advertised a "revolution," from the Beatles to Tracy Chapman, and recordings of the era began obsessively marking time: Talking Heads called their first record *77*, for the year it appeared. Prince's breakthrough album, released in 1982, was titled *1999*. That song was a joyous bop, and we sang along to it, all throughout the 1980s; but the wild night that it promised was, alas, the eve of Armageddon: "party over, oops, out of time!" Our anxiety seems so clear, looking back. Ashbery offered very good advice for the reluctant pilgrims being dragged toward the twenty-first century: "There is nothing to be done," he wrote, "you must grow up."

I am not suggesting that Bernie Sanders prophesied the arrival of social media. But he seems to have understood that he stood on the brink of something very new. Vermont's sparse population and far-flung villages made technological innovation natural and necessary. Bernie's freelance columns, his newsletter *Movement*, his bicentennial radio spots, his school filmstrips and ETV specials, his community access show, even his gospel cassette, *We Shall Overcome*, all point forward to the digital media breakthroughs of his presidential campaigns.

And Bernie's wearied-warrior persona, by the time he became a national figure, was decanted easily into the new technological vessels. For any individual who channels the "trajectory" of the times, Raymond Williams wrote, the experience can seem "private, personal, even isolating." "I am once again asking for your financial support," says a down-and-out Bernie in the viral parka pitch recorded in haste in front of his colonial on a middle-class Burlington street. The phrase "I am once again" can now be relied on in most conversations to call this image to mind.

"He'll never let up," Huck Gutman lamented, a little cheerfully, as we walked in Burlington. Huck is among the last of the people who participated in this book to remain in regular contact with Sanders, and he complained that their weekly walks have begun petering out. "I think of those lines from William Butler Yeats's 'Easter, 1916,'" Huck said, stopping to make eye contact. The poem, one of my favorites, commemorates the heroes of the Irish Easter Rebellion, even as it tallies the long-term emotional costs of political sacrifice. "Bernie has a gigantic heart," Huck said, "but sometimes I worry, you know, that it's become a little bit of a 'heart with one purpose alone.'"

I caught the reference. "Too long a sacrifice?" I replied.

Huck nodded, and finished the quote:

Too long a sacrifice
Can make a stone of the heart.
O when may it suffice?

Stannard's Fourth of July

It is hard to find evidence of the twenty-first century in Stannard, Vermont, Bernie's old mountainside town. Cell service fades north of Hardwick Village and vanishes in Greensboro Bend. Up Stannard Mountain Road, the hand-painted sign at Black Dirt Farm advertises worm castings and stewing hens. Cresting the steep rise, you come to the Stannard town hall and the old Methodist church before the road disappears into dense forest. Two hundred or so residents called this village home, back when Sanders lived here in the late '60s. The town has shrunk by a dozen or so residents since then.

By another measure, though, the twenty-first century has arrived. In August of 2011, Hurricane Irene swept through the Northeast Kingdom and wiped out hundreds of bridges and roads to villages like Stannard, which were then cut off entirely from the world. In July of 2023, the second "hundred-year storm" in a little over a decade washed these structures out all over again. Residents of one town watched their beloved covered bridge appear to genuflect as its ancient planks and pilings crumbled into the rapids. In the summer of 2024, Stannard Brook, normally a tranquil shimmer playing hide-and-seek in the roadside clearings, swelled its banks and washed out a cement bridge at the base of Stannard Mountain Road. Here in the Northeast Kingdom of Vermont, there is no ignoring the intensifying threat of climate change, or the accelerating pace of these "once in a lifetime" storms.

In July of 2024, I drove four hours from Boston to hear Bernie address a small crowd at the annual Stannard Family Picnic. Kids danced to bluegrass banjo and sucked on their juice boxes until the sides collapsed. True-blue hippies in their seventies and eighties showed up in rare early Bernie campaign buttons and T-shirts. When the skies opened, the crowd bottlenecked into a small, humid community room, where the banjo played on. Sanders, entering through the side kitchen to a light spray of applause, mixed easily with his old neighbors and friends, reminiscing about the mud, the snow, and the scandals ("There was a lot of Peyton Place–like stuff happening in Stannard, back then," he laughed) of fifty-five years ago. His son Levi, then an infant, now a tall, graying man of retirement age, filmed his father on an iPhone. I did not sense that day that "too long a sacrifice" had hardened Bernie's heart; not at all. Nor had the small crowd hardened their hearts against him. When Sanders tested a flimsy plastic table to see if it would support his weight, the room held its breath; but, with some difficulty, the eighty-two-year-old senator now relaxed into his favorite pose: stand-sitting diagonally against the table edge, legs crossed, his long arms gesticulating above his head, his index finger jabbing the air to make a point, like a conductor's baton.

Sanders had not come to Stannard only to reminisce; he was in the middle of his twenty-second, and almost certainly his last, political campaign, contending as the most favorably regarded member of the Senate as a shoo-in for a fourth term. But that weekend happened to be an inflection point in presidential politics, indeed in American history, and Bernie's message was not what many in the room expected. The issue of the hour was whether President Joe Biden, falling in the polls after a perplexed, aphasic debate performance against Donald Trump, should step aside and make way for a more effective candidate. Chatter in the room indicated near-unanimous sentiment that Biden, alas, was through.

Sanders surprised many when he argued that Biden should stay in the race. "Anybody ever hear, before last week, of Andy Beshear?" Sanders inquired. A few people nodded. "Okay," he replied. "He's the governor of Kentucky. I met him some years ago. Nice guy! Does anybody know anything about him? Probably not. But somebody has decided he's a candidate for president of the United States."

Then Sanders inquired about "a Mr. Pritzker"—J. B. Pritzker, the governor of Illinois. "He's a billionaire," Sanders cracked, "which I suppose is an asset." The point was not lost on the group: "Somebody sits around, not ordinary people, and makes these decisions." And yet, of all "the names I've heard," Sanders argued, "you know who is the most progressive? It's Joe Biden."

The ironies here could not be ignored. Sanders's second presidential campaign ended, in March of 2020, precisely when "somebody, not ordinary people," decided that the Democratic Party must unite behind Joe Biden. In a matter of days, all of Biden's former rivals had endorsed him, with Sanders, running strong in second place, conceding last. Four years earlier, Democratic superdelegates had closed ranks to stop Bernie from overtaking the Democrats' chosen candidate, Hillary Clinton. In the eyes of many of Bernie's supporters, the Democratic elite had twice overruled their own voters to install a "safe" inside choice. Now Biden's career might end according to the same mystified process. The word that weekend was that the president's fate depended on the vibes at a Sunday fund-raiser in the Hamptons, and a Monday follow-up Zoom call with top donors.

But to many in the room, the cabal of advisers protecting Biden seemed if anything more corrupt than the faction pushing him out. "Sure, it does not make you feel good about democracy," Sanders conceded, "when voters have a choice between a fascist and a guy who can't string three sentences together." This was refreshing to hear. But Sanders had found in Biden a strong and reliable ally, he said; and now, in stump speech mode, Bernie rattled off his familiar list of policy goals: Medicare for all, reproductive rights, new taxes on the wealthy, action on the environment, support for unions. "Joe Biden was the only president in American history to stand on a picket line," Sanders said. The crowd applauded, and after an hour of freewheeling debate, Sanders turned the room over to the plastic trays of ham sandwiches and hummus wraps that a hungry crowd spied behind him.

I felt weird being there—like an interloper, maybe even a flatlander. So, outside, after lining up for a picture behind men and women who'd known him for fifty-five years, I told Bernie only that I was from Burlington, and had grown up during his years as mayor. It was a thrilling place to grow up, I said. I told him it made me who I am.

"Oh boy," Sanders replied, as the guy in line behind me snapped our photo.

Stannard Family Picnic, 2024. *Courtesy the author*

Acknowledgments

I began with a regular ambition, one I'll dignify by quoting Marcel Proust: I wanted to recall "all the places and people that I had known, what I had actually experienced of them, and what others had told me." My method was to puzzle together these two types of information—what I remembered firsthand, and what people told me—as snugly as I could.

This required hundreds of hours of work from the dozens of individuals who are named in this book. Not that I was surprised to find so many who were willing: the transformation of Vermont and the political renaissance in Burlington were the fruits of their individual gifts of imagination and labor, over decades. My book—with its large cast of characters—was written in the spirit of including as many such contributions as one story would bear. As I worked, *Bernie for Burlington* branched toward information, but its roots were fed by these relationships—some new, some renewed—which often took the form of jointly remembering, of remembering together. It is a special way to spend time with a person.

Thank you, first, to Jim Rader. Jim alone can speak to the entire arc of Bernie's career, having not only observed, but often abetted his friend's rise, playing roles at every step along the way; and only Rader, a man widely loved and respected in Burlington and throughout Vermont, could invite understandably wary souls into my project. Because Jim is far too modest to tout his own importance, much of what I wrote *about* Rader was based on what others told me. Almost the best part of this process was to find one of Jim's remarkable poems in my inbox. I'm so glad, now that our Bernie project is done, that we can look forward to exchanging poems.

Thanks, too, to Meg Pond, for friendship and perspective gained from her decades of working for Vermonters, and for unbelievable dinners and wine and snacks in her home; and Emer Feeney, whom I've known since at least 1984. Reconnecting with Emer over this project, I can now call her one of my oldest friends. Meg, Jim, Emer, and I had fun adventures along the way—and it was a joy to spend time, too, with Emer's husband, Jason Pepe.

Thank you to Larry Sanders, for conversations of real scope and range about the guy that he calls "*BER*-nard." Thank you to dear Richard Sugarman—who "calls Bernie '*BER*-nard' in emulation of Larry, his brother"—for hours of personal stories, insights, and perspective. Richard is the savviest political thinker I have ever met, as well as the funniest. Thanks to Greg Guma, the true historian of Burlington's progressive past—a tradition he helped to shape—for spending an afternoon with me and supplying me with excerpts from his published and unpublished writing. Gratitude, too, to Garrison Nelson, the foremost analyst and scholar of Vermont politics—a scene that his shrewd analysis helped shape, in real time—who spoke to me for hours on his beautiful back porch in Mallets Bay. Thank you, Peter Clavelle, for an afternoon touring our home turf together, just a couple of Rice grads. Nancy Barnett was especially generous with her time. The late Stephen Terry, a great political mind and an insider par excellence, let me take him out for soup at the Middlebury Inn. Danny Lyon took my call on his dock in Maine. Peter Schumann had us up to the back cabin, where nobody ever gets to go, for strong beers. Debbie Bookchin and Jim Schumacher, recalling days in the Burlington political trenches long before they met and married, were kind to share their binocular insights. Jym Wilson, who left Burlington with an unparalleled photographic archive of the Sanders years, also acted as my unofficial photo coordinator. Huck Gutman and I spent much of our time together quoting poetry back and forth; through Huck, Modern poetry found a role in Bernie's rise. Julia Alvarez welcomed me at her home with a view of orchards, and shared wonderful stories and artifacts from her years in Burlington. It was thrilling to meet Pamela Polston, everybody's Burlington crush for decades. I'll never forget the afternoon I spent with Frank Kochman thirty feet from my childhood bedroom, over a bottle of Costco Barolo, or my conversations with Appleton King as he fed and comforted his ten-week-old puppy. George Thabault, whose family and mine go back generations, shared some of the warm, personal side of Mayor Sanders, and read several of my chapters while they were in process. Melinda and Rick Moulton welcomed me to their hand-built stone house facing Camel's Hump, and introduced me to their grandson, the poet Rowan Wilde Riggs. Joe Sherman had me up to Montgomery, where we sat by the creek and played dolls with his seven-year-old daughter. Thanks, Stu McGowan, for your stories and for your work in Burlington. Peter Smith and I struck up a friendship in our conversations: I so admire Peter's humility, his ongoing career in service to education and ordinary people, and his courageous work in the U.S. Congress.

This book began, in a kind of way, at Sneakers Bar and Grill in Winooski, Vermont, in the 1980s, when I got to know the terrific historian of Burlington and Winooski (also, Emer's father) Vince Feeney. Vince used to write in his notebooks bright and early, over yogurt and fresh fruit, before opening up his Irish imports shop, Feeney and Daughters, for the day. Inspired by his example, I wrote quite a few of my own pages at Sneakers (new space, same vibe) throughout this process.

Thank you, too, to those who filled in important gaps, or otherwise offered support: Gary De Carolis, Dennis Gilbert, John Franco, Linda Niedweske, David Clavelle, Jonathan and Roxanne Leopold, Gene Bergman, Chard de Niord, Ellen David Friedman, Nancy Hill, Clive Gray, Dan Higgins, Ruah Swennerfelt, Phil

Fiermonte, James Blumstein, Ron MacNeil, Chris Graff, Terry Bouricius, Sansea Sparling, Robin Lloyd, Chelsea Edgar, Jim Lockridge, Mike Agganis, Miciah Bay Gault, Paula Roulty, Robin Macarthur, Rick Sharp, Dug Napp, Makenna Goodman, Maria Hummel. Like many Burlingtonians, I am indebted to Bob Blanchard's marvelous archive of Burlington images and stories, "Burlington Area History," on Facebook. Murray Ngoima visited me in Wellesley, telling remarkable stories as we sorted through her boxes full of Liberty Union clippings and mementos. Brian Pine had me into the CEDO offices for warm reminiscences. Howard Dean and I talked while the governor, famously a fast walker, made the cold trek to his barber one December afternoon. Nat Winthrop hosted me at his beautiful home on College Hill in Montpelier. Mayor Emma Mulvaney-Stanak graciously welcomed me to the mayor's office, late on the Friday afternoon of a Memorial Day weekend, with the sounds and, well, the *smells* of Church Street streaming in (city hall still does not have central air). Sitting on the South Porch of Shelburne Farms one August afternoon, working on revisions, I looked up to see Senator Patrick Leahy and Marcelle Leahy strolling by after brunch. We talked for an hour on the sunny lawn—off the record, but it was mostly about all the nuns who we'd known in common.

Shelburne Farms is itself enough of a contributor to this book that I feel I should thank its sunsets and hay bales and buildings, especially the vineyard cottage back by the Breeding Barn where I wrote much of the second half of this book, in the winter of 2023–24. Thank you to Julie Eldridge Edwards for time in the beautiful archives and generous help throughout. Thanks, Tara Stetz, for hospitality throughout the seasons. Thank you, Alec Webb, for the transformative work you've done at the farms, a benefit for all Vermonters; and for sharing memories of your brother, Marshall Webb, and father, Derick Webb. And thanks, Heidi Webb, for all of your insights into your family, the property, and the region that we share and love.

If I started thanking people in Vermont, I would, alas, never stop. But my friend of some forty years, George Ewins, who is *in this* book, often met me at the end of long writing days for martinis at the Backyard Bistro in Charlotte or Trattoria in Burlington. We picked up the happy, ornery political debates we've had since the days of drinking beers at the Bourbon Street Grill, when we used to see Bernie zip by the windows on his way back to city hall. Thank you infinitely to Meghan O'Rourke of CCTV, Myles David Jewell, and Cindi and Jordan and everyone at Frankies, for the work you do on the plate, in the glass, and in the community. And I'll note two new Burlingtonians, writers I deeply admire, as especially important to this work: Noah Warren, who read the entire manuscript, and Aria Aber.

Thank you to my teachers, in and out of the classroom, for contributions direct and indirect: Robert Pinsky, who read and commented on the entire book; Jorie Graham and Peter Sacks; Frank Bidart, my mentor for thirty years; and the late Helen Vendler, who expressed bewilderment that I would write such a book, but offered kind wishes. It was important to share political gossip with my friend Margery Sabin at the start of this process. William H. Pritchard taught me to read poetry at Amherst College. Rick Griffiths makes a secret appearance in my final scene. At Rice Memorial High School, Robert Brown, RJ Noonan, and Lloyd Hulburd, all in different ways, opened my eyes to the history and landscape of Vermont.

I am grateful to two of my favorite Vermonters, both dear friends: Jamaica Kincaid and the late Louise Glück. Jamaica's garden in North Bennington is the most beautiful place in all of Vermont. It was Jamaica who first persuaded me that to write was simply a necessity for my survival, as indeed it was. And it was Jamaica who told me that writing takes courage: "What's the worst that can happen, Dan?" Jamaica once said to me. "It's not as though your period came through your new school dress." I loved reconnecting with Louise in Montpelier and looked forward to years of visits to her small, perfect cape behind the statehouse. Before she died unexpectedly in 2023, Louise read two chapters of this book, and thought I used "verbs of becoming too much." She also said that she found it "riveting" and, against her will, suspended her binge-viewing of *The Bear* to finish my pages. I miss her very much.

I am fortunate to work at Wellesley College, among friends. Thank you to my chairs, Lisa Rodensky and Yoon Sun Lee, for working so assiduously on my book's behalf. Thanks to Lisa Easley for many generosities, and Catherine O'Neill Grace for her support and friendship. Thank you to all my colleagues in the English department, for countless acts of support and expressions of curiosity. Thanks especially to Bill Cain, for reading this entire manuscript and sharing your insights. Thank you to President Paula Johnson, Provost Andy Shennan, Dean Megan Nunez, and, especially, Dean Michael Jeffries, who read early drafts of this work and generously discussed it with me in front of a crowd. Thank you to my old friend, and now my new provost, Courtney Coile, and to all of my students who tolerated my "Bernie digressions" in classes ostensibly about John Milton or James Merrill. Rory Conlin, Marty Martinage, Alice Ascoli, Jacq Roderick, Emma Sullivan, Ivy Buck, Tedi Rollins, Alina Edwards, Ahana Basu, Phoebe Zilliax Blodget, and Emily Chang were especially kind in their curiosity and encouragement.

Thank you to everyone at UVM's Silver Special Collections Reading Room, especially Prudence Doherty, who first helped me in 1988 on my AP U.S. History term paper, and, still at her post thirty-five years later, helped me with this work.

I presented an early excerpt from this manuscript at Bread Loaf's Environmental Writers' Conference: thank you, Meghan Mayhew Bergman and Jennifer Grotz. I read sections at Harvard's Woodberry Poetry Room: thank you, Christina Davis, Amanda Claybaugh, and Louis Menand. Thank you, Adam Ross, for reading parts of the book, and for your friendship and support. Thanks to the great poet Tomas Unger, my friend and former student, for thoughtful feedback. Thank you, Louisa Thomas, for reading the entire manuscript and collaborating so happily on our Harvard event. My book was influenced by the example of your fleet, brilliant prose. Speaking of "fleet": it's fun running on the Charles with you.

When I left Burlington for the first time in 1989, I realized that people were curious about my hometown—partly because of ice cream, jam bands, skiing, and beer, but mostly because of Bernie Sanders. Freshman year, Jeff Posternak borrowed my cassette of Bernie's *We Shall Overcome*, and loaned it to his dad, Chuck Posternak, who put this music—to me, I am afraid, unlistenable—in heavy rotation on the car tape deck. It was a joy to develop this project in conversation with Jeff thirty-five years later. Rob Witwer and I have merged politics and close friendship for decades. Rob's book *The Blueprint: How the Democrats Won Colorado (And Why Republicans Everywhere Should Care)*, a classic in the study of political and cultural change, was a model for this book. Rob read the entire manuscript, and passed it along to his mom and dad, Jean and John Witwer. The Witwer family spent formative years in Burlington. I think of them often when I am home.

Thanks, too, to Kyle Johnson, Bodhi Fishman, Matt Gray, Alex Ginsberg, and Ron Lieber, for friendship and conversation over all the years. Thanks to Jodi Kantor for support and advice at an important crossroads. It was an honor to share pages-in-progress with Jessica Shattuck, whose *Last House*, a beautiful novel about Vermont, influenced the writing of several sections. Thanks to our dear friends Stephanie and the late Dr. Mark Price, Jen and Bar Helzberg, and Corey and Nick Halaby. Thanks, Tyler and Hannah Wick, for friendship and laughs and Burlington stories. Thank you, Daniel Sokatch and Dana Reinhardt, for decades of friendship and for reading this manuscript with boundless curiosity. Thanks Crysalle LaCouture and Scott Stedman for friendship and curiosity. And thank you, Jimmy Wallenstein, a friend I wish I saw every day, for reading one chapter.

I was especially excited to share this book with my dear friend Chad Curlett, who drove up and spent one wild summer with me in Burlington, back in 1995. As anyone who knows Chad will confirm, I got much of my storytelling method from him. Now that Chad and Christina have moved to Burlington, I look forward to many more glasses of the *Mort du Soleil*, followed by "two large paintings"!

Thank you to my beloved friends of thirty-five years, Katie Bacon and Mark Pener. Katie edited my first five chapters at a time when I could not find the path forward, and she reviewed the completed manuscript when I was still unsure of many little things. I wrote this book with her careful attentiveness—as a reader, and as a friend so close I feel we are actually siblings—in mind. Mark and Katie's home is a place that so many of us cherish for its warmth and laughter. Thank you for welcoming us there during the hardest time in your lives. I miss Jamie every time I look across Lake Champlain at the mountains he climbed.

The idea for *Bernie for Burlington* came to me in conversation with my agent Jacqueline Ko at the Wylie Agency. Thanks, Jackie, for *getting us into this*, and for your bright encouragement throughout. It is so fun to brainstorm with you. Here I must thank Jeff Posternak a second time, along with the entire team at Wylie, for their belief in the value of writing and writers. Thank you, Andrew Wylie: the stamp you have made on contemporary literature is profound.

I had research assistance from Coby Mulliken, Sam Goorno, and Malia Chung. Special thanks to Cheynie Singleton, who helped with production, and read the whole manuscript. And my thanks to Bailey Ludwig, who coordinates our Mellon grant at Wellesley College, which provided support for my project.

Thanks to everyone at Knopf, especially Zuleima Ugalde, for guiding our production so efficiently and attentively, and Sarah New, who masterminded publicity. Thank you, Matthew Sciarappa, for your brilliant input. Thank you to Amy Stackhouse for your careful copyediting of the manuscript, and for our friendly conversations in the margins. My thanks to Jordan Pavlin and Hilary Redmon, for their enthusiastic support. I want to express my deepest gratitude to my editor, Deborah Garrison. Editors and writers so closely aligned do, I think, merge. At least I hope so. I love your poems, your energy and zest for living in the world, your belief and trust in me, and your transformative attention to so many poets and writers. It was a pure joy to do this work with you, especially through an interval when politics was worrying us both so much. Thank you, dear D.

I want to thank Philip, Mark, Paula, Susan, and Janet, for helping to raise me, and showing me so much love and support. *Bernie for Burlington* is indebted perhaps most of all to my mother, Linda Chiasson. It was a delight to share stories together about our lovable, frustrating city, and to celebrate our family's life in it. I'm especially proud of the sections on the Sisters of Mercy, the order of nuns who made such a difference in my life, and in Burlington's political renaissance. My mom has supported me as a writer and a reader from before I can remember. I love you, Mom!

This book was written in the very center of my life, surrounded by my family. Thanks to Dougie and Jena Adams, Sally Adams, and Nana and Papa; thank you all for such love and support and curiosity. Thanks to my amazing nieces, Haley and Sidney Adams, for being the people you are. Thank you, Louis and Nicholas Chiasson, for our nightly dinner check-ins about "the Bernie book," for your insights and angles, for making me laugh so much, and for tolerating the file boxes and newspapers all over our home, and in my car, and at the beach. When you were little, I used to set you up with a pile of books and Legos so that, as you used to put it, I "could go upstairs and choose words." Even then, I hung on *your* every word. Now I look forward to the mark you will put on the world. I love you guys—"to the moon and back."

I said goodbye to one writing companion during this process, our big bear, Clover, and welcomed another, our little scoundrel, Sadie. Coleridge wrote that he would have been lost in "abstruser musings" had it not been for the rhythmic gift of his "cradled infant" slumbering peacefully beside him. But babies can't compete with dogs, sorry. They require too way much; and then they go away to college.

Thank you, Annie Adams. How on earth, I really do wonder. I was so glad, that time we played "rank the New England states" on one of our long family drives, that you, a Connecticut Yankee living for thirty years in Massachusetts—you ranked Vermont first!

I sent a letter to Alison Bechdel, and before I knew it, she'd turned this book into a work of art. Vermonters, as we know from this story, turn out for each other. Thank you, Alison!

And thank you, Bernie Sanders—*for Burlington.*

Notes

Many sources are indicated in the body of the text, as part of the story. As a general rule I have not duplicated those citations in these notes. Where I have, the source seems to me rich enough to repay a reader's further curiosity, or complex enough to invite a contesting interpretation.

When I cite "interviews, conversations, and exchanges," I mean recorded interviews, on the record; unrecorded follow-up "conversations," as well as casual conversations over the course of decades in some cases; short email or text "exchanges" or quick remarks shared in person. Sources interviewed are generally indicated in the text, where, or near where, they are quoted. "Others" indicates additional sources who remain anonymous.

Prologue: Making a Scene

3 In a video that surfaced: *Bernie Sanders Interviews Mall Punks* (1988), youtube.com.
4 interviews my uncle and cousins: *Bernie Speaks with the Community*, episode 11, cctv .org.
5 In a 2020 election postmortem issue: *Jacobin* 38 (Summer 2020).
9 appeared on the *Today* show: "Socialism in New England," today.com.
10 the Diocese of Burlington: Cori Urban, vermontcatholic.org.
11 "out-Republicaned the Republicans": Debbie Bookchin, *RH*, April 4, 1982.
12 "the left wing of the possible": Matthew Zeitlin, "Bernie's Red Vermont," *New Republic*, June 13, 2019.
13 "every inch of Central Vermont": Sanders, *Our Revolution*, p. 22.

1. Welcome to Vermont!

This chapter draws on interviews, conversations, and exchanges with Larry Sanders, Jorie Graham, Jim Rader, and others.

22 "Vermont in New York: An Invitation!": *Vermont Life* 8, no. 3 (1954).
23 Vermont Information Center: Diane Rice, "The Field of Travel: Vermont Information Center Is Opened Here," *NYT*, October 25, 1953.
24 "The usual path": Ross Barkan, "Why Bernie Is Probably Not Going to Talk About His Mom as Much as Hillary Will," *New York Observer*, August 4, 2015.
25 "They did not have easy lives": *PBS NewsHour*, July 26, 2016, youtube.com.
27 "I went to the small shop": Sanders, *Our Revolution*, p. 10.
28 "builders' houses": Mimi Sheraton, *Eating My Words*, William Morrow, 2004, p. 15.

31 "The train stops somewhere in Brooklyn": Bernie Sanders, "The Revolution Is Life Versus Death," *VF*, November 15, 1969.

33 Bernie is at Cathedral Square: *Bernie Speaks with the Community*, episode 15, cctv.org.

2. *Welcome to Vermont! (Part 2)*

This chapter benefits from the historical scholarship of Paul M. Searls and Sara M. Gregg, and calls on interviews, conversations, and exchanges with Howard Dean, Vince Feeney, Stephen Terry, and others.

36 a Vermonter named William Jarvis: Unsigned, "William Jarvis & the Merino Sheep Craze," vermonthistory.org.

38 residents in their habitat: "Two Hundred Vermonters," *Rural Vermont: A Program for Its Future* (Vermont Commission on Rural Life, 1931), p. 117.

38 In 1925, Perkins: Hope Greenberg and Nancy Gallagher, *Vermont Eugenics: A Documentary History*, uvm.edu.

39 a "pirate" family": Kevin Dann, "From Degeneration to Regeneration: The Eugenics Survey of Vermont, 1925–1936," *Vermont History* 59, no. 1 (Winter 1991): 7.

40 "Vermonters with progressive leanings": Hand, *The Star That Set*, p. viii.

41 "moved to Vermont with an idea": Interview with Howard Dean, December 1, 2023.

43 interview with *Vermont Life*: Bernard Sanders, "Aiken of Vermont," *Vermont Life* 27, no. 3 (Spring 1973): 6.

44 I spoke with Stephen Terry: Interview with Stephen Terry, Wednesday, May 24, 2023.

3. *"Politics Helped"*

This chapter is informed by interviews and conversations with Danny Lyon, Ira Churgin, Jim Rader, Larry Sanders, Diana Maher, and Meg Pond.

47 an article in *Time*: Sam Frizell, "Exclusive: College Alumni Raise Doubts About Bernie Sanders Campaign Photo," *Time*, November 12, 2105.

47 a *Washington Post* columnist: Jonathan Capehart, "Stop Sending Around This Photo of 'Bernie Sanders,'" *Washington Post*, February 11, 2016.

49 "What a strange thing to happen to a little boy": Interview with Paul Auster, *Paris Review Interviews* 4 (1989).

49 Einstein's essay "Why Socialism": Albert Einstein, "Why Socialism," *Monthly Review*, reprinted 2009.

50 "the flashy young liberal": "Bernie Sanders and Rik Musty UVM Course," 1986, cctv.org.

52 a breakthrough for Sanders: Danny Lyon, "Behind the Image: Bernie Sanders at the Radical Equality Sit-In, 58 Years Ago," magnumphotos.com.

52 "these wonderful, important people had lied": "Bernie Sanders and Rik Musty UVM Course."

52 A skirmish: Isabelle Noiret, "UC CORE Meets with Local Representatives," *Chicago Maroon*, May 4, 1962.

54 "on top of everything": Sanders Mayoral Papers, University of Vermont.

54 the syndicated story: Syndicated, "University Slapped Back as Enemy of Free Love," *Dayton Daily News*, April 29, 1963.

54 in the pages of *The Chicago Maroon*: Bernard Sanders, "Sex and the Single Girl—Part Two," *Chicago Maroon* (April 1963).

55 "Marx, a lot of Freud": Rick Perlstein, "A Political Education," *University of Chicago Magazine* (January/February 2015).

55 the term *sexual revolution*: Wilhelm Reich, *The Sexual Revolution: Towards a Self-Governing Character Structure* (Farrar, Straus and Giroux, 1963).

56 "civilized living conditions": Wilhelm Reich, "The Sexual Misery of the Working Masses and the Difficulties of Sexual Reform," *New German Critique* 1 (Winter 1973).

56 while his ideas circulated freely: Christopher Turner, *Adventures in the Orgasmatron: How the Sexual Revolution Came to America* (Farrar, Straus and Giroux, 2011).

58 In the summer of 1963: Sanders, *Our Revolution*, pp. 19ff.
59 Sanders told Russell Banks: Russell Banks, "Bernie Sanders, the Socialist Mayor," *Atlantic*, October 5, 2015.

4. The Sugarhouse and the Highway

This chapter incorporates interviews and conversations with Jim Rader, Larry Sanders, Meg Pond, Emer Feeney, Stephen Terry, Garrison Nelson, Peter Schumann, and others. For in-depth study of the Vermont Republican Party, see Samuel Hand's *The Star That Set* and Stephen Terry's *Say We Won and Get Out.*

61 In February of 1964: Unsigned, "Week's Engagements Announced," *Baltimore Sun*, February 9, 1964.
62 renunciation of "all discipline": Neill, *Summerhill*, p. 27.
62 "did the tourist thing": Sanders, *Our Revolution*, p. 22.
62 severed his relationship: Ofer Aderet, "Mystery Solved: Haaretz Archive Reveals Which Kibbutz Bernie Sanders Volunteered On," *Haaretz*, February 4, 2016.
62 "structure of the community": Sanders, *Our Revolution*, p. 22.
62 ten miles from Haifa: Details in this paragraph are from the unsigned article "The Community Spirit," *Huddersfield Daily Examiner*, June 22, 1973.
64 "It was just fantastic": Russell Banks, "Bernie Sanders, the Socialist Mayor," *Atlantic*, October 5, 2015.
64 "a Republican mystique persisted": Hand, *The Star That Set*, p. 237.
65 Kennedy-like Burlington attorney: These paragraphs on Hoff draw from Stephen Terry's *Philip Hoff.*
66 In 1945: Howard Weiss-Tisman, "As Tree Falls, State Ponders How to Memorialize Romaine Tenney's Death, Legacy of Resistance," 2021, vermontpublic.org.
67 a "twilight period": Paul M. Searls, quoted in Jane Lindholm, "Interstates, Burning Farms & Eminent Domain," October 2019, vermontpublic.org.

5. "Access to Tools"

This chapter draws on interviews, conversations, and exchanges with Kate Daloz, Robin MacArthur, Gene Bergman, Joe Sherman, Larry Sanders, Jim Rader, Frank Kochman, Kip Parsons, James Blumstein, Art Spiegelman, William H. Macy, Louise Glück, Peter Schumann, Miciah Bay Gault, and others.

74 a writer for *Playboy*: Richard Pollack, "Taking Over Vermont," *Playboy* (April 1972).
75 "friends in Vermont": Email from Art Spiegelman, October 11, 2022.
75 the other end of the spectrum: Vermont Press Bureau, "Governor Allays Fears on Hippie Influx," *TA*, May 20, 1971.
77 "All aspects of life are intimately related": Bernard Sanders, "Natural Childbirth in a Vermont Commune: An Interview with Lorraine," *Movement* 1, no. 5 (1972).
78 "He was always Bernie": Lorraine Janowski, interview with the Vermont Historical Society, February 12, 2016.
79 In "Jamestown Seventy": James F. Blumstein and James Phelan, "Jamestown Seventy," *Yale Review of Law and Social Action* (1971).
80 missionary leftist named "Josh": Ginny Callan, interview with the Vermont Historical Society, July 27, 2015.
82 "The era was awash": Davis, *High Weirdness*, pp. 80ff.
83 "Elms": Louise Glück, *The First Four Books of Poems* (Ecco, 1995).
85 "drifted away": Daloz, *Going Up the Country*.
86 "kind of a frontier": Ellen David Friedman, interview with the Vermont Historical Society, September 29, 2015.

6. The Vermont Freeman

This chapter draws on interviews and conversations with Vince Feeney, Garrison Nelson, Murray Ngoima, Alec Webb, Jim Rader, Frank Kochman, and Linda Chiasson.

89 "a live bowling alley show": Betty Sproston, "WVNY Studios Are Located at Ft. Ethan Allen, Colchester," *BFP*, August 22, 1968.
91 A resident of nearby Glover: Unsigned, "Irasburg Shooting Arraignment Near," *BR*, August 1, 1968.
91 "We believe in strict law enforcement": Unsigned, "Bar Assn. Cool to Talk by Free Press Publisher," *TA*, March 1, 1969.
92 "a cooperative system": Daley, *Going Up the Country*, p. 50.
92 Free Vermont: John Douglas, interview with the Vermont Historical Society, May 13, 2016.
93 Albright's new venture: Jennifer Kochman, interview with the Vermont Historical Society, August 7, 2015.
96 seizing on the *Vermont Freeman*: Trip Gabriel, "Bernie Sanders Recants Article on Women's Fantasies of Rape," *NYT*, May 29, 2015.
100 "Keep it small": Bill Kauffman, "Bye Bye Miss American Empire," *Vermont Commons* (Summer 2011).

7. *We Americans*

This chapter draws on conversations with my family over the course of more than fifty years, as well as context provided by interviews and conversations with Vince Feeney, Garrison Nelson, Jim Rader, and others.

105 "The city rises": Anderson, *We Americans*, pp. 8–9.
106 "All of Burlington, however": Ibid., pp. 11–12.
110 a twenty-first-century American: Throughout this book, as in this passage, the early history of Burlington is informed by Vincent Feeney's *Burlington: A History of Vermont's Queen City*.

8. *The Children's Crusade*

This chapter draws on conversations and interviews with Murray Ngoima, Garrison Nelson, Richard Sugarman, Huck Gutman, John Franco, Jim Rader, Luther Martin, and others.

122 "The campuses, Cambodia": Perlstein, *Nixonland*, p. 479.
123 waving a Vietcong flag: Unsigned, "UVM Group Stages Antiwar Protest," *BFP*, April 23, 1971.
124 sending a Democrat to the Senate: Unsigned, "The Hoff Candidacy: A Man for Moderates," *VF*, March 27, 1970.
125 published Christmas verses: Frank Sullivan, "Greetings, Friends!," *New Yorker*, December 27, 1958.
125 not the Democratic Party: Martha Abbott, interview with the Vermont Historical Society, January 6, 2016.
126 "snugly cocooned": Jeffrey St. Clair, "The Trouble with Howie," *CounterPunch*, February 2, 2004.
126 eighty-five thousand Vermonters: "1970 Population," usa.ipums.org.
126 "the poor subsidize the rich": Michael Parenti, "A Third Party Emerges in Vermont," *Massachusetts Review* (Summer 1975).

9. *A Special Election*

This chapter draws on interviews, exchanges, and conversations with Jim Rader, Huck Gutman, Richard Sugarman, Debbie Bookchin, Rick Warner, and others.

129 "no organizing on college campuses": Jonathan Maslow, "Liberty Union: The Left Thrives in Vermont," *BP* 4, no. 11 (1975).
130 "bacon-and-egg diners, hardware stores, and gun shops": Biehl, *Ecology or Catastrophe*, p. 141.
133 "known meeting spot for extremists": Greg Guma, "Bernie Sanders: I Think I'd Make a Good Candidate," June 2025, globalresearch.ca.
134 "about 35 adults and children": Unsigned, "Liberty Union," *VF*, November 1, 1971.

135 in political "expediencies": Stephen Carlson, "Liberty Union Adds Woman to Ticket," *BFP*, November 16, 1971.
136 On one typical campaign day: John Lazenby, "Third Party Candidates Are Applauded at High School but Fail to Draw Any Students for Speeches at College," *RH*, December 15, 1971.
137 In third place: Robert Ward, "Stafford Wins Apathy Battle Against the Mayor," *BFP*, January 8, 1972.

10. Movement

This chapter incorporates interviews and conversations with Howard Dean, Jim Rader, Peter Smith, Alec Webb, Huck Gutman, Kate Daloz, and others.

141 "a family fiefdom": Hand, *The Star That Set*, p. 69.
142 In a 1934 strike: Mark Bushnell, "The Again: Marble Workers' Strike Was Long and Fierce," *VTD*, December 16, 2018.
142 went back a hundred years: Unsigned, "Proctor's Silent Speaker," *RH*, June 8, 1972.
143 "needed so many glasses": "Liberty Union: Where It's At," *Movement* (February 1973).
145 "the meaning of the 1960s": Perlstein, *Nixonland*, p. 608.
146 sensed an opportunity: Bernard Sanders, "Fragments of a Campaign Diary," *Chittenden Magazine* 4, no. 2 (December 1972).
153 An article in the *Burlington Free Press*: Candace Page, "Liberty Union Party Seeks Coalition of Workers," *BFP*, October 12, 1974.

11. At the Fair

This chapter was informed by conversations, interviews, and exchanges with Senator Patrick Leahy, Governor Howard Dean, Alec Webb, Heidi Webb, Julie Eldridge Edwards, Jim Rader, Stephen Terry, Murray Ngoima, Greg Guma, and John Franco.

157 Mallary hoists an enormous sausage: File photo, *BFP*, September 4, 1974.
157 had made an impression: See Baruth, *Senator Leahy*, pp. 51ff.
160 church basement in Burlington: Stuart Perry, "Liberty Union Nominates 6: Sanders Blasts Salmon," *BFP*, June 17, 1974.
161 "I can talk about the Rockefellers": Tyler Resch, "Candidate Sanders Focuses on Power of the Rockefellers," *Bennington Banner*, September 17, 1974.
162 "They are both bought": Greg LeFever, "For Sanders, Liberty Union's a Way of Life," *RH*, October 16, 1974.
163 according to Nico Baumbach: Nico Baumbach, "Sameness-Machines: On the Political Unconscious of Memes," *Representations* 168, no. 1 (Fall 2024): 153ff.

12. Vermont Vermont

This chapter draws on interviews and conversations with Alec Webb, Heidi Webb, Linda Chiasson, Susan Ford, Paula Delorme, Julie Eldridge Edwards, Jamaica Kincaid, Howard Dean, and others.

165 As Blake Harrison argues: Harrison, *The View from Vermont*, pp. 20–23.
167 The development scene: Sherman, *Fast Lane on a Dirt Road*, p. 105.

13. Bicentennial

173 in the summer of '76: Fred Bruning, "Vermont Joins the Celebration," *Vermont Life* 30, no. 4 (Summer 1976).
173 Burlington native Orson Bean: John Read, "Orson Bean Knits Holiday Crowd," *BFP*, July 4, 1976.
174 "I am having / My childhood now": Dan Chiasson, *Bicentennial* (Alfred A. Knopf, 2014).
174 a summer for origin stories: Judith Edwards, "Mozart—At Home in Vermont," *Vermont Life* 30, no. 4 (Summer 1976).

177 Barre's colorful socialist past: "Socialist Labor Party History, Pt. 1," 2022, vermont history.org.
177 Barre's two socialist mayors: Robert Weir, "Solid Men in the Granite City: Municipal Socialism in Barre, Vermont, 1916–1931," *Vermont History* 83, no. 1 (2015).
178 remote Lowell, Vermont: Rod Clarke, "Workers Buy Mine to Save Operations," *BB*, March 13, 1975.
179 wherever he was invited: Frederick Bayles, "Liberty Union's Sanders Hits Hard," *BFP*, July 4, 1976.
180 *The New Yorker* caught up with: Anthony Hiss, "Vermont Lets Off Steam," *New Yorker*, June 14, 1976.

14. Goodbye to Politics

This chapter draws extensively on interviews with Richard Sugarman, and, in addition, interviews, exchanges, and conversations with Jim Rader, Nancy Barnett, Linda Niedweske, Murray Ngoima, and John Franco. Jim Rader supplied excerpts from his journal of the period.

191 a demonstration at UVM: Frederick Stetson, "War Protestors Arrested," *BFP*, May 11, 1972.
193 Sanders called a press conference: Nick Marro, "Sanders Quits Liberty Union," *RH*, October 12, 1977.

15. The American People's Historical Society

This chapter draws on interviews, exchanges, and conversations with Nancy Barnett, Richard Sugarman, Huck Gutman, Jim Rader, Ron MacNeil, and others.

199 "Bernie the small businessman": Fintan O'Toole, "Bernie Sanders: An Outside Chance," *New York Review of Books*, April 9, 2020.
203 an embarrassing fight: Unsigned, "ETV Looking for Viewer Ideas," *BFP*, March 2, 1979.
203 "Something of a mini revolution": Unsigned, "The Public and Public TV," *RH*, January 28, 1979.

16. Eviction in a Renter's City

This chapter draws on interviews, conversations, and exchanges with Richard Sugarman, Jim Rader, John Franco, Huck Gutman, Linda Chiasson, Nancy Barnett, Gene Bergman, and others.

207 Burlington was a tenants' city: Mark Kolter and Nell Rose Smith, "Renter Blacklisting," *VP*, January 13, 1981.
208 walked by it hand in hand: Peter Freyne, "Inside Track," *VP*, May 13, 1986.
211 low-budget interview feature: "Poverty in America," youtube.com.

17. Longtime Caller

215 "It looked like a nature show": Lauper, *Cyndi Lauper*, p. 47.
216 "that Joni Mitchell song": Ibid., p. 48.
216 *The Gift of Love: A Christmas Story*: Available on youtube.com.
217 old-fashioned shopping street: Unsigned, "This Place in History: Church Street," 2016, vermonthistory.org.
217 Joe Sherman memorably captured: Sherman, *Fast Lane on a Dirt Road*, p. 172.
220 "Winooski Dome": Jodie Peck, "Winooski Puts 'Dome' Study in Request," *BFP*, November 14, 1979.

18. The Citizens Party

This chapter draws on conversations and exchanges with Nat Winthrop, Jim Rader, Nancy Barnett, Greg Guma, Robin Lloyd, and Larry Sanders.

228 Commoner went on to become: Mark Dowie, "Barry Commoner, the People's Biologist," *Nation*, October 24, 2012.
229 As Rick Perlstein describes it: Perlstein, *Reaganland*, p. 911.
229 Lloyd, heir to a cattle fortune: Susan Green, "Hyper Activist," *Seven Days*, January 24, 2001.
230 reason for both to celebrate: Nell Davis, "Jeffords Easily Wins Fourth Term in House," *BFP*, November 5, 1980.
230 tangled with Bernie for years: Greg Guma, "Through the Years with Bernie," unpublished draft, shared by author.
232 issued a position paper: Greg Guma, "Maverick Chronicles: The Mayor and the Connector," *VTD*, August 10, 2012.
233 read aloud to him an account: John Dillon, "Drunken Mayor?," letter to the editor, *Seven Days*, December 8, 2021.

19. Black Faces, White Faces

This chapter draws on interviews, conversations, and exchanges with Nancy Barnett, Linda Chiasson, Susan Ford, Janet Herrero, and others.

239 But Wanda Hines: Wanda Hines, "It Didn't Get Any Better Than That," Champlain Housing Trust, 2023, getahome.org.
240 Pearl Street at lunch hour: Fran Brock, "Woman Attacked Downtown," *BFP*, July 18, 1980.
241 "I am an old hunter": Ibid.
242 Hines suffered a nervous collapse: William Braun, "Hines: 'A Short Fuse Waiting to Explode,'" *BFP*, July 28, 1980.
244 was "everywhere": David Brooks, "The Rise of the Latte Town," *Washington Examiner*, September 15, 1997.
244 Ben and Jerry were childhood friends: Lager, *The Inside Scoop*, pp. 5ff.
245 "a particular whiteness": Vanderbeck, "Vermont and the Imaginative Geographies of American Whiteness," pp. 64ff.

20. The Downy-Filled Room

This chapter draws on interviews with Richard Sugarman, Jim Rader, John Franco, and others.

248 In the viral clip: *Bernie Speaks: The Mayor's Show*, episode 26, 2019, youtube.com.
248 "This is Bernie Sanders": Holly Otterbein, "Anyone Ever Seen Cocaine?: What We Found in the Archives of Bernie Sanders's TV Show," *Politico*, May 3, 2019.
249 first local Dunkin' Donuts: Richard Sartelle, "Lighthouse in the Dark," *BFP*, February 18, 1971.
249 the tall chain-link fence: John Gormley, "For Franklin Square's 'Caged' Residents, Robert LeFebvre Means Hope," *RH*, July 18, 1976.
252 "a Downy-filled room": Branko Marcetic, "The Bernie Sanders Origin Story," *Jacobin*, December 11, 2019.
253 Franco's name was all over the news: Mike Donoghue, "Two Jailed on Counts of Rape," *BFP*, November 7, 1979.

21. "Burlington Is Not for Sale"

This chapter draws on interviews, conversations, and exchanges with Nancy Barnett, Linda Niedweske, Richard Sugarman, Jim Rader, Huck Gutman, Phil Fiermonte, Gene Bergman, Mark Stoler, and others.

257 a press conference in the foyer: Unsigned, "Liberty Unionite to Run for City Hall," *BFP*, November 9, 1980.
258 Mark Stoler, the UVM historian, and his then wife, Jennie: Interview with Vermont Historical Society, August 3, 2015.
259 "rare" to find campus activists: Alinsky, *Rules for Radicals*, pp. 6ff.

263 after decades of turmoil: Jenny Pushner and Soph Charron, "The Demise of the Queen City Cotton Mill," March 30, 2021, storymaps.arcgis.com.
264 "It's putting us in a corner": Alan Abbey, "Paquette Promises to Support Lakeside Underpass Project," *BFP*, September 26, 1980.

22. At Bove's

This chapter draws on interviews, conversations, and exchanges with Gene Bergman, Debby Bookchin, Jim Rader, Rick Bove, Richard Sugarman, David Clavelle, Gary De Carolis, Garrison Nelson, and others.

268 fed Burlington for decades: Debbie Salomon, "50 Years Is a Lot of Meatballs," *BFP*, December 7, 1991.
270 the "pudgy" restaurateur: Robert Kingsley, "Poor Jimmy: First Came Billy, and Now There's Richard Bove," *TA*, August 11, 1980.
271 a five-page press release: Unsigned, "Liberty Unionite to Run for Mayor of Burlington," *BFP*, November 9, 1980.
272 a *Burlington Free Press* reporter: Alan D. Abbey, "I Watched Bernie Sanders Work His Magic 35 Years Ago. Nobody Should Underestimate Him Now," *Times of Israel*, February 10, 2015.
278 "ceased calling his opponent 'Saunders'": Alan Abbey, "Mayor Acknowledges Competition in Race," *BFP*, February 16, 1981.
281 the only candidate: Alan Abbey, "Burlington Police Union Gives Sanders Stamp of Approval," *BFP*, February 27, 1981.

23. Apple's House

This chapter draws on interviews, conversations, and exchanges with Appleton King, Julia Alvarez, Garrison Nelson, Gary De Carolis, Jim Rader, Richard Sugarman, Linda Niedweske, Meg Pond, Terry Bouricius, Jym Wilson, Chip Wadhams, Greg Guma, and Howard Dean.

290 told his old friend Richard Clarke: Sanders Mayoral Papers, University of Vermont.
292 "It's too early for that": Alan Abbey, "Sanders Attracted People into the Political Process," *BFP*, March 8, 1981.
293 at his friend's kitchen counter: The note was memorialized immediately by Rader; he provided me with the transcript.

24. "A Weak Mayor"

This chapter incorporates interviews, conversations, and exchanges with Greg Guma, Jim Rader, Richard Sugarman, and others.

294 In March of 1981: Sanders Mayoral Papers, University of Vermont.
295 fought off dangerous newcomers: Carlo Wolf, "Moonies Fund Raising Draws Fire," *BFP*, March 2, 1976.
296 "everyone's scared right now": Unsigned, "Sanders Aims to Help Burlington's Disadvantaged," *BR*, March 5, 1981.
297 following Appleton King's party: Debbie Bookchin, "What Happened in Burlington?," *RH*, March 5, 1981.
297 "unknowns from Oosh-Koosh": Debbie Bookchin, "Mayor Misjudged Voters, Ignored New Coalition," *TA*, March 5, 1981.
298 subject of an FBI investigation: Jeff Earle, "Bernie Sanders Campaigned for the Socialist Workers' Party," *Guardian*, May 30, 2019.
298 hovered over the tense recount: Alan Abbey, "Recount Puts Sanders Up by 10 Votes," *BFP*, March 14, 1981.
298 the *Rutland Herald*: Debbie Bookchin, "Sanders Accepts Socialist Label with a Small 'S,'" *RH*, March 16, 1981.
302 "We differ in political philosophy": Alan Abbey, "Sanders Spends Week Studying His Domain," *BFP*, March 22, 1981.

303 Students in the thousands: John Donnelly, "Coor: Five Years Later," *TA*, May 10, 1980.
304 in a state of panic: Jodie Peck, "Joint Session Held About Spring Fling," *BFP*, March 14, 1981.
305 "the freak mayor": Alan Abbey, "Bernard Sanders: Working Class Hero?" *BFP*, May 2, 1982.
306 "an offbeat individual": Marilyn Adams, "Sanders to Make His TV Debut," *BFP*, March 26, 1981.
306 "Socialism in New England": "Socialism in New England," today.com.

25. B. S. Sanders, Temporary Mayor

This chapter draws on interviews, conversations, and exchanges with Larry Sanders, Jim Rader, Richard Sugarman, David Clavelle, Chip Wadhams, Terry Bouricius, Gary De Carolis, Linda Niedweske, Meg Pond, Greg Guma, Nat Winthrop, Peter Smith, Ted Riehle, Chip Wadhams, and others.

312 delivered his inaugural address: Debbie Bookchin, "Sanders Takes Oath, and Talks of Tax Increase," *RH*, and Alan Abbey, "Sanders Takes Helm in Burlington," *BFP*, April 7, 1981.
313 paraphrased Friedrich Engels: Staff, "City File," *BFP*, June 8, 1981.
314 FBI agent arrived in Montpelier: Louis Berney, "FBI Probes Mayor to Discredit Witness," *BFP*, April 8, 1981.
315 U.S. Immigration and Naturalization Service: Alan Abbey, "Burlington Immigration Office May Get Role in Socialist Probe," *BFP*, May 21, 1981.
316 Two hundred citizens: Staff, "City File," "Brou-ha-ha or Love In?" *BFP*, and Debbie Bookchin, "Sanders, Aldermen Slugging It Out: Six Nominees Rejected," *RH*, June 2, 1981.
317 *Burlington Flea Press*: Sanders Mayoral Papers, University of Vermont.
320 the pope's rumored mistress: Nihal Thondepu, "Ex-Pope Had 32-Year Relationship with Woman," 2016, theguardian.com.
320 "The People's Republic of Burlington": Jodie Peck, "Doonesbury Comic Has Greeting for Sanders," *BFP*, July 5, 1981.
321 A confrontational memo: The memo, dated October 23, 1981, was provided to me by one of its signatories, who wished to remain anonymous.
322 "This is politics": Joe Mahoney, "Sanders Turns to Supreme Court," *BFP*, September 1, 1981.
323 Wagner intercepted a letter: Alan Abbey and Rob Eley, "Mayor Reprimands City Clerk Wagner," *BFP*, September 9, 1981.
323 six-step residency test: Joe Mahoney, "Students' Ballots Are Routinely Marked," *BFP*, November 17, 1981.

26. The People's Republic of Burlington

This Chapter incorporates interviews, conversations, and exchanges with George Ewins, Pamela Polston, Jay Strausser, Huck Gutman, and Luther Martin.

327 The next letter: Susan Green, "Raised on Music, Family Songsters Carry on Custom," *BFP*, July 2, 1981.
328 "I can't believe they elected you": Susan Green, "Comedian Youngman Gets the Red Carpet Treatment," *BFP*, May 25, 1982.
330 A woman from Belgium: Sanders Mayoral Papers, University of Vermont.
331 "had managed to locate a book": Ray Martin, "Philosopher Michel Foucault: A Man Looks Carefully at Man," *BFP*, November 2, 1982.
331 "'to be concerned with oneself'": Michel Foucault, *Technologies of the Self* (University of Massachusetts Press, 1988).
333 John Wakeling arrived: Susan Green, "Caribbean Cowboy Spices the Air with Reggae," *BFP*, June 9, 1978.
334 the enchanting Nastassja Kinski: Susan Green, "A Day on the Movie Set," *BFP*, February 6, 1982.

334 Bernie himself acted: *Sweet Hearts Dance*, youtube.com.
335 discovered in a field: "The Charlotte Whale," Perkins Museum of Geology, uvm.edu.
337 my great-uncle John Delorme: Matt Crawford, "LCI Derby Celebrates 20th Year," *BFP*, June 10, 2001.

27. City Hall

This chapter draws on interviews, conversations, and exchanges with Jim Rader, Meg Pond, Emer Feeney, Jonathan Leopold, Debbie Bookchin, Julia Alvarez, Appleton King, Greg Guma, Terry Bouricius, Pamela Polston, and others.

338 Upton's main profit stream: Deborah Weiner, "Multi-Sense Fantasy for a Quarter," *BFP*, October 17, 1976.
339 The name rang a bell: Alan Abbey, "City Says Pinball Machines, Kids Don't Mix," *BFP*, February 10, 1981.
340 The Hoosier tinkerer: Scott MacKay, "More Voting Machines Needed to Eliminate Wait," *BFP*, November 4, 1982.
340 kids of the Old North End: Staff, "City File," *BFP*, May 31, 1982.
342 city's cemetery endowment: Bernard Sanders, "It's My Turn," *BFP*, July 4, 1982.
342 city's insurance policies: Editorial, "Sanders Handles City Insurance Well," *BFP*, July 1, 1982.
343 in December, a miracle: Scott MacKay, "Burlington Uncovers Windfall," *BFP*, December 21, 1982.
346 the president "owed little": Peter Dreier, "Reagan's Legacy: Homelessness in America," May 1, 2004, shelterforce.org.
347 "to provide additional beds": John Donnelly, "City's Crying Need Is Shelter," *BFP*, March 9, 1981.
347 "Sadie White Street": Scott MacKay, "Soon Cars May Drive on Sadie White Street," *BFP*, March 29, 1983.
347 fighting an X-rated bookstore: Jodie Peck, "North Street Building Being Renovated for X-Rated Bookstore," *BFP*, November 13, 1982.
348 four "lovely young men": Susan Green, "Project Snowshovel Forging Bonds of Trust, Friendship," *BFP*, February 3, 1982.
349 "I did not burn down the Strong Theater": Scott MacKay and Ted Tedford, "Burlington Voters to Make Their Choices Today," *BFP*, March 1, 1983.

28. Lawyers, Guns, and Money

This chapter draws on interviews, conversations, and exchanges with Greg Guma, Jim Rader, Barr (Ruah) Swennerfelt, Jonathan Leopold, Rachel Nolan, Phil Fiermonte, and others.

352 glowering mill building: Staff, "Design Secrets of the General Electric Armaments Department," October 11, 2008, smallarmsreview.com.
352 a 1969 classified report: Army Concept Team in Vietnam, "Final Report: XM163 Vulcan Air Defense System," June 11, 1969, Department of the Army.
352 by 1978, GE boasted: Kyle Obenauer, "Lakeside Avenue Manufacturing," uvm.edu.
353 David Goodman, a defense analyst: "Design Secrets," smallarmsreview.
354 "How many cities of 40,000": Sanders, *Outsider in the House*, p. 66.
354 in defiance of his own aides: Memo, provided confidentially, dated July 13, 1983.
354 "just part of the package": Walter Shapiro, "I Am Not Now, Nor Have I Ever Been, a Liberal Democrat," *New England Monthly* (December 1985).
355 Crisis Relocation Program: Peter Coy, "Plattsburgh Area Plan Called Best in Nation," *BFP*, May 9, 1982.
356 "Dear Mr. Reagan" letters: Sanders Mayoral Papers, University of Vermont.
357 "We are headed": Sanders Mayoral Papers, University of Vermont.
358 "absolutely devoted sense": Mailer, *Armies of the Night*, p. 118.
364 "necessary for us to 'trespass'": Bradley, Wasserman, and Dellinger, *Por Amor Al Pueblo*, pp. 130ff.

29. Neither Out Far nor In Deep

This chapter incorporates interviews, conversations, and exchanges with Peter Clavelle, Jim Rader, Larry Sanders, Howard Dean, Ernest Pomerleau, Melinda Moulton, Rick Moulton and others.

366 "our life here in Burlington": Advertisement, *BFP*, August 1, 1980.
368 "the odd couple": Scott MacKay, "Sanders and Pomerleau: Burlington's Odd Couple," *BFP*, June 6, 1982.
369 David Sellers of Prickly Mountain: John Gittlesohn, "The 200-Year Planner," *BFP*, October 31, 1984.
370 sold minnows, nightcrawlers: "Waterfront Oral History," 1993, cctv.org.
370 had visited Burlington: Sharp, *The Burlington Bike Path and Waterfront Park*, pp. 17ff.
374 clear that Bernie intended: Scott MacKay, "Waterfront Feud Lights Up Again," *BFP*, October 26, 1983.
374 August of 1983: Debbie Bookchin, "Burlington's Big Ideas for Waterfront Stalled," *RH*, August 24, 1983.

30. Coming Out

This chapter draws on interviews, conversations, and exchanges with Peter Schumann, Debbie Bookchin, Nancy Barnett, Jonathan Leopold, Mike Agganis, Larry Sanders, Richard Sugarman, Huck Gutman, Jim Rader, David Clavelle, and Stephen Terry.

379 Bookchin and others on the left: Murray Bookchin, "The Bernie Sanders Paradox: When Socialism Grows Old," 1986, theanarchistlibrary.org.
379 White called Bernie: David Gram, "Municipalities Stymied by Reappraisal," *BFP*, July 27, 1985.
380 "wasted tremendous energy": Sherman, *Fast Lane on a Dirt Road*, pp. 201–204.
381 confided his state of mind: Sanders Mayoral Papers, University of Vermont.
382 the journalist Walter Shapiro: Walter Shapiro, *New England Monthly* (December 1985): 55.
383 "weak field of candidates": Don Melvin, "Sanders to Sit Tight," *BFP*, March 20, 1984.
383 "Longing on a large scale": DeLillo, *Underworld*, p. 11.
386 "It's a non-political thing": Peter Freyne, "Inside Track," *VP*, July 1984.
387 Sanders wrote to Agganis: Sanders Mayoral Papers, University of Vermont.
388 responded on Bernie's behalf: Ibid.
391 The mood at Pearls: Editorial, "Vermont Democrats Registered Gains Election Day," *BFP*, November 14, 1984.

31. "A Wonder of the World"

This chapter draws on interviews, conversations, and exchanges with Peter Clavelle, Bruce Seifer, Garrison Nelson, Melinda Moulton, Rick Moulton, and Howard Dean. Discussion of the Alden Plan is scattered throughout Rick Sharp, *The Burlington Bike Path and Waterfront Park*; this section draws on chapters in that book, as well as contemporary reports in *RH* and *BFP*.

393 over three hundred thousand Americans: William J. Collins and Katherine L. Shester, "Slum Clearance and Urban Renewal in the United States," *American Economic Journal: Applied Economics* (January 2013).
393 a study by Ingrid W. Reed: Ingrid W. Reed, "The Life and Death of UDAG: An Assessment Based on Eight Projects in Five New Jersey Cities," *Publius: The Journal of Federalism* (Summer 1989).
393 Urban Development Action Grants: For the best discussion of CEDO, written by one of its most important staffers, see Siefer, *Sustainable Communities*.
397 Charles Louis Heyde: Barbara Knapp Hamblett, "A View from the Past," uvm.edu/vtquarterly.

398 painted his own landscape: "Walt Whitman to Charles W. Eldridge," July 19, 1872, whitmanarchive.org.
398 Citizens for a Better Waterfront: Sharp, *The Burlington Bike Path and Waterfront Park*, p. 145.
401 On December 2, 1985: Ibid.

32. I Want My MTV

This chapter draws on interviews, conversations, and exchanges with Jim Rader, Meg Pond, Paula Delorme, Terry Bouricius, John Franco, and others.

404 Green Mountain Cable: Jim Cheng, "Cox Spokesman Hart Disputes Cable Study," *BFP*, January 4, 1984.
404 a scorching editorial: "Cable TV Takeover Is Preposterous," *BFP*, July 23, 1983.
405 "no valid cable franchise": Jim Cheng, "Attorneys Pore Over Cable Legislation," *BFP*, December 19, 1984.
406 furnished their new home: Becky Premo, "Housing Solution," letter to *BFP*, December 8, 1984.
406 Terry Bouricius was troubled: Don Melvin, "Observers Say Sanders Using Reagan's Strategy," *BFP*, December 10, 1984.
409 Dick Sartelle hammered Sanders: Don Melvin, "Sartelle Says Sanders 'Dictatorial,'" *BFP*, January 16, 1985.
409 therefore in relaxed spirits: "Sanders Mayor Campaign, 1985," cctv.org.
410 brought his handheld camcorder: Ibid.
412 changes to the city's charter: Leslie Brown, "Sanders Lobbies Lawmakers on Charter Changes," *BFP*, March 1, 1985.
412 Days after the election: Jim Cheng, "Charter Fight Goes to Supreme Court," *BFP*, March 9, 1985.

33. Sandinista!

This chapter draws on interviews, conversations, and exchanges with Peter Schumann, Don Melvin, Rachel Nolan, Peter Clavelle, Dan Higgins, David Clavelle, Debbie Bookchin, Alma Guillermoprieto, and others.

414 In January of 1985: Susan Green, "Nicaragua Diary," *VP*, February 3–10, 1985.
415 In the film: *Bread and Puppet Theater: A Song for Nicaragua*, youtube.com.
417 The pro-Sandinista left: William Braun, "Miskito Indians Face Strong Racism, Lecturer Says," *BFP*, April 16, 1985, and Maggie Hayes, "Looking the Other Way in Nicaragua," *VP*, June 2, 1985.
417 The CIA "trained and armed": Kinzer, *Blood of Brothers*, pp. 253ff.
418 On June 8, a letter: Sanders Mayoral Papers, University of Vermont.
419 "where his real interests lie": Michael Powell, "Mayor Sanders Planning to Go to Nicaragua," *BFP*, July 8, 1985
419 on a glorious July morning: "Your View," *BFP*, July 14, 1985.
420 understood that his job: Don Melvin, "US and Nicaragua: An Unhappy History," *Vermonter*, July 28, 1985.
421 A detailed account: Don Melvin, "Mayor Rails Against US Antagonism," *BFP*, July 20, 1985.
422 "most jailed, tortured people in the world": "Sanders Airport Return from Nicaragua Trip," cctv.org.
423 "long consciousness-raising sessions": Kinzer, *Blood of Brothers*, p. 21.
423 a U.S. air invasion: *BFP*, July 20, 1985.
424 ill at ease in the meeting: Melvin, "Mayor Rails," *BFP*, July 21, 1985.
424 The crowd awaiting Bernie's return: Melvin, "We Cannot Sleep . . ." cctv.org.

34. Welcome to Vermont! (Part 3)

This chapter draws on interviews with Joe Sherman, Jim Schumacher, Debbie Bookchin, Jym Wilson, Jim Rader, Garrison Nelson, Brian Pine, David Clavelle, Jonathan Leopold, Ellen David Friedman, and George Thabault.

428 Montgomery's postmistress: Sherman, *Fast Lane on a Dirt Road*, p. 51. Sherman's chapter on Burlington is especially well done.

429 The protocol with Solzhenitsyn: Jennifer Small, "Solzhenitsyns Find a Home," *BR*, April 1, 1977.

432 "complicated player in a complicated game": Ellen David Friedman, "Bernie Sanders and the Rainbow in Vermont," 1990, versobooks.com.

433 Freyne put it simply: Peter Freyne, "Inside Track," *VP*, October 28–November 4, 1984.

433 Kunin recalled run-ins: Kunin, *Living a Political Life*, p. 308.

433 mandated property reappraisal: Russell Banks, "Bernie Sanders, the Socialist Mayor of Burlington, Vermont," October 5, 2025, theatlantic.com.

434 After a spectacular overreach: Leslie Brown, "At Dawn, Officials Moved In," *BFP*, June 23, 1984.

435 as her coup de grâce: "Sanders Press Conference Response to Governor Kunin's State of the State Address," cctv.org.

436 Kunin was irate: Friedman, "Bernie Sanders and the Rainbow in Vermont."

437 "He says 'socialism'": Unsigned, "Sanders on the Stump," *SAM*, October 6, 1986.

437 At the Thunder Road Speedbowl: Freyne, "Inside Track," *VP*, October 26–November 2, 1986.

440 when Superman himself: Peter Freyne, "Inside Track," *VP*, September 28–October 5, 1986.

441 reported clearing skies: Freyne, "Inside Track," *VP*, October 26–November 2, 1986.

442 "the conservative hill towns": Chris Graff, "A Three-Way Race for Governor," *Vermont Affairs* (January 1987): 43.

35. The Same River, Twice

This chapter draws on interviews, conversations, and exchanges with Jim Lockridge, Jim Rader, Meg Pond, Emer Feeney, Richard Sugarman, Huck Gutman, and others.

445 a bulldozer operator: Don Melvin, "Burlington's Landfill Woes Aired at Hearing," *BFP*, August 3, 1984.

447 debuted in late 1986: "Intro to the Series and City Issues," cctv.org.

449 she credits the kids: Jane Sanders, interview with Jim Lockridge.

450 Bobby Hackney Jr.: Bobby Hackney, interview with Jim Lockridge.

454 "For those of you who are students": Peter Freyne, "Inside Track," *VP*, September 3–10, 1987.

455 held a group of nurses hostage: Mark Johnson, "Mayor Releases Grant for VNA," *BFP*, June 30, 1987.

456 published a lead editorial: "Common Courtesy Should Outweigh 'Right to Party,'" *BFP*, December 10, 1988.

456 handed the city of Burlington: Enrique Corredera, "Medical Center KO's City in Tac Bout," *BFP*, September 23, 1987.

457 "a chipmunk or a woman": Mary Ann Lickteig, "Mayor Sings to Beat of a Different Drummer," *BFP*, November 20, 1987.

457 Sanders told his fellow musicians: "Sanders Records 2 Songs and Talks with 30 Vt. Musicians at White Crow Music Studio," *Sanders Speaks with the Community*, November 19, 1987, cctv.org.

458 *The Bernie Sanders Christmas Album*: Peter Freyne, "Inside Track," *VP*, November 3–10, 1987.

36. *"Making History in Vermont"*

This chapter draws on interviews, conversations, and exchanges with Peter Clavelle, David Clavelle, Debbie Bookchin, Jim Schumacher, Peter Smith, Garrison Nelson, and others.

459 a hulking steel oil barge: "Burlington Waterfront Revitalization Project and Community Boathouse," sandersinstitute.org.
460 opened Burlington up to prosperity: Noble E. Whitford, "History of the Canal System of the State of New York," eriecanal.org.
460 "Waterfront Truce Disintegrates": Mark Johnson, *VP*, October 11–18, 1988.
463 C-SPAN national call-in show: "Bernie Sanders on Local and National Politics," 1988, c-span.org.
463 William F. Buckley wrote: William F. Buckley, "The Jackson Phenomenon," syndicated, March 31, 1988.
463 DeWayne Wickham: "Jesse Tries to Avoid Serious Squabbles," syndicated, December 19, 1988.
464 Sanders welcomed Jackson: "Reverend Jesse Jackson Visits Mayor Sanders," 1988, cctv.org.
466 a dramatic opportunity: Ellen David Friedman, "Bernie Sanders and the Rainbow in Vermont," 1990, versobooks.com.
467 Burlington progressives took their seats: "Reverend Jesse Jackson Visits Mayor Sanders," 1988, cctv.org.
470 this "Che Guevara type": Sherman, *Fast Lane on a Dirt Road*, p. 156.
471 last days before COVID-19: Anton Troianovski, "Behind the Story: Searching for Sanders in a Russian Archive," *NYT*, March 5, 2020.
471 a few oddities: Masha Gessen, "The Innocuous Story of Bernie Sanders's Trip to Russia," March 6, 2020, newyorker.com.

37. *"Give 'Em Hell"*

This chapter draws on interviews, conversations, and exchanges with Jim Schumacher, David Clavelle, Jim Rader, Richard Sugarman, Howard Dean, and George Thabault.

475 "Sanders in 1988": Graff, *Dateline Vermont*, p. 157.
476 attracted national attention: Ibid., pp. 157ff.
476 "After a hectic interview": Peter Freyne, "Inside Track," *VP*, October 17–24, 1988.
476 as Morley Safer once said: "Harry Reasoner," Wikipedia.
477 recalled in *Outsider in the House*: Sanders, *Outsider in the House*, p. 88.
477 Bernie was indignant: Unsigned, "Dukakis Forgoes Large Registration Drive," *BR*, October 3, 1988.
477 "the preservation of the world": Unsigned, "Conservation Society Replies to Detailed Route 7 Position," *BB*, June 7, 1972.
478 There, an old friend: Unsigned, "Ah, Politics," *Windsor Chronicle*, October 21, 1988.
481 "repetition, not variation": Fintan O'Toole, "Bernie Sanders: An Outside Chance," 2020, nybooks.com.
481 "Ideology has replaced party": James Bressor, "Sanders's Strong Showing Shakes Up Democrats," *BFP*, November 10, 1988.

38. *River Rat*

This chapter draws on interviews, conversations, and exchanges with Peter Clavelle, George Thabault, Jim Schumacher, Earl Handy, Terry Bouricius, and Debbie Bookchin.

483 A quiet civic experiment: "Resettled in Vermont," 2022, uvm.edu.
486 the apparatchiks of Yaroslavl: Enrique Corredera, "City Welcomes Mayor's Group from Yaroslavl," *BFP*, October 15, 1988.
487 a country mouse like Joe Sherman: Sherman, *Fast Lane on a Dirt Road*, p. 152.
488 as he told CCTV: "CCTV Time Machine," 2023, cctv.org.
488 In late November, Debbie Bookchin: "Sanders Looks Back on His Political Career," *RH*, November 29, 1988.

489 Peter Clavelle addressed: "CCTV Time Machine."
491 Northgate deal came together: Michael Allen, "Where Northgate Went Wrong," *BFP*, December 2, 1988.
493 "Balding, paunchy, colorless": Unsigned, "Inside Vermont," *BFP*, March 5, 1989.
494 farewell tribute to the city: "Bernie Sanders Mayoral Retirement," sandersinstitute .org

39. One Small City, One Small State

This chapter draws on interviews, conversations, and exchanges with George Thabault, Peter Smith, Huck Gutman, Dennis Gilbert, Jim Schumacher, Debbie Bookchin, Larry Sanders, Brett Mandel, Rob Witwer, and Stephen Terry.

497 Stockton, California, schoolyard shooting: "What Will Save Us? Remembering the Stockton Schoolyard Shooting," youtube.com.
498 "On the housing front this week": Peter Freyne, "Inside Track," *VP*, March 7–14, 1989.
498 local sportsmen's groups: Rosenfeld, *Making History in Vermont*, pp. 6ff.
499 practice of fish shooting: Phil Pugliese, "Pickerel Shooting Controversy Grows in State," *RH*, April 11, 1976.
500 Vermont's political playbook: Betsey Lilley, "Sanders May Run for State Office," *BFP*, May 24, 1989.
500 "the cinnamon raisin buns": Sanders, *Outsider in the House*, p. 83.
500 It did, however, in a way: For narrative flow, I mix freely throughout this section material from interviews and exchanges with Dennis Gilbert; Gilbert's "Adventures with Bernie," in *The Spectator*, students.hamilton.edu; and Gilbert's unpublished campaign diary, quoted with permission of author.
501 Brett Mandell, Bernie's student: "My Old College Professor Won the New Hampshire Primaries," brettmandel.com.
502 "I'm a weird animal": Rosenfeld, *Making History in Vermont*, p. xxviii.
503 At a Memorial Day parade: Ibid., p. xl.
504 studios of Vermont ETV: Ibid., pp. 36ff.
505 By midsummer: Dennis Gilbert's campaign diary.
507 stormed into Grant Street: Rosenfeld, *Making History in Vermont*, p. 239.
508 As a hunter from Saint Albans: Ibid., p. 358.
510 Bush was gracious: Lisa Scagliotti, "Agreeing to Disagree," *BFP*, October 24, 1990.
512 Garrison Nelson's voice: This exchange between Nelson and Barry was reconstructed from my memory, aided by news reports and interviews. No verbatim transcript of the broadcast survives.
512 Joe Sherman turns up: Sherman, *Fast Lane on a Dirt Road*, p. 160.

Epilogue: The Stannard Family Picnic

515 "As much as any political figure": Gilad Edelman, *Wired*, April 8, 2020.
515 Daniel Kreiss: Quoted in ibid.
516 "We are talking about": Williams, *Preface to Film*, p. 22.

Bibliography

Books

Aiken, George. *Speaking from Vermont*. Frederick G. Stokes, 1938.

Alinsky, Saul. *Rules for Radicals*. Random House, 1971.

Anderson, Elin L. *We Americans: A Study of Cleavage in an American City*. Harvard University Press, 1937.

Baruth, Philip. *Senator Leahy: A Life in Scenes*. University Press of New England, 2017.

Biehl, Janet, *Ecology or Catastrophe: The Life of Murray Bookchin*. Oxford University Press, 2015.

Bradley, Ben, Nancy Wasserman, and David Dellinger. *Por Amor Al Pueblo: The Trial of the Winooski 44*. Front Porch Publishing, 1986.

Brecht, Stefan. *The Bread and Puppet Theatre*. Routledge, 1988.

Bryan, Frank. *Yankee Politics in Rural Vermont*. University Press of New England, 1984.

Clavel, Pierre. *The Progressive City: Planning and Participation, 1969–1984*. Rutgers University Press, 1986.

Daley, Yvonne. *Going Up the Country: When the Hippies, Dreamers, Freaks and Radicals Moved to Vermont*. University Press of New England, 2018.

Daloz, Kate. *We Are As Gods: Back to the Land in the 1970s on the Quest for a New America*. PublicAffairs Press, 2016.

Davis, Erik. *High Weirdness: Drugs, Esoterica, and Visionary Experience in the Seventies*. MIT Press, 2019.

DeLillo, Don. *Underworld*. Scribner, 1997.

Feeney, Vince. *Burlington: A History of Vermont's Queen City*. Applewood Books, 2015.

Feeney, Vincent Edward. *The Great Falls on the Onion River: A History of Winooski, Vermont*. Winooski Historical Society, 2002.

Graff, Christopher. *Dateline Vermont*. Thistle Hill Press, 2006.

Gregg, Sarah M. *Managing the Mountains: Land Use Planning, the New Deal, and the Creation of a Federal Landscape in Appalachia*. Yale University Press, 2010.

Guma, Greg, *Strange Enough to Be True*. Unpublished manuscript.

Guma, Greg, *The People's Republic: Vermont and the Sanders Revolution*. New England Press, 1989.

Guma, Greg, *Green Mountain Politics: Restless Spirits, Popular Movements*. White River Press, 2021.

Hand, Samuel B. *The Star That Set: The Vermont Republican Party, 1854–1974*. Lexington Books, 2002.

Harrison, Blake. *The View from Vermont: Tourism and the Making of an American Rural Landscape*. University of Vermont, 2006.

Higgins, Dan. *Sister Cities: Side by Side*. Green Valley Press, 1988.

Hill, Catherine Alison. *Bernie Sanders: The Working Classes' Candidate*. Thesis, Cornell University, 1986.

Jaffe, Harry. *Why Bernie Sanders Matters*. Regan Arts, 2015.
Kinzer, Stephen. *Blood of Brothers: Life and War in Nicaragua*. Putnam, 1991.
Kunin, Madeleine. *Living a Political Life*. Knopf, 1985.
Lager, Fred. *The Inside Scoop: How Two Real Guys Built a Business with a Social Conscience and a Sense of Humor*. Crown, 1991.
Lauper, Cyndi. *Cyndi Lauper: A Memoir*. Atria Books, 2017.
Leahy, Patrick. *The Road Taken*. Simon and Schuster, 2023.
Mailer, Norman. *Armies of the Night*. New American Library, 1968.
Menand, Louis. *The Metaphysical Club*. Farrar, Straus and Giroux, 2001.
Neill, A. S. *Summerhill: A Radical Approach to Education*. Henry Hart, 1960.
Perlstein, Rick. *Nixonland: The Rise of a President and the Fracturing of America*. Scribner, 2009.
Perlstein, Rick. *Reaganland: America's Right Turn, 1976–1980*. Scribner, 2020.
Rosenfeld, Steven. *Making History in Vermont: The Election of a Socialist to Congress*. Hollowbrook Publishing, 1992.
Sanders, Bernie. *Our Revolution*. St. Martin's, 2016.
Sanders, Bernie, with Huck Gutman. *Outsider in the House*. Verso, 1997.
Searls, Paul M. *Repeopling Vermont*. Vermont Historical Society, 2019.
Sharp, Rick. *The Burlington Bike Path and Waterfront Park*. Onion River Press, 2019.
Sherman, Joe. *Fast Lane on a Dirt Road*. Chelsea Green Publishing, 1991.
Siefer, Bruce. *Sustainable Communities: Creating a Durable Local Economy*. Routledge, 2013.
Soifer, Steven. *The Socialist Mayor: Bernard Sanders in Burlington, Vermont*. Praeger, 1991.
Terry, Stephen. *Philip Hoff: How Red Turned Blue in the Green Mountain State*. Castleton Press, 2011.
Terry, Stephen. *Say We Won and Get Out: George D. Aiken and the Vietnam War*. White River Press, 2019.
Thompson, Zadoc. *History of Vermont, Natural, Civic and Statistical*. Vermont Historical Society, 1913.
Vanderbeck, Robert M. "Vermont and the Imaginative Geographies of American Whiteness," *Annals of the Association of American Geographers* 96, no. 3 (2006).
Williams, Raymond, with Michael Orrom. *Preface to Film*. Film Drama Limited, 1954.

Periodicals

The Barre-Montpelier Times Argus (*TA*)
Bennington Banner (*BB*)
The Boston Phoenix (*BP*)
Brattleboro Reformer (*BR*)
Burlington Free Press (*BFP*)
The New York Times (*NYT*)
Rutland Herald (*RH*)
Saint Albans Messenger (*SAM*)
The Vermont Cynic (*VC*)
Vermont Freeman (*VF*)
The Vermont Vanguard Press (*VP*)
VTDigger (*VTD*)

Index

Page numbers in *italics* refer to illustrations.

A NOTE ABOUT THE AUTHOR

Dan Chiasson is the author of five collections of poetry, most recently *The Math Campers*, and a book of criticism. A longtime contributor to *The New Yorker* and to *The New York Review of Books*, Chiasson is the Lorraine C. Wang Professor of English and chair of the English department at Wellesley College. He lives in Massachusetts.

A NOTE ON THE TYPE

This book was set in Janson, a typeface long thought to have been made by the Dutchman Anton Janson, who was a practicing typefounder in Leipzig during the years 1668–1687. However, it has been conclusively demonstrated that these types are actually the work of Nicholas Kis (1650–1702), a Hungarian, who most probably learned his trade from the master Dutch typefounder Dirk Voskens. The type is an excellent example of the influential and sturdy Dutch types that prevailed in England up to the time William Caslon (1692–1766) developed his own incomparable designs from them.

Composed by North Market Street Graphics,
Lancaster, Pennsylvania

Designed by Cassandra J. Pappas

The Choice is Clear
Bernie Sanders for Mayor
Vote March 1 for the People

Jym Wilson